HISTORICAL NOTES

ON

ENGLISH CATHOLIC MISSIONS

BY

BERNARD W. KELLY

AUTHOR OF 'THE LIFE OF CARDINAL YORK' 'THE CONQUEROR OF CULLODEN'
'JAMES III AND VIII' 'THE FATE OF GLENGARRY' ETC.

LONDON

KEGAN PAUL, TRENCH, TRÜBNER & CO. Ltd.

DRYDEN HOUSE, 43 GERRARD STREET, W.

1907

Originally published 1907

REPRINTED BY MICHAEL GANDY
3 Church Crescent, Whetstone, London N20 OJR
1995
with the omission of an introductory essay on the history of
Catholicism in England since the Reformation (pages 1-43 in original)
and the addition of an alphabetical index by county.

ISBN: 0 9520535 7 8

NIHIL OBSTAT.

JOSEPH WILHELM, S.T.D.

CENSOR DEPUTATUS.

IMPRIMI POTEST.

✝ GULIELMUS,

EPISCOPUS ARINDELENSIS,

VICARIUS GENERALIS.

WESTMONASTERII,

Die 24 Oct., 1906.

PREFACE

In the following pages some details have been given of the Catholic Missions in this country from the breach with the Apostolic See to our own times. The story of the English Catholics, or the ' Romance of the Recusants ' as it has been happily termed, during that long period of trial and proscription forms as interesting a narrative as any to be found in the pages of modern history.

The downfall of the great and ancient Church in these realms after the centuries of her flourishing existence is an event which Newman, in a passage of the noblest eloquence, has termed almost a miracle.[1] Tremendous, however, as was the overthrow, the rise of the ancient faith--kept alive here and there in the ancient halls and lowly cottages of the land—from generations of political oppression and social ostracism, is no less a wondrous proof of ' the vivifying principle ' of the ' old religion ' and God's protecting power. When the close of the eighteenth century ushered in such momentous changes in the state of European governments and society, the wrecked remnant of the ancient Church in England had yet within her the unquenched sparks of vitality which seemed

---

[1] ' A *great* change, an *awful* contrast, between the time-honoured Church of St. Augustine and St. Thomas, and the poor remnant of their children in the beginning of the nineteenth century ! It was a miracle, I might say, to have pulled down that lordly power ; but there was a greater and a truer one in store. No one could have prophesied its fall, but still less would anyone have ventured to prophesy its rise again.'—*The Second Spring.*

a

to say in encouragement to her scattered and dejected children, 'Resurgam'—'I shall arise.'

With regard to the historical introduction to the present work, no attempt has been made to narrate the events which marked the commencement of the Reformation in the reigns of Henry VIII. and Edward VI. or the short-lived Catholic restoration under Queen Mary. As most writers assign the final and definite establishment of Protestantism in England to the reign of Elizabeth, it is from the first year of her accession that we propose following the rapidly declining fortunes of the ancient Church. Moreover, the subject is one which deals mainly with English Catholicism in the days of its depression, far removed from the historic splendours of the mediæval religious polity.

The author is aware that many of the remarks in the ensuing notices of missions are of a scanty and fragmentary nature. Every effort has been made to exclude error, but in a work like the present it is well nigh impossible to prevent mis-statements from appearing, considering the obscurity of much of the subject and the difficulty of obtaining reliable information. Most publications of this nature are only perfected in course of time, and the writer will be grateful for any corrections that may be brought to his notice. For the rest, reliance has been placed on Catholic magazines, newspapers, county histories, private memoirs and letters of the past hundred years. By means of these auxiliaries, the author trusts that he has put forward a book which will be found useful for casual reference, and if this aspiration is realised he will feel that the labours of thirteen years have not been in vain. In conclusion, he begs to acknowledge his obligations to W. Simpson, Esq., Park Place, Mitcham, for the use so kindly afforded of a select and valuable library, to the Very Rev. Henry Canon Cafferata for several practical suggestions, and the Rev. J. Wilhelm, D.D., of Battle, for kindly supervising the proofs.

CONTENTS

The names and geographical descriptions of the missions are as in the text.

GLOUCESTERSHIRE

ESSEX

HAMPSHIRE

Aldershot	50
Andover	54
Basingstoke	67
Bishopstoke	84
Bitterne	84
Boscombe, Bournemouth	91
Bournemouth:	
Oratory	91
St Mary Immaculate	92
Christ Church	132
Eastleigh	163
Fareham	174
Farnborough	174
Fordingbridge	180
Gosport	189
Greyshott	195
Havant	207
Isle of Wight - see separate section	
Lymington	263
Lyndhurst	263
Petersfield	313
Portsmouth	319
Romsey	335
Southampton	363
Southsea	364
Tichborne	392
Waterlooville	418
Winchester	437
Woolmer, near Liphook	446
Woolston	446

HEREFORDSHIRE

Bartestree	66
Belmont, Clehonger	73
Broxwood	106
Bullingham	108
Courtfield, near Ross	143
Hereford	210
Ledbury	243
Leominster	246
Ross	335
Rotherwas	336
Weobley	421

HERTFORDSHIRE

Barnet	64
Bishop's Stortford	83
Boxmoor	93
Hadham	198
Harpenden	203
Hertford	211
Hitchin	214
Hoddesdon	214
Old Hall Green, Ware	303
Rickmansworth	332
St Albans	340
Waltham Cross	411
Ware	415
Watford	419

HUNTINGDONSHIRE

Huntingdon	223
Ramsey	327

ISLE OF WIGHT

Appuldurcombe	54
Carisbrooke	117
Cowes	144
Freshwater	181
Newport	291
Ryde	338
Shanklin	351
Ventnor	407

KENT

Abbey Wood	45
Ashford	56

LANCASHIRE

LONDON, E.

LONDON, E.C.

LONDON, N.

LONDON, N.E.

LONDON, N.W.

Kilburn	235
Marylebone Rd	273
Mill Hill	279
St John's Wood	343
Willesden	435
Willesden Green	435

LONDON, S.E.

Anerley	54
Bermondsey:	
Holy Trinity	74
(South), St Gertrude	75
Blackheath	85
Brockley	102
Camberwell	114
Catford	119
Deptford	152
Dulwich (East)	159
Forest Hill	180
Greenwich:	
OL Star of the Sea	194
(East), St Joseph	195
Herne Hill	211
Lewisham	247
Melior St, Borough	276
Newington, West	290
Norwood	297
Norwood, West	298
Nunhead	299
Peckham	311
Rotherhithe	335
Southwark:	
Precious Blood	90
Cathedral	365
Stockwell, near Clapham	374
Sydenham	387
Vauxhall	407
Walworth:	
English Martyrs	412
St Alban	413

Waterloo:	
St Patrick	418
St Thomas of Canterbury	418

LONDON, S.W.

Balham	63
Battersea:	
Sacred Heart	69
(East), OL Mt Carmel	69
Brixton	101
Brompton Oratory	103
Chelsea:	
Holy Redeemer	123
St Mary	123
Clapham:	
St Mary	133
St Vincent of Paul	456
Park	133
Fulham	182
Fulham Palace Rd	182
Mortlake	283
Parsons Green	311
Putney	325
Roehampton	334
Streatham	380
Thornton Heath	391
Tooting	394
Wandsworth:	
St Thomas	413
East Hill	414
Westminster:	
SS Peter & Edw	425
St Mary	426
Cathedral	426

LONDON, W.

Acton	48
Bayswater	71
Chiswick	131
Ealing	161

Farm St, Berkeley Square	174
Hammersmith	199
Hanwell	202
Kensington:	
OL of Mt Carmel	233
OL of Victories	233
Ogle St	302
Portman Sq.French Chapel	319
Shepherds Bush	353
Spanish Place	366
Warwick St	417

LONDON, W.C.

Hatton Garden	207
Holborn	214
Leicester Square	245
Lincoln's Inn Fields	250
Maiden Lane, Strand	266
Soho	360

MIDDLESEX

Ashford	57
Brentford	95
Edmonton	165
Enfield	167
Finchley:	
East	178
North	178
Hampton Wick	201
Harrow-on-the-Hill	203
Hounslow	220
Isleworth	228
Lower Edmonton	260
Staines	370
Sunbury	382
Twickenham	399
Uxbridge	406
Wealdstone	419
Wembley	421
West Drayton	424

MONMOUTHSHIRE

Abergavenny	46
Abertillery	47
Chepstow	124
Coedangred	137
Cwmbran	149
Ebbw Vale	164
Glen-Trothy, near Abergavenny	186
Grosmont	195
Monmouth	281
Newport:	
St Mary	291
St Michael	292
Pontypool	317
Rhymney	331
Tredegar	397
Usk	405
Whitson Court, near Newport	431

NORFOLK

Costessey Hall	142
Cromer	147
Fakenham	173
Gillingham	185
Gorleston-on-Sea	189
Hunstanton	223
King's Lynn	237
Lynford	263
Lynn	264
Norwich:	
St George	297
St John	296
Oxburgh, Stoke Ferry	308
Thetford	390
Wroxham Hall, Norwich	451
Yarmouth	453

NORTHAMPTONSHIRE

Aston-le-Walls	59

Daventry	151	Thropton	391
Great Billing	192	Tynemouth	400
Kettering	234	Walker, Newcastle-on-Tyne	409
Northampton:		Wallsend	410
SS Mary & Thomas	294	Whittingham	431
St John	295	Willington	435
Peterborough	313	Wooler	445
Wellingborough	420		

NORTHUMBERLAND

NOTTINGHAMSHIRE

		Beeston	73
Alnwick	51	Bridgford	96
Amble	52	Carlton	118
Annitsford	54	Colston Bassett	139
Ashington	57	Eastwood	164
Backworth	62	Hucknall Torkard	221
Bedlington	77	Newark	286
Bellingham	73	Nottingham:	
Bells Close, Scotswood-on-Tyne	73	OL & St Patrick	299
Berwick-on-Tweed	75	St Barnabas	298
Biddlestone	76	St Edward	299
Blyth	87	Oldcotes, Worksop	303
Byker, near Newcastle-on-Tyne	113	Retford	330
Cheeseburn Grange	122	Staunton Hall	372
Cowpen	145	West Bridgford	422
Ellingham	166	Worksop	450
Felton	177		
Gosforth	190		

OXFORDSHIRE

Haydon Bridge	208		
Hexham	212	Banbury	63
Long Horsley	258	Begbrook, near Oxford	73
Lowick	261	Bicester	76
Minsteracres	279	Caversham	120
Morpeth	282	Chipping Norton	129
Newcastle-on-Tyne:		Dorchester	156
St Andrew	287	Goring-on-Thames	188
St Lawrence	288	Henley-on-Thames	210
St Mary	288	Hethe	212
New Hartley	289	Mapledurham	270
North Shields	295	Oxford	308
Prudhoe Hall	324	Radford	326
Swinburn	385	Souldern	362

Stonor, Henley-on-Thames 376
Wroxton Abbey, near Banbury 451

RUTLANDSHIRE

Exton 172
Oakham 302

SHROPSHIRE

Acton Burnell 48
Bridgnorth 96
Market Drayton 271
Mawley 275
Newport 292
Oswestry 307
Plowden 315
Shifnal 354
Shrewsbury 356
Wellington 420
Whitchurch 430

SOMERSET

Bath:
    St John the Evangelist 67
    St Mary's, Julian Rd 68
Bonham 89
Bridgewater 97
Burnham 109
Cannington 116
Clevedon 135
Clifton Cathedral 135
Downside, near Bath 157
East Harptree 163
Frome 182
Glastonbury 186
Langport 240
Minehead 279
Prior Park, near Bath 324
Shepton Mallet 354
Shirehampton, near Bristol 355

Taunton 388
Wells 421
Weston-Super-Mare 427
Wincanton 437
Yeovil 454

STAFFORDSHIRE

Alton 51
Ashley 58
Aston, near Stone 59
Bilston 77
Bloxwich 86
Brewood 95
Brierly Hill 97
Burslem 110
Burton-on-Trent 110
Cannock 116
Caverswall, near Cheadle 120
Chasetown 121
Cheadle 121
Cobridge 136
Colwich 139
Cresswell 146
Eccleshall 165
Goldenhill 188
Great Haywood 193
Hanley:
    OL & St Patrick 202
    Sacred Heart 202
Harborne, near Birmingham 203
Haunton, Tamworth 207
Hawkesyard, near Rugeley 207
Kidsgrove 235
Leek 244
Lichfield 249
Longton 259
Maryvale 274
Newcastle-under-Lyme 288
Oakamoor 301
Oscott, near Birmingham 306
Oulton 308

Rugeley	337	Caterham	119
Sedgley	350	Cheam	122
Sedgley Park - see Oakamoor		Chertsey	125
Smethwick	360	Chilworth, near Guildford	129
Stafford	369	Croydon:	
Stoke-on-Trent	375	St Mary	148
Stone	376	(South), St Gertrude	149
Swynnerton Park	386	Dorking	156
Tamworth	388	Earlsfield, near Tooting	161
Tunstall	398	Epsom	167
Uttoxeter	406	Farnham	175
Walsall	410	Frimley	181
Wednesbury	419	Godalming	187
West Bromwich	422	Guildford	195
Willenhall, near Wolverhampton	435	Kew	235
Wolverhampton:		Kingston-on-Thames	237
SS Mary & John	442	Mitcham	280
St Patrick	442	Molesey	281
SS Peter & Paul	441	Redhill	330
Wood Lane	445	Richmond	331
		Surbiton	383

SUFFOLK

		Sutton	384
		Sutton Park, near Guildford	384
Aldeburgh	50	Walton-on-Thames	412
Beccles	71	Weybridge	428
Bungay	108	Wimbledon	436
Bury St Edmunds	112	Wimbledon (South)	437
Coldham	138	Woking:	
East Bergholt	162	Inkerman Barracks	441
Felixstowe	176	St Dunstan	441
Ipswich	228	Wonersh, near Guildford	443
Lowestoft	260	Worcester Park	449
Southwold	366		
Stoke Nayland	374		
Stowmarket	379		
Sudbury	382		

SUSSEX

SURREY

		Angmering	54
		Arundel	55
Bagshot	62	Battle	70
Camberley	114	Beeding, near Bramber	72
Carshalton	118	Bexhill-on-Sea	76
		Bognor	87
		Bolney	88

Brighton:
    Sacred Heart 99
    St John the Baptist 98
    St Joseph 99
    St Mary Magdalen 99
Burgess Hill 109
Burton Park 111
Burwash 111
Chichester 127
Crawley 145
East Grinstead 162
Eastbourne 162
Hastings 206
Haywards Heath 208
Herons Ghyll 211
Horsham 218
Hove, Brighton 220
Lewes 247
Littlehampton 252
Mark Cross nr Tunbridge Wells 271
Midhurst 278
Newhaven 290
Parkminster 311
Petworth 314
Rottingdean 337
Rye 338
St Leonards-on-Sea 343
Seaford 349
Shoreham 355
Slindon, near Arundel 359
Storrington 378
Uckfield 401
Wadhurst 409
West Grinstead 424
Worthing 450

WARWICKSHIRE

Abbots Salford, Evesham 45
Acock's Green 456
Alcester 50
Atherstone 60

Avon Dasset 60
Baddesley Clinton, Knowle 62
Bedworth 72
Birmingham:
    Holy Family 456
    St Chad 81
    St Francis 82
    St John 456
    St Michael 82
    St Patrick 82
    St Peter 80
Brailes 94
Coleshill 139
Coughton 143
Coventry 143
Edgbaston 165
Erdington 168
Foxcote 180
Hampton-on-the-Hill 201
Kenilworth 232
Kingsheath 235
Leamington 242
Newnham Paddox 291
Nuneaton 299
Olton 305
Princethorpe, near Rugby 323
Redditch 329
Rugby 337
Solihull 361
Southam, near Rugby 362
Stratford-on-Avon 379
Studley 381
Sutton Coldfield 384
Wappenbury 414
Warwick 416
Wolvey 443
Wootton Wawen nr Birmingham 448

WESTMORLAND

Ambleside 52
Dodding Green 154

Kendal	232	Filey	178
Windermere	438	Hedon, near Hull	210
		Holme-on-Spalding-Moor	216

WILTSHIRE

		Houghton Hall, Sancton	219
		Howden	220
Chippenham	129	Hull:	
Devizes	153	St Charles Borromeo	221
Malmesbury	266	St Mary	222
Salisbury	345	St Patrick	222
Swindon	386	Marton	273
Tisbury	393	Pocklington	316
Trowbridge	397	York:	
Wardour Castle, Tisbury	415	English Martyrs	455
		St George	454

WORCESTERSHIRE

		St Mary's Convent	454
		St Wilfrid	455

YORKSHIRE, N.R.

Blackmore Park	85		
Broadway	102	Aiskew	49
Bromsgrove	104	Brotton-in-Cleveland	105
Dudley	158	Brough Hall nr Catterick	105
Evesham	171	Danby - see Leyburn	
Great Malvern:		Easingwold	161
OL & St Edmund	267	Egton Bridge, Grosmont	165
St Joseph	267	Grangetown	190
Hadzor	198	Kilvington	235
Harvington	204	Lartington, near Barnard Castle	241
Kidderminster	235	Leyburn	248
Little Malvern	253	Loftus, Saltburn-by-the-Sea	258
Selly Park	351	Malton	266
Spetchley	367	Middlesbrough	277
Stanbrook Abbey	371	Northallerton	294
Stourbridge	378	Osmotherley	307
Upton-on-Severn	403	Pickering	314
Worcester	448	Redcar	329
		Richmond	332

YORKSHIRE, E.R.

		Scarborough	346
Ampleforth, Oswaldkirk	53	Scorton	348
Beverley	76	Southbank	363
Bridlington Quay	97	Staithes	370
Driffield	158	Stokesley	375
Everingham	170		

YORKSHIRE, W.R.

ABBREVIATIONS

C.J.	= Congregation of Josephites.
C.P.	= Congregation of Passionists.
C.R.L.	= Canons Regular of the Lateran.
C.SS.R.	= Congregation of the Most Holy Redeemer.
Fr.	= Father (used in this book for both secular and regular clergy).
I.S.A.	= Institute of St. Andrew.
M.R.	= Missionary Rector.
M.S.C.	= Missionaries of the Sacred Heart.
O.C.D.	= Order of Discalced Carmelites.
O.F.M.	= Order of Friars Minor.
O.P.	= Order of Preachers (Dominicans).
O.S.B.	= Order of St. Benedict.
O.S.F.	= Order of St. Francis.
O.S.F.C.	= Order of Franciscan Capuchins.
O.S.M.	= Order of Religious Servants of the Holy Virgin, Servites.
S.C.	= Salesian Congregation.
S.J.	= Society of Jesus.
V.A.	= Vicar Apostolic.
V.F.	= Vicar Foraneus, Vicar Forane, or 'Rural Dean.'
V.A.L.D.	= Vicar Apostolic of the London District.
V.A.M.D.	= Vicar Apostolic of the Midland District.
V.A.N.D.	= Vicar Apostolic of the Northern District.
V.A.W.D.	= Vicar Apostolic of the Western District.
V.G.	= Vicar-General.

BIBLIOGRAPHY

The following are the chief sources of information consulted in drawing up the present work :

1. 'Records of the English Province of the Society of Jesus,' by Brother Foley.
2. Mr. J. Orlebar Payne's 'Old English Catholic Missions' and 'Records of the English Catholics of 1715.'
3. 'The Catholic Church in England and Wales during the last two Centuries,' edited for the XV. Club (Burns and Oates, 1892).
4. 'Catholic England in Modern Times,' by Rev. J. Morris, S.J. (Burns and Oates, 1892).
5. 'Troubles of Our Catholic Forefathers,' by the same.
6. 'Historical Memoirs of the English, Irish, and Scottish Catholics,' by C. Butler (London : John Murray, 1819).
7. 'The Catholic Magazine,' 1832–35.
8. 'The Catholic Miscellany,' 1823–24.
9. The 'Orthodox Journal,' 1839–42.
10. The 'Tablet,' weekly newspaper, 1840–1906.
11. Lewis's 'Topographical Dictionary of England and Wales.'
12. Lingard's 'History of England.'
13. Challoner's 'Memoirs of Missionary Priests.'
14. 'Religious Worship Census,' 1851 (Eyre and Spottiswoode, 1853).
15. 'Bibliographical Dictionary of the English Catholics,' by Joseph Gillow, (Burns and Oates).
16. 'The Laity's Directory,' 1793 and 1824–38.
17. 'The Catholic Directory,' 1838–1906.
18. 'The London Catholic Directory and Almanac,' 1900–1906.
19. 'The Downside Review' (various numbers).
20. 'Catholic London a Century Ago,' by Mgr. Canon Ward.
21. 'The Franciscans in England,' 1600–1850, by Rev. Father Thaddeus, O.F.M. (Art and Book Co., 1898).
22. 'The History of Sedgley Park School,' by Mgr. F. C. Husenbeth (Richardson and Son, 1856).
23. 'The Catholic Times,' weekly newspaper, from about 1892.
24. 'Collections,' by George Canon Oliver, D.D. (London : Charles Dolman, 1857).

MISSIONS

N.B.—In the lists of the Clergy only the names of the head priests or 'rectors' are given. The dates of appointment are approximate.

A

ABBEY WOOD, KENT (*South-wark*).

The congregation of the Filles de Jésus, expelled from France under the Law of Associations, established a convent here in 1904. The chapel, which is open to the public, is for the present served from Plumstead.

N.B.—The name of the locality is derived from Lesnes Abbey, an Augustinian house, founded in 1178 by Richard de Lucy, and dedicated to St. Thomas of Canterbury. It was among the number of smaller monasteries suppressed by Cardinal Wolsey, 1524. The revenues were granted to New College, Oxford, as an endowment.

ABBOTS SALFORD, EVESHAM, WARWICKSHIRE (*Birmingham*).

The Jesuit Fathers occasionally visited Evesham to say Mass and administer the sacraments for the benefit of the faithful few that clung to the old religion in spite of the penal laws. Fr. T. Roper, S.J., was priest at Evesham from 1693 to about 1700. This excellent priest was a near relation of the Lords Teynham, the lineal descendants of the Blessed Thomas More. After the dissolution, Henry VIII. granted Abbots Salford and Evesham Abbey to Sir Philip Hoby. The property ultimately passed to the Stanfords, one of whom, Charles Stanford, built the Hall, 1610. Mrs. Stanford, the last of the family, lent the Hall to some Benedictine nuns expelled from France by the Revolution. The community resided here from 1807 to 1838. The property is now owned by the Eyston family.

Priests since 1727.

Rev. Francis Southcot, 1727.
„ Francis Bruning, 1730.
„ John Daniel, 1760.
„ Thos. Ballyman, 1768.
„ Edmund Hadley, 1775.
„ Richard Reeve, 1778.
„ Edw. Wright, 1781.
„ J. Conzi, 1797.
„ P. F. Chandon, 1800.
„ Chris. Louvel, 1804.
„ Ralph Shaw, ⎫
„ James Norman, ⎬ 1808–1818.
„ Stephen Barber, ⎭
„ Thos. Wassal, O.S.B., 1818.
„ Thos. Lawson, 1823.
„ L. Barber, ⎫
„ J. Kenyon, ⎬ 1830–37.
„ John Abbot, ⎭
„ Joseph Short, 1837.
„ S. Barber, O.S.B., 1838.
„ Henry Richmond, 1844.
„ Ambrose Courtenay, 1853.

Rev. Edw. Kenny, 1854.
„ Pat. Hartigan, 1858.
„ A. Crane, 1882.
„ Wm. Stoker, 1885.
„ Canon McCave, 1889.
„ John B. Caldwell, 1892.
„ A. Crane (second time), 1893.
„ F. Sutherland, 1896.
„ Canon O'Hanlon, 1901.
„ James Giblin, 1901.
„ James Bredin, 1904.

ABERFORD, WEST RIDING, YORKS (*Leeds*).

This mission, according to the statement of the Rev. John Robinson, was founded in 1786. In the later part of the eighteenth century it would appear to have been served by Benedictines. Fr. Steare, O.S.B., was priest at Aberford in 1765, but, as there was then no chapel, he resided at Parlington, a few miles distant. The registers date from 1806, but no priest's signature appears in them before 1810, when the Rev. W. Chew had charge of the mission.

Priests since 1824.
Rev. Allerton.
„ J. Robinson, 1829.
„ A. Atkinson, 1843.
„ F. Williams, O.S.B., 1866.
„ G. Fazakerley, O.S.B., 1877.
„ Jos. Warden, O.S.B., 1892.
„ Jn. Carew, O.S.B., 1893.
„ F. Hickey, O.S.B., 1896.

ABERGAVENNY, MONMOUTH-SHIRE (*Newport*). St. Michael.

A Franciscan mission was established here 1687. The house of the Order was in Frogmore Street, and was the gift of Peter Morgan, Esq., who gave it in trust to Mrs. Mary Roberts. Mrs. Gun-

ter and Mrs. F. Watkins were also early benefactresses of the foundation. The Franciscan title of the mission was that of the Immaculate Conception. The building was enlarged, 1793, owing to a bequest of Mr. Weld, of Lulworth, and other benefactions from Mr. Jones and Miss Prodger. The place ceased to be an official residence of the Preses or Guardian in 1809, though priests of the Order continued to live there till 1847. A Chapter was held here in 1835. In 1850 the Catholic population was about 400; in 1856, 600; in 1864, 800. The old chapel having long become inadequate, the present church was commenced in 1858 and finished May 1860. The cost of erection was largely defrayed by Mrs. Andrus. A fine painted window recalls the memory of Baker-Gabb, Esq., another benefactor, who died September 16, 1858. One of the lights represents Fr. Augustine Baker, O.S.B., a native of the town, who suffered at Usk for the faith in 1679, during the Titus Oates plot. The mission was taken over by the Benedictines in 1857.

' Guardians' of the Mission.
Rev. Pacificus Williams, 1687.
„ Chas. Watkins, 1701.
„ Mat. Pritchard, 1713. Bishop of the Western District, 1715–50.
„ Chas. Watkins, 1716.
„ Lewis Lewis, 1725.
„ Chas. Watkins, 1726.
„ Leo. Barker, 1738.
„ Gregory Powell, 1740.
„ Anselm Copley, 1755.
„ Gregory Powell, 1764.
„ Alexius Whalley, 1767.
„ Andrew Weetman, 1770.
„ Augustine Hickins, 1773.
„ Angelus Ingram, 1774.
„ Gregory Watkins, 1776.

Rev. Geo. Lancaster, 1779.
„ Andrew Weetman, 1781.
„ Gregory Watkins, 1782.
„ Hy. Waring, 1785.
„ Bernardine Fleet, 1787.
„ Gregory Watkins, 1788.
„ Paschal Harrison, 1791.
„ Greg. Watkins, 1794.
„ Thos. Cottrell, 1800.
„ Greg. Watkins, 1803.
„ Peter Jones, 1805.
„ Stephen Grafton, 1806.
„ Greg. Watkins, 1808.
From 1825 the priests in charge of the mission have been :
Rev. Ignatius Richards, O.S.F.
„ Francis Hendren, O.S.F., 1826, Bishop of Clifton, 1850.
„ Anselm Millward, O.S.F., 1839.
„ F. Wilfrid Price, O.S.B., 1857.
„ J. B. Caldwell.
„ A. P. Wilson, 1863.
„ J. B. Caldwell (second time), 1866.
„ Robt. Guy, 1877.
„ Henry J. O'Hare, 1885.
„ Romuald Morgan, 1888.
„ C. Wray, to date.

ABERTILLERY, MONMOUTH-SHIRE (*Newport*). St. Mary.
The town, which is engaged in the iron-smelting industry, 'lies deep in the wildest of the wild recesses among the hills.' When the Franciscans established the mission here in 1874, the place was in the utmost spiritual destitution. Occasionally ' the poor people would trudge over the hills to Pontypool or Abersychan ' to have a child baptised or get the priest to a sick call, but beyond this no signs of Catholicity were manifested. The first ' chapel ' was a club-room in a public-house. The foundation-stone of the present ' plain simple chapel' was laid by Bishop Hedley, then coadjutor of Newport, October 5, 1875. The building, which was opened 1877, was for some time served from Brynmawr, but now from Pontymister.

ABINGDON, BERKS (*Portsmouth*). SS. Mary and Edmund of Canterbury.
The mission was established through the zeal and liberality of the late Sir George Bowyer, Q.C., M.P. Mass was said on March 6, 1856, in the library of his house by Bishop Grant, of Southwark. The aisle and chancel of the present church were blessed by Mgr. Virtue, afterwards Bishop of Portsmouth, September 30, 1857. The style of the building is decorated Gothic ; architect, W. Wardell. The edifice was completed October 1865. A bell cot was added to the building in August 1884. The cemetery was consecrated by Bishop Grant, June 1, 1858.
Priests.
Rev. J. O. Toole, D.D., 1857.
„ Robert Kavanagh, 1876.
„ Edward Collins, 1881.
„ Francis Canon Kelleher, 1885 to date.

ACCRINGTON, LANCS (*Salford*). The Sacred Heart.
When the Catholic chapel was built in 1852, the Catholics of Accrington numbered 500. The new church was commenced 1867, the congregation then numbering 3,000, with 1,200 regular communicants. Fr. Maguire, who had charge of the mission about 1860, obtained the site from J. Peel, Esq., and started the church building-fund. The style of the building

which was opened in 1868, is thirteenth century Gothic, designed by Messrs. Wilson and Nichol. The accommodation is for 1,000 persons. The total cost was about £6,300.

Priests (Jesuits).

Rev. Joseph Walmesley, 1853.
  „ Edw. Whyte, 1855.
  „ Hy. Shea, 1857.
  „ James Maguire, 1860.
  „ Thos. Brindle, 1870.
  „ Thos. Swift, 1888.
  „ Edw. Lucas, 1891.
  „ Arthur Yates, 1895.
  „ Joseph Martin, 1899 to date.

ACKWORTH GRANGE, near PONTEFRACT, YORKS (*Leeds*). The Sacred Heart.

The present church was erected in 1846 by Lady Tempest, at a cost of £10,000. The church, which is described as 'a beautiful gem,' was designed by Mr. Myers. A chapel, served by the Jesuit Fathers, was opened at Pontefract (*q.v.*) in 1710. The mission does not figure as such till 1863, when it was served from Pontefract. In 1875 the mission is marked 'vacant.'

Rectors from 1883.

Rev. Joseph Schropp.
  „ Bernard Speet, 1888.
  „ James Canon Glover, 1896.
  „ Charles Walsh, 1901 to date.

ACOCK'S GREEN, WARWICKSHIRE. *See* APPENDIX.

ACTON, LONDON, W. (*Westminster*). Our Lady of Lourdes.

A Benedictine mission formerly existed at Acton, but when commenced or given up does not appear. The present mission was opened by Fr. Joseph Butt, of Hammersmith,

August 2, 1848. Bishop Morris, of Troy, officiated, and the Hon. and Rev. Fr. Spencer preached. From 1853 the chapel was served from Turnham Green (*see* CHISWICK). The district was described about this time as 'the poorest and most needy mission in the diocese,' the schools being supported by 'charitable contributions.' After 1856 Acton became part of the Chiswick 'parish,' but reappeared as an independent mission 1879, when a temporary chapel was opened at 2 Gloucester Villas, Shakespeare Road. By 1883 an iron church had been erected in Strafford Road. The present Romanesque church, designed by E. Goldie, Esq., was opened September 28, 1902, by Mgr. (now Bishop) Fenton. Seating capacity for over five hundred. Cost of church £5,000. Murillo's 'Good Shepherd' hangs in the east transept, and the sanctuary has recently been decorated with frescoes after Perugino and Benozzo Gozzoli. The magnificent high altar is in memory of Cardinal Vaughan. Number of the congregation about two thousand.

Priests.

Rev. Joseph Butt, 1848.
  „ H. Green, 1848.
  „ Thos. Heptonstall, 1849.
  „ J. Clark, 1852.
  „ John Bonus, LL.D., 1853 ; till 1879, mission served from Turnham Green and Chiswick.
  „ James O'Connell, 1879.
  „ Cornelius Bidle, 1882.
  „ H. T. Bradbee, 1885.
  „ C. E. Rivers, M.A., 1893 to date.

ACTON BURNELL (*Salop*).

Mass was said here throughout the penal times in the mansion of the ancient family of Smythe.

From 1748 till 1856 the priests lived at the Hall. In 1792 the Visitation nuns flying from the fury of the Revolution settled here for a short time before proceeding to Shepton Mallet (*q.v.*) Two years later, the Benedictines of Lambspring in Bavaria came to England and opened a college at Acton Burnell in a house presented to them by Sir Edward Smythe, Bart. They removed to Downside, near Bath, in 1814. In March 1846, a new Gothic church, dedicated to St. Peter, was opened at Acton Burnell, mainly owing to the benefactions of Mr. and Mrs. Smythe. Mr. C. Hansom was the architect; the rich stained-glass window over the high altar is the work of Wailes. Other stained-glass windows in the beautiful mortuary chapel represent various members of the Smythe family in attitudes of devotion. The high altar, dedicated to St. Edward the Confessor, was consecrated at the date of opening. The cemetery was laid out in 1858.

Priests at Acton Burnell—all Benedictines.

Rev. Francis Rookwood, 1748.
„ Ambrose Elliot, 1762.
„ Bernard Bradshaw, 1762.
„ Thomas Ballyman, 1774.
„ Peter Kendal, 1795.
„ Ralph Radcliffe, 1814 (died suddenly while going to a sick call, 1842).
„ Bernard Paillett, 1842.
„ Augustine Rolling, 1842.
„ Cuthbert Smith, 1846.
„ F. Stanislaus Giles, 1856.
„ John B. Caldwell, 1876.
„ John B. Davey, 1878.
„ James Riley, 1885.
„ James Talbot, 1886.
„ John Stutter, 1889 to date.

ADDINGHAM, WEST RIDING, YORKSHIRE (*Leeds*).

The mission was started in 1904, the first priest being Father Alfred Galli. The chapel at present consists of two rooms at the top of a private house. Addingham is famous as being the birthplace of the Blessed Richard Kirkman, priest, who suffered for the faith at York, August 22, 1582, and also of the Blessed Richard Horner, who suffered at York for the same cause, September 4, 1598.

AINSDALE, SOUTHPORT, LANCS (*Liverpool*). The Sacred Heart.

A school chapel was opened here August 15, 1878. The building, which was presented by T. Weld-Blundell, Esq., accommodates about 150.

Priests.

Rev. W. Spencer, 1878.
„ Wm. Lennon, 1888.
„ George Rigby, 1890.
„ Wm. Smith, 1892.
„ J. McFarlane, 1893.
„ F. Soden, 1902.
„ Edward O'Reilly, 1904 to date.

AISKEW, YORKS (*Middlesbrough*). SS. Mary and Joseph.

The old chapel was erected 1812, at which time the registers commence. The present chapel was opened July 4, 1878, by Bishop Cornthwaite, of Beverley, on a site presented by Lord Beaumont. The cost was bequeathed by Lady Throckmorton. Messrs. Goldie and Child were the architects; accommodation for 250; cost about £1,700. The building is described as resembling in appearance an old village church.

E

Priests.

Rev. McQuaide.
„ Jos. Sherwood, 1831.
„ Geo. Keasley, 1860.
„ Laurence McGonnell, 1863.
„ Edw. O'Leary, 1866.
„ L. McGonnell, 1870 (second time).
„ Lawrence Schoch, 1877.
„ James Griffin, 1881.
„ Wm. O'Connor, 1888.
   Mission served from North-allerton, 1891-5.
„ James Butler, 1896.
„ Richard Lewis, to date.

ALCESTER,   WARWICKSHIRE (*Birmingham*).   Our Lady and St. Joseph.

The mission was established in 1889, and served from Coughton by Fr. Francis Doyle, O.S.B. In 1896 Fr. Lawrence Larkins, O.S.B., was rector. His successors have been : Rev. Robt. Kershaw, 1897 ; David Bede Ryan, O.S.B., 1902 to date.

ALDEBURGH, SUFFOLK (*North-ampton*).

In 1904 a community of Ursuline Sisters, long established in France, acquired Thellusson Lodge at Alde-burgh, where they have commenced a boarding school. The chapel is open to the public, and for the time serves the mission. The Rev. Henry Mosnier, chaplain.

ALDERSHOT,   HANTS (*Ports-mouth*).   St. Joseph's.

In 1869 Bishop Grant, of South-wark, sent Father J. Purcill to establish a permanent mission in the town, exclusive of the existing military chapels at North and South Camps. A disused tavern was acquired, and by some archi-tectural manipulation transformed into a temporary chapel. This place of worship was opened July 29 by Bishop Morris, of Troy. By August 14 of the same year the congregation amounted to 200 re-gular attendants. Efforts are at present being made to erect 'a National Memorial Church' in memory of Catholic soldiers killed in South Africa (1899-1902).

Priests.

Rev. J. Purcill, 1869.
„ Louis Hall, 1871.
„ R. Davis, 1875.
„ Justin Mooney, 1881.
„ Edw. Riordan, 1885 to 1902.
„ Francis O'Farrell, 1902 to date.

ALFRETON, DERBYSHIRE (*Not-tingham*).   St. Mary.

The church was opened June 3, 1883, by Canon McKenna, V.G. The style is Gothic, the building consisting of nave, chancel, and sacristy. The bell turret was pre-sented by Father D. Meenagh, first priest of the mission. The seating accommodation is for about 120. On Sunday, October 20, 1901, the fine east window of painted glass was wilfully destroyed.

ALLERTON   PARK,   near KNARESBOROUGH, YORKS (*Leeds*). St. Mary.

The district was one of the many served by the Jesuit 'College' or residence of St. Michael the Arch-angel, *temp.* James I., but no records of the history of the mission are available. The foundation of the chapel is given as 1807. The registers commence in 1816. Like the neighbouring mission of Knaresborough, Allerton Park owes its preservation as a centre of Catholicity to the noble family of Stourton. The name of the place disappeared from the 'Catholic Directory' in 1853, but was again inserted in 1894. During that time the priest resided at the adjoining Stourton.

Priests.

Rev. Thos. Rolling, 1824.
„ Chas. or Thos. Weston, 1835.
„ Jn. Bridge, 1842.
„ James Canon Glover, 1894.
„ Julius de Baere, 1897.
„ Joseph Dewe, 1898.
„ Ernest Levick, 1900 to date.

ALNWICK, NORTHUMBERLAND (*Hexham and Newcastle*). St. Mary.

In 1752 Mrs. Mary Butler bequeathed some property to Fr. H. Sheldon, S.J., and from the proceeds of this the mission was established in 1755. The property in question was held in trust for the society by Ralph Clavering, Esq., of Callaly Castle. Joined to the bequest was the obligation of a monthly Mass for the Ord family. The old chapel or Mass-house was in Barliffgate Street. Fr. Francis Howard 'introduced' the people into 'the new chapel in Alnwick' August 14, 1796, and Bishop Gibson, V.A., confirmed twenty-seven persons on the 21st of the same month. The present chapel was opened September 8, 1836, and in July 1857 the Jesuits handed over the mission to the bishop of the diocese.

Priests.

Rev. H. Sheldon, 1755.
„ Nicholas Saunderson (died 1790).

Rev. Francis Howard, 1790.
„ John Beaumont, 1802.[1] This priest was a lineal descendant of Francis Beaumont the dramatist.
„ John Fishwick, 1833.
„ J. Woollett, 1853.
„ J. Gibson, 1856.
„ Edward Robert, 1891.
„ M. Forster, 1906 to date.

ALSTON, LANCS (*Liverpool*). Our Lady and St. Michael.

'Where the Wilsons, the Catons, the Edmondsons and the Cowbans, sterling good old priests—some of the last, some of the present century—laboured for the good of souls and the honour of their Heavenly Master.' (*Tablet*, September 12, 1857.) The old chapel or 'Masshouse,' dating from 1761, was superseded in September 1857 by a handsome church in the Early English style of architecture, capable of seating 600 to 700 persons. The structure is of stone, from the designs of E. Welby Pugin. The building cost about £1,500. Bishop Goss, of Liverpool, was present at the opening. The bulk of the money for the erection of the church was collected by the Rev H. Sharples, the then priest of the mission.

Priests since 1874.

Rev. Thos. Walton.
„ Thos. Bridges, 1897 to date.

ALTON, STAFFORDSHIRE (*Birmingham*). St. John.

Till 1833 Catholics in and about Alton were ministered to by the

[1] N.B. The Abbé Gautier, an émigré, assisted Fr. Beaumont for a short time.

E 2

priest at Alton Towers, the residence of the staunchly Catholic Earls of Shrewsbury. In that year a fine church in the Gothic style was erected by John, sixteenth Earl of Shrewsbury, to whose piety and munificence so many of the churches and chapels in the north and west of England are due. The church measures 90 feet by 30 feet, and is wainscoted in oak. The handsome altar of gilt-bronze stands in an oriel recess, lighted by a mullioned window adorned with figures of the four Evangelists. Copies of the 'Transfiguration' by Rafaelle and the 'Communion of St. Jerome' also adorn this church. In the sanctuary are, or were, two pictures by Pietro Perugino. In a niche outside the church, stands a pre-Reformation stone statue of St. Peter, the patron of the parish. Attached to the church are schools for boys and girls, also founded by Lord Shrewsbury. In 1834 the Catholics of Alton numbered 100. At present they exceed 400.

Priests at Alton.

Rev. Daniel Rock, D.D., 1827 ; author of 'Hierurgia' &c.; Canon of Southwark 1851 ; died 1871.

„ Henry Winter, D.D., 1840.
„ John O'Connor, 1866.
„ A. B. Gurdon, 1871.
„ W. J. Butler, 1879.
„ John Ullathorne, 1882 to date.

ALTRINCHAM, or ALTRINGHAM

(*Cheshire*). · St. Vincent of Paul.

The mission of Altrincham was started in 1847 in a small house in George Street. The number of Catholics there at that time is not recorded, but when the stone of the new church was laid on Thursday, May 27, 1858, the congregation amounted to about 400. The exiled members of Louis Philippe's family are said to have worshipped here. The new school at Hale Moss was opened February 2, 1872, and enlarged 1885.

Priests.

Rev. M. O'Reilly, 1847.
„ J. Berry, 1853.
„ W. Walton, 1855.
„ H. Alcock, 1858.
„ J. Canon O'Brien, 1876.
„ W. Stanley, 1898.
„ C. Ryder, 1903 to date.

AMBLE, NORTHUMBERLAND

(*Hexham and Newcastle*). St. Cuthbert.

The mission was served from Felton in 1877, during which year the present church was built. The Catholic population in 1890 numbered about 250, scattered over a wild district abounding in old families that had never lost the faith. One of these was the Scrowther family, of East Chevington, where a station for mission purposes was held during the eight days' mission preached at Amble in April 1890, by the late Fr. Jerome Vaughan, O.S.B.

Priests.

Rev. Edw. Robert, 1885.
„ Jn. Roth, 1888.
„ Mat. Culley, 1890.
„ M. Forster, 1893.
„ Chas. Dunne, 1897 to date.

AMBLESIDE, WESTMORLAND

(*Hexham and Newcastle*). Our Lady of Ambleside.

Mass was said here for the first time on Sunday, July 21, 1878, by Fr. J. McAuliffe, O.S.B. The chapel was an 'upper room' in a private house. In 1880 Canon Curry of Doddington said Mass here on alternate Sundays during the summer. A Gothic iron church was opened, August 1887. The altar-piece (*Mater Amabilis*) is by Sassoferrato. Fr. A. G. Brady, M.A. (Oxon.), was the first resident priest. Catholics of the district numbered eighty-five in 1890. In 1893 a Premonstratensian priory was erected, and the mission served for several years by that Order. The church is now attended on Sundays from Kirkstone Brow (1905).

AMPLEFORTH, OSWALDKIRK, YORK (*Middlesbrough*). St. Lawrence's Abbey and College.

The dilapidated and deserted church and cloister of St. Lawrence, Dieulouard, in the province of Lorraine, were offered in 1606 as a gift to the English Benedictines. The foundation from 1020 to 1602 had been an endowed canonry. The new occupants quickly raised the value of the property by skilful agricultural and brewing enterprises. In 1779, the house became the school of humanities for St. Gregory's, Douai, and so remained till suppressed by the Revolution, 1792-3. Prior Marsh, the fathers and students, after many vicissitudes, escaped to Trèves and thence to England. The community remained for some time at Acton Burnell, under the patronage of Sir E. Smythe, Bart., and after various brief sojourns at Birkenhead, Scholes, Vernon Hall, etc., finally settled at Ampleforth Lodge in 1802. This house, with thirty-two acres of land, had been given by Lady Fairfax as a place of retirement to her aged chaplain, Fr. Bolton, who made the property over to Prior Appleton. In 1803 the community consisted of two priests, five religious and nine boys. Six years later the first ordination took place at Ampleforth. The Vicar Apostolic was Bishop Gibson. The 'west wing' served as the college chapel for fifty years; the 'east wing' from 1815 till 1854 contained the old dormitories and college class-rooms. The fine Gothic church, commenced 1855, was completed in 1857. The new college block of class and lecture rooms was erected 1859-61. The much-needed monastery was started in 1894 and finished 1897. In 1900 Ampleforth was raised to the dignity of an abbey. The centenary of the college was celebrated July 21, 22, and 23, 1903.

ANDERTON, CHORLEY, LANCS (*Liverpool*). St. Joseph.

The first stone of the church was laid August 31, 1862, by Bishop Goss, of Liverpool. The style is Early English. The Stonors have a 'family tribune' in the church. The seating accommodation is for about 400 persons. At the west end of the building is erected an ancient pre-Reformation cross, which stood at Anderton some four centuries ago. The church was opened in December 1863. Charles J. Stonor, Esq., of Anderton, gave the church site and much of the materials with which the edifice is built. The schools were enlarged 1884 and again in 1894. Church and presbytery re-roofed 1889.

Priests.
Rev. Canon Greenhalgh, 1861.
„ Peter Kane, 1862.
„ Michael Donnelly, 1881.
„ J. Webster, 1883.
„ Thos. Smith, 1900 to date.

ANDOVER, HANTS (*Portsmouth*). The Rev. Dr. Val d'Eremao, of Basingstoke, opened the mission here on January 5, 1886. The chapel was at first in a private house, but afterwards temporary premises were rented. About twenty persons assembled for Mass on the first day. Fr. d'Eremao, after hearing confessions at Basingstoke on Saturday, went down to Andover by the last train, and on Sunday morning said Mass at 8.15, returning to Basingstoke to say his second mass at 11. From about 1897 the mission has been served from Winchester.

ANERLEY, LONDON, S.E. (*Southwark*). The Holy Child and St. Anthony of Padua.

Until 1878 the nearest mission was at Norwood. On October 25 of that year an iron church was opened in the Genoa Road. Canon A. Bethell, who purchased the church site, also erected the presbytery. He resigned in 1891, and shortly afterwards the temporary place of worship had to be given up. The present edifice of brick, opened May 14, 1898, consists of two stories, the upper being used as a chapel and the lower one as a school. The estimated Catholic population in 1900 was about 450.

Priests.

Rev. A. Canon Bethell, 1878.
,, Edmund Miller, 1891.
,, W. Thompson, 1900.
,, Thos. Neville, 1905 to date.

ANGMERING, SUSSEX (*Southwark*). St. Wilfrid.

The church was opened in 1872 and was the gift of the present Duke of Norfolk. The Catholic population of the district is about 100. Till the appointment of the present rector, the Rev. E. Von Orsbach, in 1902, the mission was served from Arundel.

ANGRAM, YORKSHIRE (*Leeds*).

An iron chapel costing £250 was opened here by Canon Croskell of the Cathedral, Leeds, on Sunday, May 13, 1906. The chapel, which has been mainly erected for the use of the navvies employed on the construction of a new reservoir for the Bradford Corporation, is for the present served from the Cathedral.

ANNITSFORD, NORTHUMBERLAND (*Hexham and Newcastle*). St. John the Baptist.

The mission was established in 1863 and for several years afterwards was described as being 'greatly in need of help.' A chapel was erected in 1866, and the new Church opened June 24, 1906.

Priests.

Rev. John O'Dwyer.
,, Henry Walmesley, 1881.
,, David Scott, 1899.
,, John Chapman, 1904 to date.

APPULDURCOMBE, ISLE OF WIGHT (*Portsmouth*). St. Peter's Abbey.

The Benedictines of Solesmes, near Nantes, expelled from France by the anti-christian policy of M. Combes and his government, settled here in 1900-1. The splendid Gothic abbey and church of the Order in France is represented by a moderately commodious mansion and iron chapel. A school of Gregorian or Plain Chant has been opened at the monastery, and already its influence is being felt in the liturgical world. It may be of interest to remark that the Abbey of Solesmes which was confiscated for the first time during the Great Revolution, was reoccupied by the Benedictines in 1830. The choir stalls have curious carvings representing the genealogy of Our Lord. The Community also possesses its valuable library of ancient MSS. and a sacred Thorn, which came into their possession at the time of the first Crusade.

APPLETON, LANCS (*St. Bede*). *See* Widnes.

ARNO'S COURT, CLIFTON (*Clifton*).

The church of the Convent of the Good Shepherd Order was opened March 29, 1859, by the Hon. and Rt. Rev. Dr. Clifford, Bishop of Clifton. The style is Lombardo-Byzantine. The sanctuary is lighted by a perforated arcade of five arches filled with stained glass. Mr. C. Hansom, of Clifton, was the architect.

ARUNDEL, SUSSEX (*Southwark*). St. Philip.

Owing to the adherence of the Dukes of Norfolk to the Catholic faith, a chapel was maintained here throughout a considerable portion of the penal times. The domestic chapel of St. George, within the precincts of Arundel Castle, remained the place of Catholic worship down to about 1790, when Charles, eleventh Duke of Norfolk, being then engaged in enlarging the Castle, removed the chapel to the site of the old College of the Blessed Trinity founded by Richard, Earl of Arundel, in 1380. The old ruins were restored, and the place continued to serve the purpose of

a church till the erection of the present magnificent building. The most noted priest at Arundel in recent times was the late Canon Mark A. Tierney, F.R.S., F.S.A., the well-known author of the 'History of Arundel' (2 vols., 1834), and continuator of Dodd's 'Church History from 1688 to 1800.' Canon Tierney was incumbent from 1824 till his death in February 1862. In 1873 the present cathedral church of St. Philip Neri, commenced in 1868, was opened by Bishop Danell of Southwark. The munificent donor was Henry, present Duke of Norfolk, who, it is said, expended over £100,000 on the building. The style is fourteenth century Gothic. A superb series of stations of the Cross by Messrs. Bolton have recently been erected in memory of the late Bishop Butt. Near the entrance of the church are two memorial brasses to Privates Madden and Glossop, natives of Arundel, who were killed in the great Boer War of 1899–1902. Fifty years ago the number of Catholics in Arundel is said to have amounted to only 100; at present (1904) it is over 1,200—more than half the population. By a judgment of the High Court about twenty years ago, half of the parish church, known as the 'Arundel Chapel,' was reserved for Catholic uses. Here are buried many generations of FitzAlan Howards, for the repose of whose souls Mass is offered up occasionally at the high altar. The magnificent east window depicting members of the Howard family assisting at the Holy Sacrifice was put in by the present Duke. With regard to the old chapel in use from 1791 to 1873, it measured 42 ft. by 20 ft., and had a fine altar adorned with gilt bronze, which, among the uninitiated, passed for 'real gold'! The altar-piece was a painting of the 'Adoration of the Shepherds.' A cottage school was established by Fr. Butt in King Street in 1858. The present fine schools in the Tudor style, were opened in 1885, and were the gift of the Duke of Norfolk. The sacristy of the church is rich in reliquaries and plate, including splendid Louis XV. silver candelabra, a silver relic case (Flemish, sixteenth century) embossed with scenes from the life of King David, said to have belonged to Philip II. of Spain, &c.

Priests.

Rev. Charles Cordell, 1748.
,, Joseph Addis, 1772.
,, — Fiswick, 1780.
,, Philip Wyndham, 1785.
,, Mark Canon Tierney, F.R.S., F.S.A., 1824.
,, John Butt, 1862 (assistant to Canon Tierney, 1858; Canon of Southwark, 1871; Bishop of Southwark, 1885; resigned, 1896; died, 1899).
,, John Burke, 1885.
,, A. S. MacCall, M.A., 1898 to date.

ASCOT, BERKS (*Portsmouth*). St. Francis.

The first stone of the new Franciscan church adjoining the monastery at South Ascot was laid by Bishop Virtue of Portsmouth, Tuesday, May 8, 1888. The building was opened and consecrated July 4, 1889. The style is Early English, the accommodation being for 500 persons. The Monks' choir is behind the high altar. The cost of erection was about £2,500. The site was generously given by E. F. Devenish Walsh, Esq., of Ascot. Prior to the erection of the church, Catholics in the neighbourhood of Ascot were allowed to attend Mass at the residence of C. J. Stonor, Esq., and also at the Convent of the Institute of the Blessed Virgin.

ASHBOURNE, DERBYSHIRE (*Nottingham*). All Saints.

For some time prior to 1888, the only place of Catholic worship was 'a contemptible old building.' The mission was established in 1848. As a result of numerous appeals, a plain but convenient Gothic church, designed by Simpson, was opened, August 26, 1888. Between 1850 and 1854, the mission was served from Maryvale and St. Wilfrid's.

Priests.

Rev. Wm. Daly, 1848.
,, R. Raby, 1855.
,, Jn. Cantwell, 1876.
,, Wm. O'Dwyer, 1879.
,, W. Otty, 1885.
,, J. O'Haire, 1888.
,, T. Middleton, 1892.
,, Hubert de Burgh, 1899.
,, Fredk. Brown, to date.

ASHFORD, KENT (*Southwark*). St. Teresa.

This was one of the places served by the Jesuit College or residence of St. Ignatius as far back as 1619. No record of the mission, however, has been handed down. Calehill, near Ashford, was the ancient seat of the Catholic family of Darell, and their chaplains attended Catholics in the neighbourhood till after the establishment of the Ashford mission. In 1857 Fr. Sheridan, of Calehill, hired a room in New Street, Ashford, for Mass on Sundays. The premises are now a public-house known as the 'Three Ones' (1 1 1). In 1859 a temporary chapel was opened in Chart Terrace, afterwards removed to 20 Queen Street, the residence of Mrs. Wood, whose husband was the priest's right-hand man. The mission was also greatly assisted about this time by a Mrs. Piddlesden, who 'kept the handful of Catholics together and arranged for a priest to come and give Mass on Sundays.' The present church on Barrow Hill was opened by Bishop Grant, August 22, 1865. £300 of the building expenses were contributed by Lady Tufton. Archbishop Manning preached (St. Luke i. 46). The Dover choir, under the direction of Fr. Laws, sang the Mass. A stone altar was erected in March 1867, and the sanctuary was completed 1892. The presbytery was erected 1888. A school in the Victoria Road was opened October 1, 1899, at a cost of £2,015 13s. 7d. A Convent High School, under the direction of the Sisters ' de l'Enfance de Jésus,' was established in 1903. The Darell family is now extinct, the last member, Major Darell (60th Rifles), dying in 1869. The Confirmation records at the old family chapel are as follows: confirmations by Bishop Poynter, December 8, 1812; by Bishop Bramston, July 11, 1830; by Bishop Griffiths, November 14, 1844; by Bishop Wiseman, September 23, 1849; by Bishop Grant, May 24, 1858, October 28, 1860, April 19, 1863, August 22, 1865.

Chaplains at Calehill.
Rev. John Bullock, 1791–1819.
„ John Russell, Peter Portier, Hy. Riley, James Crosby, 1819.
„ Joseph Addis, 1819-21.
„ Thos. Percy, 1821.
„ Francis Tuite, 1825.
„ John Tuomy, 1826.
„ Wm. Ryan, O.S.B., 1827.
„ John Kyne, 1842.
„ J. R. Hearn, 1845.
„ Hy. S. Philips, 1846.

Rev. Wm. Harris, 1848.
„ Jn. McDonald, 1850.
„ Jn. Butt, 1852 (Bishop of Southwark, 1885-96).
„ J. P. O'Toole, 1854.
„ H. C. Logan, 1855.
„ Edw. Sheridan, 1857.
Priests at Ashford.
Rev. Edw. Sheridan, 1857.
„ A. Oromi, 1859.
„ Thos. Moore, 1871.
„ Daniel Spillane, 1872.
„ Thos. Quinn, 188). Mission served from Ramsgate, 1884.
„ F. Reynaert, 1885.
„ C. Turner, 1897.
„ P. Mason, 1904.

ASHFORD, MIDDLESEX (*Westminster*).

In 1899 the Sisters of the Order of the Good Shepherd acquired 'Ecclesfield,' a commodious mansion and extensive estate adjoining, for use as a female inebriates' home. The chapel, which is open to the public, is so arranged as to keep the inmates unseen by the external worshippers. A site for a mission church was purchased September 1906 (£200) and the building will be opened for worship in December.
Chaplains.
Rev. R. D. Browne, 1899.
„ E. M. Daniell, 1904.
„ — Cave, 1906 to date.

ASHINGTON, NORTHUMBERLAND (*Hexham and Newcastle*).
St. Aidan.

The mission was started in 1892 and served from Morpeth till 1895. The church was opened 1895. The present rector, Fr. John O'Hear, O.S.B., was appointed the same year.

ASHLEY, STAFFORDSHIRE (*Birmingham*). Our Blessed Lady and St. John the Baptist.

The chapel, 'a neat and commodious edifice,' as the 'Catholic Miscellany' of the day described it, was opened October 29, 1823. The first title of the mission was St. Brigit. For some time it was served in conjunction with Cobridge. Fr. Egan was appointed first resident priest in 1827.

Priests.

Rev. Egan, 1827.

„　Holland, 1828.

„　Gates, 1835.

„　E. Hodson, 1840.

„　F. McGrath, 1849.

　　Mission served from Swynnerton Park, 1861, *et seq.*; at present from Eccleshall.

ASHTON-IN-MAKERFIELD (*Liverpool*).

A new chapel and altar of Our Lady of the Holy Rosary was solemnly dedicated Sunday, November 6, 1887. These additions to the church were erected by the Rev. Dean O'Reilly and the congregation, in memory of Robert Tolver, first Lord Gerard, who died March 15, 1887. Lord Gerard was a great benefactor to the mission, which was commenced in 1822, when the old chapel of St. Oswald was built. There were no Catholic schools in 1830, but fifteen years later there were both day and Sunday schools, with about 300 pupils; 145 children and adults were confirmed at the chapel on Sunday, September 14, 1845, by Bishop Sharples. The church was rebenched, refloored, and supplied with new altar rails in 1891.

ASHTON-UNDER-LYNE, LANCS (*Salford*).

Mission established 1857. In 1868 (August) the 'poor chapel' of the place was nearly destroyed by an anti-Catholic mob incited by one Murphy, a notorious Protestant lecturer. The large crucifix was injured by pistol shots, and windows and pews broken. The priest, Fr. J. Beesly, endeavoured to obtain compensation, but, after a trial of the case before the Salford Hundred Court, was non-suited on the ground that 'the mob did not intend entirely to demolish'! Several of the rioters, however, were convicted before Mr. Justice Hannen at the assizes, and sentenced to various terms of imprisonment. The chapel at Ashton-under-Lyne was built 1858–59 by the zealous Fr. W. Crombleholme, who died at Lawrence, Mass., U.S.A., in January 1884.

Priests since 1886.

Rev. Geo. Richardson.

„　Adolphus Coelcubier, 1888.

„　Martin Meagher, 1899.

„　James Murray, to date.

ASPULL, near WIGAN (*Salford*). Our Lady of the Immaculate Conception.

The foundation-stone of the church was laid March 19, 1857. The ceremony took place in the presence of about one thousand persons, mostly miners, the ground being cut and prepared by a body of Irish labourers 'as a free-will offering to the work.' The Bishop of Salford at the conclusion of the function explained to the assembled multitude the doctrine of the Immaculate Conception. Fredk. Gerard, Esq., brother of Sir R. Gerard, Bart., laid the second stone. The building was opened April 25, 1858.

Priests.

Rev. Hy. Jones, 1857.
„ P. O'Reilly.
„ T. Allen, 1874.
„ Jos. Crilly, 1882.
„ H. Schürgers, 1889.
„ Jn. Welch, 1896 to date.

ASTLEY BRIDGE, BOLTON, LAN-CASHIRE (*Salford*). The Holy Infant and St. Anthony.

The chapel was opened July 22, 1877, and served from St. Mary's, Bolton, till 1882. The congregation is now estimated at 1,000.

Priests.

Rev. Maximilian Jüttner, 1882.
„ Pius de Witte, 1885.
„ P. M. O'Reilly, 1888.
„ John Darby, 1893.
„ A. M. Vantomme, 1894 to date.

ASTON-LE-WALLS, NORTHAMP-TONSHIRE (*Northampton*).

Wm. Plowden, Esq., a staunch Jacobite and supporter of James II. at the Boyne, settled here shortly after the Revolution. He rebuilt the mansion at Aston-le-Walls, but being a Catholic soon acquired the resentment of his Whig neighbours. His coach-horses were seized by virtue of the Act against Nonjurors, and Mr. Plowden in disgust quitted the neighbourhood. The hall was pulled down with the exception of one wing, which was turned into a farmhouse. This branch of the Plowdens was connected by marriage with the Butlers, the original owners of Aston-le-Walls. One of them was Chas. Butler, of Lincoln's Inn (1750–1832), the eminent Conveyancer and Catholic publicist. It is probable that a chapel was maintained here during the eighteenth century and down to the building of the present chapel in 1827. No mention is made of the mission in the 'Laity's Directory' till 1833.

Priests.

Rev. J. Fox ; J. Perry, 1835.
„ J. B. Marsh, 1850.
„ Jn. Duff, 1853.
Rev. Wm. Canon Hammond here, 1872, and till 1901.
„ Harold Squirrell, to date.

ASTON, near **STONE, STAFFS** (*Birmingham*). St. Michael.

A very old mission. Aston Hall was for centuries the seat of the ancient Catholic family of Heveningham. The last male representative was Sir John Heveningham, whose daughter married Sir James Simeon, Bart., of Brightwell, and their only daughter married Humphrey Weld, Esq., of Lulworth Castle. In 1814 the Franciscans opened their noviciate at Aston with the full approval of Bishop Milner. In 1826 it was decided not to take any more novices in England. The estate subsequently passed into Protestant hands, but the house and a few acres were made over by the Welds to the V.A. of the Midland District for the purpose of continuing the mission. In 1842 the Passionist Fathers commenced a foundation at Aston. The chapel was still in the large room over the kitchen. The stone of the new church was laid May 21, 1847, by Bishop Walsh, V.A.M.D., Bishop (afterwards Cardinal) Wiseman preaching the inaugural sermon. The Hon. Fr. Ignatius Spencer sang the Mass. The Hon. Miss Langdale presented £100 to the building fund. The church was opened 1849. The Passionists gave up the mission 1854, after which it was served from Stone for some years. During the rectorate of Mgr. E. Hulme (1840-42) the relics of St. Chad were discovered beneath the altar of the Aston chapel. They had been removed from Lichfield Cathedral at the time of the Reformation by Prebendary Arthur Dudley, and, after being preserved by the Fitzherberts of Swynnerton, were sent to Aston for safety.

Priests since 1858.
Rev. Edward Canon Huddlestone.
„ Stuart Bathurst, 1877.
(Mission served from Stone, 1881-98.)
„ M. Glancey, 1898.
„ Jn. Price, 1900.

ATHERSTONE, WARWICKSHIRE (*Birmingham*). St. Scholastica's Priory.

The Benedictine nuns of St. Benedict's Priory, near Colwich, took over the premises from the Dominicans and opened a branch house here in May 1859. The nuns are strictly enclosed, have no schools, and a chief feature of the spiritual life of the place is the perpetual adoration of the Blessed Sacrament. The church was consecrated by Bishop Ullathorne, September 4, 1861. The house and chapel were commenced November 4, 1837, and opened as a Dominican Convent in September 1839. The chapel, which measures 58 ft. by 23½ ft., from the very first proved a great attraction, and was described as being 'crowded every Sunday' with persons mostly protestants.

ATHERTON, LANCS (*Liverpool*). St. Richard.

The mission was established at Chowbent, 1890, and for some years

served from Tyldesley. It became a separate mission 1895.
Priests.
Rev. Andrew Flynn, 1895.
„ Jules Maurus, 1899.
„ Geo. Walmsley 1904, to date.

AUGHTON, ORMSKIRK, LANCS (*Liverpool*). St. Mary.

The great growth of Catholicity in and around Aughton led to the old chapel (1784) being fitted up as schools (1850-51). The necessary alterations and extension to accommodate upwards of 1,000 children were carried out by Mr. White, architect. The chapel was built 1823, before which time Mass was said in the priest's house. Before 1784 the district was served from Moor Hall, the ancient seat of the Stanleys.

Priests.
Rev. Simeon Bordley, 1784; d. 1798, æt. 90.
„ Jas. Dennett, 1798.
„ Dr. Crook, 1845.
„ Edmund Power, 1847.
„ Peter McGrath, 1869.
„ Robt. Bridges, 1871.
„ Alf. Snow, 1878 to date.

AVON DASSET, WARWICKSHIRE (*Birmingham*). St. Joseph.

Mass was said here for the first time since the Reformation on May 10, 1852, at Bitham House, the residence of Thos. Perry, Esq.; Fr. Wm. Tandy, D.D., was the celebrant, about fourteen persons being present. The church, opened in 1855, was largely due to the munificence of the before-mentioned Mr. Perry and another convert gentleman residing in the district.

Priests.

Rev. W. O'Grady, 1855.
„ Evan Hunter, 1867.
„ Walter Norris, 1871 (?).
„ Bernard Pannier, 1877.
„ Arthur Doyle, 1892.
„ Hugh Taylor, 1896.
„ Wm. Dobell, 1899 to date.

AXMINSTER, DEVON (*Plymouth*). St. Mary.

In 1763 Mass was said at Hilary House, where a chapel was fitted up by John Knight, Esq., member of the ancient Catholic family of Knight, to whom Catholics of this place are much indebted. Mr. Knight died in 1801 *æt.* 69, and in 1830 his son Henry built the chapel of Our Lady, which was opened by Bishop Baines, V.A.W.D., August 15, 1831. The same family of Knight built the present fine church, which superseded the old chapel in May 1862. The style is fourteenth century Gothic. It contains some handsome Stations of the Cross painted in oil by M. Alcan, of Paris. The altar and pulpit are of Caen stone. A memorial tablet commemorates Mr. H. Knight, the founder of the second chapel, who died in 1858.

Priests since 1822.

Rev. Cornelius Magrath, 1822.
„ Robt. Platt, 1824.
„ Robt. Gates, 1827.
„ Henry Riley, 1828.
„ Chas. Fisher, 1834.
„ Jn. Swabrick, 1834.
„ Henry Norrington, 1837.
„ Patrick Kelly, 1849.
„ H. Keary, 1850.
„ Thos. Lynch, 1852.

Rev. Jn. Canon Toohey, 1856.
„ Michael O'Reilly, 1898 to date.

AYLESBURY, BUCKS (*Northampton*).

In 1843 Bishop Wareing, V.A., secured a room for Mass at Aylesbury. Before that time the nearest chapel was twenty miles distant. Now and then a priest from Oxfordshire would go over to Aylesbury to administer baptisms and attend to sick calls. The district in 1844 is described by Fr. Duncan, the first priest, as 'furiously anti-Catholic.' After taking up his abode at Aylesbury, Fr. Duncan opened a chapel in his house, and on a subsequent occasion went to Ireland to collect funds to build a church, but without much success. In September 1844, however, he took a larger house and fitted up a poor, but more commodious, chapel. The 'altar' was nothing more than a common deal table. Mass was only said on Sundays and holy days, the chapel being used during the week as the priest's sitting-room! Fr. Duncan died worn out with labours in 1846, and was succeeded by Fr. J. Brogan, who does not seem to have remained long. Latterly the mission of Aylesbury figures very irregularly in the 'Catholic Directory,' being some years omitted altogether. In 1880 it was served from Weston Underwood every alternate Tuesday. In 1885 the priest came from Wolverton and said Mass on the first Wednesday of every month in the house of Mr. James Roche, 2 St. Mary's Row, at 9.30 A.M. In 1890 the temporary chapel was at 33 Bicester Road; Fr. J. Collins rector. Fr. J. Mayne was his successor.

B

BACKWORTH, NEWCASTLE-ON-TYNE (*Hexham and Newcastle*). St. Edmund, Martyr.

The temporary chapel was opened 1883, the mission till recently being served from Annitsford. The present church in the Gothic style was opened 1903.

Rector.

Rev. James O'Dowd, 1902.

BACUP, LANCS (*Salford*). St. Mary, Bankside.

The mission was commenced 1852, and the church opened 1857.

Priests.

Rev. Henry Mulvany, 1852.
„ Thos. Steele, 1881.
„ John Lane, 1885.
„ Wm. Moran, 1904 to date.

BADDESLEY CLINTON, KNOWLE, WARWICKSHIRE (*Birmingham*).

The Franciscan School of Edgbaston was removed here by Fr. Ingham in 1792. Fr. Collingridge, afterwards Bishop of Thespiæ *in partibus* and V.A., was President from 1794–8. The school was closed in 1829, and now the house has been since 1850 the convent of the Poor Clares. Baddesley Clin-ton Hall was for generations the seat of the Ferrers family, a good old Catholic stock, and heirs to the barony of de Ferrers. The last of the race was Edward Marmion Ferrers, who died August 25, 1884, aged seventy. The old chapel erected by the Franciscans in 1800 was rebuilt in 1870, but not consecrated till 1894.

Priests since 1830.

Rev. Hy. Davey, 1851.
„ P. O'Farrell.
„ Barthol. Crosbie, 1853.
„ Hugh McCarten, 1870.
„ Joseph Verres, 1879.
„ Edw. Delaney, 1882.
„ Bernard Grafton, to date.

BAGSHOT, SURREY (*Southwark*). Convent of the Poor Clares.

The community opened their convent here in 1904, and their chapel for the time being serves the mission, which is attended by the chaplain.

BAKEWELL, DERBYSHIRE (*Birmingham*). The English Martyrs.

A mission was opened here Sunday, December 23, 1888, by Fr. McKey, of Hassop, when Mass was said for the first time in 300 years. The original chapel was a stable-loft, replaced by an iron church for 200 persons, in the Granby Road (February 1890). Fr. J. W. Brown was first resident priest. The mission is at present served from Hassop (1905).

BALHAM, LONDON, S.W. (Southwark). The Holy Ghost.

The mission was started in 1887, when Mass was said at 25 Ravenswood Road, by Fr. J. Simon. The present church opened April 17, 1897. It is a plain Gothic building, and is still unfinished. The Convent of the Adoration Nuns adjoins the church. Fr. J. V. Warwick, B.D., some time professor at Lisbon, has been rector since 1896. The Catholic population of the district is estimated at about 2,500.

BANBURY, OXON. (Birmingham). St. John's.

In 1629 the manor of Warkworth was purchased from the Chetwodes by Philip Holman, a London scrivener (stockbroker), whose son George became a Catholic. This latter is described by Anthony Wood as 'a melancholy and bigoted convert.' The last of the family was Wm. Holman, Esq., upon whose death in 1740 the manor of Warkworth devolved upon his nephew, Francis Eyre of Hassop. His son, Francis Eyre, became Earl of Newburgh in 1814, in succession to Anthony James Radcliffe, fourth earl. Earl Radcliffe, in 1806, built a chapel at Overthorp, near Banbury, and this continued to serve the mission till

the opening of the present church in 1838. The style is Gothic, and the interior lofty and spacious. In 1846 the Sisters of Charity opened a convent in the parish on the site of part of the premises of the Hospital of St. John of Jerusalem, suppressed by Henry VIII.

Priests at Banbury. (Early list incomplete.)

Rev. John Gother, 1689. This priest was the eminent author of the ' Papist Misrepresented and Presented,' &c.

„ Alban Butler, 1749. Author of the ' Lives of the Saints ' etc. Died President of Douai, 1774.

„ Charles Bedingfeld, O.S.F., 1756.

„ Bernard Stafford, 1761.

„ Pierre Hersent 1793.

„ Joseph Fox, 1833.

„ Wm. Canon Tandy, D.D., 1835.

„ J. H. Souter, 1864.

„ C. J. Bowen, 1873 to date.

N.B. Bishop Challoner, V.A.L.D., was, as a boy, converted to the faith at Warkworth, and received his early instruction from the Rev. J. Gother prior to proceeding to Douai. He was consecrated Bishop of Debra in 1741, and died 1781, aged ninety years.

BARKING, ESSEX (Westminster). SS. Mary and Ethelburga.

The mission of Barking was started in 1857, but the chapel was only a school room, and the priest for several years had to reserve the Blessed Sacrament in his house. He was also obliged to say a second Mass at Grays, fourteen miles distant, every Sunday. The temporary place of worship continued till 1869, when the present church was erected during the rectorate of Fr. J.

Gilligan, and on a site granted by Lord Petre. The schools, opened 1857, had an average attendance of 300 in 1900. At the opening of the church in August 1869, Archbishop Manning preached. The size of the building is 60 ft. by 30 ft. E. W. Pugin, architect. The Catholic population of the district was reckoned at 1800 in 1905. About 430 children are on the registers of the schools, which, although recently enlarged, are said to be insufficient 'to accommodate the pupils in attendance.'

Priests.

Rev. J. Gilligan, 1857 till 1887.
„ David Hickey here in 1888.
„ A. Clement, 1895 to date.

BARNARD CASTLE, DURHAM (*Hexham and Newcastle*). St. Mary.

The Catholics of Barnard Castle numbered 200 in 1847, at which time the nearest chapel was at Lartington Hall, the ancient seat of the Witham family. This latter was scarcely able to contain fifty persons. In January 1847 'a public building'—probably a room in the town hall—was hired and used as a chapel on Sundays. In March of the same year a chapel was opened and consecrated by Bishop Riddell (March 31 and April 1). Fr. W. Allen, of Ushaw, was appointed to the mission. In December 1849 a fine painting of the Crucifixion, copied from the original by Le Brun, at Lartington Hall, was placed over the altar. The sanctuary of the church was adorned and new and commodious schools commenced, December 1867. The cost of the latter was defrayed by O. Longstaff, Esq.

Priests.

Rev. W. Allen, 1847.
„ Geo. Meynell, 1857.
„ John Dunderdale, 1861.
„ Robt. Franklin, 1871.
„ Wm. Gillow, 1873.
„ E. J. Barnett, 1877.
„ James Shea, 1879.
„ Bernard Darley, 1904 to date.

BARNET, HERTS. Mary Immaculate and St. Gregory the Great, Union Street.

This locality was described nearly fifty years ago as 'one of the most bigoted places near London.' The mission dates from April 24, 1849, when Fr. Ivers, of Kentish Town, fitted up a small room as a chapel. Mass was said for the first time on Sunday, April 29, about forty persons being present. Fr. Faa di Bruno was appointed priest, and under his auspices the school was opened for the benefit of the many Catholic children in the district. Mass was said in the schoolroom on Sundays. Fr. di Bruno being summoned to the Continent to make collections for Church work in England, his place was taken by a priest from Tottenham, who, however, did not remain long. Fr. Bruno, being delayed by the Franco-Austrian war of 1859, did not return for many months, and meanwhile the mission was practically closed. In June 1860, Fr. G. Bampfield, B.A., served the chapel, and also that of Waltham Cross (*q.v.*), and in December of the same year Cardinal Wiseman confirmed about thirty candidates from the two missions. The estimated Catholic population in 1864 was 200. A new Lady Chapel was added to the church in 1877, and the interior of the building entirely redecorated. Fr. Bampfield died January 20, 1900, and was succeeded by Fr. Francis Spink, the present rector. The mission is in charge of the Institute of St. Andrew, a community of secular priests living under rule, founded by Fr. Bampfield. Large schools for 'boys of the middle and poorer classes' were commenced in June 1868, and at present have about seventy pupils. In addition to the Barnet mission, the Fathers also serve the neighbouring districts of Bushey, New Barnet, &c.

BARNOLDSWICK, YORKS (*Leeds*). St. Joseph.

At Easter 1897 Fr. H. Marchal, chaplain at Broughton Hall, the residence of the Tempest family, started the mission, and in 1901 he bought an old school for £380, which he had altered for a chapel. In 1906 a site for a church was secured in the Gisburn Road, at a cost of £636, and an iron building erected. The accommodation is for about 200. In 1897 the Catholic population of the district was about sixty, but it has since increased to over 350. The new church was opened Sunday, September 9, 1906.

BARNSLEY, WEST RIDING, YORKS (*Leeds*). Holy Cross.

The chapel was opened June 7, 1832, Fr. Tate of Sheffield, preaching at the High Mass to a large mixed congregation. The schools were erected in 1858, the stone being laid by J. Lock, Esq., M.P., a noted railway engineer.
Priests.
Rev. J. Rigby, 1832.
,, H. Cook, 1840.
,, Theophilus Cauwenberghe, D.D., 1876.
, Jn. Hill, 1895 to date.

BARNSTAPLE, DEVON (*Plymouth*). The Immaculate Conception.

In July 1827 a chapel was fitted up in the mansion of Tawstock by Sir Bourchier Wrey, Bart., who had married a Catholic lady. The same generous benefactor also erected a poor school. Bishop Baines, V.A., confirmed twenty persons in the chapel, August 26, 1832. In 1843 Sir Bourchier purchased from Chas. Roberts, Esq., a site for church and presbytery. The present handsome place of worship was consecrated by Archbishop Errington and Bishop Vaughan, October 24, 1855. Sir B. Wrey was received into the Church at Dover, September 15, 1856. The registers of the Barnstaple mission date from 1836.
Priests.
Rev. Peter Hartley, 1827.
,, Wm. O'Meara, 1829.
,, Jn. Williams, 1831.
,, Maurice O'Connor, 1833.
,, L. Calderbank, 1835.
,, M. Crowe, D.D., 1835.
,, Thos. Costello, 1837.
,, Jos. Dwyer, 1837.
,, Jn. Larkan, 1837.
,, Wm. Casey, 1839.
,, Patrick Kelly, 1840.
,, Thos. Fergusson, D.D., 1844
,, Jn. Lynch, 1846.
,, Jos. Kerrin, 1849.
,, Ralph Canon Brindle, 1850.
,, Wm. Musworth, 1890.
,, James S. Burns, 1893.
,, Wm. Unsworth, 1903 to date.

BARROW-IN-FURNESS, LANCS (*Liverpool*). St. Mary.

In 1865 the Catholic population of the district amounted to about one thousand. The nearest chapel was at

F

Ulverstone, ten miles distant. Fr. Bilsborrow, afterwards Bishop of Salford, used to come over from time to time to attend sick calls, administer baptisms, &c. A site for a church having been generously granted by the Duke of Devonshire, the present building was erected, and opened Aug. 28, 1867. E. W. Pugin was the architect, the seating capacity being for 700. A tower and spire were added 1891, and in 1894 the church was enlarged and redecorated. The Sacred Heart Convent was opened in Furness House, October 1897. In 1903 the estimated Catholic population of the mission was 3,489. St. Patrick's School Chapel, Barrow Island, opened 1877 and enlarged 1885, is served from St. Mary's.

Priests.

Rev. John Bilsborrow, 1866.
  „ James Parkinson, 1874.
  „ Wm. Gordon, 1877.
  „ Edward Caffrey, 1879.
  „ John Miller, 1899 to date.

BARROW-ON-SOAR, LEICESTER-SHIRE (*Nottingham*). St. Alban.

Some time prior to 1839 Fr. Woolfrey gave lectures on Catholic doctrine at Barrow in reply to 'a flood of anti-Catholic tracts' scattered broadcast by the Rev. Mr. Gwatkin, a protestant minister. The lectures were well attended, and many persons were received into the Church. In March 1839 the present chapel, a neat structure in the Grecian style, was opened for worship. The cost was defrayed by the contractors of the Eastern Counties Railway. The mission, which was long served from Loughborough, is now served from Sileby.

BARTESTREE, HEREFORDSHIRE (*Newport*).

The Sisters of Our Lady of Charity of Refuge, a congregation founded by the Ven. John Eudes, of Caen, in 1641, opened their convent here in 1863. Robt. Biddulph Phillips, Esq., was a great benefactor to the foundation. The work of the nuns is 'the reformation of young women and preservation of girls in danger of falling.' The chapel is open to the public.

BARTON-ON-HUMBER, LINCOLN-SHIRE (*Nottingham*). St. Augustine Apostle of England.

The mission was established in 1841–42, being served alternately from Brigg by the priest of that place. The mission, which has been an independent one since about 1843, is served by Benedictines. It owes its origin to a convert gentleman and a Mr. Aistrip of Hull.

Priests.

Rev. J. Egan (of Brigg), 1841.
  „ Jn. Taylor, 1844.
  „ P. Perry, 1845.
  „ S. Ward, 1848.
  „ Geo. Burge, 1850.
  „ J. Bernard Murphy, 1890.
  „ Ralph Pearson, 1892.
  „ J. B. Davey, 1893.
  „ Robt. Fishwick, 1894.
  „ Joseph Watmore, 1895.
  „ Thos. Feeny, 1899.
  „ Joseph Flanagan, 1900 to date.

BARTON - ON - IRWELL, MAN-CHESTER (*Salford*). All Saints.

The nucleus of this mission was the domestic chapel of the Trafford family. A school was built here in 1822 by Fr. Thomas Sadler, who in 1827 erected a public chapel at

Barton. The mission was served in conjunction with the chapel at Trafford Park. The chapel of 1827 quickly became too small for the congregation, and many years later was described as 'a wretched garret.' The present fine Gothic church —the gift of the Trafford family, the traditional patrons of the mission—was consecrated by Bishop Turner of Salford, June 9, 1868. At that time the congregation numbered 1,600. The cost of erection was £15,000.

Priests.

Rev. James Haydock, 1792.
„ Thomas Sadler, 1808.
„ Henry Newsham, 1830.
„ John Ball, 1834.
„ Joseph Westhead, 1840.
„ John Hill, 1843.
„ Mgr. John Canon 'Kershaw, 1844.
„ James Canon Hayes, M.R., 1890.
„ Monsignor Charles Canon Gadd, V.G., 1901 to date.

BASINGSTOKE, HANTS (*Portsmouth*). The Holy Ghost.

Mass was said here once a month by a priest from Woolhampton, 1869. Canon Crookhall, of the latter place, and Mr. Rivière are regarded as the two chief founders of the mission. By dint of great exertions, Fr. C. Paul erected the present small church (1878). Bishop Vertue, of Portsmouth, confirmed here for the first time, December 12, 1883. Fr. Val d'Eremao, the distinguished Oriental scholar, author of the 'Serpent of Eden' &c., was priest of the mission in 1884. The present rector is the Rev. A. S. Scoles.[1]

[1] The Marquis of Winchester, who held Basing House for Charles I. against the forces of the Parliament (1643-45),

BATH, SOMERSET (*Clifton*). Benedictines. St. John the Evangelist.

King James II. visited Bath in 1687 and while there attended Mass in the chapel served by Fr. Anselm Williams, O.S.B. This oratory was in Beltre House, rented from the Corporation at £8 a year. The priests after this were: Fr. Bernard Quinn, 1713; F. W. Banester, 1726; Francis Browning or Bruning and Dr. Lawrence York, 1730. Dr. York was consecrated Bishop of Niba *in partibus* and created V.A. of the Western district 1741. During the rebellion of 1745, an attempt was made to get his Lordship into trouble by means of a forged letter purporting to have come from Prince Charles Edward Stuart. The Mayor of Bath, who was his friend, called on him privately and advised him to withdraw for a time, which he did. Fr. Bernard Bradshaw, O.S.B., acted as Vicar-General during the Bishop's absence. Bishop York ultimately retired, worn out with labours, to St. Gregory's College, Douai, where he died April 14, 1770. Fr. Bradshaw had already given up missionary work in 1757. His successor, Fr. Placid Naylor, died at Paris, 1793, during the Revolution. Fr. John Bede Brewer, D.D. who came to Bath in 1776, built a chapel in St. James Parade. Barely had it been opened when it was burnt by a 'No Popery' mob desirous of emulating the Lord Geo. Gordon Rioters in London (June 9, 1780). Bishop Walmesley's splendid library perished in the flames, but his Lordship and the Catholics

was a devout Catholic, and patron of several missionary priests. The Basingstoke Canal now crosses the site of the historic mansion.

obtained compensation to the value of £3,734 19s. 6d. The Benedictine Fathers then built another chapel in Corn Street.[1]

Fr. Baines, afterwards Bishop, in 1817 opened another chapel in Pierrepont Street, which was numerously attended. This second was known as Portland Chapel, and before its acquisition by Fr. Baines had been a dissenting place of worship. Catholicity in Bath made great strides after 1840. Commenting on this the *Bath and Cheltenham Gazette* for January 1849 said: 'The Missionary Chapel at Brunswick Place, under the spiritual charge of the V. Rev. Dr. Bewe, has become a place of great resort to the Protestants of Bath, notwithstanding the strong Puritanical spirit there. A great number of conversions have been the result of his untiring exertions.' Among these latter were Sir T. Broadhead, Bart., and the Hon. John Sanderson, some time Chief Justice and President of the Privy Council of the Isle of Grenada. He died at 2 Nelson Place, near Bath, January 10, 1849, aged eighty-one years.

The time having arrived for a really fine Catholic church to take the place of the conventicle-like buildings of less happy times, the stone of the present church in the South Parade was laid October 2, 1862. The opening and con-

secration by Bishop Clifford, of Clifton, took place a year later, on October 7, 1863. This fine Gothic pile is of Bath stone and of commodious proportions. Mr. C. Hansom, of Bath, was the architect. Beneath the high altar, which is of marble supported by six columns of the same material, is a handsome shrine containing the *corpo santo* or body of St. Justina, presented to the Church by Prince Doria of Rome, son-in-law of the Earl of Shrewsbury. The fine spire of the building (222 ft.) was completed in September 1867.

BATH (*Clifton*). St. Mary's, Julian Road.

The first stone was laid by Archbishop Errington, June 24, 1879, and the building was opened May 3, 1881, by Cardinal Manning, who preached on Luke xvi. 8, with reference to the Bradlaugh agitation against official oaths and declarations. The style is Early Decorated from designs by Dunn and Hansom, the seating capacity being for 400.

Priests.

Rev. Francis Canon Loughnan, 1879.
„ Arnold Matthews, M.R. 1888.
„ Michael McCarthy, 1889.
„ Edward Bates 1891 to date.

BATLEY, YORKS (*Leeds*). St. Mary and the Angels.

A dirty room over a 'rag warehouse' was the first 'chapel' of this mission in 1854. For this 'horrid and disgusting room,' as the pastor, Fr. T. O'Connell, called it, a rentage of £12 per annum was charged.

The number of Catholics living at Batley was then about 600, which in five years increased to 1,000. In 1859 the Earl of Wilton generously presented a site for a school chapel, valued at about £200. In March 1859 'the first social gathering of Catholics and Protestants since the Reformation' was held at Batley, and a collection made for the schools. The 'chapel,' however, remained but 'a horrid garret' till December 15, 1870, when the church was opened. The style is thirteenth century. The accommodation is for 650. The cost of building was £2,374. The Catholic population of Batley in 1870 was about 3,500. Archbishop Manning preached at the opening on Luke i. 28. A new sanctuary and wing were added to the church in October 1884. New schools for 600 children were opened in 1897 at a cost of £4,000. The mission is much indebted to the Colbeck family for several generous benefactions.

Priests.

Rev. T. O'Connell, 1853.
„ J. Wells, 1855.
„ Patrick Lynch, 1860.
„ Thos. Rigby, 1870.
„ Wm. Gordon, 1873.
„ Chas. Gordon, 1879.
„ James Canon Gordon, 1898.
„ John Lea, 1902 to date.

BATTERSEA, EAST, LONDON, S.W.

(*Southwark*). Our Lady of Mount Carmel and St. Joseph.

The mission was founded in 1868 by the late Canon Drinkwater. A small church — now the Lady Chapel — was opened November 22, 1869 ; the rest of the building (Gothic) in 1875. The high altar, said to be one of the finest in London, was presented by the late Sir John Stuart Knill, Bart. Schools were erected 1871, and enlarged subsequently at a cost of 1,300*l.* The interior of the church was redecorated 1904. A notable feature of the church is the handsome pulpit, put up some twenty years ago in memory of the founder of the mission.

Priests.

Rev. T. Canon Drinkwater, 1868.
„ W. J. Connolly, 1881.
„ Albert Whereat, D.D., 1894.
„ Joseph Newton, 1903 to date.

BATTERSEA, LONDON, S.W.

(*Southwark*). The Sacred Heart.

Just before his death, Don Bosco, founder of the Salesian Congregation, arranged for a settlement of his Institute in England. In November 1887, some Fathers and Brothers came to London and were given charge of the Trott Street Mission, Battersea, by Bishop Butt, of Southwark. A small iron church at first sufficed, but in a short time the growth of the congregation demanded a larger building. On August 3, 1892, Bishop Butt blessed the first stone of the present church, which was opened on October 14-15, 1893. The High Mass was sung by Archbishop Cagliero, of Magida, Fr. P. Fletcher preaching in the morning and Canon G. Akers in the evening. In style the church is thirteenth century Romanesque, from design of Mr. F. A. Walters, and is an imitation of the church of St. John at Turin. The splendid high altar was presented by the late Madame Whiting. The striking scheme of decoration of the interior is the work of Fr. G. Fayers, S.C., and other members of the Salesian Congregation. The schools (primary) attached to the church were erected 1890, and now accommodate some five hundred children. In 1895 Surrey Lodge, in Surrey Lane, by Orbel Street, a large roomy mansion, was purchased for a boys' secondary school, which is now in a highly flourishing condition. New dormitories and class-rooms were added in 1898 and 1901-2. One section of the school is devoted to the teaching of arts and crafts.

Superiors.

Rev. Edward McKiernan, 1887.
„ C. B. Macey, 1889, Provincial C.S., 1903.
„ E. Rabagliati, 1903 to date.

BATTLE, SUSSEX (*Southwark*). Our Lady Immaculate and St. Michael.

The abbey was erected by William the Conqueror 1067, on the spot where Harold fell, and was dedicated to a soldier-saint, St. Martin of Tours. At the time of the dissolution, the abbey, one of the wealthiest in the land, was granted by Henry VIII. to his favourite, Sir Anthony Browne, first Lord Montague. This family remained Catholic down to the time of the seventh Viscount (1728-87), who, however, was reconciled to the Church on his death-bed, when he publicly declared 'that nothing but libertinism in theory and practice had induced him to abandon the faith of his fathers.' A local tradition narrates that after the rise of the Reformation, Catholics of Battle used occasionally to assemble by a well near the ruined abbey to recite the rosary and hear instructions from disguised priests. Fr. Thomas Pilcher, or Pilchard, who was mar-

tyred for the faith at Dorchester, March 21, 1587, was a native of Battle. Mass was not said in the district for the next 300 years. In 1882 Bertram, fifth Earl of Ashburnham, built the present church for the few Catholics of the locality, at that time estimated at about twenty. The fine presbytery was erected by his lordship in 1902, on a site obtained from the Duchess of Cleveland. It may be of interest to note that Reginald de Hesseburnham, ancestor of the present earl, gave lands to the Church at Battle in the eleventh century.

Priests.

Rev. Michael Gorman, 1882.
„ Charles Kimpé, 1893.
„ Thomas Mahon, 1899.
„ Ernest Blackborrow.
„ Enea Tozzi.
„ J. Wilhelm, D.D., 1900 to date.

BAYLIS HOUSE, SLOUGH, BUCKS.

In 1823 Mr. Wm. Henry Butt, a convert Catholic gentleman, descended from an old family in Gloucestershire, opened ' a classical academy' at Spring Terrace, Richmond, Surrey. In 1828 he removed it to its present site—Baylis House, Salt Hill, near Windsor. For nearly ninety years this excellent private school has remained under the tuition of various members of the Butt family, and it still preserves an undiminished reputation. The chaplain at this time was the Rev. J. Wilkinson, of Clewer. The present chaplain, who has also charge of the mission which the domestic chapel serves, is Fr. Raymond Colin, O.P.

BAYSWATER, LONDON, W. (*Westminster*). St. Mary of the Angels, Westmoreland Road.

The church was commenced in 1850, but, for want of funds, not completed till 1857, when it was opened by Cardinal Wiseman (July 2). A south aisle and Lady chapel, designed by J. Bentley, were added later. The style of the building is Gothic. Dr. Manning was rector till 1865, when he succeeded Cardinal Wiseman. The Oblates of St. Charles have had charge of the mission since the commencement. A splendid east window was presented to the chapel of St. Charles in 1889 by Mr. and Mrs. J. O'Grady. Among the valuable relics preserved by the community are a large green chasuble, 'constantly used by St. Charles,' and a valuable crystal sixteenth century reliquary of Italian or Spanish workmanship, containing a relic of their holy patron.

BEAUMONT COLLEGE, OLD WINDSOR (*Portsmouth*). St. Stanislaus.

Beaumont or Bowmans Lodge, near the confines of Windsor Great Park, was formerly the residence of William Duke of Cumberland, of Culloden notoriety, and Warren Hastings. In 1854 it became the noviciate of the Society of Jesus, and in 1860 was opened as a collegiate school for the sons of the upper and middle classes. The course of studies was completely reorganised in 1903, and the establishment has been lately officially recognised, in connection with preparatory military and naval studies. The junior school was completed in 1887.

Rectors (S.J.).

Rev. James Eccles.
,, Thos. Welsby.
,, Francis Cassidy, 1876.
,, Fredk. O'Hare, 1885.
,, Wm. Heathcote, 1892.
,, Jn. Lynch, 1895.
,, Gerald Tarleton, 1897.
,, J. Bampton, to date.

BECCLES, SUFFOLK (*Northampton*). St. Benet's Minster.

The mission was established from Bungay, 1888. A portion of the church was built 1889. The style is transitional Norman, consisting of nave, two side aisles, and chapels of Our Lady and St. Joseph. A tower is in course of construction. The interior is very ornate, the high altar of stone and marble being especially noteworthy. Fredk. Smith, Esq., of Bungay, bequeathed a sum sufficient for completing the church and adding the tower. The congregation — said to be mostly converts — numbers about three hundred.

Priests (O.S.B.).

Rev. Hugh Ford, 1889.
,, F. M. Fulton, 1895 to date.

N.B.—The Corpus Christi Guild, established in the mission, is a revival of the celebrated guild founded here in 1354. Like the other English guilds, numbering some 30,000, it was confiscated under Edward VI. One of the rules of the guild enacted, 'That the body of Our Lord Jesus Christ be honoured with all possible reverence, that it be placed in a gilt cup and be carried on a decorated feretory, accompanied by four priests in procession on Corpus Christi Day,' &c.—See *Downside Review*, July 1895, p. 228.

BECKENHAM, KENT (*Southwark*). The Transfiguration and St. Benedict.

The mission was commenced by Fr. W. Kirwan 1891, but does not figure in the 'Catholic Directory' till 1893. The cruciform church was commenced in October 1895 and opened by Bishop Butt 1896. Fr. Thomas Bullivant, D.D., a distinguished priest and convert, was a frequent worshipper here after his reception into the Church. He died at Rome, August 18, 1901.

Priests.

Rev. W. Kirwan, 1891.

„ W. Alton, 1902.

, W. Kilmartin, 1903.

BEDFORD (*Northampton*). Holy Child Jesus and St. Joseph.

The first Mass said at Bedford in recent times was on Christmas Day 1863, when Fr. John, afterwards Canon Warmoll, started a mission in the town. The chapel on this occasion was 'a crowded room eleven feet square.' The bigotry against Catholics in Bedford was then so great, that when, on March 27, 1865, Fr. Warmoll attended the cemetery to bury one of the congregation, a hostile crowd surrounded the grave and behaved in the most outrageous manner. A great change for the better in public opinion with regard to Catholics had taken place in October 1872, when the foundations of the new church were laid by the Bishop of Northampton. Mr. Gilbert Blount was the architect, the cost of erection being about £3,000. This beautiful church was completed during the course of 1873. A handsome carved stone and marble altar and reredos were added to the Sacred Heart Chapel by Fr. Wrigglesworth in May 1887. Messrs. Purdie and Boulton were the architects and sculptors, respectively, of this fine addition to the church.

Priests.

Rev. J. Canon Warmoll, 1863.

„ Geo. Wrigglesworth, 1885.

„ Geo. Canon Osman, 1888.

„ Robt. Middleton, 1890, to date.

BEDFORD LEIGH, LANCS. *See* Leigh, St. Joseph's.

BEDWORTH, WARWICKSHIRE (*Birmingham*). St. Francis of Assisi.

By the zeal and exertions of the Capuchin Fathers this mission was placed on a permanent footing in February 1881. On Sunday, March 5, 1881, Stations of the Cross were erected, and two sacred statues were unveiled in the chapel by the generosity of benefactors. The new Catholic Church, which was built 1882-83, accommodates some 150 persons. The schools for 100 children were erected at the same time. For several years the mission was served from Nuncaton and Weston. It is now attended by the Premonstratensians.

BEEDING, near **BRAMBER, SUSSEX.**

In 1904 the Nuns of the Congregation of the Blessed Sacrament acquired the mansion known as the 'Towers,' where they have commenced a high-class girls' school. The chapel is open to the public. Chaplain, Rev. A. Marcellin.

BEESTON, NOTTINGHAM. St. Peter.

The mission was commenced 1885 and for some time was served from the Cathedral, Nottingham. In February 1887, Fr. G. V. Bull was appointed resident rector. On the first Sunday of Lent, the same year, nine persons were confirmed by Bishop Bagshawe. The church designed by G. Hart was opened by Canon Douglas in May 1898; accommodation for 150.

BEGBROOK, near OXFORD (*Birmingham*).

A monastery—known as St. Philip's Priory—for the 'training and education' of novices for the Servite Order was opened here on Tuesday, January 5, 1897. High Mass was sung by the Rev. Bonaventure Ceirano, prior of the foundation, the sermon being preached by the Bishop of Birmingham.

BELLINGHAM, NORTHUMBERLAND (*Hexham and Newcastle*). St. Oswald.

The foundation of this mission is dated 1749. A chapel was built in 1794, from which year the baptismal register commences. That of deaths commences 1775. On June 26, 1839, 'a neat and convenient chapel in the Gothic style of architecture' was opened by Bishop Briggs. The Bishop and two Catholic gentlemen contributed liberally towards its erection. One of these was W. Charlton, Esq., High Sheriff of the County, 1838.

Priests since 1800.

Rev. Geo. Turner.
  „ Dinmore, 1832.
  „ A. Macartney, 1834.

Rev. N. Brown, 1838.
  „ E. Hothersall, 1852.
  „ Geo. Flint, 1862; till after 1900.
  „ Harold Tate, 1902.

BELLS CLOSE, SCOTSWOOD-ON-TYNE, NORTHUMBERLAND (*Hexham and Newcastle*). St. George.

The church was opened 1869.

Priests.

Rev. Thos. Clavering.
  „ Francis Kuyte, 1885.
  „ James Canon Stark, 1904 to date.

BELMONT, CLEHONGER, HEREFORD (*Newport*). Pro-Cathedral of St. Michael.

This fine church and Benedictine Priory adjoining were erected by the late F. R. Wegg-Prosser, Esq., at a cost of upwards of £17,000. The style of the church is cruciform, and, like the priory, was designed by E. Welby Pugin. From its situation on the Belmont estate, the place is often spoken of as the Benedictine Priory, Belmont, and for more than forty years it has been the noviciate of the English province of the Order. The opening of the Priory took place November 21, 1859, the anniversary of the day on which Abbot John Feckinham took possession of the Abbey of Westminster, *temp.* Queen Mary. Abbot Sweeney was superior of St. Michael at the time of the opening. He was born at Bangalore, India, 1821, his father being a British officer and one of the friends of Napoleon at St. Helena. Abbot Sweeney is the author of the well-known 'Life of Father Augustine Baker, O.S.B.,' the martyr; 'Lectures on Faith and Practice' &c. He died at St. John's Priory, Bath, April 17, 1883. The pro-Cathedral was still unfinished when the Jubilee was celebrated in September 1885.

BENTHAM, YORKS (*Leeds*). St. Boniface.

The church was opened in 1866.

Priests.

Rev. Joseph Hill, 1866.

„ Thos. Croskell, 1888.

„ S. Y. Morgan, 1898 to date.

BERMONDSEY, LONDON, S.E. The Most Holy Trinity, Parker's Row.

This mission is famous as being one of the first to be started without the aid or patronage of any of the foreign ambassadors. In May 1773 Fr. Gerard Shaw gave Bishop Talbot, coadjutor of Bishop Challoner, £500—afterwards increased to £700—to found a mission at Bermondsey. He likewise presented a silver chalice for use in the chapel. In the Latin document concerning these bequests is a clause requiring one of the chaplains at Bermondsey to be able to speak both Irish and English. The baptismal registers date from 1776, but no priest's name appears in them at that time. A Miss Byrne also endowed the mission at the outset with the sum of £200. The first chapel, or 'Mass-house,' was in East Lane. There is a tradition that during the Gordon riots in 1780 the 'No Popery' mob came to Bermondsey to destroy the chapel, but were unable to find it. Bishop Challoner is said to have preached and confirmed here. In 1799 Fr. Broderick established a

school which was supported by Irish merchants and tradesmen in London. A few years later the Baroness de Montesquieu, daughter-in-law of the author of the *L'Esprit des Lois*, who had emigrated at the Revolution, gave a site for a new school and £5,000 for a church. The double schools (for boys and girls) were in Paradise Street, Rotherhithe. Baptisms amounted to 177 in 1834; 251 in 1862; 385 in 1881. Fr. Butler, who came to Bermondsey in 1832, supplied the church with the benches that are still in use. On Monday, August 3, 1834, the first stone of the new church was laid by Bishop Bramston, V.A.L., assisted by Bishop Griffiths. The sermon by Fr. Harrington was heard with great attention by upwards of 4,000 spectators. The building was opened in June 1835. Bishop Bramstone sang the Mass, and among the choir was Madame Stockhauser, the celebrated cantatrice. Bishop Griffiths preached and in the course of the sermon he asked prayers for the Baroness de Montesquieu, then dying. This great benefactress to London Catholicity died on July 13 following, and was interred beneath the church she did so much to found. The style of the building is perpendicular Gothic with galleries above the aisles—additions which gave great offence to the architect, E. Welby Pugin.

New permanent confessionals and a large additional sacristy were added in 1900. The rich east window is the gift of the Pauling family of Effingham, Surrey. On the side walls of the church are mural tablets and brasses to past rectors of the mission, and near the entrance a fine Calvary group, in memory of Provost Bamber of

Southwark (died 1886). The Rev. E. Murnane, M.R., is the present rector. It was at this mission that the Catholic Boys' Brigade—now so widely spread over London—was first started by Fr. P. Segesser, the present rector of Deptford. The Convent of Mercy which adjoins the church was opened in 1838.⁹ Among the first sisters to be professed here was Lady Barbara Eyre, daughter of the Earl of Newburgh, a descendant of the Jacobite Earl of Derwentwater, beheaded in 1716. Several of the nuns went to the Crimea in 1854 as hospital nurses, and their services to the sick and wounded soldiers were gratefully acknowledged by Miss Florence Nightingale, whose portrait hangs in the Community room of the Convent.

N.B.—The Ven. Henry Heath, O.S.F., who suffered for the Faith at Tyburn in 1643, was arrested at the Star Inn, Bermondsey, a site now occupied, we believe, by the Star Music Hall in Abbey Street.

BERMONDSEY, SOUTH, LONDON, S.E. (*Southwark*). St. Gertrude.

The district between South Bermondsey and the Old Kent Road, which up to 1885 was mainly a waste, had by 1890 become a densely populated area. A site for a church was acquired by Bishop Butt in 1892, but the building was not erected till 1902. The style is Romanesque from design by the late F. Tasker. A generous benefactress defrayed the cost of building. Above the altar hangs a large Flemish crucifix modelled after the celebrated picture by Sir Anthony Van Dyck. Fr. Martin Gifkins was the first and the Rev. H. Evans is the present rector.

BERWICK-ON-TWEED, NORTHUMBERLAND (*Hexham and Newcastle*). Our Lady and St. Cuthbert.

The town was one of the places visited by the Jesuits of the St. John the Evangelist 'residence' after 1623. No record, however, remains of their labours. The mission afterwards passed under the care of the Benedictines, but no registers appear to have been kept till 1793. The chapel in Ravensdown Street was opened in 1829. In 1846 Fr. Witham proposed the erection of a more commodious chapel, 'neat, but not gaudy,' in the Early English style, to take the place of the existing building which was 'far too small for the accommodation of the people.' We have not, however, been able to discover if this suggestion was carried out.

Priests since 1824.

Mission vacant, 1825.
Rev. Wm. Birdsall, 1826.
„ E. Smith, 1839.
„ Thos. Witham, 1844.
„ A. Macdermott, 1848.
„ Thos. Hanegan, 1856.
„ Wm. Markland, 1858.
„ Denis Buckley, 1864.
„ John O'Connor, here 1871.
„ James Farrell, 1874.
„ Wm. Gillow, 1880.
„ James Stark, 1881.
„ Wm. Smythe, 1885 to date.

BETHNAL GREEN, LONDON, N.E. (*Westminster*). Our Lady of the Assumption.

In 1903 Cardinal Vaughan requested the Augustinian Fathers of the Assumption, expelled from France, to take charge of this newly established mission. A temporary chapel was opened at North Passage, Green Street, near the presbytery, 24 Globe Road, afterwards removed to 184 Cambridge Road. Fr. Gelase Urginet is the Superior.

BETHNAL GREEN, LONDON, N.E.
The Polish Chapel.

The mission was commenced in November 1904, Mass being said for the first time here on Sunday, December 4 following. Count Lubienski and Mr. Pace are the treasurers of the chapel, which is under the care of Fr. Gregory Domanski, of the Salesian congregation.

BEVERLEY, YORKS (*Middlesbrough*). St. John.

Before the establishment of this mission, March 1846, the nearest Catholic chapel was at Hull, some 7½ miles distant. The first chapel was a room hired by Fr. Astrop. In 1850 Beverley became the territorial See of the Bishop of the old Yorkshire district, but the occupants of it were installed at St. George's, York, in which city they resided. Owing to the growth of the diocese, it was divided into two Sees, that of Leeds and Middlesbrough, 1878.

The Lord Bishops of Beverley.
(1) Rt. Rev. John Briggs, born 1789; educated at Ushaw, and ordained July 9, 1814; president of the College, 1832–36; Bishop of *Trachis*, 1833; Vicar Apostolic of the York district, 1840; translated to Beverley, 1850; resigned November 7, 1860; died January 4, 1861.
(2) Rt. Rev. Cornthwaite, born May 9, 1818; consecrated by Cardinal Wiseman, November 10, 1861; translated to Leeds, December 20, 1878; died, June 16, 1890.

Priests.
Rev. Wm. Astrop, 1846.
  „ Bernard Branigan, 1852.
  „ Henry Walker, 1856.
  „ Thos. Smith, 1858.
  „ M. Bisenius, 1882.
  „ James Humphreys, 1885.
  „ Francis John Hall, 1891.
  „ Prosper Coppin, 1897.
  „ Thomas R. Murphy, 1905. to date.

BEXHILL - ON - SEA, SUSSEX (*Southwark*). St. Mary Magdalen.

In the spring of 1893 the Fathers of Charity opened a temporary chapel which served the mission till the erection of the present fine church.

Priests.
Rev. Richard Richardson, 1893.
  „ Alfred Knight, to date.

BICESTER, OXFORDSHIRE (*Birmingham*). St. Edith's Priory.

A school chapel was opened in 1885 and served from Hethe; later on from Souldern. The Olivetan Benedictine nuns erected a priory here in 1903.

Chaplains.
Rev. F. Venance, 1903.
  „ A. Costedloat, 1905.

BIDDLESTONE, NORTHUMBERLAND (*Hexham and Newcastle*).

Biddlestone Castle is the ancestral seat of the Selby family, who have always been staunch to the

Faith. The chapel is said to have been built in the year 1200. After the year 1623 the place was served by the Jesuit Fathers. Fr. Robt. Widdrington appears to have been the first resident missioner at Biddlestone. This worthy priest was here after the Restoration and is noteworthy for having assisted in the Conversion of James Drummond, Duke of Perth. The last Jesuit chaplain here was probably Fr. Newton 1750. The congregation at that time was returned at 'about fifty or sixty' and the remuneration as '£10 and diet.' After this the care of the missions seems to have devolved on the Benedictines. The registers date from 1767. Fr. J. Naylor, O.S.B., was here for many years and till about the end of the eighteenth century. A return set forth in 1837 gave the congregation at eighty-two, exclusive of ten converts.

Priests since 1824.

Rev. J. Abbot; Mission vacant 1832–36.
„ Jn. Fisher, 1837.
„ — Howard, 1839.
„ Thos. Hogget, 1842.
„ Henry Cartmell, 1888.
„ Wm. Drysdale, 1891.
„ Robt. Kerr, 1892 to date.

BIDEFORD, DEVONSHIRE (*Plymouth*). The Sacred Heart.
The first chapel was a mission room at the Public Rooms (1888), Fr. J. Burns being the first priest. The new church was built in the grounds attached to the priest's house, the foundation stone being laid in August 1892 by the Bishop of Plymouth. The sermon at the ceremony was preached by Fr. Langdon, of Launceston (St. Matt. vii. 24–25). The building is cruci-

form, and measures 58 ft. by 22 ft. Mr. Lethbridge of Plymouth was the architect. The church was opened in December 1892. In the autumn of 1893 the building was enriched by a new pulpit and a bell.

BEDLINGTON, NORTHUMBERLAND (*Hexham and Newcastle*). St. Bede.
A Benedictine Mission established in 1876 for the benefit of the many Catholics employed in the local colliery and nail-making industries.

Priests.

Rev. Francis Hickey, 1876.
„ Jerome Watmough, 1882.
„ Charles Wray, 1885.
„ Charles Smith, 1890.
„ James Furness, 1892.
„ Wm. Baines, 1899 to date.

BIGGLESWADE, BEDFORDSHIRE (*Northampton*).
A mission-chapel has been established here (1906), and Mass is said once a month by Fr. E. King of Shefford. An evening service is given by the same priest every Sunday, and it is hoped that a priest may soon be appointed to take charge of this growing centre of Catholicity.

BILSTON, STAFFORDSHIRE (*Birmingham*). Holy Trinity.
During the cholera epidemic of 1832 Fr. Francis, afterwards Bishop Mostyn, and Fr. O'Sullivan 'were indefatigable in their exertions to afford every spiritual and corporal assistance' to the sufferers. They

received many into the Church, and so deep was the impression made by their apostolic labours, that many protestants joined in petitioning Bishop Walsh, V.A.M.D., to erect a Catholic chapel in the town. Aided by James Wheble, Esq., and the Baroness de Montesquieu, the Bishop was enabled to open the desired chapel—to accommodate 500—in April 1834. In 1832 the Catholic population of Bilston amounted to about half a dozen families, but the number had greatly increased at the time a regular mission was established. For several years the priest had to attend Wednesbury, Darlston and Willenhall. A fine new chancel by Pugin and a window by Wailes were added to the church in August 1846.

Priests at Bilston.

Rev. F. Mostyn and O'Sullivan, 1832.
„ Thos. Sing, 1836.
„ G. Fox, 1838.
„ S. Longman, 1844.
„ M. Crewe, 1848.
„ John Sherlock and Robt. Swift, 1851.
„ P. Davies and H. Terry, 1855.
„ John O'Connor, M.R., and John Clarke, 1864.
„ James McCave, D.D., 1867.
„ M. Power in 1870.
„ W. Stone, 1889.
„ W. Waugh, 1890.
„ G. Bunce, 1898.
„ William Sutherland, 1904 to date.

BINGLEY, YORKS (*Leeds*). The Sacred Heart.

A school chapel was erected here 1873, at which time there were many Catholics engaged in the worsted, paper, and iron manufactures of the town. For some short time prior to the opening of the school chapel, a ' station ' had been established in the town and served from Shipley.

Priests.

Revs. Edmund de Thury, D.D., 1873.
„ Aloysius Puissant, 1880.
„ Alfred Watson, 1882.
„ Thos. Parkin, 1891.
„ Thos. Bradley, 1897.
„ Honoré Fové, 1903 to date.

BIRCHLEY, WIGAN, LANCS (*Liverpool*). St. Mary.

The oldest mission in Lancashire (alleged). The Hall, the residence of the Andertons, was built in 1588, and in 1618 the chapel. The family were great sufferers for the Faith. A secret printing press was set up in the house from which ' many Popish pamphlets were printed.' Fr. Robert Anderton was executed in the Isle of Wight 1586 for being a priest contrary to the laws, and two others of the race fell in the cause of Charles I. during the Civil War. Fr. Jn. Penswick, who served the mission for forty-six years and died October 30, 1864, was the last of the Douai priests. He erected the present church, opened June 20, 1828. The schools were inaugurated October 29, 1860. The chancel and presbytery were built by Fr. J. Wrennall (1872).

Priests.

Rev. Roger Anderton, 1645.
„ Thos. Jameson *alias* Sedden, 1698.
„ Richard Jameson (brother), 1717.
„ Thos. Lancaster, 1719.
„ Emerick Grimbaldestone, 1751.

Rev. Hy. Dennett, 1786.
„ Jn. Penswick, 1804.
„ Patrick Fairhurst, 1850. Died in India, May 19, 1858.
„ Jn. Hardman, 1855.
„ Thos. Walton, 1865.
„ Jos. Wrennall, 1869.
„ Austin Powell, 1872 to date.

BIRKDALE, SOUTHPORT, LANCS
(*Liverpool*). St. Joseph's.

In 1830 Birkdale was the abode of 'cormorants, seagulls, and other sea fowl.' By 1860 the place had become a city of 'stately villas and abodes of wealth.' On October 14, 1865, Bishop Goss, of Liverpool, laid the first stone of the church on a site given by T. Weld-Blundell, Esq., the Lord of the Manor, who also contributed £1,000 towards the erection. The Gothic building designed by E. W. Pugin was opened in May 1867. The seating accommodation is for about five hundred. Fr. J. Abraham, who used to attend the few Catholics of the district before the establishment of a regular mission, presented the Campanile with a fine bell. In 1883 the congregation had grown so numerous that a school room had to be used as a chapel of ease. In July 1884 a school chapel dedicated to St. Theresa was opened for worship by the Bishop of Liverpool. The chapel was provided at the expense of Mr. and Mrs. Weld-Blundell, on whose estate it is built. Fr. John Gardner was appointed priest in charge of the new mission.

Priests.

Rev. Chas. Canon Teebay, 1867.
„ Jas. Canon Taylor, 1883.
„ Jn. Canon Wallwork, M.R., 1885.

Rev. Jn. Kelly, 1891.
„ John Canon Walmsley, 1895.
„ William Canon Gordon, 1897.

BIRKENHEAD, CHESHIRE
(*Shrewsbury*). Our Lady of the Immaculate Conception.

The establishment of a chapel at Birkenhead dates from 1837. At that time the Catholic population was hardly 200 and the chapel was generally regarded as 'too large.' By 1845 the Catholics numbered 5,000! There were then 300 children in the schools. The 'Catholic life' of the place was, however, reported to be very backward, great numbers neglecting their 'duties.' Fr. Collier, of New Mills, opposite Birkenhead, did much to revive religion in the mission. New schools of Stourton stone, from the design of E. W. Pugin, were erected in 1857. In 1861 the Catholic population was estimated at 10,000. Next year (May) the church to seat about 1,000 was opened by the Bishop of Shrewsbury. The style is 'severe French Gothic.' E. W. Pugin was the architect. In 1875 a handsome pulpit was presented by Fr. Slaughter. The chancel was completed 1877. Bishop Mostyn, V.A. of Wales, was consecrated here in July 1895. The high altar of stone and marble was erected June 11, 1899.

Priests.

Rev. John Rogerson, 1857.
„ Canon Daly, 1863.
Monsignor Slaughter, 1872.
Rev. Francis Mostyn, 1891 (Bishop of Menevia, 1895).
„ Jn. Canon Barry, 1895.

BIRKENHEAD, CHESHIRE
(*Shrewsbury*). St. Werburgh.

For some notice of recent Catholicity in the town, see account of the Church of the Immaculate Conception. The mother church of the district was opened August 22, 1837, the mission having been instituted the previous year by Fr. John Platt, assisted by the Earl of Shrewsbury. A chapel for emigrants, near the docks, was established by Canon Browne, 1854.

Priests.

Rev. John Platt, 1836.
„ W. Henderson, 1840.
„ Edw. Canon Browne, 1847.
„ Robt. Canon Chapman, 1857.
„ Eugene Canon Buquet, 1882.
„ Thomas Canon Marsden, V. G., 1898 to date.

BIRKENHEAD. St. Lawrence's Church.

Erected in 1875 at a cost—including furniture, &c.—of £11,000. The congregation in 1887 numbered 5,000. In February of that year arbitration was commenced between Fr. Michael Craig, rector of the church, and the Mersey Railway Company, in consequence of the subsidence of the church due to the company's tunnelling operations. On May 16, 1886, the church showed signs of being unsafe, and the building was shortly afterwards closed. With the £7,911 paid as compensation by the Railway Company, a new church was erected between March 1889 and 1890. The architect was Edmund Kirby. In 1897 new Sacristies and Lady Chapel were added, and in 1899 a choir gallery.

Priests.

Rev. Robt. Brundrit, 1865.
„ Edward Lynch, 1876.
„ Thos. Geraghty, 1878.

Rev. Canon Marsden, 1880.
„ Michael Craig, 1885.
„ Gerald Canon Keegan, 1895 to date.

BIRMINGHAM, WARWICK-SHIRE.

On March 23, 1687, the foundation stone of a Catholic chapel at Birmingham was laid by Fr. Leo Randolph, O.S.F., 'in ye presence of many Protestants as well as Catholics.' King James II. presented twenty-five tons of timber from Needwood Forest for use in the new building, which was opened and consecrated September 4, 1688, by Bishop Giffard. His lordship ordered the anniversary of the opening to be kept on the first Sunday of September, On November 2, 1688, two days before the landing of the Prince of Orange, a protestant mob, acting under orders from Lord Delamere, razed the chapel to the ground. The building was dedicated to St. Mary Magdalen. It was 95 ft. long by 33 ft., and the high altar was adorned 'by four large pillars carved with Corinthian capitals.' The site of this chapel is, or was, called 'Mass-house Lane.' After the destruction of the chapel, Fr. Randolph retired to Edgbaston, near the town, where he opened a small chapel and started a school. The school was greatly helped by Lady Curson of Waterperry, who in 1719 bequeathed to the priest in charge some money for 'four weekly Masses.' The school and chapel always remained separate establishments, and in 1735 it was provided by the Provincial of the Franciscans in England that the incumbent of the chapel should pay the master £16 per annum for his board &c. A new house was rented for the school in 1750. The chief benefactors to the establishment after this were Mrs. Mary Weld, who left £350 to the school in 1782, and Sir James Brockholes, of Lancashire, who in 1787 presented it with £400. In 1789 the school was removed to Baddesley (*q.v.*).

St. Peter's

In 1786 Frs. J. Nutt and J. Hawley, the priests of the mission, resolved on erecting a larger chapel, and shortly afterwards a fine structure dedicated to St. Peter was opened; Fr. Joseph Berington preached on the occasion to a crowded congregation. In 1802 the chapel was enlarged, many protestants contributing to the fund. Fr. Nutt died in 1799. His successors were Messrs. Pilkington, Kimble, Summer, Hawley, and Edgeworth. In 1824 the Franciscans gave up the mission to the V.A. of the Midlands, when the Rev. J. McDonnell was appointed to the chapel. He built the presbytery, added side galleries to the chapel, and opened a Catholic burial ground. These undertakings loaded him with debt, from which he was generously relieved by the Earl of Shrewsbury. The enlarged chapel held about six hundred persons. In 1833 the Society of the Sacred Heart was established in the church. The present handsome Gothic church of St. Peter in Broad Street was opened by Bishop Ullathorne in 1871.

BIRMINGHAM. Holy Family. *See* APPENDIX.

BIRMINGHAM, WARWICKSHIRE. St. Chad's.

The old church of St. Chad was commenced in 1806 and finished 1809, during the incumbency of Fr. Edward Peach. In 1834 a meeting was held at the church when it was resolved ' that it is highly desirable that a commodious and splendid church be erected in Birmingham.' This resolution was effectively realised in June 1841, when the present magnificent Cathedral was consecrated by Bishop Walsh. The style is perpendicular Gothic, from the design of A. W. Pugin. In 1847 365 persons were confirmed here by Bishop Wiseman. Bishop Walsh, who died in 1849, *æt.* 83, is buried in the crypt. On the re-establishment of the hierarchy in 1850, Dr. Ullathorne was enthroned as Bishop of Birmingham (October 27), upon which occasion Cardinal Wiseman preached (Matt. xiv. 25, 26). The diamond jubilee of the church was celebrated in 1901. Additional sacristies were built by Canon Greaney, 1883. The St. Chad's Grammar School, opened on Summer Hill 1858, is now represented by St. Philip's Grammar School. The Chapter of the Cathedral was erected June 24, 1852, Monsignor Henry Weedall, D.D., being the first Provost. Among the benefactions to the Church may be noted: a fifteenth century brass lectern and carved oak pulpit—from the Church of St. Gertrude, Louvain—presented by John, sixteenth Earl of Shrewsbury; the rich high-altar, given by J. Hardman, Esq., &c. There are memorial windows to Thomas Canon Flanagan, the ecclesiastical historian (died July 21, 1865); George Wareing, Esq. (died 1844), &c.

Priests.

Rev. E. Peach, 1806–39.
  „ T. McDonnell, 1839.
  „ J. Moore, 1842.
  „ H. Weedall, D.D., 1849.

In 1850 the City became the See of Birmingham with Dr.

Ullathorne as first bishop. Since then the chief administrators under the bishops have been :

Rev. Geo. Canon Jeffries,V.G.,1851.

„　Michael O'Sullivan, 1866.

„　Thos. Canon Longman, 1877.

„　W. Greaney, 1885.

„　Fredk. Canon Keating, 1898.

BIRMINGHAM.　St.　Francis, Hunter Road.

Opened ' with considerable ceremony ' by Cardinal Vaughan in 1894, and has since been ' beautified by the addition of much internal decorations.' The building was consecrated by Bishop Ilsley, Thursday, June 21, 1900.

BIRMINGHAM.　St. John.　*See* APPENDIX.

BIRMINGHAM.　St. Michael's, Moor Street.

In May 1862, a Unitarian meeting house was purchased, and consecrated for use as a Catholic church by Bishop Morris, who pontificated at the High Mass and preached. The style of the building is Doric, and by a clever architectural manipulation some old vestries adjoining the church were converted into a chancel connected with the rest of the building by a Byzantine arch. These and other alterations were carried out by the architect, Mr. Bates. The ' Mass-house,' destroyed by Lord Delamere in 1688, stood near the site of this church. The celebrated natural philosopher, Dr. Priestley, often preached at the Unitarian meeting house, which is now the Catholic church. When the purchase of the place was in negotiation, the diocesan authorities received very generous treatment from the Unitarian body in Birmingham, a circumstance quite in keeping with the general good feeling existing between Catholics and the members of this persuasion arising from their suffering so long together from the operation of the penal laws.

The congregation of St. Michael numbered about 4,000 in 1865. The first priests were Frs. J. Sherlock and J. Power. Frs. J. Hanlon and W. O'Dowd are in charge of the mission at present.

BIRMINGHAM.　St.　Patrick's, Dudley Road.

This church was opened October 29, 1895, by Bishop Ilsley. The style is French Gothic. A conspicuous feature of the interior is the fine red stone columns. The accommodation of the building is for 500. Prior to the opening of the present edifice, an iron church did duty as a place of worship. The fine belfry bell was presented by Admiral Tinklar, and the alabaster font by — Brady, Esq.

BIRTLEY, DURHAM (*Hexham and Newcastle*). St. Joseph.

A Mass-house is said to have existed here in 1696. In 1820 the Jesuits had charge of the mission. Fr. Higginson, O.S.B., was rector in 1832. The Catholic population was reckoned at about one hundred, ' mostly miners.' In July 1842, the stone of the new church was laid by Fr. W. Riddell, of Newcastle, during the rectorate of Fr. Sheridan. The building (Gothic) was opened by Bishop Mostyn, May 8, 1842. Mr. Dobson was the architect. Several fine stained-glass windows were presented to the church by J. Todd, Esq., of Newcastle. The church was enlarged 1862, during the rectorate of Fr. Jn. Swale, O.S.B. Fr. F. Scannell, O.S.B., is the present rector.

BISHOP AUCKLAND, DURHAM
(*Hexham and Newcastle*).

St. Wilfrid's Church, in 'the old Gothic style,' was opened Tuesday, October 13, 1846, by Bishop Riddell, V.A. The seating capacity of the building was for 400. Before the opening of this church, Mass was said occasionally in 'a mean room,' by Fr. William, afterwards Bishop Hogarth, who, on the Sundays when no Mass was said, used to come over from his mission at Darlington, read prayers for the congregation, and catechise the children. The schools were erected in 1861. Before that time a large disused granary was kindly lent for the purpose by J. Peacock, Esq., a protestant gentleman. During the 'mission' given by the Redemptorist Fathers in August 1881, 2,300 persons approached the Sacraments, and 798 were confirmed by Bishop Chadwick, of Hexham and Newcastle.

BISHOP EATON (*Liverpool*). Our Lady of the Annunciation.

The church of the Redemptorist Fathers was opened on Thursday, July 15, 1858, by Bishop Goss of Liverpool. The style is Early Decorated. E. Welby Pugin drew the plans. A new wing was added in 1889 from designs by Messrs. Sinnott and Powell. The Preparatory College was opened 1894. The Redemptorists first came to Liverpool in 1851 at the request of Bishop Browne.

BISHOP'S STORTFORD, HERTS.
(*Westminster*). St. Joseph and the English Martyrs.

The temporary church was opened Wednesday, November 7, 1900. The number of known Catholics in the vicinity at this time did not exceed eleven. For many years prior to the opening of the church, Mass was said occasionally over the shop of a Mr. Fitzgerald, a sadler, by one of the priests from St. Edmund's, Old Hall. Then St. Mary's Convent, Wind Mill Lodge, was established, and the chapel of the institution enabled the few Catholics of the district to hear Mass on Sundays. The church of the mission was opened by the Bishop of Clifton, on behalf of Cardinal Vaughan. Since the commencement of the mission, the spiritual care of the district has been given to the Redemptorist Fathers.

N.B.—The exact date of the commencement of the mission was January 1880, and the first priest Fr. D. Nicols, of Ongar.

BISHOP THORNTON, near LEEDS
(*Yorks*). St. Joseph.

The register of baptisms commences May 7, 1803. The chapel was built about 1809. Fr. (Canon) Platt, rector here 1813–57, was popularly known as 'good old Fr. Platt.' He died at Bruges, February 1, 1862. In August 1860, two fine coloured windows were erected in the church, one of St. Joseph and the Holy Child, and the other depicting the marriage feast at Cana.

Priests.

Rev. Richard Talbot, 1803.

,, Charles Saul, died June 5, 1813.

G 2

Rev. James Canon Platt, 1813 till 1857.
„ A. Macartney, 1858.
„ Robt. Canon Thompson, 1861.
„ W. Arnold, 1863.
„ Geo. Brunner, 1870.
„ Herman Geurts, 1876 to date.

BISHOPSTOKE, HANTS (*Portsmouth*). The Holy Cross.
Prior to 1888 the mission was served from elsewhere. In May 1888, Fr. T. J. Doyle was appointed first resident priest. The church was consecrated August 1902. St. Mary's Home for ' waifs and strays ' is in the parish, and is under the direction of the Portsmouth Diocesan Rescue Society.

BISHOPSTON, near **CLIFTON.** St. Bonaventura.
The Franciscan mission was established here in 1890. Until the opening of the church on March 14, 1901, the adjoining school served as a chapel. The friary and church in Egerton Road now form a conspicuous landmark of the town. The style is thirteenth century style of Gothic (nave, chancel, side chapels, baptistery, and choir at the west end). Seats for 360. The cost of erection about £4,000.

BITTERNE, HANTS (*Portsmouth*).
Convent of the Sacred Heart of Mary, established 1904, chapel open to the public. Fr. F. Cabaret, chaplain.

BLACKBURN, LANCASHIRE (*Salford*). St. Alban.
Abram, in his history of Blackburn, says that owing to Catholic landlords and gentry, the population of Ribblesdale remained attached to the old religion throughout the penal times. When Bishop Smith, V.A., held a visitation here in July 1709, crowds of Catholics came to be confirmed at Lower Hall, Samlesbury, Blackburn, the residence of Mr. Walmesley, where his lordship resided during his stay in the district. According to a letter written about this time by the Rev. J. Holm, vicar of Blackburn, to the Archbishop of Canterbury, Catholics in this part of the country had both ' power and interest.' In 1717 Dr. Gastrell, Bishop of Chester, declared that out of 1,800 families in Blackburn 1,023 were ' avowed Papists.' The first chapel in Blackburn, between King Street and Chapel Street, was erected by Fr. Wm. Dunn, D.D., about 1783. The congregation increased so rapidly that, although the building was shortly afterwards enlarged, it was found too small. Fr. Dunn died suddenly, after Mass, October 27, 1805. In 1824 the old chapel was sold for a workshop. The second chapel was built by Fr. Albert, 1826, and enlarged 1883. It served the mission till the erection of the present church in December 1901, at a cost of £20,000. The late Mgr. Nugent, so famous for his active charities, was curate here in 1846.
The Catholic population of Blackburn has increased as follows :— 1820, 1,200 ; 1857, 12,000 ; 1882, 20,000.

BLACKBURN, LANCASHIRE (*Salford*). St. Ann's.

A new school chapel in connection with this mission was opened in the St. Silas Road, for teaching purposes, January 14, 1901, and for devotion on February 17 following. The school attendance in 1901 was about sixty. The school is dedicated to the Sacred Heart.

BLACKBURN, LANCASHIRE. St. Joseph's, Audley.

In June 1874, Bishop Vaughan sent for Fr. Maglione, of Fairfield, and said to him, 'If you take the train from Manchester to Blackburn you will find Audley. There is no church, no house, no school; you have to build all!' By August 1877 Fr. Maglione had erected ' a beautiful Italian church ' and commodious schools. A men's clubroom was inaugurated 1896. This energetic priest and learned canonist was created a monsignor, 1901, and died January 13, 1905. Canon Musseley is the present rector.

BLACKHEATH, LONDON, S.E. (*Southwark*). Our Lady Help of Christians.

About 1859, St. Mary's Orphanage for Boys was founded by Canon Todd, D.D., B.A. (d. 1877). The chapel, which was open to the public, was enlarged to accommodate an additional 300 in June 1879. The orphanage was closed 1903-4. The present fine mission church (Decorated Gothic) was built 1890-1, at the sole expense of Charles Butler, Esq., a gentleman of old Catholic family resident in the district. The accommodation is for about four hundred persons.

Mr. Purdie was the architect. The church was consecrated by Bishop Amigo of Southwark, Monday, August 13, 1906.

Priests since 1877.

Rev. Joseph Wright, 1877.
„ T. Ford.
„ Francis Shechan, to date.

BLACKHILL, DURHAM (*Hexham and Newcastle*). Our Lady Immaculate.

In 1856, Canon Kearney built a church here, but before the edifice was complete it was blown down by a storm. Aided by the Catholics of the neighbouring village of Esk, the Canon was enabled to make good the damage, and the church was opened in 1857. Fr. Thos. Smith was the next priest. Canon Gillow is the present rector.

BLACKLEY, LANCS (*Salford*). Our Lady of Mount Carmel.

The mission was started by Fr. Hubbard in 1851. The Rev. Dr. Donovan was priest in 1853. The church was opened during the rectorship of Dr. Dillon in 1855. The next priests were: Revs. P. Vermeulen, Mgr. Provost Croskell, E. Goetgeluck, R. Liptrott, J. Billington, P. Vermeulen (second time). A new infants' school and parochial hall were erected during the course of 1901.

BLACKMORE PARK, WORCESTERSHIRE (*Birmingham*). Our Blessed Lady and St. Alphonsus.

The Hornyold family received Blackmore Park and Hanby Castle by grants from Edward VI. and

Elizabeth. The old mansion, pulled down in 1861, contained many priests' hiding-places, and during the penal times parties of pursuivants and priest-hunters often visited the house. The old chapel was in the upper part of the building, and continued to serve the mission till 1846, when the splendid Gothic church and presbytery were erected by J. V. Hornyold, Esq. Dr. John Hornyold, Bishop of *Philomelia in partibus* and V.A. of the Midlands 1752-78, was a member of this family. A dukedom was conferred on the family by late Pope Leo X. about 1895.

BLACKPOOL, LANCS (*Liverpool*). Sacred Heart of Jesus and Mary.

Before the opening of the church in December 1857, the nearest Catholic chapel was at Lytham. The church was erected by Miss Monica Tempest, sister of Sir Charles Tempest, Bart., of Broughton Hall. The plans were drawn by E. Welby Pugin, the design being the decorated style of pointed architecture. Fr. G. Bampton, S.J., was the first resident priest. The schools in Talbot Road accommodate 370 children, and were opened in March 1898.

BLACKPOOL, LANCS. St. Cuthbert.

A school chapel was opened August 15, 1880. The church (Decorated Gothic), for 500 persons, was opened in June 1890. J. O'Byrne, Esq., was the architect. New sanctuary windows, representing the Adoration of the Lamb, were unveiled June 23, 1895. New infant schools were opened 1899.

The Catholic population is about 1,200.

Priest.

Rev. Edward Lupton, 1880 to date.

BLAYDON, DURHAM (*Hexham and Newcastle*). St. Joseph.

The mission was commenced 1897, and served from Stella till 1898, when the present rector, Fr. James Corboy, was appointed.

BLOXWICH, STAFFORDSHIRE (*Birmingham*). St. Peter.

Towards the end of the eighteenth century T. Purcell, Esq., proprietor of East Fields, in this district, left some money for the support of a priest here. Mass after this was said once a month at the residence of the Partridge family. The chapel was at the top of the house, the number of communicants being at this time about twenty. About 1800 the Rev. James Gordon left a sum of money for the endowment of a mission, and the Rev. J. Perry purchased a small house and shop near Bloxwich, which by some alterations was turned into a chapel for eighty persons. The Abbé J. Norman (Normand?) and the Abbé L. Bertrand were the next priests. In 1807 the number of communicants was fifty. Fr. Francis Martyn, of Oscott—the first priest wholly educated in England since the Reformation—who came here the same year, enlarged the chapel to hold 300. In 1819 this energetic priest established a second mission at Walsall (*q.v.*). The old chapel having become inadequate was superseded by the present structure, opened 1869.

Priests after Fr. Martyn.
Rev. Jn. Dunne, 1828.
„ R. Bagnall, 1831.
„ J. O'Farrell, 1842.
„ F. Turvile, 1844.
„ Thos. Longman, 1851.
„ W. Ilsley, 1853.
„ H. Davey, 1857.
„ Andreas Gauvois, 1860.
„ P. Davies, 1863.
„ L. Torond, 1888.
„ P. O'Toole, 1895 to date.

BLUNDELLSANDS, near LIVERPOOL, LANCS. St. Joseph.
The church was the gift of Col. Blundell, of Crosby, and his sister, Miss Blundell. It was opened by the Bishop of Liverpool in November 1886. The style is Early English, from the designs of A. E. Purdie. The Rosary window in the Lady Chapel was the gift of Mr. S. Sharman, Col. Blundell's agent. Dr. Paterson, Bishop of Emmaus, preached on the evening of the day of opening. The east window, in honour of St. Joseph, was erected by Mrs. Frances Taylor.
Priests.
Rev. Nugent, 1886.
„ Patrick Cahill, 1887.
„ W. Lennon, 1890 to date.

BLYTH, NORTHUMBERLAND (*Hexham and Newcastle*). Our Lady and St. Wilfrid.
The mission was commenced in 1860, and till the opening of the church in 1862 was served from Cowpen Hall, the ancestral seat of Henry Sidney, Esq. Mr. Dunn was the architect, the cost being about £2,200. The accommodation is for 600.

Priests.
Rev. P. W. Dromgoole, O.S.B., 1863.
„ Boniface Jas. MacKinlay, 1892 to date.

BODMIN, CORNWALL (*Plymouth*). St. Mary's Priory.
On July 11, 1845, the *Tablet* announced that a religious community from Brittany would shortly take up missionary work at Bodmin. The following year a suitable church in 'Early English Gothic' style was opened through the exertions of Fr. W. Young, who did much to revive Catholicity in Cornwall. Bishop Ullathorne, V.A. of the Western District, preached both on the day of opening (September 24, 1846) and the following Sunday 'to vast crowds, who assembled to witness the ceremonies.' The mission was the first in that part of Cornwall for upwards of three centuries. In June 1881 the Canons Regular of St. Augustine, expelled from France, settled at Bodmin, and took charge of the mission. They are the monastic representatives of the old canons driven from Bodmin at the Dissolution (1536-39). They transformed the old presbytery into a priory under Fr. F. Menchini. On September 3, 1882, took place the first profession of English novices since the settlement of the community in this country.

BOGNOR, SUSSEX (*Southwark*). Our Lady of Seven Dolours, Clarence Road.
The mission was established in 1880, when Mass was said in a temporary chapel between the

'Steyne' and the Railway Station by Fr. Lawrence. The new church of the Servite Order, commenced in September 1881, is in the Early English style, consisting of nave, transepts, and eight chapels. Mr. J. Hansom was the architect, the cost of erection being £5,143. The Catholic population of Bognor in 1880, including visitors, was about sixty. The building was opened Wednesday, August 16, 1882, by the Bishop of Portsmouth in place of the Bishop of Southwark. Provost Crookall, D.D., sang the Mass. The Duke of Norfolk was present as the chief representative of Sussex Catholicity.[1]

BOLDON COLLIERY, DURHAM (*Hexham and Newcastle*).

A chapel of ease was erected here by the Harton Coal Company for their Catholic employés and opened on Tuesday, May 12, 1896, by the Bishop of Hexham and Newcastle. Mass (*coram Episcopo*) was celebrated by Fr. Taylerson of the mission at Tyne Dock. At present the mission is served occasionally from Tyne Dock.

BOLLINGTON, CHESHIRE (*Shrewsbury*). St. Gregory.

In June 1830, Fr. J. Hall, of Macclesfield, fitted up two cottages as a chapel. The congregation then numbered 200. A protestant gentleman, Mr. Turner, of Shrigley Hall, generously gave a site, and

---

[1] Bognor owes its rise to Sir Richard Hotham, 'who in 1785 by an extensive erection of elegant buildings' converted an obscure fishing village into a place of fashionable resort.

---

the present church was erected 1834. The apse was adorned with panels setting forth the events of Our Lord's Passion, 1857. The mission was served from Macclesfield till 1841. A school was opened 1866.

Priests.

Rev. R. Glassbrook, 1841.
　,, 　Edw. Kenrick, 1842.
　,, 　Jn. Rich, 1845.
　,, 　Jn. Shanahan, 1846.
　,, 　Pat. Power, 1852.
　,, 　Wm. Hilton, 1858.
　,, 　Pat. Mulligan, 1860.
　,, 　Samuel Bolton, 1867.
　,, 　Wm. Fennelly, 1871.
　,, 　P. Donovan, 1876.
　,, 　P. Coleman, 1884.
　,, 　B. Thompson, 1887.
　,, 　H. Gore, 1894.
　,, 　P. Cleary, 1895.

BOLNEY, SUSSEX (*Southwark*).

The chapel is a private one attached to the residence of Lady Auckland, and is served by Fr. F. Hopper, late of Haywards Heath. The chapel, which is open to the public, was established about three years ago.

BOLTON, LANCS (*Salford*). St. Peter.

In 1800 Mass was said in a small house in Old Acres. The Catholics of the place consisted of 'seven poor families.' The Catholic population is at present estimated at over 22,000 (1906). The chapels of the city are as follows :—

(1) SS. Peter and Paul, Pilkington Street.

Opened 1800. Catholic population of the district, 5,000.

Priests.

Rev. James Shepherd.
„ Jn. Anderton, 1826.
„ Jn. Glover, 1837.
„ Jn. Dowdall, 1840.
„ E. Canon Carter, 1848.
„ Thos. Billington, 1876.
„ Henry Canon Browne, 1882.
„ John Canon Gornall, 1885.
„ Thos. Allen, 1888.
„ C. Canon Wood, 1892.
„ R. Holmes, M.R., 1901 to date.

(2) St. Mary.

The church (Gothic) was opened September 13, 1847, by Bishop Brown, V.A. The plan comprises nave, chancel, and porch. Accommodation for about 500. Catholic population about 3,800 (1906).

Priests.

Rev. Thos. Smith, 1847.
„ James Snape, 1857.
„ Wm. Taylor, 1860.
„ Denis O'Brien, 1879.
„ W. L. Fowler, 1899 to date.

(3) St. Patrick, Great Moor Street.

The church, in the Early English style, was commenced March 1860, and opened March 17, 1861. The congregation is estimated at 1,400 (1906).

Priests.

Rev. Denis Byrne, 1861.
„ Chas. McDermott Roe, 1877.
„ Joseph Canon Burke, 1889 to date.

(4) St. Joseph, Horace Street.
Founded March 30, 1879.

(5) St. Edmund, St. Edmund Street.
Opened September 15, 1861. Catholic population, 2,500.

Priests.

Rev. James Conway, 1862.
„ Angelus Dumalie, 1863.
„ Henry Browne, here 1871.
„ Peter Maringer, 1882.
„ H. Averdonk, 1885 to date.

(6) St. Ethelbert, Chapel of Ease to SS. Peter and Paul.
Opened 1905.

BOLTON-LE-SANDS, LANCS.
(*Liverpool*). St. Mary of the Angels.

Mass was first said here in 1868 in a barn lent by H. Clarkson, Esq. The present church was commenced in 1882, and consecrated by Bishop Cornthwaite, of Leeds, May 6, 1884. The style is Early Decorated. Sittings for 200. Miss Coulston, of Hawkeshead, defrayed the cost of erection. E. Simpson, Esq., of Bradford, was the architect. New schools were opened January 7, 1895.

Priests.

Rev. Geo. Braithwaite, 1868.
„ H. Gibson, 1888 to date.

BONHAM, SOMERSETSHIRE
(*Clifton*).

The manor of Bonham came into the possession of the Stourton family about the end of the fifteenth century. The mission was established there early in the eighteenth century by Lord Mowbray and Stourton. The Benedictines served the chapel. The Rev. John Panting was priest in 1783. Two years later the property was sold by Charles Philip, sixteenth Lord Stourton, who, however, reserved the chapel and presbytery for the use of the mission. In September 1801, Fr. Jos. Hawarden, O.S.B., was appointed to the mission. He opened a school, which became highly successful, but in 1823 was removed ' for breaking his vows.' He was finally reconciled to the Church on his death-bed, April 21, 1851.

Priests since 1823.

Rev. Thos. Wassall, O.S.B., 1823.
„ E. O. Davis, O.S.B., 1830.
„ Ignatius Stuart, O.S.B., 1832.
„ James Funny, O.S.B., 1888.

Rev. Henry Bulbeck, O.S.B., 1892.
„ Jn. Richards, O.S.B.
„ Thos. Matthews, O.S.B., 1901
to date.

BOOTLE, LANCS (*Liverpool*). St. Alexander.

The mission was commenced in 1862, when Mass was said in an old hay-loft. The church, in the Gothic style, was opened December 1867. E. W. Pugin was the architect. In 1878 a chapel of ease had to be erected in Brasenose Road, and six years later extensive alterations to the church were completed at a cost of £2,600, the accommodation being increased so as to raise the sittings from 500 to 800. The building was redecorated January 1898. A Catholic commercial high school was opened August 1887. The Catholic population of the district was estimated at 7,341 in 1903.

Priests.

Rev. S. Walsh, 1862.
„ Ed. Powell, 1870.
„ Michael Canon Beggan, 1885 to date.

BOOTLE, LANCS (*Liverpool*). St. James, Marsh Lane.

The mission was founded in June 1845 in an old house on the canal bank. In March 1846 a new chapel was opened in Marsh Lane. New schools were opened 1871, and enlarged at various times up to 1880. The church, presbytery, and schools were purchased by the Lancashire and Yorkshire Railway Company in 1884. In February 1886 the new church was opened by Bishop O'Reilly. New schools for 1,200 children were inaugurated the year previously. In 1890 a new marble altar and Communion rails were presented to the church by Mrs.

Lynch, of Green Lane. A new Lady altar and marble pulpit were erected in 1892 and 1893 respectively.

Priests.

Rev. Hy. Sharples, 1845.
„ Geo. Fisher, 1846.
„ J. Anderton, 1848.
„ D. Hearne, 1849.
„ Thos. Spencer, 1851.
„ Thos. Kelly, 1862.
„ P. L. Kelly, 1887 to date.

BOOTLE, LANCS. St. Winefride, Derby Road.

In 1894 Messrs. A. Wood and B. Cain secured the present building— then a Baptist chapel—for the mission. The church was opened by Bishop O'Reilly, August 11, 1895. A Catholic seamen's club is established in the mission. The estimated Catholic population is 3,400.

BOROUGH OF SOUTHWARK. Church of the Precious Blood, Red Cross Street, S.E.

Though the mission is of recent foundation, the neighbourhood abounds in some interesting Catholic memories of post-Reformation times. In Kent Street (now Tabard Street) stood in 1767 'a popish Mass-house,' where, on February 17 of the same year, the Rev. John Baptist Moloney was arrested for exercising his ecclesiastical functions. (See Croydon.) In the early part of the last century, schools for boys and girls were opened in Glasshouse Yard, Gravel Lane, and Price's Street, Southwark Street. These schools were afterwards removed to Great Guildford Street, and finally to Brent's Court, off the Borough (1872). The foundation-stone of the Church was laid by Bishop Butt of Southwark, Saturday, September 27, 1891, and the building was opened in 1892. The style is Early Italian, both the interior and exterior being very plain. The side buttresses are pierced to admit of a passage way round the church. Dimensions, 130 ft. by 42 ft.; accommodation for about 700; cost of church, site, and presbytery, £11,000; architect, F. A. Walters, Esq. The congregation is estimated at about 3,000.

Priests.

Rev. W. Canon Murnane, 1891.
„ Geo. Newton, 1898.
„ John Moynihan, 1904 to date.

BOSCOMBE, BOURNEMOUTH, HANTS (*Portsmouth*). Corpus Christi.

The mission was established in 1887, but the present church was not commenced till August 22, 1895. The opening took place the following year. The building, which is the gift of the Baroness Pauline Von Hugel, Miss Mary Yateman, &c., cost about £9,000. The style is Early English, the seating accommodation being for about 500 persons. This mission is under the spiritual charge of Fathers of the Society of Jesus.

BOSTON SPA, YORKS (*Leeds*).

The Institution of St. John of Beverley for the deaf and dumb was opened June 9, 1870, at Handsworth Woodhouse by Mgr. Canon de Haerne, D.D. The school is under the care of the Sisters of Charity, and till recently was the only foundation of its kind in England. The boys are trained in shoemaking, printing, tailoring, &c., and the girls in needlework, domestic work, &c. The support of the place mainly depends on voluntary contributions, but by the Elemen-

tary Education (Blind and Deaf Children) Act of 1893 the school authorities have power to defray cost of maintenance of children in such institutions. The Rev. E. Dawson is the chaplain and secretary.

BOSTON, LINCOLNSHIRE (*Nottingham*). St. Mary.

The district was visited occasionally during the eighteenth century by Jesuit Fathers from Lincoln. There was reported to be not a single Catholic in the town in 1781. The present church was erected by the Jesuits in 1827. It is a plain oblong building to hold about 200. The Fathers of the Society served the mission till 1858, when it was made over to the Bishop of Nottingham. Fr. A. Chépy was priest for several years after this. Canon Croft, now of Lincoln, erected the stone high altar (by penny subscriptions). Canon P. O'Donoghue, the present rector, has done much to improve the mission by building a convent and introducing the Sisters of St. Paul. The church has been entirely redecorated and the schools greatly enlarged. Much of the expense of these undertakings has been generously defrayed by Miss Smith.

BOURNEMOUTH, HANTS (*Portsmouth*). Oratory of the Sacred Heart.

In 1860, Bournemouth was little more than a large fishing village, with a population of about 5,000. The nearest Catholic mission was St. Mary's, Poole, Dorset. The only Catholic resident of Bournemouth was Mr. Maurice O'Connell, staff drill sergeant to the 4th Hants Volunteers. Between 1862 and 1865, Lady Catherine Petre supported a 'Catholic Oratory' in the Belle Vue Assembly Rooms. Mr. Thos. Long was then the only resident Catholic, Mr. O'Connell having left the place. In 1866-7 Lord Howard of Glossop had a private oratory at 'Brunstath' on the East Cliff. In 1868, Mr. Harnett, an Irish visitor, defrayed the cost of an omnibus to take the few local Catholics to Mass on Sundays at St. Mary's, Poole. In that year, however, the Jesuit Fathers opened a chapel at Astney Lodge, St. Stephen's Road. Aided by Lady Herbert of Lea and Mr. O'Connell, Fr. Maurice Mann, S.J., selected a site on Richmond Hill, where a wooden chapel was built, and this continued to serve as a place of Catholic worship till the opening of the Oratory of the Sacred Heart in 1874, during the rectorate of Fr. Augustus Dignam, S.J. In 1887 Fr. Henry Schomberg Kerr, S.J., commenced to collect funds for a new building. The foundation stone was laid in April 1896, and the first part of the structure—chancel, side chapels, and transepts —was opened in March 1900. The style is Early English, 'judiciously tempered and lightened by the delicate floral ornamentation of the massive pillars.' Alfred J. Pilkington, Esq., of Lincoln's Inn, was the architect. The Catholic population of Bournemouth was estimated at about 2,000 in 1900.

BOURNEMOUTH, HANTS. St. Mary Immaculate, Middle Road, Westbourne.

This oratory was first started at Lynnecourt, Marlborough Road, Bournemouth, on April 9, 1893, through the kindness of Mrs. Teixeira. It was removed to its present address in December of

the same year. Fr. F. M. de Zulueta, S.J., was the first priest in charge.

BOVEY TRACEY, DEVON (Plymouth).

This ancient town derives the latter part of its name from the Norman family of Tracey, one of whom, Sir William Tracey, assisted at the murder of St. Thomas à Becket.[1] He built the parish church as some sort of reparation for the sacrilege. Mass was again restored at Bovey Tracey on September 4, 1904, when the Holy Sacrifice was offered up for the first time since the Reformation by Fr. Moulinet, of St. Michael's, Newton Abbot. The 'chapel' at present is only a hired room, but it is hoped that a more convenient structure may soon take its place.

BOW COMMON, LONDON, E. (Westminster). The Holy Name and Our Lady of the Sacred Heart.

In 1891 a temporary chapel was established at 187-9 Devons Road, under the care of Fr. Gordon Thompson. The church in St. Paul's Road was consecrated by Cardinal Vaughan June 30, 1894. Congregation about 1,500.

Priests.

Rev. Gordon Thompson, 1891.
„ James Carey, 1905 to date.

BOW, LONDON, E. (Westminster). Our Lady and St. Catherine of Sienna.

This handsome church, in the

---

[1] In allusion to the ill-luck that pursued the family for the crime of their ancestor, an old rhyme says:
'All the Traceys
Have the wind in their faces!'

Early English style, designed by Geo. Blount, was opened by Archbishop Manning in 1870. The congregation is estimated at about 1,500.

Priests.

Rev. Thomas Thacker, D.D., 1370.
„ Thomas Doyle, 1899.
„ Robert Kelly, 1903 to date.

BOXMOOR, HERTS (*Westminster*).

The mission was commenced here Sunday, October 26, 1890, when Mass was said for the first time in a cottage, 37 St. John's Road. The two rooms on the ground floor were knocked into one, and the place transformed into a chapel, 'with a pretty altar surrounded with hangings and stations of the Cross.' These latter were given by Fr. Ryan, of Watford. About twenty-seven persons were present at the first Mass, which was said by the Rev. Francis Spinks, I.S.A. The Catholic population of Boxmoor in 1890 was about sixty. The mission was started by an anonymous donor, who placed £100 in the hands of the Rev. H. J. Hardy for the purpose.

BRACKNELL, BERKS (*Portsmouth*). St. Joseph, Stanley Road.

In the summer of 1881, Mrs. Roche, a Catholic lady, rented Benfield Park, Bracknell, the residence of the Dowager Lady Downshire, and converted one of the wings of the mansion into a chapel for the use of Catholics in the district. Before the opening of the mission Mass was said at Cruchfield House, Windsor Forest, the seat of Thos. Hercy, Esq., J.P., but the chapel was discontinued some time prior to 1880. The present 'roomy iron church' was erected in 1894, when Fr. G. Dolman was appointed first resident priest. For several years, however, the mission has been served from Farnborough and Wokingham. On Septuagesima Sunday, 1906, the second Mass (11 A.M.), which had been discontinued for some time, was restored, to the great satisfaction of the congregation. The mission has recently been placed in charge of the Franciscan Fathers of Ascot.

BRADFORD, YORKS (*Leeds*). St. Mary.

Early in the last century the only Catholic in Bradford was a publican in Silsbridge Lane, then a rustic thoroughfare. About 1821 some Irish woolcombers settled in the place, and on Sundays they used to go over to Chapel Lane, Leeds, to attend Mass. As the Catholics of Bradford increased, a priest was obtained from Ireland, and Mass said on Sundays at the Roebuck Inn, a site occupied in 1885 by Messrs. Brown & Muff's shop. A chapel was afterwards fitted up in a house in Well Street, but the landlady, a Wesleyan, objected, and it had to be removed to a house in Nelson Street. In 1824, a regular chapel was built on Stott Hill. Bishop Baines preached the opening sermon, on 'Faith, Hope, and Charity.' The priest of the mission was Fr. Brenan. Fr. Kay subsequently enlarged the chapel and built the presbytery. In 1826, the Catholics of Bradford numbered 400. Fr. Kay was succeeded by Canon Harrison. The Catholics of the place were now in a flourishing condition, and a new church was greatly needed. The result was that in 1852 St. Patrick's Church was erected, and a separate mission attached to it. Fr. Lynch was the first priest. He was succeeded next year by Canon Thos. Harrison, afterwards of St. George's, York. His successors have been : Rev. Jacob Illingworth, 1863 ; Canon Motler, 1865. For his work in Bradford, *see* St. Joseph's. The twenty - first anniversary of the opening of St. Mary's was celebrated in August 1846. Mass was said at five o'clock for the benefit of the mill-workers, and no fewer than 400 were present. At ten a High Mass was sung by Bishop Murphy, of Adelaide, Australia. Bishop Briggs, V.A., assisting in *cappa*. Eighty priests were present. The schools had then 160 day and 160 night scholars.

BRADFORD, YORKS. St. Joseph's.

In 1865 Canon Motler came to Bradford. In 1881 he established another mission—St. Joseph's—and erected a school chapel. The first stone of the new church, built at a cost of £7,000, was laid July 11, 1885, by the Bishop of Leeds. The building, a handsome Gothic structure capable of accommodating 800 people, was opened Wednesday, September 14, 1887, by the Bishop of Leeds and Northampton. E. Simpson, of Manningham, was the architect. The altar is a handsome structure of stone and alabaster. The cost of building the church was about £7,000.

BRADFORD. St. Peter's.

A school chapel served from St. Mary's. The site of the old schools was acquired by the Corporation for £3,500, and new buildings erected. They are 'plain and commodious' and will accommodate 600 pupils. Mgr. Motler who opened the old schools thirty-two years ago, presided at the inauguration of the new ones, September 10, 1906.

BRAILES, WARWICKSHIRE (*Birmingham*). SS. Peter and Paul.

The ancient Catholic family of Bishop kept the faith alive here during the time of persecution. Dr. William Bishop, Bishop of *Chalcedon in partibus*, the first of the Vicars Apostolic of England, 1623-4, was a scion of this house. Fr. G. Bishop served the mission of Bradford from about 1718 to 1742, when he went to Irnham. It was during his incumbency that the present mission was established (1726). The chapel was enlarged in 1836.

Priests since 1824.

Rev. Jas. Duckett.
  ,, Wm. Hilton, 1863.
  ,, James Oliver, 1871.
  ,, Jn. Nock, 1889.
  ,, J. Thompson, 1891.
  ,, Jn. Donworth, 1893.
  ,, Wm. Stoker, 1897 to date.

BRANKSOME, DORSET (*Plymouth*). St. Joseph and St. Walburga.

This mission, though only established recently, may claim to be the representative of the ancient one at Canford, in the same district. Sir John Webb purchased the Canford estate early in James I.'s reign for £14,000. This gentleman fell under suspicion of the Government on account of his religion, and in consequence endured a long imprisonment in London The chapel at Canford was long served by the Jesuits, among them by Fr. Couche, who was chaplain here in 1773. The Webb family, which later on became allied by marriage with the unfortunate Earl of Derwentwater, beheaded in 1716, became extinct on the death of Sir Henry Webb in 1874. The church at Branksome, opened in 1895, was for some years served from Poole. Fr. J. Carroll is the first and present rector.

BRAINTREE, ESSEX (Westminster).

On October 2, 1897, the late Cardinal Vaughan opened the convent of the Franciscan nuns at Bridge House, Bocking, near here. The chapel, erected 1897-8 from designs by Mr. John Bentley, is attended by the missionaries of the Sacred Heart, and serves the mission till the opening of a public church.

BRENTFORD, MIDDLESEX (Westminster).

The chapel of St. John was opened in 1856. It was formerly a Dissenting meeting house, 'devoid of architectural pretensions.' The first priest was Fr. J. Bonus, D.D. Most of the congregation then consisted of the Irish labourers on the Great Western Railway. Fr. J. H. Dale, who was the priest in 1859, acquired a house for a presbytery. The number of Catholics in 1864 was estimated at 1,000. The same year a freehold site for church, presbytery, and schools was bought for £360. The temporary chapel, which was inconveniently situated, accommodated about 100. The present church was opened by Archbishop Manning in 1866. The Catholic population then = 600; endowment, £20 a year.

Priests.
Rev. J. Bonus, D.D., 1856.
„ J. H. Dale, 1859.

Rev. G. Burder, 1861.
„ Maurice Clifford, D.D., 1863.
„ G. Burden, 1866.
„ Wm. Lloyd, 1871.
„ Victor Toenens, 1874.
„ Jos. Redman, D.D., 1879.
„ Jas. Horan.
„ Ar. Ryan, 1892.
„ Jn. Arendzen, D.D., 1903 to date.

BRENTWOOD, ESSEX (Westminster). St. Helen.

Before the establishment of this mission, the chapel was at Pilgrims' Hatch, and was served by Fr. Dias Santos. It was vacant from 1833, and finally closed 1836. Catholics then attended Lord Petre's domestic chapel at Thorndon Hall. As the inconvenience of this arrangement was very great, a Gothic church was erected, and consecrated by Bishop Griffiths October 26, 1837. The present church (64 ft. by 28 ft.) was built May 1860 and 1861, on a site given by Lord Petre, who had also liberally supported the old chapel. The building was consecrated by Archbishop Manning June 15, 1869. A burial ground adjoining the church was blessed by Bishop Griffiths 1841.

Priests.
Rev. Bernard Jarrett, 1838.
„ Thos. Molteno, 1842.
„ Eugene Reardon, 1847.
„ P. Cranshaw, 1853.
„ Joseph da Salva Tavares, D.D., 1855.
„ Jn. Kyne, M.R., here in 1870.
„ Angelo Lucas, 1881.
„ Thos. Norris, M.R., 1889 to date.

BREWOOD, STAFFS (Birmingham). St. Mary.

On the death of Thomas Giffard, Esq., of Chillington, in 1718, his widow, Mary, daughter of John

Thimelby, Esq., of Irnham, 'a lady of great piety,' retired to Longbirch, where she died February 13, 1753, aged ninety-five. She had a chapel in her house, which became the centre of a mission. Her first chaplain, Fr. John Johnson, 'a true friend of Douay College,' died in 1739. He was succeeded by Fr. J. Hornyold, who in 1752 became Bishop of *Philomelia* and V.A. of the Midland district. From this time the Vicars Apostolic of the district resided at Longbirch till 1804, when Bishop Milner removed to Wolverhampton. Fr. Hubbard in 1819 doubled the size of the chapel, which then measured 41 ft. by 20 ft. The number of communicants at this time was about ninety-six. In 1842 it was resolved to unite the two old missions of Longbirch and Black Ladies and build a new chapel at Brewood. The building was commenced 1843, and opened for worship on the Octave Day of Corpus Christi 1844. The then rector, Fr. R. Richmond, died within seven days of the opening, and was interred near the chancel end of the church. He was succeeded by his nephew, Fr. W. Richmond, who did not long survive him.

Priests (at Longbirch).
Rev. J. Johnson, 1718.
  ,, J. Hornyold, 1739.
  ,, Ed. Eyre, 1779.
  ,, — Wright, 1795.
  ,, J. Kirk, D.D., 1797.
  ,, Thos. Walsh, 1801 (Bishop of *Cambysopolis* 1825 ; died 1849).
  ,, Abbé Fautrel, 1804.
  ,, J. Bowdon, D.D., 1806.
  ,, Robt. Richmond, 1808.
  ,, R. Hubbard, 1811.
  ,, R. Richmond (2nd time), 1819.
  ,, W. Jones, 1821.

Rev. R. Hubbard (2nd time), 1831.
  ,, J. North, 1837.
At Brewood.
  ,, Robt. Richmond, 1843.
  ,, Wm. Richmond, 1843.
  ,, James Canon Jones, 1849.
  ,, Philip Kavanagh, 1856.
  ,, Michael O'Sullivan, 1858.
  ,, H. Davey, 1861.
  ,, Edw. Acton, D.D.
  ,, James Nary, 1874.
  ,, Louis Groom, 1877 to date.

BRIDGFORD, NOTTINGHAM.
The mission was commenced on Sunday, October 10, 1897, when Fr. F. C. Hays preached at the High Mass to a crowded congregation. For some months after the opening of the mission services were conducted on Sundays in the Castle Pavilion at Trent Bridge.

BRIDGNORTH, SALOP (*Shrewsbury*). St. John.
Mass was said here for the first time since the Reformation on Sunday, March 11, 1849, in a house opposite the Cross Keys Tavern, in High Street. The celebrant was Fr. P. Grey, O.M.I., who also preached at the Vespers in the evening. The chapel on this occasion is described as being ' crowded to excess.' Fr. Grey resided at Aldenham Park, as there was no presbytery at Bridgnorth. The new chapel was completed in 1857, and was well filled Sunday after Sunday. Fr. F. O'Neill was the priest then. The Bishop of Shrewsbury confirmed fifty-four persons here in October 1892, and spoke of the necessity for building a new church. In four years this desirable end was accomplished, the Church of St. John being opened

in 1896. The schools were also enlarged at the same time.

Priests.

Rev. F. O'Neill, 1855.
„ Jn. O'Callaghan, 1871.
„ Michael Brady, 1872.
„ Pat O'Reilly, 1874.
„ T. A. Crowther, 1875.
„ Jn. O'Callaghan, 1877.
„ J. G. Walsh, 1883.
„ Aug. Tremmery, 1898 to date.

BRIDGEWATER, SOMERSET (*Clifton*). St. Joseph of Arimathea.

The old church, in honour of the traditional founder of Glastonbury Abbey, was opened February 24, 1846, by Bishop Baggs. For several years Mass was said here only once a week. In March 1852 Fr. Thos. Rooker was appointed resident priest. The old building was superseded by the present structure, commenced in October 1881, and opened the following year. Fr. C. Kennard, of Cannington, laid the foundation stone.

Priests.

Rev. Thos. Canon Rooker, 1852.
„ John Bouvier, 1868.
„ John Corbishley, 1877.
„ John Archdeacon, 1879.
„ Alex. Scoles, 1887.
„ Thos. O'Meara, 1892.
„ R. Canon Wadman, 1895 to date.

BRIDLINGTON QUAY, EAST RIDING, YORKS (*Middlesbrough*). Our Lady and St. Peter.

Mass was said here in the summer of 1883. The chapel was served from Driffield by Fr. O'Halloran. Canon Fisher, Frs. J.

Murphy and Connery also laboured here. The present church, in the Early Gothic style, was commenced in August 1893, and opened 1894. At each end of the north and south aisles is a chapel, dedicated to the Sacred Heart and Our Lady respectively. The accommodation of the building is for 300 persons. Mrs. Mousley was the chief benefactress to the church.

BRIDPORT, DORSET (*Plymouth*). St. Mary and St. Catherine.

The good example given by the few local Catholics in attending Mass on Sundays at Chidiock, greatly prepossessed their fellow townsmen in their favour. This good opinion was further heightened by a discussion held at the Town Hall (June 15, 1841), when Frs. Wm. Bond, Wm. Vaughan, and F. M'Donnell explained the faith of Catholics to over 600 'influential persons.' The stone of the church was laid September 8, 1845, and the building was opened by Bishop Ullathorne, V.A.W.D., July 1, 1846. The Hon. W. Weld, Col. McDonnel, and Messrs. Thos. and Wm. Tucker were great benefactors to the mission, which for some years was served in conjunction with Chidiock.

Priests.

Rev. Jn. Dawson, 1863.
„ Remigius Canon Debbaudt, 1870.
„ Thos. Skuse, 1902 to date.

BRIERLY HILL, STAFFS (*Birmingham*). St. Mary.

The mission was established 1854, and for several years served from Stourbridge. The growth of

H

the congregation made a church imperative, and the first stone of the present building was laid in 1872 and opened by Bishop Ulla- thorne October 15, 1873. Style, Early English ; size, 80 ft. by 30 ft. ; seating for 400. A pulpit of Caen stone was presented by J. F. Has- kew, Esq., and a font by Mr. W. Bright. Architect, E. W. Pugin.

Priests.

Rev. James Oliver, 1860.
„ Thos. Revill, here in 1871.
„ Stephen Johnson, 1874.
„ Edward Plaetsir, 1877.
„ Thos. Whelahan, 1882.
„ P. Roskell, 1888.
„ J. Ellis, 1902 to date.

BRIERFIELD, LANCS (*Salford*). The Holy Trinity.

The mission was established from Nelson in 1896.

Priests.

Rev. Thos. Chronnell, 1896.
„ James Youlden, 1903 to date.

BRIGG, LINCOLNSHIRE (*Not- tingham*). The Immaculate Heart of Mary.

The Webb family had a residence at Worlaby, near Brigg. Their chapel was served by the Francis- cans. Fr. Anthony Caley, O.S.F., was here 1783, and Fr. Ignatius Casemore, O.S.F., about 1788-9. The altar picture belonging to the chapel was afterwards removed to Gainsborough. (See 'The Francis- cans in England, 1600-1850,' by Fr. Thaddeus, O.F.M.) A public chapel at Brigg was opened 1815. About 1874 Valentine Carey-Elwes, Esq., on his conversion to the Faith,

turned the stable of his residence, Billing Hall, Brigg, into a chapel and opened it to the public.

Priests.

Rev. J. Mill, 1825.
„ McDermott, 1838.
„ Richard Wall, 1841.
„ James Egan, 1843.
„ J. Naghten, 1849.
„ H. Swale, 1856; served from Gainsborough 1862 to after 1875.
„ Julian Le Quintrec, 1877.
„ Patrick Conaty, 1882.
„ Charles Carrigy, 1885.
„ Michael Kirby, 1889.
„ John Macdonnell, 1901.
„ J. Alyn Wenham, 1904.

BRIGHOUSE, YORKS (*Leeds*). St. Joseph.

This mission was served from Huddersfield from 1867 to about 1878, when Fr. Alfred Watson was appointed as resident priest. In 1882 (May) the chapel—opened July 1879—was threatened by an anti-Irish mob enraged at the recent murder of Lord F. Caven- dish and Mr. Burke in the Phœnix Park, Dublin, but happily no dam- age was done. The Catholic popu- lation of the district was estimated at 500 in 1877. Fr. Thos. Bradley is the present rector.

BRIGHTON, SUSSEX (*Southwark*). St. John the Baptist.

The mere fishing village of ' Brighthelmstone,' owing to the patronage of the Prince of Wales, afterwards George IV., became ' London-by-the-Sea ' between 1784 and 1820. Before the establish- ment of the mission in 1799, the few Catholics of the place were

ENGLISH CATHOLIC MISSIONS 99

attended occasionally by the priest of the ancient mission of West Grinstead, and by the chaplain of the Duke of Norfolk when his Grace accompanied the Prince to Brighton.[1]

In 1799 Fr. W. Barnes was appointed resident Catholic priest at Brighton by Bishop Douglas, V.A.L. In 1804 the Abbé, J. Mouchel, an *émigré*, took charge of the humble chapel in Middle Street. The Rev. Dr. Bew, of Oscott, was rector from 1811 till 1817, when Fr. E. Cullen was appointed. He was priest of the mission till his death in 1850.

In 1822 a chapel was erected in the High Street, and continued to be the Catholic place of worship till 1835, when the present church was consecrated and opened by Bishop Griffiths. The style is Classical; the marble altar and handsome altar piece were the gift of the Earl of Egremont. Mrs. FitzHerbert, the lawful wife of George IV., lies buried in this church, to which she was a great benefactress. Her death took place at Brighton in 1837. The schools in connection with the mission were established by Canon Rymer, who died at Fontainebleau in 1889. The church was lengthened in 1866, and altar rails and pulpit erected by Mgr. Johnston, the present incumbent, in 1892. The Catholic population of the mission numbered about 1,000 in 1902.

BRIGHTON, SUSSEX. St. Mary Magdalen's, Upper North Street.

[1] This was Charles, eleventh Duke of Norfolk, born 1746. He 'conformed to the Established Church' in 1780 to take his seat in the House of Lords, where he became leader of the Whig peers. He rebuilt a greater part of Arundel Castle. At his death in 1815 he was reconciled to the Church.

This, the second Brighton mission, was started in 1856 by Fr. G. Oldham, in a house called Sillwood Lodge, the residence of Mr. and Mrs. Munster. Four years later the church was built on the present site. The style is Transitional Gothic; the tower and spire were added in 1863. Fr. Oldham supplied most of the building fund, and the church is provided with three altars, and a handsome font—the gift of the late Captain Roe. Canon Bamber, who was priest here in 1885, was succeeded by the present rector, Provost Moore.

BRIGHTON, SUSSEX. St. Joseph's, Elm Grove.

The large number of Catholic soldiers in the Preston barracks made this mission necessary. A room in a small house in Elm Grove was fitted up as chapel and opened April 20, 1866. 'A rough brick building' was erected shortly afterwards, and used for worship till the opening of the present fine fourteenth-century Gothic church on a site given by Mr. Munster. Mrs. Shellice and Mrs. Haddock defrayed the cost of erection. The building was opened May 13, 1869. Number of congregation about 850 (1906).

Priests.

Rev. Neil Crispin, 1866.
  „ Nicholas Broder, 1873.
  „ Emile du Plerny, 1888.
  „ Joseph Livesey, 1899.
  „ G. B. Tatum, M.A., 1905 to date.

BRIGHTON, SUSSEX. The Sacred Heart, Norton Road, Hove.

This church was partially fin-

H 2

ished in 1881, and opened by Cardinal Manning on June 14 of the same year. The mission owes its foundation to a legacy of £6,000 left by Fr. Geo. Oldham, of St. Mary Magdalen's, who died in 1875. By the munificence of the late Charles Willock Dawes, Esq., the building was completed in October 1887. The church furniture and handsome organ were presented by the same generous benefactor. The style of the edifice is thirteenth-century Gothic. The high altar is the gift of Madame de Laski. Fr. S. A. Donnelly, the first priest, was succeeded by the present rector, Mgr. James Connelly.

BRINDLE, GREGSON LANE, PRESTON, LANCS (*Liverpool*). St. Joseph.

The Gerard family established the mission about 1680, and placed it under the Benedictines, by whom it has since been conducted. A chapel was built 1780, and greatly enlarged 1843. In 1845 much scandal was caused by one of the congregation, Mr. Eastwood, J.P., noisily refusing to pay the penny entrance fee charged for the support of the chapel. The matter finally came before Mr. Justice Wightman at the Lancaster Assizes, and his lordship upheld the legality of the admission charge on the ground that a clergyman has the right to make regulations for the conduct of his place of worship. In 1896 the Lady chapel was enlarged and a new altar erected (October). Fr. Michael Brown, O.S.B., is the present rector.

BRISTOL (*Clifton*).

Sketch of recent post-Reformation Catholicity, St. Joseph's, Trenchard Street.—A Mass-house was opened here in 1686, but at the Revolution the priest was brought to trial at the assizes. Owing to the absence of the Lord Chief Justice, Sir Edward Herbert, he was remanded to the King's Bench prison. In 1743 Messrs. Evans & Co. allowed their Flemish zinc workers the exercise of their religion. The priest in Bristol at this time was Fr. J. Lallart, S.J. He died at Boulogne the same year, aged fifty-one. His successor, Fr. Scudamore, fitted up a chapel in an upper room at Hooks Mills on Ashley Down. After a time the chapel was removed to St. James's Back. This excellent priest died April 8, 1778, aged eighty-two. The register was started about 1777 by his assistant, Fr. Jn. Fontaine. He was succeeded by Fr. Thos. Brewer, 1780. A chapel was erected by the next priest, Fr. Robert Plowden, in Trenchard Street June 27, 1790. Schools were built about the same time at a cost of £1,000. He had a dispute with Bishop Collingridge, V.A.W.D., over an alleged want of orthodoxy in one of his lordship's pastorals, 1815, and left the district for Wappenbury, where Bishop Milner gave him the charge of the mission. The priests at Trenchard Street after this were : Rev. James Tate, who, like Fr. Plowden, had a dispute with the bishop, on the subject of an appointment to a mission, and left the vicariate 1822 ; John Williams, 1821 ; John Burke, 1823 ; Francis Edgeworth, O.S.F., 1825 ; William Rowe, S.J., 1828 ; Patrick O'Ferrall, O.S.F., 1830 (these last two priests assisted Fr. Edgeworth) ; Rev. James Dawson, 1842 ; Thomas Rooker, 1843.

When Bishop Ullathorne became V.A.W.D. he wrote to Fr. Lythgoe, Provincial S.J., requesting him to again take over the Trenchard Street mission, which had been withdrawn from the care of the Jesuits by Bishop Baines, 1829-30. Fr. George Bampton, S.J., was therefore sent down as rector from October 31, 1847, but was removed to Farm Street, London, December 6, 1849. Fr. William Johnston was his successor at Trenchard Street. He remained down to about 1860. The mission was attached to St. Mary's on the Quay 1862. Fr. Peter Sherlock, S.J., was rector 1863. The mission of St. Joseph's, Trenchard Street, was shortly afterwards given up, owing to the opening of other churches and chapels, which rendered its continued existence no longer necessary.

BRISTOL. St. Mary on the Quay. About 1842 an Irvingite church came into the market, and was purchased by Fr. F. O'Ferrall, of St. Joseph's, Trenchard Street. The building was opened for Catholic worship by Bishop Baines, V.A., July 5, 1843. A gallery was added in July 1845. The mission has been served by the Jesuits from 1860.

Priests.
Rev. P. O'Ferrall, 1843.
„ Mgr. Canon English, 1857.
„ Wm. Johnson, 1860.
„ Matthew McCann, 1863.
„ Ignatius Grant, 1866.
„ Thos. Dykes, 1871.
„ Thos. Hill, 1873-93.
„ Thos. Greenan, 1893.
„ Thos. Brown, 1897.
„ Francis Grene, 1901 to date.

BRISTOL. St. Nicholas, Penny-well Road.
Founded by the Augustinians, and opened September 21, 1850. At this time only the nave was complete. A belfry and north and south aisles were added 1861. A chancel was added in October 1873, bringing the accommodation of the building up to 700. E. Hansom was the architect. During the rectorate of Canon Coxon, vestries have been added to the church and the schools improved. The church, having been freed from debt, was consecrated by Cardinal Vaughan in 1895. Present number of congregation about 700.

Priests.
Rev. N. O'Donnell, 1849.
„ Canon Illingworth, 1853.
„ Thos. Hoskins, 1857-73.
„ Septimus Canon Coxon, 1873, to date.

BRIXTON, S.W. (*Southwark*).
Corpus Christi.
The mission was opened on Sunday, June 2, 1881. The chapel was in the presbytery—a fine roomy mansion in the main road near Hayter Road. Brixton was the tenth new mission carved out of the old St. George's district. In July 1886 the first stone of the new church was laid by Bishop Butt, of Southwark. The style of the church is of the Early Second Pointed period. The plan includes a nave, aisles, side chapels, baptistery, and sacristy, but only the sanctuary and transept are now (1904) complete. The stained-glass windows, put in by Fr. E. Van Doorne, are very rich. The present incumbent, Fr. W. Curran, is making great efforts to complete the building. The opening of a por-

tion of the church took place in June 1887. The number of Catholics at Brixton amounted that year to 1,000. In 1880 it was only about 75.

BROADBOTTOM, DERBYSHIRE

(*Nottingham*). The Immaculate Conception.

Opened September 1896 by Mgr. Sabela. The site of the building, which affords sitting accommodation for about 300 persons, was presented by Lord Howard of Glossop. The day of the opening was marked by a public procession of Catholic guilds, &c., of Hadfield and vicinity. Great numbers of protestants were present in the church, where a 'short and appropriate address' was delivered by Fr. Murphy. A fine pipe organ was presented to the church at the close of the ceremony by Mr. Wyatt, of Gamesley, a protestant gentleman, who also offered the gratuitous services of an organist.

BROADSTAIRS, KENT. Our Lady Star of the Sea.

On Thursday, August 2, 1888, an iron chapel was opened at Broadstairs to take the place of a small chapel attached to a private residence (Laurel House), started 1879. A freehold site having been given to the Benedictines of Ramsgate, who serve the mission, they at once erected the above-mentioned chapel near the railway station. Fr. Swithbert Palmer, O.S.B., sang the first Mass in the new structure, the sermon being preached by Fr. Elphege Power, O.S.B. The mission is served from St. Augustine's, Ramsgate.

BROADWAY, WORCESTERSHIRE

(*Birmingham*). St. Saviour's Retreat.

This mission was established in 1827-8 by Fr. John Augustine Birdsall, O.S.B., who founded the mission at Cheltenham 1809. A burial ground, which was laid out at the same time as the church was erected, proved a great boon to local Catholics as previously the deceased faithful had to be buried in protestant churchyards with the protestant service. In 1850 the Passionists took over the mission, where they erected a monastery.

Priests.

Rev. A. T. Birdsall, 1827.
  „ C. F. Kershaw, 1839.
  „ Thos. Bonney, 1841.
  „ Jas. Kendal, 1845.
  „ F. Vincent, 1851.
  „ F. Raphael. 1855.
  „ Bernard O'Loughlin, 1857.
  „ F. Salvian Nardocci, 1863.
  „ F. Alban Cowley, 1867.
  „ Alph. O'Neill, 1874.
  „ Raymund Disano, 1877.
  „ Michael Watts Russell, 1879.
  „ Gregory Callaghan, 1882.
  „ Reginald Magee, 1885.
  „ Raymund Disano, 1888.
  „ Chrysostom Rothwell, 1890.
  „ Rd. Foy, 1897.
  „ Malachy Gavin, 1900.
  „ Michael Watts Russell, 1903 to date.

BROCKLEY, LONDON, S.E. (*Southwark*). St. Mary Magdalen.

Thirty-five years ago Brockley was a rural Kentish suburb. Now it is a region of villas. About 1864 the large cemetery was opened, and a part of this was reserved for Catholics. Sir Stuart Knill, Bart., late Lord Mayor of London, built the handsome mortuary chapel in the Catholic reserve, but no mission was established at Brockley till 1895, when the fine schools were opened by Bishop Butt (September). In 1896 the children numbered 250. A room in the school fitted up as a chapel served for Mass on Sundays. By the kindness of Bishop Bourne a sum of money was advanced sufficient to raise the structure which was opened in the Comerford Road on March 16, 1899. Bishop Bourne preached the inaugural sermon, the High Mass being sung by the Archbishop of Pario. The style of the building is Roman, the accommodation being for about 300. Over the high altar is a fine copy of Guido Reni's picture of ' Our Lady of the Seven Dolours.' The large crucifix near the entrance is in memory of Mrs. Wilson. Fr. J. Sprankling, the first priest of the mission, did much to work up local Catholicity to its present high pitch of excellence. He was called to St. George's Cathedral, Southwark, in June 1904 as administrator. Fr. J. Hayes, now of Forest Hill, was his successor.

BROMLEY, KENT (*Southwark*). St. Joseph.

The Sisters of the Holy Trinity started a convent at ' Freelands,' the Dower House of the Sundridge Park property, a spacious red-brick Georgian mansion. On Sunday, March 17, 1889, the little chapel of the convent was formally opened for public worship, Mass being said by Fr. O'Meara. Mgr. Goddard, of Chiselhurst, preached in the afternoon.

Priests.

Rev. J. O'Meara, 1889.

,, Thos. Ford, 1895 to date.

BROMPTON, LONDON, S.W. (*Westminster*). The Oratory of St. Philip Neri.

The Fathers of the Oratory of St. Philip Neri commenced their London labours in a chapel situated in King William Street, Strand, during the course of 1849. The community comprised the Revs. F. W. Faber, J. D. Dalgairns, R. M. Stanton, W. A. Hutchison, T. F. Knox, F. F. Wells. Most if not all of these were converts of the ' Oxford Movement,' and their discourses on the doctrines of the Catholic Church drew enormous crowds of listeners, which included some of the most distinguished personages of the day, as Thackeray, Charlotte Brontë, &c. In 1853 the Fathers left King William Street for Brompton, where, on March 22, 1854, a temporary but spacious church of brick was opened for worship. Of the several chapels, that of St. Mary Magdalen, containing the relics of St. Eutropius, martyr, was perhaps the most noteworthy. In July 1856, the district was canonically erected into a mission. The site chosen for the present church was a commanding one in the Brompton Road, on a spot occupied at that time by Blemmel House, a large boarding school kept by Mr. Pollard. The plan selected was that of Mr. Herbert Gribble, the design of the building being that of a cruciform Classic church, somewhat after the style of St. Peter's at Rome. The ceremony of consecration took place April 16, 1884. The gathering on this occasion was a notable one, comprising the Cardinals Manning and Newman, the Catholic hierarchy of England, and representatives of the leading laity. Until the opening of the Westminster Cathedral the Oratory was the largest

Catholic church erected in this country since the breach with the Holy See. The noble *façade* of the building was completed in 1901. The interior of the Oratory is one of extreme richness, caused by the harmonious blending of the variegated marbles used for the several columns and side altars. The high altar is adorned on either side by frescoes, one representing the famous saluting of the students of the English College, Rome, by St. Philip Neri, and the other the death of the saint. Among the other notable features of the church are the life-sized Calvary group, the Chapels of Our Lady and the Sacred Heart, &c. Adjoining the church is the residence of the Fathers of the Oratory, famous for its valuable and extensive library.

BROMPTON (NEW), CHATHAM, KENT (*Southwark*). Our Lady.

The church was opened Tuesday, May 12, 1896, by Bishop Bourne, of Southwark. The sermon was preached by Mgr. J. Vaughan. Among those present on this occasion was the late Admiral Andoe, who, in responding for the United Service at the luncheon after the ceremony, spoke of the general fair treatment meted out to Catholics in the Navy. Fr. T. McMahon is the first rector.

BROMPTON (OLD), CHATHAM, KENT (*Southwark*). St. Paulinus.

The founder of this mission was Fr. Plunkett, who in 1793 opened a small chapel which is described as being 'a very fair, creditable building for Catholics of that day.' About 1805 it was pulled down to make way for the artillery barracks, but with the money given by Government in compensation a chapel was built at the back of two small houses that formed the presbytery. By subsequent enlargements the building was made to hold about 350 persons. In 1857 the great increase of Catholicity in Chatham and the large number of Catholic soldiers always in garrison, made it necessary to erect in that town a separate mission (*q.v.*).

The Abbé Salmon, an *émigré*, who succeeded Fr. Plunkett at Old Brompton about 1802, was rector till 1830. He did a great work among his fellow-countrymen, the French prisoners of war, who were confined at Chatham and employed on fort-building. The various Irish regiments stationed at Chatham during the long French war that ended in 1815, also came in for a good share of the worthy priest's ministrations, though he never could master the spelling of Irish surnames, as the baptismal and other registers of the church prove. On his death in 1830 he was succeeded by Fr. John Meany. St. Paulinus's Church was served from Chatham 1875, and till 1892, when Fr. W. Alton was rector. Fr. Bolger was rector 1902 and subsequently.

BROMSGROVE, WORCESTERSHIRE (*Birmingham*).

The church of St. Peter, in the Worcester Road, Bromsgrove, was opened in September 1862. The building is oblong, with apsidal east end. The furniture, altar, candlesticks, and crucifix were brought from the Shrewsbury Chapel at Alton Towers. The chapel can accommodate about 400 persons. Adjoining the chapel is the school, and also presbytery. The Rev. J. Fanning was the first priest of the mission.

Priests.

Rev. J. Fanning, 1862.
„ Geo. Canon Jeffries, here in 1871.
„ Hy. Davy, 1876.
„ James Canon O'Hanlon, D.D.

BROOMS, LEADGATE, DURHAM (*Hexham and Newcastle*). SS. Mary and Joseph.

Pontop Hall, the residence of the Swinburnes, is regarded as 'the cradle of Catholicity in these parts.' Fr. Leckonby, S.J., was chaplain here in 1748, and for more than fifty years afterwards 'an old-fashioned congregation' met for Mass and prayer in an upper room of the Hall. In 1794 sixteen French *émigré* priests settled in the town, where a presbytery was generously erected for them by Sir John Lawson, Bart., Fr. Eyre, Mr. Smith, and the Silvertop family. In 1802 the first public chapel was erected. Dr. Lingard, the historian, ministered here for a time. The enormous growth of the congregation owing to the foundation and development of the Consett Ironworks about 1850, made the enlargement of the chapel an absolute necessity. This addition forms the vestry of the present Romanesque church, opened by Bishop Chadwick, of Hexham, October 25, 1869. The districts of Blackhill, Byer Moor, and Stanley, formerly served from Brooms, are now independent missions, the Catholic population of the four church areas being 9,000 in 1896.

Priests, Pontop Hall.

Rev. — Leckonby, S.J., 1748.
„ Jas. Johnson, 1778.
„ Hy. Rutter, 1791.
„ Thos. Eyre, 1791-1803.
During this time there were also :—
Rev. Jn. Worswick, 1792.
„ Thos. Storey, 1794.
„ Nicholas Gilbert, 1794-5.
„ Thos. Smith, 1795.
„ John Lingard, 1796-1803.

Priests at Brooms.

Rev. John Bell, 1803-6.
„ Jn. Yates, 1824.
„ Wm. Fletcher, 1828.
„ Thos. Gillet, 1838.
„ Jn. Ward, 1845.
„ Henry Newsham, 1845.
„ Robt. Smith, 1846.
„ Francis Canon Kearney, 1849-90.
„ Eugene McGarrity, 1890.
„ Augustine Magill, 1892, to date.

BROTTON IN CLEVELAND, YORKS, NORTH RIDING (*Middlesbrough*). St. Anthony.

Mission opened 1895 in a room over a joiner's shop. After this a miner's club room was used for Mass on Sundays, and then for some weeks in June and July 1905 a disused Salvation Army barracks. The stone of the present church was laid Wednesday, August 23, 1905, during rectorate of Fr. Gryspeert, by Mgr. Dawson. The building was opened on Easter Wednesday 1906. Mission still served from Loftus.

BROUGH HALL, near **CATTERICK, YORKS** (*Middlesbrough*). St. Paulinus.

The preservation of the Faith in

this district is mainly owing to the baronetal family of Lawson, the owners of Brough Hall. The Benedictines are said to have served the mission from about the time of the Reformation to 1700, since when it has been in the charge of the Jesuits. The church was built by the late Sir Wm. Lawson, Bart., and opened May 8, 1837. J. Bonomi, Esq., was the architect. The jubilee was observed - with much solemnity, May 1887, in the presence of the Bishop of Middlesbrough and a great assembly. The design of the building is Gothic, after that of the ancient archiepiscopal chapel at York.

Priests.

Rev. Thos. Lawson, 1700.
„ Jn. Champion, 1714.
„ Hy. Corbie, 1735.
„ Chas. Hodgkinson, 1745.
„ Fr. Blundell, 1752.
„ Robt. Knatchbul, 1758. (This priest had to leave in 1765, in consequence of the threats of the vicar of the parish, for baptising a Catholic infant.)
„ Thos. Aspinall, 1765.
„ Ralph Hoskins, 1769.
„ Thos. Ferby, 1794.
„ Jn. Laurenson, 1807.
„ Jn. Dilworth, 1830.
„ Robt. Johnson, 1834.
„ Jn. Rigby, 1841.
„ Felix Pole, 1847.
„ Jn. Rigby, 1849.
„ W. Clifford, 1852.
„ W. Smith, 1863.
„ Luke Burke, 1864.
„ Alf. Watson, 1869.
„ Wm. Canon Arnold, 1872.
„ Jas. Glancey, D.D., 1892.
„ Law. Levett, 1893.
„ John Murphy, 1895.
„ Francis Nelson, 1897.
„ Wm. Strucken, 1899 to date.

BROUGHTON HALL, YORKS (*Leeds*). The Sacred Heart.

The Tempest family have been seated here since the reign of Henry VI. The domestic chapel dates from 1453.

BROWNEDGE, PRESTON, LANCS (*Salford*). St. Mary.

Fr. Henry Brewer, O.S.B., was sent here from St. Mary's, Liverpool, 1822. He built the present church, opened 1826, and served the mission till 1846. In 1850 the schools had an average attendance of 400 pupils. The rectors after Fr. Brewer have been:—

Rev. T. Walker, 1847.
„ Austin Pozzi, 1885.
„ Thomas Clarkson, 1902 to date.

BROXWOOD, HEREFORDSHIRE (*Newport*).

The mission was founded from Hereford about 1860, the first priest being Abbot Gregory, O.S.B. In 1881 the church was redecorated and restored at the expense of Col. Cox, a member of the congregation. The Rev. R. Davis is the present rector.

Priests.

Rev. Abbot Gregory, 1860.
„ A. Van den Heuvel, 1877.
„ Athanasius Rogers, 1882.
„ Thos. Contarin, 1885.
„ Achille Ooghe, 1895.
„ R. Davis, 1902.

BUCKFASTLEIGH, DEVON (*Plymouth*). Immaculate Heart of Mary.

St. Mary's Abbey, founded in 1137 by Ethelwerd, son of William de Pomeroy, and affiliated to the Cistercian monastery of Clairvaux 1138. It is said the abbots had power to execute offenders. The abbot at the time of the dissolution was Gabriel Dunne, and he surrendered the abbey to Henry VIII.'s commissioners, February 25, 1538. In October 1882, it was purchased, 'on specially advantageous terms,' by the Benedictines of Pierre qui Vire from the proprietor, Dr. Gale, of Plymouth. Various restorations and additions were put in hand, and on April 27, 1886, the south side of the abbey was opened. Mass, however, was said at the abbey from October 29, 1882. Lord Clifford acted as chairman of the restoration committee, the plans being prepared by Mr. F. A. Walters. The old walls and buildings were skilfully incorporated with the new additions. On the day of the opening, High Mass was celebrated by the Bishop of Clifton, the sermon being preached by Fr. Jerome Vaughan, of Fort Augustus. At the *déjeuner* which followed the service in the church, the Earl of Devon in his speech assured the Abbot of Buckfastleigh of the delight it gave him at 'seeing the successors of the old monks again in their old home.' Dr. Gale, the former proprietor of the place, also expressed his pleasure at seeing the abbey once more in monastic hands.

BUCKINGHAM (*Northampton*). St. Bernardine of Sienna.

The English province of the Franciscans opened a mission at Buckingham in July 1892, when Mass was said on Sundays at 22 West Street, where a temporary chapel was fitted up in their house of residence. The town was anciently under the protection of St. Rumwald. The Rev. Fr. Thaddeus, O.S.F., was the first resident priest. The priests after him have been:

Rev. Fr. Anthony, 1895.
  „ „   Dunstan, 1897.
  „ „   Anselm, 1899.
  „ „   Norbert, 1902 to date.

BUCKLAND, FARINGDON, BERKS (*Portsmouth*). St. George.

The old domestic chapel of the Throckmorton family was built in 1725. The present fine church, erected 'by the pious munificence' of Sir Robert Throckmorton, Bart., was opened on Low Sunday 1846. The style is fourteenth-century Gothic, from designs by C. Hansom. Canon Daniel Rock, D.D., author of 'The Church of Our Fathers,' 'Hierurgia,' &c., was chaplain at Faringdon from 1840 to 1853. In 1850 the Catholic population of Faringdon numbered over 200.

Priests since 1793.

Rev. Joseph Berington (a great opponent of Bishop Milner on the 'Catholic Committee' question, and author of 'A Literary History of the Middle Ages').
  „ Jn. Hutchinson, 1828.
  „ Daniel Canon Rock, D.D., 1840 (author of 'Hierurgia,' 'The Church of Our Fathers,' &c.; died at Kensington 1871.
  „ Francis Azzopardi, 1854.
  „ Hy. Clark, 1855.
  „ E. Sheridan, 1860.
  „ Jn. Norris, 1863.
  „ R. Davis, 1881.
  „ H. Russell, 1885.
  „ J. Arundel, 1892.
  „ C. Arthur, 1903.

BULLINGHAM (*Hereford*).

In October 1862 a few Sisters of Charity came to Bullingham at the invitation of Mr. and Mrs. Bodenham, and established a boarding school. Shortly after this an elementary school was opened under Government inspection. In 1883 the children in the boarding school numbered 200, and those in the elementary school 100. The chapel of the convent served the mission. The first mention of Bullingham as a mission appears in the 'Catholic Directory' for 1883, when Fr. T. Bardet was chaplain. A new convent was erected 1885-6 to take the place of the 'old Manor House,' which had been the home of the community since its settlement at Bullingham. The Rev. D. Vendé is the present rector. A new chapel, the gift of the Superioress, the Hon. Frances Arundell, was opened by Bishop Hedley in July 1906. The style is Early English; cost, about £4,000.

BUNGAY, SUFFOLK (*Northampton*). St. Edmund.

The opening of the church on a site given by the Duke of Norfolk, June 18, 1823, attracted considerable attention in the town, and the High Mass was attended by many of the protestant local gentry. By the kind courtesy of Robt. Mann, Esq., the bells of the parish church did not ring their accustomed peal for the anniversary of Waterloo till after the service. The building was enlarged by a new chancel and sacristy in 1889— the gift of a generous benefactor, who in 1900 erected the fine schools at a cost of £2,000. He presented a baptistery to the church 1901.

Rectors.

Rev. M. Fairclough, 1822.
Hon. and Rev. E. Clifford, 1827.
Rev. Jos. Wilson, 1829.
  „ John Jenkins, 1837.
  „ A. J. Duck, 1839 or 1840.
  „ Thos. Rolling, 1846.
  „ Michael Sinnot, 1850.
  „ Patrick Leary, 1852.
  „ Thos. Brindle, 1854.
  „ Henry Sutton, 1867.
  „ Thos. Caldwell, 1874.
  „ E. Anselm Glassbrook, 1882.
  „ Ephrem Guy, 1885.
  „ Archibald Fleming, 1899 to date.

BUNHILL ROW, LONDON, E.C.
St. Joseph's, Lamb's Passage.

In April and May, 1849, Fr. Hodgson, the well-known missioner, preached here in a hired room during the evenings of several weeks, and by his exertions brought back many to the Faith. On Sunday, May 13, 1849, Bishop Wiseman concluded the sermons &c. by giving a discourse to upwards of 1,300 persons. In 1856 a semi-Gothic church was built. The accommodation was for about 400 persons. In 1854 the Catholic population of Bunhill Row was estimated at between 4,000 and 5,000 persons. A painted window over the high altar has a representation of the titular patron of the church, St. Joseph. The edifice was built on land formerly belonging to the 'Associated Catholic Charities'—a society founded about 1797 by some humble Catholics who met for the discussion of business at the 'Mariner's Arms.' They subscribed one penny a week each to a common fund for the education &c. of poor Catholic children. When Canon Keens concluded the 'mission' in December 1889 upwards of 500 persons received Holy Communion. The fine school chapel recently erected is now regarded as a chapel of ease to St. Mary's, Moorfields, from which it is served.

BURGESS HILL, SUSSEX (Southwark). St. George's Retreat.

This institution for persons suffering from mental maladies was opened in 1869 'in spacious buildings situated on an estate of 250 acres in a picturesque and healthy neighbourhood.' The patients are under the care of the Nuns of St. Augustine, a congregation founded in 1841 by the late Canon Maes, of Bruges, for the special treatment of the mentally afflicted. A highly qualified physician resides in the house. The Rev. Albert Dearn was the first and the Rev. J. O'Meara is the present rector.

BURGHWALLIS, near DONCASTER, YORKS (Leeds).

The foundation of this mission is ascribed to 'the time of the Reformation.' The Tasburghs of Flexton, Suffolk, had a hall or residence here, and it is to them that the maintenance of the Faith in the penal times is due. The chapel was served by Jesuits in the eighteenth century, the earliest Father of the Society here being Fr. J. Messenger, 1725-52. He was succeeded by Frs. James Lewis, John Shaw, and Robert Saunderson. The latter remained till his death in 1781. Later on the chaplains were French émigrés, viz. Abbé Beury, 1798; Jn. Poisnel; Peter Dubuisson,

1803. The Abbé Louis le Roux, formerly vicar of Courbevoye, diocese of Paris, was priest here from 1828 to 1845. The register dates from 1761. From 1846 to the present time the mission has been served from Doncaster.

BURNHAM, SOMERSET (Clifton). The Sacred Heart.

A community of French nuns of the Sacred Heart settled here in 1889. The convent chapel served the mission till the opening of the church. The church was consecrated by the Bishop of Clifton in June 1890. The building, a handsome and well-proportioned structure, was designed by Canon Scoles, of Bridgewater.

BURNLEY, LANCS (Salford).

St. Mary's, East Gate, Burnley, was opened March 25, 1846, and consecrated August 2, 1849. The cost of building was £16,000. The Catholic population then numbered 1,300 ; at present it is about 6,000.

Priests.

Rev. J. Worthy, 1846.
„ J. Boardman, 1849.
„ Jn. Canon Rimmer, 1851.
„ Thos. Flanagan, 1860 (?).
„ M. Dillon, here in 1871.
„ Jn. Canon Rimmer, 1874.
„ Jas. Canon Morrissey, 1891.
„ Thos. Canon Corbishley, 1904.
„ Mgr. J. B. Cooke, 1905, to date.

BURNLEY, LANCS (Salford).
St. Mary Magdalen.

A new church and presbytery in the Gannow district of the city was opened Sunday, December 11, 1904, by the Bishop of Salford. The cost of erection was about £5,000. From 1887 till 1904, a school chapel served the mission. The Catholic population of the district is about 2,000.

Priests.

Rev. Octave Raymond, 1887.
„. Thomas Harrison, B.A., 1902 to date.

BURSCOUGH, ORMSKIRK, LANCS (*Liverpool*). St. John.

The mission history dates from 1700. The schools in connection with St. John's Catholic Chapel, built in 1815, were opened in November 1850. The style of the edifice is Gothic, the accommodation at time of opening being for 120 children. The chapel was built by Fr. Coghlan. The Catholic population of Burscough in 1860 was 400; in 1901 580.

In 1568 the Earl of Derby summoned the chief Catholic gentry of the district before him at Lathom House, and the most ' obstinate ' were sent to prison. The Austin Canons had a priory in the neighbourhood until the dissolution. The Burscoughs of Lathom Hall were Catholics, and great sufferers for the Faith. The family became extinct about the end of the eighteenth century.

The upper room of Burscough Hall Farm was used as a chapel about 1732. In 1759 the chapel was improved at a cost of £80. Bishop Gibson confirmed forty-eight persons here 1793. In 1819 a new chapel and presbytery were erected. Fr. R. Hodgson added a gallery about 1855. In 1885–6 the chapel was redecorated and partly refurnished.

Priests.

Rev. James Gorsuch, 1712.
„ Rd. Walmsley, 1734 (?).
„ James Brown, 1741.
„ Hy. Kellett, 1790.
„ Wm. Coghlan, 1810.
„ Jn. Anderton, 1836.
„ Rd. Hodgson, 1850.
„ Canon Fisher, 1871.
„ Jn. Kelly, B.A., 1877.
„ Jn. Daly, 1878.
„ Pat. Cahill, 1884.
„ T. B. Allan, 1885.
„ Jas. Eager, 1885 to date.

BURSLEM, STAFFS (*Birmingham*). St. Joseph's, Hall Street.

Though many Catholics were reported to be living in the district in 1850, it was not till 1895 that a mission could be established. Mass on Sundays was said at 31 Church Square by Fr. J. Hymers. The congregation was estimated at 1,200.

BURTON - ON - TRENT, STAFFS (*Birmingham*). SS. Mary and Modwena.

When the mission was founded here, in January 1852, there was much protestant opposition, owing largely to the recent excitement over the re-establishment of the hierarchy. The Gothic school chapel (48 ft. by 20 ft.), opened on Trinity Sunday the same year, was described by a contemporary journal as ' the handsomest and most correctly ecclesiastical building in Burton.' The present Gothic church was opened by Bishop Ullathorne in 1879. It may be of interest to remark that in 1811 there was only one Catholic family in

Burton, but by 1852 the congregation was estimated at some hundreds.

Priests.

Rev. W. O'Grady, 1852.
„ T. Telford, 1856.
„ C. McCabe, 1870.
„ J. Flynn, 1877 to date.

BURTON PARK, SUSSEX (*Southwark*). SS. Anthony and George.

The ancient Catholic family of Biddulph inherited the estate of Burton Park by the marriage of Richard Biddulph, Esq., with Anne, daughter and heiress of Sir Henry Goring, of Burton. This Richard Biddulph died 1679. There was a domestic chapel at the park. The last member of this family was Anthony John Wright Biddulph, Esq. This gentleman built the present church (Gothic) on a site in the park. The building was consecrated by Archbishop Manning for Bishop Grant, August 18, 1869. The accommodation of the building is for about 100 persons. After the death of Mr. Wright Biddulph the estate passed out of Catholic hands, but the mission is administered by lay trustees. For some years past the church has been served from Crawley.

Priests from 1825.

Rev. Peter Duval.
„ Thos. Brogan, 1833.
„ Simon O'Carroll, 1841.
„ E. Hood, 1849.
„ Peter Coop, 1851.
„ Joseph McSweeny, 1857.
„ Eugene Reardon, 1861.
„ Reginald Fowler, here in 1875.
„ Thos. Canon Lalor, 1879.
„ Nicholas Broder, here in 1889 till 1895, since when the mission has been served from Crawley.

BURTONWOOD, NEWTON - LE-WILLOWS, LANCS (*Liverpool*).

A school chapel was opened October 1886 on a site generously given by John Mercer, Esq., of Alston Hall. An additional class-room for fifty children was added in 1888, and in 1890 the school was again enlarged. For twelve years after the opening, the mission was served from Sutton. The first resident priest was Fr. Peter Morgan (1898), who still retains the incumbency.

BURWASH, SUSSEX (*Southwark*). St. Joseph's.

The church and presbytery were presented to the diocese of Southwark by Madame de los Heros, of Southover Hall. The first Mass in the building was said by Bishop Butt on Tuesday, October 11, 1887. The style of the church is cruciform. Mr. B. Whelan was the architect. The mission was for several years served by secular priests of the Southwark diocese, but for some time past has been transferred to the Salesian Fathers, who have their novitiate here. The Catholic population of Burwash in 1888 was practically confined to the family and servants of Southover Hall. In 1890 it was estimated at 100.

BURY, LANCS (*Salford*). Our Blessed Lady.

In 1821 there were not more than five Catholic families in the town, when Mass was said once a month in the upper room of a wool warehouse. In 1834 the first resident priest was appointed. The church, erected 1841-2, is a Gothic structure (90 ft. by 40 ft.), with gable and octagonal tower ; east window by Wailes. Total cost of schools, church, and presbytery, about £3,000.

Priests.

Rev. Hy. Walmesley, 1834.
„ James Peacock, 1835.
„ James Canon Boardman, 1851.
„ John Canon Rimmer, 1874.
„ James Morrissey, 1891.
„ Michael Byrne, 1897.
„ David Walshe, 1902 to date.

BURY ST. EDMUNDS, SUFFOLK
(*Northampton*).   St. Edmund.

In the reign of James II. the Benedictine monks of the Rue de St. Jacques, Paris, negotiated for the purchase of a portion of the old Abbey of Bury St. Edmunds, but an outcry having been made against this, the monks, at the request of the king, desisted from the purchase.[1] About 1732 Fr. Alexius Jones, O.S.B., took up his abode at Bury St. Edmunds, and remained here as missionary priest till 1737, when he went as chaplain to Hengrave Hall. His place was taken by Fr. Howard, O.S.B., who remained at Bury St. Edmunds till his death, December 12, 1755. Fr. J. Dennett, S.J., who died here March 1, 1789, aged eighty-seven, is said to have been long on the mission at Bury St. Edmunds.

The full list of English missions, with names of clergy, hours of services, &c., was first given in the 'Laity's Directory' for 1824. The

[1] The persons who raised the outcry afterwards purchased the abbey property for themselves.

church, which is in the Classical style, was thoroughly renovated and redecorated in the autumn of 1876.

Priests since 1824.

Rev. Thos. Angier, 1824.
„ Hy. Wright, 1828.
„ J. Laurenson, 1832.
„ Jos. Tate, 1835.
„ Hy. Brigham, 1840.
„ Bernard Jarrett, 1846.
„ Jas. Brownbill, 1855.
„ Jos. Lazenby, 1874.
„ Walter Strappini, 1885.
„ Thos. Parkinson, 1888.
„ Roger Perrin, 1896.
„ F. Jones, 1898.
„ Jos. Kenny, 1904 to date.

BUXTON, DERBYSHIRE (*Nottingham*).   St. Anne.

In August 1845 Fr. O'Farrell, of Leek, started the mission of Buxton by saying Mass there every Sunday at 7.30 A.M. Up to that time, the nearest Catholic chapel was twelve miles distant. That of Buxton was a small room, into which fifty persons used to crowd. In June 1846, when Dr. Gilligan, Bishop of Raphoe, was at Buxton, he said Mass at Mr. Campbell's house in Higher Buxton. The first stone of the present church was laid in July 1860, and the solemn opening took place in July 1861. The site was obtained from the Duke of Devonshire. The style is Gothic, and the building, which is of Reeve Edge Ripping stone, cost £720, exclusive of external fittings. The patroness is St. Anne, to whom ' the holy wells ' of Buxton were dedicated in pre-Reformation times. Mgr. (afterwards Cardinal) Manning preached on the occasion of the opening. The building, which will accommodate 200 persons, is 'a neat edifice of the Early English period of architecture.' The cost of erection was defrayed by P. Hewitt, Esq., the plans being drawn by Fr. A. J. Scoles.

Priests.

Rev. Edw. McGreavy, 1861.
  ,, W. A. Margison, 1863.
  — Driscoll, here in 1872.
   (Vacant 1875).
Rev. John Power, 1876.
  ,, Theodore Canon Hoeben, 1888.
  ,, Fredk. Kind, 1902 to date.

BYER MOOR, BURNOPFIELD, DURHAM (*Hexham and Newcastle*). The Sacred Heart.

In 1830 the population of this district was under 150 inhabitants. By 1860 the place had become so greatly developed that a Catholic chapel was a necessity. A school chapel was erected here in 1869. The new church at Lintz Green was opened 1876. A cemetery was laid out at the same time.

Priests.

Rev. Patrick Mathews, 1869.
  ,, Jn. Wilson, 1879 to date.

BYKER, near NEWCASTLE-ON-TYNE (*Hexham and Newcastle*). St. Lawrence.

The new church was solemnly opened April 24, 1898. The Mass was sung by Prior Buckler, of St. Dominic's, from which mission the chapel is still served.

I

C

CAMBERLEY, SURREY (*South-wark*). St. Tarcisius.

This place was formerly known as Cambridge Town. The mission was established in 1872 by Lady Southwell, who generously gave a site for church and presbytery. The chapel is an iron building, capable of holding about 100 persons; it was opened by Bishop Coffin, of Southwark, April 27, 1884. The fine statue of Our Lady of Lourdes was presented to the church by Miss Ross. Major Stafford and the late Col. Henderson, lecturer on tactics at the Staff College, were also generous benefactors to the mission.

Priests.

Rev. John McKenna, 1872.
„ M. O'Neill, 1882.
„ John Golden, 1888.
„ Thos. Ford, 1891.
„ Alexander McAuliffe, 1895.
„ W. Fichter, 1896.
„ F. S. Bennett, 1898.
„ P. Twomey, 1906 to date.

CAMBERWELL, LONDON, S.E. (*Southwark*). The Sacred Heart.

The mission was opened on Easter Monday 1860, when Mass was said at De Crespigny Lodge, Denmark Hill, by the late Fr. Claude Bernin, of Lyons. The district was then largely one of strawberry fields and market gardens. The next chapel was at Chepstow Cottage, which also served as the presbytery. This in turn was superseded by a chapel formed out of two or three cottages in Thomas Street, now Becket Street. A lay committee ably managed the temporalities of the mission, and a flourishing school was commenced under Mr. William Geoghegan. In 1862 a temporary church was erected at a cost of £600, and opened by Bishop Morris. Fr. Bernin left in 1864, and for a time the church was served on Sundays by Fr. Power, afterwards of Canterbury. The next rector, Fr. Ed. Cahill, enlarged the church, and introduced the Sisters of Notre Dame as teachers in the girls' and infants' schools. The temporary church of 1862 was replaced by the present one in the Camberwell New Road, opened by Bishop Morris, February 16, 1870. New schools for boys and girls were shortly afterwards built in Pitman Street. A second aisle and clerestory to the church were opened by Bishop Danell, August 12, 1872, the sermon being preached by Archbishop Manning. The presbytery, for three priests, was completed in 1875. Fr. McGrath, under whom these building developments were carried out, was appointed to the mission in 1869, and in 1882 became Canon of Southwark. He removed to Weybridge 1898, when he was succeeded by Canon W. Murnane, of Red Cross Street, the present rector.

CAMBORNE, WEST CORNWALL

(*Plymouth*). St. John the Baptist.
In the eighteenth century the Catholics of Camborne were sometimes able to hear Mass at Tolfrey, the residence of the Couche family, where there was a chapel and resident chaplain. Fr. Hayman died here April 30, 1756, aged eighty-seven. The present mission dates from 1851. The number of Catholics at Camborne at that time is reported to have been scarcely fifty. Mass was said occasionally in a small hired room by a priest from Penzance. In 1853 the congregation had increased to 253. Mr. Pike, a convert gentleman, fitted up a stable loft as a chapel. In 1858 the Catholic population had risen to one thousand, owing principally to Irish immigration. The stone of the new Gothic church was blessed and laid by the Bishop of Plymouth on June 24, 1858. Fr. James Carey was priest at this time. The building was opened May 26, 1859.

Priests.

Rev. Richard Mansfield, 1853.
„ James Carey, 1857.
„ William Cassey, 1860.
„ Leo Croutelle, here in 1872.
„ Arthur McKey, 1882.
„ John McCarthy, 1885.
„ Edward Barry, 1892.
„ Laurence O'Loughlin.

CAMBRIDGE (*Northampton*).

Our Lady and the English Martyrs.
Though it was not until 1854 that the B.A. degree of the universities of Oxford and Cambridge was opened to Catholics, several distinguished adherents of the old religion, as the Duke of Norfolk, Lord Edward Howard, and Cardinal Acton, made their higher studies at Cambridge. Kenelm Digby, the well-known author of ' Mores Catholici,' joine the Church from the university in 1825, and Mr. Ambrose Lisle Philipps in 1838. Some time after 1820, when Sir Thomas Reddington was at Cambridge, his mother, who resided near his college, opened her dining-room as a chapel on Sundays to enable the Irish agricultural labourers of the district to hear Mass. In 1841 the first mission in Cambridge was established by Fr. Shenley. The chapel was in a cottage at Barnwell, a suburb of the town, the requisites for offering Mass being borrowed from the chapel at Sawston House, the residence of Major Huddlestone. Such numbers attended Mass on Sundays that Fr. Shenley resolved on building a church. Great indignation was manifested at this in the University when the project became known. On November 5 a large body of students assembled to tear up the foundations, but retreated at the prospect of an encounter with a body of burly Irishmen and a force of special constables under the command of the mayor, Thomas Fisher, Esq.

The church, designed by Pugin, was opened on the feast of St. George 1843, by Bishop Wareing, V.A. of the Eastern district. Bishop Wiseman preached to a crowded congregation. The church, dedicated to St. Andrew, Apostle, was pronounced by the Camden Society to be ' a hidden gem.' By the ' early eighties ' it was totally inadequate for the size of the congregation, and a new building was resolved on by Canon Scott, M.A., the resident priest. The cost of this new building was borne by Mrs. Lyne Stephens, a great benefactress to the Catholic Church in England. The foundation stone of the church and presbytery was laid by Bishop

I 2

Riddell, of Northampton, June 30, 1887. Messrs. Dunn and Hansom were the architects. The building was opened with much ceremony in 1890. The style of the church is Gothic. The interior of the structure is very ornate, and the belfry is provided with a fine peal of bells playing musical chimes.

CAMPDEN, GLOUCESTERSHIRE (*Clifton*).

The new church, in the Perpendicular style (*temp.* Henry IV. and V.), was opened on September 3, 1891. Fr. Lloyd, the rector, was mainly instrumental in erecting it. He was assisted to a large extent in the good work by the Earl of Gainsborough, who, in addition to monetary aid, presented the site. The stones of the old chapel at Westington were utilised for the new building. The Papal arms, with those of the Earl and Countess of Gainsborough, are displayed in the church. A statue of St. Catherine, the patroness of the church, stands in a niche over the main entrance. The altar of the Lady Chapel is in memory of Lady Constance Bellingham. W. Lunn, Esq., of Malvern, was the architect. A school chapel was opened here in September 1869, and used for worship till the opening of the present church.

Priests.

Rev. Vincent Ferreri, here in 1869 till after 1886.
  „ Bernard Lloyd, here in 1888.
  „ John Wenham, 1898.
  „ Felix May, 1902.
  „ Ignatius Gurd, 1904.

CANNINGTON, SOMERSET (*Clifton*). The Holy Name.

The mission was founded when the first Lord Clifford of Chudleigh received the estate from Charles II. in 1672. A chaplain was maintained there till about 1768, when the mission appears to have been closed, the last priest being Fr. W. Sullivan. In 1807, Charles sixth Lord Clifford gave Cannington ' Court House ' to a community of Benedictine nuns, whose chaplain attended to the spiritual welfare of the revived mission. It is interesting to note that a Benedictine convent was founded at Cannington in the troubled reign of Stephen by Robert de Courcy, the establishment consisting of an abbess and six or seven nuns.

Fr. Richard O'Meara was chaplain at Cannington in 1827. In 1831 the nuns removed to Little Heywood, in Staffordshire, but they made over the house and chapel at Cannington to the V.A. of the Western district for the use of the mission. The priests after this were :—

Rev. T. Burgess and Abbé Premord, 1832.
  „ Dr. Tuomy, 1833.
  „ T. Costello, 1835.
  „ James Platt, 1838.
  „ A. Byrne, 1841.
  „ T. Danson, 1845.
  „ E. Scully, 1845.
  „ F. English, 1851.
  „ Jn. Bouvier, 1864.
  „ Septimus Coxon, 1866.
  „ C. Kennard, 1875.

The present rector is the Rev. John Archdeacon.

CANNOCK, STAFFS (*Birmingham*). The Sacred Heart and Our Lady.

In 1876 Bishop Ullathorne, of

Birmingham, sent Fr. F. Duckett, of Rugeley, Staffordshire, to start a mission at Cannock. Aided by Sir Charles Clifford, a school and presbytery were erected at a cost of £2,000. The school children numbered 180 in 1885. In 1899, a house known as Hall Court was transformed into a church. It was opened December 8 the same year. In December 1901, the decorations of the sanctuary were completed and stations of the Cross erected.

Priests.

Rev. F. Duckett, 1876.

„ James B. Keating, 1879.

„ Thos. Dickenson, 1882.

„ James Giblin, 1891.

:, Rowley O'Keefe, 1893 to date.

CANTERBURY, KENT (*Southwark*). St. Thomas of Canterbury.

Prior to 1800, the chapel was at Hales Place (*q.v.*). In January of this year a temporary chapel was opened in a public dancing room at Canterbury. Two smaller rooms underneath served as schools for the 'scores of Catholic children' in and around the town, but no Government grant was received. A chapel was opened in White Horse Lane 1866, and used up to the opening of the present place of worship in Burgate Street, April 1875. The site of the building and £1,000 towards the expense of erection were given by Mr. and Mrs. Hart. The plan comprises 'a nave of four bays approached by a south porch, with a sacristy on the south side of the chancel.' The stone frontal displays incidents in the life of St. Thomas of Canterbury. A new Lady altar was presented by Miss Billington in December 1905.

Priests.

Rev. Thomas Richardson, 1860.

„ Richard Power, 1871.

„ Edmund Sheppard, 1905.

CARISBROOKE, ISLE OF WIGHT (*Portsmouth*).

The Dominicanesses, or Nuns of the Second Order of St. Dominic, founded 1215 by St. Dominic, had an English branch, established at Vilvorde, near Brussels, by Fr. (afterwards Cardinal) Howard in 1661. The nuns came to England 1794, and after several residences at Hartpury Court, near Gloucester, Hurst Green, Lancashire, &c., settled at Carisbrooke in a house presented to them by Elizabeth Countess of Clare in December 1866. They opened their chapel to the public, and thus a new mission was established, Fr. Peter Sablon being the first chaplain. Fr. E. G. Kelly is the present incumbent.

CARLISLE, CUMBERLAND (*Hexham and Newcastle*). St. Mary and St. Joseph.

The Catholics in the city and district were attended during the penal times by the chaplains of the Howards of Corby Castle.[1] Through the influence of Henry Howard, Esq., of Corby, a mission was established in the town in 1798, though as late as 1824 the chapel was 'an upper room.' The

[1] After the rebellion of 1745-6 many of the Jacobite prisoners at Carlisle were attended by the priest from Corby. Among these was Macdonald of Kinloch Moidart, a devout Catholic, and the only Highland chief executed for his share in the melancholy enterprise. His claymore and tartan coat are still preserved at Corby.

118   ENGLISH CATHOLIC MISSIONS

main beam gave way at Easter of
that year, and the apartment had
to be supported by ' a strong prop ' !
A site for a chapel wa obtained
from Lord Lonsdale for £400, and
a building opened, 1825.   The
presbytery was erected at the same
time.   Mainly owing to a legacy
left by Miss Lowry, of Durranthill
(died 1871), the present church
was commenced in 1891, and opened
by Bishop Wilkinson, of Hexham
and Newcastle, June 1893.   The
style is Perpendicular Gothic from
design by Dunn and Hansom, and
the structure occupies ' one of the
finest sites in the city.' A fine
oak pulpit was presented by the
Misses Fairbain, of Rugby.   The
seating accommodation of the
church is for 700.   Much of the
credit of the building of this fine
church is due to Canon Waterton,
the present rector.
Priests since 1824.
Rev. Joseph Marshall.
„ Luke Canon Curry, 1854.
„ Geo. Canon Waterton, 1879
  to date.

CARLTON, YORKS (*Leeds*). St.
Mary.
Fr. John Edisford, a Jesuit,
laboured here for many years, *i.e.*
from about 1685 till 1717. In three
years he reconciled upwards of forty
persons to the Church, and was
in consequence singled out at the
Revolution for special attack. He
succeeded in hiding the altar plate,
vestments, &c., but was so near
capture himself that on one occasion he had to lie close in a narrow
hole while his pursuers plundered
the house. He was still on the
mission in the district in 1710, en-
during every kind of hardship. The
last Jesuit missioner at Carlton was

Fr. William Allan, 1780-1. A Fr.
Charles Houghton died here 1797,
but whether a secular or religious
does not appear.
Priests since 1825.
Rev. Jn. Billington.
„ Geo. Canon Heptonstall, 1830.
„ Mgr. Edward Goldie, 1877.
„ James Canon Glover, 1882.
„ Julius de Baere, 1890.
„ Gustave Thonon, 1893.
„ J. Hubert Offermann, 1895.
„ Norman Waugh, 1903 to date.

CARLTON, NOTTINGHAM. The
Sacred Heart.
Mass was first said here in
recent times in 1877. In 1883 the
church was opened. The style is
Gothic. In April 1884 a powerful
bell for the church was consecrated
by Bishop Bagshawe. It bears the
legend : ' Ste. Joannes Baptiste ora
pro nobis.' Fr. T. Hoeben was the
first priest.
Priests.
Rev. T. Hoeben, 1877.
„ F. Kind, 1888.
„ Jn. Hardican, 1902.

CARSHALTON, SURREY (*Southwark*).
In 1793 the Dominicans of
Bornhem, Flanders, came to England after the suppression of their
monastery by the French Re-
volutionary armies. They opened
a school for boys at Carshalton, and
the establishment was known as
Bornhem House. The mansion is
now the Convent. In 1812 it
passed over to Mr. Wm. Mylius, a
well-known Catholic educationist,
who renamed it the ' Primary College.' The Abbé Chabot, who was
chaplain to the college, also at-

tended to the spiritual needs of the few local Catholics. After the removal of Mr. Mylius's establishment to Chelsea in 1830, the mission was closed. The place again became a centre of Catholicity in 1893, when the Daughters of the Cross purchased Carshalton House, a fine mansion once belonging to Dr. Radcliffe, Queen Anne's physician, and opened a highly successful boarding school. They have also a day high school and the Catholic elementary schools. The fine Gothic church of the convent was built 1899-1900, from design of C. Ingress-Bell, Esq. It was consecrated October 12, 1904, by Archbishop Bourne.

Chaplains.

Rev. James Nolan, 1893.

„ Alfred Sharpe, M.A., 1905.

CASTLEFORD, YORKS, WEST RIDING (*Leeds*). St. Joseph.

The schools erected in 1877 served the purpose of a chapel till 1890, when the present church was built. The foundations were commenced on February 27. The building is in the Gothic style, and will accommodate about 500 persons. For some years after the commencement of the mission the place was served from Pontefract.

Priests.

Rev. John Heweson, 1882 to date.

CASTLETON, LANCS (*Salford*). St. Gabriel and the Angels.

Mission established 1879. A 'very nice school chapel,' presented by a generous benefactor, was opened Sunday, January 25, 1885. A revolving wooden shutter divided the sanctuary from the class-room. Fr. W. L. Fowler had charge of the mission at the commencement.

CATERHAM, SURREY (*Southwark*).

The church of the Sacred Heart was built 1880-1 by the late Captain Roe, father of the since incumbent, Fr. F. Roe. The structure is cruciform, in the Early English style, from designs by Mr. E. Ingress-Bell. The sanctuary has been recently adorned with elegant mosaic pictures illustrative of events in the life of Our Lord. Prior to the establishment of the mission, Fr. J. McKenna, of Croydon, used to go over to Caterham occasionally to attend to the spiritual wants of Catholic soldiers in the Guards' depôt and local Catholics generally. During the building of the present church a temporary chapel was generously erected for the use of the Catholic Guardsmen by the officers of the several regiments connected with the place. The new church was solemnly opened by Cardinal Manning, Thursday, August 11, 1881.

CATFORD, LONDON, S.E. (*Southwark*).

A plain Romanesque church designed by the late F. W. Tasker, of Bedford Row, was opened for worship in Sangley Road, Catford, by Bishop Amigo, of Southwark, on Tuesday, September 13, 1904. Among the congregation present were Alderman and Sheriff Sir Stuart Knill and Lady Knill, Canon O'Halloran, &c. The building, which at present accommodates upwards of 150, is capable of being considerably enlarged. The cost of erection was defrayed by an anonymous benefactress. Fr. E. Escarguel is the first and present rector.

CATFORTH, PRESTON, LANCS (*Liverpool*). St. Robert.

This church was erected through the zeal of Fr. John Bilsborrow—afterwards Bishop of Salford. The building was opened July 29, 1877. In 1889 the interior was painted and decorated.

Priests.

Rev. J. Bilsborrow, 1877.
„ Martin Mahony, 1878.
„ Geo. Dobson, 1880.
„ Peter J. Kane, 1885.
„ Michael Ryan, 1886.
„ James Welsby, 1892.
„ John Tomlinson, 1894.
„ John Donohoe, 1903.
„ Andrew Flynn, 1904.

CAVERSHAM, OXFORDSHIRE (*Birmingham*). Our Lady and St. Anne.

Mission started in 1896. There were at this time only thirteen practical Catholics in the village, but by the time the schools of Our Lady and St. Anne were opened, Thursday August 31, 1899, the congregation had risen to 120, eighty of these being regular church-goers. Before the erection of the schools, Mass was said in the chapel of the convent belonging to the Sœurs de Miséricorde. The schools, which afford accommodation for some 114 children, were used as a chapel until the opening of the present church in 1902.

Priests.

Fr. Raymond Haskew, 1896.
Fr. W. Wells, 1902.

CAVERSWALL, near CHEADLE, STAFFS (*Birmingham*). St. Filumena.

The Benedictines of Ghent came to England in 1794, and after settling for a time at Preston, in Lancashire, they purchased Caverswall Castle and fitted it up as a monastery, about 1811. By Bishop Milner's desire, the chapel was opened to the public, and Fr. Richard Richmond placed in charge of the mission. In 1812, a larger chapel was founded, and opened on St. Polycarp's Day 1813. The Catholic population grew so rapidly that a chapel had to be erected in Lane End, near Caverswall, 1819. Fr. Richmond was succeeded by Fr. Hubbard. In 1854 the Benedictines removed to Oulton, near Stone, and the castle came into the possession of a distinguished Catholic gentleman, Mr. Radcliffe, by whom the present Gothic church was built. The stone was laid by Bishop Ullathorne on the Thursday of Easter week 1863, and the opening took place on January 28, 1864. Gilbert Blount was the architect. For some time after its opening the church was served from Longton.

CHARLTON, near WOOLWICH, KENT (*Southwark*).

In 1903 the Oblates of the Assumption, expelled from France under the law against religious associations, opened a school chapel at Charlton. The congregation as ascertained at present (1906) numbers about 250. The school, which is under the direction of the Sisters of the Assumption, gives instruction to about sixty children. The chapel was merely a large room of the convent, and was used till the opening of the present Romanesque Church, September 8, 1906. The internal decoration is very harmonious, the altar-piece being a representation of the Madonna and Child.

CHASETOWN, STAFFS (*Birmingham*). St. Joseph.

In 1881 the Catholic population of Chasetown was estimated at 350 adults and 60 children. The nearest chapel was six miles off. In the above-mentioned year an eligible site for a church was procured, and in 1883 the present edifice was opened.

Priests.

Rev. Geo. Bunce, 1883.
,, Francis McCarrick, 1888.
,, Fredk. Williams, 1895.
,, Charles Brain, 1897 to date.

CHATHAM, KENT (*Southwark*).

For the early history of Chatham *see* OLD BROMPTON. In 1859 the chapel accommodated 300. The Catholic population amounted to 1,500, including Stroud and Rochester. Of these, 500 were soldiers of the garrison. About £300 was collected to enlarge the building, but, on consideration, the rector, Fr. J. Morley, deemed it advisable to build a new church. The first stone was laid by Bishop Grant October 10, 1862. The style chosen was Lombardo-Gothic, from design by H. Clutton, Esq. The cost of the shell was about £1,700. On

June 25, 1863, the building was opened by Bishop Grant, upon which occasion Mgr. (Cardinal) Manning preached (Matt. xxvii. 19). The fine painting which forms the altar-piece was presented by the late Bishop Butt. The organ, purchased from St. John's Protestant Church, in the town, was constructed in 1829. Some few years ago the church was renovated and embellished by the late rector, Canon H. Cafferata, now of Sutton. The registers of the mission go back to about 1790, when the chapel was at Old Brompton.

CHEADLE, STAFFS (*Birmingham*). St. Giles.

This fine church was built at the sole cost of John sixteenth Earl of Shrewsbury, and was consecrated September 1, 1846. The style is Decorated Gothic, the plan comprising nave, north and south aisles, Lady Chapel, and spire (200 ft.). The east window has for subject the genealogy of Our Lord. A handsome rood-screen separates the sanctuary from the body of the church. The opening ceremony was attended by all the Vicars-Apostolic, the Earl and Countess of Shrewsbury, the Archbishops of Sydney and Damascus, the Austrian Ambassador, &c. Bishop Gillis, of Edinburgh, preached (Ps. cxxii. 1, 2).

The mission formerly formed part of that of Cresswell. Fr. Wareing, the priest of that place, finding many Catholics at Cheadle in danger of losing their faith, opened a chapel there in a private house. This place of worship proving inadequate, a disused Militia storehouse (60 ft. by 20 ft.) was purchased and turned into a chapel.

In 1834 the number of communicants at Cheadle numbered ninety. The establishment of the mission, erection of the schools, &c., is entirely due to the sixteenth Earl of Shrewsbury.

Priests.

Mission served from Cresswell 1818–23 by Frs. Wareing and Baddeley.

Rev. — Gates, 1824.

  „ — Jeffries (first resident priest), 1827.

  „ Francis Fairfax, 1834.

  „ Wm. Gubbins, 1848.

  „ James Canon Jones, 1856.

  „ Stuart Eyre Bathurst, 1860.

  „ E. H. Hunter, here 1871.

  „ Walter Morris, 1876 to date.

CHEAM, SURREY. St. Anthony's Hospital.

A mission was established here in the reign of Charles I., and served from the chapel of Queen Henrietta Maria. In 1755 the place was attended by the chaplains from the Portuguese Embassy. The register dates from about this time. During this period, Fr. Wm. Heatley, O.S.B., was instrumental in converting over fifty protestants to the Faith, which led to a prosecution being instituted against him by the Rev. J. King, rector of the parish. The chapel would appear to have been in the house of the Dowager Lady Petre, who long resided here. It was searched in 1745—the year of the Jacobite rising—for a secret supply of arms which it was alleged existed there. In 1780, one Wm. Bryant, a Catholic, was 'hounded to his grave in the parish churchyard by the hellish rabble' of Lower Cheam. The mission would appear

to have been closed shortly after 1788.

In 1904 the Daughters of the Cross Nuns acquired North Cheam House from F. Burdett, Esq., and on June 21 of the same year opened a hospital for convalescents. The chapel serves the mission, which, exclusive of the hospital, has a Catholic population of about sixty, mostly resident at Worcester Park, *q.v.*, some two miles distant.

Some Priests of the Old Mission.

Rev. Joseph Hansbie, 1742.

  „ — Heathe, 1753.

  „ Wm. Heatley, O.S.B., 1755.

  „ B. Bradshaw, 1761.

  „ R. Harris, 1772.

  „ J. Brewer, O.S.B., 1776.

  „ J. Placid Naylor, O.S.B., 1776.

  „ Benedict Short, O.P., 1785.

Priests of the Modern Mission of North Cheam.

Rev. G. Gallea, 1904.

  „ Marmaduke Langdale, 1905.

  „ Bernard W. Kelly, 1905.

CHEESEBURN GRANGE, NORTHUMBERLAND (*Hexham and Newcastle*). St. Francis Xavier.

Cheeseburn Grange is the ancestral seat of the Riddells, who inherited the estate from the Widdringtons. The date of the establishment of the mission is 1768. The Dominicans had charge of the chapel, Fr. James Sharp, O.P., being the first priest. He was probably the Fr. J. Sharp who 'died the enviable death of charity on the 28th February, 1801, by attending the infected at Coventry' (Oliver). Another priest, Fr. Phillips, died at the Grange August 7, 1783. The baptismal list commences 1775. The public chapel of Cheeseburn Grange 'was duly certified as a place of public religious worship in the year of Our Lord 1792,' in pursuance of the Catholic Relief Act of the previous year. The church underwent extensive renovation and redecoration in 1852.

Priests from 1792.

Rev. John Tate.
„ J. Fleet.
„ John Leadbitter, 1815.
„ Thos. Cock, 1817.
„ Thos. Gillett, 1850.
„ Edward Gosford, 1856.
„ Francis Trappes, 1858, *et seq.* (Vacant 1875).
„ Wm. Baron, here in 1883, till 1892.
„ Hy. Blake, 1892.
„ M. P. Horgan, 1893.
„ Patrick Matthews, 1896.
„ Henry Walmesley, 1899 to date.

CHELMSFORD, ESSEX (*Westminster*).

The church here was the first in England to be dedicated to the Immaculate Conception. It was opened by Bishop Wiseman October 21, 1847. Before this time, Mass was said in one of the rooms of the schools erected in 1845, in which year the mission was started. The building was consecrated October 20, 1866. The architect of the church, which accommodates 1,000, was J. J. Scoles. The Catholic population of the place in 1860 was about 500. The new Lady altar, presented by Mrs. C. Wells, was blessed October 9, 1904.

Priests.

Rev. C. P. King, 1845.
„ C. Batt, 1867.
„ J. Padbury, M.R., 1885.
„ C. Shepherd, 1901 to date.

CHELSEA, LONDON, S.W. (*Westminster*). The Holy Redeemer, Cheyne Row, Chelsea.

The church was opened by Cardinal Vaughan October 23, 1895. The style is ' Italian of the English type.' There is a spacious gallery at the west end. This church is the eighth erected by Canon Keens, M.R., the late incumbent. Fr. D. Skrimshire is the present rector.

CHELSEA, LONDON, S.W.

St. Mary's Church owes its foundation to the Abbé Voyaux, one of the most distinguished of the *émigré* clergy. He was, at the time of the Revolution, professor of the Sorbonne, hon. canon of the Royal Chapel of St. Denis, and president of the College of Trenecinque. His first chapel at Chelsea was ' a poor room over a shop in a back street,' but his zeal subsequently enabled him to erect in 1812 the recent Church of St. Mary. The Abbé had chiefly in view the spiritual needs of the hundreds of Catholic veterans in the Royal Hospital of Chelsea, many of whom had lost some or other of their limbs in fighting their pastor's countrymen in Spain or Flanders. The cost of the church was £6,000, of which a considerable portion was subscribed by Louis XVIII. and the exiled nobility of France. Sir Robert Peel, the great statesman, gave £300. The building was very plain until 1856, when extensive improvements were effected by Messrs. Barff & Co. These consisted of three fresco altar pieces in the Italian style. The pilasters of the church were adorned with paintings of the Apostles. Cardinal Weld, after his ordination to the priesthood in 1821, was curate at

Chelsea for some years till his health gave way. He was consecrated Bishop of Amycla in 1826, and created cardinal at Rome by Pius VIII. in March 1830. Notwithstanding his having been twice solicited to return to France by Louis XVIII. and Charles X., the Abbé Voyaux refused to leave ' his beloved flock at Chelsea,' though it is certain that an archbishopric and a cardinal's hat awaited him in his native country. He died in November 1840, aged eighty-one. The old church having long outlived its capabilities, Canon Macmullen, in June 1876, appealed for funds for a new building. The first stone of the present structure—designed by J. F. Bentley—was laid in July 1877 by Cardinal Manning, who employed for the purpose the silver trowel used at the founding of Moorfields Church in 1817. The building, which is a fine specimen of the Early English style, was opened in May 1879.

CHELTENHAM, GLOUCESTERSHIRE (*Clifton*). St. Gregory the Great.

In October 1809, Fr. Aug. Birdsall, O.S.B., came to Cheltenham from Bath and started the mission. He was assisted by Richard Rawe, Esq., and on June 3, 1810, he opened the old chapel, which was several times enlarged. During the riot in November 1850, aroused by the restoration of the hierarchy, the building was much damaged, but all the loss was made good by the Hundred, and also from the private subscriptions of distinguished individuals, as Mr. Grenville Berkeley, M.P., Colonel the Hon. — Browne, &c. The present cruciform church, designed by C. Hansom, was opened

by Bishop Clifford, of Clifton, in the presence of Cardinal Wiseman, the mayor and corporation, &c., May 1857. The east window is the gift of J. Fitzherbert, Esq., of Swynerton. The building was consecrated November 6, 1877.

Priests.

Rev. Aug. Birdsall, O.S.B., 1809.
  „ Christopher Shann, 1834.
  „ Hy. Paillet, 1843.
  „ A. Glassbrook, 1849.
  „ Ambrose Cotham, 1851.
  „ Robt. Wilkinson, 1874.
  „ E. Anselm O'Gorman, 1889.
  „ Robt. Wilkinson, 1890 to date.

CHEPSTOW, MONMOUTHSHIRE (*Newport*). St. Mary.

Mr. Gunter, of Chepstow Grange, was the chief Catholic in the district at the end of the seventeenth century. The chapel in the house was served by the Jesuits (1685). Fr. W. Gunter, who suffered for the Faith 1588, was probably a member of this family. The mission was afterwards served by the Franciscans. Bishop Collingridge, V.A.W.D., resided here for some time after 1807. Forty years later the mission was in a very precarious condition, being in want of a school and presbytery, and having but an income of £80 for all purposes. Catholics then numbered 147, and in 1864 250.

Priests since 1824.

Rev. Jn. Williams, —.
  „ P. Yates, 1831.
  „ — Kelly, 1833.
  „ J. Carbery, 1835.
  „ R. Hartley, 1837.
  „ W. Woolett, 1841.
  „ Thos. Cody, 1843.
  „ P. Millea, 1850.
  „ John Dawson, 1852.
  „ Francis Trapper, 1854.

Rev. Thos. Fenn, 1857.
„ David Lambe, 1861.
„ John B. Quaid, here 1867, and till 1895.
„ M. Vandenberghe, 1895.
„ H. E. Stuart Mills, 1897.
„ J. B. Conway, 1903 to date.

CHERTSEY, SURREY (*Southwark*).

On the conversion of Lord and Lady Holland to the Catholic faith in 1850, a domestic chapel was opened at St. Anne's Hill, Chertsey, the country seat of the Holland family. For many years, Fr. Charles Comberbach was chaplain. This excellent priest was a convert to Catholicity, and for some years before going to St. Anne's Hill was stationed at the Priory, Princethorpe. He died in 1890, aged ninety-two. Lady Holland died in 1889, when the estate passed to her kinsman, Lord Ilchester, a protestant, but the chapel was kept up till the death of Fr. Comberbach. For some years subsequent to this, a small basilica-shaped chapel on the Woburn Park estate (St. George's College) did duty as a place of worship for Chertsey Catholics, who were under the spiritual care of Fr. O. Turner, prefect of studies at the college. About 1893 the mission of Chertsey was served every Sunday from the diocesan seminary, Wonersh, by Fr. S. Banfi, D.D. Fr. Banfi succeeded by the present Fr. Dominic Brownrigg, of the Salesian congregation. The chapel is an iron building in the Eastwood Road, and adjoins the Convent of Our Lady Help of Christians. The congregation is about 100. The Marquis of Ruvigny and Raineval, the distinguished historian and heraldist, is the most noted member of the congregation.

CHESTER (*Shrewsbury*). St. Werburgh, Grove Park Road.

The mission appears to have been once served by the Jesuits. Fr. J. Cuffaud, S.J., died there March 19, 1715, 'a martyr of charity in attending the sick prisoners.' These were probably Jacobites who had taken part in the rebellion on behalf of James III., the 'Old Pretender.' The chapel at Chester, dedicated to St. Werburgh, was founded by Bishop Penswick in Queen's Street in 1799. The seating capacity was for 210. In Lent 1846, Fr. Gaudentius gave a mission here, when the chapel was 'crowded to suffocation' at all three daily services. In 1850 the Catholics of Chester numbered between 3,000 and 4,000. The school room adjoined the chapel, and by cutting holes in the dividing wall 400 children were enabled to hear Mass on Sundays. In addition to the civilians, large numbers of the garrison were Catholics. In November 1850, Fr. E. Carbery, the priest of the mission, appealed to Mr. Wilbraham, formerly M.P. for South Cheshire, for help in building a school, but that gentleman declined on the ground of the 'insolent usurpations' of Pius IX. and Cardinal Wiseman in the matter of the restored hierarchy.

The old church of St. Werburgh in Queen Street was replaced by another and larger structure in the Gothic style in the Grosvenor Park Road, 1873-5. Between 1883-6 nearly £700 was expended in improving the interior of this handsome church. In April of the last named year the windows of the apse were filled in with stained glass, the designs being subjects taken from Our Lord's Passion. The window at the back of the altar—given by G. Hostage, Esq.—has a representation of the Crucifixion, with a lower medallion of St. George. A third window represents the Resurrection, with lower and separate views of the old and new St. Werburgh's.

Priests.

Rev. Jas. Lancaster, 1794.
,, Thos. Penswick, 1796.
,, Jn. Ashurst, 1815.
,, Jn. Briggs (Bishop of Beverley 1850), 1818.
,, Jn. Wilcock, 1833.
,, Edw. Canon Carbery, 1838.
,, Hy. Hopkins, 1861.
,, P. Lahaye, 1865.
,, W. Walton, 1867.
,, Canon Buquet, 1868.
,, Wilfrid Dallow, 1882.
,, Canon Lynch, 1883.

CHESTER. St. Francis, Grosvenor Street, Franciscans.

In 1858, Mass was said at Bishop Lloyd's house, Water Gate Row. In 1860 a shed at 25 Watergate Row was fitted up as a chapel. On June 16, 1864, a temporary wooden chapel for 500 persons was opened on the present church site. The present Gothic church was opened April 29, 1875, by Bishop Hedley, of Newport; Cardinal Manning preached. The debt on the building was paid off by the Tatlock family in September 1899, and the edifice consecrated by Bishop Allen, of Shrewsbury, June 3, 1900. The monastery was opened in 1876 and the schools in 1882.

Priests (O.S.F.)

Fr. Seraphin, 1858.
,, Elzear, 1858.
,, Venantius, 1859.
,, Pacificus, 1873.
,, Nicholas, 1879.
" Pacificus, 1882.
,, Modestus, 1885.
,, Bernard, 1888.
,, Anthony, 1889.
,, Fidelis, 1892.
,, Bernardine, 1895.
,, Ambrose, 1897.
,, Seraphin, 1898.

CHESTER-LE-STREET, DURHAM (*Hexham and Newcastle*). St. Cuthbert.

The Recusants of the district paid £11,650—about £60,000 of modern money—in fines for non-attendance at the parish church in 1632. In 1847 Fr. Jos. Sheridan, O.S.B., of Birtley, had charge of the few Catholics here. The present mission dates from 1881, when the chapel—' a small brick building in a back lane '—was opened in Lumley Terrace. A site for a large church has recently, it is said, been given by the Earl of Durham. A school chapel (73 ft. by 24 ft.) was completed towards the end of 1888.

Priests.

Rev. Hy. Blunden, 1881.
,, Michael Greene, 1888.
,, E. Barnett, 1889.
,, Geo. Mendham, 1891.
,, Ignatius Beale, 1893.
,, Francis Holmes, 1895.
,, Patrick Kearney, 1902 to date.

CHESTERFIELD, DERBYSHIRE (*Nottingham*). Mount St. Mary's.

Spinkhill, near Chesterfield, was the ancient seat of the Pole family, and ' one of the earliest centres of labour of the English Jesuits.' It is not quite certain when the Fathers first made the place their abode, but we read of a Fr. John Pole, S.J., being sent from here to Valladolid in 1600 to teach theology. The last of the family was John Pole, Esq., who died in 1718. His widow, Madame Ursula Pole, survived till 1751, and after her death the estates passed to the Jesuits, under her husband's will. There is a tradition that Fr. Robert Parsons (1546–1610) lived at the hall for some time. In 1721 the chapel is described as containing, among other items, a green silk vestment, two velvet antependiums, gilt silver chalice and paten, two pyxes, missal, four lacquered candlesticks, etc. Forty-seven baptisms are recorded at Spinkhill between 1757 and 1766. Many local Catholics were interred in the burial ground attached to the mission, which was used down to about 1835. Till the building of the new church in 1845, the chapel was a room at the top of the house. The residence of the Jesuits was known in the registers of the Society as the ' College of the Immaculate Conception,' but there is still some doubt whether the place during the penal times was not also a real school where Catholic boys were secretly instructed. The present College was commenced in 1842. Between 1844–6 was erected the first portion of the fine block of buildings of the College of Mount St. Mary's, ' to prepare youths '—so the first prospectus ran—' for the higher ecclesiastical studies or for commercial pursuits.' The Church was opened by Bishop Walsh, V.A., September 21, 1846. The building was redecorated and a new Gothic altar erected, 1896. A sacristy and south tribune

were added 1864. The old Spinkhill chapel is now used for sodality meetings. The new college buildings were erected 1876-7. Like Stonyhurst, St. Edmund's, and other Catholic foundations of a similar nature, the college has long since outgrown its original dimensions, and now ranks as one of the most complete educational establishments in England. The number of students is about 150.

Rectors of the College (S.J.)

Rev. Wm. Cobb, 1846.
  ,, Francis Clough, 1847.
  ,, John Baron, 1848.
  ,, Maurice Mann, 1854.
  ,, Geo. Tickell, 1859.
  ,, Thos. Williams, 1862.
  ,, Thos. Dykes, 1873.
  ,, John Clayton, 1879.
  ,, Henry Parker, 1888.
  ,, Geo. Haggins, 1893.
  ,, Francis Payne, 1901 to date.

CHICHESTER, SUSSEX (*Southwark*). St. Richard.

The first priest to reside at Chichester was Fr. John McDonald, in 1854, during which year the church was commenced. The opening took place in 1855. The style is Early English. The structure comprises a nave, chancel, and sacristy from the design by Wardell. Fr. J. F. Wilkinson was incumbent from 1855 till his death in October 1866. While a priest at Clewer Green, near Windsor, he had ' the somewhat unusual honour ' of being presented to King William IV. by Lord Melbourne. He lies interred in the church near the vault of the late Lady Newburgh, who died in 1860.

Priests.

Rev. Jn. McDonald, 1854.
  ,, J. F. Wilkinson, 1855.
  ,, Victor Duke, 1866

Rev. Thos. Lalor, 1874.
,, Edward Clery, 1878.
,, W. Bolger, 1897.
,, Edmund Miller, 1900 to date.

CHIDEOCK, DORSET (*Plymouth*).
Our Lady of Martyrs and St. Ignatius.

Chideock Castle, once the possession of the noble family of Arundell of Wardour, and now belonging to the Welds, was noted during the penal times as a refuge for priests, of whom some three were apprehended here.[1] The castle was held for Charles I. in the Civil War, and appears after that to have fallen into decay. The gateway was taken down in 1741, and the tower was in ruins in 1756. After the dismantling of the castle, the chapel was removed to the upper room of a cottage in North Chideock. Another was opened on Easter Sunday 1811. The pious wish for a really fine church was finally realised in 1884, when the present building was opened by Bishop Vaughan, of Plymouth.

Priests at Chideock (early list incomplete).

Rev. T. Pilchard, *martyr*, 1584-7.
,, J. Cornelius, *martyr*, prior to 1594.
,, Hugh Green, 1605. Martyred 1642.
,, — Higgs, 1680.
,, F. Wm. Byfleet, about 1695 till 1746.

[1] (1) Rev. Thos. Pilchard, M.A. (Balliol Coll., Oxon.), suffered at Dorchester for the Faith, March 21, 1587; (2) Rev. J. Cornelius at the same place, July 4, 1594; (3) Rev. Hugh Green, executed at Dorchester, August 19, 1642, for exercising his functions as a priest. He had been at Chideock upwards of thirty-seven years.

Rev. Charles and Richard Shimmell, 1762-3.
,, Joseph Clossette, 1779 (?).
,, Philip Compton, d. 1788.
,, Thos. Lewis, 1788-1809.
,, Thos. Tilbury, 1809-40.
,, Wm. Bond, 1840.
,, Robt. Platt, 1844.
,, M. Ryan, 1844-50.
Mission vacant 1850-3.
,, Thos. Basil, O.S B., 1853.
,, Jn. Gallagher, 1853-4.
,, Charles W. Price, O.S.B., 1854.
,, John Sinnot, O.S.B., 1855.
,, J. B. Caldwell, O.S.B., 1857.
,, C. W. Price (second time), 1861.
,, T. Fenn, 1866.
,, Henry Blunden, here 1872.
,, Joseph Toohey, 1874.
,, Francis Rotterman, 1877.
,, Joseph Verres, D.D., 1885.
,, Richard Canon Mansfield, 1888.
,, Joseph Randal Hurley, 1895.
,, Hugh C. Briggs, 1899.
,, Charles Gandy, 1903 to date.

CHILD'S HILL, HAMPSTEAD, N.W. (*Westminster*).

This mission—an offshoot from that of Hampstead—was opened by Canon Purcel. The temporary chapel of the Convent of Franciscan Sisters was blessed, and Mass said there for the first time on November 14, 1883. A house belonging to the Sisters was used as a temporary chapel and school. The Catholic population in 1883 was about 100. For some time the mission was served by the Passionist Fathers of Highgate, Mass being said in the house of a Catholic resident. The church was solemnly opened May 22, 1888, by Dr. Weathers, Bishop of Amycla. The building can accommodate about 250. Among those who assisted the building fund were Miss Mary Anderson (Madame Navarro), the celebrated actress, Madame Schumann, the Baroness Von Hugel, Major Gape, &c.

CHILWORTH, near GUILDFORD, SURREY (*Southwark*). The Holy Ghost.

The Franciscan priory and church, in the Gothic style, were opened on Thursday, June 31, 1892, by Bishop Patterson. The cost of erection (£7,000) was defrayed by Mgr. Wells, who further made a gift of £5,000 to the Fathers to free the church, etc., from debt. The monastery serves as the novitiate for the English Franciscans. The Rev. Fr. Bede, the first guardian or superior of the place, did much to draw a congregation to the church, and would no doubt have formed the nucleus of a permanent one, when he was recalled to take up important mission work in the East End of London. The architect of the friary was F. A. Walters, Esq., of Westminster. The interior of the church is very striking, the chief objects of interest being a handsome rood, carved oak choir stalls, and mortuary chapel adorned with a handsome triptych of the Flemish school.

CHIPPENHAM, WILTS (*Clifton*). St. Mary.

The mission was started 1854. The chapel was erected by Jn. Pollen, Esq., of Radbourne, and opened August 22, 1855. For some years the place was served from Bath, Frome, and Devizes, but became an independent mission about 1870.

Priests since 1870.
Rev. Hy. Hancock.
„ Jn. Corbishley, 1882.
„ Geo. Bailey, 1888.
„ Ignatius Gurd, 1897.
„ Francis McElmail, 1904.

CHIPPING, LANCS (*Salford*). St. Mary, School Lane.

James Dewhurst, Esq., of Leagram Hall, was prosecuted in 1586 for harbouring one Guile, 'a Popish priest.' The hall afterwards came into the possession of the Welds, and at the 'Lawnd' or lodge of the estate lived Fr. Richard Pencoth, or Penketh, S.J., who died here in August 1721 after many years' missionary labour. A chapel appears to have been built some time prior to the accession of James II., and another in 1787 by Thos. Weld, Esq. This latter edifice measured 60 ft. by 25 ft., and was of very plain style. A third chapel was erected in 1827-8, and was served by the Jesuits till 1857. The site was presented by Mr. Weld.

Priests since 1825.
Rev. J. Reeve.
„ P. Morrin, 1828.
„ Edw. Morrin, 1832.
„ — Peacock, 1834.
„ Edw. Morrin, 1836.
„ Felix Poole, 1840.
„ Jn. Middlehurst, 1842.
„ Jas. Bateman, 1846.
„ Peter de Blon, 1857.
„ Jn. Canon Rimmer, 1860.
„ Isidore de Gryse, 1866 to date.

CHIPPING NORTON, OXFORDSHIRE (*Birmingham*).
The mission was established in

K

1834, mainly through a bequest of one Mary Bowden, and the chapel, in the Classical style, erected 1837. An endowment was settled upon the incumbent by Miss Mary Bowden. To commemorate the jubilee of the church a new chapel, sacristy, and organ loft were built by subscription in 1888.

Priests.

Rev. Patrick Heffernan, 1834.

„ Canon Mitchell, 1838.

„ Joseph Abbott, 1854.

„ Samuel Sole, 1879 to date.

CHIPPING-SODBURY, GLOUCESTERSHIRE (*Clifton*). St. Laurence.

A mission was established at Horton in 1708, when John Paston, Esq., of Norfolk, came 'to reside on his Gloucestershire estates.' On the death of Wm. Paston, Esq., in 1763, the estate was sold. Fr. Jas. Placid Waters, O.S.B., was chaplain 1772-7. As late as 1855 there was living at Horton a very old man who remembered Mass being said at the 'Manor House' in Mr. Wm. Paston's time. After the selling of the estate, F. F. Pembridge and Ainsworth attended the mission. In 1815, during Fr. Birdsall's time, the chapel was an upper room of a poor thatched cottage. A deal table served as an altar, and the congregation consisted of about ten persons. The chapel at the old hall remained intact as late as 1833, and contained, *inter alia*, ' a well carved oak altar, a mahogany tabernacle, two old candlesticks, and a little bell on the altar steps on the epistle side with Ave Maria round the rim.' The place is now the village school. The mission at Chipping-Sodbury proper was started in 1838, the foundress being Mrs.

Sarah Neve, widow of the Rev. Egerton Neve, a clergyman of the Established Church. She was the sister of the Countess de Front, wife of Philip Count de Front, the Sardinian minister to the Court of St. James's (d. 1812), and known as a great benefactress to the Dover mission. Mrs. Neve purchased the largest inn at Chipping-Sodbury for £1,300, and converted it into a chapel and presbytery. The priests there were Fr. Thos. Rolling, O.S.B. (October 26, 1838-40); Fr. Jerome Jenkins, O.S.B. (1840-1); Fr. Bernard Paillet (1841); Fr. Ignatius Sutton (1841-5); Fr. Ambrose Duck (1845-6); Fr. Maurus Cooper (1846-January 1, 1869). Since his death the chief incumbents have been Fr. Placid Sinnot; Fr. Edmund Caldwell, Fr. Ignatius Stuart. The Catholic population of the place was about sixty in February 1897.

CHISLEHURST, KENT (*Southwark*). St. Mary.

This mission dates from 1852. The present cruciform church was opened August 8, 1854, mainly owing to the munificence of Captain Bowden, of the Scots Guards. Local Catholicity made great strides under Canon Todd, the well-known founder of the Boys' Orphanage, Blackheath. Most of the congregation in his time (1855-60) consisted of poor Irish employed in the mills at Crayford, St. Mary Cray, and adjoining districts. During Canon Todd's incumbency, the present fine presbytery, in the Gothic style, was erected and opened. The mission will always be associated with the exile of Napoleon III., Emperor of the French, who, after the Franco-German war, resided at Camden

House, Chislehurst, from 1871 till his death in 1873 (January 9). Her Imperial Majesty the Empress Eugénie, and their son, the ill-fated Prince Imperial, were familiar figures in the neighbourhood. The Prince Imperial, after completing his studies at Woolwich, joined the Artillery (1875), and in March 1879 proceeded to Zululand as a volunteer on Lord Chelmsford's staff. On June 1 he was slain while on reconnaissance. His obsequies at Chislehurst were attended by the Prince of Wales and a crowd of notables (July 12, 1879). Bishop Danell, of Southwark, sang the Mass, assisted by Canons Wenham Moore, Mgr. Goddard, Fr. Sammons, &c. In 1888 the bodies of Napoleon III. and the prince were removed to the Imperial Mausoleum, Farnborough (Hants), since 1881 the residence of the Empress Eugénie—'the sole remnant of a shipwreck which proves how fragile and vain are the grandeurs of this world.'[1] Mgr. Goddard, rector since 1870, was succeeded by Fr. A. Boone, the present incumbent. A notable feature of the church is the beautiful recumbent monument to the Prince Imperial, erected by Mgr. Goddard shortly before he left the mission. A fine stained glass window and wrought iron screen were added to the Sacred Heart Chapel in October 1906.

CHISWICK, W. (*Westminster*).
Our Lady of Grace and St. Edward.

Mission established at Turnham Green May 3, 1864, by Fr. Ryan. Countess Tasker built the school, opened February 2, 1865. By 1880 the district, which hitherto had been

[1] Letter of H.I. Majesty to Mgr. Goddard on his jubilee, June 1885.

one of market gardens, was built over. The present church, in the basilica style, was opened in October 1886 by Cardinal Manning. The accommodation is for about 600; cost of erection, £3,400.
Priests.
Rev. M. Ryan, 1864.
„ John Doherty, 1869.
„ Reginald Canon Tuke, 1881.
„ J. Keating.

CHORLEY, WELD BANK, LANCS
(*Liverpool*). St. Gregory the Great.

The present mission is the representative of an ancient one at Burgh Hall, the seat of the Rigby family. After the death of the last member, Sir Alex. Rigby, about 1700, the estate passed to the Chadwicks. In 1774 Mr. Thomas Weld, father of Cardinald Weld, presented the mission with a chapel site at Chorley, and the priest, Fr. J. Chadwick, V.G. to Bishop Gibson, removed thither. From this time the place was known as Weld Bank. His successor, Fr. R. Thompson, V.G., erected the present chapel (1815). The high altar was put up by Fr. Lennon (1870-96). In 1854 the congregation numbered 1,000. When the church was enlarged (1877) Catholics of the district were estimated at 5,000.

CHORLTON, LANCS (*Salford*). St. Augustine.

St. Peter's Priory (Gregorians) was opened here 1892. The institute appears to have been discontinued after 1896, when the mission was continued by seculars.
Priests.
Rev. Jerome Vaughan, 1892.
„ Paul Klootson, 1896.
„ Fredk. Holt, 1897 to date.

CHRIST CHURCH, HANTS (*Portsmouth*). The Immaculate Conception and St. Joseph.

A mission was opened at Burton Green, near Christ Church at the commencement of the last century by the Abbé A. Cochet, an *émigré* priest. As the congregation was very poor, the Abbé supplemented his income by taking pupils. The Abbé would appear to have returned to France at the restoration of Louis XVIII. (1815). In 1822 the priest at Burton Green was Fr. J. Stapleton, and in 1835 Fr. R. Kelly. In 1864 (November) Bishop Grant, of Southwark, authorised by letter the Rev. B. Van Reeth, the priest of the mission, 'to collect funds towards building a small church in the town.' The last priest at Burton Green was Fr. Van Reeth, who transferred the mission to Christ Church. The present church was opened December 1866. A reredos and organ were added October 1878. Mr. Sperati, of Highbury, London, presented ground for a cemetery, which was consecrated, June 1880.

CHUDLEIGH, UGBROOKE, DEVON (*Plymouth*). St. Cyprian.

Thomas first Lord Clifford erected a domestic chapel at Ugbrooke Park 1671. After his conversion he fitted it up in a splendid manner for Catholic worship (1672). The altar plate cost upwards of £227. Next year the Test Act ousted Lord Clifford from his position as Lord Treasurer (1673), an event which his lordship only survived a few months. He was buried ' in his owne chappell.' A cemetery for Catholics was afterwards opened at the rear of the building.

Priests.

Rev. Thos. Risdon, 1701.
„ Dominic Derbyshire, O.P., 1735.
„ James Price, O.S.B., 1757.
„ Jas. Frost, O.S.F., 1758.
„ Wm. Strickland, S.J., 1766.
„ Jos. Reeve, S.J., 1767 (died here 1820, æt. 87).
„ Felix Vauquelin, 1794.
„ Jas. Laurenson, S.J., 1816.
„ Jas. Brownbill, S.J., 1830.
„ Wm. Cotham, S.J., 1834.
„ Chas. Lomax, S.J., 1845.
„ Hy. Brigham, S.J., 1856.
„ Pat. Walsh, 1867.
„ Mgr. Thos. Reekie, 1877.
„ Hy. Dowsett, 1901 to date.

CIRENCESTER, GLOUCESTERSHIRE (*Clifton*). St. Peter.

Fr. Anselm Glassbrook, O.S.B., fitted up ' a neat little chapel capable of holding 100 persons,' which was opened January 23, 1855. This was the first time that Mass had been said in the town since the reign of Elizabeth. A larger chapel was opened in 1862. This continued till the completion of the present fine church in 1896. For some years after the mission was commenced it was served from Fairford and Stroud. In 1875 it was served from Woodchester, but only at ' the Eight Indulgences,' and this state of dependence still continued in 1883. By 1891 the mission had a resident priest, Fr. Jas. O'Shaughnessy. Fr. J. Martin is the present rector.

CLACTON-ON-SEA, ESSEX (*Westminster*). Our Lady of Light.

For some time prior to 1884 Fr. King used to come over once a month and say Mass in a disused Martello tower. The only Catholics at Clacton at that time were some coastguards and their families. In 1884 Fr. Beale hired the Town Hall for Mass on Sundays. Owing to the generosity of two Catholic ladies, a chapel was opened at Montfort House, in the Church Road, in June 1895. Mass was said here on June 27 by Fr. Beale, the sermon being preached by Fr. Lucas. The mission is now in charge of the Oblates of St. Charles.

CLAPHAM, LONDON, S.W. (*Southwark*). St. Mary.
On August 1, 1848, the Redemptorist Fathers took possession of the old mansion which had formerly belonged to Lord Teignmouth, and in which the famous ' Clapham sect ' had so often met. One of the rooms was converted into a chapel," and continued to serve the mission till the opening of the present church, which was consecrated by Cardinal Wiseman, October 13, 1852. Since that time no fewer than eight missions have been formed out of the wide area formerly served by the Redemptorist Fathers. The old house has recently been supplanted by a new monastery. The church, which was used for the first time on May 14, 1851, was designed by Wardell. Above the chancel arch is a fine fresco by Settegast, of Coblentz, representing the ' Last Judgment.' The accommodation is for about 600 persons. The jubilee of the establishment of the mission was celebrated in the summer of 1898. The first Fathers to reside in the locality were the Rev. Frs. de Held and Petcherine, C.S.S.R. Not far from the monastery stands the mother house of the Notre Dame Order, which also

dates its commencement in this country from 1848.

CLAPHAM, S.W. St. Vincent of Paul. *See* APPENDIX.

CLAPHAM PARK, LONDON, S.W. St. Bede, Thornton Road.
In September 1903 a large mansion in the Thornton Road was opened as a preparatory school to St. John's Seminary, Wonersh. The number of students in residence is about sixteen. The church adjoining is a plain commodious building in the Romanesque style, opened early in 1906. The school is dedicated to St. John Berchmans.
Rectors.
Rev. G. Fitzgibbon, 1903.
,, M. P. Hanlon, 1905.
,, A. Armstrong, 1906.

CLAPTON, LONDON, N.E. (*Westminster*). St. Scholastica's.
The mission was founded in 1862 by the Fathers of Charity from Kingsland. Till 1877 the chapel was a rented room in the London Road. In the November of the last-named year, Canon Bamber, of Thorndon, Essex, presided at a meeting to consider the erection of a permanent chapel. Fr. R. Swift was the priest in charge of the mission. As an outcome of the meeting a permanent chapel was opened about 1880. Fr. Swift was succeeded by Fr. Biale, the present rector.

CLAUGHTON-ON-BROCK, GARSTANG, LANCS (*Liverpool*). St. Thomas.
' Claughton Chapel,' near Garstang, was the subject of a public inquiry in 1591. The regular succession of priests here dates

from the time of Charles I. Fr. T. Whittaker, who suffered for the Faith August 7, 1646, was priest here. His portrait was preserved at the English College, Douai, till the time of the Revolution, and a life-size statue was erected to the memory of the martyr at Claughton-on-Brock Church in September 1882. The next priests were:— Frs. T. Walmsley (1665), E. Blackburn (1683), T. Taylor (1726), R. Birtwistle (1727), Brockholes (1740). Under Fr. J. Parkinson the chapel was opened over the presbytery, 1744. It was enlarged in 1794 by Fr. Jn. Barrow, and again in 1805 by Fr. H. Gradwell. Mgr. Robt. Gradwell, who was priest from 1811, was appointed rector of the English College, Rome, in 1818. His brother Henry succeeded at Claughton-on-Brock, where he continued till his death in 1860. The schools, which date from 1840, are due to a bequest from Mrs. Catherine Gill. A baptistery and confessional were added to the church in 1883. The cemetery, opened in 1873, was given by T. F. Brockholes, Esq. The belfry was erected in 1897 in memory of the late Queen's jubilee. In December 1899 the late rector, Mgr. Gradwell, nephew of the bishop, celebrated the golden jubilee of his priesthood.

CLAY CROSS, NORTH DERBYSHIRE (*Nottingham*). SS. Patrick and Bridget.

On the death of the last member of the ancient Catholic family of Hunloke, the chapel at Birdholme was discontinued (1859?). In 1862, when the estimated Catholic population of Clay Cross was upwards of 450, the Bishop of Nottingham caused a plain but commodious

chapel in the Gothic style to be erected. It was opened on June 1 of the same year, but for some time Mass was only said there occasionally. Fr. A. McKenna, of Ilkeston, had charge of the mission in 1863. He came over once a fortnight, said Mass at Clay Cross, and attended sick calls. The new church was opened by the Bishop of Nottingham, Thursday, November 9, 1882. The building is Gothic, consisting of nave, chancel, and Lady Chapel. The accommodation is for 200. The site and much of the cost of the new church were provided by W. Arkwright, Esq.

CLAYTON GREEN, LANCS (*Liverpool*). St. Bede.

There were many ' schismatic Catholicks ' reported to be living in this district, 1590. No mission, however, was founded here till 1822, when Fr. S. Day commenced the chapel opened in 1824. The mission is served by the Benedictines.

Priests.

Rev. S. Day, 1822.

„　Thos. Caldwell, 1836.

„　James Dowding, 1840.

„　Wilfrid Phillipson, 1876.

„　Jn. Placid O'Brien, 1879.

„　Augustine (Abbot) Bury, 1885.

„　Leonard Davies, 1895 to date.

CLEATOR, CUMBERLAND (*Hexham and Newcastle*). Sacred Heart of Our Lady.

A chapel was established here 1853–4, under the title of St. Bega. The accommodation was for 500–600. Owing to the working of the rich hematite iron mines in the district, the population greatly increased, so that by 1869 the

Catholic section alone was estimated at 5,000. On October 3 of the last-named year, the first stone of the present church was laid by Bishop Chadwick, of Hexham, and the building was opened 1872. The style is cruciform and Gothic ; architect, E. W. Pugin ; cost, about £5,000 ; dimensions, 130 ft. by 50 ft.

Priests (O.S.B.).

Rev. W. Holden, 1853.
„ Francis Williams, 1860 *et seq.*
„ Matthew Brierley, here in 1871.
„ Jn. Burchall, 1877.
„ Essington Ross, 1888.
„ Joseph Warden, 1890.
„ Thos. McCabe, 1891.
„ Edward Ward, 1893.
„ Robt. Kershaw, 1902 to date.

CLERKENWELL, LONDON, E.C. (*Westminster*). SS. Peter and Paul, Rosoman Street.

This mission was established in 1843 by Fr. J. Hearne, and was for some time known as the Saffron Hill Mission. The first chapel was a room of No. 1 Leicester Place, Saffron Hill. In 1847 ' a spacious Baptist chapel' in Upper Rosoman Street was purchased for £2,300 and fitted up as a Catholic church. The style of the building is Grecian, and the accommodation is for about 1,000 persons. Various improvements were effected in 1856, when the galleries were reduced and open seats provided. The first priests of the mission were Spanish—Frs. Herera and Farria. The next to succeed were the Revs. P. McClean and C. Woolett. Fr. McClean died in 1850, when Fr. J. Kyne was appointed. In 1864 the priests were the Revs. Walter McAvila and Cyriacus Herdel. Fr. Zsilkay was

rector 1875, Fr. Biemans in 1885, Fr. A. Pownall 1898, Fr. G. Curtis 1904.

CLEVEDON, SOMERSET (*Clifton*). The Immaculate Conception.

The Franciscans, expelled from France by the Jules Ferry laws of 1881-82, settled in Clevedon and acquired the premises formerly known as the Royal Hotel. Here they established a monastery and chapel. On January 17, 1884, the structure was seriously injured by a fire, but the rest of the building was happily saved from destruction, though much church furniture was destroyed. A new bell, weighing over 400 cwt., was hung in the belfry of the new church during the course of its erection, September 1886.

CLIFFORD, YORKS (*Leeds*).

The town is considered by some to give its name to the ancient Catholic family of Clifford-Constable. The church was opened January 18, 1842. A great ' mission ' was given here in December 1849 by Fr. Furlong, which was attended by ' vast crowds.'

Priests.

Rev. Edw. Clifford, 1842.
„ James Cullimore, 1860.
„ Matthew Gosse, 1904.

CLIFTON, SOMERSET. Pro-Cathedral of the Apostles.

The site of the church was purchased in 1833 by Fr. Edgeworth, one of the priests at St. Joseph's, Trenchard Street. This excellent missioner greatly distinguished himself by his ' humanity and courage ' during the terrible Reform riots at Bristol in 1831. A temporary chapel was opened on the ground in 1842, but the expenses incurred were too much for Fr. Edgeworth, and, becoming bankrupt, he had to retire to Antwerp (1844). The old title of the church was St. Augustine Apostle of England. Bishop Ullathorne, after his consecration as V.A.W.D. in June 1846, made this his vicarial church.

Priests.

Rev. F. Edgeworth, 1842.
„ T. M. Macdonnell, 1844.
„ Bishop Ullathorne, administrator, 1846.
„ Wm. J. Vaughan, 1849 (Bishop of Plymouth in succession to Bishop Errington, 1855 ; *d.* October 25, 1902).
„ F. R. Canon Neve, 1855.
„ John Canon Bonomi, 1863.
„ Provost F. Neve (second time), 1870.
„ Mgr. John Clarke, D.D., V.G.
„ Arthur Canon Russell, V.G., 1893.
„ David Canon O'Brien, 1904 to date.

CLIFTON HILL, near GARSTANG, LANCS (*Liverpool*).

The church of SS. Catharine and Barbara was erected between 1878 and June 1880 by Mrs. Fitzherbert-Brockholes. The congregation in 1880 numbered fifty-two, and the seating capacity of the church is for double that number. The mission was formerly served by the domestic chapel at Clifton Hill, the residence of the Gillows.

Priests.

Rev. E. Swarbrick, 1878.
„ Alf. Walmsley, 1885.
„ Jn. Crilly, 1889.
„ Rd. Barton, 1891.
„ Pat. Delany, 1901 to date.

CLITHEROE, LANCS (*Salford*). SS. Michael and John.

In 1797 the congregation consisted of 'twelve poor Catholics.' Fr. John Laurenson, of Stonyhurst, hired a small outbuilding, and said Mass there for the first time in November 1797. The congregation increased and a larger chapel was erected. Till 1842 the mission was served from Stonyhurst. In 1843 Fr. J. Holden was resident priest at Clitheroe. On Thursday the octave of Corpus Christi, 1850, the new church was opened by Bishop Brown, V.A. The congregation at this time numbered 800. The church, which was designed by Hansom, cost £2,500. Fr. T. Seed, of Stonyhurst, had charge of the mission at this time. The new Lady Chapel of the building was opened in September 1884. It contains a beautiful alabaster statue of Our Lady and three paintings by Mr. Joseph Bonvier.

CLOWN, near CHESTERFIELD, DERBYSHIRE (*Nottingham*).

The mission was commenced 1903, when a chapel was established at Southgate House under the title of the Sacred Heart and Our Lady of Victories. The chapel is now (1905) in Mill Street.

Priests.

Rev. Charles Froes.
„ Alfred L. Barry, 1905.

COBRIDGE, STAFFS (*Birmingham*).

In the eighteenth century, the Biddulphs and Macclesfields were the chief Catholic families in north-west Staffordshire. Mass was sometimes said at Chesterton Hall, the residence of the Macclesfield family, prior to 1752. Fr. Flynn was the first resident priest (1752). In 1780 or 1781 the Rev. John Corne built a chapel and presbytery. Messrs. Bucknell and Blackwell, two wealthy Catholic potters, in conjunction with another Catholic, Mr. Dadford, architect and agent to the Grand Trunk Canal Company, contributed largely to the cost of building. Fr. Prendergast and Fr. Lewis Gerard subsequently enlarged the building by galleries and wings (1817-18). They likewise erected schools for 250 children. In 1832 the Catholic population = 300. Fr. Leith restored the chapel about 1853. In 1858 he became M.R.

Priests from 1780.

Rev. J. Corne, 1780.
„ F. Hartley, 1784.
„ R. Prendergast, 1794.
„ Abbé Louis Giraud or Gerard, 1813.
„ Roger J. O. Higgin, O.S.F., 1842.
„ Jos. Abbot, 1845.
„ Thos. Matthias, 1851.
„ Phil. Hendren, 1873.
„ Alf. Mulligan, 1903.

COCKERMOUTH, CUMBERLAND (*Hexham and Newcastle*). St. Joseph.

Land for a church was purchased in 1847, but as late as 1853 the Catholics of the place were compelled 'to assemble for Divine worship in a hayloft open to the tiles and immediately over public stables.' At first, the mission was served from Wigton once a month, but by 1850 Fr. Joseph Watson had come as resident priest. The church was commenced early in 1856, and opened November 26 the same year. Schools were erected and the church enlarged during the incumbency of Fr. Smits. The Mission passed over to the Benedictines in 1902. The Jubilee of the church was celebrated, September 15 and 16, 1906.

Priests.

Rev. Joseph Canon Humble, 1848.
„ Joseph Watson, 1849.
„ Robt. Orrell, 1854.
„ R. Canon Smith, 1857.
„ Wm. Farmery, 1858.
„ — Hanigan, 1861.
„ Pat. Bourke, 1863.
„ Edw. O'Dwyer, 1867.
„ — O'Connor, 1869.
„ — M'Cartney, 1870.
„ James Corboy, 1870.
„ James Smits, 1871.
„ Thos. Clavering, 1885.
„ James Smits (second time), 1897.
„ Robt. Fishwick, O.S.B., 1902 to date.

COEDANGRED, MONMOUTHSHIRE (*Newport*).

The Church of the Immaculate Conception was built in 1847, when Fr. Thos. Abbot was priest. The mission was started in 1845 by Fr. Burgess, of Monmouth, 'for the sake of the remnants of three former congregations in this part of Monmouthshire.' The first 'mission' ever given in the church concluded on September 12, 1880, when Fr. Seraphim, O.S.F.C., of Chester, had the happiness of bringing back 'many stray Catholics' to their religious duties.

Priests.

Rev. Burgess, 1845.
„ Thos. Abbot, 1847.
„ Austin Neary, 1852.
„ J. Arquis, 1854.
„ Edw. Glassbrooke, here in 1871.
„ F. Marianus, 1877.
„ John Higgins, 1882.
„ P. Capron, 1885.

Rev. Clement Matthews, 1888.
„ F. Tierney, 1891.
„ P. Cardinael, 1893.
„ Isidore Heneka, 1899.
„ J. Murphy, 1902 to date.

COLCHESTER, ESSEX (*Westminster*). St. James.

Sir George Mannock, Jesuit and last baronet, lived at Bromley Hall, near Colchester, from about 1775 to 1782. He used to say Mass in a private chapel and attend to the few Catholics in the district. The present mission was established in 1837, when the church in Priory Street was opened, on November 3 of that year. Before this time the nearest chapel was at Thorndon Hall, Lord Petre's residence. About 1867 a separate camp-chapel for the Catholic soldiers at Colchester was opened by Fr. J. Vertue, afterwards first Bishop of Portsmouth. Cardinal Manning confirmed sixty-eight persons in the church September 1886, and administered the pledge to many civilians and soldiers.

Priests.
Rev. C. King, 1837.
„ J. Kaye, 1845.
„ Julius Picquot, D.D., 1848.
„ R. Canon Shepherd, 1857.
„ C. Woolett, 1867.
„ E. Meyer, 1885.
„ C. P. Collingridge, 1889.
„ Cornelius Biale, 1892.
„ Mgr. Vincent Coletti, D.D., 1896.
„ Angelo Lucas, 1899.
„ Jn. Bloomfield, 1903 to date.

COLDHAM, SUFFOLK (*Northampton*). Our Lady and St. Joseph.

Coldham Hall was the ancestral seat of the Rookwood and Gage families. Edward Gage, Esq., third son of Sir John Gage, of Firle, was created a baronet by Charles II. 1662. The last of this ancient Catholic stock was Sir John Gage, Major, Scots Guards, who died in 1879. The mission of Coldham was early served by the Jesuit Fathers. The martyr, Fr. Thos. Garnett, nephew of Fr. Henry Garnett, was seized near Coldham in 1608. Fr. James Dennett, provincial of the Society in England, was missioner at Coldham for many years, and travelling tutor to Sir Thos. Rookwood Gage, fifth baronet. The last Jesuit chaplain at Coldham was Fr. Edward Baptist Newton, who died here 1787. After this the place was served from Bury St. Edmunds, but the congregation rapidly declined, so that what had once been a body of eighty communicants had by 1834 fallen to thirteen. The old mission was, however, served, like that of Hengrave, the other residence of the Gages, at the Eight Indulgences. The above-mentioned Fr. Newton in his correspondence gives a sad picture of the state of Catholicity in the neighbourhood at the close of the eighteenth century. This zealous missioner had often to traverse a district of some fifty miles, visiting Sudbury, Chilton, Clare, Melford, 'where nothing is to be met with but ignorance, stupidity, and sometimes a total neglect of religion.' In one place the Catholics had fallen from 100 to four! The mission was apparently closed from 1856 to 1860, when it again figures in the 'Catholic Directory.' The church was opened in 1870.

Priests of the Mission since 1800.
Rev. L. Simon (served from Bury, 1836–40).
„ James O'Neill, 1840.
„ Bernard Shanley, 1843.
„ P. Gates, 1844–55.

Rev. Wm. Poole, 1860.

„ Christopher Scott, 1863.

„ Patrick Canon Rogers, 1867.

„ George Miles, 1885.

„ Augustine Wilkinson, 1890 to date.

Priests.

Rev. Jones, 1872.

„ Pierce Griffith, 1873.

„ D. Reynders, 1879.

„ Henry Mom, 1885.

„ A. Van der Beek, 1904 to date.

COLESHILL, WARWICKSHIRE (*Birmingham*). The Sacred Heart and St. John.

Mission established February 1880. Fr. C. Wheatley, the first priest, said Mass 'in a rented room over a stable.' The congregation at that time was 'small and very poor.' In addition to these, Fr. Wheatley had also charge of the Catholic children in the Marston Green Homes.

Priests.

Rev. C. Wheatley, 1880.

„ James Giblin, 1885.

„ C. Gottwaltz, 1888.

„ Geo. Hudson, 1899 to date.

COLNE LANCS (*Salford*).

The Rev. Dean Jones, who came to reside at Colne in 1872, was the first priest in the district since the Reformation. The neighbourhood was once a stronghold of Catholicity, as the numerous ruins of churches &c. show. A new school and chapel were commenced in December 1887, and opened July 15, 1888. The number of Catholic children then attending the school was about sixty. The adult population was over 400. Before the opening of the school chapel, the place of worship was a shed over a chemist's shop.

COLSTON BASSETT, NOTTS (*Nottingham*).

The 'beautiful little Gothic structure,' as the chapel was described, was opened in October 1840. Francis Martin, Esq., of Colston Hall, gave the site.

Priests.

Rev. J. Bick, 1840. Served from Eastwell 1860 *et seq.* At present served from Carlton.

COLWICH, STAFFS (*Birmingham*). St. Benedict's Priory.

In 1652 a filiation of the Benedictine Nuns of Cambray opened a convent in Paris for the purpose of devoting themselves to the perpetual adoration of the Blessed Sacrament. At the general upheaval consequent on the Revolution, the community came to England, and were settled at Marnhull, Dorset, under the protection of the Hussey family (1795). In 1807 they removed to Cannington, near Bridgewater, where Lord and Lady Clifford afforded them 'a very comfortable and conventual asylum at Cannington Court House.' On leaving this retreat in 1835 for Colwich, their 'large and beautiful chapel,' opened July 7, 1831, became the church of the Cannington Mission (*q.v.*). The convent at Colwich is a strictly enclosed community, and receives neither boarders or pupils. The church is open to the public.

COMMERCIAL ROAD, LONDON, E. (*Westminster*). SS. Mary and Michael.

The history of the old Virginia Street mission—the forerunner of the church in Commercial Road—is buried in obscurity. In 1768 Fr. James Webb, the priest of the chapel, was tried before the Court of King's Bench at Westminster for saying Mass. The infamous Payne was the informer on this occasion, but Lord Chief Justice Mansfield at the trial laid down the important rule that before a priest could be convicted it was necessary to prove, first, that he was really a priest, and, secondly, that he had actually said Mass. The jury acquitted the accused. In January 1770, the Hon. and Rt. Rev. Bishop Talbot, brother of the Earl of Shrewsbury, was committed for trial for having exercised his priestly functions at Virginia Street. He was tried at the Old Bailey (February), but acquitted on the same grounds as Fr. Webb. He was the last Catholic clergyman to be indicted for saying Mass. In 1773 he took a lease of the chapel in Virginia Street for eighty-four years. The property was acquired from the London Dock Company, the bishop being mentioned in the document as plain Mr. James Talbot. The old chapel or Mass House was one of those destroyed by Lord George Gordon's mob in 1780. The priest of the mission, Fr. M. Coen, might have defended the place with upwards of 3,000 Irish labourers, but he yielded to the wishes of the magistrates, who dreaded the results of so terrible a conflict.[1] The priest, however, re-

ceived compensation from the Government, and a chapel, 'totally devoid of ornament,' was subsequently erected at a cost of £1,500. By 1820 the Catholic population of Commercial Road had increased to 20,000. About 1815 a collection for a new church was set on foot by Fr. Horrabin, and after many years a site in Commercial Road was purchased in 1842 at a cost of £3,000. Fr. Horrabin died in 1846, and in 1851 the foundation of the new church for which he had so ardently longed was laid. The new building was opened by Cardinal Wiseman on December 8, 1856, in the presence of the Bishops of Northampton, Nottingham, and Troy. The church is Gothic of the Decorated period. The total length is 185 ft., breadth 75 ft., and in appearance the inside of the church much resembles St. George's Cathedral. The total cost was about £30,000. The Catholic schools were founded in 1778 by a few Irishmen resident in Wapping. In 1810 a similar establishment for girls was opened by Fr. J. Delaney. The Christian Brothers taught the boys in 1838, and in December 1849 the new Catholic schools were opened by Bishop Wiseman, assisted by Bishop Morris and the Hon. Charles Langdale. The total number of children receiving education there in 1858 was about 2,000.

Priests since 1856.

Rev. W. Kelly.
  ,, Pat. Canon O'Callaghan, M.R., 1877.
  ,, Geo. Canon Akers, 1897.
  ,, Peter E. Amigo, 1899, Bishop of Southwark, 1904.
  ,, Andrew Dooley, Dean, M.R., 1902.

[1] One of the rioters who helped to burn the chapel, and who was fearfully mangled by the bullets and bayonets of the troops in the repression of the riots on June 6, 1780, was long supported by the congregation of Commercial Road after the chapel had been rebuilt.

Rev. Timothy Ring Dean, 1905 to date.

CONGLETON, CHESHIRE (*Shrewsbury*). St. Mary.

On December 21, 1821, Mass was said here in a cottage in Moody Street by Fr. J. Hall, of Macclesfield. The club room of the Angel Hotel was afterwards hired on Sundays, and this served as a place of worship till the opening of a chapel in 1826. The underneath portions of the building were used as schools.

Priests.
Rev. J. Hall, 1821.
„ C. Brigham, 1831.
„ J. Pratt, 1834.
„ J. Fisher, 1840.
„ J. Hill, 1850.
„ J. Anderton, 1853.
„ H. Lynch, 1855.
„ J. Daly, 1861.
„ G. Clegg, 1863.
„ F. O'Neil, 1872.
„ F. Waterhouse, 1873.
„ P. Power, 1880.
„ G. Carton, 1884.
„ P. Coleman, 1887.
„ C. Hooghe, 1888.
„ J. Haskett, 1889.
„ W. Kelly, 1891.
„ H. Donlevy, 1894.
„ Wm. Reade, 1903 to date.

CONISTON, LANCS (*Liverpool*). The Sacred Heart.

The want of a chapel in this district was advertised in the *Tablet* for September 17, 1859. The ex-Queen of the French (Amélie), who spent the autumn of that year at Coniston, threw open her domestic chapel to the neighbouring Catholics, and before her departure is reported to have forwarded a substantial sum to the Bishop of Liverpool towards the erection of a church. This was opened by Bishop Goss on September 29, 1872, the Sunday preceding his death.

Priests.
Rev. Pat. M'Aroy, 1867.
„ Hy. Gibson, 1874.
„ Peter Laverty, 1889 to date.

CORBY, near GRANTHAM, LINCS (*Nottingham*). Our Lady of Mount Carmel.

Irnham Hall, the seat of the Thimelby family, is considered by some to have preserved the Faith in these parts from Catholic times. Fr. Richard Thimelby, S.J., one of those accused by Oates as privy to the concocted 'Plot,' was a member of this family. The last of the race was John Thimelby, Esq., who died 1720, æt. 86. His property passed to the Lords Clifford, with whose descendants it still remains. The chapel was served by the Jesuits down to 1845, when the mission was handed over to the Vicar Apostolic. The same year, the old chapel at Irnham was demolished and the stones used for building a small church at Corby. A handsome school-house was opened September 1881 on a site given by Henry Clifford, Esq.

Secular Priests since 1845.
Rev. Canon Gascoyne, 1845.
„ Joseph Canon Baron, 1880.
„ John Brown, 1901.
„ A. Howarth, 1905 to date.

CORNFORTH, WEST. *See* **WEST CORNFORTH.**

COSSEY, or COSTESSEY, HALL, NORFOLK (*Northampton*). St. Wulstane.

Cossey Hall, the ancient seat of the Jerningham family, remained a centre of Catholic faith and endurance throughout the penal times. About 1805 the number of Catholics in the district is said to have only amounted to about thirty. In 1832 it had risen to 400. Two years later, the fine church was commenced by George Jerningham, Baron Stafford. The architect was Mr. Buckler, of Oxford. The height is 40 ft.; length, 100 ft.; width, 25 ft. A considerable portion of the building fund was collected by Mgr. Husenbeth, chaplain to the family, and famous as the biographer of Bishop Milner. Some of the windows contain specimens of mediæval glass rescued from various French churches at the time of the Revolution. At the opening, May 26, 1841, an ancient pre-Reformation Missal was used by Mgr. Husenbeth, who sang the Mass. This great scholar is the well-known author of the 'Life of Bishop Milner,' and was chaplain at Cossey till his death, October 31, 1872. 'The Royal Hotel Guide to Norwich,' 1898, thus speaks of Cossey:—'The Roman Catholic body is very strong in Cossey, and probably Mgr. Davies, the present occupant of the Roman Catholic presbytery here, has one of the largest flocks professing Papal tenets of any village in England.'

Priests.

Rev. Geo. Chamberlayne, 1784. This gentleman, an M.A. of King's College, Cambridge, was received into the Church at the Sardinian Chapel, Lincoln's Inn Fields, 1780. Dr. Johnson, on hearing of the sacrifice involved by this step, exclaimed, with reference to Mr. Chamberlayne, 'God bless him!' (Boswell). Mr. Chamberlayne was ordained priest at Douai 1783, and served the Cossey Mission from 1784 till 1798. He died February 4, 1815, aged seventy-seven.

Rev. Samuel Jones.
  ,, Mgr. Husenbeth, 1820, till his death, October 31, 1872.
  ,, Mgr. Geo. Davies, 1872 to date.

COTTAM, near PRESTON, LANCS (*Liverpool*).

This mission was for generations served by the domestic chapel of the Haydock family. Fifteen years before the death of the last Squire Haydock Fr. John Kendal rented a barn and four acres at Cottam from Wil. Bilsborrow, yeoman, and fitted up a chapel and presbytery. In 1745, after the retreat of Prince Charles Edward and the Highlanders from Derby, the chapel was burnt by a ' No Popery ' mob from Preston. The priest at Cottam at this time was Fr. John Harrison, who took the mission oath at Douai November 3, 1734. After the burning of the chapel, Fr. Harrison went to Townely, where he served as priest till about 1775. He died January 16, 1780, at the house of his brother Lawrence, in the Friargate, Preston. The successor of Fr. Harrison at Cottam was Fr. J. Cowban, who afterwards went to Crathorne, where he died October 6, 1777. Fr. Smith was priest at Cottam in 1763, and either he or Fr. Cowban restored the chapel. During the great election riot at Preston in 1768, the chapel was again in danger. In 1769 Fr. J. Lund was priest. He built the present chapel in 1793, and was rector till his death in 1812. Fr. Thos. Berry, who was priest till 1845, built the presbytery. Fr. Dixon was the next priest till 1852. Fr. Geo. Corless, D.D., his successor, laid out the cemetery and enlarged the sacristy. He died November 1, 1865. The next priests were:— The Revs. Roger Taylor (resigned 1867), H. J. Throwner (1868), F. Gillow. At present (1904) the incumbent of the mission is Fr. Joseph Barker.

COUGHTON, WARWICKSHIRE (*Birmingham*). SS. Peter, Paul, and Elizabeth.

Coughton Castle is one of the historic residences of the Throckmortons. It has several priests' hiding-places, and in one of these, in an 'angle turret,' an altar-stone was discovered some years back. Fr. Garnett, S.J., who suffered for the Gunpowder Plot, 1606, was here in November 1604, and it was afterwards alleged that an exhortation he used 'to be rid of heresy' was in connection with the impending conspiracy. The words, however, were those of a prayer in use for centuries. Fr. Pope was chaplain here in 1824, and Fr. Davis, O.S.B., from 1835 to 1889! The present Gothic church superseded the old chapel, 1857.

COURTFIELD, near ROSS, HEREFORDSHIRE (*Newport*).

The ancestral seat of the Vaughan family, whose domestic chapel has for generations served the Catholics of the district. Fr. Thomas Vaughan, who died of ill-usage at the hands of the persecutors during the per-

secution in 1646, was a member of this family. In 1688 the mansion was invaded by an anti-Catholic Whig mob and much damage done. In more recent times the chapel became a centre from which many of the surrounding missions were either started or supplied. Thus in 1836, when Fr. J. Reeve was chaplain, the chapel of Hatherop was dependent on Courtfield for a monthly Mass. The chaplain at Courtfield in 1825 was Fr. J. Knight. In 1881 the chapel was redecorated and reopened by Bishop Hedley, of Newport. Archbishop Kenelm Vaughan, who died at Ince Blundell in 1883, was interred at Courtfield pending the removal of his remains to his metropolitan cathedral of Sydney.

COVENTRY, WARWICKSHIRE (*Birmingham*). St. Osburg, Hill Street.

When the mission was started, 1757 – 60, there were only four Catholics in the city—Mrs. Bruckfield, Ann Short, Mr. and Mrs. Lane. The nearest chapel was at Wappenbury. About 1757, Fr. Hy. Bishop used to come once a month 'to say prayers' (? Mass) at Mrs. Bruckfield's, near St. Michael's Churchyard. In 1764 Fr. Diconson, O.S.F., came to reside permanently at Mr. Bruckfield's house, that gentleman having been converted to the faith with a Mr. Whittingham. In 1775 a permanent chapel was established in Miss Latham's house in Little Park Street. This chapel was finally shut up 'on account of the faithful not subscribing in a proper manner.' A chapel was then opened in Mitford (Smithford) Street, 1795; but, owing to some difference among the congregation, all did not attend, till, 'by order of the Bishop,' the Smithford Street chapel was declared that of the mission, when the irritation ceased, January 31, 1796.[1] The labours of the missioners were well rewarded. In spite of the penal laws the number of Catholics increased from the four of 1757 to nearly one hundred in 1770. The chapel in Smithford Street was transferred to Hill Street 1807. An 'unliquidated debt' was still on the building in 1825. Bishop Ullathorne, who resided here from 1841, was, on his consecration in 1846, presented by the congregation with a splendid set of silver Mass cruets of ancient design. The present church was commenced 1843, on the highest part of the city. The Gothic building (115 ft. by 50 ft.) designed by C. Hansom, was opened September 10, 1845, by Bishop Wiseman, assisted by Bishops Sharples, Briggs, Griffiths, Morris, and Brady (West Australia). A set of fine stained-glass windows was presented by the Blount family.

Priests.

Rev. Henry Bishop, 1757 or 1758.
„ M. Diconson, or Dickinson, O.S.F., 1764.
„ Alexius Whalley, O.S.F., 1766.
„ Geo. Baynham, O.S.F., 1769.
„ Bernardine Fleet, O.S.F., 1776.
„ John Bonaventure Pilling, O.S.F., 1779.
„ Anselm Millward, O.S.F., 1794.
„ — Angier, O.P., May 22, 1795, to August 27, 1795.
„ Peter Bernardine Collingridge, 1795 ; Bishop of *Thespiæ*, 1807 ; died 1829.
„ James Vincent Sharp, O.P., 1795.

[1] The other chapel at this time, 1795, was at Mr. Whittingham's. The origin of the dispute is not clear, but it probably arose from the payment difficulty referred to above.

Rev. Richard Anthony Sumner, 1801. (The Abbé Messinge 'supplied' till his arrival.)
„ — Dawber, —.
„ C. Ferand, here in 1824.
„ — Bretherton, 1826.
„ Richard Marsh, 1828.
„ Thos. Cockshoot, 1831.
„ R. Pope, 1840.
„ W. B. Ullathorne, 1841 ; Bishop of *Hetalona* and V.A.C.D., 1846 ; of Birmingham, 1850 ; died 1889.
„ J. A. Clarkson, 1846.
„ Thos. Heptonstall, 1852.
„ Ralph Pratt, 1854.
„ Cuthbert Smith, here in 1871.
„ Henry Moore, here in 1875 (Abbot 1890) till 1892.
„ Antonio Ambrose Pereira, 1892.
„ John Clement Fowler, 1896 to date.

COWES, ISLE OF WIGHT (*Portsmouth*). St. Thomas of Canterbury.

About 1795, Mrs. Heneage, a wealthy Catholic lady, proposed the erection of the chapel, the plans of which were drawn by Fr. Thos. Gabb, a skilful amateur architect. The building was opened in 1796 at a cost of £3,000. more than half of which might have been saved had the chaplain's advice been attended to ! Fr. Gabb, nevertheless, was most unjustly blamed for the waste of money and dismissed. He died on the mission at Worksop Manor, April 17, 1817, aged 75. A Catholic circulating library in connection with the Cowes mission was formed 1850-51.

Priests from 1825.

Rev. W. Pierrepont, —.
„ Jos. Rathbone, 1832.
„ W. Fryer, 1842.

Rev. C. D'Arcy, 1849.
„ J. Canon Bower, 1853.
„ R. Davis, 1885 (?) to date.

COWPEN, NORTHUMBERLAND (*Hexham and Newcastle*). St. Cuthbert.

About 1771 Mr. Marlow Sidney became a Catholic while a student at Cambridge. The immediate cause of his conversion was the strong Gospel argument for the Real Presence as compared with protestant denial.[1] In 1804 he succeeded to the family estate at Cowpen, where he opened a chapel and encouraged Catholicity in every way. The present chapel was erected by his son, Marlow John Sidney, Esq., 1842. Schools were opened 1844. A gallery was added, 1860, thus increasing the accommodation by sixty sittings. The mission is served by Benedictines. New schools were opened November 1898.

Priests.

Rev. J. B. Thomas, 1840.
„ W. Burchall, 1846.
„ J. B. Caldwell, 1852.
„ J. Burchall, 1854.
„ Percy Anderson, 1867.
„ Jos. Murphy, 1873.
„ Ralph Pearson, 1879.
„ Wm. Farrant, 1885.
„ Jn. Oswald Burchall, 1892.
„ Joseph Kershaw, to date.

CRAWCROOK, DURHAM (*Hexham and Newcastle*). St. Agnes.

A mission established in 1892

[1] An interesting account of his conversion was written by his granddaughter and published under the title of *A Hundred Years Ago*. (Burns and Oates, 1877.)

for the benefit of the many Catholics of this mining centre.

Priests.

Rev. Philip Fitzgerald, 1892.
„ Edw. Beech, 1893.
„ Francis Holmes, to date.

CRAWLEY, SUSSEX (*Southwark*). St. Francis.

About 1858 the Hon. Mrs. Montgomery went to live near Crawley. At that time it is said there was not a Catholic in the place. Mrs. Montgomery turned her coach-house and stable into a chapel and school-room and so a mission was formed. In 1861 there were about twenty-five children in the school and an adult congregation of over thirty. The Capuchin Fathers, who had charge of the mission, commenced the present church and monastery in 1860, on a site presented by Captain Francis Blunt, 60th Rifles, a near relation of Mrs. Montgomery's, who also most generously gave £2,000 towards the erection of the buildings. The solemn opening took place on the feast of St. Seraphim, October 12, 1861. Canon Oakeley preached at the Pontifical High Mass (St. Luke xix. 9). Of recent years a philosophical society for the discussion of religio-scientific subjects was established at the monastery and the meetings attended by some of the first scholars and thinkers of the day.

CRAYFORD, KENT (*Southwark*). St. Mary of the Crays.

Many Catholics were reported to be living in the neighbourhood in 1841, at which time Mass was said once a month by Fr. Nightingale

L

in the house of Aug. Applegarth, Esq. In May 1842, the chapel was opened. Fr. Aug. Applegarth, son of the above-named gentleman, was the first resident priest (1843–1855). Bishop Griffiths confirmed thirty persons here, December 1, 1844. The school and presbytery were erected in Fr. Donovan's time (1856–60?).

Recent Priests.

Rev. Jos. Alberry.

„ Jn. Boase, 1877.

„ Wm. Hogan, 1887 to date.

CRESSWELL, STAFFS (*Birmingham*).

A chapel was maintained at Draycott Hall, Cresswell, by the Lords Langdale during a great portion of the penal times. On the death of the fifth Lord Langdale, in 1777, the property went to his sister and finally to the Stourtons. Shortly after the death of Lord Langdale, the chapel was removed to Cresswell. A larger chapel was built in 1782. Fr. Edward Coyney, who was at Draycott during the early part of the eighteenth century, did much to keep Catholicity alive in those parts. He used to visit his scattered flock disguised as a pedlar. Fr. Alban Butler was priest at Cresswell for a time and here he completed his 'Lives of the Saints.' In 1815 Fr. T. Baddeley built 'a handsome Gothic chapel' at Cresswell and opened a secondary school. He died in 1823. The Draycott and Cresswell missions may be called the cradle of North Staffordshire Catholicity in recent times. In 1834 the Catholics at Cresswell numbered 120.

Priests after Fr. Cresswell.

Rev. J. Canon Dunne (he was rector till 1881), 1824.

„ S. E. Canon Bathurst, 1881.

„ Thos. Scott, 1883 to date.

CREWE, CHESHIRE.

In 1830 Crewe contained less than 250 inhabitants and indeed was no more, topographically speaking, than 'a village in Cheshire.' By 1846, owing to the L. & N. W. Railway having established their engine and rolling-stock works here, the village had become a town with many thousands of inhabitants. The mission was established here that year 'in an inconvenient building,' which later on gave place to a commodious school chapel. At a meeting of the congregation in November 1888 proposals were made for the erection of a church. After some delay the present building was commenced in 1890 and opened in 1891.

Priests.

Rev. Jn. Quealy, 1846.

„ Martin Brodrick, 1848.

„ — Foster, 1851.

„ Rd. Doyle, 1852.

„ Hy. Alcock, 1853.

„ Roger McCarte, 1857.

„ Thos. Canon Marsden, 1871.

„ Fredk Waterhouse, 1882.

„ Jn. Barry, 1884.

„ Michael Canon Craig, 1895 to date.

CRICKLEWOOD, LONDON, N.W. (*Westminster*). St. Agnes.

The mission was established in 1901, at Westcroft Villas, Cricklewood Lane. The Catholic population is estimated at 800. New schools have been commenced and will be opened shortly ; cost about £3,000.

Priests.

Rev. Osmund Cooke, 1901.
„ Owen G. Fitzgerald, 1905 to date.

CROFT, LANCS (*Liverpool*).
St. Lewis.

The chapel was built by the Jesuits, the first stone being laid by the Abbé Louis Le Richebec, an *émigré*, June 29, 1826. The building was opened May 29, 1827. Before the establishment of the mission at Croft the chapel appears to have been at Culchetch, the ancient seat of the family of that name. Several of its members entered the Society of Jesus, and two, William and John Culchetch, captains in the Royal Army, lost their lives for Charles I. in the Civil War. The family became extinct on the death of Thos. Culchetch, 1747. When the chapel at the Hall was closed, a Mass house was opened in the district, and so continued till the erection of the chapel as above. The Jesuits gave up the mission to seculars in 1855.

Priests (S.J.).

Rev. Jn. Penkith, 1670.
„ Edward Scarisbrick, 1690.
„ Richard Smith, 1724.

At Croft.

Rev. Richard Reeve, 1780.
„ Abbé Le Richebec, 1798.
„ James Clough, 1845.
„ Wm. Waterton, 1848.
„ Henry Shea, 1849.
„ Fredk. Muller, 1851.

Seculars.

Rev. Wm. Gillett, 1855.
„ Thos. Gibson, 1857.
„ Wm. Wells, 1860.
„ James Parkinson, 1875.
„ Jn. Dorran, 1882.

Rev. Francis Blake, 1885.
„ Patrick Monaghan, 1888.
„ Charles Reynolds, 1899.
„ Francis Blake, to date.

CROMER, NORFOLK (*Northampton*). Our Lady of Refuge, Overstrand Road.

In 1893 Mass was said at the Assembly Rooms adjoining the Red Lion Inn. In September of that year the site was acquired for a new church. Canon Duckett had charge of the mission. The neighbourhood abounds in ruined churches and other vestiges of bygone Catholicity. Fr. T. Carter was appointed to the mission in October 1902. The church was opened August 25, 1895 : accommodation for about one hundred.

CROOK, DURHAM. Our Lady Immaculate and St. Cuthbert.

For historical notice of Crook Hall, see Ushaw. The mission of Crook was started in 1853, when the present Bishop of Hexham and Newcastle, then Fr. Thos. Wilkinson, took a house in the town and laboured for the spiritual good of the rapidly increasing mining population. Fr. J. Rook was the first resident priest of the place, which also had the benefit of the zeal of Fr. Richard Ward, formerly an Anglican clergyman and superior of St. Saviour's, Leeds. The church was commenced in 1853, and opened 1854. In July 1860, Fr. Wilkinson took up his abode at Crook, and in a few years he had added to the church a presbytery, school-house and convent. In 1865 he was elected a canon of Hexham. On July 25, 1888, he was consecrated

L 2

bishop at Ushaw College by Bishop Clifford of Clifton, and next year (September 1889) succeeded Bishop O'Callaghan in the see of Hexham and Newcastle. His successor at Crook was Fr. Austin Pippet, who still retains the mission.

CROWLE, LINCS (*Nottingham*). The Blessed Sacrament and St. Norbert.

Mission opened August 10, 1863, by Fr. W. Harris, of Gainsborough, who said Mass on Sundays in the Assembly Rooms. The congregation is described as being 'large and attentive' (*Retford and Gainsborough News*, August 1863). In 1872 the Premonstratensian Fathers took over the mission, and the new church was opened October 15, the same year, by the Abbot of St. Bernard's Abbey, Leicester. The donor of the church and presbytery was T. A. Young, Esq., K.S.G. By 1882 the congregation had greatly increased, no fewer than fifty-five persons being confirmed at Crowle in the November of that year.

CROXDALE HALL, DURHAM (*Hexham and Newcastle*). St. Herbert.

The mission is described as founded 'from time immemorial. The register dates from 1801. Thos. Salvin, Esq., lord of the manor, erected the chapel (Gothic). For many years, the priest at Croxdale had also to serve the mission at Bishop Auckland. The estimated number of Catholics in 1834 was about two hundred.

Priests.
Rev. Kendal, 1730.
„ Hankin, —.
„ Waram, —.
„ Dunn, —.
„ Taylor, —.
„ Talbot, —.
„ Storey, 1771.
„ Thos. Smith, 1808.
„ John Smith, 1854.
„ Robt. Laing, 1897.
„ Geo. Fehrenbach, 1904 to date.

CROYDON, SURREY (*Southwark*). St. Mary.

Mass was said occasionally here during the eighteenth century by priests from the several ambassadors' chapels in London. On August 23, 1767, Fr. John Baptist Maloney was convicted at the Surrey Summer Assizes, held at Croydon, of saying Mass and exercising his priestly functions. He was condemned to perpetual imprisonment, but shortly afterwards banished. The present mission dates from 1837. Next year, Fr. Patrick O'Moore, a Spanish priest of Irish descent, who had left Spain in consequence of the Carlist troubles, opened a chapel first at Duppas Hill and afterwards at Broad Green, London Road (1841). As he could not speak English, catechetical instruction was given by Dr. Lashmar, a Catholic physician of the town. From 1850 to 1857 the mission was served from Norwood. In the latter year, Fr. Alphonse, afterwards Canon David, came to reside as permanent rector. The Catholic population, estimated at about 1,400 in 1861, is now about four times that number. Lady Vanstruser—afterwards a Dominican nun at Stone, Staffordshire—defrayed the cost of erection of the present Gothic church, opened by Bishop Grant, 1864. Adjoining the church and presbytery in the Wellesley Road are fine schools, under the direction of the Sisters of Mercy. The Josephite establishment, St. George's College, founded in the Wellesley Road, 1869, was removed to Woburn Park, Weybridge, 1884. The premises are now the St. Mary's Industrial School (Sisters of Mercy).

Priests.

Revs. Abbé Chabot, 1837.

„ Patrick O'Moore or More, 1838.

„ J. Bradshaw, 1849.

„ Michael Vesque, 1850 (Bishop of Roseau, West Indies, 1857).

„ Alphonse Canon David, 1851; resident 1857.

„ John McKenna, M.R.; curate 1874, rector 1894 to date.

CROYDON, SOUTH. St. Gertrude, Purley Road.

The church, a plain building in the Romanesque style, was opened 1903, and for some time served from St. Mary's. In May 1904 Fr. C. Turner, the present rector, was appointed to the mission from Ashford (Kent).

CUSTOM HOUSE, E. (*Westminster*). Our Lady and St. Edward.

A few years ago, the Custom House district was a marsh, but now it contains a dense population of hundreds of thousands of working people. Until the opening of the church in December 1899 by Cardinal Vaughan, Catholics had to go to Mass at Silvertown or Stratford, while 'hundreds of children were swept into Board Schools.' The sacred edifice, as well as the fine Catholic schools for some 500 children, are almost entirely due to the energetic rector, Fr. Timothy Ring. The church is Pointed Gothic in style, designed by Mr. Curtiss, who also presented the handsome high altar. Seats for about three hundred.

CWMBRAN, MONMOUTHSHIRE (*Newport*). Our Lady of the Angels.

When the Franciscans undertook to establish the mission here in 1864 Catholics of the place numbered about 380, ' sunk into a state of utter indifference to religion, or indeed to anything beyond their daily or nightly toil.' The first chapel was the club-room of a public-house, the altar and furniture being of the poorest description. The congregation subscribed £30 from their hard-earned wages and with about £200 from other sources the present chapel was built, the opening taking place January 1, 1867. Prior, afterwards Archbishop Vaughan of Sydney, preached ; schools, under government inspection, were inaugurated 1868. A chancel was added to the church about 1870. The mission has for many years been served from Pontypool.

D

DALTON-IN-FURNESS, LANCS (*Liverpool*). Our Lady of the Rosary.

A school chapel was opened here by Bishop O'Reilly, December 16, 1879. It was served from Barrow till 1893.

Priests.

Rev. Edward Kelly, 1893 to date.

DANBY, YORKSHIRE. *See* **LEYBURN.**

DARLINGTON, DURHAM (*Hexham and Newcastle*). St. Augustine's.

The baptismal register of this mission dates from 1783. The priests in charge of the chapel from that year to 1848 were Revs. J. Daniel, Wm. Coghlan, Lewis le Crornier (*émigré*), Thos. Story, Jos. Curr, and Wm. Hogarth, afterwards first Bishop of Hexham (1850-66). The old chapel was pulled down when the new one was built, in 1826, from designs by J. Bonomi, Esq. The mission was formerly served from Cliffe, the seat of the Witham family, whose arms appear over the chapel door. On the sale of the Cliffe estates Fr. Hogarth—'at great sacrifice and expense'—built the Darlington chapel. The number of regular communicants in 1832 was 200. In December 1865, the chapel underwent considerable improvements and alterations. The side windows were enlarged and a Gothic tower added. The interior was adorned with several fine stained-glass windows. For several years after the establishment of the hierarchy, St. Augustine's presbytery was the residence of the bishop of the diocese.

Priests since 1850.

Rev. Thos. Crowe, 1849–50.
„ Robt. Tate, D.D., 1850.
„ Bishop Hogarth of Hexham and Newcastle, 1852.
„ Hy. Coll, 1867.
„ Jas. Canon Rooney, here in 1877 and to date.

DARTFORD, KENT (*Southwark*). St. Anselm, Spital Street.

The mission was opened March 8, 1866, but in November 1884 when Fr. E. Buckley was priest of the place, the 'chapel' was still 'a damp inconvenient room,' barely accommodating sixty people. It possessed neither tabernacle, vestments, nor sacred vessels. Mass was only said on Sundays. The cottage which did duty as the Catholic school was so ill-adapted for the purpose that the Government grant was withdrawn. The first stone of the new church was laid March 3, 1900. The style is Early English. Accommodation for 300. F. A. Walters, Esq., architect. St. Vincent's Industrial School, under the direction of Brothers of the Presentation, was removed here from Deptford in August 1878. Fr. W. Thompson, rector of the mission, was succeeded by Fr. James Mahoney, August 1906.

DARTMOOR, DEVON (*Plymouth*). Convict Prison, Prince Town.

The prison was built 1806-9, and was used at first for the incarceration of French and American prisoners of war. After the downfall of Napoleon in 1815, the building was converted into a naphtha and ammonia factory, but in 1850 again became a prison for the reception of persons sentenced to penal servitude. The Catholic chapel is said to be one of the finest in the county, the altar, &c., being the work of the convicts. Mass on Sundays at 10 A.M. for prisoners, warders, and other Catholics of the place.

Catholic Chaplains.

Rev. Geo. Green, 1863.
„ David A. Coleman, 1891.
„ Michael Laurenson, 1900 to date.

DARTMOUTH, DEVON (*Plymouth*). St. John the Baptist.

The mission was started 1860, and for some years was served from Torquay. The Gothic church was opened 1869. A fine altar of Malplaquet stone was erected in March 1887.

Priests.

Rev. J. Jolly, 1863.
„ J. B. Laborie Rey, 1867.
„ Wm. Downing, 1885.
„ Jn. McCarthy, 1893 to date.

DARWEN, LANCS (*Salford*). Church of the Sacred Heart, Blackburn Road.

From 1878, when the mission was started, to 1882, Fr. J. Lathouwers had to conduct the Divine services in a damp and leaky building quite unsuited for use as a chapel. The first stone of the present church was laid on August 19, 1882, by the Bishop of Salford, afterwards Cardinal Vaughan. Several of the town councillors and magistrates contributed to the building fund. The style of the building is Early English Gothic, and the seating capacity for 400 persons. The cost of erection was about £2,000.

DAVENTRY, NORTHAMPTON-SHIRE (*Northampton*). St. Mark's.

This church was opened on Low Sunday, 1882, by Bishop Riddell, of Northampton. The building was originally a stable, but by the ingenuity of Fr. Walstan Smith, the incumbent, was converted into 'a small, neat, and tasteful church.' Lord Braye, of Stanford Park, and Sir Charles Tempest, of Ashby Lodge, generously defrayed the expense of alteration.

Priests.

Rev. Walstan Smith, 1882 till after 1898.
„ Jas. Purcell, to date.

DAWLISH, DEVONSHIRE (*Plymouth*).

A room was hired for a chapel, and Mass said for the first time of late years by Fr. W. Dawson, Sunday, February 11, 1906. The temporary chapel is close to the station, and can accommodate about fifty persons. Major-General Laye and Mr. Eccles, of Teignmouth—from which town the chapel is at present served — have greatly assisted in the establishment of the mission.

DEAL, KENT (*Southwark*). St. Thomas of Canterbury.

The first resident priest of this mission was Fr. Cuthbert Downey, O.S.B., of St. Augustine's, Ramsgate. The first chapel was in the schoolroom, and had 'little in its four whitewashed walls to inspire devotion in the faithful.' Mass was said there for the first time in March 1865. Fr. J. Scratton, who laboured here from 1869 to January 1884, was, on leaving the mission, presented by his grateful congregation with a handsome chalice and paten. He was succeeded by Mgr. Daniewski. Fr. A. Limpens is the present rector.

DEEPCAR, YORKS (*Leeds*). St. Anne.

A chapel was opened here 1860 for the benefit of the many Catholics engaged in the local terracotta works and collieries. It was served from St. Vincent of Paul's, Sheffield, till about 1876.

Priests.
Rev. Patrick Keating, 1876.
,, Patrick Kiernan, 1882; served from Mortomly, 1898.
,, John Carr, 1899 to date.

DENABY MAIN, ROTHERHAM, YORKS (*Leeds*). St. Alban.

The mission was commenced 1894, the chapel being in the priest's house, No. 1 Wood View. Fr. T. B. Kavanagh is the first and present rector.

DENTON, LANCS (*Salford*). St. Mary.

A school chapel was opened 1870 (?) and served from St. Anne's, Ashton-under-Lyne, till 1889, when the mission became separate. Catholic population about 300.

Priests.
Rev. Thos. Twomey, 1889.
,, Jn. Welch, 1895.
,, H. Schurgers, 1897.
,, Patrick Joyner, 1898.
,, J. M. Willemse, 1904 to date.

DEPTFORD, LONDON, S.E. (*Southwark*). The Assumption.

Fr. Green, of St. George's, Southwark, laboured here 1795–1815, and Fr. Stewart 1815–23, Fr. McCabe 1823–27. A temporary chapel was opened in King Street in 1842. The schools accommodated about 200 children. The present church in the High Street was opened 1846, and enlarged by a chancel (December 15, 1859). The fine reredos (1884) was exhibited at the Paris Exhibition 1878. The church was redecorated 1904. The style is geometrical Gothic. In May 1906, a fine hall adjoining the church, formerly used for concerts &c., was acquired by the present rector Fr. Segesser, for the use of the mission.

Priests since 1843.

Rev. W. Marshall, 1843.

„ E. North, M.R., 1850.

„ J. Norris, 1860.

„ J. Canon Glenie, M.A., 1862.

„ Michael Canon Fannan (curate since May 1865), 1871.

„ Felix Segesser, 1905.

The Catholic population of the district is estimated at about 7,000.

DERBY (*Nottingham*). St. Mary's.
The church was designed by E. Welby Pugin, and the first stone laid by the Hon. and Rev. Fr. Ignatius Spencer. The dedication took place October 9, 1839, when the sermon was preached by Bishop Wiseman. The decorations, stained-glass windows, &c., were added in 1853. The church was beautifully redecorated in November 1892. The reredos at the back of the high altar is sculptured with reliefs of the Adoration of the Magi, the Annunciation, &c. The Lady Chapel, built in 1853 from a design by Hansom, has an altar piece dating from 1462. In 1829 the number of Catholic families in Derby was twenty. On the Third Sunday of Advent, 1849, Bishop Ullathorne confirmed 180 persons at St. Mary's. The Catholic population of Derby and vicinity was then reckoned at 3,000. Fr. Sing built the Convent of Mercy, and the nuns took over the teaching of the Catholic schools. In June 1849 a great Corpus Christi procession took place round the enclosure of the church, which was attended by many protestants, whose attitude was most reverential.

DERBY. St. Joseph's, Mill Hill.
The growth of Catholicity in Derby necessitated the opening of a temporary chapel (Gothic) in Moore Street, November 1878. The accommodation was for seventy, the cost of the building being about £400. In 1897 the present fine church superseded the old chapel, and there are now two priests in charge of the mission.

DEVIZES, WILTS (*Clifton*). Immaculate Conception. St. Joseph's Place.
Mission opened 1861, the first chapel being a disused warehouse. Captain Jewel built the church and endowed it. He also established the mission at Malmesbury. Devizes was long a centre of intense protestantism, and great animus was shown against Catholics when the chapel was first opened. The Congregation of St. Francis of Sales have had charge of the mission from the commencement.

N.B.—When some of Lord George Gordon's emissaries were hurrying to Bath in 1780 to stir up a 'No Popery' riot there, they asked if there were any Papists at Devizes. On being informed that the only one was a cobbler, they said 'he was beneath their notice' and rode on! (Tradition.)

DEVONPORT (*Plymouth*). SS. Michael and Joseph.
In 1860 there were neither chapel nor schools at Devonport. The nearest Catholic place of worship was the Cathedral, Plymouth, separated from Devonport by an inlet of the sea crossed by a toll

bridge. The congregation, mostly composed of soldiers, sailors, and others in her Majesty's service, amounted to 1,500. About 1859 Government granted a commodious site for a church on condition that one was built within two years. On December 19, 1861, the church was opened by Bishop Vaughan, of Plymouth—though only the nave and south aisle were complete at that time. The style is Early English, from the plans of C. Hansom. The civilian Catholic population of Devonport in 1861 was about 500.

Priests.

Rev. Geo. Hobson, 1861.

„ Bernard Verdon, here in 1871.

„ Jn. Canon Lapôtre, here in 1883.

„ Thos. Kent, 1891 to date.

DEWSBURY, YORKS (*Leeds*). Our Lady and St. Paulinus.

Mass was first said at Dewsbury in ' a cloth hall ' in the spring of 1841 by Fr. E. O'Leary. This chapel proving very inconvenient, Fr. O'Leary went to Ireland to collect funds to build, but returned without much success. The present church was opened Tuesday, May 30, 1871. The cost of erection was £9,000, the architect being E. W. Pugin. In 1881 another mission, dedicated to St. Joseph, was started at Batley Carr, a suburb of Dewsbury, and by October of the same year the school chapel had proved ' wholly inadequate to the congregation.' Fr. Thos. Parkin was the first priest of the new foundation.

DITTON HALL, LANCS (*Liverpool*). St. Michael.

The Jesuit fathers expelled from Prussia by the ' May Laws ' opened a mission here about 1875. A fine church presented by the Marchioness Stapleton-Bretherton was erected in 1879, and a large congregation gradually formed round it. A pulpit of Caen stone was set up in September 1882. The schools were built in 1886 by the noble foundress of the church. Fr. Anthony de Haza Radlitz, S.J., was the first priest in charge of the mission. The German Jesuits quitted charge of the place in August 1895, when Fr. Dupuy, S.J., of the English Province, was appointed. Fr. T. Dawson is the present rector.

DODDING, or DODDIN GREEN, KENDAL, WESTMORLAND (*Hexham and Newcastle*). SS. Robert and Alice.

This mission was founded by Robert and Alice Stevenson in 1724. The first priest of the mission, Fr. Thomas Roydon, had prior to this been chaplain to John Leyburne, Esq., of Nateby. This gentleman joined the forces of the Chevalier de St. George (James Francis Stuart ' the Old Pretender') during the rising of 1715, and lost several fine estates in consequence. Fr. Roydon was what was known as ' a riding priest,' *i.e.* one whose duty it was to ride round the country and visit the Catholics on the various estates of his patron—in this case, Mr. Leyburne. After the disaster of 1715, Fr. Roydon went to live with Mr. Stevenson who at his death left him his estate. Fr. Roydon died in 1741 and was succeeded in the estate by his nephew, Mr. Thomas Roydon, who died October 17, 1764. Doddin Green was said to be the best mission in the northern vicariate in 1803. Owing to an unhappy dispute there was no incumbent from 1812 till 1834. Two other vacancies have since occurred, viz. 1844-60 and 1874-79. The chapel is still a room in the priest's house, and the congregation is regarded as the second smallest in England.

Priests.

Rev. Thos. Roydon, 1724.
„ Robt. Johnson, 1764.
„ John Lonsdale, 1799.
„ R. Bannister, 1802-12.
(Mission vacant till 1834.)
„ Henry Bannister or Rutter, 1834. This priest was a nephew of the preceding and held the mission till his death in 1838. He was an uncle of Bishop Goss of Liverpool.
Rev. C. Brigham, 1838.
(Mission vacant 1844-60.)
„ Robt. Canon Hogarth.
„ Ralph Canon Platt, 1868— ' a classical scholar, an antiquarian, a philosopher, and a theologian.'
(Mission vacant 1874-79.)
„ Canon Curry, 1879.
„ Henry Brettargh, 1892 to date.

DONCASTER, YORKS (*Leeds*). St. Peter's Chains.

In 1833 the Catholic population of Doncaster is said not to have exceeded twelve. The chapel in Princes Street was opened 1835. and three years later Confirmation was given here for the first time since the Reformation by Bishop Briggs, V.A. On November 12, 1843, sixty-eight persons were confirmed at Doncaster, and in 1864 the Catholic population of the place was estimated at about 900. By this time the chapel, which only accommodated 200, had become old and dilapidated, and the priest, Fr. E. Pearson, appealed for funds to build. The present church was built between October 1866 and August 1867. The style is thirteenth century Gothic. The cost was £1,500, of which £1,000 was contributed by Charles Cholmondeley, Esq., of Doncaster.

Priests.

Rev. J. Furniss, 1835.
„ J. Ball, 1840.
„ Robt. Gibson, 1848.
„ Wm. Scruton, 1857.
„ Jos. Hill, here 1862.
„ Edward Pearson, 1863.
„ Chas. Burke, here 1871 till 1892.
„ Andrew Leonard, 1892 to date.

DORCHESTER, DORSET (*Plymouth*). Our Lady of the Martyrs.

A Gothic school-chapel was erected in the High Street, Dorchester, in November 1867. Bishop Vaughan, of Plymouth, remarked in his sermon, on the occasion of the solemn opening, that the holy sacrifice of the Mass had not been offered in Dorchester since the martyrdom of Fr. Hugh Green, of Chideock there in 1642. At first the chapel was served by Fr. John Charles, of Weymouth.

N.B.—The Ven. Hugh Green, of Douai, served the mission at Chideock in Dorsetshire, as chaplain to Lord and Lady Arundell of Wardour. He was arrested at Lyme while proceeding to France, and sentenced to death at the Dorchester assizes ' for being a priest contrary to the laws.' He suffered at Dorchester August 19, 1642. Fr. Thomas Pritchard suffered for the Faith here March 21, 1587.

DORCHESTER, OXFORDSHIRE
(*Birmingham*). St. Birinus.

The mission was re-established from Oxford by Fr. Robt. Newsham, 1823. He served the place till 1834, when apparently he was forced to relinquish it for some years. The church was opened by Bishop Ullathorne, V.A., August 21, 1849. John Davey, Esq., defrayed the cost of erection of the building, which was designed by W. Wardell. Fr. Newsham took up permanent residence in the mission this year and added a fine rood-screen to the church. He was incumbent till his death in October 1859, aged 76. The interior of the church is adorned with some fine coloured windows illustrating events in the life of St. Birinus.

Recent Priests.

Rev. Henry James Green, 1860.
„ Henry Davey, 1863.
„ James Narey, 1876.
„ Wm. Barry, D.D., 1885. The distinguished littérateur.

DORKING, SURREY (*Southwark*).
St. Joseph's.

In the eighteenth century the few Catholics of the district were attended by the chaplains of the Dukes of Norfolk, who possess much property in the neighbourhood. In the record of a baptism at Reigate on June 4, 1779, one Edward Menzies, ' in service of the Duke of Norfolk at Dorking,' is mentioned as sponsor. Fr. M. Pembridge, O.S.B., was here 1786-91. The

present mission dates from 1871, when an unpretentious chapel was opened in Coldharbour Lane. Schools were inaugurated March 1877, about which time the chapel was redecorated. The present church in the thirteenth century style of Gothic was opened June 26, 1895, and is in memory of Mina Duchess of Norfolk. The accommodation is for 500. Mr. F. A. Walters, architect.

Priests.

Rev. Geo. Ballard, 1871.
„ J. F. Volckeryck, 1878.
„ W. B. Alexander, 1903.

DOVER, KENT (*Southwark*). St. Paul.

The mission registers date from 1822. Early in the nineteenth century Mass was said at various private houses in the town, *e.g.* at 45 Snargate Street. The visiting priest about this time was the zealous Fr. Costigan, of Margate. In 1824 Fr. Patrick Portal became resident priest. He left in 1826, when the mission was again periodically served by Fr. Costigan. In 1834 Fr. F. Jarrett, chaplain to the Robinson family, who lived in Dover, used to say Mass over a carpenter's shop. After a time a Methodist chapel in Queen Elizabeth Square was purchased by Mr. H. Robinson and fitted up as a chapel (1835). Tradition says that Wesley preached here. A house close by was also purchased for £315 for use as a presbytery. Fr. Jarrett was succeeded by Frs. J. B. Hearn and J. L. Savage. In 1861 a site for a new church was purchased through Major Molyneux Seel. At this time the Catholic population of Dover, exclusive of the military, numbered 190. The site in the Ashentree Lane was found to be unsuitable, and another was purchased in the Maison Dieu Road. The new church—designed by E. Welby Pugin—was commenced June 1, 1867, and opened May 15, 1868. Archbishop Manning preached at the Mass of inauguration. The style of the building is thirteenth century Gothic. Its erection was largely due to the untiring exertions of Fr. James Laws, priest at Dover from 1863 till his retirement in 1891. Much of the money expended on the fabric came from the bequest of the Countess de Front, wife of the Sardinian Minister to the Court of St. James. This lady died in London, January 7, 1830; and on the death of her brother, Sir Thomas Fleetwood, the money came into the hands of Bishop Grant, of Southwark. The church at Dover was enlarged by thirty feet and re-opened in 1873. The building was consecrated by Bishop Bourne in 1897.

DOWNALL GREEN, WIGAN, LANCS (*Liverpool*).
Mission established 1896.
Priests.
Rev. James Smith, 1896.
„ John Smith, to date.

DOWNSIDE, near BATH, SOMER-SET (*Clifton*). St. Gregory's Abbey.
In 1605 an English Benedictine monk, named Dom Augustine Bradshaw, opened a school, for the sons of his fellow-countrymen, at Douai. The foundation was greatly fostered by the Archduke Albert and Dom Philip Cavarel, Abbot of the Benedictine monastery of St.

Vedast at Arras. The school grew into the monastery of St. Gregory the Great, opened at Douai, October 11, 1611. Swept away with the other Catholic institutions of France during the fury of the Revolution in 1793, the Fathers and students escaped to England, where Sir John Smythe, Bart., of Acton Burnell (Shropshire), an old pupil of the Benedictines, gave the fugitives hospitality. The college re-established at Acton Burnell continued till 1814, when the purchase of the manor house and estate of Downside enabled the community to settle there. In 1823 the old manor house—still standing—was supplemented by a new chapel and college, in the Gothic style, designed by Goodridge of Bath. The chapel was opened by Bishop Baines, V.A.W.D., July 10, 1823. The 'new' college block, by C. Hansom, was erected 1853-56, during the presidency of Prior Sweeney. The monastery and college extension—the plans of which were drawn up by Messrs. Dunn and Hansom—were commenced on October 1, 1873, and opened in September 1876, the foundation stone being laid by Cardinal Manning. The splendid Decorated Gothic church, begun at the same time, is only now approaching completion. The transepts were opened in 1882, and the 'series of chapels, forming a corona round sanctuary and choir,' between 1885 and 1901. Beneath the high altar reposes the body of the Ven. Archbishop Oliver Plunket, of Armagh, one of the victims of the Titus Oates Plot (1681), formerly preserved at the Benedictine monastery of Lambspring in Bavaria. The priory of Downside was created an abbey in 1900, the Right Rev. Hugh Ford, O.S.B., being the first abbot. It is impossible in a brief notice like this to refer to the college further. Since its foundation, it has held a distinguished place in the educational field of English Catholicity. It was affiliated to the London University by Royal Charter in 1841. Quite recently a foundation, known as St. Benet's, for Benedictine University candidates, has been opened at Cambridge. From the point of view of the present work, Downside is one of ·the most important centres of Catholicity in England, and during its existence of almost a century on' English soil has become the mother of not a few of the chief neighbouring missions, as St. Benedict's, Stratton-on-the-Fosse, erected in 1857.

DRIFFIELD, YORKS (*Middlesbrough*). Our Lady and St. Edward.

The mission was opened about the end of January 1883. Mass was at first said in a large private house and afterwards in the Corn Exchange. The number of Catholics in the town was then about 100. When the Bishop of Middlesbrough visited the chapel in February 1883, some 600 protestants were drawn to the extemporised place of worship ' to hear a Catholic Bishop preach and witness the ceremony.' The feeling of the town at the outset of the mission is described as having been ' exceedingly favourable.'

Recent Priests.
Rev. Francis Gerrard, 1889.
„ Wm. Storey, 1893 to date.

DUDLEY, WORCESTERSHIRE (*Birmingham*). Our Blessed Lady and St. Thomas of Canterbury.

The mission was established 1835 from West Bromwich. The site of the church was acquired 1837. The church was consecrated by Bishop Wiseman on Easter Monday 1842.

Priests.
Rev. J. O'Neill, 1837.
„ Henry Elwes, 1840.
„ M. Horgan, 1842.
„ Geo. Fox, 1848.
„ Thos. Moore, 1857.
„ Jas. Bond, here in 1862.
„ Thos. Keates, here in 1888 and to date.

DUKINFIELD, CHESHIRE (*Shrewsbury*). St. Mary.

A hired room in Cricket's Lane served as a chapel in 1822. A regular mission was established three years later, when a church was erected in Astley Street. Owing to signs of collapse, in consequence of the church being built over a coal-mine, the services were transferred to a room of the ' Old General' Inn hard by in 1847. The present church was commenced 1854 and finished in March 1856. Schools were erected in 1872.

Priests.
Rev. J. Fisher, 1825.
„ T. Gillett, 1835.
„ R. Brown, 1837.
„ W. Henderson, 1839.
„ G. Fisher, 1840.
    (Served from Aston-under-Lyne, 1848–56.)
„ W. Fennelly, 1856.
„ H. England, 1857.
„ P. Power, 1858.
„ J. Jones, 1859.
„ R. Hilton, 1863.
„ P. Lyons, 1869.

Rev. M. Craig, 1876.
„   A. Tremmery, 1883.
„   T. Ratcliffe, 1886.
„   C. Collenbier, 1888.
„   P. Cleary, 1900.

DULWICH (EAST), LONDON, S.E. (*Southwark*).   St. Anthony of Padua.

Mass was said here in the temporary chapel, Lordship Lane, for the first time on Whit Sunday, June 1, 1879.   In 1882 the average attendance at Mass on Sundays was about 200.   The number of Catholic children was about 180. Schools for boys and girls were opened in November 1883.   The new schools were opened in April 1885, and in May of the same year the new church.   The High Mass was sung by the Bishop of Melos. The mission was subsequently taken over by the English Benedictines, who took formal possession of the chapel on Sunday, July 10, 1892.   Fr. Wulstan Richards, O.S.B., preached on the history of the Benedictines in England in recent times.

DUNMOW, ESSEX (*Westminster*). Our Lady.

The little church was opened in 1853, and served for years from Ongar.   Owing, we believe, to financial difficulties, it had to be closed about 1878, when Mass was only said at irregular intervals on week-days.   In June 1898 the church was again opened for regular services at the initiative of the late Cardinal Vaughan.   At present (1904) the mission is served from Braintree.

DUNSTON, DURHAM (*Hexham and Newcastle*).   St. Philip Neri.

Mass has been said here regularly since February 1880, when Fr. Arnold Matthews fitted up a chapel at 4 Brompton Place.   'The new and elegant school chapel' was opened for service on Advent Sunday 1882.   On Christmas Day the same year a magnificent altar of inlaid wood and reredos containing an elegant portrait of St. Philip were exposed for the first time.   The chapel accommodation is for 500 persons.   A large iron church, to accommodate 700, was opened Sunday, June 4, 1905, on a site granted by the late Lady Ravensworth, who also presented a fine Madonna picture as altarpiece.

DURHAM, ST. CUTHBERT'S, OLD ELVET (*Hexham and Newcastle*).

The Durham mission is stated to have been 'founded from time immemorial.'   During the penal times it was long known among missioners as ' Mrs. Durham.' Bishop Leyburn confirmed 1,024 persons here in 1687.   Fr. Thos. Pearson, S.J., was the priest at this time.   In 1688 the Mass-house and presbytery were burnt by the mob, but Fr. Pearson continued his labours and died at Durham, 1732, aged 87.   The register dates from about 1708 with an entry of the death of Margaret Carnaby, ' Ob. 11 Jan., 1708-9.'   After the baptism of Sarah Watson, January 20, 1746, the following words occur : ' Not continued for yᵗ year, probably on accᵗ of ye difficulty of ye Times.'   The Jacobite rebellion of 1745-46 was then at its height, and the laws against ' Papists ' were were being strictly enforced.   Frs.

Edward Walsh and John Scott were priests here in 1768 and Fr. Nicholas Clavering in 1778. In 1826 the Jesuits, who had hitherto served the mission, made over the chapel to Bishop Smith, V.A.N.D. The old chapel would appear to have become dilapidated or insufficient at this time, for in 1827 'an elegant Gothic chapel, from a design by Ignatius Bonomi, Esq.,' was announced as being erected. It was opened the same year.

Priests since 1825.

Rev. W. Croskell, V.G. (and John Scott).

„ Wm. Fletcher, D.D., 1840.
„ Provost Platt, V.G., 1857.
„ Provost Edward Consitt, M.R., 1868.
„ Wm. Canon Brown, rector here in 1889 to date.

DURHAM (*Hexham and New-castle*). St. Godric.

This church was not completed till 1864. In 1859 (June) a tem-porary chapel was opened in Fram-wellgate in a house formerly be-longing to a Miss Williams. The drawing-room was fitted up as a chapel capable of holding 500 per-sons. The room is described as being 'a very elegant one,' adorned with some splendid wood-carving by Catisi. The first Mass was said by Provost Platt. The Catholics of Durham numbered about 3,000 in 1863, when the present church of St. Godric was commenced. The style is Decorated Gothic. The stone was laid by Bishop Hogarth, of Hexham. Most of the money (£3,000) for the erection of the church was collected by Canon Smith ('Durham Chronicle'). The solemn opening of the building took place on November 15, 1864. The seating capacity is for about 500 persons.

Priests.

Rev. Robt. Pattison.
„ John Nolan, 1871.
„ Wm. Perrin, 1874.
„ G. Jones, 1885.
„ Robt. Thornton, 1895 to date.

E

EALING, LONDON, W. (*Westminster*). SS. Joseph and Peter.

The mission was established in 1893. At first Mass was said in a small room of a private house in Windsor Road. Afterwards a chapel was opened in the drawing-room of Mattock Lodge, Mattock Lane. A large temporary chapel was subsequently erected by the first priest of the mission. In March 1899, the Benedictine Fathers took over the mission, and by this time a handsome church (St. Benedict's) had been erected in the Blakesley Avenue. Early in 1901, the nuns of the Holy Child established a convent school at Castlehill House, a fine old mansion formerly occupied by the Visitation Nuns, now of Harrow. The style of the church, opened November 26, 1899, is fifteenth century Gothic, the design comprising, when complete, wide nave, two aisles, choir, sanctuary, seven side chapels, and crypt. F. A. Walters, F.S.A., architect.

At the commencement of the eighteenth century, the Catholic Earl Rivers had a mansion at Ealing. Fr. John Savage, his nephew, was there as chaplain, 1712. He succeeded the earl as fifth and last of the title 1715. He conformed to the Established Church, and entered the House of Lords, but soon repented, and retiring abroad, died Canon of Seclin, near Douai, 1737.

EARLSFIELD, near TOOTING, SURREY (*Southwark*). St. Gregory the Great.

A plain church, in the Romanesque style, was opened in November 1904, and Mass said for the first time on Sunday, the 20th of the same month. The church is the gift of an anonymous benefactress. The Catholics of the district, to the number of about 800, had formerly to go for Mass to Wandsworth and Tooting. The Rev. F. Laurence, now of Horsham, was the first rector of the mission, which is at present served by the Salesian Fathers of Battersea.

EASINGTON, DURHAM (*Hexham and Newcastle*). Our Lady of Victories.

The mission was established from Hutton House (*q.v.*) in 1863. Two years later the present church was opened on Ferry Hill.

Priests.

Rev. William Markland.

„ Lawrence Boland, 1878.

„ Geo. Gregson, 1895 to date.

EASINGWOLD, YORKS (*Middlesbrough*).

The mission was originally served from the domestic chapel at Gilling

M

Castle, the seat of the Catholic Lords Fairfax. The last of this ancient family was Lady Anne Fairfax, who died unmarried in 1793. A house which she built for her chaplain, Dom Anselm Bolton, O.S.B., became the nucleus of Ampleforth College in 1802. After her death, the mission of Gilling was removed to Craike, and thence to Easingwold in 1830. The register only dates from 1819. In 1898 the old chapel was superseded by the present church. The mission has always been under the care of the Benedictines.

Priests from 1824.

Rev. T. Croupe.

„ J. Tyrer, 1827.

„ J. Dowding, 1835.

„ Michael Brown, 1877.

„ Sir John Swale, Bart., 1879.

„ Ralph Pearson, 1885 to date.

EAST BERGHOLT, SUFFOLK (*Northampton*). St. Mary's Abbey.

After the destruction of English religious houses under Henry VIII., a convent was founded in Brussels under the title of the Glorious Assumption (1598). The foundress of this abbey was Lady Mary Percy, kinswoman of the Duke of Northumberland, assisted by the Ladies Dorothy and Gertrude Arundell, of the noble house of Wardour. Dame Joanna Berkeley, daughter of Sir John Berkeley, of Beveston Castle, Gloucestershire, was the first abbess, and Lady Mary Percy, a niece of the foundress, the second. When the French Revolutionists invaded Belgium in 1794, the nuns were forced to seek refuge in England, after witnessing the loss of the bulk of their property. With the assistance of Bishop Milner they opened a house at Winchester, where the

community remained till 1857, when they removed to East Bergholt. A high-class ladies' school was maintained here till 1877, when it was discontinued, both on account of the many schools of the kind in England and for the more perfect accomplishment of a chief duty of the rule, *i.e.* the singing of divine office in choir.

EASTBOURNE, SUSSEX (*Southwark*). Our Lady of Ransom.

The mission was established 1869, when Fr. Charles King opened a temporary chapel in Terminus Place. Another brick building was afterwards erected in the Junction Road, under the title of Stella Maris. Fr. Charles Stapley commenced the existing handsome Gothic church in 1890, and it was completed 1903, during the rectorate of the present incumbent, Fr. Paul Lynch, B.A. St. Joseph's School Chapel, Whitley Road was opened as a chapel-of-ease to the mother church in September 1895 by Canon E. St. John. A church, dedicated to St. Agnes, is in course of erection. It is the gift of a lady, and will cost about £1,500.

EAST GRINSTEAD, SUSSEX (*Southwark*). Our Lady and St. Peter.

The mission was served by the Jesuits during the 'troubled times.' The chapel appears to have been at Edge Court till about 1774, when the place was sold. Among the items of 'Church stuff' at this time were included 'five silver candlesticks, silver thurible, two cruets of silver, four sets of vestments, Massbook, and large crucifix.' Fr. Hy. Molyneux, S.J., priest here from 1721 to 1733, was paid £30 a year from 'Mrs. Hants.' The existing mission was commenced in 1879, under the title of SS. Edward and Louis, and was served from Crawley. The present church was consecrated August 1, 1899.

Priests.

Rev. Fredk. Edwards, 1885 ; served from Crawley 1889–99
„ John Burke, 1899.

EAST HAM, PLAISTOW, LONDON, E. (*Westminster*).

This mission was formerly known as Upton Park and Plaistow. In 1878 it was served by a temporary chapel dedicated to St. Anthony and attended from Stratford (*q.v.*). When St. Edward's Orphanage for Boys was established here in 1878, under the care of the Brothers of Mercy, a chapel was attached for the use of the community, and this temporarily served the mission from 1891 to 1903. The premises occupied by the Orphanage were formerly known as Greenstead House, in the garden of which Henry VIII. erected a tower 50 feet high for Anne Boleyn ; hence the place is often called Boleyn Castle. Fr. Joseph Zsilkay, who was chaplain here 1879–99, did much to extend Catholicity in the neighbourhood. He was succeeded by Fr. E. Walsh and A. Maes. The mission has now its own church, situated in Castle Street.

EASTLEIGH, HANTS (*Portsmouth*). The Holy Cross.

The mission was established 1885 and served from Winchester till 1888, when the Rev. T. Ryan was appointed resident priest. The church, in the Gothic style, was consecrated by Bishop Cahill in August 1902.

Priests.

Rev. T. Ryan, 1888.
„ Jn. Molloy, 1891.
„ Joseph Hayes, 1893.
„ J. E. McCarthy, 1896.
„ Albert Clarke, 1899.
„ Thos. Hickey, D.D., 1903 to date.

EAST HARPTREE, SOMERSET (*Clifton*).

The Faith lived on in this district after the Reformation owing to the protection of the Waldegrave family of East Harptree Court. In 1722 James, second Earl Waldegrave, 'conformed to the Established Church,' after which Mass was only said occasionally in the neighbourhood. In 1794 the Rev. Joseph Hunt, assisted by his family, commenced a regular mission at Shortwood, in this district. The old chapel, dedicated to St. Michael, was opened May 15, 1806. Fr. Hunt's father took the name of Beaumont on succeeding to some property, but his son always retained the older patronymic. Among the benefactors to the Shortwood mission was the Rev. Jn. Brookes, rector of Hinton Bluett, who embraced the Catholic faith about 1804. In or about 1883, the old territorial title of Shortwood was altered to that of East Harptree.

Priests.

Rev. Joseph Hunt, 1794.
„ Jn. Swarbrick, 1838.
„ Jn. Larkan, 1838.
„ James Dawson, 1841.
„ Moses Furlong, 1842.
„ Thos. Dawson, 1842.
„ Thos. Fergusson, D.D., 1844.
„ Patrick Kelly, 1844.
„ Thos. Rooker, 1845.
„ Thos. M'Donnell, 1852.
„ Jn. B. Morris, 1861.

Rev. Robt. Platt, here 1871.
„   Hon. Everard Arundell, 1878.
„   Wm. Walsh, 1880.
„   Robt. Dunham, 1883.
„   Geo. Johnson, 1886.
„   Cornelius Carroll, to date.

EAST HENDRED, BERKS (Portsmouth). St. Mary.

This parish is inseparably associated with the ancient Catholic family of Eyston, the patrons of the mission. In 1688 the domestic chaplain of the Eystons was plundered by a party of Orange soldiers on their way to Oxford, and among the list of recusants for the county of Berks assessed at the double land tax, pursuant to the Act of 1722, appear the names of Charles and Robert Eyston, Esquires. The old chapel of St. Amand served the mission prior to the present one, opened in 1865. In July 1849 Bishop Wiseman confirmed thirty-six persons in the chapel, and on Sunday, August 30, 1862, Bishop Grant, of Southwark, consecrated a new altar. The whole of the ancient fabric was thoroughly restored the same year by Mr. C. Buckler, of Oxford. The church of East Hendred was made over to the diocese of Southwark in 1865 by Charles Eyston, Esq., and consecrated by Bishop Grant on August 17 of the same year. The mission is now in the Portsmouth diocese.

EASTWELL, LEICESTERSHIRE (Nottingham). The Holy Family.

Described as a very old mission, 'The secret chapel in Eastwell Hall' served the district in penal times. The public chapel was opened in 1798. The place was at various times in subsequent years served from Nottingham and Melton Mowbray. In June 1904 the mission became independent. Fr. Hendricks is the incumbent.

EASTWOOD, NOTTINGHAMSHIRE (Nottingham). Our Lady of Good Counsel.

In 1889 the mission was started by the Rev. Isaac Hanks, the temporary chapel being in the Langley Mill Road. The present Gothic church in the Eastwood Road was erected shortly afterwards. From 1892 to 1894 the mission was served from the Seminary, since when the rectors have been Rev. Ar. Howarth, 1895; Michael Kirby, 1903 to date.

EBBW VALE, MONMOUTHSHIRE (Newport). All Saints'.

This mission may be considered as one of the results of the revival of Catholicism in the country owing to the zeal of the Franciscan missionaries in the district half a century ago. The present school chapel was opened October 8, 1865.

Priests.

Rev. E. J. Sheehy, 1865 (?).
„   P. J. Capron, 1875.
„   E. O'Dwyer, 1880.
„   Augustine Fritz, 1883.
„   D. Hallahan, 1903 to date.

ECCLES, LANCS (Salford). St. Mary.

In 1875 the mission was served from Barton. The church was opened July 30, 1879. Catholic population about 1,900 (1906).

Priests.

Rev. Thos. Sharrock, 1879.

„ Francis Newton, 1894 to date.

ECCLESHALL, STAFFORDSHIRE
(*Birmingham*). SS. Peter and Paul.

A chapel was commenced here in 1882, and served from Swynnerton every other Sunday. In 1889 the Rev. Alfred Hall was resident priest. Fr. Michael Glancey was here 1894. In 1898 the Fathers of the Institute of the Sacred Heart took over the mission, which they have since served.

EDGBASTON (*Birmingham*). The Oratory. The Immaculate Conception, Hagley Road, Edgbaston.

When the Fathers of the Oratory settled here in 1849–50, it was the great wish of Dr. Newman to erect a church after the style of that of San Martino at Rome. Owing to lack of funds the idea was not carried out and a smaller church was built from designs of M. Viollet-le-Duc. When the jubilee of the Oratory was celebrated in 1898, the memory of the great Cardinal's life and labours inspired Catholics to erect such a church as he had desired to see built. The foundation stone of the building was laid by Bishop Ilsley in 1903. Owing to the fact that the new edifice has been built over the old one, which was used as long as possible during the work of construction, the operations have been considerably retarded thereby. The style of the new building is that of the Church of San Martino at Rome, and the plan comprises sanctuary, nave, transepts, and several chapels, including a fine

one to St. Philip Neri. A barrel dome roof is a notable feature of the interior. Mr. Doran Webb is the architect of the church, which will probably cost over £30,000. During the removal of the old church from the interior, the congregation worshipped at the chapel of Ladywood Hall. The solemn opening by Bishop Ilsley took place October 9, 1906, Archbishop Bourne preaching (Eccles. xlix. 13) to a large and distinguished congregation.

EDMONTON, MIDDLESEX (*Westminster*).

In the July of 1903, the Redemptorists started the mission by purchasing a site sufficient for church, monastery, and schools. An iron building capable of accommodating about 200 persons will soon be superseded by the new church, the foundation stone of which was laid by Archbishop Bourne on Easter Monday, April 24, 1905. The architect is Mr. E. Doran Webb, F.S.A.

EGREMONT, CUMBERLAND (*Hexham and Newcastle*). St. Mary.

The mission was founded as a chapel of ease to the church at Cleator (*q.v.*) in 1878.

Priests.

Rev. John Fr. Kerin, 1879.

„ Francis Sumner, 1882.

„ Joseph Worden, 1885.

„ Leonard Davies, 1891.

„ Simon Finch, 1893 to date.

EGTON BRIDGE, GROSMONT, YORKS (*Middlesbrough*). St. Hedda.

Missionary priests were here

some time before 1679. Fr. Nicholas Postgate, one of them, was hanged at York, August 7, 1679, ' for the Faith.' His head is preserved at Ushaw.[1] After this, Mass was said in various neighbouring farmhouses. Also at Ugthorpe Old Hall, where, in one of the hiding-places, images of SS. Michael and John the Baptist were recently found. The chapel at Egton Bridge, built in 1790 by Fr. Hy. Greenhalgh, is now used as a school. The church, opened August 21, 1867, at a cost of £4,000, was consecrated July 14, 1885. It may be worthy of remark that Thomas Ward, author of 'England's Reformation,' was a native of the parish. Lord Herries and Major Scrope-Danby were great benefactors of the mission. The church was redecorated at a cost of £700 in 1877, the walls of the interior being beautifully adorned with paintings of saints. A new oak pulpit was set up in July 1880.

Priests since 1824.

Rev. J. Woodcock, 1824.
„   N. Rigby, 1827.
„   H. Greenhalgh, 1835.
„   Wm. Parsons, 1842.
„   A. Macartney, 1844.
„   Thos. Middlehurst, 1857.
„   F. Callebert, 1860 to date.

ELLINGHAM, NORTHUMBERLAND (*Hexham and Newcastle*).

The preservation of the faith here is mainly due to the Haggerston family, whose ancestral residence is in the district. Sir Thos. Haggerston, a distinguished royalist officer, was created a baronet by Charles I. in 1643. Fr. Francis

[1] One of the chief witnesses against Fr. Postgate was a person who deposed to having seen him baptise a child.

Mannock, S.J., son of Sir F. Mannock, Bart., was chaplain here in 1710. The mission registers date from 1775, when Fr. Mathew Joy, S.J., was priest. He died ' much respected,' February 21, 1798, *æt.* 56. Bishop Gibson—referred to as ' Mr. Gibson ' in the registers—confirmed twenty-two persons here July 17, 1783. The Easter communions at Ellingham in 1796 were eighty-three ; twenty-five persons were confirmed there on August 25 of the same year, and thirty-two in August 1809. Fr. John Forshaw, probably a Benedictine, was priest at Ellingham from 1805 to 1810. Between 1810 and 1840 the priests were : Wm. Birdsall, John Beaumont, S.J., Thos. Lawson, O.S.B., Ric. Albott, John Parsons, Edw. Crane, Thos. Parker. From this date (1840) the priests are as follows : Revs. E. Smith, 1844 ; Geo. Meynell, 1849–57 ; mission vacant, 1858 ; A. Macartney, 1862 ; Aloysius Hosten, 1875 ; Gregory Jones, 1879 ; Joseph Fawell, 1881 ; Edmund Barnett, 1884 ; Bernard Darley, 1889 ; Wm. Baron, 1891 ; Wm. Toner, 1900 ; Henry Cartmell, 1903.

ELTHAM, NEAR LONDON, KENT (*Southwark*). St Mary.

Well Hall, near Eltham, formerly belonged to John Roper, Esq., attorney-general *temp.* Henry VIII., and son-in-law of the Blessed Thos. More. In 1616 Christopher Roper was raised to the peerage as Baron Teynham of Linstead and Well Hall, Kent. The old Well Hall, a moated grange, was burnt down about 1706. The present edifice, built shortly after the fire, is in the Georgian style of architecture. It is still surrounded on three sides by a moat. The property is at present leased by Herbert Bland, Esq. The Teynham family, who possessed Well Hall for upwards of two centuries, were Catholics till February 1716, when Henry Roper, eighth Baron Teynham, 'conformed to the Established Church.' The old Hall possessed a chapel where Mass was occasionally said, probably down to the time of the aforesaid lamentable apostasy. The present mission of Eltham dates from 1871, when the temporary chapel was served from Woolwich. In November 1890 a new church in the classical style was opened by Bishop Butt of Southwark. High Mass, *coram episcopo*, was sung by Fr. Sheehan of Blackheath, the sermon being preached by Canon Murnane, V.G. St. Mary's Poor Law school for little boys and girls adjoins the church and is under the care of the Sisters of Mercy.

ELY, CAMBRIDGESHIRE (*Northampton*). St. Etheldreda.

In 1859 Fr. Thomas McDonald, who had charge of this mission and also that of Newmarket, fitted up a disused stable as a chapel. The first resident priest was sent to Ely in July 1890. Even as late as this the chapel was but a hired room. A temporary chapel was opened in July 1891, when Mass was sung by Fr. Freeland, the priest of the mission. Fr. King of St. Thomas's Seminary preached on the fall and rise of the Church in England. The patron of the mission, St. Etheldreda, lived, died, and was buried at Ely. Her shrine 'covered with gems' was reported to be hidden at the time of the

Dissolution and is at present (September 1906) being diligently sought for by the authorities of Ely Cathedral.

ENFIELD, HERTFORDSHIRE (*Westminster*). Our Lady and St. George.

Mission founded by the late Fr. G. Bampfield, B.A., in 1862. The old chapel erected shortly after held sixty persons and was situated in Cecil Road. The next priests were Frs. Bronsgeest and Murphy. In 1900 Fr. A. O'Gorman, D.D., commenced the present church, which was opened in April 1901 by Cardinal Vaughan. The old chapel is now the school. In September 1905 Fr. Geo. Cox became rector.

EPSOM, SURREY (*Southwark*). St. Joseph, South Parade.

In April 1859 Fr. J. B. Hearn opened the mission at a cottage in Woodcote Road, hired at £14 per annum. The 'church stuff' consisted of an altar, chalice, cross, candlesticks, altar linen, and three chasubles. In 1860 (February) Fr. (Canon) David, of Croydon, said Mass at Epsom every other Friday, and catechised the children, besides attending sick calls. The first resident priest was Fr. Patrick Kelly, 1861. The church, 'a neat Gothic structure,' was erected 1865–66. Lord Russell of Killowen, Lord Chief Justice of England, was for many years the chief Catholic resident at Epsom, and a generous patron of the mission. Fr. T. Morrissey is the present incumbent of the church.

N.B.—The few Catholics about

Epsom were attended during the middle part of the eighteenth century by the Benedictine missioners attached to Lady Petre's Chapel at Cheam (*q.v.*). At the time of the French Revolution the priest at the Dominican College at Bornhem House, Carshalton, undertook this duty. When Mr. Mylius established his school in the same house after the departure of the Dominicans (1812) the Abbé Chabot, his chaplain, continued to attend to the Catholics at Epsom for some years.

ERDINGTON, WARWICKSHIRE (*Birmingham*). St.Thomas's Priory.

A chapel was erected by 'the zealous exertions of several gentlemen,' and opened Sunday, April 9, 1842. The new church was consecrated June 11, 1850, by Bishop Ullathorne, V.A. Fr. D. Haigh, M.A., the incumbent, defrayed the cost of erection. The church is well described as 'a perfect revival of an old English parish church.' In 1876 some of the Benedictine monks, expelled from Beuron, Germany, by the Kulturkampf of Prince Bismarck, were invited to take charge of the mission at Erdington, vacated by Fr. Haigh on account of old age. For some years the monks lived 'in a small and incommodious cottage,' but in July 1880 the present monastery of St. Thomas was commenced 'by the assistance and generosity of friends abroad.'

ERITH, KENT (*Southwark*). Our Lady of the Angels.

The Capuchin Fathers of Peckham opened a church and mon-astery here in 1870. The place was served from Northfleet 1875. In 1903 the new church and monastery was opened in the Carlton Road, the old church of St. Fidelis now serving as a chapel of ease.

Father Guardians.

Rev. F. Louis, 1870.

  ,, F. Cherubino, 1878.

  ,, F. Lewis, 1880.

  ,, F. Pelicetti, 1882.

  ,, Nicholas Mazzarini, 1889.

  ,, Clement David, 1892.

  ,, F. Bernardine, 1900 to date.

N.B.—Fr. H. Garnet, S.J., who was executed 1606 for alleged complicity in the Gunpowder Plot, had a house at Erith, but it does not appear that there was any mission in the town.

ERRWOOD HALL, BUXTON, CHESHIRE (*Shrewsbury*).

The domestic chapel of the Grimshawe family, opened in October 1851, serves the mission. In the sacristy are preserved many antique vestments of great beauty, while the reliquary contains a portion of the Crown of Thorns.

Priests.

Rev. H. Alcock, 1851.

  ,, E. W. Nightingale, 1851.

  ,, R. Maurice, 1852.

  ,, D. Organ, 1852.

  ,, B. O'Donnell and E. Maggreevy, 1852-59.

  ,, J. Quinn, 1859.

    (Served from Gorton, 1863-69).

  ,, C. Bell, 1869.

  ,, H. Wood, 1877.

  ,, W. McAuliffe, 1877.

  ,, M. Gérin, 1889.

  ,, J. Bérard, 1896.

  ,, H. Welch, 1890.

ESH LAUDE, DURHAM (*Hexham and Newcastle*). St. Michael. According to the registers preserved at the presbytery, this mission 'was founded in 1790.' It was served from 1795 (June) till May 1827 by Fr. John Yates, V.G. to Bishop Smith, V.A. Fr. Yates died June 1, 1827, and was buried at Ushaw, his place at Esh being taken by Fr. W. Fletcher of the same college. Fr. Roger Glassbrook succeeded in 1839. The present chapel of 'massive stone and slate' was erected in 1832, on a site presented by Sir Edward Smythe, Bart., of Acton Burnell. This ancient Catholic family has an ancestral residence at Esh Laude. The old chapel was built about 1799. It was served for some time by Fr. Ashmell, who lived to be 105. This excellent priest, during his missionary labours in the north of England about the middle of the eighteenth century, used to go about disguised as a farmer in 'leather gaiters, grey coat, check cloak, and slouched hat.' In recent times the priests at Esh have been Revs. Wm. Canon Thompson, 1841–80; Samuel Harris, 1880; Matthew Culley, 1902.

EUXTON, near CHORLEY, LANCS (*Liverpool*). St. Mary. Euxton is one of the many places in Lancashire where the Faith has survived the long ordeal of the penal times, thanks in great measure to the fostering care of the Andertons of Euxton and the Molyneuxes of Sefton. In 1524 James Anderton, of Euxton, built a chantrey in the parish and established a priest there 'to pray for himself and his wife.' The chapel wherein the chantrey was placed was built eleven years earlier by Sir W. Molyneux, and his descendant Lord Molyneux retained possession of it as late as 1687. In 1718 his son gave up the chapel, and then one was constructed at Euxton Hall 'in a room open to the public.' In the preceding century Sir Hugh Anderton, of Euxton, a devoted Royalist, had afforded hospitality to Charles II. on his march to Worcester. In the 'Mercurius Politicus' for August 16 of that year, Sir Hugh is described as 'a bloody Papist.' In 1715 another branch of the Andertons, the Andertons of Lostock, 'lost a good estate for being with the rebels but one day.' The 'rebels,' of course, being Lord Derwentwater, Mr. Foster, Lord Carnwath, &c., in arms for James III. The old Catholic chapel at Euxton was enlarged at different times till 1817, when a new one was built. The domestic oratory at the Hall was bought back by Colonel Anderton, the money being left to accumulate in the hands of the trustees till such time as a new chapel should be required. This came about in 1864, when the first stone of the present church was solemnly laid on a site given by Geo. Garstang, Esq. Captain Anderton of Euxton Hall contributed £1,000. The building was opened October 29, 1865, by Bishop Goss, assisted by Bishop Grant of Southwark. The accommodation is for about 4,000. The total cost was £3,000. The style of the building is Early Decorated Gothic.

Priests.

Rev. Thos. Townley, 1718 (?).
„ Hon. W. Molyneux, 1734.
„ Thos. Anderton, 1735.
„ Cuthbert Haydock, 1741.
„ Jn. White, 1750 (?).
„ Robt. Swarbrick, 1778.
„ Jn. Bell, 1815.

Rev. Higginson, 1817.
„ R. Gillow, 1846.
„ John Canon Worthy, 1851.
„ Francis Soden, 1893.
„ Thos. Keely, 1896 to date.

EVERINGHAM, YORKSHIRE
(*Middlesbrough*). St. Mary.
The chapel is described as founded in the reign of Edward VI. The Constable family of Everingham long kept the Faith alive in these parts, and it is satisfactory to note that the estate has always been in Catholic hands. The property passed to the family of the present Lord Herries by the marriage about 1780 of Winifrid Maxwell—granddaughter of the Jacobite Lord Nithsdale—with Wm. Haggerston Constable, Esq., of Everingham. The register of baptisms dates from 1771, with the baptism of John Dolman. The present fine church was erected by W. Constable Maxwell, Esq., who in 1858 succeeded to the Herries peerage. The style of the building—opened July 10, 1839—is cruciform, after the plan of the Maison Dieu at Nismes. Size 70 ft. by 30 ft.; interior decorated by fluted Corinthian columns, and altar of rich Italian marbles.

Priests at Everingham.
Rev. John Bennet, here 1771.
The next priests were Frs. T. Gurnall, Edward Clarkson, and S. Hodgson (1814).
Rev. Matthew Newsham, 1824.
„ J. Brown, 1844.
„ Richard Browne, 1845.
„ Matthew Newsham, 1848.
„ Robt. Cook, 1849.
„ Joseph Arnoux, 1852.
„ Henry Walker, 1858.
„ Edward Riddell, 1862.
„ Wm. Gordon, 1864.
„ Thos. Knight, S.J., 1874.

Rev. Joseph Dodds, 1882.
„ Chas. Donovan, 1885.
„ Wm. McNaughton, 1888.
„ Jn. Murphy, 1892.
„ Jn. Willemse, 1895.
„ Cornelius English, 1900 to date.

EVERTON, LIVERPOOL. St. Edward's College.
This well-known seat of learning was established in 1842 under the auspices of Bishop Brown, V.A. It was opened for students, January 16, 1843. Though mainly intended for those desirous of pursuing 'commerce or any of the learned secular professions,' it had also a course of studies for the ecclesiastical state. Alexander Goss, D.D., afterwards second Bishop of Liverpool, was vice-president, and it was while spending the vacation with some of the students at Ardrishaig, Argyllshire, that he received news of his appointment as coadjutor to Bishop Brown (July 1856). The college was, perhaps, the first Catholic one in England which allowed pupils to go home at Christmas. It was early affiliated to the London University, and many of its students have since taken high places in the arts and science examinations. From about 1885 to 1896 the college was an episcopal one, presumably for the sole education of Church students.

Presidents.
Rev. Mgr. John Canon Fisher, D.D., 1843.
„ Mgr. Canon Carr, V.G., 1885.
„ Evan Canon Banks, B.A., 1895 to date.

EVESHAM, WORCESTERSHIRE (*Birmingham*).

This place was among the number served by the Jesuit Fathers of St. George, Worcester, 1633 *et seq.* Fr. Oldcorne is said to have had a conference with Fr. Garnet, at Evesham, a short time before the Gunpowder Plot. Fr. Thomas Roper, S.J., son of the fourth Lord Teynham, was here 1693-1700. After this, Evesham disappears as a mission till 1887-88, when the Passionists started a foundation here under Fr. Alban Cowley. The chapel, an iron one, was served from Broadway, 1896, and by Fr. Robert Patten, 1897 to date. Schools erected 1900. The iron church was removed from Magpie Lane to the High Street the same year. Presbytery built 1900.

N.B.—In 1865 the late Duke d'Aumale opened his private oratory at Wood Norton to the public, and this chapel was the only Catholic one in the district until the re-establishment of the Evesham mission by the Passionists.

EXETER, DEVON (*Plymouth*).
The Sacred Heart.

The Exeter mission dates from 1745, when Mass was said in Mr. Flashman's house, known as King John's Tavern, in South Street. In the reign of James II. a chapel had been opened in the city, but it was destroyed by an Orange mob at the Revolution. Fr. Richard Norris was priest at the time, and he continued to act as such down to 1717. After this the mission was served by different priests, as follows:—Revs. J. Beaumont, O.S.F. (1733 ?), E. Williams (1776),

E. Hussey, O.S.B. (*d.* September 25, 1785), — Parry, and — Rigby (1790 ?), W. Sutton (*d.* 1800). Most of these priests seem to have only occasionally ministered at Exeter, for about 1762 the Jesuits offered to serve the mission, and their services were accepted by Bishop Walmesley, V.A., of the Western District. Fr. W. Gilibrand was here from 1762-67. He lived with the Truscot family. Fr. J. Edisford, who came in 1772, died of gaol fever caught while attending the prisoners in the old county gaol (November 20, 1789). The old chapel, erected in 1790, in the Mint, was dedicated to St. Nicholas. It was built by the Jesuits on the site of the Old Priory of St. Nicholas, and was opened in 1792 and enlarged in the summer of 1859 by Fr. A. Eccles, S.J. This zealous missioner also built the Catholic schools. Under him the chapel was enriched with a fine pulpit, an altar of Caen stone, and a Norman altar screen. The Rev. Geo. Oliver, D.D., the distinguished antiquary, was appointed to the Exeter mission in 1807. Most of his learned works and 'Collectanea' were composed here. He died March 23, 1862, and was succeeded by Fr. James Eccles, S.J. In December 1871, the mission was taken over by the Bishop of Plymouth, who appointed Fr. G. Hobson to Exeter. The first stone of the present church of the Sacred Heart was laid, Wednesday, March 20, 1883. The church is in the thirteenth century Gothic style, from designs by C. Ware, Esq., of Exeter, and L. Stokes, Esq., of London. The total cost was about £10,000. The accommodation is for 600. An old fifteenth century window lights the staircase to the choir. The reredos contains statues of the Apostles, and is otherwise richly carved. The 'stately church' was opened Tuesday, November 18, 1884, 'with all the ceremonial and ritual which form the glory of the Church.' Bishops Vaughan, Errington, and Clifford took part in the imposing function.

EXMOUTH, DEVON (*Plymouth*).

Mission established 1888, about which time the church—a Gothic iron structure for 200 persons—was erected. The congregation is about 130. The church was enlarged in April 1905.

Priests.

Very Rev. Mgr. John Grainger, 1888.

Rev. Bernard Palmer, 1900 to date.

EXTON, RUTLAND (*Nottingham*).

St. Thomas of Canterbury.

The thirteenth century Gothic church (60 ft. × 20 ft.) was commenced December 29, 1867, and opened 1868, by the Bishop of Nottingham. C. A. Buckler was the architect. In 1870, a school was in existence and reported to be 'fairly attended.' The church at Exton was the first Catholic place of worship opened in Rutland since the Reformation.

Priests.

Rev. Philip Munro.

„   Charles Gey, 1877.

„   John Burns, 1879.

„   E. Van Dale, 1882.

„   J. Thompson, 1885.

„   Francis Busch, 1890 to date.

F

FAILSWORTH, LANCS (*Salford*).
The Immaculate Conception.
A portion of the present church was opened October 1865. A new sanctuary was opened 1892, at a cost of £1,240. The style of the building is decorated Gothic. The mission started by the erection of a temporary chapel 1851.
Priests.
Rev. W. Daly, 1851.
  „ John Hennessey, 1890.
  „ John Canon Boulaye, 1902.
  „ John Morris, 1904.

FAIRFORD, GLOUCESTERSHIRE (*Clifton*). St. Thomas of Canterbury.
In 1823 Fr. Glassbrook used to say Mass here, and it is said that he had a pension of £40 per annum from Lord de Mauley. The church was opened in October 1845. The ceremony was performed by Fr. J. Mitchell, of Chipping Norton, on behalf of the V.A. Fr. P. O'Farrell preached at the High Mass, and Dr. Rock in the evening.
Priests since 1845.
Rev. J. Mitchell.
  „ W. Goodwin, 1851.
  „ E. A. Glassbrook, 1853.
  „ Peter Seddon, here in 1864.
  „ John Dickenson, 1867.
  „ Jas. Dawson, here in 1872.

Rev. Francis Coopman, 1877.
  „ James Lonergan, here in 1891.
  „ George Canon Crook, 1892.
Very Rev. Mgr. E. English, D.D., 1896 to date.

FAKENHAM, NORFOLK (*Northampton*). St. Anthony of Padua.
Mission founded 1905. The present place of worship is a garret in the Hempton Road.
Priest.
Fr. Gray.

FALMOUTH, CORNWALL (*Plymouth*). St. Mary.
This mission owes its origin to Rowland Conyers, Esq., who died April 28, 1803. A room was fitted up and opened as a chapel in January 1805. A larger chapel was opened October 24, 1821, through the exertions of the Abbé Grezille, who collected £500 towards the purpose from the Royal Family of France. The Redemptorists were in charge of the mission from 1843 to 1845, when they left for Clapham. Mr. Andrews, a resident in the town at this time, was a great benefactor to the mission. The old chapel was superseded by the present Gothic structure opened 1869.

Priests.

Rev. Ignatius Casemore, O.S.F., 1803.
„ Abbé Grezille, 1805.
„ Thaddeus O'Meally, 1822.
„ Peter Hartley, 1823.
„ Robt. Gates, 1827.
„ Robt. Platt, 1832.
„ M. O'Connor, 1831.
„ Robt. Platt, 1832.
„ Fredk. Held, C.SS.R., 1843.
„ Michael Carroll, 1845.
„ Jn. Ryan, 1846.
„ Tiberius Soderini, 1852.
„ James Carey, 1854.
„ Wm. Laffan, 1857.
„ Denys Byrne, 1863.
„ Wm. Cassey, 1866.
„ James Burns, 1903 to date.

FAREHAM, HANTS (*Portsmouth*).

The mission dates from 1873, when a temporary chapel was erected and placed under the charge of Fr. T. Foran, Acting Chaplain to the Forces. The present church, in the Decorated style, was opened by Bishop Danell, of Southwark—in which diocese Fareham then lay—September 1878. Mr. J. Crawley was the architect, the accommodation of the church being for about 300.

Recent Rectors.

Rev. T. Doyle, 1885.
„ E. Canon Collins, 1888 to date.

FARM STREET, BERKELEY SQUARE, LONDON, W. (*Westminster*). The Immaculate Conception.

The foundation-stone was laid on the Feast of St. Ignatius Loyola, July 31, 1844, by Fr. Randall

Lythgoe, S.J., in the place of Bishop Griffiths, V.A.L.D., and the building was opened in 1845. For some years (1845-49) the clergy residence was at 25 Bolton Street, Piccadilly. Mention is first made of Farm Street Church in the 'Catholic Directory' in 1850. The style of the building is 'Gothic of the Third Period,' from the design of Scholes. Since the opening of the church two handsome aisles have been added, one of them as recently as 1904-5. The east window is by Wailes and the high altar by A. W. Pugin. The several side altars are dedicated to SS. Ignatius, Francis Xavier, and other canonised members of the Society of Jesus, the fathers of which have charge of the church.

FARNBOROUGH, HANTS (*Portsmouth*). St. Michael's Priory.

On her return from Zululand in May 1881, where she had been to visit the scene of the death of her son, the Prince Imperial, the Empress Eugénie took up her residence at Farnborough Hill. Here Her Majesty built the monastery and church. On Monday, January 8, 1888, the bodies of Napoleon III. and the Prince Imperial were removed from Chislehurst(*q.v.*) and deposited in the crypt of the newly erected church. The style of this building is Flamboyant Gothic. The altar and sanctuary are of richly inlaid marbles, many of the varieties used being from Corsica, the cradle of the Napoleonic race. In the sacristy are kept some splendid copes and chasubles made from the Coronation robes of the Empress, who has richly endowed the church and adjoining monastery. A staircase leads from the

Gospel side of the sanctuary to the crypt—a fine underground chapel, with a handsome marble altar and richly embossed bronze fittings. The Imperial remains repose in handsome red granite sarcophagi, the gift of Queen Victoria. That of the Emperor bears the inscription : 'Napoleon III. R.I.P.' On the one containing the remains of the Prince Imperial appear the words : ' Napoleon Eugène Louis Jean Joseph, Prince Impérial, né à Paris 16 Mars 1856; mort en soldat à Itrotrotiozy (Afrique Australe) 1 Juin 1879. R.I.P.' Mural tablets, wreaths, and funereal banners adorn the chapel. The church and monastery of St. Michael were first placed under the care of the Premonstratensian Canons from St. Michael's, Frigolet (France). These were supplanted a few years ago by the Benedictines of Solesmes, who divide their time between the zealous discharge of their religious and liturgical duties and the composition of learned works, thus ably maintaining in their English home the best traditions of the renowned Order of St. Benedict.

FARNHAM, SURREY (*Southwark*). St. Polycarp's, Park Lane, Farnham.

The mission was opened on the Feast of St. Polycarp (January 26), 1890. Among the congregation were Lady Wood and Capt. Wood, wife and son of Field-Marshal Sir Evelyn Wood. Bishop Butt, of Southwark, made his first visitation of Farnham in September 1890. Fine schools have been since erected by Fr. Gérin, the first priest of the mission, who is making great efforts to provide his increasing congregation with a church.

FARNWORTH, LANCS (*Salford*). St. Gregory's.

A mission was started here in June 1852, by Fr. W. Taylor, who remained till January 1861. The Sisters of the Most Holy Cross took over the teaching of the schools in 1871. The present church was commenced August 16, 1873, the foundation-stone being laid by Bishop (afterwards Cardinal) Vaughan. The Rev. F. Schneider, a German priest of Treves, who had been expelled by the May Laws, was priest here in 1876. A new organ by Benson was installed 1901-2.

FAVERSHAM, KENT (*Southwark*). Our Lady of Compassion and St. Theodore.

The district was formerly served by the chapel at Linsted Lodge, the residence of the Lords Teynham. The family (Roper) was descended from Thos. Roper, son-in-law of the Blessed Thomas More, and remained Catholic till about the end of the eighteenth century. The last Catholic holder of the title appears to have been Henry, 10th Baron, who died in 1781, though in 1831 the ' People's Book ' erroneously asserted that the Lord Teynham of the day (Henry, 15th Baron) was a Catholic. Fr. Chas. Forrester, S.J., was chaplain here 1767-75. His calm expostulation with the local protestant clergyman, the Rev. Mr. Fox, not only disarmed the hostile opposition of that gentleman, but even led to him sending his two sons to Douai College ! (*See* Oliver's 'Collections,' p. 306.) The present mission of Faversham was founded in 1899, and is served by the Oblates of St. Francis of Sales.

The temporary chapel is at Plantation House. The Rev. F. Mahoney was the first rector. Confirmation was administered here for the first time since the Reformation by a Catholic bishop, August 26, 1906. Great efforts are being made to erect a permanent church.

Priests.

Rev. F. Mahoney.

,, L. Dubruyer, 1904 to date.

Note. — Linsted Lodge was served by the Jesuits at an early date. In 1688 an Orange mob threatened the mansion and fearfully ill-used the priest, Fr. Thos. Kingsley, *alias* de Bois, who narrowly escaped death. Concerning the first apostasy of the family, that of Henry, 8th Lord Teynham, Fr. Jn. Clare, S.J., thus wrote, March 3, 1715: 'Our chief families fall off; Lord Teynham, Sir Joseph Shelley, Mr. Cotton, and two or three more are talked of,' &c.

FELIXSTOWE, SUFFOLK (*Northampton*). St. Felix.

The locality having grown from a fishing village to ' a smart watering-place,' it was found necessary to establish a mission in the town in July 1899. The chapel is in the Gainsborough Road. In pre-Reformation times the church pertained to the Benedictines of Rochester.

Priests.

Rev. Fr. W. Cooper, 1899.

FELLING, DURHAM (*Hexham and Newcastle*). St. Patrick.

A chapel was opened at Felling, January 25, 1841. At that time there were many Catholics in the district, mostly employed in the chemical works of Messrs. Lee, Patterson & Co. This firm generously made ' a handsome annual allowance' to the priest of St. Patrick's Chapel. In 1850 the Catholic children who attended ' the mixed school ' at Friars Goose in the vicinity were taught their catechism by the mistress who was a Catholic. Separate Catholic schools were not erected till later. At the retreat given by the Redemptorists in September-October 1859, 1,400 persons received Holy Communion. In March 1860 Fr. Kelly, priest of the Felling mission, was committed to prison by Mr. Justice Hill for contempt of court in refusing at the Durham assizes to answer certain questions as to a fact known under the seal of confession. He was, however, soon liberated, the conduct of the learned judge being made the subject for some severe comments in the general press. The old presbytery was burnt January 1877, but afterwards rebuilt on an enlarged scale. The present fine Gothic church was erected 1893-94, during the rectorate of Fr. J. Murphy, D.D.

N.B.—The Brandlings 'an ancient Catholic family of great possessions' acquired Felling from the Places, *temp.* Henry VIII. In 1729 Ralph Brandling, Esq., married Eleanor Ogle, a protestant, and after his death in 1749 she brought up their only son, Charles, in her own religion. The family was thus lost to the Faith, and the chapel which had hitherto served the mission was closed.

Priests of the present Mission.

Rev. Fr. J. Kelly, 1847.

,, Fr. T. Carroll, 1882.

,, Fr. J. Murphy, D.D., 1892 to date.

FELTON, NORTHUMBERLAND (*Hexham and Newcastle*). St. Mary.

Felton Castle has been the seat of the Riddell family since about 1720, and Mass was said here throughout the penal times. The registers date from 1792. The domestic chapel was served occasionally by the Jesuits, but no particulars of their ministrations are forthcoming. The present church for 220 persons, opened June 16, 1857, is situated on the west side of the mansion, and is well described as 'a beautiful specimen of the revival of ancient ecclesiastical architecture.' Mr. Gilbert Blount was the architect.

Priests since 1820.

Rev. J. Robinson; J. Orrell, 1828.
  „ J. B. Swale, 1846.
  „ W. A. Brindle, 1847.
  „ S. Day, 1850.
  „ Charles Smith, O.S.B., 1870 (?).
  „ Peter Dorn, 1884.
  „ Adam Wilkinson, 1888.
  „ M. P. Horgan, 1895.
  „ Edmund J. Barnet, 1897 to date.

FERNYHALGH, LANCASHIRE (*Liverpool*). St. Mary.

Called also Ladywell and in old documents Sanctæ Mariæ ad Fontem. The Lady Chapel close by the holy well dates from 1348, being erected by a merchant in thanksgiving for deliverance from shipwreck. The place has always been a stronghold of Catholicity even during the worst period of the penal laws. A school was kept here early in the eighteenth century by one 'Dame Alice.' She was originally a protestant, but by reading books of controversy and apologetics was led to embrace the Catholic faith. On being turned adrift by her father, she opened a Catholic school. Her pupils boarded at the various cottages in the district. She took the children to chapel every day, and on the way the party always recited a Pater, Ave, and Gloria at the 'Lady well.' Her school became very famous locally, so that even many protestants entrusted their children to her for their education. Dame Alice Harrison retired to end her days with the Gerards of Garswood, where she died about 1760. In 1684–85 a new chapel or 'house of prayer' was built by Mr. Cuthbert Hesketh, of White Hill, Goosnargh. His cousin, Fr. Charles Tootell, was priest at Fernyhalgh and Vicar-General of Lancashire and Cumberland in 1719. During the Jacobite troubles of 1715, Fr. Tootell was sought for by the priest-hunters and for days lay concealed in a barn. He was 'much troubled' down to 1719, when the persecution ceased. Later, he records thus: 'We began to pray at Our Lady's well privately, August 5, 1723, and publicly, August 15 in the same year.' He died at Fernyhalgh, November 13, 1727, leaving behind him a curious didactic work entitled 'The Layman's Ritual for the Instruction of his Flock.' Fr. Melling, who succeeded, died April 17, 1733. His successor was Fr. Oliver Tootell, nephew of Fr. C. Tootell. When Prince Charles Edward Stuart and the Highlanders retreated from Derby in December 1745, a protestant mob burned the chapel at Fernyhalgh to the ground. An account of this act of destruction has been left by Fr. Oliver Tootell. The chapel was subsequently rebuilt. In 1793 a larger chapel was

N

erected by Fr. Anthony Lund, one of the Douai professors. The consecration took place August 12 of the same year. Another restoration and re-opening took place in August 1847. Mr. Anderton, of Haighton, gave a handsome lamp in honour of the event.

Priests.

Rev. Robt. Bannister, 1770.
„ A. Lund, 1773.
„ R. Blacoe, 1811.
„ R. Gillow, 1823.
„ Mgr. Cookson, 1864.
(Administered, 1878–80.)
„ W. Gordon, 1880.
„ Daniel O'Hare, 1888.
„ John O'Reilly, 1893 to date.

FILEY, NORTH RIDING, YORKS
(*Middlesbrough*).

The Sisters of Charity of Notre Dame acquired Clarence House as a convent in 1905, and till the opening of the present handsome church on May 10, 1906, by the Bishop of Middlesbrough, the temporary chapel of the community was open to the public. The style of the church is Roman of the first century, the plan comprising nave and sanctuary; accommodation for about 250 persons. The altar is supported by a single thick pillar. A fine bell has been presented by Mr. Wake, of Sheffield. A. Pretia, Esq., was the architect. Fr. E. Roulin, O.S.B., is the first and present rector of the mission.

FINCHLEY EAST, MIDDLESEX
(*Westminster*). St. Mary.

Towards the end of the eighteenth century Mr. William Mawhood, a wealthy Catholic gentleman and army contractor, had his residence at Finchley, and in his house Bishop Challoner stayed during the Gordon riots, June 1-6, 1780. Two of Mr. Mawhood's sons were at the Old Hall Green Academy (St. Edmund's College) in 1769. It is probable that this family had a chapel in their house. From 1796, the nearest mission was St. Mary's, Holly Place, Hampstead, founded by the Abbé J. Morel (*see* Hampstead). After the establishment of St. Joseph's Retreat, Highgate, by the Passionist Fathers, in June 1858, the few Catholics in and around Finchley went there to Mass. In 1864, the nuns of the Good Shepherd Order at Hammersmith opened a branch convent at East End, Finchley, in a large mansion formerly belonging to a protestant gentleman. Here they have continued to carry on their work of active charity. Till the recent establishment of the mission of St. Mary's (1898), High Road, East Finchley, the convent church was open to the public. A small day school was opened November 6, 1899. The average daily attendance that year was fifteen.

Priest.

Rev. A. C. Day.

FINCHLEY NORTH, MIDDLESEX
(*Westminster*).

Until 1903 North Finchley and its adjunct, Whetstone, were administered to from Barnet. A new mission was established in the former place in June 1903, Fr. M. St. John Sellon being placed in charge. Mass was said in a small hired loft over a stable-yard, the Blessed Sacrament being reserved in the priest's house, Nether Street, where Mass was said on weekdays. In 1903 the chapel was at 4 Percy

Road, near Tally-ho Corner, the mission being served from Barnet.

FLEETWOOD, LANCS (*Liverpool*). St. Mary.

On Thursday, September 29, 1841, a grand concert was given at the Whitworth Institute, Fleetwood, to augment the building-fund of the church. Many of the officers attached to the School of Musketry attended, and subscribed liberally. The edifice was opened in November of the same year. The sermon was preached by Dr. Butler, of St. Anthony's, Liverpool. The new church was erected 1867, from a design by Pugin, jun. The site was given by Sir P. Fleetwood. In 1877 the presbytery was built, and in 1896 new schools. In 1903 the Catholic population was 1727.

Priests.

Rev. R. Carroll, 1841.
,, E. Carter, 1847.
,, Thos. Gibson, 1849.
,, Hy. Cook, 1857.
,, Thomas Canon Newsham, 1860 (?).
,, Thos. Bridges, 1867.
,, Wm. Rockliff, 1897.

FOLKESTONE, KENT (*Southwark*). Our Lady Help of Christians and St. Aloysius.

As late as 1863 Folkestone was described as 'a destitute mission,' with no better chapel than 'a bare room.' About seventy Catholic children of the place were said to be attending protestant schools. Fr. E. Sheridan, of Hythe, served the chapel on Sundays. The present church in Guildhall Street was opened July 19, 1889, by Bishop Butt, during the rectorate of Fr. F.

Dennan. The old 'Towns End' cottages formerly stood on the site. The church is a substantial building in the Early Gothic style; the architect was Mr. Leonard Stokes. The seating capacity is for about 750 people. The cost of erection was between £5,000 and £6,000. The sermon at the opening was preached by Mgr. Harrington Moore (Jeremias vi. 16). Mr. C. Santley, the celebrated vocalist, sang the 'Veni, Sancte Spiritus' at the offertory. The present incumbent of Folkestone is Mgr. C. Coote, successor to Fr. T. Scannell, now of Weybridge.

FORD, LIVERPOOL, LANCS. The Holy Sepulchre.

The Earl of Sefton in October 1846 gave an acre of land at Ford as a site for the Catholic schools. In 1858 a piece of ground was purchased from the same noble landlord and consecrated as a cemetery. The church in the centre of this burial-ground was opened by the Bishop of Liverpool in September 1861. The style is Modern Gothic, and the building will accommodate about 200 persons. Fr. T. Kelly was the first resident priest. The Church of the Good Shepherd Convent—dedicated to the Sacred Heart—was commenced in May 1886. The style is Gothic. The building is divided into three sections—for nuns, penitents, and people.

Priests.

Rev. — Kelby, 1861.
,, Moses Doon, 1863.
,, Richard O'Neill, 1871.
,, M. Aylward, 1874.
,, Thos. Browne, 1885.
,, E. O'Reilly, 1893.
,, C. Reynolds, 1895.
,, P. Monaghan, 1899.

N 2

FORDINGBRIDGE, HANTS (*Portsmouth*). Our Lady of Seven Dolours.

A mission established by the Servite Fathers in 1872.

Priests.

None mentioned 1875.
Rev. Mgr. Carter, 1878.
„ Edw. Sheridan, 1880.
„ Edw. Collins, 1885.

Servites.

Priors. Rev. P. M. Simoni, 1889.
„ A. Brugnoli, 1890.
„ John Angelo Price, 1891.
„ A. Brugnoli, 1892.
„ P. Mullarky, 1895.
„ S. Barry, 1897.
„ Leo Graty, 1900.
„ Ambrose McGrath, 1903 to date.

FOREST GATE, LONDON, E. (*Westminster*). St. Anthony of Padua.

A school chapel was opened by the Franciscans, Wednesday, October 8, 1884. High Mass was sung by Dr. Weathers, Bishop of Amycla. In the afternoon of the same day the foundation of the Friary was laid by the Bishop of Emmaus. It forms the house of studies of the Order in England. The church was opened in 1887. Catholic population of the district, about 4,000.

FOREST HILL, LONDON, S.E. (*Southwark*). St. William.

The church, in the Romanesque style of architecture, was opened by Bishop Amigo, May 3, 1906. The building, which is the gift of an anonymous benefactress, will accommodate about 200 persons.

Fr. James Hayes, late of the neighbouring mission of Brockley, is the first rector.

FORMBY, LANCS (*Liverpool*). Our Lady of Compassion.

The ancient Catholic family of Formby lost the faith shortly after 1720. Up to this time the chapel served the mission. Fr. R. Forster, S.J., was priest 1701-7, and after him Fr. Beaumont. Fr. C. Burton, 1709-19, Fr. W. Clifton, 1719-49, Fr. F. Blundell, 1749-79, were the next priests. A public chapel was commenced about 1686. At the Revolution it was seized and used as a tithe-barn. About 1794 it returned to its original purpose, and was enlarged for 150. By 1860, the Catholic population had risen to 1,100. The church was opened in August 1864 on a site given by Mr. Weld-Blundell, who also contributed £1,000. The design is Romanesque, from design by Clutton. Seats are arranged for 600. The schools were enlarged in 1898.

Priests since 1779.

Rev. Hy. Blundell, S.J., 1779.
„ F. Blundell, 1784.
„ Thos. Caton, 1787.
„ — Parkinson, 1791.
„ — Wheldon, 1791.
„ F. Craythorne, 1795.
„ Hy. Carter, 1796.
„ Jos. Maini, 1805.
„ Jn. Smith, 1834.
„ Thos. Crowe, 1853.
„ Mgr. Canon Carr, 1862 to date (1905).

FOXCOTE, WARWICKSHIRE, (*Birmingham*). The Immaculate Conception.

The ancient Catholic family of

Canning—descended from Thos. Canynges, Lord Mayor of London 1456—were seated here till their extinction in January 1857. The estate now belongs to the Howards of Corby. Mass was said in the chapel at the Hall down to 1813, when the present edifice was erected.

Priests.

Rev. W. Mannock, O.S.B., 1709-59.
„ Louvel, 1794 (?) ; served by Fr. J. Ducket of Brailes, 1833-36.
„ Geo. Burge, 1837.
„ A. Lempfried, 1849.
„ D. F. Mascot, 1867.
„ Jn. Smith, here 1871.
„ W. Timothy, 1876.
„ W. Stoker, 1882.
„ Patrick Reynolds, 1885.
„ Michael Hourigan, 1888.
„ J. Kennedy, 1903.

FRESHFIELD, near LIVERPOOL (*Liverpool*).

St. Peter's school for foreign missions was started here June 29, 1884, in a house formerly used as a boys' school under the direction of a protestant clergyman. The church adjoining is in a mixed style of architecture, and will accommodate about 100. The interior has recently been adorned under the direction of the present rector. The students, who number about fifty, go through their course of Humanities at this college prior to their philosophical studies at Rozendaal (Holland), after which they proceed to Mill Hill, London, for theology, Canon law, &c. A fine quadrangle was added to the school in 1903.

Presidents.

Rev. Francis Henry, 1884.
„ Joseph Rettori, 1892.

Rev. John Sala, 1893.
„ Edmund Farmer, 1901 to date.

FRESHWATER, ISLE of WIGHT (*Portsmouth*).

The domestic chapel of Weston Manor, the seat of the Ward family, was opened for public worship September 14, 1871. In December 1892 Fr. Bernard Vaughan preached a mission here, during which time about forty persons were received into the Church.

Priests.

Rev. P. Haythornthwaite, 1871.
„ Patrick Curtiss, 1899.
„ L. Doran, 1902 to date.

FRIMLEY, SURREY (*Southwark*).

A wooden chapel, for the use of the Catholic soldiers, was commenced here, Oct. 1906. The building, which will probably be finished by Christmas, is for about 300. Architect, B. Williamson, Esq. The mission, which was commenced in June 1906, is under the care of the Rev. Geo. Boniface.

FRIZINGTON, CUMBERLAND (*Hexham and Newcastle*). St. Joseph.

The mission was founded in 1875. The present church, to accommodate 400, was opened January 27, 1897. The reredos has finely carved figures of SS. Benedict, Edmund, and other English Saints. The Lady Altar is in memory of Fr. Brierley.

Priests.

Rev. Matthew Brierley, O.S.B.
„ Hy. Perkins, 1879.
„ Ralph Pearson, 1889.

Rev. Wm. Hurley, 1891.
„   Thos. Bamford, 1899.
„   Wm. Hurley, 1904.
„   A. Prior, 1906.

FROME, SOMERSETSHIRE (*Clifton*). St. Catherine.

In 1850 the Benedictine Fathers of Downside visited Frome and laboured assiduously among the poor Catholics of the district. Mass was said on Sundays in the house of a Mr. Downing, a grocer. In June 1854, Fr. Richard Ward, formerly a protestant clergyman, fitted up an old building, known as St. Catherine's Tower, as a church and presbytery, after which time Catholicism in the district greatly increased.

Priests.
Rev. R. Canon Ward, 1854.
„   Maurice Power, 1860.
„   Robt. Wadman, 1863.
„   Alex. Ryan, 1871.
„   F. Bartley, 1874.
„   J. Fanning, 1879.
„   J. Archdeacon, 1885.
„   Albert Williams, 1892 to date.

FULHAM, LONDON, S.W. (*Westminster*).

When Pugin's beautiful church of St. Thomas of Canterbury was erected in 1847 — through the munificence of a convert lady—the congregation mainly consisted of poor market gardeners who laboured in the 'Fulham Fields.' In 1884 thousands of houses covered the once rural expanse. In January of that year, a large school chapel was erected by Fr. C. J. Keens, formerly of Maiden Lane church, for the benefit of the many Catholic poor 'crowded out' to Fulham from the West End. The number of children of school age was estimated at about 700. The high altar of the church is adorned by a richly carved reredos, and the windows are filled with stained glass. The first incumbent was Fr. T. T. Ferguson, D.D. He was succeeded in 1856 by Canon John Morris, who in 1861 entered the Society of Jesus. The Catholic population of the mission is about 4,000.

Priests since 1862.
Rev. Geo. Canon Rolfe, 1861.
„   Wm. Bond, 1866.
„   Alexius Mills, 1874.
„   Mgr. Fenton, Bishop of Amycla 1904, Bishop Auxiliary of Westminster.
„   John Crowley, 1899 to date.

FULHAM PALACE RD., LONDON, S.W. (*Westminster*).

The mission, which is under the care of the Augustinians, was commenced, 1903, in 'a little house-chapel' in Comeragh Rd., West Kensington. The present iron church of the mission was opened Sunday, September 16, 1906; accommodation for about 250 ; Very Rev. Patrick Raleigh, prior.

G

GAINFORD, DURHAM (*Hexham and Newcastle*). St. Osmund.

The mission was founded as a chapel of ease to St. Augustine's, Darlington, in 1852.

Priests.

Rev. Thos. Witham, 1855.
„ James Rodgers, 1860.
„ Michael Birgen, 1891.
„ Henry Dix, 1895.
„ Thos. H. Knuckey, to date.

GAINSBOROUGH, LINCOLNSHIRE, (*Nottingham*). St. Thomas of Canterbury.

The mission was set on foot in 1866, and on Wednesday, June 3, 1868, the new church was opened by Bishop Roskell, of Nottingham. The edifice, which was built at the cost of T. A. Young, Esq., of Kingerby, is in the twelfth century style of Gothic. Mr. Hadfield was the architect. The accommodation is for about 150. Cost of erection about £1,250. The convent and schools were built later.

Priests.

Rev. Michael Scully, 1866.
„ Michael Gorman, 1877.
„ John Wenham, 1888.
„ Herbert Beale, 1889.
„ Thos. Bolton, 1890.
„ Michael O'Reilly, 1893.

Rev. Geo. Hawkins, 1897.
„ Redmond Walsh, 1898.
„ Alf. Bowen, 1899.
„ Owen J. Scully, 1901 (?).

GARSTANG, LANCS (*Liverpool*). SS. Mary and Michael.

Prior to 1788, Catholics at Garstang had to attend Mass at Claughton or Scorton. In the spring of that year, a chapel was opened, Fr. Shuttleworth being the first priest. In 1790 he went to Aston-le-Willows and was succeeded by Fr. J. Barrow. Fr. Barrow died in 1812. Fr. A. Story, who had kept ' a young gentlemen's academy ' at Tudhoe, was the next incumbent. He retired about 1823 and died in Yorkshire aged eighty-seven. In 1820 the Catholic population of Garstang numbered 530. In 1857 it was 1,000, by which time the old chapel had become almost unfit for use. A fine site at Barnacre was purchased from Mr. Bashall, of Farrington Lodge, and the foundation stone of the new church laid by Bishop Goss, of Liverpool, in June 1857. Fr. M. Hickey, resident priest at Garstang from 1827 to 1871, collected most of the £3,000 required for the contract. The style of the church, which was solemnly opened in August 1858 by Bishop Goss, is geometrical, and the building will hold over 600 persons. New marble altar and rails before the High and Lady Altars were erected by 'the pastor and people' in June 1898.

Priests.

Rev. Wm. Foster, 1741.

„ Edw. Daniel, 1745.

„ Shuttleworth, 1788.

„ J. Barrow, 1789.

„ Wm. Barnes, 1796.

„ J. Worswick, 1796.

„ Jn. Rickaby, 1798.

„ Rd. Sumner, 1800.

„ J. Barrow, 1800.

„ J. Burnard, 1807.

„ Ar. Story, 1813.

„ Dan. Hearne, 1824.

„ M. Hickey, 1825.

(T. Wells, assistant.)

„ Canon Seed, 1871.

„ Jn. Nixon, 1872.

„ Jas. Hennessy, 1874 to date.

GARSTON, LIVERPOOL. St. Francis of Assisi.

In 1874 the trustees of the Liverpool Mission Fund granted £100 towards a school chapel in this district. The mission, however, was not started till 1883, when a Congregational chapel was purchased and opened for worship (July). New schools were inaugurated October 1884.

Priest.

Rev. Fredk. Smith, 1883 to date.

GATESHEAD, DURHAM (*Hexham and Newcastle*). St. Joseph.

The town was formerly known as Gateside. During the reign of James II., Fr. Philip Leigh, S.J., had a large 'classical academy' and 'spacious chapel' in the town. Bishop Leyburn confirmed 360 persons here August 10 and 11, 1687. Fr. Leigh was still here in 1704. There is no mention of a mission after this, but when the Duke of Cumberland was hurrying north to suppress the Scotch rebellion in 1746, 'the old Catholic Church of St. Edmund' at Gateshead was burnt by the mob. Whether this was an old pre-Reformation church or a 'Mass-house' does not appear. The foundation of the present mission is due to Fr. Robert Suffield, who in 1851 hired a loft at Hillgate and fitted up a chapel. The 'Long Room' of the Queen's Hotel was afterwards hired for the same purpose. A site for a new church was secured in 1850 at 'Jackson's Chare' near the centre of the town. The first stone of the building was laid by Bishop Hogarth, of Hexham, June 1, 1858, and the church was opened July 5, 1859. A liberal portion of the building fund was subscribed by the congregation, including many of the employés of Messrs. Allhusen & Co. In November 1883, the church was reopened after a thorough course of renovation. Several fine stained-glass windows were added to the clerestory about this time.

Catholic population, 1854, 2,008.

Priests.

Rev. R. Suffield, occasionally, 1851.

„ F. Betham, 1852.

(Mission served from Hexham 1855-56.)

„ Edward Consitt, 1857.

„ Hy. Wrennall, 1860.

„ Hy. Riley, 1867.

„ John Wilson, 1874.

„ Patrick Thomas Mathews, 1879 till 1895.

„ Canon Michael Greene, 1895 to date.

GATESHEAD, DURHAM (*Hexham and Newcastle*). 'Our Lady and St. Wilfrid.'
This mission was initiated temporarily about fifty years ago by Fr. Beetham, of Newcastle, but the project was shortly afterwards given up. In 1886 the effort was again renewed, when Mass was said every Sunday in the district by a priest from St. Joseph's, Gateshead (*q.v.*). A new iron church to accommodate about 500 persons was opened on Sunday September 18, 1904. High Mass was sung on this occasion by Fr. G. Wheatley, D.D., of Ushaw. The Catholic population of the neighbourhood is estimated at 2,000.
Priests.
(Mission served from St. Joseph's 1886-1901.)
Rev. James Kay, to date.

GILLINGHAM, NORFOLK (*Northampton*). Our Lady of Perpetual Succour.
The church in the Roman style was opened in August 1898, the stone having been laid in February of that year by Fr. M. Fulton, O.S.B. Size, 77 ft. by 22 ft.; campanile 60 ft. high. The nave and aisles are separated by handsome Doric columns. J. G. Kenyon, Esq., of Gillingham Hall, defrayed the cost of erection. The mission is at present served from Beccles.

GILLMOSS, WEST DERBY, (*Liverpool*). St. Swithin.
This mission originated about 1700 at Croxteth Hall, the residence of the Lords Molyneux. When the

1st Earl of Sefton (Charles 9th Viscount Molyneux) conformed to the Established Church in 1768, he had some rooms in a farmhouse near Croxteth Hall turned into a Catholic chapel and also erected a residence for the priest. The incumbent at this time was Fr. B. Bolas, O.S.B., who died in 1773. His predecessor had been the Rt. Hon. and Rev. Charles 6th Lord Dormer, of the Society of Jesus. Fr. Joseph Emmott, S.J., came in 1773 at the special request, it is said, of the conforming Lord Sefton, who had been one of his pupils at St. Omer's. This story, however, is denied, as the Earl's guardians being protestants would not let him have a Catholic education. The present church was opened July 21, 1824, and the presbytery in 1836. In 1887 the Jesuit Fathers severed their connection with the mission, which has since been served by seculars. Fr. John Kelly was the first of these. He renovated the church in 1891. Fr. Taylor succeeded him in November 1891. The church contains some valuable sacred pictures and is justly considered ' a very beautiful country church.' A fine school and parish hall add greatly to the efficiency of the mission.
Priests.
Rev. Albert Babthorpe, S.J., 1701.
„ Richard Hitchmough, 1709. He apostatised, 1714, and became a priest-hunter. He received from the Government the small living of Whenby, Yorkshire, where he died in 1724.
„ Thos. Worthington, O.P., 1713.
„ Richard Jameson, 1725.
„ Robt. Kendal, 1733.
„ Wm. Molyneux, 1746, became 7th Viscount Molyneux, 1756.

Rev. Chas. Dormer (6th Baron Dormer), 1747.
„ Jn. Bodenham, 1750.
„ Bernard Bolas, O.S.B., 1756.
„ Jos. Emmott, S.J., 1773.
„ Nicholas Sewell, S.J., 1816.
„ Jos. Cope, S.J., 1818.
„ Thos. Clarke, S.J., 1834.
„ Jos. Johnson, 1841.
„ Edw. Morron, 1844.
„ John Milner, 1862.
„. Bernard Jarrett, 1863.
„ James Walker, 1880.
„ Geo. Noble, 1881.
„ John Young, 1882 (last Jesuit rector).
„ John Kelly, 1887.
„ Thos. Taylor, 1891.

GLASTONBURY, SOMERSET. Our Lady of the Sacred Heart.

This town, so famous in the ecclesiastical annals of England for its renowned abbey, dissolved in 1539, was without a mission till the autumn of 1886, when the Fathers of the Sacred Heart from Issoudun (France) opened a small chapel. They also served the mission of Highbridge, which till then had only the privilege of Mass on the first and third Sundays of each month.

GLEN-TROTHY, near ABERGA-VENNY (*Monmouth*). The Sacred Heart.

The chapel was opened in October 1885. The building, which was erected at the sole cost of Reginald Vaughan, Esq., of Glen-Trothy, consists of nave, chancel, porch, and sacristy. The high altar is adorned by a carved group of the Crucifixion, the whole being lighted by a rich east window. High Mass on the occasion of opening

was sung by Bishop Hedley, of Newport. Mr. E. Kirby, of Liverpool, was the architect of the chapel.

Priests.

Rev. Henry Clark, 1885.
„ Sidney Nicholls, 1888.
„ Hyacinth Skerrett, 1890.
„ James Phelan, 1892.
„ P. Larkin, 1893.
„ Edmond Mottay, 1895 to date.

GLOSSOP, DERBYSHIRE (*Nottingham*). St. Mary.
1. All Saints.

Fr. Nicholas Garlick, priest, who suffered for the Faith at Derby, 1588, was a native of Glossop. The place was one of the seats of the ducal family of Norfolk, who maintained a chapel here which served the mission till the opening of a small church in 1837. The stone was laid by Mr. Ellison on behalf of the Duke of Norfolk, February 13, 1835. Schools for 300 children were erected about the same time. Edward Fitzalan Howard, first Baron Howard of Glossop (December 9, 1869), was a generous benefactor to the mission.

Priests.

Rev. M. Barbe, 1824.
„ T. Lakin, 1828.
„ T. Canon Fauvel, 1835.
„ C. Tasker, 1866.
„ Henry Koerfer, 1882.
„ W. Baigent, 1892.
„ Francis Ffrench, 1897.
„ J. A. Wenham, 1901.
„ Owen Scully, 1903 to date.
2. St. Mary.

The present mission was formed 1882, by the Rev. Charles Tasker of All Saints, who left that church to be first incumbent of St. Mary's. The site of the new church—begun in July 1884—was given by Lord

Howard of Glossop, the building expenses (£12,000) being defrayed by the late Francis Sumner, Esq. A handsome presbytery was erected by the same generous benefactor. The church was opened by Bishop Bagshawe, August 16, 1887. Canon Tasker, who was created a domestic prelate (Monsignor) in 1893, died August 1906.

GLOUCESTER (Clifton). St. Peter.

The mission owes its rise to the munificence of Miss Mary Webb, daughter of Sir Jn. Webb, Bart. The first priest was Fr. Geo. Gildart, but he did not remain long. His successor, Fr. Jn. Greenaway, erected the chapel in 1789. This excellent priest also carried on a highly successful ' academy for young gentlemen' and gained the respect of all classes. He died November 29, 1800, aged fifty, and is buried in the chapel. His successor appears to have been the Abbé Giraud. During the incumbency of the Abbé Jossé (1833) some valuable church plate was stolen from the sacristy (October 21). The chapel was rebuilt and reopened March 22, 1860 ; much internal decoration was carried out October and November 1886 under the direction of Senor Dastis, of the Academy of Madrid. The carved oak stalls of the sanctuary were erected at the same time.

Priests.

Rev. George Gildart, 1788.
   „ John Greenaway, 1789.
   „ Abbé Giraud, 1800.
   „ John Burke, 1825.
   ., Abbé L. Jossé,

Rev. P. Hartley, 1841. Died of contagion, caught while visiting the sick, 1847.
   „ Henry Godwin, 1847.
   „ T. Macdonnell, 1848.
   „ Leonard Canon Calderbank, 1850.
   „ George Canon Case, D.D. 1866.
   „ M. Bouvier, 1877.
   „ Eustace Canon Barron, 1879.
   „ Joseph Chard, 1896 to date.

GODALMING, SURREY (Southwark).

This mission was started in 1899 and for some time was served on Sundays from the Franciscan Priory of Chilworth (q.v.). The Rushbrooks and Flemings are the most considerable Catholics of the place. The new church in the Early English style (98½ ft. × 26½ ft.) designed by Mr. F. Walters was opened by Bishop Amigo, June 27, 1906. Cost of the building together with the ' commodious presbytery' £4,700. Fr. St. George Hyland has charge of the mission.

GOLBORNE, NEWTON-LE-WIL-LOWS (Liverpool). All Saints.

The mission was established 1863.

Priests.

Rev. Francis A. Dunham.
   „ Thos. Carroll, here 1871.
   „ Francis A. Soden, 1876.
   „ Thos. Carroll, 1879.
   „ Rd. Baynes, 1882.
   „ Wm. Hy. Byrne, 1885.
   „ Thos. O'Donnell, 1895.
   „ Michael Quirke, 1902 to date.

GOLDENHILL, STAFFORDSHIRE
(*Birmingham*). St. Joseph.

A school chapel was erected in 1873, and served from Tunstall till the opening of the church (Gothic) in 1883.

Priests.

Rev. Thos. Kenny, 1885.
„ Bernard Grafton, 1893.
„ Wm. Hopkins, 1894.
„ Thos. Hanley, 1904.
„ Willibrord Buscot 1905 to date.

GOOLE, YORKS (*Leeds*). St. Thomas of Canterbury.

The mission was established in 1864. A school chapel was opened in July 1870, and the present church September 22, 1877, by Cardinal Manning. Style, Early English; accommodation for about 350; cost about £1,200.

Priests.

Rev. James Atkins, 1864.
„ Geo. Pearson, 1887 to date.

GOOSNARGH, PRESTON, LANCS
(*Liverpool*). St. Francis.

Fr. Thaddeus, O.S.M.F in his 'Franciscans in England' gives the date of the foundation of this mission as 1687. The ground and a small endowment (£10 per annum) were given by Cuthbert Hesketh, Esq. The chapel was dismantled at the Revolution next year, but 'soon rose out of its ruins.' The estate on which the chapel stood was sold in 1757 to Thos. Starkie, Esq., but a portion of the property was secured for the mission. The baptismal registers date from about 1770. Fr. Dinmore, O.S.B., who succeeded the last Franciscan incumbent, Fr. Bonaventure, 1833,

enlarged the chapel (1834). New schools were opened in August 1880.

Priests.

Rev. Michael Jackson, 1687.
„ Hy. Appleton, 1710.
„ Chas. Tootell, 1738.
„ Jn. Tootell, 1752.
„ Robt. Painter, 1753.
„ Chas. Tootell, 1755.
„ Leo. Francis, 1767.
„ Bernardine Fleet, 1770.
„ Lawrence Eccles, 1773.
„ Bernard Yates, 1776.
„ Alex. Whalley, 1778.
„ Peter Wilcock, 1779.
„ Anthony Caley, 1782.
„ P. Wilcock, 1784.
„ Ig. Casemore, 1785.
„ Jas. Howse, 1787.
„ Nich. Knight, 1788.
„ Ig. Casemore, 1790.
„ P. Wilcock, 1791.
„ Hy. Waring, 1794.
„ Pacif. Kington, 1800.
„ Jos. Tate, 1803.
„ Bonaventure Martin, 1805.
„ Jos. Tate, 1808.
„ Anselm Millward, 1809.
„ B. Martin, left 1833.
„ Edw. Dinmore, O.S.B., 1834.
„ Mat. Brierley, O.S.B., 1879.
„ Joseph Worden, 1895 to date.

GORING-ON-THAMES, OXFORD-SHIRE (*Birmingham*). Our Lady and St. John.

Mass was said here in the summer of 1895 by various priests for the benefit of Catholic visitors to the place. Goring was established as a permanent mission with resident priest in April 1896. The site for church and presbytery was secured about this time, but for some months Mass was said on Sundays in the house-boat of W. B. Hallet,

Esq. The foundation stone of the present church was laid by the Bishop of Birmingham on November 3, 1897, and the building was opened in 1898. The edifice, which stands in Ferry Lane, consists of a sanctuary and half the intended nave. The style is Perpendicular Gothic, designed by W. Ravenscroft, F.S.A., of Reading. The site was presented by Mr. W. Hallet.

GORLESTON-ON-SEA, SUFFOLK *Norfolk* (*Northampton*).

The temporary chapel was opened June 1889. The building, which was formerly a malthouse, will accommodate about 150. Estimated number of congregation, about 70. Gorleston-on-Sea is a growing seaside resort well known for its 'beautiful cliffs and bracing air.' A site for a future church has been secured by the present rector.

Priests.

Rev. Edward Scott, 1889.

„ Henry Stanley, 1905.

GORTON, MANCHESTER, LANCS (*Salford*). St. Francis of Assisi.

The Franciscans purchased a house and piece of land here in February 1863. It was occupied by the Fathers after Easter of the same year. The cruciform Gothic church designed by E. W. Pugin was commenced in May 1863, and consecrated 1872. Till its opening, the schools served as a temporary chapel. The church and the adjoining monastery cost upwards of £10,000. A splendid marble high altar was erected in July 1885. When Cardinal Manning visited the church in September 1885, he could congratulate the Fathers on their work, for there were 700 children in the schools and 'a multitude of people who received the sacraments.'

GOSPORT, HANTS (*Portsmouth*). Our Lady of the Sacred Heart.

The foundation of this mission is set down at 1750, but we have been unable to discover anything of its early history. As late as 1851 the chapel in Middle Street was 'a mean wooden structure' at the back of the presbytery, affording 'most inadequate accommodation for the congregation.' Fr. Baldacconi, D.D., erected the present church, opened about 1855. Donna Maria Francisca, wife of the Spanish royal claimant Don Carlos, was buried here in 1835.

Priests.

Rev. Abbé Delarue, 1800 (?).

„ Silveira, 1827.

„ O'Meara, 1829.

„ Jn. Clarke, 1830.

„ A. M. Baldacconi, 1850.

„ Thos. Canon Doyle, here in 1871 and till 1896.

„ Mgr. Cahill, administrator, 1896 *et seq.*

„ Jn. Canon Watson, to date.

GOUDHURST, KENT (*Southwark*). The Sacred Heart.

A home for cripples was founded here, at Oakleigh House, in 1880 (?) by Miss Dashwood, of Slindon, the chapel being open to the public. The home was subsequently closed, but the mission still continues, the Catholic population of the place being about thirty (1905).

Priests.

Rev. Ar. Cumberlege.

„ E. Palmer.

Rev. John Brady.
„ Geo. Mendham, 1895 to date.

GOSFORTH, NEWCASTLE-ON-TYNE (*Hexham and Newcastle*).
The Sacred Heart and St. Charles.

The mission was commenced in 1868, Mass being said at Cox Lodge. The chapel was dedicated to St. Charles and served from the cathedral till about 1876, when a resident priest was appointed. The Bishop Chadwick Memorial Schools (Industrial) were inaugurated October 1882 and the cemetery of the Holy Sepulchre opened 1891. The church was erected 1896.

Priests.
Rev. Michael Birgen, 1876.
„ Peter Perrin, 1882.
„ Wm. Stevenson, 1892.
„ Adam Wilkinson, 1895.
„ Thomas Reilly, 1897 to date.

GRANGE-OVER-SANDS, LANCS (*Liverpool*).
Mass was offered for the first time here on Sunday, August 26, 1882, at Kent Ford House, the residence of J. Sutcliffe Witham, Esq., by Fr. J. Bilsborow, afterwards Bishop of Salford. Till that time there was no Catholic chapel nearer than Carnforth, about ten miles distant. The foundations of the present church were laid May 29, 1883. The style of the building, designed by E. Simpson of Bradford, is Early English, the structure comprising nave, chancel, and side chapels. The accommodation is for 150 persons. The site was purchased by Fr. W. Massey, of Ulverston. The opening took place

January 22, 1884. Cartmel Priory belonging to the Canons Regular of St. Augustine before the dissolution, is situated in the neighbourhood.

GRANGETOWN, NORTH RIDING, YORKS (*Middlesbrough*). Our Lady of Perpetual Succour.
What was formerly a small village had by 1883 become a town with 4,000 inhabitants. The school chapel at the entrance of the town was opened in the summer of 1885, mainly owing to the efforts of Canon Holland, of Southbank. For some years after 1885 the mission was served from Southbank.

Priests.
Rev. James Nolan, 1888.
„ Patrick Cronin, 1899.
„ Bernard Kelly, 1902 to date.

GRANTHAM, LINCS (*Nottingham*). St. Mary's.
The Thimelbys of Irnham Hall were the support of this mission during the greater part of the eighteenth century. Bishop Hornyold was chaplain here about 1740. On one occasion when the pursuivants came to arrest him for saying Mass, he escaped detection by disguising himself in a long cloak. Fr. R. Thimelby, S.J., laboured in the district during the preceding century from about 1649 to 1665. Owing to the influx of Irish labourers the congregation greatly increased about 1820, and thirteen years later a chapel was opened (May 1833) by Fr. Tempest. A mural tablet was erected to his memory after his death (November 19, 1861). The chapel was

enlarged and decorated in 1884. Fr. P. Sabela has been rector since 1882.

GRASSENDALE, LIVERPOOL.
St. Austin.

In 1835 Charles Challoner, Esq., offered £50 a year to support a priest, and all the timber requisite for building, if a church were erected in the neighbourhood. The building was opened in July 1837, the cost of the structure having been £2,800. The rectors of the mission—Benedictines—since that time have been :

Rev. R. A. Prest, 1837-41.
„ C. A. Shann, 1843.
„ James Carr, 1845.
„ S. B. Day, 1849.
„ W. A. Brindle, 1850.
„ C. Shann, 1853.
„ R. A. Prest, 1857.
., J. H. Dowding, 1864.
„ W. A. Bulbeck, 1872.
„ J. P. Hall, 1882.
„ J. C. Murphy, 1883.
„ J. J. Brown, 1891.
„ J. P. O'Brien and T. A. Burge, 1898.

GRAVESEND, KENT (Southwark).
St. John the Evangelist.

The mission was started about 1840 by Fr. Gregory Stasiewiecz, a refugee Polish priest who opened a humble chapel in Windmill Street. By dint of great exertions he erected a larger chapel in the Chatham Road, under the patronage of St. Gregory the Great. He was succeeded by Fr. A. Ritort. In 1850 the priest was Fr. Hearne, of Moorfields. He repaired the walls of the chapel. In July 1851 a fine proprietary (Gothic) chapel belonging to the Rev. Mr. Blew, a convert Anglican clergyman, was purchased, and con-

secrated by Bishop Grant on October 30 following. Mr. L. Raphael generously advanced the purchase money (£2,000). This church was erected in 1838. It accommodates 1,200 persons. The aisles are adorned with a series of well-executed statues of the principal English saints. In July 1861 Bishop Grant consecrated a Catholic cemetery at Gravesend, 'hundreds falling on their knees in response to his entreaty that they would say a De Profundis and a Hail Mary for the Souls in Purgatory.'

Priests since 1853.

Rev. Amadeus Guidez.
„ Michael Driscoll, 1855.
„ M. O'Sullivan, 1860.
„ Joseph Wyatt, here in 1871, and till 1906.
„ Fr. M. Gifkins, 1906.

GRAYS, ESSEX (Westminster).
St. Thomas of Canterbury.

This mission was commenced in March or April 1862, by Fr. J. Gilligan. The 'chapel' was a closed-up shop and the altar a deal table. The vestments are described as 'unfit for use.' Fr. Gilligan had also charge of the mission of Barking, fourteen miles distant. The 'chapel' of Grays only accommodated some forty persons and the congregation numbered nearly 200. Fr. Geo. Sparks appealed for funds to build (December 1880). As late as 1885, when Canon Keens had charge of the mission, the 'chapel' was a disused butcher's shop. A school chapel was commenced in April 1886, the stone being laid by Cardinal Manning. The new building, which was opened in October the same year, is capable of accommodating 400 children. The chapel is in the upper storey with seating capacity for 500. The style is Early Gothic. F. Pownall was the architect.

GREAT BILLING, NORTHAMPTONSHIRE (*Northampton*). The Immaculate Heart of Mary.

In 1874 V. Carey-Elwes, Esq., fitted up a chapel in his house and opened it to the public. It was served by a priest from Northampton, but at that time the only Catholics in the place were the members of the Elwes family, numbering about five. By 1878, there was a resident priest and upwards of fifty Catholics, mostly converts. A large temporary church—the gift of Mr. Elwes—was opened the same year (September 8).

Priests.

Rev. W. Blackman, 1878.
  „ Chas. Mull, 1882.
  „ Patrick Murphy, 1885.
  „ Fredk. Maples, 1888.
  „ W. Canon Blackman (second time), 1893 to date.

GREAT CROSBY, LANCS (*Liverpool*). SS. Peter and Paul.

The mission was started in 1826 in a temporary chapel which was superseded by 'a neat commodious structure,' opened in 1832. The congregation then numbered 400. Schools were erected by Canon Fisher, and the present fine Gothic church opened 1894.

Priests.

Rev. Wm. Brown, 1826.
  „ James Canon Fisher, 1850.
  „ Jn. Canon Wallwork, 1871.
  „ Jn. Nixon, 1885 to date.

GREAT ECCLESTON, LANCS. St. Mary.

The first chapel, founded in 1760, was situated at 'the Raikes,' about quarter of a mile from Great Eccleston. The baptismal registers date from 1771. The school built in 1780 served as a chapel on Sundays till the completion of the present church, opened in July 1835. In 1869 an altar and reredos were erected in the church in memory of the last of the Leckonbys 'a fine old Catholic family of the Fylde.'

Priests since 1824.

Rev. Hy. Parkinson.
  „ Ralph Platt, 1833.
  „ Thos. Pinnington, 1837.
  „ Randolph Frith, 1840.
  „ Edw. Brown, 1844.
  „ Walter Maddocks, 1846.
  „ E. Swarbrick, 1860 till 1878.
  „ Thos. Wells, 1879.
  „ Thos. Smith, 1889.
  „ Hy. Roberts, 1896 to date.

GREAT GRIMSBY, LINCS (*Nottingham*). St. Mary.

When Mass was first said at Great Grimsby in 1857 by Fr. G. Bent, there was neither 'chapel, mission house, nor school' in the place. In 1871 a site for church and schools was given 'by a noble benefactor.' The church was opened Sunday, August 19, 1883, by Bishop Bagshawe, of Nottingham. The 'noble benefactor' referred to above was T. A. Young, Esq., K.S.G., who also built the Gothic church. In July 1883 a splendid altar, designed in the Early Decorated style, like the Angel Choir at Lincoln Cathedral, was consecrated by the Bishop of Nottingham. The schools adjoining the church were built at the cost of Sir John Sutton and the Hon. Mrs. Fraser. This latter benefactress gave a handsomely carved reredos and altar to the Sacred Heart chapel of the church in January 1884. In November 1887 a beautiful altar was erected in the Young Chantry by the Hon. Mrs. Fraser, in memory of her deceased husband, Col. the Hon. Alexander Fraser. In March and April 1888 T. A. Young, Esq., K.S.G., presented the church with carved oak stalls for the sanctuary and a handsome *sedile* for the officiating priest.

Priests.
Rev. G. Bent, 1857.
„ George Canon Johnson, 1861.
„ Joseph Hawkins, 1885 to date.

GREAT HARWOOD, LANCS (*Salford*). St. Hubert.
This mission was established in June 1857 by James Lomax, Esq., of Clayton Hall. Mass was said there for the first time on June 29. The church, erected by the munificence of James Lomax, Esq., was opened for worship by Bishop Turner, of Salford, November 1859. The style of the church, which cost about £6,000, is of the Decorated period, and will accommodate some 700 persons. The high altar, which rests on marble columns, is adorned with figures emblematic of the Synagogue and the Church. The several windows of the church in stained glass are very fine. The whole edifice was redecorated in September 1864 at the expense of the Lomax family.

Priests.
Rev. W. Canon Dunderdale, 1857 till after 1883.
„ Arnold Nohlmanns, 1885.
„ Hy. Hill, M.A. ,1888 to date.

GREAT HAYWOOD, STAFFS. (*Birmingham*). St. John the Baptist.
The church was dedicated October 21, 1846. Bishop Wiseman officiated, assisted by the Hon. and Rev. G. Spencer, F. Searle, J. Keon Dunn, &c. G. Clifford, Esq., of Wycliffe, Yorks, gave £20 towards the expenses of opening. The neighbourhood teems with associations connected with such old Catholic families as Tixall, Aston, Clifford, &c. In May 1847 a solemn requiem Mass was sung in the church for the repose of the soul of Col. Sir Charles Chichester, 61st Regiment, who died at Toronto, Canada, while in command there. His family was among the early patrons of the mission of Great Haywood.

Priests.
Rev. Jn. Levy, 1845.
„ B. J. Butland, 1851 to date.

GREAT MARLOW, BUCKS (*Northamptonshire*). St. Peter's.
When the foundation stone of the church was laid July 2, 1845, the Catholics of Great Marlow totalled six out of a population of 6,000. Bishop Wareing laid the stone in the presence of 1,500 spectators. Mr. Scott-Murray acted as crossbearer in the procession to the site. Mr. E. Wheble was M.C. The religious ceremony concluded with a banquet at the town hall, while shillings and loaves were distributed to a number of the deserving poor. Among the distinguished company present were Lord and Lady Camoys, Lady Bedingfeld, Lady Russell, P. Howard, Esq., M.P., The O'Conor Don, &c. The church was designed by Pugin and built at the sole expense of Mr. Scott-

O

Murray. The spire is seventy feet high. In August 1846 a collection plate and set of altar cruets were stolen from the sacristy. Fr. Peter Coop was the first priest in charge of the mission. In 1851, when Fr. J. Morris was chaplain to Mr. Scott-Murray, High Sheriff of Bucks, Lord Campbell, the Assize-judge, objected to riding in the same carriage with a ' Popish chaplain.' The incident was much commented upon at the time, and in the sequel the learned judge wrote apologising for his want of courtesy.

Priests.

Rev. P. Coop, 1845.

„ Jn. B. Ludwig, 1849.

„ J. Morris, 1851.

„ Bernard Canon Smith, 1854 to 1903.

„ H. Squirrell, 1903 to date.

GREENGATE, LANCS (*Salford*). St. Peter.

A chapel was opened Sunday, January 4, 1863, and in 1874 the church was erected. In July 1883 a new stone altar and reredos were added. The general design consists of a series of ornamental arcadings supported by columns of Irish marbles, and flanked on either side by statues of SS. Peter and Paul.

Priests.

Rev. Henry Beswick.

„ Aemilius Goetgeluck, 1882.

„ Martin Meagher, 1893.

„ David Power, 1895.

„ John Moore, 1902.

„ Henry Hunt, 1904 to date.

GREENHITHE, KENT (*Southwark*). Our Lady of Mt. Carmel.

This mission was started at Galley Hill in the spring of 1859 by Fr. F. W. Faber of the Oratory. The chapel at first was a small room opening out into an uncovered yard. The number of Catholics was set down at about 300. The first resident priest of Greenhithe was Fr. F. Maurice, O.C., who was succeeded by Fr. M. O'Sullivan, O.C., in 1861. The chapel was so crowded on Sundays that the children who were placed near the altar actually touched the priest while saying Mass. The church was opened 1875, and for some time was served from Northfleet. In 1904 it was attended on Sundays by a priest from Walworth.

GREENWICH,   LONDON,   S.E. (*Southwark*). Our Lady Star of the Sea.

The old Catholic chapel situated in East Street dates from shortly after the commencement of the last century. About 1830, the congregation numbered 1,500—1,000 civilians and 500 naval pensioners. The bulk of the former were very poor. Fr. R. North, who was appointed to Greenwich in 1828, started collecting funds for a new church. It is said that when in danger of death by shipwreck as a lad, he made a vow to become a priest and build a church in honour of Our Lady, both of which promises he fulfilled. His congregation responded cheerfully to his appeal, one old Trafalgar veteran giving all his life's savings (£25) to the fund. The Lords of the Admiralty, in consideration of the great work done by Fr. North among the old sailors, contributed £200. In October 1846, the present Gothic church was commenced on Croom's Hill, and opened December 8,

1851. Bishop Grant sang the Mass, and Cardinal Wiseman preached. At the golden jubilee of the church, December 8, 1901, Bishop Bourne preached, and Fr. Oswald Turner, C.J., of St. George's College, Weybridge, sang the Mass. About £600 was collected for the decoration of the church in memory of the event. Canon R. North died in February 1860. Over 1,100 persons attended his funeral, which was 'strictly Gothic.' He was buried in the chancel, where a monument has been erected to his memory. His brother, Canon Joseph North, died in 1886. He was the beau-idéal of the old type of English Catholic priest. Since then the rector has been Canon O'Halloran, who came to the church as a curate in 1859. We may add that the mission is indebted for much of its present flourishing condition to such generous benefactors as the late Sir Stuart Knill, sometime Lord Mayor of London, and his son, the present Alderman Sir John Knill. The estimated number of the congregation—owing to the establishment of local missions—is now about 700.

GREENWICH (EAST) (Southwark). St. Joseph's Church, Pelton Road.

Opened Wednesday, May 25, 1881. Style, Early Decorated. Cost about £4,350. Seating capacity of church, 500. Architect, A. J. Hansom. Fr. A. M. Boone was priest at the time of opening, when Mass was sung by Bishop Patterson, of Emmaus. Cardinal Manning preached (St. Matt. xxviii. 20). Present rector, Fr. Thomas Nolan.

GREYSHOTT, HANTS (Portsmouth).

The mission was commenced in 1893 when the temporary chapel was served during the summer months by one of the Premonstratensian Canons from Farnborough. Fr. Jerome O'Callaghan was appointed 1896; J. D. Breen, 1899; Henry L. P. Kelly is the present rector.

GROSMONT, MONMOUTHSHIRE (Newport).

An iron chapel was opened here August 8, 1906. The mission was established conjointly by Godfrey Radcliffe, Esq., of Dan-y-Craig, and Count Keyes O'Clery, in memory of Major Joseph Radcliffe, 'a gallant soldier and a staunch Catholic.' The beautiful oak altar of the chapel was carved by Mr. Radcliffe.

GROVE FERRY, KENT (Southwark).

In 1903 the Marist Brothers acquired a large mansion known as 'Shrublands,' formerly used as a boarding establishment, and by the addition of some adjoining houses transformed the entire block into a college. At present, the number of pupils is about 100. An iron chapel to accommodate about 130 has been erected, and for the time being serves as the mission church of the district.

GUILDFORD (Surrey). St. Joseph, Chertsey Street.

From 1792 to 1801 a certain émigré, Abbé Goudemetz, resided

o 2

at Guildford and said Mass in a temporary chapel, probably in Friary Street, where some 120 fellow *émigrés* were accustomed to worship. The present mission of Guildford was, however, started from Sutton Place (*q.v.*), about 1857, by Fr. Joseph Sidden, who opened a temporary chapel in a room in Spital Street. Already, in November 1846, a site for a church had been secured in Chertsey Street by Bishops Wiseman and Griffiths. The purchase was effected by a Mr. Edward Collen, of Postford Mill, Albury. In 1860 a wooden military hut was erected on the site and fitted up as a chapel. The cost of this structure was largely met by the Catholic Scotch and Irish bargemen who worked on the river Wey. The military hut did duty till the opening of the present church by Canon Crookall, V.G., October 19, 1881. The style of the building is Geometric Gothic, the structure being designed for 200 persons. The church was completed in August 1884, and on the 19th of that month the event was celebrated by a solemn High Mass, at which Cardinal Manning pontificated and preached. The pulpit was presented by Mrs. Byrne, the altar by Mrs. Littledale, and the five stations by Albert Sibeth, Esq. Col. and Mrs. Tredcroft were also generous benefactors to the church. A fine presbytery was built in 1890. The priests at Guildford, since the establishment of the mission, have been :—Rev. E. Clery, 1860-64; Rev. T. Richardson, 1864-65; E. Sheridan, 1865-78; R. Fowler, 1878, the present incumbent.

H

HACKNEY, LONDON, N.E. (*Westminster*).

In 1840, Hackney, though a fairly populous district, 'lay open to the fields and intersected by country lanes.' The Catholics of the locality had to go as far as Moorfields for Mass, but in 1843 they were accustomed to meet in an obscure room on Sunday evenings to recite the rosary, read one of Challoner's meditations, and sometimes hear a sermon from one of the Moorfields priests. In 1844 a temporary chapel behind 'The Black Boys' brewery in Elsdale Street, was occupied, and in June 1845 a site 'for a chapel and nunnery' was purchased in the Triangle for £700. The church, consisting of a nave, north aisle, chancel, sacristy, and bell-cot, was built in 1848, from a design by Wardell. The accommodation was for 500 persons, the cost of the building being about £2,000. A baptistery was subsequently added by Miss Harrison. Father Kaye gave the beautiful Lady Altar of marble and alabaster to the church, the funds being supplied by the Confraternity of the Living Rosary. The church, after being thoroughly cleaned and renovated for the occasion, was solemnly consecrated by Bishop Brindle, D.S.O., on Tuesday, November 21, 1899. The congregation at that time was estimated at 800 effective members, the average school attendance being about 230.

Priests.

Fr. J. Lecuona, 1844.
„ John Vertue (Bishop of Portsmouth 1882–1900).
„ J. P. Kaye, M.R.
„ Padbury.
„ W. Fleming.
„ T. Denny, M.R.
„ Geo. Cox, to date.

HADFIELD, near GLOSSOP (*Nottingham*).

St. Charles' Church was built in 1858-60. During the mission given there by the Franciscan Fathers of Gorton Brook, near Manchester, in September 1865, no less than 1,000 members of the congregation received Holy Communion. The mission is largely indebted to the munificence of Lord Edward Howard of Glossop, the donor of the church. The church and congregation were solemnly 'consecrated to the Sacred Heart September 6, 1873.'

Priests.

Rev. Bryan O'Donnell, here in 1862.

Rev. C. L. Monahan, 1863.
„ Charles Hickey, 1877.
„ Wm. Yates, 1882.
„ Herman Canon Sabela, 1888 to date.

HADHAM, HERTS (*Westminster*). The school for epileptic children, under the care of the Daughters of the Cross, was opened September 22, 1903. The Gothic church and convent were designed by Mr. J. F. Bentley, architect of the Westminster Cathedral. The church is so arranged that the inmates of the place, who number about fifty, cannot be seen by those who attend the services from outside. The Catholics of the district are estimated at about a dozen.
Priests.
Rev. O'Doherty, 1903.
„ E. Schmitt, 1904.
„ W. J. Smullen, 1905.

HADZOR, WORCESTERSHIRE (*Birmingham*). SS. Richard and Hubert.
This mission was started from Broadway early in 1878. On July 16 of that year, the present little church, in the Flemish style, was opened by Bishop Ullathorne (C. Buckler, architect). The altar and furniture were the gift of Joseph Whitehouse, Esq. ' An elegant and spacious gallery ' was added to the church in the autumn of 1884.
Priests.
Rev. James Rigby, 1878.
„ Edward Dorr, 1882.
„ Terence Fitzpatrick, 1885.
„ Wm. Stoker, 1889.
„ Joseph Lillis, 1891.
„ John Kelly, 1892.

Rev. Henry Gregson, 1895.
„ Clement Gottwaltz, 1899 to date.

HAINTON, or HANTON, LINCOLNSHIRE (*Nottingham*). St. Francis of Sales.
Priests.
Rev. Jn. Abbot, 1836.
„ James Canon Simkiss, 1837.
„ Francis Canon Cheadle, 1857.
„ M. P. Horgan, 1885.
(Mission served from Market Rasen, 1892-3.)
„ W. Yates, 1894.
„ Joseph Feakens, 1899 to date.

HALES PLACE, CANTERBURY (*Southwark*).
Sir Edward Hales, Bart., became a Catholic about the time of the accession of James II., and he it was against whom the collusive action was brought to ascertain if the courts would allow a Catholic to hold a commission in the army by royal license. The judges after trial in 1686, gave their opinion in favour of the ' dispensing power ' by which the king could suspend the operation of the penal laws. The family of Hales clung to their newly adopted faith, and till the opening of the Canterbury mission their chapel was the only Catholic one for miles round. Sir Edward Hales, last baronet, died in 1829, leaving his daughter, Mary Barbara, a ward in Chancery. This lady subsequently entered the Carmelite Order, but obtained, after a few years, a Papal dispensation from her vows. She then commenced building a monastery on her estate at Hales Place, but her intentions were never fully realised. In

1881-2 the French Jesuits, expelled from France, acquired the estate, and built on it a college for their novices. Miss Hales died Saturday, April 18, 1885, and was buried among her ancestors in the chapel at Hales.

HALIFAX, YORKS, WEST RIDING (*Leeds*). St. Mary.

The date of the foundation of this mission is given as 1827, but no mention of it occurs in the 'Laity's Directory' till 1830, when the priest in charge of the place was Fr. F. Keily. The congregation is described as made up of a 'number of poor Catholics,' who 'have only a temporary room in which they hear Mass on Sundays, which on weekdays is used for every profane purpose.' By 1837, this depressing state of things had not changed, but next year 'a new Catholic church' was erected in the town. This structure made way for the present Church of St. Mary, opened in 1865.

Priests.
Rev. Thos. Keily, 1827 (?).
,, Joseph Fairclough, 1837.
,, John Rigby, 1840.
,, James Hostage, 1849.
,, Matthew Kavanagh, 1856.
,, Jacob Illingworth, as second priest, 1858.
,, J. Kelly and J. Atkinson, 1864.
,, J. Geary, 1871.
,, B. Wake, 1882.
,, Canon Gordon, 1891.
,, P. Mulcahy, 1898.

HALLIWELL, BOLTON, LANCS (*Salford*). St. Joseph.

On Sunday, August 21, 1881, the school chapel of the mission was opened by the Bishop of Salford. It accommodates 400 people on Sundays and 300 children on weekdays. The cost of the building was £980. The present fine church was opened by the Bishop of Salford in 1900. Canon Boulaye, V.G., is the present rector.

HALSTEAD, ESSEX (*Westminster*).

A regular mission was started here in March 1898, when a wooden building in Rosemary Lane—formerly used by a firm of printers—was fitted up as a chapel. Mass was said here for the first time on Sunday, March 27, by Mgr. Canon Moyes, D.D., who in the course of his sermon gave a lucid explanation of the Catholic doctrine of the Holy Eucharist. The mission is at present (1906) served from Braintree. On Tuesday, October 26, 1897, Cardinal Vaughan lectured on the Catholic Church in the Town Hall of Halstead, which was densely crowded. The next evening his Eminence lectured on devotion to Our Lady, and on the conclusion of the address a vote of thanks was unanimously passed at the suggestion of the Rev. R. H. Fuller, a Unitarian minister, who described the lecture as 'an intellectual treat.' The bulk of the large audience present were the most 'dissident of dissenters.'

HAMMERSMITH, LONDON, W. (*Westminster*). The Most Holy Trinity.

From its retired situation, Hammersmith was during the penal times chosen by many Catholics as a suitable place of residence.

In 1685, Mrs. Frances Bedingfeld, sister of Sir Henry Paston Bedingfeld, Bart., established a community of Benedictine nuns, from Munich, at Hammersmith in a spacious house surrounded by a large garden. The nuns wore the ordinary dress of the period, and devoted themselves to teaching the daughters of the Catholic nobility and gentry. For the sake of protection, the property was nominally held by the Portuguese ambassadors, who had their country house at Hammersmith. The Vicars Apostolic of the London District also had a residence in the neighbourhood. Their house afforded the blessings of Mass and the Sacraments to the proscribed Catholics in the district. Bishop Gifford died here in 1734, and Bishop Talbot (brother of the Earl of Shrewsbury) in 1790. In 1795, the English Benedictine nuns of Dunkirk came to England after suffering much ill-usage at the hands of the Revolutionists, and were settled by the V.A. of London, Bishop Douglass, at the Hammersmith convent, which at this time contained only three nuns of the old community. The spacious chapel of the house, built in 1812 by Joseph Gillow, Esq., served the mission down to 1853, when the church at Brook Green was built. The present church was commenced May 8, 1851, and opened July 26, 1853. The style is Decorated Gothic, from design by Wardell. Fr. Joseph Butt, who died September 27, 1854, was the founder. The spire was added 1867, and a peal of bells in 1871. The Chapel of the Blessed Sacrament was built by the late Countess Tasker in 1854. Fr. D. O'Keefe succeeded as rector in 1854, and in 1881 Canon Alfred White, formerly curate to Fr. Butt. Canon White was elected an alderman of the borough of Hammersmith in 1900, and died at an advanced age in 1904. The church was cleaned and redecorated both in 1880 and 1898 through the generosity of Mr. and Mrs. H. Kearsley, who also defrayed the cost of lighting the building by electricity. Near the church are the St. Joseph's Almshouses, the foundation stone of which was laid by the Duchess of Norfolk, May 28, 1851.

Priests.

Rev. Wm. Maire, 1697–1739.

. . . . . .

„ Joseph Bolton, 1770 (?)

„ James Barnard, V.G., 1783–1803.

(The Rev. Joseph Lee, 1790-1800, appears to have been his assistant.)

„ Abbé F. Bellissent, 1803. His assistant was the Abbé Nicholas Jacquin.

„ Wm. Kelly, 1840.

„ Joseph Butt, 1847.

„ D. O'Keefe, 1854.

„ Alfred Canon White, 1851.

„ Alfred Canon Clements, 1904 to date.

HAMPSTEAD, LONDON, N. (*Westminster*).

The founder of this mission was the Abbé Morel, an *émigré* of the Great Revolution. After teaching French for a few months in Sussex (1792–3) he went to Reading, and in 1796 came to Hampstead as chaplain to a number of French refugees resident in the then beautiful village. He fitted up a chapel in Oriel House, Church Row, recently pulled down, and there administered the Sacraments and said Mass till the opening of the present 'tasteful and artistic little church' in Holly Place in 1816. The good Abbé died in 1852, and his remains repose under the porch of the church where he laboured so long. An altar tomb was erected to his memory in March 1857. The centenary of the mission was celebrated July 2, 1896, the Feast of the Visitation, in the presence of Cardinal Vaughan, the Bishop of Emmaus, and a large congregation. The entire church was redecorated at a cost of £400 in November and December 1892.

Priests.

Rev. Abbé J. Morel, 1796.
„ Jn. Walsh, M.R., 1852.
„ Mgr. V. Eyre, here 1862.
„ Ar. Dillon Canon Purcell, here in 1871 till 1901.
„ Michael FitzGerald, M.R., 1901 to date.

HAMPTON-ON-THE-HILL, WARWICKSHIRE (*Birmingham*). St. Charles.

Until 1819, Catholics in the vicinity of Hampton-on-the-Hill worshipped at Grove Park, the ancestral seat of the Lords Dormer. In the above-named year, Charles Lord Dormer built the present chapel at Hampton-on-the-Hill, and handed it over to the V.A. of the Midland District. In spite of the difficulties of the time, Catholics increased very considerably at Hampton-on-the-Hill during the first few decades of the nineteenth century, but they are said to have lately declined owing to Grove Park having been let to protestant tenants. In 1860 the present Catholic chapel was founded at Warwick by Mgr. Longman,

priest of Leamington, then incumbent of Hampton-on-the-Hill.'

Priests since 1820.

Rev. Francis Turvile, 1820. During his rectorate of over twenty years the old chapel was enlarged, 1830.
„ W. Foley, 1841.
„ D. Bagnall, 1843.
„ T. Revill, 1847.
„ W. Ilsley, 1851.
„ Mgr. Thos. Longman, 1853.
„ Jn. Gibbons, here in 1862.
„ Charles Hipwood, 1867.
„ Charles Ryder, 1872.
„ J. Robinson, here in 1874.
„ A. Delerue, 1879.
„ Jos. Daly, 1888 to date.

HAMPTON WICK, MIDDLESEX (*Westminster*). The Sacred Heart of Jesus.

The temporary chapel was opened in November 1882. Canon George Akers, M.A. (Oxon.) was the first priest. About the same time he hired a room at South Teddington for Mass on Sundays. The extemporised chapel accommodated about 150 persons. In 1893 a large 'oblong church' was opened in the Teddington Road. The present incumbent is Fr. J. Hazell.

N.B.—The Hon. Mrs. Porter (Petre ?), who lived at Hampton Wick in 1734, had a chapel in her house. Her chaplain was Fr. Peter Brailsford, a Lisbonian.

[1] In 1742 it was decided that the incumbent of Grove Park must say Mass weekly for the repose of the soul of Lady Anne Curson, so long as he received the alms. In 1758 Fr. Arnold, O.S.F., resided here. See Thaddeus, *Franciscans in England.*

**HANDSWORTH, near SHEF-
FIELD, YORKS** (*Leeds*). St. Joseph.

Mass was first said at Handsworth in 1867, and in 1870 a Catholic deaf and dumb institution was
opened in the parish. After its
subsequent removal to Boston Spa,
the wooden chapel of the place was
used by Catholics of the district.
It quickly became too small, and
on August 27, 1879, the first stone
of the new church was laid by the
Bishop of Leeds. The Duke of
Norfolk generously defrayed the
cost of erection—between £8,000
and £9,000. The opening took
place on June 7, 1881. The style
is that of the 'late rectilinear
period,' like that of the old parish
churches of Rotherham and Laugh-
ton. There is also a crypt with
mortuary chapel. The seating
capacity is for 800 persons. M. E.
Hadfield & Son were the architects.

HANLEY, STAFFS (*Birmingham*). Our Blessed Lady and St.
Patrick.

In 1836 the only Catholic chapels
in the Potteries were at Cobridge
(built 1717) and Longton. The
priests of these missions served
Hanley alternately. In 1860 the
Catholic population was 2,000, and
in June the same year the first
stone of the new church was laid
by Fr. F. Sullivan, of Revel Grange,
and the building was opened November 22, 1860. The style is
simple Gothic, and the total cost
was about £1,000. The accommodation is for 800.

N.B.—Hanley Castle, Hill End,
was the seat of the ancient Catholic family of Bartlett. In 1765 Fr.
Felix Bartlett, brother of the

squire, was chaplain. He died at
Worcester in 1777.[1]

Priests.

Rev. W. Molloy, 1861 till 1890.
„ Jas. B. Keating, 1891.
„ M. O'Rourke, M.R., 1899.

HANLEY, STAFFS. The Sacred
Heart.

This church was commenced
August 1889, and opened September 21, 1891. It has been since
1893-4 the chief church of the district, and the older foundation of
Our Lady and St. Patrick (*q.v.*) are
served from it.

Rev. M. O'Rourke, present rector.

HANWELL, LONDON, W. (*Westminster*). Our Lady and St.
Joseph.

A chapel was opened at Clifton
Lodge, the residence of Miss Rabnett, May 1853. The present
Gothic church was opened June
1864 by Cardinal Wiseman, on a
site presented by Miss Rabnett.
E. Pugin was the architect. A
new Lady Chapel—the gift of an
anonymous benefactor—was opened
December 11, 1904. The Catholic
population of the district is about
800.

Priests.

Rev. F. Lang, 1853.
„ John Bonus, D.D., 1855.
„ J. Staples, 1860.
„ Aemilian Kirner, 1863.
„ Francis Laing, D.D., 1867.
„ Henry Karslake, 1890.
„ C. Clarke, 1893.
„ Donald Skrimshire, 1895.
„ M. Brannigan, 1905 to date.

[1] Foley Records, Society of Jesus, xii.

HARBERTON, DEVON (*Plymouth*). St. Rose of Lima.

The chapel at Dundridge House, the residence of Robt. Harvey, Esq., was blessed by Bishop Graham on Wednesday, September 6, 1893. Dom Adam Hamilton, O.S.B., preached on the triumph of the Mass against all its enemies in England since the Reformation. He referred to the massacre of the Devon peasantry by Lord Russell's German troops for defending the old religion in 1549, and also to Dorothy Risdon of Harberton, whose estates were confiscated about 1640 for her adherence to the ancient faith.

HARBORNE, near BIRMINGHAM. St. Mary.

Mission established by the Passionist Fathers 1870. In 1876 the church attached to the monastery or 'Retreat' was opened.

HARPENDEN, HERTS (*Westminster*). Our Lady of the Sacred Heart, Rothamsted Avenue.

A church of wood and iron was blessed and opened by Canon Carter, Sunday, June 4, 1905. Fr. Marten, M.S.C., is the incumbent.

HARRINGTON, CUMBERLAND (*Hexham and Newcastle*). St. Mary.

A school chapel was opened 1874, and the present Gothic church May 14, 1893. C. Walker was the architect. Seating accommodation for 300. In September 1881 a stone Calvary was erected in the adjacent cemetery to the memory of Fr. Francis Wall, an Apostolic Franciscan missioner in this district, who suffered for the Faith August 15, 1679, during the Titus Oates plot. The mission was long served from Workington.

Priests (O.S.B.).

Rev. Francis Hutchinson, 1885.
,, Francis Hickey, 1892.
,, Austin Firth, 1896 to date.

HARROGATE, YORKS (*Leeds*). Our Lady and St. Robert.

Though the mineral springs of Harrogate had long made the place one of the fashionable spas of England, no Catholic chapel was established in the town till May 1861, when Mass was said for the first time in a room of the Crescent Hotel, by Fr. F. Goldie. Before this, the nearest mission was Stourton Park, the seat of Lord Mowbray and Stourton. In September 1864 a school chapel and presbytery, were opened. The present church dates from 1873. A site for schools was acquired 1863, and buildings erected shortly afterwards.

Priests.

Rev. F. Goldie, 1861 *et seq.*
,, Jas. Glover, here in 1871.
,, Michael O'Donnell, 1877.
,, James Downes, 1888.
,, Wm. Canon Pope, 1889 to date.

HARROW-ON-THE-HILL, MIDDLESEX (*Westminster*). Our Lady and St. Thomas of Canterbury.

A temporary chapel was opened in the Roxborough Road 1873, and served on Sundays by the late Fr. Joseph Redman, D.D., professor at St. Thomas's Seminary, Hammersmith. The new church was opened 1894. The stained-glass window in the sanctuary was erected by Mr. and Mrs. Philip Thornton, of Douglas Lodge, to the memory of their five children. A new Gothic reredos was added to the Lady Chapel 1900.

N.B.—About 1793, a Catholic boys' school was opened in the district by Fr. Collins, D.D., and removed to Southall Park 1806. The school existed till about 1830, and was 'held in high estimation.' Fr. Jn. Chetwode Eustace, author of the celebrated 'Classical Tour through Italy,' was sometime a master here.

HARROW ROAD, LONDON, N.W. (*Westminster*). Our Lady of Lourdes and St. Vincent of Paul.

The church was opened in January 1883. The cost of erection was defrayed by the Rev. Lord Archibald Douglas, so well known in the cause of rescue work. The style is of the Transition period, between Early English and Decorated. J. Hall, Esq., was the architect. The stained-glass windows are by Lavers, Westlake, and Barraud. The solemn opening of the church did not take place till Tuesday, December 12, 1893, when the debt on the building had been paid off. Cardinal Vaughan preached on this occasion. Fr. E. Banns is the rector.

HARTLEPOOL, DURHAM (*Hexham and Newcastle*). The Immaculate Conception.

In 1820 Mass was said in a private house, the congregation amounting, it is said, to only six persons. In 1832 Fr. W. Knight was appointed to Hartlepool, where he built a small chapel. After eighteen years of labour in the district, he was able to purchase the site of a new church, and in June 1850 the stone was laid by Bishop Hogarth. The style is Early English Gothic, the seating capacity being for 900 persons. The building was opened in 1851 by Cardinal Wiseman. Fr. Knight became Canon of Hexham the next year, and served the mission till his death in March 1874.

Priests since 1874.

Rev. Francis Moverley.

„ Gerard Van-Hoof, 1879 and to date.

HARVINGTON, WORCESTERSHIRE (*Birmingham*). St. Mary.

Harvington Hall, near Kidderminster, was in the possession of the Packington family, *temp.* James I. The estate came to the Throckmortons through the Yates, and the old mansion is described as possessing a curious priests' hiding-place under the staircase. Fr. Sylvester Jenks was chaplain to the Yates family here from 1686 to about 1688, when James II. made him one of his preachers and brought him to London. In 1713 he was chosen by Propaganda to be Vicar Apostolic of the Northern District, with the title of Bishop of *Callipolis, in partibus*, but died before consecration. On, June 19, 1832, Fr. Brownlow, priest, of the mission, was unanimously chosen to preside at a 'Reform Gala' by the local Whig association, in place of the Anglican rector, who declined. The church was handsomely decorated with medallions of the prophets, and a wrought-iron screen erected November 1888. The Ven. John Wall, O.S.F., who suffered for the Faith at Red Hill, near Worcester, August 22, 1679, laboured in this district. A stone Calvary group in the church was blessed by Bishop Ullathorne September 1881. The Rev. Hugh Tootel, *alias* Chas. Dodd, wrote his 'Church History' while a priest here—from 1726 till his death in 1743.

Priests since 1794.

Rev. Rd. Cornthwaite, died 1803.

. . . . . .

,, J. Brownlow, 1824.
,, W. H. Wilson, 1877.
,, Clement Harris, 1885.
,, Philip Roskell, 1902 to date.

HARWICH, ESSEX (*Westminster*). Our Lady of Mount Carmel.

A chapel was opened in ' an upper room ' of 10 King Street in July 1864. The ' dingy and worn ' chasubles in use were described as ' unfit for elsewhere.' The present Gothic church, designed by E. Pugin, was opened by Archbishop Manning November 3, 1869. Confirmation was first administered in the mission by Bishop Weathers March 23, 1881.

Priests.

Rev. Thos. Parkinson, 1864.
,, C. Moncrieff Smyth, 1879.
,, John Davis, 1882.
,, Alf. Roche, 1885.
,, Joseph O'Sullivan, 1888.
,, Robt. Kelly, 1889.
,, Thos. Walsh, 1901.
,, T. O'Sullivan, 1905 to date.

HASLINGDEN, LANCS (*Salford*).

Fr. Thos. Marten was the first resident priest at Haslingden since the Reformation. Mass was said there in ' a wretched garret ' in the September of 1854. Catholics then numbered about 200. The beautiful silver chalice and paten used in the ' chapel ' were the gift of an anonymous benefactress. After several years Fr. T. Martin and his parishioners contrived to erect the present church, in the Gothic style. The first stone was laid Wednesday, June 22, 1859, by Bishop Turner. The same year the edifice was complete (November 13). The number of Catholics at the time of opening was about 1,400, but in 1864, owing to the cotton famine, it had fallen to 1,050.

Priests.

Rev. T. Martin, 1854.
,, M. E. Dillon, 1882.
,, Michael Buckley, 1895 to date.

HASSOP, DERBYSHIRE (*Nottingham*). All Saints.

This village was formerly the principal seat of the ancient Catholic family the Eyres of Hassop. Fr. Godfrey Cuffaud, S.J., was chaplain here in 1672. Two of the Eyre family entered the Society of Jesus —(*a*) Thomas, who died November 9, 1715, *æt.* 45 ; and (*b*) William, who served as priest in the Eastern Counties. He died in 1724. The last of the Eyres of Hassop died in 1853. They also possessed Warkworth Hall, in Northamptonshire, which was pulled down in 1804, and the estate sold. The family is now represented by the Leslies of Slindon. The present mission of Hassop dates from 1818. Fr. J. Jones was then resident priest. He served the mission till 1852, when Canon Nickolds succeeded. He celebrated the golden jubilee of his priesthood April 1885. In September 1887, through the exertions of Fr. McKey, a school was opened at Hassop. The old schools were closed about 1872. Fr. McKey did much to beautify the church, adding new altar rails, stations of the Cross, &c. It may be interesting to note that the marble altar of the church was presented by the Earl of Newburgh, who died in 1814.

Priests since 1889.

Rev. J. Browne, 1889.
„   W. Baigent, 1896.
„   J. Young, 1903.

HASTINGS, SUSSEX (*Southwark*). Our Lady Star of the Sea.

The Fathers of the Pious Society of Missions opened a temporary chapel in the High Street in March 1881. The poet, Coventry Patmore, most munificently gave £5,000 towards the building of the present church, on condition that a similar sum was subscribed by the Catholic public. Mr. Basil Champneys was the architect. The total cost was about £1,500. The handsome oak rood screen was given to the church in June 1883 by Mr. C. Patmore, in memory of his only son, Henry, who died the preceding February. In July of the same year the church was opened by Bishop Coffin, of Southwark. A lofty and well-lighted crypt runs beneath the building.

HATHERSAGE,   DERBYSHIRE *Nottingham*).   St. Michael.

A remote populous village near the Peak. The Furniss family, resident here for generations, kept the Faith alive throughout the penal times. The author was informed by the late Fr. H. Furniss, of the Josephite Congregation, that during the times of persecution a priest disguised as a prosperous yeoman used to visit his family at stated intervals. Mass was said in the best room of the farmhouse, and here the proscribed missioner would spiritually counsel and instruct the few Catholics of the district. The present chapel, a square-shaped Classical building for about 100 persons, was opened in 1806. The Eyre family also had a mansion and chapel in this district (at North Sees), both of which were plundered by Orange mobs at the Revolution.

Priests since 1825.

Rev. Edward Eyre.
„   John Ross, 1837.
„   B. Hulme, 1849.
„   Edward Whitehouse, 1853.
„   M. Le Dreau, 1855.
„   Joseph Canon Daniel, 1867.
„   Hugh O'Neill, 1879.
„   Thos. McNamee, 1883.
„   Henry Geo. Canon Dobson,
     here in 1889 to date.

N.B.—At Padley Hall, Hathersage, the then residence of John Fitzherbert, Esq., Fr. Nicholas Garlick, priest, was arrested, January 1587. He was concealed in ' a buttress-like chimney ' near the chapel, but was betrayed by John, son of his patron, Thomas Fitzherbert. Thomas was imprisoned, and only saved by his son-in-law, Thos. Eyre, Esq., paying the Queen (Elizabeth) £20,000 as ransom. Fr. Garlick was executed at Derby together with Frs. Ludlam and Simpson, July 24, 1588, ' for being ordained by authority of the Holy See and coming into the country.' —*Nicholas Garlick, martyr,* by the Rev. Edward King, S.J. (Burns & Oates, 1904).

HATTON GARDEN, LONDON, W.C. (*Westminster*). St. Peter.

The Italian Church. This fine structure is mainly due to the late Revs. Joseph Faa di Bruno and Raphael Melia, who collected upwards of £15,000 for its erection. The edifice is in the Roman Basilica style. The altar is adorned with columns of black and white marble and figures of the four Evangelists. The church, which was opened April 16, 1863, can accommodate about 3,400 persons. The interior of the church was beautifully decorated in April 1886 by Signors Arnaud and Gauthier. The sanctuary was embellished with paintings of the Holy Trinity, Our Lady, and the four Doctors of the Latin Church. The roof of the nave is painted with a picture of St. Peter bearing the Keys and Cross. The solemn reopening of the church was celebrated on Sunday, May 16, 1886; Bishop Patterson, of Emmaus, preached.

HAUNTON, TAMWORTH, STAFFS (*Birmingham*). SS. Michael and James.

Till this mission became an independent one, in 1862, it was served by the Dominicans of Hinckley. The first chapel was built at the expense of C. E. Mousley, Esq., and opened July 28, 1863. The present church was built between 1901-2 by Mr. Pye, of Clifton Hall. The style is Early English, the materials used being Hollington stone. A quaint porch adorns the north end, and an oak bell-turret the west gable.

HAVANT, HANTS (*Portsmouth*). St. Joseph.

The mission was started at Brock-

hampton, near here, in 1730. Fr. Jn. Frankland, a Lisbonian, was priest here 1734-42. He was the author of 'A Memorial of a Clerical and Missionary Life' (MS.), and died in London July 16, 1752. The chapel was erected 1790. The Sone family were the chief supporters of the mission, and one of them, Mr. John Sone, a wealthy miller, gave Bishop Douglass, V.A.L.D., £10,000 towards the building of St. Edmund's College (1795). Catholics numbered 150 in 1810. The old chapel was replaced by a Norman church for 240 persons 1839. A third structure was erected 1875. Adjoining the church is a Catholic cemetery.

Priests since 1824.

Rev. Jos. Kimbell.
  „ Jn. Kearns, 1826.
  „ D. Donovan, 1853.
  „ A. Retort, 1855.
  „ E. Reardon, 1867.
  „ W. Stone, 1884.
  „ Jn. Horegan, here in 1871.
  „ Joseph Hayes, M.R., 1895.
  „ Albert Clarke, M.R., 1903 to date.

HAWKESYARD, near RUGELEY, STAFFS (*Birmingham*). St. Thomas's Priory.

A Dominican priory and church were erected here in 1894, but the latter was not consecrated till July 1899. A fine modern example of the fifteenth-century Perpendicular reredos was inaugurated Sunday, December 23, 1900. This ornamental addition to the church was the gift of Miss Gulson.

HAYDOCK, ST. HELENS, LANCS (*Liverpool*).

The school chapel, in honour of

the English martyrs, was opened August 10, 1879, and till 1887 was served from Blackburn. In that year, a presbytery was erected 'through the energy and self-sacrifice' of Fr. E. O'Sullivan. As far back as November 1892 a fund for building a new church was started by Fr. W. Moore, and when erected the edifice will stand in a district where once laboured Fr. Edmund Arrowsmith, S.J., who died for the Faith at Lancaster August 28, 1628. Fr. T. Walmsley is the present incumbent.

HAYDON BRIDGE, NORTHUMBERLAND (*Hexham and Newcastle*). St. John of Beverley.

In 1860 a large number of Catholics were attracted to the district owing to the increasing importance of the brass and iron foundries established in the town. In 1861 a temporary chapel was opened here by Fr. Francis Kirsopp, of Haltwhistle, from which mission Haydon Bridge was served once a month. A school chapel was erected in 1873.

Priests.
Rev. Nicholas Darnell, 1873.
„ Henry Brettargh, 1885.
„ Peter Perrin, 1892.
„ Geo. Silvertop, 1903 to date.

HAYWARDS HEATH, SUSSEX (*Southwark*). Priory of Our Lady of Good Counsel.

On Monday, May 5, 1890, Bishop Butt, of Southwark, solemnly blessed the first stone of the convent church. The convent is an affiliation of the English Convent of Nazareth at Bruges, connected with the old convent at Louvain

for English ladies, founded in 1609. The first superioress of this latter foundation was Mother Margaret Clement, daughter of Margaret Giggs, the adopted daughter of the Blessed Thomas More. The nuns of Bruges fled to England in 1794 during the invasion of the Low Countries by the French, and were hospitably received by Sir Rookwood Gage, Bart., at Hengrave *a* Hall. In 1802, they returned to Bruges. The convent at Haywards Heath was established in 1886. The first chapel of the community was a room in the house, where Mass was said by their chaplain, Fr. L. Laevens. The handsome Gothic church which has taken its place is open to the public. The nuns recite the Divine office daily in choir, and also attend to the education of a limited number of young ladies.

HAZELWOOD, YORKS (*Leeds*). St. Leonard.

Sir Thos. Vavasour, of Hazelwood Hall, so distinguished himself in raising troops against the Spanish Armada that Queen Elizabeth 'would never suffer the chapel at Hazelwood to be molested where the Roman Catholic rites still continue to be celebrated.' In spite of this temporary protection, the family were great sufferers during the penal times for the Faith, Wm. Vavasour, Esq., being imprisoned and fined for having a priest in his house. Several members of the house were priests or nuns, and one of the family, Major Thomas Vavasour, fell at Marston Moor 1644, *ex parte regis.*[1] A baronetcy was

[1] Among the priests of the family were: Fr. Francis Vavasour, Franciscan, 1672; Henry Vavasour, died at Antwerp

conferred on the family 1628. During the Oates plot, 1679–80, one of the family, Jn. Vavasour, Esq., was prosecuted for publicly denying the fabrication. We have come upon but few facts relating to the mission. The chapel is a pre-Reformation one, and dates from 1290; the registers only from 1772.

Priests.

Rev. Wm. Daniel, 1772.
„ James Melling, 1780.
„ Wm. Chew, 1806.
„ Robt. Tate, 1832.
„ J. C. Fisher, 1840.
„ Robt. Canon Tate, 1853.
„ Michael Fryer, 1863.
„ Philip Vavasour, 1866.
„ Xavier de Vacht, 1874.
„ Augustin Collingwood, 1877.
„ Gustave Thonon, 1885.
„ John Bradley, 1892.
Mission served from Tadcaster since 1898.

HEATON NORRIS, LANCS (*Salford*).
The district, like the other 'Heatons' of Lancashire, is said to have given its name to the ancient Catholic family of Heaton, the owners of Lastock Hall (*q.v.*). This mansion was taken from them by a ruse of the Andertons, who in turn lost the property for their share in the rising of 1715. The mission, however, is purely modern. The first chapel, opened August 18, 1867, did duty till the erection of the existing church, in the Gothic style, opened by Bishop Bilsborrow in 1897.

1660; Fr. Wm. Vavasour, S.J., *alias* Thwinge, died 1683. Among the nuns were: Theresa Vavasour, Abbess of St. Clare at Rouen, died 1779; Mary, Abbess at Brussels, 1660, &c., &c.

Priests.
Rev. Jn. Tracy, 1867.
„ Wm. Malone, 1874.
„ Michael Morris, 1877.
„ Francis Reichart, 1885 to date.

HEBBURN, DURHAM. St. Aloysius.
Founded 1871. This mission is due to Fr. Geo. Meynell (1817–97). The present church was opened in 1888.
Priests.
Rev. James Corboy, 1871.
„ Peter Ward, 1879.
„ Matthew Toner, D.D., 1882 to date.

HEBDEN BRIDGE, YORKS (*Leeds*). St. Thomas of Canterbury.
Mission commenced from Halifax in 1885, and served by the priests there till 1889, when the present rector, Fr. Max. Tillmann, was appointed. The small but sufficient church was opened in 1897.

HECKMONDWIKE, YORKS (*Leeds*).
In 1859 Fr. O'Leary, of Dewsbury, finding a large number of poor Catholics engaged in the woollen and carpet manufactures in the town, hired a room for a chapel. It continued to be served from the parent mission till about 1870, when Fr. Stephen Dolan was appointed. A school chapel was erected 1873. Subsequent rectors:
Rev. Thos. Parkin, 1885.
„ D. O'Sullivan, 1890.
„ Patrick Hickey, 1898.
„ Joseph Russell, 1903 to date.

P

HEDON, near HULL, YORKS (*Middlesbrough*). SS. Mary and Joseph.

The chapel was built in 1803 by Fr. Joseph Swinburne, who received a sum of money for the purpose from Francis Constable, Esq. Fr. Swinburne was at Douai at the time of the Revolution, and was among the number of English students imprisoned at Dourlens. Ordained at Crook Hall in 1800, he resided as pastor at Hedon till 1838, when he retired to a small house near the chapel. His successor was Fr. W. Parsons.

Priests.
Rev. J. Swinburne, 1800.
„ W. Parsons, 1838.
„ Hy. Newsham, 1840.
„ Wm. Parsons, 1844.
„ Robt. Canon Tate, D.D., 1852.
„ J. C. Fisher, 1854.
„ John Leadbitter, 1885.
„ David Smith, 1889 to date.

HEMSWORTH, YORKS (*Leeds*).
Mission served from Ackworth 1893-5.

Priests.
Rev. J. Speet, 1896.
„ L. Leteux, 1898 to date.

HENDON, LONDON, N.W. (*Westminster*). Our Lady of Dolours.

The first stone was laid in July 1861 by Dr. Morris, Bishop of *Troy.* Mgr. Manning preached on the occasion. It was opened for worship in 1862. The high altar was erected and the walls of the nave decorated with paintings from the designs of Mr. Redmond Doran September 1865.

Priests.
Rev. Mgr. Edward Clifford, 1861.
„ Geo. Carter, here in 1871 and to date.

HENLEY-ON-THAMES, OXFORDSHIRE (*Birmingham*).

For some remarks on the early history of Catholicity in this district, *see* STONOR. In 1888 a mission-house, No. 6 Caxton Terrace, was acquired as chapel and presbytery, and placed under the care of Fr. J. Bacchus, the present rector.

HEREFORD, HEREFORDSHIRE (*Newport*). St. Francis Xavier.

In the reign of James I. ' Fawn Hope,' an old mansion a few miles south-east of Hereford, was the occasional resting-place of a few missionary priests. During the course of 1626, the then Bishop of Hereford was instructed to effect the arrest of George Berrington, O.S.B., and Geo. Hanmer, S.J., ' two Romish priests who do lurk near Hereford.' Both priests, however, escaped the pursuivants, the former, Fr. Berrington, surviving till May 1664. Fr. Walter Kemble, O.S.B.—a relative of the martyr Fr. John Kemble—died at Fawn Hope in 1633. The first Catholic chapel at Hereford since the Reformation was built by Fr. Wm. Horne, 1790, and licensed by order of Quarter Sessions October 17, 1791. This structure was in Broad Street, and continued ' as a public chapel or place of worship for the exercise of the Popish religion ' till 1838, when the Jesuits built the present handsome church, in the Classical style, at a cost of over £16,000. The architect was

Mr. C. Day, but the splendid high altar is the work of Fr. Geo. Jenkins, S.J. The congregation numbered 400 in 1856.

Priests of the Mission.

Fr. Wm. Clarke, S.J. (died at Hereford February 6, 1734, *æt.* 65).

„ T. Butler, S.J. (died at Hereford 1774).

Hon. and Rev. John Butler, S.J. (Lord Cahir) (died 1786, *æt.* 59).

Fr. Wm. Horne, S.J. (died November 13, 1799).

„ Wm. Anderton (died September 28, 1823).

„ W. Cotham, 1823.

„ Lovet, 1828.

„ Hy. Brigham, 1830.

„ Richard Boyle, 1836.

„ Wm. Waterworth, 1843.

„ Francis Jarrett, 1855.

„ W. Scarisbrick, O.S.B., 1858.

Rev. F. V. Canon Spears, 1862.

„ Chas. Dolman, O.S.B., here in 1875 to date.

HERNE BAY, KENT. Our Lady of the Sacred Heart.

The foundation stone of the Passionist Church was laid in June 1889, and the building was solemnly dedicated by Bishop Butt, of Southwark, Thursday, June 26, 1890. The style is Early Gothic, the seating capacity of the church being for 400 persons. The sermon on the occasion of the opening was preached by Canon Murnane, who took for his subject 'Christ Crucified.' The church was consecrated August 10, 1897.

HERNE HILL, LONDON, S.E. SS. Philip and James.

A plain Romanesque church, in Poplar Walk, was opened the end of May 1906. Fr. James Lonergan, late of Eltham, is the rector.

HERONS GHYLL, SUSSEX. St. John's.

A chapel, with elementary school attached, was solemnly opened on Sunday, October 3, 1880. The buildings were the munificent gift of the Duke of Norfolk. The present church, in the Early English style, was erected in 1897, and consecrated September 7, 1904, by Bishop Amigo, of Southwark. The building stands on the estate of Jas. Hope-Scott, Esq., M.P., who defrayed the cost of erection.

HERTFORD (*Westminster*). The Immaculate Conception and St. Joseph.

The site of this church, which stands on that of the old Benedictine Priory of St. Mary's, was acquired in August 1858. The mission, which was started in the autumn of the same year by Fr. Herbert, afterwards Cardinal Vaughan, was at the time of its foundation the only one in the county after St. Edmund's, Old Hall. At first, Mass was said in a stable loft, the number of Catholics being about 300. The stone of the present church was laid October 18, 1858, by Cardinal Wiseman. The consecration of the building by Archbishop Manning took place on Friday, October 16, 1866, amidst a distinguished Catholic gathering. The mission of Hertford is greatly indebted to Fr. Francis Stanfield, who collected funds for the building of the church and otherwise consolidated the good work initiated by Fr. Vaughan.

P 2

HETHE, OXON. (*Birmingham*).
Holy Trinity.

The Fermors of Hethe House, Tusmore, in this parish were long the mainstay of Catholicity in this district. Like the rest of the Catholic nobility and gentry, they endured constant persecution for the old religion. The old mansion contained an ingenious hiding-place for the priest, the entrance to which was a trapdoor concealed by a dummy window-sill. The last of the family, Wm. Fermor, Esq., died November 28, 1828, aged fifty-seven. The estate passed to protestants, and the chapel was closed. The last chaplain there was Fr. Corbishley. A new mission was then started by Fr. A. Maguire, who appealed to the public for funds, and so successfully that the present chapel was opened, May 22, 1832, by Bishop Walsh. A large congregation attended, upwards of £62 being subscribed towards the building fund.

Priests.

Rev. Alfred Maguire, 1831.
„ Joseph Robson, 1847.
„ P. Sweeny, here in 1872.
„ J. Bonner, 1888 to date.

HEXHAM, NORTHUMBERLAND (*Hexham and Newcastle*). St. Mary.

A mission has long been in existence here. In 1687 a Franciscan residence was established under the title of St. Anthony of Padua. Mr. Ben Carr, a gentleman residing in the town, gave the site. The presides or superiors in succession were :

Fr. Geo. Golding, 1687–95.
„ Geo. Goodyer, 1695.
Bernardine Metcalfe, 1698.

Fr. Constantine Jackson, 1701.
„ B. Metcalfe, 1717.
„ Gregory Jones, 1719.
„ Bonaventure Hutchinson, 1725.
„ Peter Gordon, 1729.
„ B. Metcalfe, 1731.
„ Pacificus Baker, 1734.
„ Lawrence Robinson, 1737.
„ Bernard Yates, 1743.
„ P. Gordon, 1746.
„ B. Hutchinson, 1749.
„ Leo Francis, 1752.
„ Paul Dixon, 1758.
„ Robt. Painter, 1761.
„ Bernard Yates, 1764.
„ Henry Bishop, 1767.
„ Joachim Arnold, 1770.
„ Alexius Whalley, 1771.
„ Chas. Juliaeus, 1773.
„ Thos. Cottrell, 1776.
„ Hy. Bishop, 1779.
„ Bruno Babe, 1781.
„ Lawrence Hall, 1782.
„ Angelus Ravenhill, 1791.
„ Bernardine Fleet, 1793.
„ Andrew Weetman, 1794.
„ Paschal Harrison, 1800.
„ Alex. Whalley, 1805.
„ Thos. Cottrell, 1806.
„ Alex. Whalley, 1808.
„ B. Fleet, 1809–12.

No further appointments.

Concerning the early history of the secular mission of Hexham we have not been able to obtain any information. Fr. Geo. Gibson was here about 1751. He also assisted many of the Catholics about Nafferton, and in order to give employment to a number of poor boys and girls of the district established a woollen spinning manufactory at Hexham. This excellent priest died at Hexham December 3, 1778, 'universally regretted.' In 1762 he was assisted for a short time by Fr. N. Leadbitter, O.P., and afterwards by Fr. Francis Houghton, of the same Order. Long before this the priest at Hexham was 'Mr. Thompson,' who resided at the house of Mr. Rymer, a merchant of the town, about 1716. Fr. Aug. Noel died 1812.

HEYWOOD, LANCS (*Salford*). St. Joseph.

Mission inaugurated 1854; church opened by Bishop Turner 1856. Catholic population, 2,200.

Priests.

Rev. R. Hubbersty, 1854.

„ Arthur MacCann, 1855.

„ Wm. Bradley, 1892.

„ C. W. Poole, 1898 to date.

HIGHGATE, LONDON, N. (*Westminster*). St. Joseph's Retreat.

On January 29, 1849, Fr. Ivers, of St. Alexis' Church, Kentish Town, gave a lecture on Catholic doctrine at 17 High Street, Highgate, but the meeting was broken up by 'a vile rabble.' In June 1858, the Passionist Fathers acquired a house and site for a church in Highgate, which was commenced in 1860. In January 1859 the temporary chapel was already too small for the wants of the congregation. The church was completed in 1863, and handsomely decorated August–September 1880, under the direction of Mr. A. Vicars. On Sunday, August 28, 1887, a meeting of gentlemen of the congregation, presided over by Fr. Gerrard, C.P., was held to consider the subject of a new church. It was unanimously resolved that 'a new church be built, and that an iron building be used for worship till it should be completed.' In 1863 the Catholics of Highgate comprised forty-three families; and in 1886 the Catholic population amounted to 1,500, notwithstanding that

missions had been opened at Hendon, Finchley, and other places formerly served by St. Joseph's. When the present church was commenced, Pope Leo XIII. 'signed with his own hand a special Benediction for all who helped in the good work.' The building was opened in September 1889. It provides seating accommodation for 1,000 persons. On each side of the nave are processional aisles 6 ft. wide. There are six side chapels. The dome, walls, and ceiling are richly painted with scenes from the Sacred Passion, death of St. Joseph, &c., the latter by M. Laby. The high altar was exhibited at the Paris Exhibition of 1889.

HIGH WYCOMBE, BUCKS (*Northampton*). St. Augustine Archbishop of England.

Fr. Herbert Beale, of Dawsfield, commenced this mission in September 1889. On Sunday evening, September 21, of that year, he gave a lecture on 'Roman Catholics' in the South Bucks Auction Mart to a large audience, almost entirely protestant. The lecture was much appreciated. Mass was said for the first time in a room fitted up as a chapel on Sunday, November 10, 1889. The chalice used by Fr. Beale was a jubilee offering to Pope Leo XIII., who gave it to the Bishop of Northampton for missionary purposes. The church, in the Perpendicular Gothic style, was opened recently. Fr. J. Flint is the present rector.

HINCKLEY, LEICESTERSHIRE (*Nottingham*). St. Peter's Priory.

The domestic chapel of the Turvilles at Aston Flamville Hall, near Hinckley, served the mission during the penal times. Fr. J. Clarkson, O.P., was priest here from 1734 to 1747, and again from 1757-8. Fr. Mat. Norton, also a Dominican, who was here in 1759, removed the mission to Hinckley in 1765. When the Revolution drove the English Dominicans from Bornhem (Belgium) to England Hinckley became a priory. Fr. C. Caestrick, O.P., built a chapel on a scale then considered 'preposterously large.' The present church and priory were erected 1824-5. Till 1852 the house was a school for Catholic boys. In 1885 it was reconstituted as the Dominican novitiate. A tower, chancel, and sacristies were added to the church the same year.

HINDLEY, WIGAN, LANCS (*Liverpool*). St. Benedict.

The mission commenced in 1727 in a chapel at Lowe Hall. It was removed to Strangeways 1773. In 1789 Peter and Nicholas Marsh, father and son, subscribed a handsome sum for the establishment of a new mission at Hindley. In consideration of the gift, the Marsh family was assigned seats near the altar rails. The family is now represented by the Marsh-Carrs. The chapel, with various additions and improvements, served down to 1869, when the present church was opened.

Priests.
Rev. Rowland Lacon, 1789.
  ,, Thos. Appleton, —.
  ,, Wm. Corlett, 1837.
  ,, Richard Cyprian Tyrer, 1863.
  ,, John Brown, here in 1871.
  ,, John Cuthbert Murphy, 1874.
  ,, Francis Hickey, 1882.
  ,, James Sanders, 1888.

Rev. John Cody, 1890.
  ,, Arthur O'Hare, 1892.
  ,, Hubert Murphy, 1893.
  ,, Geo. Clarke, 1895 to date.

HITCHIN, HERTS (*Westminster*).

This mission was commenced by the Fathers of the Institute of St. Andrew at Barnet, who opened a temporary chapel here at 46 Old Park Road in 1893. The present church, in the Nightingale Road, was opened in 1902. The same year Cardinal Vaughan gave the charge of the district to the congregation of St. Edmund of Pontigny, Fr. T. M. Aubin being the first and present superior.

HODDESDON, HERTS (*Westminster*). St. Monica's Priory.

For some notice of the English Augustinian Canonesses Regular of St. John Lateran, *see* NEWTON ABBOT. In 1886 a house of the Order was established at South Mimms, near Barnet. In 1898 Rawdon House, Hoddesdon, was acquired, and the community removed to here from South Mimms the same year. The Rev. E. Tunstall is the chaplain.

HOLBORN, LONDON, W.C. (*Westminster*). St. Etheldreda's, Ely Place.

John de Kirkeby, Bishop of Ely 1286-90, left by will to his successors 'a messuage' in the parish of St. Andrew's, Holborn. During the episcopate of William de Luda, who came after him, the chapel of Ely Place was built, between 1290 and 1299. The London palace of the Bishops of Ely, which adjoined, was frequently the scene of sumptuous feasts, given during term time to such personages as the serjeants-at-law, benchers of Gray's Inn, &c. In the cloisters of Ely Place, Henry VIII. is said to have first met Cranmer. After the Reformation, the palace was little used by the protestant occupants of the See of Ely, and, with the chapel, was leased about 1608 to Gondomar, the famous Spanish ambassador. Mass was once more restored, to the great delight of the persecuted Catholics of London. Here died the saintly Louisa de Caravajal, who left her country, Spain, to assist the long-suffering faithful in England ; and here, too, was celebrated before James I., Gondomar, and their suites, the last passion play ever given in England. Bishop Wren, of Ely, uncle of the famous architect, suffered a long confinement from 1640 to 1660 at Ely Place for introducing Catholic practices into his diocese. In 1772, the then Bishop of Ely was empowered to sell the estate, which passed to Mr. C. Cole, an architect, who built the houses in Ely Place, the chapel being preserved as a place of worship for the residents. In 1844 the chapel passed into the hands of the Welsh Episcopalians. About thirty years later, in consequence of a lawsuit, the whole of the property was sold, when the church was bought by Fr. Lockheart, of the Order of Charity, for £5,400. Thus was the place again restored to Catholic hands. After considerable restoration, the building was reopened for worship by Cardinal Manning on June 23, 1879. The church, which, as we have remarked, was founded at the close of the thirteenth century, is one of the most beautiful in England. It is lighted by mag-

nificent east and west windows, the former presented by the Duke of Norfolk, the latter by E. Bellasis, Esq., Lancaster Herald, E. de Lisle, and other benefactors. The east window displays Our Lord robed as High Priest and King, attended by Our Lady, St. Joseph, St. Etheldreda, and St. Bridget. That to the west depicts Cardinal John Fisher, Thomas More, and the monks of the Charterhouse, who suffered under Henry VIII. Beneath the high altar is a jewelled reliquary containing a portion of the hand of St. Etheldreda, Abbess of Ely, who died 679. It was discovered in a priests' hiding-place in a Sussex farmhouse on the estate of the Duke of Norfolk. The choir at the end of the church is supported by a beautiful Gothic screen, the work of the late Mr. Bentley. In the sanctuary, near the south entrance, is a brass tablet in memory of Fr. W. Lockhart, B.A. (Oxon.), rector of St. Etheldreda's from 1879 till his death in August 1892. Beneath the church is a dark and spacious crypt, which serves as a chapel for daily Mass, confessions, &c. The congregation of the church, which before the pulling down of neighbouring courts and alleys to make way for business houses, &c., was very numerous, is now only about 1,000.

HOLLINWOOD, LANCS (Salford).

The church was opened December 21, 1878. Before the opening of the church, the temporary chapel was in Maple Street. Catholic population about 1,336.

Priests.

Rev. Christian Müller.
  ,, Thomas Walsh, 1880.
  ,, Bartholomew Flynn, 1888.
  ,, Francis Oakes, 1904 to date.

HOLLOWAY, LONDON, N. (*Westminster*). The Sacred Heart of Jesus.

A mission was established at 5 Albany Place in 1854 by Canon Oakeley, of Islington. After a few months, a larger chapel was established at 19 Cornwall Place, and opened June 11, 1855, by Canon Maguire, V.G. A fine bell was presented by J. Mears, Esq., and much material assistance rendered to the mission by the Countess of Shrewsbury. The chapel, however, was merely a front and back parlour thrown into one, and was described in 1868 as the most wretched place of Catholic worship in the Westminster diocese. The late Canon Keens, who came as rector that year, managed to secure a site for church and schools by March 1869, at a cost of £1,500. The present church, in the Geometrical Gothic style, was opened by Cardinal Manning on August 18, 1870. Nave and chancel measure about 90 ft. Schools for 200 children were opened about the same time. F. H. Pownall was the architect. The Catholic population in 1868 was estimated at 3,000. New schools were built in 1905 at a total cost of £5,500. Electric light installed in church and schools 1900.

Priests.

Rev. — Dale, 1855 (first resident priest).

„ Emeric Podolski, 1856 (chaplain to the British Polish Legion during the Crimean war, 1854–6; again at Holloway 1856).

„ Cornelius Canon Keens, 1868.

„ Wm. Dolan, 1871.

„ Thos. Carey, M.R., 1901.

HOLME-ON-SPALDING MOOR, YORKS (*Middlesbrough*). St. John the Baptist.

The date of the foundation of this mission is set down as 1743, though chaplains were here as early as 1670. The place is one of the residences of the noble family of Stourton. Lewis in his 'Topographical Dictionary' says that the Vavasours in Catholic times established cells on the moor for two monks to act as guides to travellers. Fr. J. Le Grand, O.S.B., established a permanent chapel and commenced the register 1743. A new chapel was opened May 1766. The Canonesses of the Holy Sepulchre had a convent here from 1794 to 1796, when they removed to Dean House, Salisbury.

Priests.

Rev. Edw. Booth, 1670.

„ Lawrence Ireland, S.J., 1673.

„ Gervase Littleton, 1698.

„ — Price, 1723.

„ Ar. Baker, O.S.F., left 1743.

„ Jos. Le Grand, O.S.B., 1743.

„ Jn. Fisher, O.S.B., 1743.

„ Andrew Ryding, O.S.B., 1788.

„ Jn. Storey, O.S.B., 1792.

„ Thos. Marsh, O.S.B., 1795.

„ Edw. Clarkson, O.S.B., 1798.

„ Jn. Turner, O.S.B., 1815.

„ Edw. Glassbrook, O.S.B., 1843.

„ Thos. Cockshoot, O.S.B., 1846.

„ Nicholas Hodgson, O.S.B., 1858.

„ Thos. Shepherd, O.S.B., 1860 (?).

„ Chas. Holohan, O.S.B., 1862.

Seculars.

„ Gerald Shanahan, 1864.

„ Jas. Dolan, 1876.

„ Jn. Doud, 1881.

„ S. O'Hare, 1884.

„ Aloysius Maes, 1897.

„ Geo. de Stoop, 1901 to date.

HOMERTON, LONDON, N.E. (*Westminster*). Immaculate Heart and St. Dominic.

A chapel was opened in Sidney Terrace by Fr. (Canon) G. Akers, M.A., 1873. The present church, in the Italian style, was opened by Cardinal Manning October 29, 1877. Captain Salvin, of Sutton Place, Guildford, presented the marble altar. In April 1878, a new stone altar was erected in the side chapel dedicated to St. George. The building was consecrated by Bishop Weathers, of Amycla, July 2, 1884. It may be interesting to state that the edifice is modelled after that of SS. Nereus and Achilles at Rome. The church was consecrated 1884.

Priests.

Rev. G. Akers, 1873.
„ G. Langton Vere, 1877.
„ Thos. Hogan, 1885.
„ E. Meyer, 1891.
„ Clement Dunn, 1892 to date.

HONITON, DEVONSHIRE (*Plymouth*). The Holy Family.

Through the generosity of the Ladies Mary and Margaret Howard, an iron church, formerly at Heron's Ghyll, Uckfield, was removed to Honiton and erected on a site acquired from W. H. Fowler, Esq., February 1898. Before the opening of the iron chapel, Catholics worshipped at the domestic oratory in Deer Park, the residence of Lady Lindsay. Mass on the day of opening was celebrated by Fr. Allaria, C.R.L., rector of the mission, the plain chant of the service being sung by the choir from Spettisbury Priory. It may not be uninteresting to remark that a certain Dr. Marwood, who died at Honiton in 1617, was 'a good and faithful Catholic,' and one who did much to preserve the remnants of the old religion in the district during a particularly severe epoch of the penal laws.

N.B.—The mission at Deer Park was founded by the Hon. Colin Lindsay 1877. He was the author of the well-known 'Evidences for the Papacy' (Longmans 1870). Mr. Lindsay died 1892, *æt.* 73.

HOOTON, CHESHIRE (*Shrewsbury*). St. Mary of the Angels.

This mission, under the patronage of the Stanley family, was served by the Jesuits from about the reign of James I. till 1854. Fr. Stanislaus Green was priest at Hooton in 1701; Fr. M. Tichborne about 1735; Fr. J. Porter in 1750; Fr. J. Shaw in 1773. The new church, erected by Sir John Stanley Errington, Bart., was opened August 21, 1879. The Stanley Chantry, dedicated to the Sacred Heart, is lighted by eight handsome stained-glass windows by Meyer, of Munich. The church, which will accommodate about 250 persons, was consecrated July 1883. The design was planned by Mr. E. G. Tarvor, of London.

Priests since 1805.

Rev. Thos. Collingridge, 1803.
„ Thos. Crowe, 1849.
„ P. F. Baron, 1851.
„ Wm. Canon Hilton, V.G., 1866.
„ Geo. Canon Clegg, 1876.
„ Chas. Langdon, 1888.
„ G. B. Provost Clegg, 1903 to date.

HORNBY, LANCS (*Liverpool*). St. Mary.

From about the reign of James I.

to 1762, the chapel at Robert Hall, the seat of the Cansfields, served the districts of Hornby, Claughton, and Caton. The Cansfields were staunch supporters of Charles I., and suffered much in the cause of that monarch. The priest at Robert Hall from 1699 to 1740 was Fr. Edward Gilpin. His successor was Fr. Jas. Gandy. Fr. E. Bennett, who was chaplain in 1745, showed such partiality for the cause of Prince Charles Edward Stuart during the rebellion of that year, that he had to retire abroad for some time. He afterwards returned to his pastoral duties at Hornby, dying at Scarborough in 1765. In 1762 Mrs. Ann Fenwick, relict of John Fenwick, Esq., got leave of Bishop Petre, V.A., to fit up a chapel at her residence, Hornby Hall. Fr. Thos. Butler was appointed priest of the mission, which then numbered 115 persons. After Mrs. Fenwick's death in 1777, the Hall passed into other hands ; but Fr. Butler, with the funds she had placed at his disposal, purchased a house as chapel and presbytery, and continued his ministrations till his decease in 1795. The mission of Hornby is indissolubly connected with the Rev. John Lingard, D.D., the Catholic historian of England, who was priest of the place from 1811 till his death in July 1851, aged eighty-one. Much of his well-known history was written at Hornby, and here he was wont to entertain Brougham, Scarlett, Pollock, and the other leaders of the Bar whom the Northern Assizes brought into his district (Tierney's ' Memoir,' Lingard's ' History,' vol. i.). Fr. Geo. Gibson was the next priest after Dr. Lingard. The chapel was rebuilt in 1819. Fr. Gibson was succeeded in 1875 by Fr. Geo. Fisher, who was followed in 1897

by Mgr. Wm. Wrennall. In conclusion, it may be added that from the death of Fr. Butler in 1795 till the appointment of Dr. Lingard in 1811 the priests were : Abbé A. J. Legaigneur, an *émigré*, 1795-8 ; Rev. J. Worswick, 1798-1809 ; Rev. Ar. Story, 1809-11.

HORNSEY. *See* **STROUD GREEN, N.**

HORSEFORTH, YORKS (*Leeds*). Our Lady of Good Counsel.

Mission commenced 1892, and served from the Church of the Sacred Heart, Leeds, by Fr. Chas. Croskell. In 1893 it was supplied by a priest from the cathedral, and in 1895-6 from the seminary. In the last year Fr. E. Walsh was appointed rector. His successors have been: Rev. John Kalb ; Rev. Thos. Shine, to date.

HORSHAM, SUSSEX (*Southwark*). St. John, Springfield Road.

The old chapel in West Street was founded by Charles, eleventh Duke of Norfolk, about the commencement of the last century. This nobleman, although he ' conformed to the Established Church ' in 1780, was always secretly attached to the religion of his forefathers, and at his death in 1815 abjured the tenets of protestantism. The bodies of the Dukes of Norfolk always rested at the Horsham Chapel for one night when being brought from London to Arundel for interment. The last time that the old custom of bringing the ducal remains by road was observed took place at the funeral of Bernard, seventh Duke, in April 1842. For many years after the foundation of the Horsham mission it was served in conjunction with West Grinstead. The priest in charge of the place in 1827 was the Abbé Adrien Grémare. He left in 1835. The next priest was Fr. Edward Fowler. The mission was marked 'vacant' in 1850, but in 1853 the incumbent was Fr. Joseph Sidden. The services even at this time continued to be only occasional, Mass being said at Horsham on the first Sunday of each month. In 1864 it was served by the Franciscan Fathers from Crawley. The following year saw the opening of the present Gothic church (December 27), by Bishop Grant. The edifice is due to the pious munificence of the late Mina Duchess of Norfolk. Fr. H. Lawrence is the present rector.

HORWICH, LANCS (*Salford*). Our Lady of the Rosary.

The Gothic school chapel was opened by the Bishop of Salford on Sunday, July 11, 1886. The chapel is of brick, with stone dressings, and has a neat presbytery adjoining. Bishop Vaughan, at the opening, preached an effective sermon on the Rosary, which his lordship described as 'a summary of the whole Gospel.'

Priests.

Rev. Joseph Crilly, 1886.
  ,, Henry Hunt, 1899.
  ,, Michael McGrath, 1903.

HOUGHTON HALL, SANCTON, YORKS (*Middlesbrough*). The Holy Family.

There was a chapel at this, the ancient seat of the Langdale family, about the time of the accession of Elizabeth. Anthony Langdale, Esq., who died at Rome, April 10, 1577, is regarded as 'an exile on account of his faith.' Fr. John May, an alumnus of St. Omer and Valladolid, served the mission from about 1652 till his death, some time after 1690. The old chapel was built 1780, and the registers date from 1787. The Benedictines ceased to serve the mission 1805. The new chapel, near the Hall, was erected by the Hon. Charles Langdale, and opened February 25, 1829—the year of Catholic emancipation.

Priests.

Rev. John May, 1652 till after 1690 (immediate successors not known).
  ,, Edw. Hatton, 1730
  ,, John Holme, 1739.
  ,, Archibald Macdonald, 1766.
  ,, Edward Howard, S.J., 1770.
  ,, Thos. Slater, 1787.
  ,, Jn. Rigby, 1803.
  ,, Jas. Wrennall, 1805 (?) till 1827.
  ,, Jn. Ball, 1827.
  ,, Jn. Glover, 1830.
  ,, Henry Newsham, 1836.
  ,, Geo. Keasley, 1838.
  ,, Jn. Glover, 1842 (second time).
  ,, Robt. Canon Thompson, 1860.
  ,, Laurence McGonnell, 1861.
  ,, James Canon Wells, 1862.
  ,, Herbert Davies, 1897.

HOUGHTON - LE - SPRING, DURHAM (*Hexham and Newcastle*). St. Michael.

The mission was started 1831, Fr. Macevoy, of Maynooth, being the first resident priest. Mass was first said in a hired room, the number of Catholics in the town being estimated at between eighty and a hundred. The church was opened November 9, 1837, and in 1844 the chancel end was decorated. The site of the building was rented from Lord Durham. When Catholicity first reared its head at Houghton-le-Spring, the place was described as a locality of 'all-pervading bigotry.' The stipend of the priest was at the outset only £40 a year, and he had to struggle against a heavy mission debt. A cemetery was laid out and schools built in 1842.

Priests.
Rev. J. Macevoy, 1831.
(Served from Sunderland 1845.)
„ A. Watson, 1846.
„ Joseph Canon Browne, 1857.
„ John O'Brien, 1889 and to date.

HOUNSLOW, MIDDLESEX. SS. Michael and Marten, Burdett Lodge.

An important meeting, presided over by Mgr. Weld, was held at Hounslow early in June 1883 to consider the ways and means for building a church. The collection amounted to over £20. The new school chapel was opened by Cardinal Manning, Tuesday, August 24 1886. As far back as 1862, Mass was said for the Catholic soldiers every Sunday at the barracks. The first chaplain was Fr. C. Herdel, who resided at 6 Belgrave Terrace. The military chapel was open to civilians.

HOVE, BRIGHTON (*Southwark*). St. Peter's.

This church was opened as a chapel of ease to the mission of the Sacred Heart, Brighton, 1902. The style is Gothic. Sittings for about 200 persons. Fr. Joseph Ward has charge of the district served by the chapel.

HOWDEN, YORKS, EAST RIDING (*Middlesbrough*). The Sacred Heart.

There were about 150 Catholics at Howden in 1850, when the mission was started by Fr. R. Cook. For several years it was served from Everingham. The 'beautiful little Gothic church' was built in 1852. At the conclusion of the mission given in March 1885 by Fr. G. Seadon, C.R.P., over sixty persons enrolled themselves as associates of the Perpetual Adoration Sodality. [When Fr. Cook first went to Howden he applied for the use of the Town Hall for Mass on Sundays, but was refused. He then preached to the people from the town cross, and with such success that he was enabled to erect a temporary chapel.]

Priests.
Rev. R. Cook, 1850.
„ Thos. Danson, 1855.
„ James Butler, 1882.
„ C. Donovan, 1888.
„ Patrick O'Brien, 1890.
„ Wm. McNaughten, 1892.
„ Patrick Cronin, 1896.
„ Chas. Van Poucke, 1897 to date.

HOXTON, LONDON, N. (*Westminster*). St. Monica's Priory.

In 1863 the Augustinians returned to London at the invitation of Cardinal Wiseman. The old pre-Reformation house of the Order in London was Austin Friars, City, founded 1423. The present priory was opened by Mgr. (afterwards Cardinal) Manning, August 15, 1864, and the Decorated Gothic church two years later. Schools were erected 1870. The average attendance in 1905 was 344.

HOYLAND, NETHER BARNSLEY. YORKS (Leeds). St. Helen's Chapel.

The mission was commenced in 1864, and on Easter Monday 1865 the first stone of the school chapel was laid. The opening took place Sunday, April 22, 1865, by the Bishop of Beverley. The style is twelfth-century Gothic. The building is of stone after designs by Hadfield. Fr. C. J. Locke was priest of the mission in 1865. At the mission given at St. Helens in June 1866, by Fr. Bertrand, O.S.F., over 600 persons renewed the baptismal vows, and about eighty-three were confirmed. In 1891 the mission was served from Mortomley.

Recent Priests.

Rev. Wm. Smith, here in 1883.
„ W. J. Smith, 1892.

HUCKNALL TORKARD, NOTTINGHAMSHIRE (Nottingham). Holy Cross.

From 1879, when the mission was started, 'a building of a temporary character' served as a chapel. In September 1886, owing to the liberality of Mr. O'Hanlon, who gave £1,000, and Major Worswick, who gave £500, the new church was founded, and completed in April 1887. The style is Early Decorated Gothic. The schools adjoining, built by Major Worswick, accom-

modate about 100 pupils. The congregation was estimated at about 200 at the time of opening. The seating capacity of the building is for about 250 persons. R. C. Clarke was the architect. Fr. Rupert Macaulay, present rector.

HUDDERSFIELD, YORKS (Leeds). St. Patrick.

The mission at Huddersfield dates from 1828, when Mass was said on Sundays in a hired room over a workshop. The baptismal registers were irregularly kept for the first two or three years, owing probably to the fact that the priest baptised in private houses and entered the names later. In 1835, the chapel was commenced in the Halifax Road, Huddersfield, by Fr. James Keily, but the debt on the building was not paid off till 1861. Between October 1859 and September 1861, about £400 was collected by Fr. S. L. Wells towards new schools. These were commenced in September 1862, and opened during the course of 1863. The cost was about £800, the accommodation being for 108 boys, 128 girls, and 60 infants.

Recent Priests.

Rev. Stephen Canon Dolan, here 1891 and to date.

HULL, YORKSHIRE (Middlesbrough). St. Charles Borromeo, Jarratt Street.

In 1780, the Catholic chapel was at Posterngate. Fierce 'No Popery' riots—in imitation of the Gordon riots—broke out in June the same year, and the chapel was destroyed. The Jews afterwards obtained a lease of the site for a synagogue. The Catholics of the town, who then numbered about forty, next set up a chapel in a private house. In 1798, the Abbé Peter Francis Foucher, formerly vicar general of Aix, came to Hull from Pocklington, and built the house and chapel, opened July 26, 1799. Monseigneur de Boisgelin, Archbishop of Aix, sang High Mass in the chapel on September 22 following. The Abbé Foucher spent about £2,000 of his own money on the mission, and on returning to France in 1820 bequeathed a silver chalice, ciborium, and some fine vestments to the chapel. Miss Anne Heatley, who died 1803, was also a great benefactress to the mission. Seventy-two persons were confirmed here by Bishop Gibson, V.A., in 1808, and eighty-three by the same prelate, in October 1815. The old chapel having become inadequate was supplanted by the present handsome structure opened by Bishop Penswick in 1835. The handsome screen by Scholes is a copy of the one in the church of the *Gesu* at Rome. The title of the church was changed from that of St. Augustine to St. Charles Borromeo, 1850-1. The congregation was then estimated at 6,500. The children attending school 240 ; Baptisms, 247 ; Marriages, 47 ; Converts, 41.

Priests.

Rev. Robert Johnson, 1780.
„ Abbé P. F. Foucher, 1798. Became Canon and V.G. of Aix on returning to France, 1820.
„ John Smith, 1820.
„ Joseph Render, 1830.
„ Michael Trappes, 1848.
„ Benjamin Canon Randerson, 1874.
„ William Canon Sullivan, 1887.
„ Francis Canon Hall, V.G., 1901 to date.

HULL. St. Mary, Wilton Street.
The growth of Catholicity in Hull made a second mission necessary shortly after 1850. In January 1857, schools were opened in Dansom Lane and placed under the care of the Sisters of Mercy. A school chapel was inaugurated, March 7, 1858. The number of children attending school in 1859 was about 600. The present church superseded the chapel 1890. In August of the following year, a chapel of St. Francis was opened ' over the vault of Sir Francis Turville, K.C.M.G.,' by his widow, Baroness Lisgar.

Priests.

Rev. Luke Burke, 1858.
„ Joseph Geary, 1866.
„ George Browne, 1871.
„ Charles H. Wood, 1885.
„ James Canon Griffin, 1889 to date.

HULL, YORKS, EAST RIDING (*Middlesbrough*).
St. Patrick's Church was built in Mill Street 1871. The present church in Spring Street was opened on Thursday, September 8, 1904. The style is Romanesque. The accommodation is for 500 persons. The Bishop of Middlesbrough presided at the throne on the occasion of the opening, the sermon being preached by the Very Rev. Placid Conway, O.P. (1 Kings ix. 3).

HUNSLET, LEEDS. St. Joseph.
Erected 1859-60. The number of Catholics then at Hunslet was over 1,000. The St. Joseph's Building Society was formed that year to further the erection of the

church. The first stone was laid by the bishop of the diocese November 16, 1859. The style of the church is 'mixed Gothic'; to accommodate about 600 persons. The site formed part of the Brandling estate, and the cost of the building was about £1,600. In 1884 the Catholic population of the district was about 2,500. At the 'mission' given by the Jesuit Fathers in April 1884 upwards of 1,000 confessions were heard, 221 persons brought back to the practice of their religious duties, and 500 Holy Communions administered.

HUNSTANTON, WEST NORFOLK (Northampton). SS. Mary and Edmund, K.M.

The chapel of St. Edmund House, the convent of the Dominican nuns, who settled here in 1903, served as a place of worship for local Catholics for some time. In January 1904, Fr. E. Garnett, the chaplain, obtained a site for the badly-needed church from Alderman Hamon Le Strange, the lord of the manor, who generously gave the land free of cost. In August 1904, a temporary building—the sacristies of the future church—was opened for worship by Bishop Riddell, of Northampton. Mass was celebrated by Mgr. Scott, D.D., V.G. of Cambridge, the sermon being preached by Fr. J. Freeland (Isaiah iv. 5). At the conclusion of the Mass, the Bishop confirmed the Hon. Otway Plunket, son of Lord Louth, and two little girls—the Misses Harriet and Mary Cole.

HUNTINGDON (Northampton). St. Hubert.

The establishment of this mission in 1869 is due to some Irish horse-

dealers, who, finding no Catholic church at Huntingdon, which town they were obliged to attend every year at fair time, clubbed together and built a temporary iron chapel. Soon after its erection, the chapel was almost destroyed by a violent gale, and as early as 1882 was 'in a deplorably leaky state.' In 1901 the present handsome church was erected by George Temple Layton, Esq., late of The Croft, Mitcham, Surrey, at a cost of about £5,000. Fr. Patrick Duffy has been rector of the mission since its establishment.

HUSBANDS BOSWORTH, LEICESTERSHIRE (Nottingham). St. Mary.

In 1763, the ancient Catholic family of Turville of Aston Flamville came into the property of Husbands Bosworth, on the decease of their cousin, Maria Fortescue. The chapel at Bosworth Hall served the mission for upwards of a century. The present church was built in 1874 at the cost of Sir Francis Turville, K.C.M.G. The style is Gothic. In the chapel of St. Joseph, opening out of the north wall, repose the remains of the founder, and also the relics of his ancestor, the blessed Sir Adrian Fortescue, a Knight of St. John of Jerusalem, who suffered for the Papal supremacy, July 10, 1539. The church was redecorated August and September 1900 in a style resembling that of St. Stephen's Chapel, Westminster.

Priests of the Mission since 1825.
(1825, vacant.)
Rev. — Wilford, 1826.
  „ J. Ross, 1827.
  „ R. Bagnall, 1829.
  „ J. Jones, 1831.

Rev. E. Whitehouse, 1849.
„ Richard Raby, 1853.
„ E. Whitehouse, 1854.
In 1874 the mission was served from Market Harborough by the Rev. Richard Vandepitte.
„ Fr. A. Ryan, 1879.
„ Fredk. Wehn, 1880.
„ Wm. Farmery, 1885.
„ Jn. Salins, 1887.
„ W. Otty, 1891.
„ Jos. Fagan, 1893.

HUTTON HOUSE, CASTLE EDEN, DURHAM (*Hexham and Newcastle*). SS. Peter and Paul.

Fr. J. A. Slater, of Uskaw College, started the mission here in 1825. Before this time, the few local Catholics heard Mass at Hardwick House, long the seat of the ancient family the Maires of Hutton. The property was sold in 1824.[1] Fr. Slater built a Gothic chapel in 1832, at which time the number of communicants amounted to eighty. The old chapel did duty till 1895, when it was supplemented by a handsome church. Schools were advertised as greatly needed in October 1901, and Fr. Jackson, C.SS.R., appealed for funds to build them Sunday, October 26, the same year.

HUYTON, LANCS (*Liverpool*). St. Agnes.

A small chapel was opened here in 1856. In 1860 upwards of £200

[1] Mr. Maire was a distinguished Catholic conveyancer about 1770, when all other branches of the legal profession were closed against Catholics. The famous Charles Butler of Lincoln's Inn studied under him. Near Hardwick House was a retired cave where Mass was often said during the penal times.

was raised towards the expense of a new church. Major Molyneux-Seel gave the site in 1861. The church, which was commenced in May the same year, is in the French Gothic style, and cost £2,500. It was opened 1861.

Priests.

Rev. Canon Walmsley, 1856.
„ P. Holmes, 1859.
„ Hy. Lamon, 1882.
„ Jn. Smith, 1884.
„ Canon Holden, 1885 to date.

HYDE, CHESHIRE (*Shrewsbury*). St. Paul.

The chapel was founded 1848, in a room over a blacksmith's forge. Six years afterwards the church was opened on a site presented by Robt. Ashton, Esq., a Unitarian (July 1854). In April 1862, the church was completed, a belfry and peal of bells being added to the structure. The late M. Harnett, Esq., gave £1,000 towards the schools.

Priests.

Rev. Canon Jn. Reah, 1848.
„ Jn. Hill, 1853.
„ Hy. Hopkins, 1869.
„ Patrick Tracy, 1879.
„ Chas. Langdon, 1882.
„ Thos. Ratcliffe, 1888.
„ Jn. Thompson, 1889.
„ Jas. Hennelly, 1896.

HYTHE, KENT (*Southwark*).

As far back as 1860 Fr. Sheridan opened a mission here, assisted by the brothers Edmund and Arthur Robinson, to whom Catholicity at Dover is so much indebted. In March 1865 Fr. (now Mgr.) Goddard took up his residence at Hythe, where he laboured with much success till 1867, when the first Army chaplain was appointed to the place. From this date till 1891 the various chaplains ' made them-selves responsible for the Catholic soldiers at the School of Musketry,' the civilians being regarded as under the clergy of the neighbour-ing mission of Folkestone. In 1891 the Austin Friars settled in Hythe.

Their church was solemnly opened and dedicated by Bishop Butt, August 6, 1894. The building, which was designed by A. E. Purdie, is ' large and not ungraceful,' and is capable of accommodating at least 300 people.

Q

I

ILFORD, ESSEX (*Westminster*). SS. Peter and Paul.

The foundation stone of the church was laid by Cardinal Vaughan, May 14, 1898, and the building was opened in June 1899. Style, Perpendicular Gothic; architect, Mr. Curtis Prior; seating capacity, about 560. Prior to the opening of the church, a temporary iron building was used. In 1895 Fr. A. S. Barnes estimated the number of Catholics in the district at about six or eight. The same year, Fr. Bede, O.S.F., was sent to establish the mission, and he opened a chapel in 'a humble tenement' in Ilford Lane. Fr. Palmer is the present rector. The church was completed, and opened by Archbishop Bourne, May 31, 1906. A notable feature of the interior is the fine oak pulpit, presented by the congregation. The average school attendance is 278.

ILFRACOMBE, DEVONSHIRE (*Plymouth*). Our Lady Star of the Sea.

Fr. Walter Keily was the first to open the mission, 1874. There was no resident priest till 1876. The present church was commenced October 12, 1892, and opened January 18, 1893. A new chapel, added to the main building, was completed May 1895.

Priests.
Rev. Francis Higgins, 1876.
„ Thos. Spencer, 1879.
„ Walter Baggaley, 1888.
„ H. Bromley, 1890.
„ G. Graham.

ILKESTON, DERBYSHIRE (*Nottingham*). Our Lady and St. Thomas of Hereford.

Mass was said occasionally here from 1857 till 1861, when the mission became a permanent one. The priest at this time was Fr. C. Tasker of Glossop. The 'chapel,' however, was merely 'a room in an empty lace factory.' Ilkeston is spoken of at the time the mission was started as 'a long-neglected place.' The Catholics in 1861 numbered about 600. Three years later the chapel was served from Derby by Fr. Ar. McKenna.

Priests.
Rev. Hugh O'Neill, here in 1872.
„ Thos. Revill, 1879.
„ Patrick Conaty, 1885.
„ Philip Canon McCarthy, 1888 and to date.

ILKLEY, YORKS, WEST RIDING (*Leeds*). The Sacred Heart of Jesus.

For some time prior to August

1878, Mass was said on Sundays at Myddelton Lodge, the seat of W. Middleton, Esq. In the above-named month and year a church and school were commenced on a site near the Wharfe, presented by Mr. Middleton. The style is 'purely Old English,' with open roof. Adjoining is a cemetery. The accommodation of the church is for 220; of the school 120.

Priests since 1892.

Rev. Alf. Watson.

„ Alf. Galli, 1896 to date.

INCE BLUNDELL, LANCS (*Liverpool*). The Holy Family.

The Faith was supported here throughout the dreary time of persecution by the protection of the Ince Blundell family, many of whose members figure in the recusant rolls between 1633 and 1679. In addition to being a focus of Catholicity, Ince Blundell Hall acquired, about the middle of the eighteenth century, a deserved reputation for its fine collection of sculptures and paintings, brought together by Henry Blundell, Esq. The estates passed to the Weld family in 1837. The present Gothic church was erected in 1858.

Priests since 1824.

Rev. Thos. Berry.

„ P. Greenough, 1827.

„ Jules Maurus, 1867 (?).

„ Thos. Murphy, 1899.

„ James Hughes, 1903 to date.

INCE WIGAN, LANCS (*Liverpool*). St. William.

A chapel attached to Ince New Hall was built 1760. The chaplain from 1786 to 1818 was Fr. Joseph Higginson. The present mission was established in 1873. A temporary iron church was opened by Bishop O'Reilly, of Liverpool, in April 1881. Seating accommodation for about 620; cost of erection, £1,500. The opening of the chapel was deferred from February to April on account of the colliers' strike.

Priests.

Rev. P. Clarke, 1873.

„ Michael Naughten, 1877.

„ Jeremiah Dowling, 1879.

„ John Hanly, 1885.

„ Geo. Swarbrick, 1904 to date.

INGATESTONE HALL, ESSEX (*Westminster*). SS. Erconwald and Aedilburga.

Ingatestone Hall came into the possession of the Petre family at the time of the suppression of the religious houses (1536-9). The domestic chapel was described in 1857 as being 'a small building with a gallery over the entrance.' It was redecorated in 1852. In 1855 a priests' hiding-place was discovered. Fr. A. Paige was chaplain at Ingatestone Hall prior to his execution for the Faith at Chelmsford in 1590. Fr. R. Manning, D.D., wrote his famous 'Discourses' at Ingatestone when chaplain there early in the eighteenth century. Before the opening of missions at Southend, Shoebury, &c., these places were served by the priest at Ingatestone. The church of Ingatestone Hall, after being closed some months for the purpose of enlargement, was solemnly reopened on Sunday, October 18, 1863. The alterations were all skilfully carried out by D. C. Nicholls, Esq., of London.

N.B.—The body of the unfortunate Earl of Derwentwater rested for one night at Ingatestone Hall after his execution on February 24, 1716, for participation in the Jacobite rebellion of the preceding year. The Earl's remains were interred at his ancestral home, Dilston, in Northumberland, but in 1874 were removed to Thorndon Hall (*q.v.*).

IPSWICH (*Northampton*). St. Pancras.

In 1793 the Abbé Louis Pierre Simon, an *émigré*, came to Ipswich, where he hired a house and turned one of the rooms into a chapel. For a time this small place of worship sufficed for the few Catholics of the town. By 1820, the congregation had so increased that he found it necessary to build a chapel for 150 persons. This structure formed the transepts of a still larger church consecrated by Bishop Walsh, V.A.M.D., October 10, 1838. The style was Perpendicular Gothic; accommodation for about 600. The building stood on the site of the Black Friars' monastery, plundered in the reign of Edward VI. A school for children was opened about the same time. In consequence of the growth of Catholicity in and around Ipswich, a still larger church became necessary, and the present building was opened by Bishop Amherst, of Northampton, June 12, 1861. The building, which was designed by Hadfield & Goldie, after the Geometric style, will accommodate about 1,000.

Priests.

Rev. Louis Simon, 1793.
„ Ignatius Collingridge, 1840.
„ James O'Neill, 1842.
„ M. Lane, 1849.
„ W. Marshall, 1851.
„ J. C. Kemp, 1855.

Rev. Joseph Faa di Bruno, here 1871.
„ Aemilianus Kirner, 1874.
„ Joseph Bannin, 1879.
„ Wm. Canon Blackman, 1882.
„ Patrick Canon Rogers, 1885 to date.

IRLAM, MANCHESTER, LANCS (*Salford*). St. Theresa, Liverpool Road.

This became a separate mission in 1900. The new schools, which were built 1901-2, will accommodate about 100 children. The old school chapel has been fitted up as a church, and is under the spiritual direction of Fr. A. Van der Beek.

ISLEWORTH, MIDDLESEX (*Westminster*). The Immaculate Conception and St. Bridget.

The noble family of Shrewsbury, premier Earls of England, long owned a residence here on the site of the present mission in Shrewsbury Place. Being staunch Catholics, they had a chapel in the mansion, which was attended by the few local adherents of the ancient Faith. The baptismal register dates from 1675. The house was a residence of the family as late as 1761, but was probably sold soon after. A portion of the premises was reserved for a chapel and priest's house. This old chapel (40 ft. by 16 ft.) was 'badly constructed and scantily supplied.' The present building was erected at the expense of the late Mgr. Weld. It consists of a nave and galleries, the style being Romanesque and the accommodation for about 200. The old chapel forms the sacristy. Schools were built about the same time by the same reverend benefactor. The Catholic population of the district is about

500. In March 1841, the nuns of the Faithful Companions of Jesus Congregation opened a high-class convent school at Gumley House, Isleworth, a fine old mansion, formerly the residence of General Gumley. The convent has since been in great repute as an educational establishment.

N.B.—Mgr. Weld, who did so much for the mission, was a near kinsman and former secretary of Cardinal Weld (died 1837). The Monsignor was a man of saintly life, and the well-known author of the treatise on 'The Love of God.'

Priests since 1790.

Rev. Geo. Bruning, 1790 (?), *d.* 1902.

„ Anthony Warcing, 1810 (died 1855).

„ S. Faenza, 1855.

„ Mgr. Francis Weld, 1855.

„ Thos. Francis Gorman, 1897 to date.

ISLINGTON, LONDON, N. (*Westminster*). St. John the Evangelist.

The church, a Norman structure, designed by Scoles, was opened June 26, 1843, by Bishop Wiseman. Upwards of 2,000 persons were present, including the Earl of Arundel and the Hon. E. Petre, Hon. E. Jerningham, the Ladies Camoys, Lovat, &c., &c. Bishop Wiseman preached a powerful sermon on the progress of Catholicity in England since the penal times. Canon Oakeley, M.A., was appointed priest of the mission in 1850. The church was consecrated in June 1873. The apse was adorned by Mr. Armitage, R.A., with frescoes representing Our Lord and the Apostles – a design characterised by the *Athenæum* as 'a work of great merit.' The church, which had become somewhat dilapidated, was thoroughly restored and beautified in the autumn of 1884. New stations of the Cross were erected, and a handsome screen under the choir gallery set up. In August 1887, Mr. Armitage's great picture, 'The Institution of the Franciscan Order,' replaced a fresco of the same subject set up in 1859. Canon Oakeley died January 29, 1880, and was succeeded by Canon Leopold Pycke, the present incumbent.

J

JARROW-ON-TYNE, DURHAM (*Hexham and Newcastle*). St. Bede's.

The stone was laid, November 1860, by the Bishop of Hexham. The building of this fine church was largely due to Fr. Kelly, who collected much of the money required. The church was opened early in 1862. In 1883 the Catholics of Jarrow had increased to 6,000. To meet the growth of the congregation the church was enlarged to double its original size. A new high altar and exquisitely carved reredos were erected in the church in April 1885. The reredos is said to contain no fewer than 2,000 pieces of stone, each symbolically carved.

Priests.

Rev. Geo. Meynell, 1862.

,, Martin Hayes, 1885 and to date.

K

KEIGHLEY, YORKS (*Leeds*). St. Anne.

The mission was established 1835, and the church—described at the time as 'by far the handsomest building in Yorkshire'—was opened by Bishop Briggs, V.A., November 21, 1840. Some stained-glass windows were presented to the church in 1841.

Priests.

Rev. Wm. Hampson, 1835.
„ Robt. Gibson, 1836.
„ T. Walsh, 1844.
„ James Cullimore, 1854.
„ Timothy O'Connell, 1860.
„ Patrick Kiernan, here 1871.
„ Herbert Duke, 1881.
„ Edw. Canon Watson, 1888 to date.

KELVEDON, ESSEX (*Westminster*). St. Mary Immaculate and the Holy Angels.

The present mission was established in 1875, mainly owing to the munificence of the late R. Rann, Esq., J.P.—formerly an Anglican clergyman—who built the church. The building was consecrated October 24, 1891. A series of fine stained-glass windows which light the church commemorate the deceased relatives of the donor. Prior to the opening of the mission, the domestic chapel of the Wright family of Kelvedon Hall was attended by local Catholics. Fr. John Mannock, O.S.B., the well-known author of 'The Poor Man's Catechism,' was chaplain here from 1759 till his death, November 30, 1764, aged eighty-three. One of his predecessors was Fr. Sebastian Redford, S.J. (1756-8), author of 'An Important Enquiry.'

KEMERTON, GLOUCESTERSHIRE (*Clifton*). St. Bennet.

This mission can claim descent from the ancient one at Beckford, where the Lee family maintained a chapel. Fr. Isaac Gibson, S.J., died here in November 1738. The Hon. and Rev. R. Dormer was also here for a time. Other priests were Fr. Placid Bennett, O.S.B. (1783), Abbé Louvelle (1795?), Thos. Kenyon, J. Harrison (—), and Wm. Jolly (1825). After the opening of the church at Kemerton, July 19, 1843, the Catholics of Beckford became absorbed in the new congregation. The erection is due to the pious munificence of the Eystons, Tidmarshes, and Throckmortons. Fr. Samuel Day was the first rector, being followed in 1848 by Fr. Peter Ridgeway, who was here till 1896, when Fr. Alph. Thomas, O.S.B., the present rector, was appointed.

KENDAL, WESTMORLAND (*Hexham and Newcastle*). Holy Trinity and St. George.

The mission was established 'about 1724' through the efforts of the Roydon family (*see* DODDING GREEN). The register dates from 1762. In 1800 Fr. Thos. Wilkinson founded schools in Stramongate. These were rebuilt by Dean Gibson to accommodate 500 scholars, and are said to be among the finest of their kind in the North of England.

Priests since 1800.

Rev. T. Wilkinson (assisted by various curates after 1840; died 1857).

„ James Gibson, 1857.

„ Wm. Stevenson, 1895 to date.

KENILWORTH, WARWICKSHIRE (*Birmingham*). St. Augustine.

This church, which is one of Pugin's 'earliest attempts at Gothic revival,' was commenced in 1841, but not completed till the summer of 1852. It was built at the expense of the Amherst family, then resident at Fieldgate House. The last member of this family was Fr. W. J. Amherst, S.J., author of the 'History of Catholic Emancipation,' who died in April 1904. He was brother of Bishop Amherst, of Northampton (1858–79). The building was restored during the summer of 1904, and consecrated by Bishop Ilsley, of Birmingham, on September 1 of the same year. The handsome brass sconces for the candles used in the consecration were presented by Major Berkeley and family, of Fieldgate House.

KENSAL GREEN, LONDON, N.W. (*Westminster*).

Thirty acres of land, adjoining the celebrated protestant burial ground, were consecrated as a Catholic cemetery in June 1858 by Bishop Morris, of *Troy*, assisted by the Hon. and Rev. E. Stonor, now Archbishop of *Trebizond*, Canon O'Neal, &c. The mission appears to have been started in the district about 1860, the first priest being the Rev. John Moore. His successor in 1863 was the Rev. Richard Bennett. When the Church of Our Lady of the Holy Souls was opened in 1872, the mission had for some time been under the care of the Oblates of St. Charles. Owing to the construction of the Great Central Railway, 1893-6, large numbers of poor people were compelled to leave Marylebone and contiguous districts and settle in Kensal Green, where it soon became necessary to build new Catholic schools, at a cost of nearly £4,000. The buildings were opened Tuesday, November 28, 1899, by Cardinal Vaughan, who paid a warm tribute to the Rev. Frs. Wyndham and Green for their 'great courage' in surmounting the local educational difficulty. The schools accommodate about 900 children. At the time of the opening of the schools, the Catholic population was estimated at 5,000.

KENSAL NEW TOWN, LONDON, N.W. (*Westminster*). Our Lady of the Holy Souls.

The church was opened April 13, 1882, 'amidst a poor and thickly populated district.' A new reredos was added to the sanctuary March 1889. The altar-piece is a copy of the famous triptych by Stephen Loethener in Cologne Cathedral.

New schools were opened 1892. The mission was commenced by the opening of a school chapel in November 1872.

Priests.

Rev. Henry Karslake, 1872.
„   Francis Kirk, 1877.
„   Septimus Andrews, 1879.
„   Joseph Greene, 1882 to date.

KENSINGTON, LONDON, W. (*Westminster*). Our Lady of Victories.

Mr. More, a Catholic gentleman who resided 'in Kensington Gore, by London,' about 1730, presumably had a chapel in his house, as a 'Mr. Burgis' is given as resident chaplain at this time. This priest was probably a Jesuit. About 1794 some exiled French Jesuits opened a school at Kensington House, and the few Catholics of the district were enabled to hear Mass in the adjoining chapel. Richard Lalor Sheil, the great barrister and Parliamentary orator, was one of their pupils before proceeding to Stonyhurst. The school was closed about 1806, but the chapel was continued owing to the liberality of Richard Gillow, Esq., and Mr. Kendall, the latter giving £100 towards the mission and 'many requisites for the altar.' Mr. Gillow and some friends contributed £500, with which sum a site was purchased and a chapel erected in Holland Street. Elementary schools were established about 1830, and the chapel enlarged by a sanctuary a little later. The structure, with a few subsequent improvements, served till the opening of the present handsome Decorated Gothic church by Archbishop Manning, 1869. The building consists of a nave, sanctuary,

and two aisles, the interior being lighted by a clerestory and east windows. For over thirty years the church 'played the honourable *rôle* of pro-cathedral.' The building was consecrated by Cardinal Vaughan, May 1, 1901. A new boys' school, to accommodate ninety pupils, was opened in Warwick Road by Archbishop Bourne, April 21, 1906. Mr. Goldie was the architect ; cost about £4,000.

Priests.

Rev. Gilles Vielle, 1806.
„   Dominic Le Houx, 1823.
„   Wm. Bugden, 1840.
„   Charles Woolett, 1851.
„   James Foley, 1860.
„   Mgr. J. Rouse, D.D., 1879.
„   Mgr. C. Harrington Moore, 1885.
„   Michael Canon Fanning, 1889 to date.

KENSINGTON, LONDON, W. (*Westminster*). Our Lady of Mount Carmel and St. Simon Stock.

The Order of Mount Carmel (White Friars) was introduced into England by St. Simon Stock (1240). After the Reformation many of the fathers laboured on the English mission. In 1861, Fr. Herman Cohen, who had been converted from Judaism at Rome, opened a house of the Order in Kensington Square. It was afterwards removed to Vicarage Place. Here an old schoolroom was turned into an oratory, and opened October 15, 1861. Mgr. Manning preached on the glories of the Carmelite Order. The relics of St. Simon Stock were solemnly deposited in a shrine beneath the high altar by Cardinal Wiseman May 16, 1864. The present church, by E. Pugin, was built 1866.

KENTISH TOWN, LONDON, N. (*Westminster*). Our Lady Help of Christians.

A chapel was opened in Kentish Town by Fr. Harding Ivers in November 1846. The Count de Montemolin subscribed £20 towards the expenses of the new mission. In July 1847, a learned Jewish gentleman lectured in the chapel on the corruptions and interpolations of the authorised version of the Scriptures, and advised the many protestants present to use the Douai Bible. Great sensation was caused by this incident, and the report was, of course, circulated that the Rabbi was 'a Jesuit in disguise'! About this time Fr. Ignatius Grant, of the Passionist Order, gave £100 towards the fund that had been started for a new church. Soon the little chapel in Fitzroy Terrace, which only accommodated 150 persons, had to be exchanged for a larger building in Gospel Terrace, where Fr. Ivers had the assistance of Fr. Faa di Bruno, author of 'Catholic Belief.' In 1856 Fr. Robt. Swift was the priest at Kentish Town. Two years later (August 1858), the stone of the church was blessed and laid by Cardinal Wiseman. The opening took place in August 1859. In the autumn of 1876 the church was quite transformed by several improvements, amongst which may be noted the high altar of stone and alabaster and a carved reredos.

N.B.—Fr. William Prichard, a Lisbonian, died at Kentish Town October 22, 1734, whence it may be inferred that even at this date there were some Catholics in the district.

KESWICK, CUMBERLAND (*Hexham and Newcastle*).

In the summer of 1861 a room was fitted up as a chapel and Mass said 'by any priest who happened to be staying there.' At that time there were fifty 'very poor Catholics' in Keswick, and no mission nearer than Cockermouth, about thirteen miles off. No further mention is made of the place in the 'Catholic Directory' after this till about 1903, when the mission is described as served from Cockermouth.

KETTERING, NORTHAMPTON (*Northampton*). St. Edward.

A new mission was started here in October 1891, when the temporary chapel was served by Fr. H. Stanley, of the Bishops' House, Northampton. A site for church and presbytery was secured about this time. The chapel was at first in a shoe factory in Church Walk, near the parish church. In November 1891 Fr. Stanley went to live permanently at Kettering, his residence being 13 The Grove, Kettering. The new church was opened in January 1893. It is a large and commanding structure, 'fitted up in most excellent fashion.' The cost of erection was about £1,300. In the parish of Kettering stands Rushton Hall, an old Elizabethan mansion, formerly the residence of the Treshams. It contains many priests' hiding-places, and in one of these some interesting family documents and rare controversial tracts—among them 'The Spiritual Conflict,' by Hierome Count of Portia — were accidentally discovered in 1828. The house is now leased by Mr. James Van Allen, an American gentleman.

KEW, SURREY (*Southwark*). The Rev. M. Cummins, of the Marist Congregation, was appointed to this newly formed mission in 1898. The chapel is a temporary one at the clergy house, 14 Kew Gardens Road. The congregation at the time the mission was started was described as 'a small and scattered flock,' and the character of the neighbourhood as 'indifferent.'

KIDDERMINSTER, WORCESTERSHIRE (*Birmingham*). St. Ambrose.

In 1831, Bishop Walsh, V.A., sent Fr. C. J. O'Connor to found the mission. Fr. O'Connor brought the congregation up to 100. Mass was said in a hired Methodist chapel, the first being offered up on Trinity Sunday 1831. John Jeffreys, Esq., a Unitarian gentleman, was a great benefactor to the mission, as were also James Mackrell, Esq., of Harvington, and Sir Edward Blount, Bart. A chapel was built, and opened November 15, 1834, when the Mass was sung by the Hon. and Rev. G. Spencer. Fr. O'Sullivan, of Wolverhampton, preached on the authority of the Church. Seating capacity of the building for 300. Much interest was evoked in the neighbourhood, and several protestant clergymen attended the inaugural Mass. The chapel of 1834 was replaced in 1858 by a church in the Geometrical style. Messrs. Meredith and Pritchard designed the spire, which was finished December 11, 1901. The opening ceremony was attended by the mayor and corporation of Kidderminster.

KIDSGROVE, STAFFS (*Birmingham*). St. John the Evangelist. The mission was established 1892.

Priests.

Rev. Thomas Kenny, 1892.
„ Raymond Haskew, 1901.
„ Francis J. Swift, 1903 to date.

KILBURN, LONDON, N.W. (*Westminster*). The Sacred Heart of Jesus.

In 1800 Kilburn was in the country, and famous for its hot springs. Half a century later, it was part of London. In 1864, Cardinal Wiseman asked the Oblates of Mary Immaculate to take spiritual charge of the district. From that date till 1868 Mass said on Sundays and festivals in a house in Greville Place. In the last-named year the priory was opened in Quex Road, and the library served for a chapel. The fine church, in the Early Decorated style, was opened by Cardinal Manning, May 8, 1879. The accommodation is for about 500. Messrs. Pugin were the architects.

KILVINGTON, THIRSK, YORKS (*Middlesbrough*). St. Anne.

Kilvington Hall has been for generations the seat of the Meynell family, great sufferers in times past for the Faith. This mission has existed from about the end of the sixteenth century. Colonel Thos. Meynell commanded a regiment of horse for Charles I., and was slain in an encounter with the Parliamentarians near Pontefract Castle, 1644. Several other members of the family have been priests of the

Society of Jesus. The registers date from 1775.

Priests of the Mission.

Rev. Geo. Grange, or Carnaby, O.S.B., about 1633–73.
„ Thos. Helme, O.S.B., 1704.
:, Wm. Davis, O.S.B., 1728.
„ Robt. Stanfield, S.J., 1731.
„ Joseph Wright, S.J., 1741.
„ Francis Digges, S.J., 1743.
„ Jn. Rigmayden, *alias* Roth-well, S.J., 1749.
„ Jn. Jones, 1782.
„ Robt. Tindall, 1788.
(Seculars served mission 1811–18.)
„ Thos. Austin Lawson, O.S.B., 1818.
„ Edw. Metcalfe, 1822.
„ Joseph Orrell, 1824.
„ James Blundell, 1827.
„ Richard Brown, 1834.
„ Chas. Brigham, 1834.
„ Edw. Canon Crane, 1835.
„ Jas. Canon Sherwood, 1859.
„ Henry Walker, 1862.
„ Thos. Rigby, 1863.
„ Michael Fryer, 1864.
„ Luke Burke, 1869.
„ Gerald Shanahan, 1876.
„ Alfred Galli, 1877.
„ Jas. Atkinson, 1878.
„ Maurice Trant, 1879.
„ Edmund Kennedy, 1882.
„ Richard Howley, D.D., 1883.
„ Charles Donovan, 1884.
„ Thos. Canon Holland, 1885.
„ Lawrence McGonnell, 1888.
„ Chas. Donovan, 1890.
„ J. Dewe, 1898.

KINGSBRIDGE, DEVON (*Plymouth*).

Woods Farm House, three miles from Kingsbridge, was taken by the Trappist Fathers expelled from France, December 1901. They came from Mount Melleraye, and are the same Order that occupied the monastery of St. Susanna, Lulworth, 1800–15.

KINGSHEATH, BIRMINGHAM (*Birmingham*). St. Dunstan.

The church was opened 1896. Fr. Michael Dolan, first and present rector.

KINGSLAND, LONDON, N. (*Westminster*). Our Lady and St. Joseph.

'The mission was begun in October 1854 by the Fathers of Charity.' Mass was first said in the house of Thomas Kelly, Esq., resident in the Tottenham Road. The church, 'a spacious brick edifice,' was originally intended for a factory, but was altered into a place of worship by the skill of Wardell, the eminent architect. The building was opened September 29, 1856, by Cardinal Wiseman. The chancel is conspicuous by a splendid reredos displaying pictures, by Barff, of Our Lord, St. Augustine of Hippo, and St. Thomas Aquinas. The golden jubilee of the mission was celebrated Sunday, October 16, 1904, when an impressive sermon was preached by Archbishop Bourne, of Westminster. At the first Mass offered up in the parish, about fifteen persons are recorded to have been present. During the fifty years of the church's existence, upwards of 3,750 persons had received holy baptism from its several pastors. The well-known Father Lockheart, of the Institute of Charity, was for upwards of twenty years rector of the mission. During the ten years that Mgr. Howlett, D.D., held the incumbency (1895-1905) the mission debt was reduced from £3,800 to £1,800, apart from an expenditure of £2,000 on various repairs and improvements. Fr. Thos. Walsh in the present rector.

KING'S LYNN, NORFOLK (Northampton).
The church was erected in 1845 by Fr. John Dalton. The nave, built at a cost of £650, was the first part of the church opened. Fr. George Rigby, afterwards Canon of Northampton, succeeded Fr. Dalton in 1847. Strangely enough, when Canon Rigby died, Fr. Dalton, now a canon, took his place. Fr. G. Wrigglesworth about 1887 thoroughly restored the altar. Some candelabra and sanctuary lamps were presented to the church at this time by Mr. Blake. The old building being declared unsafe, a new church was commenced in October 1896, and opened in 1897. The style is Decorated Gothic. Some of the candlesticks used in the church are old pre-Reformation ones from the priory of Walsingham, in the neighbourhood.

KINGSTON-ON-THAMES, SURREY (Southwark). St. Agatha.
The church was opened Thursday, December 21, 1899, by Bishop Bourne, of Southwark. The building, which was erected at the cost of Mrs. Currie, of Kingston Hill, is in the Roman style of about the fifth century. The edifice comprises a sanctuary, terminating in a semicircular apse, nave, two aisles,

and two side chapels. The interior is lighted during the day by twelve clerestory windows and at night by electricity. In addition to defraying the building expenses (£6,000) Mrs. Currie generously presented the church with an organ. Fr. Caspar Lutz, who has been at Kingston since 1894, has erected the presbytery and schools adjoining.

KINGSWOOD, BRISTOL (Clifton). St. Joseph.
The Redemptorist monastery was founded 1901, Fr. George Nicholson, C.SS.R., being first superior. The late Fr. P. Lasseter succeeded him in 1904.

KIRKDALE, LIVERPOOL. St. John.
In 1870, a Nonconformist chapel in Claremont Grove (now Fountains Road) was purchased, and early in 1871 opened for Catholic worship. In 1883 the old chapel was far too small for the congregation. By multiplying Masses, 1,200 persons could attend to their duties on Sundays. The new Gothic church was opened Sunday, November 21, 1885. The seating accommodation is for 800; total cost about £6,700. In 1875 the congregation numbered 2,700. In 1882 it had increased to 7,500. In 1885, when another mission had taken away 2,000, the congregation numbered 6,700. Fr. P. Power was priest at the time of opening. New and handsome stations of the Cross by Ball, of Dublin, were erected in the church in January 1887. Messrs. J. and B. Sinnott were the architects of the church.

KIRTLING TOWER, CAMBRIDGE- SHIRE (*Northampton*). Mary Immaculate and St. Philip.

The mission was started in 1871, Mass being said in an iron chapel on the estate of the Hon. W. North. The present church was opened April 17, 1877, on nearly the same site. C. Buckler was the architect. For many years the mission was served from New-market, but in 1896 Fr. F. Donovan was appointed resident priest. He commenced his pastorate by a series of lectures on Catholic faith and practice, which were very well attended.

KNARESBORO', YORKS (*Leeds*). St. Mary.

The mission is a continuation of that at Follifoot, where the Plumpton family possessed considerable property. They became extinct in the male line 1755. The district was then, as it is now, served by Benedictines. The mission register dates from 1765, but no priest's signature appears till January 4, 1797. Knaresboro' Chapel, in Briggate, was built in 1790 by Mr. Thornton, a cotton manufacturer, who became bankrupt owing to losses during the French war. About sixty persons were confirmed here by Bishop Gibson, V.A., November 9, 1808. Fr. Denis Allerton, O.S.B., was priest at this time. He probably succeeded Fr. T. Appleton.

Priests from 1824.

Rev. J. Barber, 1824.
,, J. Prest, 1826.
,, Robt. Bretherton, 1828.
,, Ralph Pratt, 1830.
,, Wm. Hampson, 1839 or 1840.
,, Geo. Gillett, 1857.
,, Edw. Lynass, O.S.B., 1874.
,, Charles G. Smith, O.S.B., 1885.
,, Essington Ross, O.S.B., 1890.
,, Charles Smith, O.S.B., 1892 *et seq.*
,, Alf. Wilson, O.S.B., 1896 and to date.

KNUTSFORD, CHESHIRE (*Shrewsbury*). St. Vincent of Paul, Queen Street.

Until the starting of this mission, in October 1862, the nearest Catholic chapel was at Altrincham. In 1862 the Catholic population of Knutsford amounted to about 400. The church was opened by Fr. Alcock, of Altrincham, on Sunday, September 16, 1866. The building was used as a school on week-days. In 1860-1 Mass was said at various places, first at Caldwell's Farm, Over Tabley, then in a room of a public-house in the Manchester Road, Knutsford, and lastly in the hired room in King Street.

Priests.

Rev. Hugh Lynch, 1861.
(1865-7 served from Altrincham.)
,, Daniel Casey, 1867.
,, Patrick O'Reilly, 1876.
,, Robert Maurice, 1879.
,, John St. Roche, 1903.

L

LANCASTER (*Liverpool*). St. Peter.

In the reign of Elizabeth the country round Lancaster is described as being 'full of Seminary priests and gentlemen recusants who harbour them.' The Ven. Thos. Woodcock, O.S.F., suffered for the Faith at Liverpool August 7, 1646. His head was kept at St. Bonaventure's, Douai, prior to the Revolution, and an arm-bone of the martyr is now preserved by the Franciscan nuns at Taunton. In 1710 the V.G. of the Lancashire clergy resided in the town. About 1753, Fr. Nicholas Skelton, who had 'assisted' the Catholics of the place for over forty years, erected a 'retired chapel' at the back of his house. This worthy priest died 1775, 'full of years.' He was for a long time befriended and protected by the Duchess of Hamilton. When Bishop Gibson came to confirm in 1790, it was not thought prudent to have the rite administered in the town, and the candidates had to go to the chapel of the Daltons, two miles away! In 1799 a large chapel was erected by subscription in Dalton Square. Richard Gillow, Esq., founder of the Margate mission, was a generous contributor to the fund. The present Gothic church was commenced 1857, and consecrated by Bishop Goss, of Liverpool, October 4, 1859. A splendid high altar was presented by Mrs. Gabriel Coulston, and a Lady Chapel by Miss Elizabeth Dalton, the last of that ancient family. The north transept is lighted by a beautiful stained-glass window representing the English martyrs. New sacristies were erected 1887, the church redecorated 1895, and the presbytery enlarged 1896.

Priests.

Rev. Thos. Hays, 1678 (?).
,, Peter Gooden, 1692.
,, Edw. Hawarden, 1694. ('A glorious preacher.' He refuted the Unitarian Dr. Clarke in the presence of Queen Caroline, consort of George II., and received the public thanks of the University of Oxford for the same.)
,, Nicholas Skelton, 1714.
,, James Tyrer, 1766.
,, Jn. Rigby, D.D. (Sorbonne), 1784.
,, Geo. Brown, 1818 (Bishop of Liverpool 1850).
,, Richard Brown, 1840.
,, Wm. Canon Walker, 1869.
,, Richard Billington, 1893.

LANCASTER. St. Joseph's, *see* **SKERTON.**

LANCHESTER, DURHAM (*Hexham and Newcastle*). All Saints.

The mission was founded 1748 at Pontop Hall. The register of deaths was in existence November 1778. Some names entered are as follows: 'Margarita Punshon, obiit 18 January, 1780'; 'Joa. Winship, obiit die 19 January, 1781'; 'Ric. Carrick, obiit 20 April, 1781.' Fr. John Lingard, the historian, was here for a time, 1796; Fr. John Jones about 1797; Fr. Thomas Eyre about 1803. Fr. John Bell came April 1, 1803. No mention is made of the mission from 1824 till 1901. In the autumn of 1899 Fr. Samuel Harris commenced appealing for a church in this district, which contained many Catholics. The church was commenced in the spring of 1900, and opened 1901. Cost of erection about £1,500.

LANGLEY MOOR, DURHAM. (*Hexham and Newcastle*). St. Patrick.

Mission established 1876, and chapel erected the same year.

Priests.

Rev. James Hanley, 1876.
„ Richard Hannan, 1882.
„ James Thorman, 1899 to date.

LANGPORT, SOMERSETSHIRE (*Clifton*).

In 1904 the Sœurs de St. Gildas acquired Hill House for a convent. The chapel is open to the public. Fr. E. Trébeden, chaplain.

LANHERNE, CORNWALL (*Plymouth*). SS. Joseph and Anne.

The manor of Lanherne came into the possession of the Lords Arundell of Wardour about 1690, but the family did not often reside in this remote place. In August 1794, Henry eighth Lord Arundell gave the manor house to the Carmelite nuns fleeing from the French Revolution. In gratitude for the hospitality afforded them by England the nuns have since daily recited the prayer for the Sovereign, 'Domine salvum fac,' &c., in their office. Though strictly enclosed by their rule, the nuns threw open their chapel to the few neighbouring Catholics, mostly tenants of Lord Arundell, and so numerous did the congregation become, that in 1797 the drawing-room of the mansion had to be fitted up as an oratory. A church has long since taken the place of the domestic chapel. In virtue of the gift of Lord Arundell, the nuns obtained certain rights over a chapel in the parish church, and here several of the community were interred among the deceased members of their noble patron's family, until a private cemetery was opened in the convent grounds. A splendid high altar, designed by Canon Scoles, was consecrated in the convent church August 1893.

Priests at Lanherne (*list incomplete*).

Rev. Boniface Hall, 1756.
„ Thos. Lodge, 1758.
„ Lorymer, 1762.
„ Wilfrid Strutt, 1770.
„ Placid Bennet, 1780.
„ Abbé Riout, 1794.
„ John de la Fosse, 1802 till 1817.
„ Charles Lengronne, 1806.
„ Maurice Connor, 1823.
„ Louis Dourlens, 1827.

Rev. Wm. Cooke, 1839.
„ Mgr. Weld, 1844.
„ Joseph Prost, 1849.
„ M. Oleron, 1850.
„ Patrick Walsh, 1852.
„ Joseph Bunn, 1860.
„ R. W. Meager, here 1872.
„ David Coleman, 1877.
„ John Kennedy, 1879.
„ Wm. Dawson, 1882.
„ John Corbishley, 1891 to date.

LARTINGTON, near BARNARD CASTLE, YORKS (*Middlesbrough*).

Lartington Hall is the seat of the ancient Catholic family of Maire. A mission has existed here since 1700. After the opening of the Barnard Castle chapel, in the vicinity, by Bishop Riddell, V.A., in March 1847, Lartington ceased to serve the Durham district. The Catholic cemetery of Lartington was provided by Fr. T. Witham, and in January 1882 a mortuary chapel was erected contiguous to it by the same family. There are memorial tablets on the walls to Bishop George Witham, V.A. († April 16, 1725), Bishop William Maire († July 25, 1725), Sir H. Lawson, Bart., of Brough (1750-1834), &c.

LATCHFORD, CHESHIRE (*Shrewsbury*). Our Lady of the Assumption.

Until 1866 the nearest chapel was at Warrington. On Sunday, October 2, 1869, Mass was said for the first time in a building known as 'the Old Factory.' In September 1871, a school chapel was opened. In 1901 a new church

was commenced, and opened in 1902. The presbytery was built in 1898.

Priests.

Rev. H. Alcock, 1866.
„ T. Mulvanny, 1870.
„ W. Dallow, 1881.
„ J. Thompson, 1882.
„ E. Hanlon, 1889.
„ J. Hennelly, 1891.
„ W. Stanley, 1896.
„ J. McGrath, 1898.

LAUNCESTON, CORNWALL (*Plymouth*).

This town will ever be famous as the scene of the martyrdom of the blessed Cuthbert Maine, the protomartyr of Douai College. He was arrested in the house of Mr. Tregian, owner of Tremolla and other large estates in Cornwall, and on November 29, 1577, hanged and quartered at Launceston for denying the spiritual supremacy of Queen Elizabeth and for having said Mass. A mission was started here in September 1886—the year of the beatification of the English martyrs—and placed in charge of Fr. Chas. B. Langdon, M.A. (Oxon.), sometime a clergyman in the Church of England. The first chapel was in a house called Kensey View, on St. Stephen's Hill, formerly occupied by Fr. Langdon's family. As the congregation increased, he built a small wooden church, opened November 28, 1887. The design of the building was drawn up by his brother Arthur. The accommodation is for 120. The altar was decorated by Mr. Bolger, of Devonport.

LAWKLAND, YORKS. St. Oswald.

The mission was anciently served from Lawkland Hall, till 1790,

R

when the chapel was 'removed to its present locality.' The registers commence June 29, 1745, with the baptism of Ann Taylor by Fr. James Legrand, O.S.B., who resided with John Stephen Ingleby, Esq. This gentleman was either a son or nephew of Sir Charles Ingleby, serjeant-at-law, who died 1720. The last of this branch of the family died 1844.

Priests since 1824.

Rev. Jn. Clarkson.
„ Jn. Barber, 1826.
„ R. Marsh, 1833.
„ H. Sutton, 1840.
„ C. F. Kershaw, 1842.
„ J. Dewhurst, 1846.
„ C. Kershaw, 1848.
„ Geo. Gillet, 1852.
„ Wm. Hampson, 1857.
„ Robt. Garstang, 1863.
„ Wm. Smith, here 1871 till 1881.

Mission served from Bentham 1883-90 ; now from Settle.

LEA, PRESTON, LANCS (*Liverpool*). St. Mary.

The old chapel was at Salwick Hall, the baptismal registers dating from 1775. The Cliftons of Lytham were the ancient patrons of the mission, and did much to keep alive the Faith in the district during 'the dismal times of persecution.' (letter of Bishop Goss to Rev. W. S. Maddocks, 1866). When the chapel at Salwick Hall was shut up the congregation built the present chapel and presbytery (1799–1800). The schools were erected in 1860. Bishop Gradwell of Lydda and Bishop Brown of Liverpool were natives of Lea. In 1888 the church and presbytery were re-roofed and a stone belfry erected.

Priests since 1808.

Rev. J. Haydock.
„ Jn. Anderton.
„ Richard Albot, 1826.
„ Chas. Walker, 1837.
„ Richard Doyle, 1871.
„ Henry Clements, 1874.
„ James Eager, 1882.
„ John O'Reilly, 1885.
„ Fredk. D'Heuter, 1895.
„ James Gardner, 1897 to date.

LEAMINGTON, WARWICKSHIRE (*Birmingham*). St. Peter.

Before the establishment of the mission the place was visited by the priest at Wappenbury. In 1822, an Irish prelate who had visited the spa induced Bishop Milner to establish a mission in the town. In October 1828 'an elegant and commodious chapel' was opened and 'a resident and exclusive pastor' provided. Major Patrick Bisshop (40th Regiment) was the chief Catholic resident at this time. A large church in the Lombardic style was consecrated by Bishop Ullathorne August 17, 1864. The interior was very ornate, the tabernacle being enriched with gems and the dome of the sanctuary painted. On the night of Wednesday, December 19, 1883, the main building was accidentally destroyed by fire, but much valuable furniture was saved. Until the opening of the new church by Bishop Ilsley, November 11, 1884, Mass was said in the schools. Mrs. Bennet, widow of Major Bennet, was a great benefactress to the building fund.

Priests.

Rev. B. Crosbie, 1824 (?).
„ James McDonnell, 1831.
„ Wm. Cunningham, 1840.
„ Hy. Weedall, D.D., 1844.
„ Francis Fairfax, 1850.
„ James Canon Jeffries, 1852.

Rev. Verney Cave Brown, 1882.
„ Thos. Canon Longman, 1885.
„ James Nary, 1892.
„ Mgr. Canon Souter, 1895.
„ Wm. Canon Greaney, 1901 to date.

LEDBURY, HEREFORDSHIRE
(*Newport*). St. Thomas of Hereford.

The Benedictines, assisted by Edw. Hanford, Esq., opened a boys' school near here about 1733. Owing to the penal laws it had to be closed about 1740. The present mission dates from about 1900. Fr. C. Begley, rector.

LEE HOUSE, PRESTON, LANCS
(*Salford*). St. William.

The chapel was founded 1738 by Thos. Eccles, Esq., who endowed the mission with three farms at Thornley. The mission was made over to the Franciscans, 'the founder's' church stuff for priests and altar' and 'books of religion' being part of the gift. In return for these the 'chaplain' was to 'serve the mission for the Catholics in Thornley, Chipping, and all other Catholic people thereabouts.' During the rebellion of 1745, Fr. Germanus Holmes was arrested and thrown into Lancaster Castle, where he died the following year. Some other priests here were Fr. Leo. Francis, 1758; Fr. Jos. Tate, 1808; Fr. Bernardine Davison, 1820-5. Next year the Franciscans handed the mission over to Bishop Smith, V.A., who appointed Fr. P. Orrell rector. His successor, Fr. F. Trappes, had a dispute with the authorities, and the mission was in consequence closed 1840. In

October 1859, the chapel — a new structure, erected by Fr. Trappes —was reopened for worship by the Bishop of Salford, 'to the great satisfaction of the Catholics in that locality.' The Benedictines have had charge of the mission since this time.

Priests since 1860.

Rev. G. Caldwell.
„ Joseph Murphy, 1871.
„ T. Atkinson, 1874.
„ Wm. Watmough, 1877.
„ J. Procter, 1882.
„ J. Dewhurst, 1885.
„ F. Roche, 1888.
„ J. Carew, 1892.
„ J. Morgan, 1895 to date

LEEDS (*Leeds*). Our Lady of the Rosary, Barrack Street.

This church, a plain substantial structure in the Gothic style of architecture, was opened Sunday, October 3, 1886. The accommodation is for 400 people. The cost of erection was £3,000. Messrs. Kelly and Birchall were the architects. The Bishops of Liverpool and Leeds were present at the opening. The mission is still served from the Cathedral.

LEEDS. St. Mary.

The Order of Mary Immaculate opened a foundation at Leeds in 1851, but it was not till May 1853 that the first stone of their new church was laid by the Bishop of Beverley. The building was opened on Wednesday, July 29, 1857, by Cardinal Wiseman. Thousands of persons filled the streets, and in Mill Street, near the church, three immense triumphal arches were erected. The Bishop of Marseilles

R 2

celebrated the Mass, and there was a large attendance of clergy, and an 'immense congregation.' The powerful sermon of the Cardinal on Ps. lxxxix. 17, made a great impression. Only the nave and aisles were completed at the time of the opening, the north and south transepts and the other portions of the church not being finished till 1686.

Priests.

Rev. Robt. Cooke, 1851.

„ Thos. Pinet, 1863.

„ Lawrence Roche, 1892 to date.

LEEK, STAFFS (*Birmingham*).

About the time of the Peace of Amiens (1803) the Abbé Gerard said Mass for the French prisoners confined at Leek and the few Irish labourers of the district, in the house of Mr. Ward, a solicitor in King Street. The Abbé Gerard at the same time served Cobridge. Fr. Jeffries, of Cheadle, about 1825, hired a room here and said Mass for the benefit of the few Catholics in and around Leek. In 1828 he commenced building a chapel, with the assistance of the Earl of Shrewsbury. The opening took place May 1829—the year of Catholic Emancipation. In 1830 a presbytery was added. Fr. Whitaker was priest here in 1832 ; Fr. B. Ivers in 1838. Fr. J. F. Anderson, who came to the chapel in 1860, founded the convent and in 1864 a new chapel, on a site generously given by the Messrs. Bermingham. He died suddenly Thursday, May 15, 1884. Bishop Ullathorne summed up his work and life in one sentence : 'No debts and living on 17s. a week.' The foundation stone of the new church was laid on Thursday, October 15, 1885, by Bishop Ilsley.

His Lordship gave a public discourse on the meaning of the ritual, which was listened to with great attention. About £760 was deposited on the stone, including £700 from Mrs. James Bermingham. The plan consists of a nave and two aisles, chancel for choir, side chapels and baptistery. The opening by the Bishop of Birmingham (Dr. Ullathorne) took place in May 1887. The accommodation is for 600. Three of the bells in the belfry were presented by Fr. W. Waugh and Mr. J. H. Sperling. The sanctuary window by Mayes & Co. is the gift of Mrs. J. Bermingham. The building was erected at the cost of Messrs. John and Alfred Sperling.

LEES, LANCASHIRE (*Salford*). St. Edward.

This district is a suburb of Oldham, in the prosperity of which it shares. The church was opened 1874 and served from St. Mary's, Oldham, till about 1877, when Fr. M. O'Callaghan was appointed. The successive rectors have been :

Rev. Pierce Griffith, 1880.

„ Timothy Burke, 1882.

„ James Brady, 1885.

„ J. Lathouwers, 1888.

„ M. A. Holohan, 1893.

„ James Hanrahan, 1894.

„ P. Ryan, 1899 to date.

LEICESTER, HOLY CROSS (*Nottingham*).

The Dominican Priory was built by Fr. Chas. Caestryck, O.P., 1817, and some years later he added the house. He died at Hinckley, June 2, 1844, aged eighty-three and is buried in the church at Leicester. A pleasing etched portrait of this excellent priest is preserved at Woodchester. It may be remarked that the pre-Reformation Dominican Priory at Leicester, dedicated to St. Clement, P.M., was founded in 1247.

Priors.

Rev. Chas. Caestryck, 1817.
„ B. Hulme, 1831.
„ H. Oxley, 1833.
„ W. Nickolds, 1842.
„ Pius Cavanagh, 1876.
„ Ceslas Fletcher, 1882.
„ John Procter, 1885.
„ Lewis Thompson, 1888.
„ Ceslas Fletcher, 1890.
„ Thos. Laws, 1894.
„ Joseph Mandy, 1897 to date.

LEICESTER (*Nottingham*). St. Patrick's.

The mission was established from Holy Cross Church, Leicester, 1854, by Provost Nickolds, but no mention is made of it till after 1856. The temporary chapel made way for the present church in 1867. A stone altar was erected January 1879.

Priests.

Rev. Provost Nickolds, 1854.
(Served from Holy Cross for many years.)
„ Cyril Bunce, O.P., 1874.
„ P. Stapleton, 1885.
„ T. Ambrose Smith, D.D., 1888.
„ Wm. Hawkins, 1895 to date.

LEICESTER. St. Peter, Noble Street.

Mission established in the town in February 1896, when a portion of the parish, hitherto served by the Dominican Fathers, was entrusted to the spiritual charge of Fr. J. Rear-

don Kane. For some months Mass was said on Sundays in one of the class rooms of the local Board School.

Priests.

Rev. J. Reardon Kane, 1896.
„ Fr. Ellison, 1896 (May).
„ H. Fitzgerald, 1897.
„ Felix May, 1899.
„ M. Griffin, 1902.

LEICESTER SQUARE, LONDON, W.C. (*Westminster*). Notre Dame de France.

A temporary chapel was opened December 8, 1866, and the present church June 11, 1868. The style is Gothic, the accommodation being for about 400. Since the foundation the mission has been under the care of the Marist Fathers. The French Hospital under the Nuns of the Sacred Heart is close by.

LEIGH, LANCS (*Liverpool*). St. Joseph.

Prior to 1670, the domestic chapel at Culcheth House served the mission. Fr. John Penketh, S.J., who was here in 1678, was condemned to death during the Oates plot, but reprieved and released from prison 1685. Prior to the erection of the chapel in 1778, Mass was said at Hopcar, in the house of the Sale family, one of whom, Fr. John Sale, served the mission. Mass was also said at Parsonage, the seat of the Urmstons, and at Hall House. Fr. Shaw built the chapel 1778, and presbytery 1789. Bishop Gibson, V.A., confirmed 135 persons at Leigh in 1784. The school was erected 1829. The present church (Gothic) was erected 1855 from designs by Mr. Hampden.

Being injured by a furious gale, it was repaired 1865. The church tower was added subsequently. A new infant school was opened, and the girls' school enlarged 1902. The Catholic population is about 4,628.

Priests.

Rev. J. Penketh, 1678 (died August 1, 1701, *æt.* 71).
„ Sebastian Needham, 1699.
„ Robt. Petre, 1728.
„ Jn. Sale, 1733.
„ Jn. Shaw. 1776 (died at Stonyhurst 1808).
„ Wm. Poole, 1807.
„ Edw. Morron, 1828.
„ Jn. Reeve, 1828.
„ Jas. Brownbill, 1840.
„ Felix Poole, 1841.
„ Hy. Beeston, 1843.
„ Francis West, 1843.
„ J. McClune, 1844.
„ Jn. Middlehurst, 1846.
„ Anthony Butler, 1877 (V.A. of Demerara 1878).
„ Jas. Fanning, 1878.
„ Hy. Cowell, 1886.
„ Edward Porter, 1898.
Henry Martin, 1899 to date.

LEIGHTON BUZZARD, BEDFORD-SHIRE (*Northampton*). The Sacred Heart.

Mainly owing to assistance from the late Mrs. White, a room was fitted up as a chapel over a general shop in North Street, 1894. Two years later the present iron chapel was erected on a freehold site in Beaudesert ; the building was blessed December 15, 1897, by Canon Duckett. Catholics of the district number about forty. At first protestant feeling ran very high, and when the presbytery was built by

Fr. C. E. Reilly the windows were broken by an angry 'No Popery' crowd.

Priests.

Rev. H. Parker (occasionally), 1894.
„ Chas. Ed. Reilly, 1895.
„ Canon Stokes, to date.

LEOMINSTER, HEREFORD (*Newport*). St. Ethelbert.

The Blessed Roger Cadwallador, who laboured here as a missionary priest for some sixteen years, suffered for the faith at Leominster, August 27, 1610. There is a memorial tablet to the martyred priest in the church, which was erected here between September 1887 and May 1888. Prior to the opening of the church, Catholics of the place had to worship in an old brick building, originally a Dissenters' chapel. The site for the new church was obtained by Fr. A. Rogers. The building is in the Perpendicular style ; architects, Messrs. Pugin. The cost of erection was about £1,300.

Priest.

Rev. Athanasius Rogers, 1887 to date.

LEVENSHULME, LANCS (*Salford*). St. Mary of the Angels and St. Clare.

The mission was started 1853, the chapel being opened August 21 of that year. 'A very plain but lofty' Gothic church, designed by Tijou, took the place of this structure March 3, 1882. The accommodation is for about 200.

Priests.

Rev. T. Unsworth, 1853.
„ H. Marshall, 1855.
„ H. Browne, 1857.
„ T. Fox, 1861.
„ Wm. Corry, 1863.
„ Provost Croskell, 1871.
„ C. McDermott Roe, 1904 to date.

LEWES, SUSSEX (*Southwark*). The Sacred Heart and St. Pancras.

The revival of Catholicity in Lewes is due to the late Canon Thos. Drinkwater, who, at the suggestion of Bishop Grant of Southwark, started the mission in 1865. Aided by Major and Mrs. Fletcher-Gordon, of the Manor House, St. George's Retreat, he opened a chapel on the second floor of his house at Priory Crescent, Lewes. Before this time, the nearest mission was at Brighton. In 1868 Fr. Hubert Wood, one of Canon Wenham's curates at Mortlake, was appointed to Lewes in succession to Canon Drinkwater, who went to Battersea. Rev. H. Wood's father—a protestant—erected the present chapel and clergy house in 1870. The style is 'pure Victorian carpenter's Gothic,' but the building was never intended to be a church, only a school chapel. The transfer of the mission from Priory Crescent to the present building took place on January 25, 1870. Since the establishment of the Reformation, Lewes has been notorious for its anti-Catholic feeling. We have been informed by Canon W. McAuliffe, the priest of the place, to whom we are indebted for the above details of the mission, that an effigy of the Pope continues to be religiously burned on each succeeding Guy Fawkes day. The number of Catholics at Lewes is about 150, but the mission could not be supported were it not for the endowment left for the purpose by Fr. Wood. Bishop Challoner, Vicar Apostolic of the London district (1758-81), was born here in 1691. He was probably converted to the Faith in the family of Sir Thomas Gage of Firle, a village about five miles from Lewes. The Gages long kept the lamp of Catholicity burning in the district, but after the defection of Sir William Gage, about 1720, the chapel at Firle, which had for generations been served by the Jesuits, was closed. Sir Henry Gage, governor of Oxford for Charles I. in 1644, and Fr. John Gage, S.J. (1720-90), who introduced the *greengage* into England, were members of this family. The Jesuit Fathers served the mission of Firle till as late as 1766.

Priests at Lewes.

Rev. Canon Drinkwater, 1865-68.
„ Hubert James Wood, 1868 (died December 14, 1882).
„ William Canon McAuliffe, 1882 to date.

LEWISHAM, LONDON, S.E. (*Southwark*). St. Saviour and SS. John the Baptist and Evangelist.

A committee, presided over by Captain Everard, was held on Sunday, October 27, 1893, to consider the possibility of establishing a chapel in the district. Up to this time the nearest mission was at Sydenham. Shortly afterwards a chapel was fitted up at No. 157 Lewisham High Street, and Mass said here on Sundays by Fr. McCalmont. In 1895, Fr. G. B.

Tatum, M.A., formerly an Anglican clergyman, was appointed priest of the mission. In 1897, the present school chapel for 200 persons was built on part of the site secured for a church, and it may be of interest to remark that the ground was once occupied by the country house of John Wesley, the founder of Methodism. A convent conducted by Ursuline nuns was opened near the church in 1901. Fr. Connell is the present rector of the mission.

LEYBURN, YORKS (*Middlesbrough*).

Danby Hall, in the North Riding, has been the residence of the Scrope family since the commencement of the seventeenth century. The domestic chapel was served by the Jesuit Fathers from about 1730 to 1785. The register dates from 1742. Fr. Edward Boone, S.J., the last priest of the Society at Danby, was particularly zealous in his missionary labours, and in 1771 he established a centre of Catholicity at Leyburn. Before this time, the few faithful depended for spiritual assistance on the chaplain, at Danby Hall.[1] The chapel, which was long a mere room, was superseded in 1836 by the present building erected mainly at the expense of Simon Scrope, Esq. (1790-1872), who claimed for his family the earldom of Wilts.

[1] 'Died at Leyburn, Christopher Barker. I administered to him the extreme unction. He died of an apoplexy' (May 29, 1759). Note by Fr. Wappeler, S.J., chaplain at Danby, 1758-64.

Priests.
Rev. — Oakley, S.J., 1742.
„ Wm. Wappeler, S.J., 1758.
„ Edward Boone, S.J., 1764-85.
„ Abbé C. Devienne, 1793.
„ Richard Billington.
„ T. Middlehurst, 1831.
„ Rd. Bolton, 1845.
„ Lawrence McGonnell, 1867.
„ Thos. Loughran, 1870.
„ Edward Canon Pearson, 1877.
„ Wm. Maher, 1894.
„ Joseph Canon Dodds, 1896 to date.

LEYLAND, LANCS (*Liverpool*). St. Mary.

In 1845 a school house belonging to Mrs. Buchanan was purchased by Catholics for a chapel. The first priest of the mission was Fr. Shepherd. Fr. J. Kirshaw, who was missionary rector in 1855, built a chapel in the Gothic style. Fr. E. G. Lynass, O.S.B., added the sanctuary, which in February 1857 was adorned by a handsome reredos. Schools for 256 children were opened November 6, 1897. The Catholic population of Leyland in 1903 was 570. In the sacristy of the church is preserved a curious pre-Reformation silver chalice inscribed with the words, 'Restore me to Leyland in Lancashire.'

LEYTON, ESSEX (*Westminster*). St. Joseph.

The mission was established in 1897, the chapel being that of St. Agnes Orphanage, Church Road, Leyton. In 1900 St. Joseph's school chapel, Vicarage Road, was erected and continued to serve as a place of worship till the opening of the present church, Sunday

November 27, 1904. The structure is a simple one of wood and iron. The opening ceremony was attended by Archbishop Bourne, of Westminster, the sermon being preached by Mgr. Croke Robinson, M.A. (Matt. xxviii. 19). St. Joseph's mission was founded by Fr. Francis C. Brown, late of the Catholic Church, Tottenham, who is still the rector.

LICHFIELD, STAFFS (*Birmingham*). Holy Cross.

Pipe Hall, near Lichfield, was the ancient seat of the Heveningham family, and on the death of Sir Walter Heveningham, Knt., it passed to the Simeons. At the death of Sir Edw. Simeon in 1768 the property went to the Welds of Lulworth. Mass, which had only been said occasionally at Pipe Hall, now became regular. Fr. Robt. Tindall was the priest about 1786. In 1788 he went to Kilvington, in Yorkshire. Fr. John Kirk succeeded. He added a new sanctuary to the old chapel. During the régime of the next priests, Fr. Charles Clements and Fr. Isaac Milward, O.S.F., the estate was sold to protestants and the chapel closed. The altar plate, vestments, &c., were made over to Thos. Clifford, Esq., afterwards Sir Thos. Clifford-Constable, Bart., who purchased an old house in Lichfield and reopened a chapel there. At the request of Bishop Stapleton, Fr. Kirk took charge of the mission, his Lordship allowing him £60 a year from the bequest of a Mr. Munford, formerly of St. Omer's College. Fr. Kirk built a chapel on the London Road, Lichfield, and opened it November 11, 1803.

The Catholics of the town numbered about fifty at this time. Mr. Thos. Weld, of Lulworth, father of Cardinal Weld, presented the chapel with a handsome altar-piece representing the Crucifixion by De Bruyn. By 1810 the Catholics of Lichfield and Hopewas, a neighbouring village, had increased to seventy-five and in 1833 to 145. The next year (1834) Fr. Kirk, then in the seventy-fifth year of his age, erected a simple Gothic church at Lichfield, which was opened by Bishop Walsh, V.A.; Dr. Weedal, of Oscott, sang the Mass (September 23).[1] Fr. J. Parke succeeded Dr. Kirke at Lichfield in 1851. The mission was greatly hampered for resources in 1865 by the death of a generous benefactress who had hitherto subsidised the schools, and the priest of the time, Fr. F. Magrath, was compelled to solicit support. The present church was opened 1895, during the rectorate of Fr. McCarten.

LIMEHOUSE, LONDON, E. (*Westminster*). Our Lady Immaculate.

The mission was started here in February 1881 for the benefit of the large Irish population. Mass was first said in a room over a chandler's shop and then in a large room in the priest's house, No. 9 Turner's Road. Fr. F. G. Maples was the first priest. The extemporised chapel was so crowded on Sundays that numbers had to kneel on the stairs. The number of children attending the school in August

[1] The Rev. John Kirk, 1760–1851, was a distinguished scholar. His notes formed the basis of Canon Tierney's continuation of Dod's 'Church History.'

1881 was sixty. Fr. F. H. Higley, the present rector, succeeded to the mission about 1890.

LINCOLN (Nottingham). St. Hugh.

The Jesuit Fathers opened a school at Lincoln for a short time in the reign of James II. In 1781 Fr. Richard Knight, S.J., served the mission. The Catholic chapel, 'a plain Romanesque building terminating in an apse,' was opened in — and redecorated in August 1863. The present fine Gothic church was opened by his Eminence Cardinal Vaughan on Tuesday, December 18, 1893. Most of the money necessary for the purpose was collected by the incumbent, Canon Croft The Carthusian monks of Parkminster, Sussex, contributed very largely to the fund. The o d title of the church, SS. John the Baptist and John the Evangelist, was retained till after 1898, when that of the present patron was adopted.

LINCOLN'S INN FIELDS, LONDON, W.C. (Westminster). SS. Anselm and Cecilia.

This mission has been rightly termed 'the Mother Church of the Catholic Faith in the Archdiocese of Westminster.' There is evidence that Mass was said 'in the house of a widow on the left-hand side of Duke Street,' 1648. In 1687 Fr. Jn. Cross, Provincial O.S.F., leased the house near the arches in Lincoln's Inn Fields and opened a chapel there. Bishop Ellis, V.A.W.D., and afterwards of Segni, Italy, often preached here. At the Revolution the Franciscans were compelled to retire at a loss of £3,000. After this the Sardinian Ambassador acquired the chapel, and it remained attached to the Embassy for nearly a century. Nollekens, the sculptor, was baptised here in 1737. On October 30, 1759, serious damage was caused by a fire, but the loss was repaired by the Count de Virey, the then Ambassador. The whole chapel, with the exception of the sanctuary end, was destroyed by the Gordon rioters in June 1780, but the loss was made good by Government, who also presented the new chapel with a fine altar-piece. The old sanctuary end is said to be the work of Inigo Jones, and is shown in the familiar prints of Bishop Challoner preaching. The building was enlarged 1811. The schools were established by a Catholic Society about 1764. In 1838 about one thousand children were enrolled on the books. Mr. Chas. Butler, the eminent barrister (1750–1832), was long a noted member of the congregation. In 1857 the roof of the church was raised and the interior painted. A new gallery was added 1851. King Victor Emmanuel, of Sardinia, attended Mass in state here Sunday, December 3, 1855. Prayers for the House of Sardinia ceased about 1861, when His Majesty invaded the States of the Church. Owing to the Strand to Holborn 'improvements' recently undertaken by the London County Council, the old Church of SS. Anselm and Cecilia will soon be numbered with the past, but another church not far from its site will, it is reported, arise to perpetuate its history and work.

Priests.

Rev. Wm. Barrow, S.J., 1677.
„ Jn. Cross, 1687.
„ Wm. Pouce, 1729.
„ Patrick Bradley, O.P., 1741–1760, subsequently Bishop of Londonderry.
„ Hy. Peach, 1761.
„ Robt. Smelt, 1771.
„ Jas. Archer, D.D., 1781–89.
„ Thos. Rigby, D.D., 1783.
„ Francis Tuite, 1810.
„ Thos. Percy, 1816.
„ Angelo Baldacconi, D.D., M.R., 1824.
„ Jn. Hearne, 1843.
„ W. O'Connor, 1845.
„ Patrick O'Connor, rector in 1875.
„ P. Cavanagh, rector in 1883.
„ Michael FitzGerald, rector 1891.
„ Jn. Dunford, 1901 to date.

A large number of priests have been attached to the mission as 'chaplains' at various times, but we have only named those first in seniority or superiority.

LISCARD, CHESHIRE (*Shrewsbury*). St. Alban.

In 1842 the Catholics of Liscard and vicinity numbered 300. The same year a room at Egremont was secured by Fr. Dawber, 'where he celebrated the Divine mysteries and ministered to the spiritual wants of the Catholics of the neighbourhood.' The school, chapel, and house were erected in 1842, and the church opened in the presence of Cardinal Wiseman, September 8, 1853. A large bell, costing £220, was consecrated October 10, 1858. Bishop Knight opened the Catholic club-room February 13, 1888.

Priests.

Rev. Jn. Dawber, 1841.
„ Ambrose Canon Lennon, V.G., 1843.
„ Wm. Walton, 1868.
„ Joseph Canon Daly, 1872.
„ T. Geraghty, 1876.
„ Wm. Stanton, 1878.
„ Thomas Canon Marsden, V.G 1887.
„ C. Ryder, 1898.
„ J. G. Walsh, 1898.

LISKEARD, CORNWALL (*Plymouth*). St. Neot.

The chapel was erected 1862-63 by Fr. T. Francis. Sir Paul Molesworth was one of the most notable contributors to the building fund. The cost of the building, which in style is 'plain underrated Gothic,' was about £400; the seating capacity is for 400 persons. Bishop Vaughan, of Plymouth, pontificated at the opening ceremony in May 1863. A fine granite octagonal font was erected in the church in June 1882 from the legacy of Mr. James Carroll, many years resident at Bodmin. The new organ was inaugurated the following Christmas. For several years after the opening the mission was served from Sclerder.

Priests.

Rev. T. Francis, 1862.
„ H. Dobbelaire, 1866.
„ F. Gallini, here in 1871.
„ W. Keily, 1877.
„ Geo. Graham, 1879.
„ R. W. Meager, 1893.
„ Norbert Woolfrey, here in 1897.
„ Joseph Hurley, to date.

LITHERLAND, LANCS (Liverpool). St. Elizabeth.

A church was opened here by the Bishop of Liverpool on Sunday, October 9, 1904. The sermon both at the morning and evening service was preached by Canon Gordon.

chaplains of the Blundells of Crosby served the mission during the times of persecution. In 1896 the Catholic cemetery was enlarged, and a new window and south side of chancel added to the church.

LITTLEBOROUGH, LANCS (Salford). The Annunciation.

A temporary chapel was opened in 1879, and on Saturday, June 4, 1881, the foundation stone of the present church was laid by Canon Sheehan, V.G., assisted by Fr. L. Schreiber, priest of the mission. The school and presbytery were built at the same time. The church was opened January 1, 1882, by Bishop Vaughan, of Salford. The style is Byzantine.

Priests.

Revs. Conrad Kaelin, 1879.
„ Laurence Schreiber, 1882.
„ W. Fowler, 1885 ; served from Buckley Hall, Todmorden, &c., 1890-93.
„ James Manning, 1893.
„ Michael Cahill, 1897.
„ Pius de Witte, 1899.
„ Henry Egbers, 1902.
„ Octave Raymond, 1904 to date.

LITTLEHAMPTON, SUSSEX (Southwark). St. Catherine.

In the summer of 1859, Mass was said here on Sundays at eleven for the benefit of the Catholic visitors. The temporary chapel was a room in the Beach Hotel and was served by Fr. John Butt of Arundel. The handsome Gothic church, situated on the common, is one of the five churches built in honour of the Five Precious Wounds of Our Lord, by Mina Duchess of Norfolk, mother of the present duke. It was opened May 26, 1863. The handsome Lady Altar of variegated marbles was erected in 1883. The church was again considerably enlarged in the summer of 1904 by the lengthening of the nave and aisles. Fr. R. L. Irvine Neave has been priest of the mission since 1875. His predecessor was Fr. Thos. Dixon, O.P.

LITTLE CROSBY, LANCS (Liverpool). St. Mary's.

The stone of the church was laid March 25, 1845, by Nicholas Blundell, Esq., who defrayed the cost of erection. The style is Decorated Gothic. Messrs. Weightman and Hadfield were the architects. The building was consecrated by Bishop Brown, V.A., September 7, 1847. The domestic

LITTLE HULTON, LANCS (Salford). St. Edmund.

The church was opened 1876, and was served from Farnworth till 1890, when Fr. Wilfrid Hampson was appointed.

Subsequent Priests.

Rev. Peter Grobel, 1895.
„ Godric Kean, 1901.
„ Henry Joseph Hunt, 1905.

LITTLE MALVERN, WORCESTER-SHIRE (*Birmingham*).

This beautiful estate came to the Beringtons from the Russells. The Beringtons have always been staunch to the Faith, and in the days of persecution their mansion was 'a city of refuge' for priests. One or two hiding-places in the roof were probably the work of the martyr, Brother Nicholas Owen, S.J. In 1641 the house was searched by order of the House of Commons 'for Jesuites and Romish priestes; also Massing stuffe, Popish relics, Popish books and warlike ammunition, but did not find any such.' The Rev. Joseph Berington (1743–1827), author of ' The Literary History of the Middle Ages,' and a supporter of the Catholic Committee on the subject of the famous oath, was a member of this family, as was also his brother, Bishop Berington, V.A. The ancient domestic chapel of the house is still kept open for the purpose of serving the mission.

LIVERPOOL. All Saints, Oak-field.

Till 1885 this district was partly in the mission of St. Michael's, and partly in that of Our Lady Immaculate. In October 1888, a school chapel, capable of accommodating 480 children on the ground floor, and 500 adults on the chapel storey above, was commenced, and opened September 2, 1889. A stone belfry surmounts the west gable of the nave. The cost of erection was about £4,000.

Priests.
Rev. Wm. Smith, 1889.
  „ R. Etherington, 1891.
  „ R. Baynes, 1894.
  „ James Cross, 1899.
  „ W. Gregson, 1900.

LIVERPOOL. St. Alphonsus.

In 1877 a disused Masonic Hall was acquired for use as a chapel. New schools were erected 1888 at a cost of £3,000.

Priests.
Rev. Edward Birchall, 1878.
  „ Wm. Pennington, 1888 to date.

LIVERPOOL. St. Augustine's, Great Howard Street.

The mission of St. Augustine was founded ' in poverty and want ' in September 1849, when it was served from St. Mary's. The church was erected a little later. It had little architectural merit till decorated in 1885 by Mr. Hopkins, of Abergavenny. The church was enriched with two new altars, a screen of carved stone, and marble altar rails. The high altar was further adorned by a Calvary group with angels. On the day of opening, Sunday, August 9, 1885, Fr. W. O'Brien, a former priest of the mission, preached an eloquent sermon describing the work of the Catholic Church throughout the world, and incidently sketching the history of St. Augustine's from its foundation. New schools were opened February 21, 1897.

Priests.
Rev. F. Cook, 1849.
  „ W. Bulbeck, 1858.
  „ Ralph Cooper, 1864.
  „ E. Ross, 1875.
  „ J. Potter, 1881.
  „ C. O'Neill, 1882.
  „ W. Rigby, 1882.
  „ T. V. Murphy, 1889.
  „ A. D. Firth, 1890.
  „ T. Murphy, 1889.
  „ — Sanders, 1892.
  „ Hugh Larkin, 1892.
  „ T. Rathe, 1895.

LIVERPOOL. St. Alban, Athol Street.

In 1848, Fr. Thos. Newsham purchased a site for a church for the spiritual benefit of the large number of Irish labourers employed on the Liverpool docks extension. The building was designed by C. Hadfield, and opened for worship, Sunday, August 19, 1849, by Bishop Brown, V.A. Fr. Thos. Kelly (1849-62) completed the church, gave a fine bell to the belfry and erected the organ. He likewise built the sacristy and presbytery. His successor, Fr. R. Seed (1862-71), built magnificent schools to accommodate 1,000 children. These were enlarged by Fr. Patrick Kelly, rector from 1871 to 1887. Fr. Kelly enriched the church with a handsome altar of the Sacred Heart and fine pulpit. In 1890 the Albany Club for young men was opened, and the year following the sacristies were improved and fitted with new presses, &c. The church was redecorated 1893. To commemorate the jubilee of the mission, new marble and alabaster altar rails, by Hardman, were added to the sanctuary in 1899. Fr. J. Buckley, appointed in 1898, is the present rector.

LIVERPOOL (*Liverpool*). St. Clare, Sefton Park.

This church was started in April 1889, and consecrated June 3, 1890. The design is Decorated Gothic. The accommodation is for 600. The cost, including the schools for 400 children, was £10,779. The church was erected at the sole cost of two benefactors, Messrs. Francis William and James F. Reynolds. The Catholic population of the parish is about 1,500.

LIVERPOOL (*Liverpool*). Edge Hill, St. Ann's.

Mass was said in the presbytery in 1843 by Fr. Maurus Margison, the founder of the mission. The church (Late Gothic) was opened August 5, 1846, by Bishop Brown, V.A.N.D., assisted by Archbishop Polding and Bishops Sharples and Morris. The chancel was added in 1887. A new priory was erected 1893. Two fine windows in the church commemorate Fr. Basil Feeny (1893-97), and the oak choir stalls serve as a memorial to Fr. Egbert Turner (September 1897). The Catholic population of the district is estimated at about 5,500. The church is largely due to the zeal and exertions of Fr. H. Brewer, Provincial of the English Benedictines, Northern Province, from 1837 to 1846. Fr. Jn. Darby is the present superior (1904).

LIVERPOOL (*Liverpool*). St. Joseph, Grosvenor Street, N.

In 1846 a former protestant place of worship was purchased for use as a Catholic church. Schools in connection with the mission were founded in Edgar Street in 1852 by Thomas Gillow, Esq., of Mexico. On January 23, 1870, a false alarm of fire led to a fatal panic in the church. Six years later the building became unsafe, and was replaced by the present church, opened March 19, 1878. The Bishop Goss Memorial Schools were opened about the same time. A handsome marble altar was erected in the church and consecrated December 1881. The Lady Altar, by Messrs. Pugin, was put up in 1890 in memory of Fr. Robert Bridges, who died in 1888. New altar-rails were added to the sanctuary to commemorate the jubilee of the mission, April 1896.

Priests.

Rev. John Murphy, 1846 ; died Archdeacon of Cork, 1885.
„ W. Carter, 1847–53.
„ Maurice Duggan, 1853-October 1879.
„ Robt. Bridges, 1878 ; Professor of Moral Philosophy at St. Joseph's College, 1885; died 1888.
„ T. B. Allen, 1885.
„ H. Roberts, 1885 ; appointed M.R. 1891.
„ Joseph Rigby, 1896.

LIVERPOOL (*Liverpool*). Holy Cross, Great Crosshall Street.

This mission was founded in 1842 by Fr. F. McDonnell, whose first chapel was a room over a cow-house in Standish Street, The Oblate Fathers took over the mission in 1850, and shortly after this the schools were erected by Fr. Noble. Bishop Jolivet, of Natal, was one of the priests here till about 1867. Dr. Jolivet built the church, which was opened October 30, 1860, by Bishop Goss, the sermon being preached by Cardinal Wiseman. The new chancel was opened August 31, 1875. A new altar was erected in 1882. The schools underwent extensive alterations in 1895.

Priests since 1875.

Rev. F. M. Gaughren, now bishop.
„ T. G. Roche, 1876.
„ D. Madden, 1883.
„ B. O'Dwyer, 1883.
„ L. G. Roche, 1887.
„ A. Coyle, 1890.
„ J. McSherry, 1895.
„ C. Byrne, 1904.

LIVERPOOL (*Liverpool*). St. Anthony, Scotland Road, N.

Fr. Jean Baptist Girardot, an *émigré*, erected a chapel in the Scotland Road about 1804. The chapel was afterwards sold, and a new church erected by Fr. P. Wilcock, and opened September 29, 1833. The Abbé Girardot was greatly esteemed in Liverpool for his amiable qualities and for his skill in curing the dropsy. He died at Liverpool in October 1825, aged seventy-five years. Since then the rectors of the mission have been :—

Fr. P. Wilcock, 1825. His assistants in 1837 were Frs. A. Lennon and J. Peduzzi.
„ J. Dawber, for public institutions, 1840.
„ T. Newsham (rector), 1844.
„ P. Power, 1860 (?).
„ P. Murphy, 1875.
„ J. Dowling, 1884.
„ Wm. Newsham, 1894 to date.

LIVERPOOL (*Liverpool*). St. Peter's, Seel Street.

This church was founded from St. Mary's, then the only Catholic place of worship in Liverpool, in 1788 by Fr. Archibald Macdonald, O.S.B. The building was opened on September 7 of the above-named year. The baptismal register dates from 1789, during which year fifty children were baptised. A school in connection with the church was not started till 1817. In 1843 the old presbytery was added to the church to form the sanctuary and sacristy. New schools for girls and infants were erected about 1870 ; they were enlarged in 1889. The interior of the church was renovated and redecorated in 1902 at a cost of £300.

Priests of the Mission.

Rev. A. Macdonald, 1788-1814.
„ Dunstan Tarlton, 1814-16.
„ Gregory Robinson, 1816-35.
„ Vincent Glover, 1835-38.
„ Ephraim Platt, 1838-41.
„ J. F. Appleton, D.D., 1842 ; died of typhus caught during his sacred ministrations, 1847.
„ Thomas Bonney, 1847-64.
„ — Davey, 1864-67.
„ W. B. Scarisbrick, 1867, consecrated Archbishop of Mauritius, 1871.
„ J. Brown, 1872-74.
„ P. M. Anderson, 1874-1900.
„ Robert Corlett, 1901.

The church has always been under the care of Benedictines.

LIVERPOOL (*Liverpool*). St. Sylvester, Scotland Road.

On March 11, 1888, the foundation of the present Gothic church was laid by the Bishop of Liverpool, and the building was opened September 2, 1889. The seating capacity is for about seven hundred. The old chapel was opened in a 'converted wooden shed' in 1875. The schools were built, 1872-73. In May 1896 a new Lady Altar, by Pugin, was erected, and two years later the church was cleaned and decorated. The congregation is estimated at about 7,200.

LIVERPOOL. Our Lady of Lourdes and St. Bernard, Kingsley Road.

Cardinal Manning preached on behalf of this, then recently founded, mission, Sunday, September 9, 1882. A chapel was erected 1884. The new church was opened by the Bishop of Liverpool on Whit Sunday, 1901. The building cost about £8,000. Messrs. Pugin, of London, were the architects. The first rector of the church was Fr. Billington, afterwards Dean of Lancaster. His curate, Fr. James Hayes, succeeded in 1885. The rector in 1901 was Fr. Harris. Catholic population about 1,800.

LIVERPOOL. St. Vincent of Paul.

On February 5, 1843, Mass was celebrated in an upper room in Blundell Street; and on the 7th of the same month a boys' school, taught by a Christian Brother, was opened in the same room. This arrangement continued till January 1848. Fr. Edward Walmesley was the first priest. St. Vincent's was served from St. Patrick's till it became an independent mission, August 1852. On January 23, 1849, a large wooden shed was hired for a chapel, and in April 1856 the first stone of the new church was laid by the Bishop of Liverpool. E. Welby-Pugin designed the building, which is in 'the purest style of Geometrical Gothic.' The opening by Bishop Goss took place in August 1857. The schools, presented by E. Challoner, Esq., were opened 1862, and greatly enlarged 1893. Bishop O'Reilly, of Liverpool, was rector of the mission 1852-73. He was consecrated in St. Vincent's Church March 19 of the last-named year.

LIVERPOOL. The Sacred Heart, Mount Vernon.

Till 1885, a small convent chapel did duty for missionary purposes, but by that year the vast increase of the congregation made a new church absolutely necessary. A church in the Early Decorated style was commenced that year, and opened in December 1886. The accommodation is for 800. The imposing character of the front is enhanced by an octagonal turret. The handsome stone pulpit of the church was presented by Mr. T. Poulton, the large bell by Mr. Michael Byrne, and the carved oak tabernacle with silver embossed door by Mr. J. Collier. The silver-plated lamps in the sanctuary were the gift of W. Yates, Esq. The marble high altar, by Messrs. Pugin, was unveiled by the Bishop of Liverpool, Sunday, October 11, 1891. New schools for 400 children were erected 1898.

LIVERPOOL. Our Lady of Reconciliation, Eldon Street.

Foundation stone laid by Bishop Goss, Wednesday, February 2, 1859. The old chapel in Blackstock Street was opened in 1854 by Fr. R. Vandepitte, a missionary from Flanders. The building was merely a wooden shed. The Catholics of the district then numbered about eleven thousand. The new church, opened in 1860, is in the French style of Gothic. The presbytery and schools, erected about 1886, cost upwards of £10,000. There are many Poles in the neighbourhood, and a 'Polish service' is given on the first and third Sunday of each month. A new altar to Our Lady of Wilna was opened September 17, 1893, and the organ February 4, 1894.

LIVERPOOL. St. Mary's, Hadfield Street.

The old chapel was founded in 1736. In 1701, Fr. W. Gillibrand, S.J., served the Liverpool mission, which had then no regular chapel. In 1736, Fr. John Harvesty, S.J., built St. Mary's. In December 1745, when Prince Charles Edward Stuart and the Highlanders retreated from Derby, the mob burnt the chapel to the ground. They behaved 'with the greatest respect' to the priests—Fr. Hermengild Carpenter, S.J., and Fr. Thos. Stanley, allowing them to remove the ciborium and other consecrated vessels. Henry Pippard, Esq., a Catholic, and one of the chief merchants of the town, rebuilt the chapel 1758, in a secluded part of the city. The new building looked exactly like a warehouse. In spite of this safeguard, the Catholics could only enter the chapel with the greatest caution. In 1783 the mission was transferred to the Benedictines. In 1844 a fine new church, designed by A. W. Pugin, was commenced to take the place of the old ugly chapel. The opening took place July 1, 1845. The sermon was preached by Bishop Morris. The church, 'a new and spacious building,' occupied the site of the old chapel, and accommodated 3,000. In 1883–84 the site of the building was bought by the Lancashire and Yorkshire Railway Company, and a new church—a reproduction of the old one—was built in Hadfield Street. P. P. Pugin was the architect. The solemn opening took place July 7, 1885. In 1895 the sanctuary was beautifully decorated by Mr. Pippet. The schools were enlarged 1898.

Priests.

Rev. — Williams and — Harris, S.J., 1773.
 „ A. Macdonald, 1773.
 „ E. Pennington, 1788.
 „ Jos. Collins, 1794.

S

Rev. Alexis Pope, 1797.
„ Wilfrid Fisher, 1802.
„ James Wilkinson, 1847.
„ S. Giles, 1850.
„ Jos. Sheridan, 1850.
„ Bede Almond, 1860.
„ P. O'Brien, 1873.
„ Benedict Snow, 1878.
„ George Bede Cox, 1894.

LOFTUS, SALTBURN - BY - THE - SEA, YORKS (*Middlesbrough*). SS. Joseph and Cuthbert.

The Catholics of Loftus, after having worshipped for some years 'in a small room over a shop,' acquired a site for a school-chapel near the market-place. The building, to hold some three hundred persons, was erected from designs by Mr. Martin Carr. Fr. W. Sullivan was the priest at the time the chapel was built. The opening took place on March 8, 1883. The building will hold over three hundred. The altar, of Corinthian design, was decorated by Dominic Mazzotti, of Saltburn. The stone baptismal font was carved by Mr. Robt. Moody, of Loftus. Before the opening of this mission the nearest chapel was at Ugthorpe, eight miles distant.

LONG EATON, DERBYSHIRE (*Nottingham*). St. Francis of Assisi.

Mission established 1884.
Priests.
Rev. J. McCarthy, 1884.
(Mission served from Cathedral &c., 1889 *et seq.*)
„ Frederick Begue, 1896.
„ Emile Van Dale, 1897.
(Served from West Bridgford, 1900.)
„ T. B. Birmingham, 1901 to date.

LONG HORSELEY, NORTHUMBER- LAND (*Hexham and Newcastle*). St. Thomas of Canterbury.

This mission was served by the Jesuit Fathers for many years. Gorton in his 'Topographical Dictionary' says : 'Here is a strong ancient tower, which formerly belonged to the Horseleys, but is now (1833) converted into a Catholic chapel, with a house for the priest. It is a plain square building with a deer park adjoining it.' In 1733 the Hon. Mrs. Widdrington endowed the mission with £400, which sum was many years ago handed over by the Jesuits to the bishop of the district. In 1750 the following note was made by one of the Fathers of the Society which well expresses the concealment required during the existence of the penal laws :

'Horseley (Mr. Howe) no salary from the place, but £30 from the factory, and £5 to pay house rent. Customers to shop about one hundred and twenty-five. Of my own gaining about ten.' The 'shop' and 'customers' are of course the chapel and congregation, and the 'gaining' the number of persons reconciled to the Church.

A new Gothic church took the place of the tower-chapel in 1843. Confirmation was given here on November 8, 1891, for the first time in thirty-one years, when, strange to say, exactly thirty-one persons received that Sacrament, from the Bishop of Hexham and Newcastle.

Priests since 1824.
Rev. John Sharrock, 1824.
„ N. Brown, 1835.
„ W. Fletcher, 1837.
„ James Hubbersty, 1848.
„ J. Rogerson, 1854.
„ Thos. Clavering, 1860.
„ Robert Orrell, 1871.
„ James Smits, 1885.
„ W. Farmery, 1888.

Rev. Matthew Culley, 1892.

„ George Dover, 1897.

„ George Silvertop, 1899.

„ Francis Kuyte, 1904 to date.

LONGRIDGE, near **PRESTON, LANCS** (*Salford*). St. Wilfrid, Pitt Street.

The mission was established, 1869. By 1884 the congregation had become too large for the chapel. The main portion of the present church was opened Sunday, July 4, 1886, by Bishop Vaughan, of Salford. The cost of the completed portion was about £3,000 ; style, Early English ; seating capacity about 500.

Priests.

Rev. Charles Boardman, D.D., here in 1871.

„ J. Wissink, 1895 to date.

LONGTON, STAFFS (*Birmingham*). St. Gregory.

The mission was formerly known as Lane End. In 1819, through the exertions of Bishop Milner, a site was obtained and a good chapel erected for the benefit of the many Catholics of these parts. Before this time, the nearest chapel was at Caverswall Castle (*q.v.*). For some months after the opening, Longton was attended by Frs. Thomas Baddeley and William Wareing, but in 1820 Fr. Edw. Daniel was appointed resident priest. This zealous pastor built a school and provided the chapel with an organ. The chapel itself he enlarged in 1834. In 1850 the building was enlarged by transepts added at the expense of Messrs. Hamilton and Moore, two members of the congregation. The old chapel having long

become inadequate for the largely increasing congregation, the present church (140 ft. × 50 ft.) was erected, and opened by Bishop Ullathorne, July 20, 1869. His Lordship referred to the new structure as likely to prove ' a great boon to the poor Catholics in this dreary town of sin and mud.'

Priests.

Rev. E. Daniel, 1820.

„ James Massam, M.R., 1857.

„ John Stringfellow, 1877 to date.

LOSTOCK HALL, LANCS (*Salford*). St. Paulinus.

The Hall, the ancient seat of the Anderton family, was built 1591, and enlarged 1702. James Anderton (1557–1613) appears to have conformed to protestantism for a time, but later is said to have assisted his brother Roger in setting up a secret press at the Hall. Dingley, the apostate priest and informer, deposed to saying Mass at the Hall during 1592. Fr. Lawrence Anderton, S.J., nephew of James, and author of the ' Liturgy of the Mass,' ' Life of Luther,' &c., laboured in the district for several years after 1610. The Hall was lost to the Andertons in 1716, owing to Francis Anderton, Esq., having espoused the cause of James III. (Prince James Francis Stuart). The mansion is now a ruin and has passed to the Blundells of Ince. The place, which was originally served by the Jesuits, was till quite recently included in the Brownedge Mission. In 1892 a chapel was opened at Lostock and served from St. Mary's till it became an independent mission under Dom Francis Turner, O.S.B., in 1902. Fr. Turner, by dint of

s 2

much labour, raised £450 and so reduced the heavy debt on the mission. He died at Ampleforth, December 2, 1905.

Priests at Lostock.

Rev. Henry Holland, S.J., 1610–1643. Was tried and condemned for his priesthood 1648, but ultimately banished. Died at Liège, 1656.

„ John Turberville, 1700. The district in modern times included in the St. Mary's, Brownedge mission. A chapel opened at Lostock 1901 and served from the former place 1891–1902.

„ Dom Francis Ambrose Turner, O.S.B., appointed priest 1902. Died 1905.

LOUGHBOROUGH, LEICESTERSHIRE (*Nottingham*). St. Mary.

The opening of the Catholic chapel at Loughborough through the exertions of the Rev. B. Hulme in December 1835, was made the subject of a furious anti-Catholic 'Address' in the *Times* which, however, was ably answered by a 'Counter Address' in the then widely circulated *Andrews' Weekly Orthodox Journal* (March 8, 1836). The Brothers of Charity opened their college in the town on the feast of the Presentation 1844, when the ceremony was marked by a grand Catholic procession. The famous Fr. Gentili preached at the High Mass. In May 1881, Bishop Riddell, of Northampton, confirmed eighty-three persons in the church.

Priests.

Rev. B. Hulme, 1835.·

„ Norbert Woolfrey, 1840.

„ Dr. Pagani, 1842.

„ Dr. Gentili, 1844.

Rev. A. Rinolfi, 1846.

„ Bartholomew Crosbie, 1848.

„ Andrew Egan, 1851.

„ Andrew McGuire, here in 1888 and to date.

LOUTH, LINCOLNSHIRE (*Nottingham*). St. Mary.

This mission is one of considerable antiquity. Fr. R. Stuthard succeeded Fr. Fromont here 1795, and remained till January 1806, when Fr. F. Martyn was appointed. The Abbé L. Bertrand was incumbent in 1824 and till 1831. The mission was marked vacant 1832, but by 1833 Fr. H. Hall had been appointed. This worthy priest was rector of the mission till after 1875. The church in Upgate was altered and redecorated in August and September 1882, the chancel roof being adorned with emblems of the Passion, and the north wall decorated by a full-length picture of St. Hugh of Lincoln. Fr. A. Rowley was rector in 1883, and to date (1904).

LOWER EDMONTON, HERTS (*Westminster*). Church of the Most Precious Blood.

The mission was opened in the summer of 1903, Fr. MacMullen being the first priest.

LOWESTOFT, SUFFOLK (*Northampton*). Our Lady Star of the Sea.

In August 1881, Mass was said in a house in Upper Raglan Street by a priest from Yarmouth. Fr. Geoffrey Brennan was the first resident missioner, 1882–84. His successor, Fr. Alex. Scott, purchased a site in the Gordon Road, and the first stone of the new building was laid by Bishop Riddell, August 23, 1900. The structure, which accommodates about six hundred, was opened in the course of 1902. The cost of erection—or a considerable portion of it—was defrayed by an anonymous benefactor.

LOWICK, NORTHUMBERLAND
(Hexham and Newcastle). St. Edward.

The mission was established here, 1862, in a temporary chapel, served every alternate Sunday from St. Ninian's, Wooler.
Priests.
Rev. C. Dunn, 1863.
,, Jeremiah Connolly, 1873.
,, James Stark, 1877.
,, Joseph Wilhelm, 1882.
,, C. Hergenroether, 1885.
,, Edward Rigby, 1888.
,, Alex. Gerry, 1901 to date.

LULWORTH CASTLE, DORSET
(Plymouth). St. Mary.

The ancestral seat of the Weld family. A chaplain has been maintained here since 1641, when Humphrey Weld, Esq., of Holdwell, bought the estate. St. Mary's Chapel was erected in 1786. The style is Classical. King George III. and his consort, Queen Charlotte, visited the Castle in 1789, when his Majesty began that warm friendship for the Weld family which has become one of the matters of history. In 1790 Fr. James Carroll was consecrated first Bishop of Baltimore, U.S.A., in the chapel of Lulworth Castle (August 15, 1790). Thomas

(afterwards Cardinal) Weld (1773–1837) was one of the acolytes on this occasion. The consecrating prelate was Bishop Walmesley, V.A. of the Western District. The Trappist monks of Mount Melleraye occupied a house at Lulworth from about 1794 till 1815, when they returned to France. Owing to the recent expulsion of the French religious orders, the Fathers have again settled in England, at Kingsbridge, Devon (*q.v.*).

LUTON, BEDFORDSHIRE *(Northampton).* Our Lady Help of Christians.

For several years Luton was served on Sundays from Bedford. In December 1883, the Bishop of Northampton secured a house in Rothsay Road as temporary presbytery and chapel. In January 1884, Fr. Joseph O'Connor was appointed to the mission as resident priest. In 1892 Fr. John Hy. Ashmole became rector. Fr. Hy. O'Connor is the present incumbent.

LUTTERWORTH, LEICESTERSHIRE *(Nottingham).* Our Lady of Victories and St. Alphonsus.

The mission is described as being started by Fr. Martin, chaplain to Lord Denbigh, 1874, and for some time was served from Monks Kirby. After this Fr. Hazeland, chaplain to Lord Braye, and the present incumbent, fitted up a temporary chapel near the Denbigh Arms Hotel. The site of the present church was presented by Lord Denbigh, who also gave £200 towards the cost of building (£1,200). The opening, by the Bishop of Nottingham, took place in August 1881.

LYDD, KENT (*Southwark*).

An ancient town near Romney. It is famous of late years for its artillery range and also for the fearful explosive *lyddite* which was first experimented upon here. The chapel of wood and iron, dedicated to St. Martin of Tours, was erected in 1890 for the accommodation of the many Catholic soldiers of the garrison. It was long served by the Rev. E. St. John of St. George's Cathedral, but since 1898 the Canons Regular of St. Augustine have been in charge of the mission.

LYDIATE, near LIVERPOOL, LANCS (*Liverpool*). Our Lady.

The foundation of the new church of Our Lady was laid on the Thursday of Easter week 1854 by Francis Weld Blundell, Esq., of Ince Blundell Hall, who generously presented the site. The endowment of the church was left in the form of bequest by Charles Robt. Blundell, Esq. The church—designed by J. Scoles—is provided with a tower and steeple. The building was opened in 1854. The schools were erected 1862, and enlarged 1887. The church was consecrated October 11, 1892. Lydiate Hall, in the parish of Halsall, is situated about ten miles from Liverpool, on the Southport Road. It was built between 1451 and 1485, and subsequently came into the possession of the Andertons, and after them the Blundells. The old chapel was disused after the opening of the church in 1854. During some alterations made in the place in 1841 a secret hiding-place behind a sliding panel was discovered by a workman. An old pewter chalice and paten are still preserved at the Hall. This species of altar plate was permitted during the penal times 'as less likely to attract the cupidity of pursuivants.' The priests at Lydiate for nearly two centuries were Jesuits. Some of them were as follows:—F. Waldegrave, cousin or brother of Lord Waldegrave (†1701); J. Draper (†1703); Rev. J. Mostyn (†1721); J. Blackbourne (†1728). The mission of Lydiate was made over to the Bishop of Liverpool by the Society of Jesus in 1860. Fr. Thos. S. Gibson was the first priest appointed after the transference.

Recent Priests.

Rev. Thos. Gibson, 1860.
„ Wm. Johnson, 1879.
„ Edward Powell, 1885.
„ John Hanly, here in 1904.

LYME REGIS, DORSET (*Plymouth*). St. George.

The church was built 1835-37 during the rectorate of Fr. C. Fisher. E. Goodridge was the architect. Fr. William Vaughan, afterwards Bishop of Plymouth (1855–1902), completed the church and built the presbytery. The Lady chapel, described as a 'bijou,' was finished 1851. The style of the church is Gothic. In 1882 the whole interior of the edifice was completely transformed by Messrs. Westlake & Co. The high altar was lighted by a handsome stained-glass window, the gift of a venerable member of the congregation. Some idea of the growth of Catholicity in Lyme Regis over sixty years ago may be gathered from the early confirmation returns. In 1836 it was ten, and in 1849 twenty-three. Fr. J. Hurst, founder of Sedgley Park School, is said to have been here in 1771, but probably only as a visitor, as prior to

1830 the few Catholics of the district 'were in the habit of attending Axminster for prayers.'

Priests.

Rev. Chas. Fisher, 1835.
„ W. Swarbrick, 1837.
„ Wm. Vaughan, 1840.
„ W. Agar, 1845.
„ J. Conolly, 1854.
„ Joseph Bunn, 1855.
„ Joseph O'Dwyer, 1857.
„ James Canon Dawson, 1860.
„ Richard Meagar, 1863.
„ Wm. Walsh, 1867.
„ W. Downing, here 1871.
„ L. Croutelle, 1882 to date.

LYMINGTON, HANTS (*Portsmouth*). Our Lady of Mercy and St. Joseph.

The mission was established in 1800, mainly, it appears, for the benefit of the many French emigrants who settled in and around this old seaport town at the time of the Revolution. The chapel was at Pylewell House, the residence of a branch of the Weld family of Lulworth Castle. The old chapel was superseded by the present church, opened May 18, 1859. The Pylewell property afterwards passed to Wm. Ingham Whitaker, Esq., the millionaire. The baptismal registers date from about 1803.

Priests since 1800.

Rev. J. Blot, 1800.
„ John Alleway, —.
„ Thos. Tilbury, 1807.
„ Abbé Le Tellier, 1809.
„ John Brown, —.
„ John Leadbetter, —.
„ Wm. Waterton, S.J., 1823.
„ Richard Norris, S.J., 1824.
„ J. Leadbetter, 1827.
„ W. Waterton, 1833.
„ J. Clough, 1841.
„ Wm. O'Brien, 1846.

Rev. Ralph Cooper, 1853.
„ Joseph Holden, 1856.
„ Jn. Milner, 1858.
„ Patrick O'Connell, 1866.
„ Cuthbert Winder, 1904 to date.

LYNDHURST, HANTS (*Portsmouth*). Our Lady of the Assumption.

In November 1886, Fr. P. O'Connell, of Lymington, established a chapel at Wellands Hall where Mass might be said on Sundays. In this work he was ably seconded by Mr. J. Maxwell, the well-known publisher. According to one account there have long been a number of Catholics in the vicinity. The new church, capable of accommodating about one hundred persons, was built at the expense of M. Edward de Souberbielle in memory of his wife Marie Louise. The style is of the eleventh and twelfth centuries; the architect was Sir Arthur Blomfield. The building, a gem of its kind, was consecrated by the Bishop of Portsmouth July 28, 1896.

LYNFORD, NORFOLK (*Northampton*). Our Lady of Consolation and St. Stephen.

This church, erected by the 'pious munificence' of Mrs. Lyne-Stephens, was commenced in 1878 and consecrated Tuesday, October 7, 1884, by the Bishop of Northampton, Dr. Riddell.

Priests.

Rev. Michael Canon Dwane, 1882 and to date.

LYNMOUTH, DEVON.

Prospect House was opened as a convent of the Poor Clare nuns August 1904. Rev. Anatole Durand, O.F.M., is the chaplain.

LYNN, NORFOLK (*Northampton*).
St. Mary's.

The mission was founded in 1810 by the Abbé P. Dacheux, an *émigré*. At his death, May 12, 1843, aged eighty-three, he left his property to the poor of the district. Two years later (May 8, 1845) the present church was opened by Bishop Wareing. Only the chancel and nave (costing £650) were complete at this time ; the rest was added later. The fine east window was designed by Wailes. In 1847 the congregation presented the rector, Fr. Dallas, with a silver chalice of antique pattern for the use of the mission.

Priests.

Rev. Abbé P. Dacheux, 1810.
  ,, John Dalton, 1843.
  ,, Geo. Canon Rigby, 1847.
  ,, T. McDonald, 1860.
  ,, Wm. Poole, 1863.
  ,, Andrew Walshe, 1866.
  ,, Stodart Macdonald, 1877.
  ,, Geo. Wrigglesworth, 1888.
  ,, Chas. Eeles, 1901 to date.

LYNTON, NORTH DEVON (*Plymouth*).

A recently established mission served from Lynmouth.

LYTHAM, LANCS (*Liverpool*).
St. Peter.

The handsome church was re-opened after redecoration, Sunday, September 9, 1888. The Lady and St. Joseph chapels were adorned after the Gothic style, and the entire church wainscoted in oak. New stations of the Cross and an oak pulpit were given by the congregation. Mass was formerly said at Clifton Hall, where a regular chapel was built 1764 and used till 1800. A tithe-barn was then fitted up for worship, and used till the opening of the church in 1839. The tower was added in 1878 by the late Jn. Talbot Clifton, Esq., who also presented the present rectory. The church was newly benched in 1893, and a peal of bells hung 1894. The congregation is about 1,000.

Priests.

Rev. W. Westby, 1712.
  ,, C. Burton, S.J., 1740.
  ,, — Mansell, S.J., 1750.
  ,, — Blacow, O.S.B., 1790.
  ,, — Pope, O.S.B., 1802.
  ,, Thos. Dawson, 1804.
  ,, Jos. Walmesley, 1829.
  ,, Roger Taylor, 1873.
  ,, James Canon Taylor, 1885.

M

MACCLESFIELD, CHESHIRE (*Shrewsbury*). St. Alban's.

From 1716 till the apostasy of Viscount Fauconberg in 1732, Mass was said at his residence of Sutton Hall. After this time a chapel was opened at Lane Ends. In 1792, a larger chapel was erected at Blackwall Gate. Another and still larger chapel, dedicated to St. Michael, was built in Chester Road 1810, a room partitioned off serving as the priest's residence! Fr. J. Hall, D.D., came here in 1821, at which time the congregation numbered about 300. He did much for the Catholicity of the place, and also attended one or two other missions besides. In 1839 he commenced the present fine example of 'an old English parochial church,' designed by Pugin, and opened in May 1841. The splendid east window was the gift of the Earl of Shrewsbury. A Catholic cemetery was blessed in 1866.

Priests.

Rev. Edw. Kenyon, 1792.
,, Abbé Louis Robin, 1796 (?).
,, J. Provost Hall, D.D., 1821.
,, Hy. Alcock, 1857.
,, Wm. Walton, 1858.
,, Geo. Clegg, 1862.
,, M. Rogerson, 1863.
,, Hy. Canon Walker, 1872.
,, Jas. Robinson, 1889.

MAGHALL, LIVERPOOL (*Liverpool*). St. George.

The mission was founded in 1887, and was served from the Bishops' House till 1892, when Canon Charles Green was appointed rector. He was succeeded by the present incumbent, Fr. Wm. Dennet, in 1902.

MAIDENHEAD, BERKS (*Portsmouth*). St. Joseph, Market Place.

The mission was started in 1867 by Fr. J. C. Robertson, who opened a temporary chapel in St. Ives Place. In March 1879, a fine site was procured for £1,116, and in August 1884 the first stone was laid. The church is cruciform, of flint and brick. The style is of the Transition period. The cost of the building was £1,500. Fr. J. Scannell was the priest at the time the new church was built. The building was opened in December 1884.

Recent Priests.

Rev. Jn. Watson, here in 1891.
,, Louis Canon Hall, 1893.
,, Jn. Watson, here (second time) 1897.
,, P. Curtin, 1903 to date.

MAIDEN LANE, STRAND, LONDON, W.C. (*Westminster*).

The Church of Corpus Christi was commenced August 1874 by the late Canon Keens. The site of the building is on that of the ' Cyder Cellars ' music-hall, made famous by Thackeray and Sam Hall's gruesome song. The building, which is of red brick and Gothic in style, was opened by Cardinal Manning in 1875. Present rector, Fr. Jn. Subra.

MAIDSTONE, KENT (*Southwark*). St. Francis of Assisi.

At the initiation of Bishop Grant a mission was opened here in 1859, Mass being said in ' a poor dwelling-house in an obscure street.' A large mansion, known as Grove House, was purchased in 1860, where a temporary chapel was fitted up. The schools, designed by E. W. Pugin, were opened by Bishop Grant in March 1863. On October 4, 1880, the present church, designed by C. Wray, was opened by Bishop Danell. The style is Geometric Gothic; dimensions, 60 ft. by 40 ft.

Priests.

Rev. R. Emanuele, 1859.

,, James Purdon, 1866.

,, A. Cumberlege, 1869.

,, M. Duggan, 1877.

,, J. Warner, 1885.

,, James Duggan, 1893.

,, Geo. Le Bosquet, 1899 to date.

MALDON, ESSEX (*Westminster*). Our Lady.

The mission was commenced in 1890, and served on Sundays from Witham till 1901. The first chapel (temporary) was in Silver Street, and was replaced by the present one in the Victoria Road 1898. Catholic population about seventy.

Priests.

Rev. M. Fitzpatrick.

,, A. Fortescue, D.D.

MALMESBURY, WILTS (*Clifton*). St. Aldhelm, Cross Hays.

The mission was started in 1867, ' with just means sufficient to support the missionary priest-in-charge and a lay brother.' In 1868, a school was opened; the attendance in 1880 was about fifty. The church, a Gothic stone-faced brick structure, was built in 1875. Fr. F. Larive, of the Congregation of St. Francis of Sales, who was priest here in 1881, did much to spread the Faith in and around Malmesbury. The wealthy silk manufacturer, Mr. Davenport, ' a good Catholic proprietor,' was a great benefactor to the mission. Fr. F. Decompoix, here since 1891, is the present rector.

MALTON, YORKS (*Middlesbrough*). St. Mary.

Fr. John Taylor, S.J., who laboured in the Yorkshire district, was arrested here June 7, 1642, and in March following was indicted at the York assizes for his priesthood. He was sentenced to death, but subsequently released. After a long life spent on the mission he died in Hampshire 1675. The present mission dates from 1837, in which year the chapel was built.

Priests.

Rev. Robert Garstang, 1837.

,, Thos. Middlehurst, 1851.

,, Stephen Wells, 1857.

,, Thos. Middlehurst (second time), 1860.

,, James Redding, 1881.

,, Patrick Clarke, 1885.

,, Wm. Murray, 1888.

,, James Coghlan, 1890.

Rev. Edmund Hickey, 1893.

„ Augustine D'Hooghe, 1902 to date.

MALVERN, GREAT (Birmingham). St. Joseph's.

The church, in the Early English style, was opened October 26, 1876. The site was given by Mr. Hornyold, of Blackmore Park ; T. R. Donelly, architect. Although so comparatively long established, the church is still served from the Benedictine monastery at Great Malvern.

MALVERN, GREAT, WORCESTERSHIRE. Our Lady and St. Edmund.

The Benedictine monastery was established here in 1891, but by 1904 the chapel had become so dilapidated that it was resolved to erect a new church. The foundation stone of the building was laid Tuesday, September 6, 1904, by the Bishop of Birmingham. A statue of St. Edmund, king and martyr, the secondary patron, stands on a niche to the left of the porch. The seating accommodation is for about 300. This church was one of the last designed by the late Peter Paul Pugin, K.S.G. The opening took place in the summer of 1905.

The mission of Great Malvern was established in 1871 by Fr. Henry Bernard Bulbeck at Aldwyn Tower. He died in 1901.

MANCHESTER, LANCASHIRE (Salford). St. Alban's, Fawcett Street, Ancoats.

The first chapel was opened November 15, 1863, the present church in 1878. Before the erection of a separate mission the district was served from St. Anne's.

Priests.

Rev. John Gornall, 1863.

Rev. P. Hennebery, 1884.

„ F. Timony, 1888 to date.

MANCHESTER. St. Aloysius.

As the congregation, between four and five hundred in number, was leaving the church after the last Mass on Sunday, October 2, 1880, the floor gave way, with the result that one person was killed and six injured. The accident was caused by a subsidence of the foundations. The new church, in Park Place, Ardwick Green, was opened March 15, 1884, by Bishop Vaughan, of Salford. The building is Gothic and cruciform. The accommodation is for 800, the cost of the building, of which Mr. Healy, of Manchester, was the architect, being about £3,200. Fr. J. M. O'Callaghan was priest at the time the church was built. The mission was established 1852, and for some years was served from St. Augustine's.

MANCHESTER. St. Anne's.

The church was opened August 31, 1847, and completed June 7, 1848. The first priest of the mission was Fr. Geo. Green, afterwards Catholic chaplain at Dartmoor Prison for many years. The church debt was greatly reduced (£5,000 to £2,000) by Canon Liptrott, who also made several valuable additions to the schools and presbytery. Congregation about 6,000 (1906).

Priests.

Rev. Geo. Green, 1847.

„ Thos. Allen, 1855.

„ Peter Canon Liptrott, 1865.

„ M. Buckley (administrator), 1894.

„ Lionel Canon O'Kelly, 1895 to date.

MANCHESTER. St. Augustine's.

The old church was built 1818-1820 at the suggestion of Fr. Broomhead. The site was in Granby Row. The ground was recently acquired by the Corporation for £39,000. The present church in York Street was opened by the Bishop of Salford, September 8, 1896. See under St. Chad's.

MANCHESTER. St. Bridget, Mill Street, Bradford.

When, in 1877, it became necessary to establish a mission for the largely increasing Catholic population here, a site was obtained by the late Canon Liptrott, of St. Anne's, Manchester, from Townley-Parker, Esq., upon which a school chapel was erected at a cost of £2,000. The building was opened in 1879, and by 1880 the district served by it had become an independent mission. The estimated congregation is over 4,000 (1906). An iron church took the place of the chapel in the school May 18, 1884.

Priests.

Rev. Wm. Sassen, 1880 to date.

MANCHESTER. St. Chad's.

Catholics are said to have been very numerous in Manchester during the seventeenth and eighteenth centuries, but on account of the laws numbers were compelled to disguise their religion. Chapels near the town existed at Crumpsall Hall, Trafford, &c., and Catholics were frequently visited in their own homes by peripatetic priests. No records of baptisms were kept till about 1772, when they numbered seventy. In 1781, the Catholic population was reckoned at 1,100. Fr. Rowland Broomhead, an alumnus of Sedgley Park and the English College, Rome, who came to Manchester in 1778, made the old religion a power. The priests immediately before him were Fr. Edw. Helme (died 1773) and Fr. Orrell, who in 1776 built the old St. Chad's Chapel in Rook Street. This place of worship supplanted an older chapel down a passage known as 'Roman Entry.' After sixteen years' labour Fr. Broomhead found it necessary to erect another chapel (St. Mary's) in Mulberry Street. A third, St. Augustine's, was consecrated a few days before his death in 1820, at which time the Catholic population had risen from 1,000 in 1778 to over 40,000! The old St. Chad's, in Rook Street, was sold in February 1846, and the foundations of the new church commenced in York Street, Cheetham, the following April. The building was opened by Bishop Browne, August 4, 1847, upon which occasion a relic of St. Chad was presented to the church by Bishop (afterwards Cardinal) Wiseman.

MANCHESTER. St. Edward, Rusholme.

The church was opened in December 1861. Style, Early English, from design by A. W. Pugin; size, 90 ft. by 44 ft.; cost of erection, about £3,000.

Priests.

Rev. J. Fox, 1861.
„ Peter Vermeulen, 1874.
„ Cornelius Vervoort, 1877.
„ Thos. Croskell, 1879 and to date.

MANCHESTER. St. Francis of Assisi, Gorton.

The Franciscan Recollect Fathers established a mission here in 1862, the first church being opened October 4, 1863, and the present structure September 26, 1872. Fr. F. Verhaegen was the first Guardian.

MANCHESTER. The Holy Name.

The mission was founded 1867 by Fr. Thos. Porter, S.J. The church was built out of a legacy left by Miss Harriet Walton, of Worcester. A splendid Chapel of the Sacred Heart was added to the church May 1888. The altarpiece represents the vision of Our Saviour to the Blessed Margaret Mary.

Priests.
Rev. Thos. Porter, 1867.
„ Henry Birch, 1871.
„ Wm. Lawson, 1877.
„ Joseph Jackson, 1885.
„ Bernard Vaughan, 1888.
„ Thos. Brown, 1902 to date.

MANCHESTER. St. Mary's, Mulberry Street.

The old chapel, as has been already mentioned, was erected by Fr. R. Broomhead, and was opened November 30, 1794. The fabric was built by subscriptions from Catholics and Protestants, the annual ground rent, payable to Jn. Leaf, Esq., being £49 10s. Fr. H. Gillow, rector 1821-37 is said to have been the last priest in Manchester to wear hair powder, knee breeches, and silver buckles. The old chapel, having long become inadequate, was replaced by the present Gothic church, opened by Bishop Brown October 19, 1848.

Priests.
Rev. E. Kenyon, 1794-1816.
„ Henry Gillow, 1821-37.
„ J. Billington, 1837.
„ Jas. Boardman, 1844.
„ Mathias Canon Formby, 1846.

Rev Jn. Newton, 1863.
„ John Burke, M.R., 1884.
„ Edward O'Dwyer, 1888.
„ Thos. Buckley, 1897.
„ Thos. Walsh, 1898 to date.

MANCHESTER. St. Michael's.

The church (style Early English), for 1,000, was opened August 1, 1869. Wm. Nicholson, Esq., was the architect. The sanctuary is lighted by a fine east window representing the Crucifixion. Until the opening of the church the mission was served by a temporary chapel, opened July 1859.

Priests.
Mission served from St. Patrick's from 1859 till after 1875.
Rev. Henry Hill, 1877.
„ John Bramer, 1882.
„ Thos. Canon Byrne, 1888 and to date.

MANCHESTER. St. Patrick's, Livesey Street.

The church was opened February 29, 1832, by Bishop Penswick, V.A. The style is Grecian and cruciform. In 1846, much scandal was caused by the affair of Fr. Daniel Hearne, the rector. This priest did not get on well with his curates, and to prevent further difficulty Bishop Brown replaced him by Fr. (afterwards Bishop) Roskell. The largely Irish congregation made a great disturbance at this, denouncing the Bishop and English clergy, and even brawling in the church during service time! Thanks to the intervention of Frs. Gentili and Furlong, the deplorable state of things ended November 12, 1846. Fr. Hearne died on the mission in the United States some time after 1851. In 1854, the mission had two flourishing elementary schools, with an average attendance of 900 pupils. The Sunday-school attendance was upwards of 1,000.

Priests after Fr. Roskell.

Rev. Edmund Cantwell, 1851 to after 1875.

„ Bishop Vaughan (administrator), 1877.

„ D. Forbes (administrator, 1891).

„ J. Canon Mussely (rector), 1894 and to date.

MANCHESTER. St. William.

This chapel is in Simpson Street, close to Rochdale Road. The style is plain Gothic, and the building will accommodate about 750. The cost, £1,200, was almost entirely contributed by the congregation of St. Chad's. The architect of the chapel—opened in December 1865—was Mr. E. Tijou. The mission was served from St. Chad's till 1895, and again from 1903-5.

Priests.

Rev. James Thomson, 1895.

„ M. Holohan, 1899.

MAPLEDURHAM, OXON. (*Birmingham*). St. Michael.

The place is associated with the ancestral seat of the ancient Catholic family of Blount, who have been resident here since 1489. Fr. Richard Blount, first Provincial of the Jesuits in England, 1623, was a member of this family, which has given several members to the Society. Mapledurham was one of the places served by the Jesuit Fathers of the Oxford Circuit of St. Mary, but the records, if existing, are 'now lost to memory.' The house, like all those of the recusants, has 'a good specimen of a priests' hiding-place.' In the eighteenth century Mapledurham

would appear to have been served for some time by Franciscans. It is mentioned in the correspondence of Fr. Felix Englefield, O.S.F. (died 1767), and in 1758 Fr. Edward Madew was resident here. In 1766 Mrs. Mary Blount, of Mapledurham, gave a donation of £30 to the Order for anniversary and other Masses. The mission is at present served from Reading.

MARGATE (*Southwark*). SS. Austin and Gregory, Victoria Road.

From the time of James II. to the close of the eighteenth century, the few Catholics in Margate and Ramsgate had to resort to the ancient mansion of the Hales family, near Canterbury, for 'the ordinances and sacraments of the Church.' About 1793, the wealthy Lancashire Catholic family of Gillow had Mass said privately for them by their chaplain in a small building in Prospect Place. In 1800, Bishop Douglass, aided by Mr. Kebbel-White, bought the site of a chapel, which was erected in Prospect Place 1801-4. The external appearance was very much like a Methodist meeting-house. The chapel was 70 ft. long by 20 ft. wide, with a gallery at one end, and was capable of seating 250 persons. The first baptism is recorded March 9, 1823. The Abbé François Bellisant, an *émigré*, was the first resident priest (1804-8). He afterwards became chaplain to the Benedictine nuns at Hammersmith. Fr. Joseph Anson succeeded him. He was followed by Fr. J. Costigan, from Webb Street, Bermondsey. From 1803-21 the baptisms at Margate numbered 129; from 1822-37, 130. The old chapel in later times was adorned with a stone font presented by

Pugin and a copy of Guido's picture of the Crucifixion.[1] This picture was rescued from the old chapel of Moorfields when it was burnt by the Gordon rioters in 1780. Fr. Costigan opened a small school shortly after his arrival, but owing to lack of funds it had to be soon closed. Upon his arrival, Fr. Costigan found himself the only priest upon the coast of Kent. He had in consequence to visit from time to time such remote districts as St. Leonards and Hastings. He sometimes celebrated Mass at Rye, Romney, Deal, Hythe, and Dover, for such scattered congregations as he could collect. Once when going on a sick call a great distance off, Dr. Phillpotts, protestant Bishop of Exeter, kindly drove him to his destination in his coach, and, the evening being very stormy, the great Duke of Wellington put him up for the night at Walmer Castle. In 1860, Fr. H. Whiteside, O.S.B., of Ramsgate, who had succeeded Fr. Costigan after his retirement in 1856, started a day school for children in his own house. In three years the number increased to forty, and in 1863 a school-house was erected on a piece of ground adjoining the church. In June 1866, the church was reopened by Bishop Grant, after having undergone much-needed repair. In 1878 what was practically a new church was opened at Ramsgate by extensive additions to the old building. A new pulpit of Caen stone was

[1] During the French Revolution, a ship freighted with sacred pictures and 'church stuff' was wrecked off the coast of Kent, and such portions of the cargo as got ashore were sold by auction. Hence, half a century ago, good copies of religious pictures were common in the neighbourhood of Ramsgate, Deal, Sandwich, &c.

presented in October 1882, and in November 1884 a fine new altar was erected in the church by Captain Chambers, British consul at Guayaquil. Finally in August 1891 a new side chapel was built in honour of St. Joseph. Fr. T. Elphege Power, O.S.B., is the present rector.

MARK CROSS, near TUNBRIDGE WELLS, SUSSEX (Southwark). The Holy Trinity.

The convent boarding school of the Holy Child Jesus nuns, a fine Gothic structure designed by A. W. Pugin, was erected and partially endowed by the late Dowager Duchess of Leeds, 1866. The endowment is mainly for the maintenance of a certain number of orphans of a superior class who hold the same status as the 'foundation scholars' at the public schools. The church—a handsome Decorated Gothic structure—was completed 1875, and is open to the public. Accommodation for about 250.

Priests.

Rev. J. Baron, S.J., 1866.
„ T. Maher, 1874.
„ John Warner, 1877.
„ Michael Cotter, 1885.
„ Charles Stapley, 1888.
„ C. Ellison, 1891.
„ Vincent Placid Wray, O.S.B., 1893.
„ James Duggan, 1900.
„ A. Wright, 1906 to date.

MARKET DRAYTON, SALOP (Shrewsbury). SS. Thomas and Stephen.

The mission was founded from Whitchurch in 1857. The new church was opened by Bishop

Knight, of Shrewsbury, in November 1886, the cost of the building being defrayed by Egerton Harding, Esq., of Old Springs. Mr. Edmund Kirby, of Liverpool, was the architect. The style is Early English.

Priests.

Rev. Jas. Kenny, 1857.
„ H. Walker, 1858.
„ J. Robinson, 1864.
„ L. Levett, 1884 (first resident priest).
„ D. Williams, 1890.
„ H. Lynch, 1894.

MARKET HARBOROUGH, LEICESTERSHIRE (*Nottingham*). Our Lady of Victories.

The mission was started in 1859, being served from Leicester once a fortnight. By 1874, a temporary chapel had been erected and placed under the care of Fr. Richard Vandepitte, during whose rectorate the present church was built. As late as 1893, the 'presbytery' was miserably furnished, the schools were not recognised by Government, and had only eighteen children. By 1897, things had greatly altered for the better. The schools had an average attendance of fifty-two and were 'under inspection,' while the attendance at Mass on Sundays had risen from thirty or forty to nearly a hundred. The total number of the congregation was then about 300.

Priests.

Rev. Fr. R. Vandepitte, 1873.
„ Fr. H. Kavanagh, 1893.

N.B.—A considerable portion of the church and school building fund (£700) was bequeathed by the Abbé Malvoisin, who died 1847. He was chaplain to the Nevilles of Holt.

MARKET RASEN, LINCS (*Nottingham*). Holy Rood.

The place was occasionally visited by Fr. Johnson, S.J., prior to the year 1782. In that year, Fr. Richard Knight, chaplain at Kingerby, built a commodious edifice at Market Rasen which served both for chapel and presbytery. Fr. James Lesley was here till 1793, and the Abbé Allaine from this latter year till 1798. Fr. W. Brewster, 'the last of the Carmelite Order in England,' served the mission from this last date till 1848. This worthy priest, aided by some of the congregation, erected the present chapel, opened September 14, 1824. On retiring from the mission, Fr. Brewster resided at an adjacent cottage till his death in 1849, aged seventy-nine. When Bishop Roskell visited the place in 1849, the mission was in a very flourishing condition, with schools, efficient choir, &c. New north and south aisles were opened in September 1868, the church being remodelled after the style of twelfth-century Gothic by Messrs. Hadfield. The Young family of Kingerby, an ancient Catholic stock, have been great benefactors to the mission. The 122nd anniversary of the establishment of the mission was celebrated Sunday, September 18, 1904.

Priests since 1848.

Rev. James Walker, 1848.
„ Thos. Clarke, 1851.
„ Thos. Canon Sing, 1860.
„ Algernon Moore, here 1871.
„ James Canon Dwyer, 1876.
„ Francis Hays, 1901 to date.

MARNHULL, DORSET (*Plymouth*).

The Hussey family purchased the manor of Marnhull and

established the mission 1651. The priest of the place resided either there or at Stour Provost. A chapel was erected 1772, and continued in use till the opening of the present one, July 3, 1832. The English Benedictine nuns of Paris took refuge here at the time of the great Revolution, but retired to Cannington 1807.

Priests.

Rev. — Smith, 1720.
„ T. Cornforth (died 1748; he founded a fund for the support of his successors).
„ Rd. Molyneux, 1749.
„ Jn. Englefield, 1761 (?).
„ Geo. Bishop, 1768.
„ R. Molyneux, junr., 1769.
„ Jn. Smith, 1770.
„ C. Fryer, 1774.
„ Edw. Hussey, O.S.B., 1785.
„ Abbé Chas. Primord, 1802.
„ Wm. Casey, 1824.
„ Thos. Spencer, 1866 (?).
„ Walter Keily, 1879.
„ John McCarthy, 1882.
„ Augustine White, C.R.L., 1885.
„ B. Grillet, 1892.
„ Urban Rouvière, 1897.
„ Alex. C. Dodard, 1898 to date.

MARPLE BRIDGE, near STOCK-PORT, DERBYSHIRE (*Nottingham*).
Mass was said here for the first time in recent years on December 21, 1859. The church, which is a neat structure, was mainly founded by Lord Howard of Glossop and Edward Ross, Esq., of this locality.

Priests.

Rev. James Luke, 1859.
„ Michael Canon Scully, 1876.
„ C. McSweeny, 1890.
In August 1900 Fr. McSweeny was raised to the dignity of missionary rector.

MARTON, YORKS (*Middlesbrough*). Most Holy Sacrament.
The mission was started in 1774 by Fr. Chas. Howard, D.D., who ministered here till July 1815. Fr. Hogarth, in forwarding the registers to the Commissioners of Records at Somerset House in 1840, implies that the mission has a much older date of foundation than the one given above (1774), but no details are forthcoming. The priest in 1816 was Fr. Thos. Hodgson. After 1824 Canon Robert Hogarth, V.G., was appointed. He was succeeded in 1863 by Fr. Geo. Keasley. The mission was vacant in 1875, 1883, and 1889. After this it was served from Hedon till 1896. In 1897 Fr. Patrick Ryan was rector, and till after 1900. Fr. Christopher Flanagan is the present rector.

MARYLEBONE ROAD, LONDON, N.W. (*Westminster*). Our Lady of the Rosary.
In 1848, the Count de Torre Diaz, a Spanish nobleman resident in London, hired a hall in Cato Street, where Fr. Hodgson, the devoted priest-missioner, said Mass and preached Sunday after Sunday to a numerous congregation drawn from the slums and alleys of the neighbourhood. The chapel having become unsafe, Fr. Hodgson continued his ministry by preaching vigorous open-air sermons in the courts behind Portland Street. In 1849 the Count de Torre Diaz and some other Catholic gentlemen bought land for church and schools in Homer Row, Marylebone Road. After six years, the church was opened in Winchester Row, New Road, afterwards called the Marylebone Road.

T

The building was blessed by Cardinal Wiseman August 9, 1855. The Catholic population of the district at this time was reckoned at 2,500. For several years a portion of the edifice was used as a school. The church, designed by Blount, was enlarged in 1870.

Priests.

Rev. J. Bamber, 1855.
„ W. J. Fielding, 1856.
„ Alfred White, 1860 (?).

In 1884 Fr. White was made rector of the church at Brook Green, Hammersmith, and subsequently was created a canon of Westminster and alderman of the borough. He died in 1904. His successor at Marylebone, the Very Rev. John Canon Brennan, still holds the incumbency.

MARYVALE, near BIRMINGHAM. St. Mary's.

The mission was founded about †1675 by Fr. Andrew Bromwich, he last priest sentenced to death for the Faith in England. In 1794, St. Mary's College, Oscott, was founded in the old house at Maryvale built by Bishop Hornyold as a residence for the Vicars Apostolic of the Midlands. After the transference of the college to the new building in 1838 the house was occupied by Fr. John Henry (Cardinal) Newman and Fr. Faber, who called the place ' Maryvale ' to distinguish it from New Oscott. In 1850, the Sisters of Mercy opened their orphanage within its walls. The chapel was built in 1816 by Bishop Milner, who placed in it a painted window of the Sacred Heart. In 1873, the Sisters established the Association of the Perpetual Lamp in honour of the

Sacred Heart, and the jubilee of the devotion was celebrated in February 1898.

MARYPORT, CUMBERLAND (*Hexham and Newcastle*). Our Lady and St. Patrick.

The mission was commenced in 1838, and the church built 1844–45 at a cost of £1,400. The number of Catholics then was about 300. The dedication of the church was celebrated with great solemnity in May 1846, when Bishop Briggs preached at the High Mass. On Sunday, February 4, 1882, the church was reopened after having undergone an enlargement of some 15 ft. in order to accommodate the increased congregation that had arisen owing to the commencement of the new docks. Fr. J. J. Cummins, O.S.B., the incumbent, acted as architect. Fr. Murphy during his rectorate greatly adorned the church, and introduced several improvements. In 1889, the Catholic population of Maryport was 1,700. In January of 1889, the jubilee of the mission was celebrated by Fr. J. Cummins, O.S.B., the then incumbent. A new Lady Altar was erected in memory of the event.

MATLOCK, DERBYSHIRE (*Nottingham*). Our Lady and St. Joseph.

On May 2, 1880, Mass was said in a house in Holt Lane and the same year a church site was acquired by Canon McKenna, V.G. The church, in the Gothic style, was opened in July 1883; seating capacity for about 200. In the church there is a chapel dedicated to St. Dismas, 'the good thief,' whose *cultus* was popular in early Christian times. For some years after the opening, the church was served from St. Mary's, Derby. The first resident priest was appointed in 1890.

Priests.

Rev. Robert Browne, 1890.
„ Thomas Parkinson, 1892. (Served from Tideswell 1894.)
„ George Le Roy, here in 1897 and to date.

MAWDESLEY, ORMSKIRK, LANCS (*Liverpool*). SS. Peter and Paul.

The Finch family of Mawdesley were great sufferers for the Catholic Faith, one of them, John Finch, being executed at Lancaster, April 20, 1584, for affirming 'that the Pope hath power or jurisdiction in the Kingdom of England.' Another of the family, the Rev. James Finch, was prior of a Carthusian monastery in Austria. After its suppression by Joseph II., he came to England, and died at Fernyhalgh, March 3, 1821, aged seventy-two. The old mansion at Mawdesley contains many hiding-places, and, among other relics of the past, the skull of William Haydock, of Whalley Abbey, martyred 1537. The actual mission was established 1831, when the church was built and opened by Bishop Penswick, V.A.

Rectors.

Rev. J. Lawson, 1831.
„ J. Dawber, 1843 till after 1864.
„ Jn. Hardman, 1871.
„ Jn. Nixon, 1874.
„ John Irish, 1885.
„ Jules Maurus, 1902 to date.

MAWLEY, SHROPSHIRE (*Shrewsbury*). St. Mary.

An entry in the missal used at Mawley states that the chapel was blessed by Bishop Thomas Talbot October 31, 1776. Before this time, Mass was said secretly at the top of Mawley Hall, the residence of the Blounts. The chapel, opened in 1776, was for some time called the 'servants' hall' to hide its real purpose. It was enlarged in 1825 and 1850. The centenary of the chapel was celebrated November 7, 1876. The priests at Mawley from 1763 were:

Rev. James Chester.
„ Jn. Manning.
„ R. Gibson, 1784.
„ Menard, Dodomb, Broderick, 1800.
„ J. Appleton, 1801.
„ Pierre Chardon, 1805.
„ Jos. Bowden, 1806.
„ Denis Fortin, 1807.
„ Ch. Blake, 1813.
„ W. Jones, 1815.
„ T. Percy, 1824.
„ R. Gates, 1825.
„ P. Vergy, 1826.
„ J. Egan, 1829.
„ B. Crosbie, 1830.
„ Mgr. Hulme, 1843.
„ J. Spencer, 1847.
„ L. Acquaoni, 1848.
„ T. Green, 1849.
„ W. Molloy, 1859.
„ Pat. Power, 1860.
„ J. Quin, 1864.
„ H. Lynch, 1865.
„ T. Crowther, 1870.
„ T. Donovan, 1875.
„ J. Millward, 1876.
„ T. Ratcliffe, 1877.
„ D. Williams, 1881.
„ J. Hackett, 1883.
„ D. Fitzgerald, 1885.
„ H. Gregson, 1887.
„ F. de Vos, 1895.
„ J. McGrath, 1898.

Rev. G. de Stoop, 1900.
„ A. Devine, 1900.

Leics.

MEASHAM, ~~DERBYSHIRE~~ (St. Charles Borromeo).

The chapel, erected by the Countess of Loudoun, was opened in December 1881. The interior is adorned by an altar of Caen stone and several painted windows. Mr. C. Wray was the architect.

Priests.

Rev. Hubert de Burgh, 1885.
„ Joseph Fagan, 1888.
„ W. J. Otty, 1893 and to date.

MELBOURNE, DERBYSHIRE (*Nottingham*).

On Sunday, May 6, 1906, Mass was said here for the first time since the Reformation. A disused laundry serves for a chapel at present, and, on the occasion of the opening, a large congregation attended. Lord Walter Kerr is the patron of the mission, which is under the care of Fr. Francis Richmond.

MELIOR STREET, BOROUGH, LONDON, S.E. (*Southwark*). Our Lady of La Salette and St. Joseph.

This mission originated in 1847, when Fr. Robert Hodgson hired an old coach-house and said Mass there for the benefit of the poor Catholics of the place. Such crowds flocked there on Sundays, that Fr. Hodgson had to rent from Guy's Hospital an old dissecting room in Webb Street, Borough. After clearing away 'nearly two cartloads of human bones' and dis-

lodging legions of rats, Fr. Hodgson turned the upper portion of the building into a chapel and the lower part into a school. Bishop Wiseman attended the opening of this poor place of worship in 1848. Within three months, 4,000 persons went to Holy Communion. The mission being firmly established, Fr. Wenham and Fr. McMullen were appointed to carry on the work. The first mention of the mission in the 'Catholic Directory' appears in 1858, when the resident clergy were the Rev. F. Lawrence and the Rev. S. McDaniel. The humble chapel, which could barely accommodate one-fifth of the congregation, was replaced by the present Gothic church, opened May 2, 1861. A large portion of the once very considerable Catholic resident population has left the district, owing to the pulling down of whole streets and courts to make way for huge warehouses and railway offices. The present rector of the mission is Fr. S. Buckley.

MELTON MOWBRAY, LEICESTER-SHIRE (*Nottingham*). St. John the Baptist.

The foundation of this mission is chiefly due to two generous benefactors, Fr. Thos. P. Tempest and John Exton, Esq. The chapel was commenced 1840, and opened 1842 by Bishop Walsh, V.A. For some time after the opening, the priest had to live at two miles' distance, but by 1844 a presbytery was provided. At the outset a considerable amount of protestant opposition was aroused by the notorious 'no Popery' lecturer Dr. Cumming, but the ill-will soon subsided. A small school was started in 1843. The mission was served from Eastwell some time prior to 1875, and in 1898 from the Nottingham seminary.

Priests.

Rev. A. McDermott, 1843.
„ E. Belisy, 1845.
„ Andrew Eagan, 1849.
„ Geo. Bent, 1850.
„ Jeremiah Donovan, D.D., 1857.
„ J. Birmingham, 1860 (?).
„ Geo. Newton, 1871.
„ Rev. H. Swale, 1874.
„ A. Pol, 1877.
„ E. Van Dale, 1879.
„ J. Neligan, 1882.
„ T. O'Reilly, 1885.
„ C. Holland, 1898.
„ G. W. Hendriks, 1903.

MIDDLESBROUGH, YORKS. St. Mary.

In 1825 there was but one farmhouse on the spot now covered by a large city. In 1857, the Catholic population in and around Middlesbrough was 1,500. The old church of St. Mary was opened by Bishop Briggs, V.A., October 1847, and the church was enlarged (February–March 1866) 'to meet the wants of the rapidly increasing mission.' The present fine cathedral was opened in August 1878 on the site of the old building. In December following, it became the cathedral of the newly erected diocese of Middlesbrough. A fine altar-piece of the Madonna and Child, by Cottignola (died 1528), was presented to the church by H. W. Bolckow, Esq. Mr. Goldie was the architect.

Priests.

Rev. Bernard Branigan, 1847.
„ Jos. McPhillips, 1849.
„ Andrew Burns, 1854.

Rev. Richard Lacy, 1874.

In 1878 Middlesbrough became the see of the new diocese which, with Leeds, was formed out of Beverley, and from that time the bishops have been the *ex-officio* rectors of St. Mary's.

MIDDLETON, LANCS (*Salford*). St. Peter, Taylor Street.

The school chapel was opened in 1867, at which time the Catholic population numbered 400. Fr. E. Goetgeluck was the first priest placed in charge of the mission. He was rector here till after 1875. Fr. J. Wigman, appointed prior to 1883, is still the incumbent (1904).

MIDDLEWICH, CHESHIRE (*Shrewsbury*). St. Mary.

About 1847, Mass was said at Winsford Hall, the residence of the Waltington family, by Canon Carter, of Bolton. The Waltingtons subsequently left the Hall, and then Mass was said in a cottage belonging to a family named McDonald by Frs. Pope, Foster, Waltington, Doyle, Alcock, Gibbons, Power, and Fennelly. In August 1865, a dissenting chapel was purchased by Fr. Fennelly and fitted up for Catholic worship. The building was enlarged 1869. The present church, designed by E. Kirby, was opened May 31, 1891. The Catholic population in 1903 was 300.

Priests.

Rev. Jn. Moore, 1866.
„ Chas. Coelenbier, 1872.
„ Aug. Tremmery, 1876.
„ Denis Cregan, 1883.
„ Jas. O'Grady, 1891.
„ Jn. Ryan, 1898.

MIDHURST, SUSSEX (*Southwark*). St. Francis.

Cowdray House, near Midhurst, was formerly the seat of the Catholic Lords Montague. During the reign of Elizabeth upwards of sixty priests are said to have been sheltered here. In 1625, the Lord Montague of the day gave St. Cuthbert's ring to Bishop Smith, V.A., who bequeathed it to the English nuns at Paris, from whom Cardinal Wiseman obtained it for Ushaw College (1858). The seventh Lord Montague 'conformed to the Established Church' 1778, but was reconciled on his death-bed, declaring that 'libertinism in theory and practice' had alone seduced him away. George, the next and last Viscount, was drowned at Schaffhausen, Switzerland, 1793, on the very day that Cowdray House was destroyed by fire. After this a chapel was opened in the adjoining village of Midhurst, and used by the few local Catholics till 1861. Unfortunately, for some reason, the lease was not renewed, and the building ultimately became a club. We have been informed that the piscina, in what was the sanctuary, is now used as a receptacle for billiard balls. The present church was opened, November 7, 1869, by Bishop Brown, of Newport, on behalf of Bishop Grant. The style is Early English; C. A. Buckler, architect. For several years after the opening, the church was served from Burton Park. Confirmation was given here in December 1888 for the first time in fifty years.

Some Priests of the Cowdray Mission.

Rev. Dom Edward Ash, O.S.B., 1630.
  ,, J. Sheppard, 1745.

Rev. J. Barnard (V.G. to Bishop Talbot, V.A.L.D.), 1762.
  ,, J. Blevin, 1767.
  ,, Richard Antrobus, 1779. (This priest recommenced the registers.)

Priests at Midhurst since 1824.

Rev. Geo. Halsey.
  ,, Thos. Molteno, 1834.
  ,, Francis Bowland, 1840.
  ,, Peter Coop, 1857. (Mission closed 1860–69. Mission served from Burton Park 1869–79.)
  ,, Mgr. James Carter, 1879 to date.

MILE END, LONDON, E. (*Westminster*). The Guardian Angels.

A dissenting meeting - house known as 'Salem Chapel' was purchased and converted into a Catholic church about 1870. The 'bare and comfortless' interior was decorated and adorned with stations of the Cross in the autumn of 1876. In May 1901, the old church was pulled down to make way for the present structure, the gift of the Lady Mary Howard. The style is Perpendicular Gothic. During the rebuilding of the church a temporary structure, No. 381 Mile End Road, served as a chapel. The cost of the church was £11,000.

MILLFIELD, DURHAM (*Hexham and Newcastle*). St. Joseph's.

A recently established mission. The first stone of the new church was laid July 23, 1906, by Bishop Collins. The design is Romanesque, the materials used being blocks of concrete. Accommodation for about 700. Cost £3,000.

MILL HILL, LONDON, N.W. (*Westminster*).

St. Mary's Franciscan Abbey was opened by Cardinal Manning about 1887, and the church in October 1889. The style is simple Gothic. On either side of the high altar are chapels of St. Joseph and Our Lady. The seating capacity is for 200.

MILLOM, CUMBERLAND (*Hexham and Newcastle*). Our Lady and St. James.

The chapel was opened in 1867, and enlarged in October 1881. The same year the Catholic schools were sanctioned by the Education Department after much local opposition. The church was built between May 1886 and the early part of 1887. A great procession of clergy and people, headed by Fr. Perrin, priest of the mission, inaugurated the ceremony of laying the foundation stone. The church is a very handsome one, in old French Gothic, from the design of H. V. Krolow, of Liverpool. Millom was once the seat of the Neville family, and, by an heiress, passed to the Huddlestones, also staunch Catholics. Fr. Huddlestone, of this family, reconciled Charles II. to the Church on his death-bed in February 1685.

MILLWALL, ISLE OF DOGS, LONDON, E. (*Westminster*). St. Edmund.

The church in the West Ferry Road was opened in 1846. It is described as 'a neat Gothic building, consisting of a nave and chancel.' It is lighted by six lancet windows, 'deeply splayed.' Mr. Wardell was the architect. For many years after its erection, the mission was served from the church of Our Lady and St. Joseph, Poplar. Schools were opened 1870. Average daily attendance 1899, 270.

Priests.

Rev. Joseph Biemans, here in 1871.
„ Geo. Smith, 1877.
„ Wm. Lloyd, 1879.
„ Nicholas Drew, 1882.
„ Emile Van Dale, 1892.
„ A. J. Egglemeers, here in 1897.
„ Thos. Dunphy, 1897.
„ Bartholomew Doherty, 1904.

MINEHEAD, SOMERSETSHIRE (*Clifton*). The Sacred Heart.

The temporary chapel in Salborne Place was opened in December 1890. by Bishop Brownlow, of Clifton. Fr. Wilberforce preached (Cor. iv. 1–6) on the unity of the Church. The present church, in the Gothic style, was opened August 1898.

Priests.

Rev. J. Davis, 1890.
„ Richard Chichester, here in 1897 and to date.

MINISTERACRES, NORTHUMBERLAND (*Hexham and Newcastle*). St. Elizabeth.

A chapel was opened here in 1766 by John Silvertop, Esq., the lord of the manor. A more public one seems to have been established in 1790. This latter continued in use down to 1834, when ' a new Catholic chapel ' was built by Geo. Silvertop, Esq., and 'opened by a solemn Mass June 22 of the same year. On the death of this gentleman, February 20, 1849, without issue, he was succeeded by his nephew, the Hon. Charles Englefield, who took the name of Silvertop. The new Lord of Ministeracres proved himself a munificent patron of the mission, the present fine Gothic church, designed by J. Hansom and opened August 24, 1854, being erected at his expense. The registers of the mission date from 1795.

Priests since 1820.

Rev. T. Douthwaite, —.
„ T. Danson, 1838.
„ Edw. Browne, 1839.
„ J. S. Rogerson, 1843.
„ R. Orrell, 1854.
„ Joseph Watson, 1856.
„ Lawrence Boland, 1866.
„ Peter Perrin, 1876.
„ Michael Birgen, 1882.
„ Edmund Barnett, 1891.
„ M. P. Horgan, 1897 to date.

MINSTER, ISLE OF THANET, KENT (*Southwark*). St. Mildred.

The Catholic faith was strong here down to the time of Charles I. During the Civil War, Cromwell sent down ‘a religious enthusiast,’ who, after making most of the population ‘drunk with new wine,’ persuaded them to pull down the ancient cross that stood in the market-place. The poor people were so ashamed of this act that when they came to their senses they emigrated *en masse* to Belgium as the only means of preserving their holy religion. In the vicarage of Minster were long preserved a number of Catholic books, the property, no doubt, of some priests who officiated there before the Civil War. Among these was a complete copy of Cornelius à Lapide’s ‘Commentary on the Scriptures’ (Lewis’s ‘History of Thanet’). In August 1878, a community of Benedictine nuns was established at Minster by Prior Bergh, of St. Augustine’s, Ramsgate. They continued to occupy the convent till about 1891, when they were supplanted by the Sisters of Mercy, who have a laundry for the maintenance of a number of poor girls whom they supervise. The chapel, a plain cruciform Gothic structure, was consecrated by Bishop Bourne, of Southwark, in July 1901. The patron saint of the convent is St. Mildred, Abbess of Minster, who died A.D. 725.

MITCHAM, SURREY (*Southwark*). SS. Peter and Paul.

Mass is said to have been occasionally offered up during the penal times in a house in Church Lane (Road). The Hon. C. Langdale, whose distillery on Holborn Hill was burnt by the Gordon rioters, June 1780, owned Elmwood House, Mitcham. His domestic chapel here was long served by the Abbé L. Le Grip, an *émigré*, who died November 6, 1819. After this the place was served from Croydon. About 1839, Fr. O’Moore, of Croydon, used to say Mass occasionally in a house of a Mr. Kiernan, a pawnbroker. In 1853 a disused stable belonging to W. Simpson, Esq., was fitted up as a chapel. It was served by Frs. David Morel and other priests from Croydon and Norwood. The school chapel was opened in 1862 on a site presented by W. Simpson, Esq. Fr. Robt. Simpson, M.A., formerly Anglican rector of the parish church, was priest-in-charge for a few months. Fr. F. Whyte served the mission from 1865 till 1879. The present church, erected in 1889 on a site given by W. Simpson, Esq., is a neat structure in the Romanesque style. A stained-glass window and pulpit were presented by G. Temple-Layton, Esq. The seating capacity of the church is for about 250. The congregation numbers about 600. Fr. J. Pooley is the present rector.

MOLESEY, SURREY (*Southwark*).

This mission was founded through the efforts of Fr. E. du Plerney, of Surbiton. A house bearing the somewhat appropriate name of ' Stonyhurst,' in the Vine Road, was acquired for the purpose of a mission centre, and Mass said here for the first time in September 1905. The chapel was at first served every Sunday from Surbiton. Catholics of the district are estimated at about 250. Rev. H. Willaert, rector Sept. 1906.

MONMOUTH (*Newport*). St. Mary's.

Fr. William Dormer was at the ' Priory,' Monmouth, about 1730-32 as priest of the mission. He died at Staplehill in June 1758. In 1737 Fr. Robt. Garbott was chaplain. The present chapel was built in 1795, at which time the Catholics of the place numbered about 120. In 1845, the congregation numbered about 200. Four years later, Catholics were estimated at 300. A new chapel was opened 1837. In 1864, the Catholic population was 350.

Priests since 1824.

Rev. J. Jones.
  „ T. Burgess, 1836.
  „ T. Abbot, 1852.
  „ James Moore, 1895.
  „ Sidney Nicholls, 1897 to date.

MONKWEARMOUTH, DURHAM (*Hexham and Newcastle*). St. Benet.

The mission was established in 1864. The present church was consecrated in July 1889 by Bishop Wilkinson, upon which occasion the Blessed Sacrament was carried in procession amidst a vast concourse of Catholics and protestants. The style of the church is Early Decorated ; accommodation for about 800. New schools, of Gothic design, were opened September 1870.

Priests.

Rev. D. Macartney, 1867.
  „ Jules Du Flöer, here in 1871 and till 1897.
  „ Henry Canon Gillow, 1897.

MOORFIELDS, LONDON, E.C. (*Westminster*). St. Mary's.

In 1736—some say 1733—there existed a Mass-house in this neighbourhood, which for security's sake was known as the ' Penny Hotel.' This place of worship was in Ropemakers' Alley. During the renewed persecution of London Catholics in 1765, ' two Romish priests were taken out of a private Mass-house near Moorfields to be dealt with according to law ' (' Universal Museum,' October 21, 1765). During the Gordon riots of 1780, the chapel or Mass-house was among the number destroyed by the mob. Fr. Richard Dillon, who had been priest of the place since 1749, was so severely maltreated by the rioters that he shortly afterwards died. With the money obtained from Government in compensation, another and larger chapel was erected in White Street 1781. This continued in use till the building of the large and imposing church, opened with great pomp April 20, 1820, in the presence of a large gathering of ambassadors, nobility, and gentry. By this time the congregation was reckoned at over 6,000. The style of the building was Classical, with a Greek façade, the interior being remarkable for a large picture of the Crucifixion, painted on stucco by Signor Aglio, and arranged as a background to the high altar. The architect of the church was Mr. John Newman; total cost of erection, £26,000. Pope Pius VII. presented a splendid gold chalice, paten, and cruets to the church on the occasion of the opening, the gift being valued at 10,000 Roman crowns. The vaults beneath the church were a favourite burial-place with London Catholics till 1853, when they were closed. On the demolition of the church, upwards of 5,000 coffins were reinterred at Wembley, but the remains of Bishops Poynter, Bramston, and Gradwell were removed to St. Edmund's Old Hall. It was at St. Mary's that Dr. (afterwards Cardinal) Wiseman delivered his famous lectures on 'The Truths of the Catholic Faith' to crowds of persons during the course of 1836. Owing to a variety of circumstances, it was found necessary to close the old church, which was demolished during November and December 1899. A smaller edifice was opened in the adjoining Eldon Street March 25, 1903, in which most of the features of the former imposing building have been reproduced.

Priests.

Rev. R. Dillon, 1749–81.
,, Fuller, 1781.
,, Bernard, —.
,, Dunn, —.

Rev. Joseph Hunt, here 1816 *et seq.*
,, R. Horrabin, 1839–41.
,, Jn. Rolfe, 1841.
,, Provost Robt. Whitty, 1851.
,, Mgr. Daniel Gilbert, 1858.
,, Wm. Canon Fleming, 1895 to date.

MORECAMBE, LANCS (*Liverpool*). St. Mary.
Mission started from Lancaster 1895.

Priests.

Rev. John Smith, 1897.
,, Chas. Reynolds, 1901 to date.

MORLEY, YORKS (*Leeds*). St. Francis of Assisi, Westfield Road.
The Oddfellows' Hall was hired as a Catholic place of worship, and Masses said here for the first time Sunday, May 15, 1898, by Fr. John Brennan, chaplain to the Marquis of Ripon, and Fr. Dobson, of Batley. Fr. Augustus, O.S.F.C., preached · in the evening to a crowded congregation. Fr. Francis Mitchell is the present rector.

MORPETH, NORTHUMBERLAND (*Hexham and Newcastle*). St. Robert.
In 1768 a room in a tenement building in Bowlers' Green was fitted up as a chapel. Mr. Hy. Clark, a convert, used to keep watch while Mass was being said to give warning to the congregation if strangers approached. Shortly after this, the chapel of St. Bede was erected in Oldgate (1778). Fr. How was the first priest. His successor, Fr. Turner, was a practical

chemist, and added to his income by supplying the local gentry with soda-water! He died 1802. The next priests were Fr. Lawson (1802–29); Fr. Shann and Fr. H. Flinn (1830 and 1834); Fr. Geo. Lowe, O.S.B. (1837). By this time the old chapel had become quite inadequate, and in 1849 'a neat and commodious church' in the Early English style was erected. The opening ceremony was regarded with much friendly sympathy in the town. Mr. T. Gibson was the architect. In 1850, the presbytery and church were renamed St. Robert's Abbey in consideration of the Benedictines, by whom the mission has since been attended.

MORTLAKE, LONDON, S.W. (*Southwark*). St. Mary Magdalen.

For some time prior to the erection of the present church, a disused hayloft at the residence of Lady Mostyn served as a chapel for Mass. About 1849, Fr. Robt. Hodgson, of Richmond, came to Mortlake, sought out numbers of lapsed Catholics, and opened a school, where 'he said Mass, preached, and heard confessions.' He was nobly aided in his labours by Lady Mostyn, to whom is largely due the fine church of St. Mary Magdalen, opened May 12, 1852. The style is Decorated Gothic, from designs by Gilbert Blount, Esq. The priests' residence was at first a mere cottage, but a good presbytery was built not long after the opening of the church. Adjoining the mission is a cemetery. A tablet on one of the walls of the nave records the reception into the Church of Lieut. Augustus H. Law, R.N., afterwards the well-known Jesuit missioner. The church was consecrated 1869.

Canon Wenham, Provost of Southwark, was priest of Mortlake from 1851 till his death in March 1895. He was succeeded by Fr. C. Hogan, the present incumbent.

MORTOMLEY, near SHEFFIELD, YORKS (*Leeds*).

The mission was opened 1888, there being at this time a considerable Catholic population in the neighbourhood. Fr. W. J. Smith was the first priest. After his departure, 1892, the chapel was served from Elsecar till 1897, when Fr. A. McDonagh was appointed. Fr. Julius de Baere has been incumbent since 1899.

MOSSLEY, LANCS (*Salford*). St. Joseph's.

In 1863 the Catholics of this district are described as 'numerous and poor.' Thanks to the efforts of Frs. Conway and Grymonprez, schools were erected in the last-named year. For several years after the opening, the building was used also as a chapel. In 1864 the congregation was reckoned at 700.

Recent Priests.

Rev. P. Cardinael, here in 1871.

„ Jn. Kass, 1879.

„ Jas. Brady, 1888 and to date.

MOTTINGHAM, near ELTHAM, KENT (*Southwark*).

An old mansion, known as Mottingham House, was opened as a preparatory college for military education (Woolwich and Sandhurst) in 1883 by the Rev. E. Von Orsbach, late tutor to the Princes of Thurn and Taxis. After a successful career, the school was acquired by the diocese of Southwark as an orphanage for little boys under the care of the Sisters of Charity (1903). A large stable-house adjoining the establishment has been altered and fitted up as a chapel for the use of the inmates and the Catholics of the district. For some time after the opening the place was attended by a priest from Sidcup. The Rev. G. Leidig is the present rector (January 1906).

MOUNT ST. BERNARD'S ABBEY, COALVILLE, near LEICESTER (*Nottingham*).

This abbey is a filiation from Mount Melleray, Waterford, and was founded 1837 by the assistance of Ambrose Phillipps-De-Lisle, Esq., of Grace Dieu Manor, Leicestershire, and John sixteenth Earl of Shrewsbury. The fine pile of buildings was designed by A. W. Pugin, and much of the labour of stone-cutting, building, &c., was done by the monks after the manner of their predecessors during the Middle Ages. Adjoining the abbey is a spacious guest-house, with reception room, bedrooms, &c., also a house for the entertainment of the casual poor, regardless of creed. The monks are engaged in prayer, study, and manual labour, and much of the waste land round the monastery has been reclaimed by them and brought under cultivation. An interesting account of the place has been published by Llewellynn Jewitt, F.S.A., in his ' Guide to the Abbey of Mount St. Bernard.'

N

NANTWICH, CHESHIRE (*Shrewsbury*).

In 1832 Mass was said once a month by Fr. J. Briggs at Beam Heath, an old farmhouse two miles from Nantwich. The Catholics of the place then numbered five families and fourteen other persons. In 1843 a Methodist chapel was rented by Fr. E. Carberry, but given up four years later. In 1852 Fr. H. Alcock, of Crewe, hired an old salt-shed on the north bank of the river Weaver at Crewe, and fitted it up as a chapel. The 'No Popery' feeling generated by the recent restoration of the hierarchy was then very strong in the town, and Sunday after Sunday hostile crowds assembled before the chapel yelling and hooting. The present church was built 1855-56, and was partly paid for by W. Houlgrave, Esq., of Liverpool. The presbytery was built 1875-80.

Priests.

Rev. J. Robinson, 1868.
„ D. Williams, 1871.
„ E. Byrne, 1875.
„ P. Deery, 1880 to date.

NELSON, LANCS (*Salford*). St. Joseph.

The foundation stone of the school chapel was laid Saturday, August 4, 1883, and the building was opened early the following year.

Priests.

Rev. Jn. Bramer, 1891.
„ Robt. Smith, 1895 to date.

NESTON, CHESHIRE (*Shrewsbury*). St. Winifride.

The chapel was opened November 29, 1843. A. Pugin was the architect. A cemetery was laid out 1851, and next year an extension and gallery were added to the church. Schools were opened 1857.

Priests.

Rev. J. Kershaw, 1843.
„ Jas. Canon Pemberton, 1845.
„ Joseph Canon Daly, 1876.
„ Geo. Provost Clegg, 1890.
N.B.—For many years the chapels of Hooton and Puddington, belonging to the Stanley family, were the only Catholic places of worship in the district. Fr. Ralph Platt, who died February 13, 1837, bequeathed his savings for the establishment of a mission at Neston.

NETHERTON, near LIVERPOOL, LANCS. St. Benet.

This mission is an offshoot of that at Sefton. In 1792, Fr.

Richard Vincent Gregson, O.S.B., the chaplain at the last place, got the ex-Catholic Viscount Molyneux to grant a site for a chapel at Netherton. Next year 'a commodious house and chapel' were erected, towards the expense of which the Hon. Mrs. Mary Molyneux liberally contributed. The school was not started till 1871. Another and larger building was opened in August 1888.

Priests at Sefton Hall.

Rev. Thurston Anderton, O.S.B., 1672 (?).
„ Richard Helme, or Holme, O.S.B., 1697.
„ — Cuerden, 1716.
„ James Kaye, 1742.
„ Richard Gregson, 1754.

Priests at Netherton.

Rev. Richard Gregson, 1792.
„ Stephen Hodgson, 1800.
„ Richard Pope, 1804.
„ Edw. Clifford, 1828.
„ Abraham Abram, 1830.
„ Geo. Caldwell, 1867.
„ Thos. Shepherd, 1870.
„ John Burchall, 1887.

NEWARK, NOTTINGHAMSHIRE (*Nottingham*). The Holy Trinity.

The church was erected about 1840 by the late James Provost Waterworth, of Nottingham. The style is Tudor; sittings for 200. An endowment of about £80 per annum was settled on the mission by the founder. The two fine altars of the Sacred Heart and Our Lady are the gift of Redmond Cafferata, Esq., present occupier of Staunton Hall, and nephew of the Provost. The mission of Newark was apparently founded about 1820 by Fr. J. Yvers. The old chapel in Parliament Street was a humble unecclesiastical building, like the other Catholic chapels of the time, and for some years Mass was only said there on the first and fifth Sunday of each month.

Rectors.

Rev. J. Yvers.
„ James Provost Waterworth, D.D., 1836. (This learned ecclesiastic was the author of a 'History of the Reformation,' mainly derived from non-Catholic sources, and several other well-known works. Died 1876.)
„ Edmund Smith, M.R., 1876 to date.

NEW BRIGHTON, CHESHIRE (*Shrewsbury*). SS. Peter and Paul.

In 1879 a room was hired for a chapel in Egerton Street, and in January 1880 the Bishop of Shrewsbury appointed Canon Frith to take charge of the mission. There was at that time neither church nor school, but a site for a church had been generously given when the mission was started. The Catholic population in 1880 numbered about 250. In June 1881 the present church was opened for worship. The late Mrs. Santa Maria gave £500 towards the building expenses. E. Kirby was the architect.

Priests.

Rev. Randolph Canon Frith, 1879.
„ William Canon Stanton, 1887 to date.

NEWBURY, BERKS (*Portsmouth*). St. Joseph's.

This mission owes its establishment to the apostolic zeal of Fr. Robert Hodgson. In 1852, when spiritual director at the adjacent College of St. Mary, Wolverhampton, he was struck by the religious destitution of the few Catholics at Newbury, and resolved to start a mission there. He accordingly went over to Newbury on Sundays, said Mass for the congregation, and catechised the children. After a time he was enabled to build church and schools. He had a most enthusiastic helper in the young Earl of Arundel and Surrey, then residing at Dorrington Lodge, near the town. This young nobleman, among other things, used to act as doorkeeper of the chapel on Sundays! Fr. Hodgson laboured for about twelve years at Newbury, when he retired to Holloway. He died there December 27, aged seventy-one. The present rector of the mission is Fr. H. L. Kelly, M.R.

NEWCASTLE-ON-TYNE, NORTH-UMBERLAND (*Hexham and Newcastle*). St. Andrew's.

In the reign of James II. a Mass-house was opened in the Flesh Market, but closed at the Revolution (1688). A chapel was then fitted up in a room in Nuns' Lane. This was broken up by a 'No Popery' and anti-Jacobite mob January 28, 1746, shortly after the victory of Prince Charles Edward Stuart at Falkirk. A third chapel was then established in Bell Court, Newgate Street, by the pastor, Fr. Thos. Gibson, uncle of Bishop Gibson, V.A. About 1792 a second chapel was opened in the Close, and served by regulars. Fr. Worswick in 1797 collected funds for the erec-

tion of a large church in Pilgrim Street. Thos. Riddell, Esq., gave £100, Sir Jn. Lawson £80, and Bishop Gibson £80 towards the building fund. The opening took place February 11, 1798, when High Mass was sung for the first time since the Reformation. Schools were erected near the church in 1830, at a cost of £2,000. The Dominicans had charge of the mission for a few years after 1860. A new church was erected in Worswick Street, and opened by Bishop Chadwick September 26, 1875.

Priests.

Rev. Aug. Janneson, —.
„ Thos. Maire, 1731.
„ Thos. Gibson, —.
„ C. Cardell, 1765.
„ J. Jones, 1791. (N.B.—Fr. J. Cotes died at Newcastle-on-Tyne July 8, 1794, aged ninety-four.)
„ H. Potts, 1792 (?) (he died 1800).
„ Jas. Worswick, 1797.
„ W. Riddell, curate to preceding 1830; rector 1843; D.shop and Vicar Apostolic N.D. 1844; died 1847 of typhus, contracted while attending the sick.
„ Robt. Smith, 1845.
„ Jas. Standen, 1846.
„ Jos. Cullen, 1848.
„ Jos. Browne, 1852.
„ Jos. Canon Humble, 1857.
Very Rev. J. Bernard Morewood, O.P.
Very Rev. Dominic Aylward, O.P., 1863.
Rev. Geo. King, O.P., here 1871.
„ Edw. Rigby, 1874.
„ Hy. Berry, 1879.
„ Richard Collins, 1882.
„ Jos. Newsham, 1896.
„ Rd. Vaughan, 1897 to date.

NEWCASTLE-ON-TYNE, NORTH-UMBERLAND. St. Mary, Clayton Street West.

The opening of this church on August 21, 1844, was the occasion for a great Catholic demonstration. The bishops present were : Dr. Riddell, Dr. Griffiths, Briggs, Morris (of Mauritius), Baggs, Brown, Sharples, and Collier. Bishop Riddell pontificated at the High Mass, the sermon being preached by Bishop Gilles, of Edinburgh. A great 'mission' was given here in January 1846 by the Passionist Fathers Gentili and Furlong, during the course of which 1,800 persons received Holy Communion and forty-nine were reconciled to the Church. During the typhus pestilence of 1847 Bishop Riddell, who resided at St. Mary's, exerted himself to have a suitable temporary hospital erected for the sufferers. Before the end of the year this excellent prelate departed this life, and his mortal remains were interred beneath the church. His friend Bishop Gilles, of Edinburgh, pronounced the funeral oration (November 1847). In the autumn of 1881 the church was completely redecorated by Messrs. Westlake & Co., new stations being erected, the roof adorned with *fleurs de lys*, stars, &c. The high altar was adorned by a fine painting of the Annunciation, the patronal title of the church.

NEWCASTLE-ON-TYNE. St. Lawrence, Byker.

In 1877 Bishop Chadwick, of Hexham and Newcastle, opened the old school chapel. By 1884 most of the Catholic population had shifted to the opposite end of the district, and in January of that year Bishop Bewick opened the new school chapel in Felton Street, Byker. The cost of the building was £1,000. The style is Early English. The Bishop, in his opening discourse, referred to Dame Dorothy Lawson, of Heaton, who in the dark times of the penal days did so much to keep the Faith alive about the Tyneside. The mission is served from St. Dominic's.

NEWCASTLE-UNDER-LYME, STAFFS (*Birmingham*). Holy Trinity.

The church was opened May 13, 1834, by the Vicar-Apostolic (Bishop Walsh). The priest of the mission, Fr. Egan, erected the church ; his congregation at this time amounted to about three hundred. The mission, which formerly formed part of that of Cobridge (*q.v.*), made great advances after the opening of the church, so that when Bishop Walsh visited it on November 16 there were 132 for confirmation, while 250 received Holy Communion. A splendid organ was presented to the church by the congregation in November 1846. Fr. Gaudentius, the Passionist, preached on this occasion.

Priests since 1846.

Rev. James O'Donnell.

„ James O'Farrell, 1848.

„ James Massam, 1849.

„ Jn. O'Connor, 1857.

„ Jas Terry, 1863.

„ Martin Maguire, here in 1882 and to date.

NEW FERRY, CHESHIRE (*Shrewsbury*). St. John Evangelist.

The mission was established 1903. A room was hired in the Assembly Hall, and Mass said there on Sundays at 8.30 and 10, and on weekdays at the presbytery, 12 Stanley Road. Fr. Wm. Baines, rector.

NEWHALL, DERBYSHIRE (*Nottingham*). St. Edward.

The large Gothic chapel, erected in this village at the expense of the Countess of Loudoun, was opened on the Feast of Corpus Christi 1886. Pontifical High Mass was sung by Bishop Bagshawe. The front gable contains a statue of St. Edward the Confessor. The seating accommodation of the building, which cost about £1,500, is for 300 persons.

Priests.

Rev. Hubert de Burgh, 1886.
,, Thos. Middleton, 1899.
,, D. Hengel, 1902.
,, Maurice Parmentier, 1903 to date.

NEW HALL, ESSEX (*Westminster*). Holy Sepulchre of Our Lord.

The English branch of the Canonesses of the Holy Sepulchre was founded at Liège in 1642 by Miss Susanna Hawley, daughter of Thomas Hawley, Esq., of New Brentford, Essex, and cousin of Francis H. Lord Donamore. The rule, which was approved by Pope Urban VIII., unites active work with the contemplative. The pious foundress died 1706, aged eighty-three. In 1794 the community, being threatened by the French Revolutionists, retired under the escort of some French gentlemen *émigrés* to Maestricht, and from thence proceeded to London. They were kindly assisted by Lord Clifford and Sir Wm. Gerard, Bart., and about October of the same year took possession of Holme Hall, Yorkshire, at the invitation of Lord Stourton. In 1796 the nuns removed to Dean House, Wilts, and finally in January 1799 to their present abode at New Hall. The mansion on the estate had formerly been the favourite residence of Henry VIII., who called the place Beaulieu. It afterwards became the residence of the Duke of Buckingham—James I.'s ' Steenie '—and later on of Geo. Monk, Duke of Albemarle. The property was purchased for the nuns by a Mr. Michael McEvoy from the son of Baron Waltham. Since the establishment of the Order in England, the convent under their direction has achieved a wide and well-deserved reputation as an excellent place of education for young ladies. The chapel of the convent is a handsome piece of architecture which in former days served as the ' great hall ' of the historic mansion.

NEW HARTLEY, NORTHUMBERLAND (*Hexham and Newcastle*).

A recent Benedictine mission, founded from Blyth in 1895. Fr. Augustus Gregory Green, O.S.B., was appointed rector in 1902.

U

NEWHAVEN, SUSSEX (*Southwark*). The Sacred Heart.

The church was opened by Bishop Bourne, January 2, 1898. The style is Romanesque, from a design by Mr. W. Romaine. The first Mass was sung by Mgr. C. Coote. Mr. Justice Day was among the congregation present on this occasion. The building accommodates 120 sons, but provision has been made for future extension. Fr. R. Collinson, the first resident priest, was transferred to Putney in 1902, since which time the Newhaven mission has been under the Assumptionist Fathers. From about 1895 till the establishment of a regular mission Canon W. McAuliffe, of Lewes, used to come over to the town once a month to say Mass at Albion Villa and visit the few Catholics.

NEW HOUSE, WATERHOUSES, DURHAM (*Hexham and Newcastle*). Queen of Martyrs.

The Ven. John Bost, or Boast, who suffered for the Faith at Durham, July 24, 1594, laboured in this district prior to his seizure at Waterhouses, September 10, 1593. He was chiefly charged with having said 'Masse att ye Waterhouse,' and it was probably to this ancient chapel that the Bishop of Hexham and Newcastle referred when opening the present church, October 26, 1871. The structure was reconstituted 1882, and opened March 1883. In August 1885, 186 persons were confirmed here. The building was freed from debt and consecrated 1894.

Priests.

Rev. P. Fortin, 1871.
,,   Edward Beech, 1902 to date.

NEWINGTON (WEST), LONDON, S.E. (*Southwark*). St. Wilfrid.

On Rosary Sunday 1904 a chapel was opened in the Lorrimore Road by Bishop Amigo, of Southwark. For some time the mission was served from St. George's Cathedral, Southwark, but since 1905 the Rev. Geo. Palmer has been the rector.

NEWMARKET, CAMBRIDGE-SHIRE (*Northampton*). Our Lady and St. Etheldreda.

As late as 1859, the only Catholic chapel at Newmarket was a room kindly lent by a protestant gentleman. Fr. Thomas McDonald, who served the mission, had also to do duty at Ely, but a site for a church was purchased for £300 in July 1859. The same month, the Catholics of Newmarket and Ely presented Fr. McDonald with a handsome gold watch, 'as a tribute of their affectionate regard.' The church was commenced October 1861, and opened April 5, 1863. Fr. McDonald was rector here till 1877, when he was succeeded by Fr. Joseph Van den Dries. In 1891 it was Fr. Henry Stanley. His successor, Rev. Patrick Grogan, 1892, is the present rector.

NEWMILLS, DERBYSHIRE (*Nottingham*). St. Mary.

The church was erected 1840. Style, Gothic ; accommodation for about 250. The congregation numbers 235. The district served by the church is described as 'one of the poorest missions in England, scattered over ten miles.'

Priests.

Rev. J. Collins, 1840.
„ Bryan O'Donnell, 1855.
„ F. Pauline, 1858.
„ C. L. Monahan, 1861.
„ Albert Op Broek, 1864.
„ H. T. Sabela, 1877.
„ J. Prendergast, 1880.
„ Michael Kirby, 1885.
„ Charles Carrigy, 1888.
„ Wm. C. McKenna, 1893 to date.

NEWNHAM PADDOX, WARWICK-SHIRE (*Birmingham*). The Sacred Heart.

The church of the Sacred Heart —the gift of the Earl of Denbigh— was opened Wednesday, May 26, 1880, by Bishop Hedley. The structure was designed by Wyatt. On either side of the reredos are statues of St. Augustine and St. Clare. At the solemn procession of the Blessed Sacrament on the occasion of the opening the richly adorned canopy was borne by the Earls of Denbigh and Gainsborough and the Lords Herries and Campden.

Priests.

Rev. Jos. Sweeney, here in 1883.
„ Bernard Murphy, 1892.
„ Archibald Fleming, 1896.
„ Marmaduke Langdale, 1904.

NEWPORT, ISLE OF WIGHT, (*Portsmouth*). St. Thomas of Canterbury.

This mission, like that of Cowes, owes its origin to Mrs. Heneage, relict of James Heneage, Esq., of Cadeby, Lincoln, and Gatcombe, Isle of Wight. The chapel at Newport was built at the suggestion of her chaplain, Fr. Simon Lucas,

1791. Fr. Gandolphy was priest here in 1804. The Abbé de Grenthc, an *émigré*, was also missioner at Newport, either after the departure of Fr. Lucas or Fr. Gandolphy. He died March 31, 1842, and is buried beneath the sanctuary of the church. His name does not appear in the clergy list of the 'Catholic Directory,' 1838-43, but it does among those of the French clergy annually published as having signed the 'Form of Declaration of Catholic Communion' against Blanchardism.

Priests.

Rev. John Russell.
„ Joseph Robson, 1838.
„ Thos. Canon Fryer, 1840 (retired 1889).
„ J. D. Mooney, 1889.
„ James Murtough, 1892.
„ James Canon Conway, 1899 to date.

NEWPORT, MONMOUTHSHIRE (*Newport*). St. Mary.

In 1790 there were four Catholics in Newport, who used to attend Mass at Caerleon, where there was a small room fitted up as a chapel. A chapel was erected at Newport in 1812, but the priest, who had several missions to attend to, could only officiate there occasionally. By 1840, the Catholic population had increased to about 1,600. The accommodation of the old chapel was for 200. Assisted by the distinguished Catholic families of Llanarth and Clytha, Fr. E. Metcalfe, the priest of Newport, undertook the erection of the present thirteenth-century Gothic church (106 ft. by 42 ft.), designed by J. Scoles and opened in November 1840. A mission preached here in Lent

1846 by Frs. Gentili and Furlong caused a great revival of Catholic fervour in the town, which had been much edified by the excellent conduct of the large number of Irish soldiers of the 37th Regiment, which left for India the same year. Schools were erected in 1849–50, and in the latter year 300 children were being educated. In 1858 Catholics in and about Newport were reckoned at 4,500.

Rectors since 1843.

Rev. A. Baldacconi, LL.D.
„ P. Hutton.
„ Dominic Cavalli, 1849.
„ Richard Richardson, here in 1862.
„ Dominic Cavalli, 1863.
„ Michael Bailey, 1892 to date.

NEWPORT, MONMOUTHSHIRE.
St. Michael, High Street, Pillgwenlly.

This mission was established in 1872 from St. Mary's. The fine Gothic church was opened September 29, 1887, by Bishop Hedley. Among the congregation present were the mayor and corporation, General Sir A. Herbert, K.C.B., &c. Exclusive of the gallery, the building will accommodate about 600 ; cost of erection, about £3,377 ; architect, W. Gardner, Esq.

Priests.

Rev. Michael Bailey, 1888 to date.

NEWPORT, SALOP (*Shrewsbury*). SS. Peter and Paul.

An obscure mission was established at Longford, a village one mile from Newport, *temp.* James II. The Mass-house was an old mansion of the Talbots, and stood 'far

from the observation of passengers along the road.' In 1785 the property of Longford Hall was sold by Charles Earl of Shrewsbury to a protestant gentleman named Leeke. The priest then was Fr. Houghton, and when the old chapel was closed he opened an oratory in Newport, where he went to live. This humble place of worship was afterwards exchanged for Salters' Hall, in the High Street, which was given by the Earl of Shrewsbury. The baptismal registers of Newport commence with four names in 1785. Fr. J. Wilkes (January 1796–May 1798) kept a mission school for the sons of the Catholic gentry. Among his pupils were Sir H. Tichborne, Bart., Mr. Swinburne, of Capheator, &c. When Fr. Trovell came in 1838 he found the congregation less than 100 ; the Easter communions were about forty or fifty. By 1856 the Catholics had risen to over 600, and the Easter communicants to between 300 and 350. The schools were formerly in the stables of the Hall, but in 1840 a convenient school-house for about 100 children was erected. About the year 1828, most of the old chapel was pulled down to make way for the new Gothic church, the gift of the Earl of Shrewsbury. It was opened for worship Tuesday, July 3, 1832, by Bishop Walsh, V.A. of the Midland District. Mr. Potter, of Lichfield, was the architect. It was ' beautified internally' about the year 1842, and again in 1851 from the designs of Mr. C. Hansom. In the chancel are two stained-glass windows by Wailes, representing SS. Peter and Paul, the patrons of the church. In the library of the presbytery are preserved an old tabernacle used at Longford Hall in the days of persecution, portraits of some members of the

Talbot family, and also of Fr. John Duckett, who suffered for the Faith at Tyburn 1644, aged thirty-one. There is also an old 'Ordo Baptizandi' containing some interesting Catholic memoranda, as: 'His Grace the Duke of Norfolk died 1777, September 20, aged ninety-two.'

Priests.

Rev. Jn. Wright, 1785.
„ Jn. Wilkes, 1795.
„ Wm. Goff, or Le Goff, 1800.
„ Jn. Reeve, 1801.
„ Geo. Howe, 1806.
„ Michael Canon Trovell, V.G., 1837.
„ Eugene Canon Buquet, 1867.
„ Gerard Lamb, O.S.F.C., 1868.
„ Ambrose Canon Lennon, 1868.
„ Jn. Canon Rogerson, 1872.
„ David Williams, 1894.

NEWQUAY, CORNWALL (*Plymouth*).

St. Augustine's opened on Trinity Sunday 1903. The site—close to the headland—was given by Lady Molesworth. The style is Early English, from the design of Canon Scoles. Like several of the other Cornish missions, the church is served by the Canons Regular of St. Augustine.

NEWSHAM, LANCS (*Liverpool*). St. Mary.

The mission was founded at The Hough about 1700. Fr. F. Kirk was priest there in 1716. The estate known as, The Hough belonged to the Hesketh family. Fr. Roger Brockholes succeeded Fr. Kirk. During the march of Prince Charles Edward Stuart into England, 1745,

the priest of Newsham, Fr. J. Carter, received an assurance of protection from the Prince. It was probably this priest who built 'the small, ill-made chapel,' on a piece of ground given him by E. Fishwick, Esq. During the election riots of 1768 the Newsham mission was nearly destroyed. Fr. Carter died October 18, 1789, but his nephew, Fr. R. Carter, succeeded him in the mission, and erected the chapel near the site of the old one, 1806. He served the mission till his retirement, 1818. Fr. Jos. Marsh, the next priest, was here from 1818 to 1854. Canon R. Gillow, who came in 1856, erected the schools. He was a very accomplished scholar, and served the mission till his death on November 3, 1867.

Recent Priests.

Rev. W. Bradshaw, 1867.
„ Austin Powell, 1871.
„ J. Bilsborrow, 1874.
„ Thos. Carroll, 1882.
„ Edmund Kearney, 1895 and to date.

NEW SPRINGS, WIGAN (*Salford*). The Holy Family.

Mission established and chapel opened 1898 by Fr. Owen McNulty, the present rector. Catholic population of the district, 550.

NEWTON ABBOT, DEVON (*Plymouth*). St. Joseph's.

The mission was established 1871. Fr. Thos. Reckie was priest in 1875; Fr. J. Higgins, 1883; Jos. Atkins, 1891 and to date.

NEWTON ABBOT, DEVON. St. Augustine's Priory.

The church was consecrated by Bishop Clifford September 9, 1863. The building is Gothic, from design by J. Hansom ; accommodation for about sixty. The English Augustinian Canonesses of the Lateran formed a convent at Louvain, Belgium, in 1609. At the time of the Revolution, 1794, they returned to England, settling first at Hammersmith, and next at Amesbury, Wilts, and Spetisbury House, Dorset. On October 2, 1861, they commenced residence at Newton Abbot. Until 1860 the Canonesses carried on a school for young ladies, but since that time the principal object of the rule has been the Perpetual Adoration of the Blessed Sacrament.

NEWTON-LE-WILLOWS, LANCS (*Liverpool*). SS. Mary and John.

Mission opened November 1861. By August 1862, many lapsed Catholics had returned to their duties. Fr. J. Lennon was the first priest, the chapel at the outset being a hired room in the glass works. Assisted by Sir Robt. Gerrard, Bart., Fr. Lennon in 1863-64 built the church, to accommodate about 600 persons. The style is Gothic. In 1903 the Catholic population was about 2,360.

Priests.
Rev. J. Lennon, 1861.
„ Wm. O'Reilly, 1898 to date (1904).

NEW WHITTINGTON, DERBYSHIRE (*Nottingham*). St. Patrick.

The church was opened March 17, 1906. The style is Gothic, comprising nave, chancel, and sacristy; accommodation for 300. The opening ceremony was marked by a great procession, over 1,000 strong, through the streets of the town. During the afternoon, the architect was presented by the clergy and congregation with a handsome silver crucifix in appreciation of his work. Fr. J. McKearney, of Staveley, is at present in charge of the mission.

NORDEN, LANCS (*Salford*). St. Mary.

The mission was established by the Redemptorists, and the church opened 1904. The Catholic population is about fifty. Rev. Chas. McNeiry, superior.

NORTHALLERTON, YORKS (*Middlesbrough*). The Sacred Heart.

Until the school chapel was opened, May 23, 1870, the nearest mission was at Thirsk. The style is Gothic ; architect, G. Goldie. Till 1890 the chapel was served from Aiskew.

Priests.
Rev. James Butler, 1890.
(From 1895 to 1904 served from Aiskew.)
„ L. Tills rector 1904, to date.

NORTHAMPTON. Cathedral of St. Mary and St. Thomas.

In 1820, there was no Catholic chapel in the whole of Northamptonshire. Bishop Milner, who was anxious to establish one, sent Fr. W. Foley from Oscott to Northampton on October 22, 1823. The number of Catholics in the town was then about eighty, visited occasionally by the chaplain from Weston Underwood. Bishop Milner and Fr. Foley gave £600 for the erection of presbytery and chapel, opened October 25, 1825. A small boys' school was started shortly afterwards. Bishop Wareing, at his own expense, added a gallery to the church in 1849. Next year Northampton became the cathedral town of the newly erected see. The present cathedral was commenced on October 1, 1862. Mgr. Husenbeth preached at the inaugural ceremony, which was attended by a large concourse, including a number of the 5th Lancers. In 1881 the high altar was enlarged, and a fine pulpit of Caen stone erected in memory of Mgr. Oleron, V.G. (1807-80).

NORTHAMPTON. St. John.

The old building on the east side of Bridge Street, Northampton, known as St. John's Hospital, was opened as a Catholic chapel on Saturday, August 18, 1882. The 'Hospital' was built in the twelfth century, and at the Reformation was among the few charitable institutions allowed to retain its endowments. It ultimately came into the possession of the Midland Railway Company, who let it to a Mr. Mold for use as a timber store. In 1882 it was purchased by Catholics, on the sale of the property, pursuant to an order in Chancery. The church was restored at a cost of £600, and opened for worship by Canon Scott, V.G. Bishop Riddell, of Northampton, sang the Mass, and Cardinal Manning preached on St. Thomas of Canterbury and the ancient fidelity of England to the Holy See. The mayor and corporation attended the inaugural service in state.

NORTHFLEET, KENT (Southwark). Our Lady and St. Joseph.

The establishment of this mission dates from August 15, 1867, when Fr. M. O'Sullivan, of Gravesend, said Mass in a house which served as presbytery and chapel. The number of Catholics in Northfleet was about 143. In 1875 it was served by Capuchins, Fr. Anthony being superior. The mission was served from Greenhithe from 1885 till after 1898. Fr. John Fletcher then became incumbent. In 1906 he went to Tulse Hill as priest. Fr. S. Wray is the present rector of Northfleet.

NORTH SHIELDS, NORTHUMBERLAND (Hexham and Newcastle). St. Cuthbert's.

On July 15, 1784, Fr. Jas. Johnson, of Pontop, Durham, opened a chapel in a room in Milburn Place. Mass was said here once a month for the Catholics, who numbered at the most thirty. The next priest was Fr. P. Willcox. About 1793, the Abbé Duboison hired a room in Norfolk Street, and officiated as priest of the place till his return to France about 1803. Before leaving he publicly thanked the inhabitants of the town for their kindness to him during his stay among them. In 1796 an Irish regiment was quartered in the town, and Fr. J. Worswick, of Newcastle, opened a chapel, mainly for the accommodation of the men, in Union Street. Crowds of protestants used to attend the soldiers to Mass, and nurses would promise to take their charges to 'the Catholic chapel for a treat'!

After the military left, the chapel was moved, first to Camden Street, and then to Perry Street. In 1817, mainly owing to the energy of Fr. Thos. Gillow, the present fine church was commenced, and opened June 14, 1821, by Bishop Smith, V.A. Among the notable benefactors to the church were Lady Clifford (£500), Geo. Silvertop, Esq. (£200), Geo. Dunn, Esq. (£200). Great numbers of persons attended the inaugural ceremony, and the whole day after the service was spent by them in inspecting the building. Commodious schools were opened in 1842, and six years later the church was decorated by Bulmer. Next year (1847) 147 persons were confirmed here by Bishop Riddell, V.A.

Priests since 1817.

Rev. T. Gillow (died March 1857, aged eighty-eight).
„ J. Bewick. Bishop of Hexham, 1882.
„ Wm. Gillow, 1871 (?).
„ Robt. Franklin, 1874.
„ Jn. Nolan, 1879.
„ Jas. Canon Stark, 1885.
„ Michael Haggarty, 1903.

NORTHWICH, CHESHIRE (*Shrewsbury*). St. Wilfrid.

About 1856, a Methodist chapel, capable of holding some 500 persons, was rented as a Catholic place of worship, and so continued till March 1865, when it was turned into a co-operative store. After much difficulty, the priest of the place, Fr. Joseph Fennelly, secured a site for a church and presbytery, the services being meanwhile performed in a hired building in Witton Street. The estimated Catholic population in 1862 was about 900. The present church was built be-

tween September 1864 and August 8, 1866. The style is Early English Gothic. The sitting accommodation is for 400. E. Kirby was the architect. The mission dates from 1840, when Mass was occasionally said in a cottage near Pump Stile.

Priests.

Rev. Jos. Fennelly, 1854.
„ Michael Power, 1855.
„ John Gibbon, 1857.
„ Jos. Fennelly, 1859.
„ Wm. Stanton, 1868.
„ Jn. Barry, 1878.
„ Gerard Boen, 1885.
„ Denis Cregan, 1891.

NORWICH, NORFOLK (*Northampton*). St. John.

The palace of the Duke of Norfolk, built in 1602, was abandoned by Thomas Earl of Arundel and Surrey about the time of Charles I., because the mayor, T. Havers, Esq., would not allow him to have a private theatre. The palace fell into decay, and part of it was ultimately let as a workhouse. A priests' residence and chapel were attached to the building, and when the place was sold in 1801 these portions were excepted from the sale. The chapel attached to the Duke's residence was served by several eminent priests, notably Fr. Alban Butler, author of the 'Lives of the Saints,' and Fr. Edward Beaumont, a descendant of Beaumont the poet and colleague of Fletcher. He was at Norwich in 1758. In 1791 the old chapel mentioned above was closed, and another erected in the Maddermarket. Among the contributors to the building fund were Sir W. Jerningham, Bart., of Cossy Hall, Norris Suffield, and Pitchford Bokenham, Esqrs. The altar plate, vestments, furniture, &c., were removed from the old chapel. Fr. Beaumont died August 1, 1820, aged eighty-eight. He was buried beneath the chapel of St. John, where a marble tablet recalls his memory. The fine church which took the place of the old chapel, founded in 1791, was commenced in July 1884, and consecrated ten years later. It is one of the largest erected in England since the Reformation. The central tower can be seen from the Yarmouth Roads, over twenty miles off. The Duke of Norfolk, E.M., was the munificent founder. A new guild-room was opened in November 1896.

NORWICH, NORFOLK. St. George's, Fishergate.

The Jesuit Fathers had a mission at Norwich 'very early.' Fr. F. Sankey, S.J., was priest here in 1647, and Fr. J. Mumford, S.J., in 1650. In the reign of James II. Fr. C. Gage, S.J., 'effected wonderful conversions by his sermons.' The chapel was attacked by an 'insolent rabble' at the Revolution (1688), but, thanks to the courage of the sheriffs, very little damage appears to have been done. The old Mass-house, which stood originally in Chapelfield, was removed to St. Swithin's Lane about 1775 by Fr. Galloway, S.J. The Catholic school was also carried on there, and was attended by the sons of the first Catholic families in the vicinity, as the Gages of Hengrave, Mannocks, &c. Fr. T. Angier, S.J., succeeded Fr. Galloway in 1775, and served the mission till his death in 1788. The chapel of the Holy Apostles was opened in August 1829. The bells of the protestant church of St. Giles were rung in honour of the event, most likely at the instigation of the liberal-minded Bishop Bathurst, of Norwich, whose descendants are now Catholics. The mission was served by the Jesuit Fathers down to January 1881, when it was handed over to the Bishop of Northampton. The retiring priests, Fr. Williams, S.J., and Fr. Perrin, S.J., were presented with a gold chalice and silver pyx by the congregation as a mark of gratitude for their zealous ministrations.

Secular Priests since 1881.

Rev. Thos. Fitzgerald.

„ Henry Long, 1899.

NORWOOD, LONDON, S.E. (*Southwark*).

A dissenting chapel was hired and opened for Catholic worship July 10, 1842. On the first day that Mass was said there, a number of persons walked over from St. George's Chapel, Southwark, and, on approaching the temporary mission-house, formed a sort of procession, with banners &c. At first, Mass was only said once a month, but a Mass was promised every Sunday 'if many Catholic families settled in the neighbourhood.' The Norwood chapel first appears as an independent mission in 1849, when Fr. Quiblier was incumbent. The convent of the 'Daughters of the Faithful Virgin' was founded here in 1848. The Sisters conduct a high-class boarding school for girls, and also a large and flourishing orphanage, which is certified for the reception of Poor Law children. In 1851 no mention is made in the 'Catholic Directory' of the Norwood mission as such, but the Abbé Vesque is given as chaplain to the convent. In 1852 Fr. (afterwards Canon) David came as assistant priest, and for some five years had to serve the neighbouring mission of Croydon. In 1857 Fr. David went to Croydon permanently. The priests at Norwood that year were Frs. J. B. Morel, F. Maillard, and P. Rouelle. Finally the present fine church, in the Middle Gothic style, was opened June 1, 1871, as a memorial of Bishop Grant, of Southwark, who had always shown a keen interest in the welfare of the Norwood convent, within the precincts of which he is buried. The rectors of the mission in late years have been the before-mentioned Fr. J. B. Morel (died 1881), Francis O'Callaghan (1881–96), John Warner (1896), F. Wilderspin (1900), Joseph Haynes (1903 to date).

NORWOOD (WEST), LONDON, S.E.
(Southwark). St. Matthew.

This plain church, in the Romanesque style, was opened March 30, 1905. The accommodation is for about 200. Fr. W. Fichter is the first and present rector.

NOTTINGHAM   *(Nottingham).*
Cathedral of St. Barnabas.

The first public place of Catholic worship in Nottingham was a plain, unecclesiastical building, in King's Place, Stoney Street. In 1831 another chapel, in George Street, dedicated to St. John, was opened. It was at the time thought ' preposterously large,' but a few years proved it to be quite insufficient, and on May 10, 1842, the first stone of the present cathedral was laid by Bishop Wiseman. The building, which was consecrated August 27, 1844, is a Gothic cruciform structure some 200 ft. in length. A large sum towards the building expenses was contributed by John sixteenth Earl of Shrewsbury, who also greatly assisted in the foundation of the Catholic schools, opened 1832. A. W. Pugin was the architect both of the cathedral and the adjoining house, the residence of the Bishops of Nottingham since the restoration of the hierarchy in 1850. Fr. Robt. Wilson, for many years priest of the Nottingham mission, was mainly instrumental in the erection of what a contemporary journal described as ' this stately Gothic fane.'

The Lord Bishops of Nottingham.

(1) Rt. Rev. Joseph Hendren, O.S.F. Born at Birmingham October 19, 1791 ; educated at the Franciscan academy of Baddesley Clinton ; a zealous missioner at Courtfield, Aston, Swynnerton, &c., 1816–39 ; Vicar-Apostolic, Western District, 1848 ; translated to Clifton 1850 ; to Nottingham 1851 ; resigned 1852 ; died 1866.

(2) Richard Roskell. Born 1817 ; D.D. Rome 1842 ; rector of St. Patrick's, Manchester, 1842 ; V.G. of Salford 1851 ; Bishop of Nottingham September 21, 1853 ; resigned 1874 ; died at Whitewell, near Clitheroe, January 27, 1883.

(3) Edward Bagshawe. Born January 12, 1829 ; Bishop of Nottingham November 12, 1874 ; resigned 1901 ; Archbishop of *Seleucia,* 1904.

(4) Robt. Brindle, D.S.O. Born in Liverpool, November 4, 1837 ; educated at the English College, Lisbon ; for many years an Army chaplain of great distinction, and as such took part in the Egyptian and Soudan

campaigns ; consecrated by Cardinal Satolli March 12, 1899, as Bishop Auxiliary for Westminster ; translated to Nottingham December 6, 1901 ; received Princess Ena—Queen Victoria Eugénie of Spain—into the Catholic Church 1906.

NOTTINGHAM. Our Lady and St. Patrick.

This handsome church, in the London Road, was opened Monday, September 24, 1883, by Bishop Bagshawe. It took the place of the old chapel, opened in 1867. The building is in the Early English style of Gothic of the Lancet period. The accommodation is for 600 people. The reredos, which is of oak, handsomely carved, contains figures of Our Lady, St. Joseph, and St. Patrick. Mgr. Provost Harnett, the incumbent of the church at the time of opening, is still the rector (1905).

NOTTINGHAM. St. Edward's, Blue Bell Hill.

When the mission was erected in 1886, the once rural district had become a region of streets and houses. Two years earlier St. Joseph's Convent was opened, and, as the chapel was semi-public, a congregation was quickly formed. The present church was opened in July 1886 by Cardinal Manning ; cost of erection, about £1,200. A portion of the building serves, or served, the mission for a school, the sanctuary being ingeniously screened off. The erection of St. Edward's is largely due to Canon

Monahan, the first rector. Fr. Ig. Beale has been incumbent since about 1896.

NUNEATON, WARWICKSHIRE (*Birmingham*). Our Lady of the Angels.

The chapel was opened July 25, 1838, and completed 1840. Fr. W. Nickolds was the first resident priest. Before this, the mission was served on Sundays from Hinckley. Fr. Alwyrd was priest in 1847, Fr. P. Sablon in 1855, and Fr. W. Hilton in 1872. Fr. William, O.S.F.C., celebrated his silver jubilee here in June 1886. He improved the interior of the church, ' making it perfect of its kind,' and also founded the neighbouring mission of Bedworth. The schools and presbytery were built by Fr. Sablon, who subsequently acted as chaplain to the Dominican nuns at Hurst Green and Carisbrooke.

NUNHEAD, LONDON, S.E. (*Southwark*). St. Thomas the Apostle, Hollydale Road.

The present church was opened for Mass, November 5, 1905. Fr. P. Ryan, D.D., rector. The sanctuary has recently been fully decorated, and altars of brass and bronze erected. During Passion Week 1906 the first mission was conducted by Fr. Athanasius Ryan, C.P., both morning and evening services being well attended.

NUN MONKTON, YORKS (*Leeds*). St. Joseph.

The mission was anciently established at Linton-on-Ouse 1700, but its history is said to have been un-eventful. The register dates from 1771. In 1856 the lease of the old chapel expired, and efforts to get another site in the district were frustrated by anti-Catholic preju-dice. The mission was consequently removed to Nun Monkton in 1862. During the interval, 1856–62, Mass was said at Linton in a private house by a priest who came from York on Sundays. The present church at Nun Monkton was opened in October 1870. The style is Gothic; with seating for about 160.

Priests since 1810.

Rev. Peter Thebault (*émigré*), 1810.
„ P. Chatelais (*émigré*), 1813.
„ Louis de Henne, 1816.
(No mention of mission till 1829.)
„ James Wrennall, 1829.
„ Arthur Wilson, 1852.
„ Henry Walker, 1854.

At Nun Monkton.

Rev. Robt. Canon Thompson, 1862 and till after 1875.
„ Wm. Wilson, 1877.
„ Charles Burke, 1891.
„ Joseph Locke, 1899.

O

OAKAMOOR, STAFFS (*Birmingham*). St. Wilfrid's College.

This is the lineal descendant of Sedgeley Park School, founded in 1763 in an old mansion rented from Viscount Dudley and Ward. This nobleman was a firm friend of the long-persecuted Catholics, and more than once defended in Parliament his conduct in letting his mansion 'for a Popish school.' The school flourished, and by 1770 there were about one hundred pupils, most of them destined for mercantile and commercial pursuits and living under a *régime* of Spartan simplicity. Various additions were made to the building from time to time, notably in 1793 and 1794. A new chapel, of Classical design, was erected (1800-1) from plans by Dadford. The altar-piece was a copy of West's 'Last Supper,' and the altar an 'oblong square,' with 'an antependium of painted and gilt leather.' High Mass up to this time seems to have been conspicuous by its absence, and Benediction only given on the greater festivals. Even then the priest wore no cope—a vestment at that period rarely seen in England outside the embassy chapels in London. After Bishop Milner became Vicar Apostolic (1803) great improvements took place in the services not only at Sedgeley, but throughout the vicariate, Gregorian chant being introduced and more elaborate ritual adopted. The Bishop took great interest in the school, presiding at the annual 'exhibitions' and giving the students correct notions of English history—a subject then and long after a mere farrago of doubtful assertions and anti-Catholic prejudice as far as the vast majority of text-books was concerned. Owing to the establishment of other Catholic schools, the number of students at 'The Park' gradually declined, though it rarely fell below 100 and sometimes rose above 120. Among its students are numbered Bishops Milner, Wareing, Smith, and Brown, a large number of priests, John and Charles Kemble, the famous actors, &c. Mgr. Husenbeth, the eminent biographer of Bishop Milner, who was a student here from 1803 to 1810, published a detailed history of the school in 1856. The centenary of the college was celebrated with much rejoicing in 1863. Ten years later, however, partly owing to the decayed state of the fabric and partly on account of the falling in of the lease, the school was transferred to St. Wilfrid's, Coton Hall, in the same county. This latter place had been a residence of the Oratorians from 1847 to 1849. The church was opened April 25, 1848. In its new home, historic Sedgeley has worthily upheld its great reputation as the loved *alma mater* of zealous clergy and worthy laymen, and maintained to the full those happy traditions which are the guide of present conduct and the subject of pleasing recollections.

Presidents of Sedgeley Park and St. Wilfrid's.

Rev. Hugh Kendal, 1763.
„ Thos. Southworth, 1781.
„ John Kirk, 1793 (*d.* 1851, *æt.* 91).
„ Thos. Southworth (second time), 1797.
„ Joseph. Birch, 1816.
„ Walter Blount, 1821.
„ Jos. Bowdon, D.D., 1836.
„ Henry Smith, 1845.
„ James Brown, 1848 (Bishop of Shrewsbury July 1851).
„ Thos. Canon Flanagan, 1851.
„ Geo. Canon Rolfe, 1853.
„ James Canon Moore, 1860.
„ Joseph Canon Souter, 1873.
„ John Canon Hawksford, D.D., 1885.
„ E. Hymers, 1904 to date.

OAKHAM, RUTLAND (*Nottingham*). SS. Joseph and Edith.

The foundation stone of the first Catholic church in Oakham since the Reformation, was laid by the Earl of Gainsborough, Lord Lieutenant of the county, July 7, 1883. The church was erected in memory of Charles George second Earl of Gainsborough. Lady Edith Noel, of the same family, and at that time a Sister of Charity at Leyton, Essex, endowed the mission with £40 a year 'for ever.' The first priest at Oakham was Fr. Van Dale. The town is said at that time (1883) to have been 'the centre of a very protestant district in the Midlands teeming with dissenters and Low Churchmen.' The dedication of the church by the Bishop of Nottingham took place on Tuesday, October 16, 1883. The structure is a neat building in the Gothic style, capable of holding about 120 persons. The Bishop of *Emmaus*, Mgr. Patterson, preached at the opening from the text, 'The just man lives by faith.'

OAKHAMPTON, or OKEHAMPTON, DEVONSHIRE (*Plymouth*).

The mission has only recently been established, and is under the care of Fr. Burns (1906). A site for a church has been acquired in the Slater Road, and £100 contributed towards the new building by two anonymous benefactors.

OGLE STREET, LANGHAM PLACE, LONDON, W. (*Westminster*).

The church of St. Charles Borromeo was opened in Lent 1863 by Cardinal Wiseman, but the usual solemnities were postponed till Wednesday, May 20, of the same year. The style of the church, designed by Messrs. Willson & Nichol, is Gothic. The side altar of the Sacred Heart was presented by Mrs. Grace and T. H. Galton, Esq. The handsome sanctuary lamp suspended before the side altar was given by Lord Edward Howard.

Priests.

Rev. Cornelius Keens, 1863.
„ Daniel Canty, here in 1871.
„ Reginald Tuke, 1877.
„ Thos. Regan, 1879.
„ Edmund Egan, 1895 to date.

OLDCOTES, WORKSOP, NOTTS (*Nottingham*). St. Helen.

Before the commencement of the mission, the district was served by the priest at Worksop (*q.v.*). The foundation stone of the church was laid September 15, 1868, and the building (Gothic) was opened 1869. The fabric is of cedar-wood, and was the gift of a wealthy timber merchant of Liverpool. Accommodation for about 120.

Priests.

Rev. Jn. Power, 1867.
„ B. Douglass, 1874.
„ C. L. Monahan, 1877.
„ Patrick Conaty, 1879.
„ Michael Fryer, 1882.
„ Wm. O'Dwyer, 1885.
„ Joseph Stourton, 1888 to date.

OLD HALL GREEN, WARE, HERTS (*Westminster*). St. Edmund's College.

In 1769 a school, called the 'Old Hall Green Academy,' was opened through the efforts of Bishop Challoner, V.A.L., and his coadjutor, the Hon. and Right Rev. Bishop Talbot. In spite of the then existing penal laws, the obscure academy flourished under the presidency of Fr. James Willacy. Like Sedgeley Park, the institution was long regarded as a place of preparation for Douai. On the breaking up of this latter college at the time of the French Revolution (1792-93), the professors and students escaped to England. A number of these were established at Old Hall Green by Bishop Douglass, V.A.L.D., and the place renamed St. Edmund's College (November 16, 1793). New college buildings were erected 1795, mainly at the expense of Mr. Sone, of Bedhampton, Hants. The history of the college is practically that of Catholicity in the South of England, large numbers of the nobility and gentry and clergy having been educated here. In 1869 the 'Church students' were removed to St. Thomas's Seminary, Hammersmith, for their theological studies, but in 1903 St. Edmund's again became the divinity *alma mater* for the archdiocese. The number of students, clerical and lay, is about two hundred. The college church — a splendid example of Gothic architecture — was consecrated by Cardinal Wiseman May 16, 1853. Within the precincts of the college repose the remains of several bishops, notably Bishop Talbot, V.A.L.D. (*d.* 1790), Bishop Poynter (*d.* 1827), &c.

Presidents of St. Edmund's.

Rev. James Willacy, 1769.
„ John Potier, 1792.
„ Gregory Stapleton, 1795. Bishop of *Hierocæsarea*, 1801. Died 1802.
„ Bishop Poynter, D.D., 1801.
„ Joseph Kimbell, 1813.
„ John Bew, D.D., 1817.
„ Thomas Griffiths, D.D., 1818. Bishop of *Olena*, 1833. Died 1847.
„ Richard Newell, D.D., 1834.
„ John Rolfe, 1838.
„ Edward Cox, D.D., 1840.
„ Mgr. Weathers, D.D., 1851. Bishop of *Amycla*, 1872. Died 1895.
„ Mgr. Fredk. Rymer, D.D., 1868.
„ Mgr. James Patterson, M.A. ; 1870. Bishop of *Emmaus*, 1880. Died 1902.
„ Geo. Akers, M.A., 1880.
„ Mgr. Patrick Fenton, 1882. Bishop of *Amycla*, 1904.
„ Mgr. J. Crook, 1887.
„ Mgr. Bernard Ward, D.D., 1893 to date.

OLDHAM, LANCS (*Salford*). Our Lady of Mount Carmel and St. Patrick.

In 1862 Fr. J. Conway, of St. Mary's, Oldham, opened a school chapel in John Street. Fr. P. Cardinael was first priest-in-charge. In 1868 Fr. R. Brindle received a site for a new church from the Ainsworth family, then recent converts. The building was opened in 1870. Fr. T. Byrne was the next priest after Fr. Brindle.

Recent Priests.

Rev. Jn. White, 1883.

„ Richard Canon Brindle, 1891 to after 1894.

„ Thos. O'Callaghan, 1897 and to date.

OLDHAM, LANCS. St. Ann's, Greenacres.

The old school chapel was opened November 1880, to accommodate some 400 persons on Sundays and 250 pupils on weekdays. A new school chapel, costing £6,000, was opened here in the summer of 1903.

OLDHAM, LANCS. St. Mary.

A chapel was opened in Lord Street by Fr. E. Hogan in 1838. In June 1861, an anti-Catholic mob attacked the chapel, and did considerable damage. Mr. Abraham Leach, the mayor, behaved with great courage, and the riot was soon quelled. Several of the rioters were tried at the quarter sessions, but released on their own recognisances at the request of Fr. Conway, the priest of St. Mary's. The building subsequently underwent extensive alterations, and was reopened in

September 1867. Mr. Buller gave £100 of the £500 required for builders' charges.

Recent Priests.

Rev. Thos. Wrennall, 1862.

„ Chas. Grymonprez, here in 1871.

„ Jn. White, 1879.

„ Jn. Cooke, 1897.

„ Jn. Lane, 1903.

„ M. Buckley, 1904.

OLD SWAN, LIVERPOOL (*Liverpool*). St. Oswald's.

When the first stone of the church was laid, in 1840, Old Swan was 'a country place far away from Liverpool.' The building was opened August 7, 1842; cost of erection, £5,000. The presbytery was completed May 7, 1858.

Priests.

Rev. Canon Maddocks, 1842.

„ Thomas Bennett, 1864.

„ Richard Canon Holden, 1867.

„ Peter Canon Van Hee, 1882.

„ M. Gallagher, 1894.

„ J. E. Clarkson, 1898.

OLNEY, BUCKS (*Northampton*). Our Lady Help of Christians and St. Lawrence.

The mission was served till recent times by the chapel at Weston Underwood, the seat of the Throckmorton family. When the old hall was removed in 1826 several hiding-places were discovered. The chapel of St. Lawrence at Newport Pagnell was superseded by the present church in 1901.

Priests (until 1837 these were Benedictines).

Rev. A. W. Blakey, 1715.
  „ J. Bernard Wythie, 1727.
  „ Jn. Placid Rigby, 1736.
  „ J. B. Daniel, or Simpson, 1747.
  „ Wm. P. Metcalfe, 1769.
  „ Wm. Gregson, 1770.
  „ Michael Lorymer, 1800.
  „ Jos. Anson, 1803.
  „ Jas. Calderbank, 1805.
  „ J. B. Rigby, 1806.
  „ Seth Canon Eccles, 1826.
  „ Geo. Stokes, 1884.
  „ Fr. M. Carton de Wiart, 1899 to date.

OLTON, WARWICKSHIRE (*Birmingham*). Immaculate Conception.

This house of studies of the Franciscan Capuchins was established 1883, Fr. Bernard Devlin, being the first superior.

ORPINGTON, KENT (*Southwark*). St. Joseph's and St. Anne's Orphanage.

This institution, which is a Poor Law school for Catholic children, under the management of the Southwark Rescue Society, was opened by the late Bishop Butt in 1894. The building, of two stories, which was designed by Mr. Walters, F.S.A., is spacious and well adapted to the purpose for which it was intended. About three hundred orphan boys are educated here under the care of the Presentation Brothers. About half of each day is devoted to ' the three R's,' whilst the remainder is set aside for technical instruction in a trade. Much attention also is devoted to physical exercises, and the school band is considered by experienced judges to be one of the best of its kind in England. Farming, stabling, and gardening are also well attended to, with a view to the emigration of many of the lads to Canada. The chapel, which is still only a temporary one, is open to the public, and, though simple in character, has been adorned with considerable taste and skill by Brother Stephens. The Rev. W. Linnett is the priest of the mission.

N.B.—The Roper family (Barons Teynham) had a residence at Orpington, *temp.* James I., but we can find no trace of it or the secret chapel which existed there. It was probably served by the Jesuits.

St. Anne's Orphanage.—Adjacent to St. Joseph's is St. Anne's Orphanage, for girls, under the care of the Sisters of Mercy. Originally what is now St. Joseph's did duty for both boys and girls, the wing, &c., occupied by the former, being separated from the latter by internal and external walls. Since the opening of the separate convent school (1901) the work has greatly expanded, upwards of four hundred orphan and destitute girls being now provided for. The elementary school is apart from the rest of the building, so as to keep the home and scholastic life of the place quite separate.

ORRELL, WIGAN, LANCS (*Liverpool*). St. James.

The Leigh family appear to have been the founders of this mission. John Leigh, Esq., was fined and imprisoned 1584 'for recusancy.' Another of the line, Alexander Leigh, was on the list of recusants 1662. The Rev. Jn. Thulis, hanged and quartered at Lancaster for the

X

Faith 1616, was a native of the parish. The chapel was started at Crossbank 1699, and removed to Moor Ditch 1805. Mrs. Ann Sandford endowed it with £100 in 1740. The building was enlarged 1841, and a bell tower added 1882. Schools were erected at Roby Mill 1875. The Benedictine nuns of Heath (Yorks) settled here for a time (1821) before removing to their present convent at Princethorpe (1833).

Priests since 1824.

Rev. — Hawley, —.
„   J. Cotham, 1826.
„   Thos. Pennington, 1831.
„   Robt. Hubbersty, 1841.
„   Thos. Adamson, 1849.
„   Hy. O'Bryen, D.D., here 1871
„   Moses Doon, 1874.
„   Wm. Parkinson, 1899 to date.

OSBALDESTON, LANCS (*Salford*). St. Mary.

The church, in the Henry VII. style of Tudor, was opened by Bishop Briggs in October 1837, having been built by W. Heatley, Esq., of Brindle Lodge.

Priests.

Rev. Thos. Canon Irving, 1837.
„   T. Smith, 1857.
„   E. Tunstall, 1879.
„   Laurence Johnson, 1894.
„   John Canon Boulaye, 1897.
„   Michael Cahill, 1902.
„   James Manning, 1904 to date.

OSCOTT,   near   BIRMINGHAM. St. Mary's.

Fr. Andrew Bromwich, a 'Lisbonian,' was priest here in 1678. During the Titus Oates plot he was tried before Justice Scroggs, and sentenced to death for being 'a Popish priest contrary to the law,' but reprieved by King Charles II. He returned to Oscott, and continued his ministry till his death in 1706. Curiously enough, he was succeeded here as priest by his aged uncle, also a Lisbonian, who served the mission till his death in 1711, aged eighty-nine. In 1752 Fr. Pierce Parry built a new presbytery. The chapel occupied the front floor of the upper story. In 1778 a new chapel was erected near the clergy-house, which was let as a school to a Mrs. Johnson, of Harvington, in Worcestershire. Fr. Joseph Berington, author of the 'Literary History of the Middle Ages,' was priest at Oscott for a short time, but left 1793. Next year the Rev. Dr. Bew, who had been president of St. Gregory's Seminary in Paris, commenced 'Oscott College' at the request of the English Vicars-Apostolic. Dr. Bew did not long retain the presidency of Oscott, but went to Brighton as priest of St. John the Baptist's Chapel. He was president of St. Edmund's College, Old Hall, from 1817 to 1818, and died at Brockhampton October 25, 1819. The college, after the usual initial difficulties, flourished exceedingly, and soon became a perfect stronghold of Catholicity in the Midlands. The old building was abandoned in 1838 for the splendid Gothic pile that, in a sermon now historic, inspired one of Newman's most eloquent passages. The college became exclusively an ecclesiastical seminary in 1889.

OSGODBY, LINCOLNSHIRE (*Nottingham*). St. Joseph.

This mission, like that of Kingerby (*q.v.*) owes its establishment and preservation to the Young family of the latter place. The priests' house, and chapel over it, were erected 1793, the building forming a good specimen of a Catholic mission-house at the close of the penal times. The registers date from 1799.

Priests since 1824.

Rev. M. Gilbert.
„ J. Abbot, 1837.
„ James Egan, 1839.
„ James Canon King, 1841.
„ Thos. Jackson, 1863.
„ Amadeus Gavois, 1866, and till 1892.
„ Robt. Brown, 1892.
(Mission served from Market Rasen 1894.)
„ A. Lepère, 1895.
„ Jn. Wenham, 1897.
„ Redmond Walsh, 1899.
„ Gilbert Bull, 1901 to date.

OSMOTHERLEY, YORKS (*Middlesbrough*).

A school kept by Franciscans was set up here about 1672, but was closed for a time, probably during the Oates plot (1679–81). In 1702, the Provincial appointed a Mrs. Jennison as matron or manageress. At the time of the Jacobite rising, 1714–15, Fr. Ambrose Ogle, the chaplain, 'was much persecuted' by the justices for recusancy. Shortly after 1723 the school was removed to Edgbaston, but Osmotherley was continued as a 'residence' of the Order. In 1799 it was decided to make the place the novitiate, but the venture did not succeed, and in 1823 it was resolved to admit no more aspirants. The register dates from about 1771. For nearly forty years the mission has been served from Stokesley.

Priests since 1812.

Rev. P. Kington, 1812.[1]
„ John Davison, 1828.
(Mission vacant 1834–36.)
„ A. Macartney, 1837.
(Mission served occasionally 1841. No mention of mission for nearly thirty years. From 1875 till the present time the place has been served from Stokesley.)

OSWESTRY, SALOP (*Shrewsbury*). Our Lady Help of Christians and St. Oswald.

In 1839 Mass was said occasionally in an upper room of the White Hart Inn by Fr. Jn. Collins, of Wrexham. In 1864 a chapel was opened in Cripplegate Street by Fr. W. Barry, of Welshpool. Fr. P. Tracy, who came in 1865, was the first resident priest. In 1879 an iron church was presented to the mission by T. Longueville, Esq., of Llanforda Hall. Eleven years later, the same generous patron built the present church in Brook Street. The sanctuary was beautifully decorated in 1897 from designs of Mr. J. Pippett, and a porch added 1899.

OTLEY, YORKS, WEST RIDING (*Leeds*).

The mission was commenced about 1850, the church, in the Gothic style, being opened in 1851.

[1] Fr. Pacificus Kington, O.S.F., was Confessor to the Poor Clares at Aire in Artois, 1786–91. He would have been guillotined, July 28, 1794, had not Robespierre been executed the day before.

x 2

The architect was the late Mr. T. Constable. During the rectorate of Fr. Martin Kelly, the present priest of the church, the St. Joseph schools, which existed as 'a mere shell' when he first came (1871), have been 'properly equipped and brought into a full state of efficiency.' Fr. Wm. Macdonnell was the first priest at Otley.

OULTON, STAFFS (*Birmingham*). St. Mary's Abbey.

In 1853 the Benedictine nuns from Caverswall Castle, which they had occupied from 1811, came to Oulton, where the Lady Abbess (Juliana Forster) found means to erect the church of St. Mary. The architect was Mr. Edward Pugin, then only nineteen years of age. The building was consecrated November 24, 1854, by Bishop Ullathorne. The style of the edifice is Gothic. The chapter-house, sacristy, and presbytery were built during the reign of the second Lady Abbess (Catherine Beech), 1869–1900. The handsome oak stalls in the sanctuary were given by Mrs. Waterton. The jubilee of the foundation at Oulton was celebrated on Thursday November 24, 1904. The Bishop of Birmingham, Dr. Ilsley, pontificated at the High Mass, the sermon being preached by Mgr. Ward of St. Edmund's College, Ware. Among the many persons present were eight ladies who had been pupils at the convent when the church was consecrated in 1854.

OXBURGH, STOKE FERRY, NORFOLK (*Northampton*). Our Lady and St. Margaret.

The church was erected at the expense of Sir Henry Paston Bedingfeld, Bart., and opened July 10, 1836. Style, fourteenth-century; size, 72 ft. by 20 ft. ; open roof. The sanctuary is lighted by coloured windows dating from 1521. The communion rails are splendidly carved with representations of Isaac, Melchisedech, &c. Before the opening of the church, the mission was served by the chapel at the Hall, which has been a focus of Catholicity throughout the penal times. In the turret of the east tower is a curious priests' hiding-place, built in the solid wall. The mansion contains some fine specimens of ancient armour, old portraits, &c. In the library is a MS. history of the Passion of Our Saviour, written by Sir Henry Bedingfeld when a prisoner in the Tower for loyalty to Charles I. The Jesuit Fathers formerly served the mission.

Priests since 1824.

Rev. J. Gascoyne, —.
„ Wm. Gubbins, 1845.
„ Stephen Longman, 1847.
„ Wm. Bodley, 1873.
„ Henry Parkes, 1902.
„ Joseph Prince, 1904 to date.

OXFORD (*Birmingham*). St. Aloysius, St. Giles.

In 1577 a bookseller was tried at the Oxford Assizes for printing and distributing Catholic books. Fr. Wm. Lacy, S.J., according to Anthony Wood, is said to have ministered to the Catholics of Oxford during nearly half of the seventeenth century. He was a B.A. of the university, and had been converted to the Catholic faith by Fr. Doulton, a secular priest. Sir Henry Gage, governor of Oxford for Charles I. during the Civil War, used to attend Fr. Lacy's Mass nearly every day.[1] After Fr. Lacy's death, in or about 1680, Catholics of Oxford were dependent on the priests at Dorchester (Oxon.), Brightwell, &c. In 1793 Fr. Leslie built a chapel for Catholics of the city and vicinity, who then numbered about sixty. In 1842 a meeting was held at the house of the resident priest, Fr. Newsham, to consider the erection of a church worthy the antiquity and splendour of Catholic worship. Nothing, apparently, was done, and in 1862 Bishop Ullathorne sent Fr. A. Comberbach to Oxford for the purpose of erecting a new church, 'as the old chapel was only fit for a school.' The first stone of the present building was laid May 20, 1873, by Bishop Ullathorne in the presence of a large and distinguished gathering. Fr. John Morris, S.J., preached. The style of the building—opened 1875—is Perpendicular Gothic, from design by J. Hansom. Seating accommodation for 800. The Jesuit Fathers have charge of the mission.

[1] Sir Henry Gage was killed in a skirmish with the Roundheads at Culham Bridge, January 11, 1644. He had some time prior to this relieved Basing House, then held for the King by the Catholic Marquis of Winchester. Sir Henry was a very devout Catholic, and, where possible, heard Mass every day. He was much esteemed by King Charles I., who attended his funeral in state.

P

PADIHAM, BURNLEY, LANCS (Salford). St. John the Baptist.

The school chapel, for 300 persons, was erected in the autumn of 1863, the first stone being laid by Canon Rimmer. Mr. Welby Pugin was the architect. The mission was served from Burnley for some years, until it became capable of supporting a priest. The new church was opened the end of March 1881. It is erected on a site on the borders of the Townley estate. Seating accommodation for 600 persons. The cost, without the chancel (erected subsequently), was £2,100.

Priests.

Rev. Hy. Jones, here in 1875 and till 1892.

„ E. Goetgeluck, 1892.

„ Francis Hart, 1901 to date.

PAIGNTON, DEVON (Plymouth). St. Mary.

The Marist Congregation started their novitiate house here in September 1882. The church, commenced about the same time, was opened in the course of 1883. Till the completion of the building the little oratory of the Fathers was ' literally crowded week by week ' with Catholics, and also many protestants anxious to witness the Sacrifice of the Mass, then offered at Paignton for the first time since the Reformation. The new church was opened Thursday, June 14, 1883. It is a small but lofty Gothic structure in the thirteenth-century style. The building was designed by Fr. Rosier, and built by Mr. F. Vanstone, at a cost of about £2,000. Bishop Vaughan, of Plymouth, preached at the opening, which was attended by a very large congregation. The church was beautifully decorated at the cost of one of the congregation in August and September 1886. The number of Catholics in Paignton, which in 1880 was but a dozen, had increased to 100 in 1886.

PARBOLD, LANCS (Liverpool). Our Lady and All Saints.

The church, the gift of Mr. H. Ainscough, was opened May 29, 1884. The building, which cost £15,000, is in the Gothic style, surmounted by a lofty steeple. The altar and reredos of alabaster are beautifully carved. The seating capacity of the church is for 500. Fr. J. O'Brien was the first rector. A new Lady Altar was erected 1893. Fr. J. Brown, O.S.B., is the present incumbent.

PARKMINSTER, SUSSEX (*Southwark*). St. Hugh's Monastery.

In 1873 the Carthusian Order acquired Parknowle estate, near Horsham, and upon it the splendid church and monastery — covering 640 acres—were erected, 1876-82. The imposing entrance is crowned by statues of Our Lady, St. John the Baptist, and St. Bruno. The style of the buildings is Romanesque. In the chapter-house are life-sized wall-paintings of the martyrdom of the Carthusian Fathers of the London Charterhouse for refusing to abjure the Papal supremacy, 1535. The chapel of relics contains, among others, the stole of St. Hugh of Lincoln, and portions of the bones of St. Thomas of Canterbury and St. Bruno. The original mansion of the estate is now the guesthouse. St. Hugh's was built with the view of becoming a refuge for the Order in the event of revolution and spoliation in France. The wisdom of this determination has recently become apparent, since, owing to the expulsion of the religious orders under the Associations law of M. Combes and his party the whole of the Carthusian Order in France were compelled to take refuge abroad.

PARSONS GREEN, LONDON, S.W. (*Westminster*). Holy Cross.

A mission was started here in 1843, and continued till 1848. Mass was said on Sundays and holy days at 9 A.M. A second mission was established in 1884, when a school chapel was opened in the Cassingley Road. The present chapel, still only a temporary one, is in the Ashington Road, but great efforts are being made to erect a church.

Priests.
Rev. W. Kelly, 1843.
„ Joseph Butt, 1847.
„ C. Moncrieff Smyth, 1884.
„ Rd. Conway, 1888.
„ Rd. Galvan, 1903 to date.

PEASLEY CROSS. *See* **ST. HELENS**, St. Joseph's.

PECKHAM, LONDON, S.E. (*Southwark*).

The Catholic population was estimated at 1,000 in 1849. On August 9 of that year Mr. J. Gilbert called a meeting to consider the erection of a public chapel. Some reference was made to an old bequest of 1492 for perpetual lights before the statues of Our Lady and St. Nicholas—the ancient patrons of the locality—in the parish church. A mission would appear to have been commenced about 1850 by Fr. J. Furniss, member of an old Catholic family at Hathersage(*q.v.*) He joined the Redemptorists at Clapham in 1851. The same year the Capuchin Fathers came to Peckham, Fr. Louis being placed in charge of the mission. He apparently resided at the convent of the Christian Retreat, Kennington, during this time. Upwards of £300 was collected by him for the Peckham mission before his removal to Toronto, Canada, where he died March 17, 1857. By this time the Catholic congregation had nearly doubled. Fr. Anthony, the pupil and successor of Fr. Louis, opened a chapel in a stable in Stafford Street, known to the inhabitants as ' The Hole in the Wall' ! On July 6, 1859, the first stone of the present fine church and monastery was laid

by Bishop Grant, of Southwark. E.
Welby Pugin was the architect.
The clergy - house was then at
4 Carlton Place, New Peckham,
S.E. The solemn opening by Archbishop Manning and Bishop Grant
took place on Thursday, October 4,
1866. The building consists of a
nave and two aisles, which termi-
nate at the eastern end in a chancel
and two lateral chapels. The altar
of the Lady Chapel is of Irish
marbles, curiously carved. A fine
Calvary towers above the high
altar, the gift of the late Miss
Hales, of Canterbury. The cost of
erecting the church was £6,000.
Fr. Emidius, O.S.F., was guardian
of the Peckham monastery at the
time the church was opened.

PEMBERTON, near **WIGAN**,
LANCS (*Liverpool*).   St. Cuthbert.
In 1870-71 schools were erected,
one of the larger class-rooms serving
as a chapel. Fr. W. Brady was
the first priest. A church to accom-
modate 500 was announced as likely
to be built (1878), but nothing,
apparently, was done till 1887, when
an iron church was opened by
Bishop O'Reilly (February 13). The
Catholic population of the district
is about 2,000.
Priests.
Rev. Bernard Brady, 1871.
„ J. Manning, 1885.
„ Francis Blake, 1888.
„ Edward Smith, 1902 to date.

PENRITH, CUMBERLAND (*Hex-
ham and Newcastle*). St. Catherine.
In 1681 five Catholics and thirteen
Quakers were cited before the chan-
cellor of the diocese of Carlisle at
Penrith for not attending the parish

church. In 1833 a room was hired
in the town by J. Smith, Esq., and
fitted up as a Catholic chapel. The
mission was described as 'wretchedly
poor,' the priest, Fr. H. Newsham,
having 'to lodge as best he could
with protestants.' In November
1839 the Rev. G. Haydock, the
Biblical commentator, was appointed to Penrith. Though he
did not live to see the opening of
the present thirteenth - century-
Gothic church—opened on June 11,
1850—it was mainly owing to his
exertions that the building was
erected. Lady Throckmorton, Mr.
Howard, of Corby, and others were
notable benefactors. In October
1860, the structure was nearly
doubled by the addition of apse and
transepts.
Priests at Penrith.
Rev. H. Newsham, 1833.
„ James Seddon, 1838.
„ Geo. Haydock, 1841.
„ Robt. Smith, 1850 (after the
restoration of the hierarchy
in that year he was made
Canon of Hexham).
„ Geo. Flint, 1857.
„ Robt. Canon Smith (second
time), 1862.
„ Wm. Smith, 1867.
„ E. O'Dwyer, here 1871.
„ Geo. Meynell, 1884.
„ John Chapman, 1897.
„ Jeremiah Foran, 1901.

PENZANCE, CORNWALL (*Plymouth*). The Immaculate Conception.
In 1837, Fr. W. Ivers attempted
to found a mission here, but failed.
In July 1840, Fr. W. Young came
to the town and built the church.
The schools were situated underneath. The opening took place
October 26, 1843. The care of the

place was made over to the French Conceptionist Order. The mission having fallen into financial difficulties, bankruptcy was averted by Bishop Errington, of Plymouth, who advanced the sum of £950 to the rector. Most of the funds for building the new church were collected by Fr. Young in London. The Bishop of Marseilles, Superior-General of the Conceptionists, also liberally subscribed. A Catholic lending library was established in connection with the church in 1847, and proved very useful. Among the many converts who were received into the Church at Penzance was Miss Elizabeth Peel, cousin of the great statesman Sir Robert Peel. Sir Paul Molesworth, Bart., of Keneggie, was the chief Catholic in the neighbourhood of Penzance at this time. In October 1884 a splendid new organ, by G. Tucker, of Plymouth, was installed in the church. The cost of the instrument was £350, of which £100 was given by John McAlister, Esq., a member of the congregation. Canon Shortland was priest at Penzance from 1859 till his 'terribly sudden death' in July 1889.[1] In 1892 new schools were erected at a cost of £1,300 on a site given by James Runnalls, Esq. The jubilee of the Penzance mission was celebrated with much ceremony in November 1893.

Catholics was then less than twenty. In 1858 they numbered 150. In the districts of Whittlesea, Thorney, Crowland, and Huntingdon, which were then served from Peterborough, the number of the faithful was about 350, 'almost all poor agricultural labourers.' From 1848-50, Mass was celebrated in a private house, barely accommodating thirty persons. A house was next purchased for £450, and here a temporary chapel was fitted up. This was sold in 1856, and a school chapel erected for 200 persons. This building, together with the adjoining presbytery, was opened on Rosary Sunday 1856. It may be of interest to note that the Ven. Henry Heath, O.S.F., who suffered at Tyburn for the Faith, April 17, 1643, was a native of Peterborough. In 1890 (January) a splendid gold and jewelled monstrance was presented to the church by an anonymous benefactor. At Norman Cross, near Peterborough, are buried many of the French prisoners of war who died here during the early part of the last century. A chapel to their memory has been added to the church of All Souls, opened in the summer of 1896, from the design of Mr. L. Stokes. Mr. L. Dold gave £200 towards the high altar, and Mr. H. Walters a handsome statue of St. Peter.

PETERBOROUGH, NORTH-AMPTONSHIRE (*Northampton*). All Souls.

The mission was established in 1848, Canon Thomas Seed being the first priest. The number of

PETERSFIELD, HANTS (*Portsmouth*). St. Lawrence.

The church, in the Roman style, was built by Mr. Cave, of Ditcham Park, and opened 1890. Prior to this, the mission was served by Mr. Cave's domestic chapel. The Salesian Fathers had charge of the place till August 1893, when

[1] Canon Shortland was formerly protestant rector of Penzance

they were supplanted by the Benedictines from Ampleforth. Fr. Ildephonsus Cummins, O.S.B., was the first resident priest of this latter Order. There were no Catholics in the district in 1885, but ten years later in addition to the church there was a school attended by seventy children.

PETWORTH, SUSSEX (*Southwark*). The Sacred Heart.

Until the establishment of the present mission, the nearest chapel was at Burton Park (*q.v.*). The handsome Decorated Gothic church, to accommodate about three hundred persons, was built at the expense of the late Willock Dawes, Esq., of Brighton, and was consecrated by Bishop Bourne June 19, 1901. Mr. F. A. Walters, F.S.A., was the architect.

Priests.
Rev. Thomas Canon Lalor.
„ Edward Martin, 1901.

PICKERING, YORKS, NORTH RIDING (*Middlesbrough*).

In 1901, the few Catholics of the place met in a hired room in a narrow lane for devotions. Fr. E. Bryan was sent down to attend the incipient mission, and in answer to appeals for funds sufficient money was collected to purchase a house and site for a church (1902). Three rooms of the house serve as a chapel, and another as a schoolroom.

PILLING, GARSTANG, LANCS (*Liverpool*). St. William of York.

Mission founded from Garstang 1891.

Priests.
Rev. Edw. Smith, 1891.
„ Rev. Jn. Smith, 1901 to date.

PLAISTOW. *See* EAST HAM, E.

PLATT BRIDGE, WIGAN, LANCS (*Liverpool*). The Holy Family.

The school chapel was opened for worship on the fourth Sunday of Advent 1893, when Mass was said by Dean Kelly, of Bootle. The average attendance at the school in 1894 was about 125. In 1898 the schools were increased. An iron church was put up in 1900 by Fr. Louis Verbrugghe. The handsome Gothic stations of the Cross were erected November 1901.

PLEASINGTON, LANCS (*Salford*). SS. Mary and John the Baptist.

The mission was commenced 1816 by John F. Butler, Esq., who erected the church, at a cost of £20,000, as a thank-offering for recovery from dropsy. It was opened August 24, 1819. The first priest was Fr. Edw. Kenyon, who had been a fellow-student of Mr. Butler's at Douai. He left the mission for that of St. Alban's, Blackburn, 1828. The present congregation numbers about 280.

Priests since 1828.
Rev. P. Orrell, 1828.
„ Thos. Holding, 1835.
:, Hy. Sharples, 1840.
„ Jn. Lawson, 1845.
„ Jn. Peduzzi, 1847.
„ Thos. Quick, 1879.
„ H. Mulvany, 1881.
„ Jas. Lawless, 1892 to date.

PLOWDEN, SHROPSHIRE (*Shrewsbury*). St. Walburga.

Plowden Hall, the seat of the ancient Catholic family of Plowden, was for generations the mainstay of the Faith in this part of the district. Sir Edmund Plowden, who lost the Chancellorship under Elizabeth for being a Catholic, was the author of the celebrated dictum, 'No priest, no Mass,' which subsequently proved fatal to many a prosecution for 'recusancy.' From about 1729, the chaplains at Plowden were mostly Jesuits. From 1784 to 1787, the Benedictines of Acton Burnell served the mission. During the incumbency of Fr. Richard Colgan, 1827-67, the present chapel and presbytery were built by Wm. Plowden, Esq. (1862). The school was added in 1874, and enlarged 1896, by Wm. Francis Plowden, Esq. There is still a domestic chapel at the Hall, which contains several priests' hiding-places. Some ancient vestments, &c., are carefully preserved there, including a chalice-veil said to have belonged to the Blessed Thomas More.

Priests since 1868.

Rev. Canon Tobin, 1868.
„ F. O'Neil, 1873.
„ W. Kelly, 1887.
„ Mgr. Slaughter, 1891.
„ A. Tremmery, 1895.
„ C. Ryder, 1898.
„ E. Byrne, 1899.
„ G. Gastaldi, D.D., 1900.

PLUMSTEAD, near WOOLWICH (*Southwark*). St. Patrick.

A site for a school chapel was purchased in 1890, and plans for the intended building prepared by Mr. F. A. Walters. Until the chapel was opened Mass was said in a hired hall by Fr. T. Whelahan. The chapel was opened in August 1893 by the Bishop of Southwark. Canon Murnane preached. Fr. A. Staunton is the present rector.

PLYMOUTH, TOTHILL LANE (*Plymouth*). Holy Cross.

This church was solemnly opened, December 20, 1881, by Bishop Vaughan, of Plymouth, who also preached (Heb. xiii. 10). The church, which is a neat Gothic structure, capable of holding about two hundred persons, was built from designs of Messrs. Hansom. It was originally erected at Plymouth, but, owing to operations of the Great Western Railway Company, had to be removed. Mr. Dillon, of Plymouth, was a noted benefactor of the new church. Fr. W. F. Traies, M.A., on leaving the mission, after a pastorate of four years, in April 1885, was presented by his sorrowing congregation with a massive chalice and paten, burnished with gold and set with gems. Fr. Traies spent the last five years of his all too short life as a priest at St. George's Cathedral, Southwark, London, S.E. He died at Exeter in November 1890. The Rev. Canon John Keily, rector here in 1891, is the present incumbent.

PLYMOUTH, DEVONSHIRE. SS. Mary and Boniface.

In 1803, Rowland Conyers, Esq., a Catholic, gave a sum of money sufficient to open a chapel in the town. Mass was said at first over the stable of the George Inn, Devonport. In 1806 the Abbé L. Guilbert, an *émigré* priest, built a chapel at Stonehouse, some little distance from Plymouth. Fr. Alexander Lun, the next priest, died suddenly in 1821. He was succeeded by Fr. T. Costello, who settled at Plymouth at the earnest request of Bishop Collingridge, Vicar Apostolic of the Western District. There were many Irish soldiers in the garrison at Plymouth at this time, and Fr. Costello did much for their spiritual welfare. On quitting the town in 1834 to take up his duties as chaplain to Lady Wrey at Tawstock Court Fr. Costello was publicly presented with a piece of plate by all sections of the inhabitants, ' as a token of respect and esteem.' Plymouth became a see at the restoration of the hierarchy in 1850, and the first stone of the new cathedral was laid in June 1856. The building was nearing completion when, in August 1857, the roof fell in with a tremendous crash. Happily no lives were lost, but the fabric of the church was damaged to the extent of about £640. Upon examination, Mr. Hansom, the architect, discovered that the roof had proved too heavy for the Bath stone supports. In spite of the delay caused by the accident, the cathedral was ready for opening on March 25, 1858. The tower and spire, 205 ft. high, were completed from designs by Hansom June 5, 1866.

Administrators.

Rev. Mark Canon Oleron, V.G., 1850.
  „   Hon. W. Clifford, D.D., 1854.
  „   W. Buckle, 1856.
  „   H. Canon Woollett, 1862.
  „   W. R. Canon Brownlow, 1888.
  „   Thos. Canon Courtenay, 1897 and to date.

POCKLINGTON, YORKS (*Middlesbrough*). St. Mary and St. Joseph.

The Abbé Pierre Foucher, formerly Vicar-General of Aix, was sent here by Bishop Gibson in March 1790. His successor, Fr. J. Hodgson, erected the old chapel. The mission is not given in the ' Laity's Directory ' for 1825 and some succeeding years, and, indeed, is said to have been in an almost moribund state. It was revived by Fr. R. Cook, and in 1852 was served from Everingham. The present church was opened by Bishop Cornthwaite, of Beverley, July 29, 1863. A new school, for fifty children, was inaugurated by Lord Herries, 1877.

Recent Priests.

Rev. Edward Riddell, 1863.
  „   Edward Pearson, here in 1871.
  „   Geo. Brunner, here in 1877.
  „   James Murphy, 1885.
  „   P. O'Brien, 1888.
  „   Wm. Desmond, 1890.
  „   Richard Lewis, 1892.
  „   Richard Shennick, 1893.
  „   Jn. Carr, here in 1897.
  „   Matthew O'Donohoe, 1898.
  „   Gabriel Ryan, 1904.

PONTEFRACT, YORKS (*Leeds*). St. Joseph.

Fr. Hy. Hamerton, S.J., established here a boys' school, for fifty to sixty scholars, in 1685. By 1688 the congregation attracted by the chapel had reached 300, of whom some 280 were confirmed by Bishop Leyburn. At the Revolution (1688), the school was closed, and Fr. Hamerton imprisoned for some time in York Castle. The present mission is reported to have been ' founded about the year 1800,' but there was an older chapel in the parish from which the congregation removed. The register dates from 1787. The Abbé Jean Beurcy served the mission from about 1794 till his death, February 11, 1800, aged forty. Fr. J. B. Fountaine, S.J., was here 1812, and Fr. Reeve, S.J., about 1817. Mr. B. Boothroyd, in his 'History of Pontefract' (1807), gives the following facts about Catholics in the town: 'Their number in this place has never exceeded thirty or forty persons. Their place of worship till lately was a room in the house occupied by their *teacher*. They have now erected a place of worship on a more enlarged scale. . . . The building is a neat structure, and its interior well finished.' This chapel was built 1800, and is still in use.

Priests (S.J.) since 1825.

Rev. W. Waterton, —.
„ Wm. Ibbotson, 1827.
„ E. G. Pugh, 1828.
„ J. Bird, 1837.
„ Jas. Etheridge, 1838.
„ Jos. Holden, 1841.
„ John Bird, 1843.
„ J. Brigham, 1848.
„ Wm. Lomax, 1851.
„ J. S. Woollett, 1858.
„ Jn. Rigby, 1862.
„ Geo. Pearson, 1867.
„ Walter Clifford, here in 1871.
„ James Maguire, 1888.
„ Martin Brey, 1891.
„ Cyril de Cuyper, 1895 to date.

PONTYPOOL, MONMOUTHSHIRE (*Newport*). St. Alban.

When the mission was started here in 1844, the Catholics of the place were reckoned at 492. Mass was said in a room, and as late as the commencement of 1845 there was still no chapel, school, or presbytery. The average weekly income of the mission at this time was 11s. 4d. A 'neat church' was erected and opened July 23, 1846, and a presbytery in 1849. The congregation by this time had increased to 870, 'almost without exception the lowest class of labourers.' The place was in a state of terrible spiritual destitution. In 1864, the Catholic population had increased to over two thousand. The Franciscan Capuchin Fathers took over the mission in May 1860, and here they continued till 1891, when the spiritual care of the district again returned to the seculars. When a school was started by the Franciscans about September 1860, 'scarcely half-a-dozen children had seen a book, and, worse still, not more than three or four could make the sign of the cross, repeat the simplest prayer, or tell who made them!' [1]

Priests.

Rev. Wm. Woollett, 1845.
„ A. Clarkson, 1855.
„ F. Elzear Torrigiani, 1859.
„ F. Joachim, 1877.
„ Evangelist de Milia, 1882.
„ Seraphin Bolger, 1885.
„ Rudolph McCarthy, 1888.
„ P. Degen, 1892 to date.

POOLE, DORSET (*Plymouth*). St. Mary's.

The mission was founded by the Abbé Pierre Lanquetuit, assisted by Mr. Weld, of Lulworth, and Lady Anastasia Mannock. This lady was the daughter of Lord Montague and sister of the last Viscount. In 1820, the Abbé returned to France. The church was opened July 16, 1839, when Lady Mannock again showed her

[1] *Franciscan Missions in Monmouthshire* (London: Burns & Oates, 1876).

interest in the mission by contributing £800 towards the expenses of building. The organ gallery and organ were erected 1848-49. By 1850 the congregation had so increased that it was found necessary to convert the existing sacristy into a schoolroom.

Priests.

Rev. Abbé Pierre Lanquetuit, 1793.
„ Jean Coupé, 1820.
„ D. Morton, 1828.
„ Jos. Dwyer, 1831.
„ Wm. Casey, 1837.
„ Jn. O'Brien, 1840.
„ R. Tower, 1842.
„ Edward Kenny, 1844.
„ H. Canon Woollett, 1846.
„ Jos. Parke, 1857.
„ Denis Byrne, 1860.
„ Desiderius de Smet, 1863.
„ R. Meagar, 1867.
„ Henry Dobbelaere, here 1871.
„ Jos. Higgins, 1874.
„ Robt. Browne, 1879.
„ Aug. Morford, here in 1888 and till after.
„ H. J. Dowsett, 1893.
„ Timothy Hannigan, 1902.

POPLAR, LONDON, E. (*Westminster*). St. Mary and St. Joseph.

The church was opened by Cardinal Wiseman September 24, 1856. The style is thirteenth-century Gothic (cruciform), the seating capacity being for about 1,100. There are two chapels, and the sanctuary is lighted by a splendid east window displaying events in the life of Our Lady. The reredos has carvings representing the Gifts of the Holy Ghost. In 1880, the interior of the church was thoroughly redecorated. Prior to the opening of the present church, the congregation worshipped in 'a miserable chapel' in Wade Street, erected in 1818. The

Catholic population was estimated at 5,000 in 1840.

The church was consecrated by the Bishop of *Amycla* (Dr. Fenton) Wednesday September 26, 1906, and the building solemnly reopened in the presence of Archbishop Bourne, the Sunday following.

Priests.

Rev. R. Barber, here in 1825 and till 1839.
„ J. Hearsnep, 1839 till after 1858.
„ Jn. Stanton, 1860.
„ Jas. Lawless, M.R., 1879.
„ Thos. Doyle, M.R., 1903 to date.

PORT CLARENCE, DURHAM, (*Hexham and Newcastle*). St. Thomas of Canterbury.

Before 1830, Port Clarence was merely a coal station. Owing to railway extension, a town had risen up by 1866. The Catholic population at that time was reckoned at 200. In the spring of the same year, a room over an old dissenting chapel was hired for Mass and Sunday school. Fr. Michael Bourke, who had charge of the mission, was compelled to lodge at nearly two miles' distance from the scene of his labours. In 1875, the place was served from Haverton Hill. A school chapel was erected 1879. Fr. Robt. Harris was rector in 1883 and to date (1904).

PORTICO, near PRESCOT, LANCS (*Liverpool*). Our Lady Help of Christians.

The chapel was built in 1790 by Fr. N. Sewall, S.J., but, long before this, Mass was said regularly at Schole's Farm, close to the present church. The nearest Catholic day schools are at Thatto Heath. St.

Nicholas was the title of the church till after 1864. The mission has always been served by Jesuits.

Priests from 1824.

Rev. J. Hughes.
„ Bernard Addis, 1828.
„ Jos. Newsham, 1830.
„ Hy. Beeston, 1832.
„ Jn. McClune, 1842.
„ Matt. McCann, 1844.
„ Felix Poole, 1850.
„ Wm. Cotham, 1852.
(Mission served from Prescot 1864 *et seq.*)
„ Matthew M'Cann, 1870.
„ Jn. Milner, here in 1875.
„ Bernard Beiderlinden, 1877.
„ James Henry, 1879.
„ Augustine Oswald, 1882.
„ Bernard Winkler, 1885.
„ Joseph Imhassly, 1889.
„ Thos. Hill, 1895 to date.

PORTMAN SQUARE, LONDON, W.
(*Westminster*). The French Chapel.
At the immigration of the French clergy and nobility in 1793, they used as a chapel a miserable room beneath a poulterer's shop in Dorset Street Mews. The Abbé Bouret was the first priest. Later on, a small chapel was opened in Little George Street. During the building it was a common sight to see the princes of the royal house of France assisting the workmen! The Comte de Provence (Louis XVIII.), the Comte d'Artois (Charles X.), the Duc de Berry (assassinated 1820), &c., &c., heard Mass regularly at this little place of worship, which, after the restoration in 1815, was known as the Chapel Royal, from the support (25,000 frs.) it received from the French monarchy. The Abbé Latel succeeded the Abbé Bouret. The

other chief priests in succession were: Abbé Chenel (—), Abbé de Laporte (—), Abbé Mailly (1840), Abbé Toursel (1845–80). Government support was suspended after the July revolution of 1830, but later on a grant was made by King Louis Philippe for that portion of the chapel occupied by the French ambassador and suite. In 1850, the young Comte de Paris made his first communion in the chapel, in the presence of a distinguished gathering. Under the Second Empire, the chapel received from Napoleon III. an annual allowance of 3,500 frs. It was to the Abbé Toursel of this church that the Emperor's son, the ill-fated Prince Imperial, went to confession prior to leaving for Zululand, in February 1879. In March 1881 the infidel Government of France suppressed the official stipend of the church, thus 'accomplishing,' as the Paris *Union* sarcastically said, 'one of those acts of generosity and greatness of soul which raises its prestige in the eyes of the foreigner!' Mgr. L. Toursel is the present rector.

PORTSMOUTH, HANTS (*Portsmouth*).
The mission was founded in 1793 by the Abbé de la Rue, who opened a chapel in Prince George Street, Portsea. The Abbé continued to serve the mission till his death at Gosport, May 14, 1827. Before the Revolution he was a priest of the diocese of Bayeux. Fr. J. Welch succeeded him, and was rector till 1841. The estimated Catholic population of Portsmouth in 1866, both civil and military, was 5,640. The old chapel has sittings for only 500, so

that on Sundays the congregation was most inconveniently crowded. The military had their own chapel from about 1863. Frs. Woolett and Horan commenced collecting for a new church in 1866, when some £470 was subscribed. The foundation stone of the present St. John's Cathedral was laid by Bishop Danell, December 1879. The style is Geometrical Gothic, a lofty tower and spire being the chief features. Large schools occupy the rear. At the time of the opening, August 10, 1882, Portsmouth had become a diocese (1881), and St. John's was now its cathedral church.

POULTON - LE - FYLDE, LANCS (*Liverpool*). St. John the Evangelist.

The old Singleton chapel, dedicated to Our Lady, passed out of Catholic hands shortly after the accession of Elizabeth. At the visitation of the Archbishop of York, 1578, the place is described as 'full of disorders.' In 1650 it would seem to have returned to the Catholics, and was used as a priests' residence. The mission was largely supported by the Gillows. Between 1650 and 1680, the priests here were Frs. Hy. Holden, Matthews, and Jas. Swarbrick. The last incumbent was arrested after the Jacobite rising of 1715, and died in Lancaster Castle, 1717. The chapel, 'a poor, thatched dwelling,' was seized by the protestants at the conclusion of Prince Charles Edward's abortive rising of 1745-46. Fr. Jn. Cooling, or Cowling, the incumbent, was forcibly ejected, and the building converted into a chapel of ease to the parish church at Kirkham. One of Fr. Cowling's successors, Fr. Watts, conformed to the Established Church and ' finished his days ingloriously as the curate of Wray Green,' 1773. He was probably reconciled to the Church before he died. Curliff Shaw, Esq., lord of the manor of Singleton, protected the Catholics, who, when deprived of the old chapel, erected a presbytery and place of worship at their own expense. Fr. Cliff, from Great Eccleston, and Fr. Husband were the priests between 1768 and 1799. Fr. A. Story came in 1800 for a few years, and after him Fr. Joseph Orrell, who died at Blackbrook, 1820. In 1826, during Fr. E. Kenyon's pastorate, the Catholics of Singleton numbered two-thirds of the population. Fr. J. Anderton, an alumnus of Crook and Ushaw, died at Singleton in August 1857. When Fr. Orrell retired in 1814 a new chapel was erected at Poulton. Fr. Orrell gave the priest the ancient silver crucifix and reliquary used in the chapel at Singleton during the penal times. The Singleton property was sold in 1860 by Bishop Goss, of Liverpool, to Mr. Thos. Miller, of Preston.

Priests at Poulton-le-Fylde since 1862.

Rev. Fr. Wm. Johnson, 1862.
„   Roger Arrowsmith, 1879.
„   Thos. Grimes, 1885.
„   W. Vaughan, 1900.

PRESCOT, LANCS (*Liverpool*). Our Lady Immaculate and St. Joseph.

This mission has often been confounded with that of Portico (*q.v.*), which lies near it. In 1782

Fr. Wm. Molyneux, S.J., last Catholic Viscount Molyneux, established a mission either at or near Prescot. In 1745, during the progress of the Jacobite rebellion under Prince Charles Edward Stuart, Fr. Wm. Green, who had charge of the chapel, was committed to York Castle as ' a very dangerous person.' In recent times the spiritual care of the local Catholics was undertaken by the priest at Portico. In 1857 a church was built at Prescot by Fr. Wm. Cotham, S.J., and opened on October 21 of the same year. It was served from Portico till about 1863, when the Revs. Joseph Walmesley, S.J., and Geo. Harper, S.J., were appointed resident priests. The Catholic schools attached to the mission were enlarged 1894.

Recent Priests.

Rev. Thos. Cooper, here 1871.
„ P. Sherlock, S.J., 1874.
„ Ralph Brindle, S.J., 1877.
„ Thos. Musworth, 1902.

PRESTON, LANCS (*Liverpool*).

From copies of memoranda made by Fr. J. Dunn, it appears that a brick chapel, roofed with thatch, was opened in the Friargate, Preston, in 1605, and dedicated to St. Mary Magdalen, the patroness of the old parish church, erected in 1293 (Edward I.). Fr. Joseph Banister, ' a learned Jesuit,' was the first priest of this chapel. From the time of James II.'s accession, 1685, the Jesuits had charge of the Preston mission. On September 7, 1687, Bishop Leyburn confirmed 1,153 persons at Preston and Tulketh. Mass was then said in a barn at Fisherwick. In 1761 Fr. Patrick Barnewall, S.J., opened the first public Catholic chapel in Preston, on the site of the old Grey Friars' monastery. Under his successor, Fr. Joseph Smith, this chapel was destroyed by ' an election mob ' (1768). This misfortune so preyed on the good priest that he died shortly afterwards of a ' broken heart.' When Fr. Joseph Dunn came to Preston, in 1775, the Catholics numbered less than 500, and many of these did all they could to hide their religion because of the ' sharp lookout that was kept for Popish recusants.' Fr. Dunn did much by his conciliatory manners to disarm protestant prejudice. In June 1793 he and his colleague, Fr. Richard Morgan, officiated in the old chapel for the last time. This building became a cotton warehouse of Messrs. Sidgreaves & Leighton till about 1815, when it again became a place of Catholic worship. Some improvements were undertaken, and the chapel served down to 1856, when it was rebuilt on an enlarged scale. The style is Romanesque. Above the altar hangs a copy of Carracci's ' Ascension,' from the original at Stonyhurst. The seating accommodation is for about 1,000. The following are the priests who have served the mission :

Priests at St. Wilfrid's, Preston.

Rev. Patrick Barnewall, 1761.
„ Joseph Smith, 1767.
„ Joseph Dunn, 1776. A man of great public spirit and one of the pioneers of gas lighting in Preston. Died 1827, aged 81.
„ — Morgan, 1828.
„ John Bird, 1829.
„ F. West, 1834.
„ G. Connell, 1836.
„ Thos. Weston, 1842.
„ R. Norris, 1844.
„ Thos. Weston, 1846.

Y

Rev. Henry Walmesley, 1851.
„ James Etheridge, 1855.
„ Joseph Bateman, 1857.
„ Wm. Cobb, 1860.
„ Robt. Whitty, 1873.
„ Joseph Jackson, 1877.
„ Thos. Dykes, 1882.
„ Thos. Splaine, 1888.
„ Fredk. O'Hare, 1894.
„ Francis Scoles, 1901 to date.

PRESTON, LANCS. St. Augustine.
At the invitation of Joseph Gillow, Esq., a meeting was held at the 'Shelley's Arms,' March 9, 1836, to consider the erection of a new church. A site was given by Wm. Heatley, Esq., of Brindle Lodge, and in November 1838 the church was commenced, the stone being laid by Alderman Gradwell, a kinsman of the bishop. The building was opened by Bishop Briggs, V.A., July 30, 1840.

Priests.
Rev. T. Canon Cookson, 1840.
„ Fr. E. Swarbrick, 1856.
„ Fr. W. Walker, 1860.
„ J. Canon Walker, 1869.
„ Canon Taylor, 1874.
„ Lawrence Canon Cosgrave, 1883 to date.

PRESTON, LANCS. St. Joseph.
As far back as 1853, two acres of land were purchased in Rigby Street, Ribbleton Lane, for the purpose of a chapel. The first stone, however, was not laid till July 1860, and in May 1862 the spacious school chapel was opened. The cost was about £740, the style adopted being Early English. The architect was R. W. Hughes. The church (Gothic) was opened in 1874, and in 1896-97 the chancel and

side chapels were decorated and 'stations' by De Beaule added. Two years later a handsome rood screen was erected. The schools were improved the same year.

PRESTON, LANCS (*Liverpool*).
The English Martyrs, Moor Park.
The school chapel was opened Sunday, January 22, 1865. The accommodation was for about 150 persons. Fr. J. Taylor was the first priest in charge of this mission. The church of the same title was completed in December 1867. The style is Gothic, from the plans of E. W. Pugin, and the building will accommodate about 850 persons. The cost was about £8,000. Two bays, a transept, and a chancel were added to the church early in 1887-88. These additions were found necessary owing to the large increase of the Catholic population. Fr. J. A. Pyke was chiefly instrumental in bringing the enlargements about. The infant school was enlarged 1892. In 1895 new stations of the Cross were erected. The Catholic population of the parish is about 6,700.

PRESTON, LANCS. St. Walburga, Maudlands.
A site for a church was purchased in March 1846 from the Preston and Wyre Railway Company by the rector of Stonyhurst College. Upon this 'a handsome, commodious, and elegant' church (Early English style) was erected, and opened by Bishop Brown August 3, 1854. The accommodation is for 2,000. A tower was erected by subscription and completed Sept. 14, 1866. The mission is indebted for its

completeness to such benefactors as Mr. W. Talbot, Mr. Robt. Arrowsmith, J. Anderton, &c. A new wing was added to the schools 1894, and additional class-rooms 1901-2.

Priests from 1861.

Rev. Thos. Weston.
„ Chas. Henry, 1863.
„ Geo. Lambert, 1867.
„ Joseph Johnson, 1871.
„ Nicholas Papall, 1874.
„ Jn. O'Neil, 1902 to date.

PRESTON, LANCS. St. Wilfrid's.

In June 1793 the 'spacious chapel' of St. Wilfrid was opened with much solemnity. It was enlarged in the autumn of 1843. A Lady Chapel was added 1844. This latter is adorned with pilasters, designed by H. T. Bulmer, after 'the style of ancient churches in Rome.' The church was redecorated 1891.

Priests since 1824.

Rev. — Trappes, 1824.
„ — Lythgoe, 1827.
„ G. Rogerson, 1833.
„ G. Connell, 1836.
„ J. Bird, 1841.
„ Richard Norris, 1843.
„ Thos. Weston, 1845.
„ Henry Walmesley, 1851.
„ James Etheridge, 1855.
„ James Bateman, 1857.
„ Wm. Cobb, 1861.
„ Robt. Whitty, 1874.
„ Joseph Jackson, 1877.
„ Thos. Dykes, 1882.
„ James Splaine, 1888.
„ Fredk. O'Hare, 1895.
„ Francis Scoles, 1901 to date.

PRESTON, LANCS. St. Ignatius.

The church was opened by Bishop Briggs May 5, 1836. On July 31, 1887, a new chancel, reredos, and altar were added to the building, which had been considerably enlarged 1858.

Priests.

Rev. F. West, 1836.
„ Francis Daniel, 1842.
„ Henry Walmesley, 1844.
„ Wm. Knight, 1846.
„ Thos. Clarke, 1850.
„ Francis Daniel, 1852.
„ Wm. Mitchell, 1855.
„ Richard Cooper, 1857.
„ James Walker, 1867.
„ Vincent Bond, 1879.
„ James Fanning, 1890.
„ Ignatius Gartlan, 1895.
„ Francis Payne, 1899.
„ Francis Dobson 1902 to date.

PRESTWICH, LANCS (*Salford*). Our Lady of Grace.

This mission was formed in August 1889 out of the existing missions of St. Mary's, Bury, and St. Thomas, Radcliffe. The first place of worship was the Co-operative Hall, where Mass was said weekly from Sunday, June 9, till the erection of the large school chapel in August 1891, during the incumbency of Fr. D. Walsh, who also built the handsome presbytery. Fr. Joseph Hayes is the present rector.

PRINCETHORPE, near RUGBY, WARWICKSHIRE (*Birmingham*). St. Mary's Priory.

In 1792 the English Benedictine nuns of Montargis were compelled by the French Revolution to come to England for safety. They landed at Shoreham March 16 of the above year, and proceeded to Brighton, where they were met by the Prince of Wales, afterwards George IV., who had heard of them through Mrs. Fitzherbert. The nuns thought of retiring to Holland, but the Prince said, 'Stay where you are, and I will protect you.' They accordingly proceeded to Rodney Hall, Norfolk. The educational establishment for young ladies which they continued from the one in France having outgrown the exigencies of the place, they removed to Heath Hall, Yorkshire, and finally in 1833 to Princethorpe, near Rugby, where they still remain. The chapel of the community was consecrated October 17, 1843. When the Order removed to Princethorpe in 1833 there were still two choir nuns and one lay sister alive who had made their profession at Montargis. The centenary of the English foundation was celebrated in July 1893.

PRIOR PARK, near BATH, SOMERSET (*Clifton*).

In the early part of the eighteenth century, Ralph Allen, Esq., the philanthropist, who made a fortune by devising a system of cross posts for England and Wales, erected the magnificent mansion, which, after a variety of vicissitudes common to such buildings, was purchased by Bishop Baines, V.A.W.D., in December 1829. Two fine wings, under the title of St. Peter's and St. Paul's, were added to the original house, and the whole opened as a mixed ecclesiastical and lay college in July 1830. In 1836 a large part of the pile of buildings was accidentally destroyed by fire, and although the damage was quickly repaired the calamity is said to

have hastened the death of the founder, who died at the college July 6, 1843. He was much blamed by his contemporaries for founding a college so near to that of Downside, and at a time when there was certainly no need of such an establishment. His withdrawal of certain funds, professors, and students from Ampleforth as a nucleus for the new college was also most detrimental to that college, and, indeed, well nigh caused its ruin. For the rest, Prior Park has had a singularly chequered career. It reached perhaps its highest pitch of efficiency under the late Mgr. Canon E. Williams (*d.* 1891), although its standard as a teaching institution has always ranked high. In 1895-96, the Christian Brothers replaced the secular clergy as professors, and continued to conduct the college till 1902, when the place was again made over to the secular clergy for a short time, Mgr. E. Nolan, M.A. (Cantab.), being the president. The college is at present under the care of the Fathers of the Society of the Holy Ghost.

PRUDHOE HALL, NORTHUMBERLAND (*Hexham and Newcastle*). Our Lady and St. Cuthbert.

A Catholic church and school were built in 1870 by Matthew Liddell, Esq., of Prudhoe Hall, who died October 20, 1881. His remains lie buried in a vault beneath the north end of the chapel. The present church was erected in 1891 by Mrs. Liddell, widow of the above-named Matthew Liddell. The style of the building, which was designed by Messrs. Dunn & Hansom, is Early Perpendicular. The altar and reredos, by Peall, of Newcastle, are beautifully carved. The font is a copy of the ancient one at Shaddingfield, Norfolk.

Priests.

Rev. Wilfrid Lescher, O.P., here in 1875.
„ Geo. King, 1882.
„ Wm. Stevenson, 1888.
„ Wm. Drysdale, 1892.
„ Austin Simmons, 1893 to date.

PUDDINGTON, CHESHIRE (*Shrewsbury*). St. Mary.

The Ven. Wm. Plessington, a priest of the English College at Valladolid, was chaplain to Mr. Massey, of Puddington, at the time of his arrest in 1679. He was condemned to death at Chester for his priesthood, and suffered with great constancy on July 19 of the same year. Down to 1757, Mass was said ' very privately ' in the old hall, but about this time the Massey family built a new hall and chapel. The latter had a passage leading to it from the house. The hall was destroyed by fire in December 1867, but the chapel was saved. The priests at Puddington since 1785 have been :

Rev. Jn. Shuttleworth, —.
„ W. Blacoe, 1786–91.
„ R. Platt, 1792–1837.
„ Jn. Carter (curate), 1834–36.
„ R. Gillow, 1837–45.
„ P. Perry, 1845–49.
„ Thos. Crowe, 1849–51.
„ P. F. Baron, 1851–94.

The mission has since been closed, but it is hoped that so historic a centre of Catholicity as this may shortly be revived.

PUDSEY, YORKS (*Leeds*). St. Joseph.

When the school chapel was opened here in 1883, many Catholics were said to be living in the town and district, which is engaged in the woollen manufacture. The chapel was served from St. Mary's, Bradford, till 1901, when the mission was taken over by the Calced Carmelites. Fr. Paul Hurlmans and Fr. Vitalis Felix are the priests in charge.

N.B.—This locality gave its name to the Pudsey family of Bolton and Barford, great sufferers in the cause of religion and loyalty. Thos. Pudsey, Esq., of Bolton, died in York Castle 1571, a prisoner for the Catholic Faith. His grandson, Michael Pudsey, had his estates forfeited by the Parliament for devotion to the cause of Charles I. Another grandson, Stephen, was a priest of Douai. The family became extinct early in the eighteenth century.

PUTNEY, LONDON, S.W. (*Southwark*).

This mission was commenced at Christmas 1902, the place of worship being a disused Methodist chapel hired for the purpose. In 1903 a fine site was given for a church in the Chelverton Road by Lady Westbury, and on this piece of ground a temporary iron building was erected. The estimated Catholic population of the district is about 450. Fr. Robt. Collinson, late of Newhaven, is the incumbent. A permanent church in the Florentine style of architecture was opened by Bishop Amigo of Southwark, Sept. 2, 1906.

R

RADCLIFFE, LANCS (*Salford*). St. Mary and St. Philip Neri.

First chapel opened 1863. The old pre-Reformation chapel of ease attached to Prestwich Church was in 1879 used as a stable. For some time after the opening, the mission was served from Ramsbottom. A second chapel was opened in 1878, and the present church in 1894. Catholic population about 1,600.

Priests.

Rev. Malachy O'Callaghan, 1867.
„ Richard Gerrard, here 1871.
„ John Mussiley, 1877.
„ James Gerity, 1882.
„ Hugh Carroll, 1885.
„ W. L. Fowler, 1890.
„ J. Aukes, 1897.
„ J. Murtagh, here in 1904.

RADFORD, OXON. (*Birmingham*). Fr. W. O'Grady, who died February 18, 1888, was priest at Radford from 1864. The church was opened January 21, 1841, but no information as to the origin of the mission has been forthcoming.

Priests.

Rev. M. Gannon, 1841.
„ E. Winter, 1843.
„ W. O'Grady, 1864-88.
„ P. Sweeny, D.D., here in 1891 and to date.

RAINFORD, ST. HELEN'S, LANCS (*Liverpool*). Corpus Christi.

In 1676 Mrs. Anne Singleton, of Crank, left £40 as ' Mass money ' to Fr. Thurstan Anderton, of Lostock, priest. For many years Mass was said at Crank Hall, the seat of the Singletons, and even after they left it, about 1691, Mass continued to be offered there. Fr. Wm. Barton, *alias* Gerard, served the mission 1702–11. The estate probably passed out of Catholic hands shortly after the rebellion of 1745–46.

After this the focus of Catholicity at Rainford was at Mosborough Hall, the ancient seat of the Lathoms, which passed by marriage to the Molyneux family in 1715. In 1718 the apostate Richard Barker, in his account of the ' church stuff' at Mosborough, notices ' one large silver chalice and paten.' After the purchase of the estate by the Earl of Derby, in or about 1752, a priest was still maintained in the district by the Blounts of Sodington, co. Worcester, but the present mission at Rainford was not started till 1873, when the site of the church was purchased, and the building was opened for worship October 17, 1875. The presbytery was built in 1878.

Recent Priests.
Rev. Jos. Barker, 1877 and till after 1894.
„ Thos. Carroll, 1895 and to date.

RAINHAM, near BARKING, ESSEX (*Westminster*).
Dean Clements, of Barking, opened an iron chapel here in October 1901. The money for starting the mission was given by an anonymous benefactor. The Catholic population at the time was about 100. Before the establishment of the mission there is no record of Holy Mass ever having been offered at Rainham since the time of the Reformation.

RAINHILL, LANCS (*Liverpool*).
St. Bartholomew.
The church, in the Grecian style of architecture, was built 1832-40 by the munificence of B. Bretherton, Esq. There is a memorial brass in the church to William Gerard, Esq., of Ditton, who died 1844. This gentleman was a great benefactor of the mission. The new Catholic Club was opened 1897. The schools have an endowment from the Marchioness Stapleton-Bretherton.
Priests.
Rev. Fr. Worsley, 1840.
„ J. Mason, 1842.
„ Dean Kiernan, 1844.
„ G. Holden, 1885.
„ R. F. Carr, 1888 to date.

RAMSBOTTOM, LANCS (*Salford*).
St. Joseph, Bolton Street.
The first priest of this mission, which was started in 1861, was

Fr. Laurence Schneider. Mass was said in a room not capable of holding one-half of those who wished to attend. The Catholics of the place amounted to about 400. The new church was opened September 30, 1880, during the rectorate of Fr. B. de Mullewie. The old chapel was opened August 17, 1862. Catholic population, 900.
Priests.
Rev. L. Schneider, 1861.
„ Michael Keating, 1863.
„ Bernard de Mullewie, here 1871 and till 1893.
„ James O'Riordan, 1893 to date.

RAMSEY, HUNTINGDONSHIRE (*Northampton*). The Sacred Heart.
The 'chapel' of Ramsey in 1863 was in a cottage, where, Sunday after Sunday, 'about a hundred poor creatures were obliged to crush into the small, unbecoming kitchen.' Many of these are reported to have scarcely known the rudiments of their religion. The priest at this time was Fr. Thomas Seed, who, for lack of accommodation at Ramsey, was compelled to live at Peterborough, fourteen miles distant. At first, Fr. Seed could only say Mass at Ramsey on weekdays, when he used to offer the Holy Sacrifice as early as four or five in the morning to enable the hard-working people to be present. The mission is served from Huntingdon.

RATCLIFFE COLLEGE, near LEICESTER (*Nottingham*). The Immaculate Conception.
The Fathers of Charity, founded by the Ideologist Abbate Antonio Rosmini-Serbati, came to England 1835. In 1845 the college at Rat-

cliffe was founded for those 'who find the larger colleges too expensive, but who wish for their children a thoroughly refined Christian, classical, and commercial education.' For many years the house was also the novitiate, till its transference to Wadhurst, Sussex, in 1881. Fr. J. B. Pagani was the first rector. The jubilee of the foundation was celebrated 1895.

RAWTENSTALL, near MANCHESTER (*Salford*). St. James the Less.

When the mission was started in 1835 by Fr. Hodgson the only Catholics in the town were the Ashworth family and a few poor persons employed by Mr. Brooks, of Sunnyside. This gentleman kindly lent a small building for use as a chapel. By the generous assistance of Mrs. Ashworth, of Lawnd House, Mr. Brooks, Mrs. Collinge, and other benefactors, a site was obtained for a church, which was opened on September 24, 1845. The building was consecrated by Bishop Sharples. The Rev. Dr. Roskell preached at the inaugural Mass. In style the church is Early English.

Priests.

Rev. Thos. Rimmer, 1845.
,,   Thos. Unsworth, 1849.
,,   Hy. Swale, 1853.
,,   Joseph Scott, 1855.
,,   Denis Byrne, 1877.
,,   M. McCormack, 1879.
,,   John Mussely, 1882.
,,   Peter Klein, 1893 to date.

READING, BERKS (*Portsmouth*). St. James.

After the accomplishment of the Reformation in England, the nearest Catholic chapel to Reading was at White Knights, the residence of the ancient family of Englefield. The mission was served 'for a very considerable time' by Franciscans. Fr. Clifton, O.S.F., on leaving White Knights in 1734 made the following curious behest : ' My bridle, saddle, whip, boots, spurs, and spatterdashes I leave to my successor, if a Brother of our Province, who may have the use of them ; of my two tomes in folio of Père Henno's Divinity, and of all the other books in my closet, all of which belong to the body of the English Franciscans, or to some particular members thereof, whose names are in them, or else R.A.' (' Recollectorum Anglorum '). Fr. Healy, O.S.F., was priest at White Knights 1773-75. ' He was a man of truly seraphic science and piety, who won all hearts by his affability and kindness. In 1780 the chapel of the ' Resurrection ' was built in Vastirn Lane, Reading, most probably at the expense of Sir Henry Englefield, Bart. In 1824 the chapel is set down as ' St. Lawrence's Church' in the ' Laity's Directory.' Fr. F. Bowland was priest at that time. The Englefield family became extinct in 1822 by the death of the learned Sir Henry Englefield, since 1777 president of the Antiquarian Society. In him the Reading mission lost a great patron, and henceforth the chapel was advertised as 'wholly supported by subscription.' Between 1837 and 1840, during the rectorate of Fr. John Ringrose, the present church was built, as well as a commodious school. The stones used in erecting the church came from the adjacent ruins of St. Mary's Abbey, which was consecrated by St. Thomas of Canterbury in 1164. On the restoration of the Catholic hierarchy in 1850, Fr. Ringrose was nominated Canon of Southwark. The church is in the Norman style. In the autumn of 1883 it underwent considerable improvements under the direction of Messrs. Westlake. Canon Hall was rector at this time.

Recent Priests.

Rev. Francis Weale, here in 1891 and to date.

READING, BERKS. St. William, Upper Redlands Road.

The mission of East Reading was started in 1904 by the present rector, Fr. Wm. Le Grave, D.S.O., a distinguished Army chaplain. The foundation stone of the church was laid July 12, 1905, and the building opened Wednesday, February 14, 1906. The structure, when complete, will be 90 ft. by 50 ft.; seating capacity for 450. Canon Scoles and Mr. G. Rayment, of Basingstoke, were the architects. Mr. and Mrs. F. Lonergan gave the site, Mr. Oliver Dixon the cost of the foundations, and Fr. Le Grave £750 towards the expense of erection. During his sermon on the occasion of the opening, Bishop Cahill, of Portsmouth, referred to Mrs. Lonergan as 'a generous benefactress who had for a great number of years thrown open her own private chapel for the use of the people close at hand, and who had defrayed the cost of the site.'

REDCAR, YORKS, NORTH RIDING (*Middlesbrough*). The Sacred Heart.

The mission was established 1877, when a temporary chapel was fitted up at 16 Newcomen Street, Coatham. A school chapel was erected 1879. The Nuns of the Faithful Companion opened a convent boarding school at Coatham in 1882, which in 1896-97 became the property of the Dominican Nuns.

Priests.

Rev. Edw. Canon Riddell, 1877.
„ Sylvester McMahon, 1895 to date.

REDDISH, near **STOCKPORT, LANCS** (*Salford*). St. Joseph.

The church, with schools adjoining, opened December 24, 1882, are due to the munificence of Joseph Higginson, Esq. The church, which is in the Gothic style, cost about £2,000, and will accommodate some 250 persons. The schools when first built were for 220 children. Mr. Herbert Tijou was the architect. Before the opening of St. Joseph's, Catholics were forced to go as far as Levenshulme or Heaton Norris on Sundays. The Lady Chapel contains a fine representation of the Annunciation. Catholic population 430.

Recent Priests.

Rev. Pius De Witte, here in 1888.
„ C. McDermott Roe, 1899.
„ Paul Dootson, 1906.

REDDITCH, WARWICKSHIRE (*Birmingham*). Our Lady of Mount Carmel.

The site of the Catholic schools was generously presented to Fr. J.

Kendal, of Mount Carmel Church, by a protestant lady, Mrs. Haywood, of Sillens House, near Redditch, in August 1867. The mission was started as far back as 1834, when Fr. R. Pope was appointed first resident priest. The old chapel was not supplanted by the new Gothic church till 1881. In December 1884 a fine reredos, designed by Fr. Dunstan Breen, was erected to celebrate the golden jubilee of the mission. The screen is adorned with figures of St. Dunstan and St. John. The altar was also remodelled and fitted with a tabernacle of carved oak and brasswork, the chancel decorated, and the church rebenched. Fr. Breen was succeeded by Fr. Isidore Green, O.S.B., 1892, who was here till after 1898. Fr. Bernard Suter, O.S.B., is the present rector.

REDHILL, SURREY (*Southwark*). St. Joseph's.
The first stone was laid in August 1897 by the Bishop of Southwark ; the Catholic population of Redhill was then reckoned at about 300. The style of the building, which was designed by A. E. Purdie, Esq., is Late Decorated Gothic. The plan comprises a nave, two aisles, chapels of Our Lady and St. Joseph, baptistery, sacristy, and organ chamber. During the rectorate of the late priest of the mission, Fr. T. Smith, a fine new presbytery, adjoining the church, has taken the place of the dilapidated old house that formerly served that purpose. The Catholicity of the place has also made great strides, owing in large measure to the zeal and energy of Fr. T. Smith, who was known as a strenuous defender of

the Holy Faith against all adversaries. The church of Redhill was opened and consecrated October 27, 1898. The cost of erection was about £6,400. The mission of Redhill—classed under the head of Reigate in the 'Catholic Directories ' of forty years ago—dates from about 1851, when the Rev. Dr. (afterwards Cardinal) Manning first said Mass in the oratory of Prudell Court, the residence of his brother, Charles Manning, Esq. The old church, opened in October 1861, owes its origin to some extent to Lady Mostyn, who made a permanent mission in the town possible by opening a chapel in her grounds. In 1857 the Catholic population numbered about 150, mostly agricultural labourers.[1]

Priests.
Rev. Andrew Reinaud, D.D., 1861.
„ G. Edwards, 1872 (?) to 1896.
„ J. Kavanagh, 1896-99.
„ Thomas Smith, 1899.
„ F. S. Bennett, 1906 to date.

RETFORD (*Nottingham*). St. Joseph.
Many Catholics were reported to be here 1827. Mass was said here occasionally by Fr. Patrick O'Gorman, of Worksop. After this no mention is made of a mission till 1861, when the place was served from Oldcoates and Worksop. In 1875, Canon Douglass, of Nottingham, purchased a disused Wesleyan chapel, and for a time the place was attended regularly by the priest from Gainsborough. The congregation, however, dwindled,

---

[1] At the beginning of the last century a Catholic family lived at Merstham, near Redhill, but it does not appear that there was a chapel in their house.

and the chapel was sold about 1882. In July 1895, an iron chapel, to accommodate about 200, was opened by Bishop Bagshawe. It was served from Gainsborough till 1898, when Fr. Michael O'Reilly, the present incumbent, was placed in charge of the mission.

RHYMNEY, MONMOUTHSHIRE (Newport). St. John.

This mission was commenced on August 1, 1861. The first two priests were Frs. J. Dawson and J. M. Phillips. The chapel was for a time served by the Benedictines. In 1885 it was transferred to the diocesan clergy, Fr. A. Van den Heuvel being the first secular priest. He was succeeded in 1892 by Fr. Jn. Crawford. Fr. F. Dent, who was here in 1897, is still the incumbent.

RIBCHESTER, PRESTON, LANCS (Salford). SS. Peter and Paul, Stydd Lodge.

'Twas written on a wall at Rome
That Ribchester is rich as any town
in Christendom.

So runs an old legend, but in 1859 Ribchester was only 'a poor, obscure village.' The ancient chapel of Stydd, which belonged to the Knights of St. John of Jerusalem, though almost in ruins, was used as an extra parochial chapel in connection with the parish church as late as 1859. Beneath the communion table is buried the Hon. and Right Rev. Bishop Petre, V.A. of the Northern District, who died at Showley, in the parish, 1775. The Catholic chapel, opened 1789, is not far from the ancient one, and

there are also some almshouses for the aged Catholic poor of the place. The Bishop of Salford confirmed sixty-six persons here in July 1882. Catholic population of the town, 318.

Recent Priests.

Rev. Michael Byrne, 1875.
,, Thos. Martin, 1882.
,, Hy. Newton, 1890.
,, Francis Daniel, here in 1897 and to date.

RICHMOND, SURREY (Southwark). St. Elizabeth's.

The first chapel of the mission was in Newark House, Vineyard, and was opened Easter Sunday, March 30, 1793. A colony of French exiles lived in the town and district of Richmond at this time, and the first entry in the baptismal register is that of Gaston Francis Christopher Victor, infant son of Gaston Duc de Levis, colonel in the French royal army. The sponsors were the Duke of Spinola, Genoese minister to England, and Rose d'Emry, relict of the governor-general of the French islands in America. Fr. Thos. Monk was priest of the mission at this time, but the before-mentioned baptismal ceremony was performed by Philip d'Albignac, Bishop of Angoulême. The present church, in the Classical style, was built in 1822 by Miss Elizabeth Doughty. Tradition says that builders and architects managed to spend the enormous sum of £24,000 on what was, till lately, a small and inconvenient building. It is also said that the foundress was so disgusted with the result of her outlay that she never entered the church again after her first inspection. It is but fair to state, however, that the foundations were discovered to be far more costly than at first antici-pated. The opening by Bishop Poynter, V.A.L.D., took place July 6, 1824. The high altar was sur-mounted by a dark window in stained glass representing the Ad-oration of the Shepherds. During 1902-4 the church was greatly en-larged and the presbytery entirely rebuilt.

Priests.

Rev. Thos. Monk, 1793.
„　James Peters, 1797-1839.
„　R. S. Hodgson, 1839.
„　J. B. Hearn, 1848.
„　J. B. Wenham, 1850.
„　R. S. Hodgson, ⎫
„　Sebastian Faenza, ⎬ Jan.-Aug. 1851.
„　W. MacHarron, ⎭
„　John Tilt, 1851.
„　John Bernard Canon Bag-shawe, 1859. (Canon Bag-shawe was Chaplain to the Forces in the Crimean war, 1854-56. He was the author of 'The Threshold of the Catholic Church' and seve-ral other well-known works. Died October 31, 1901.)
„　George Barrett, D.D., 1901 to date.

RICHMOND, YORKS (*Middles-brough*). St. Joseph and St. Francis Xavier.

The origin of this mission is lost in obscurity. The register dates from 1748. The first priest's name to appear is that of Fr. James Nelson, 1765. Whoever was the missioner between 1748 and the last date, he was very active, for the register is full of entries of persons reconciled to the Church. Among these was James Peacock, 'son to a protestant parson.' From 1794 to 1814 Fr. Thomas Lawson was incumbent, but he had the assistance

of the Abbé Perrot, an *émigré*. Fr. Robt. Johnson came 1815. Between this date and 1825 upwards of sixty persons are noted down as *in ecclesiam recepti*. The old chapel was built by Sir John Lawson, Bart., of Brough Hall, in 1806. Among the presentations to it appear the following : A cope from Lady Lawson, June 1814 ; a white vestment from Mrs. Errington ; Miss F. Scroope, an alb and com-munion cloth, &c. A Sunday school was opened 1818. Fifty-six per-sons, of whom twenty-seven were converts, were confirmed here by Bishop Briggs, V.A.N.D., May 7, 1837. This was the first Catholic confirmation in the town since the Reformation. Fr. Robt. Johnson was succeeded 1863 by Fr. Geo. Noble. The old chapel of 1806 made way in 1868 for the present church.

Recent Priests.

Rev. John Meagher, here in 1875 till 1883.
„　Joseph Foxwell, here in 1889.
„　Thos. Swift, 1894.
„　Richard Cardwell, 1896.
„　Hy. Farmer, 1898 to date.

RICKMANSWORTH, HERTS (*Westminster*).

On All Saints' Day, November 1, 1887, Mass was said here in an old cottage in the High Street, which had been fitted up as a chapel. The room beneath the chapel was used as a Sunday school. At the outset Mass was only said occa-sionally, but from Whit Sunday 1890 it was offered up regularly every Sunday. Fr. H. J. Hardy was visiting priest at this time. In October 1890, an iron building for about sixty persons was opened as a chapel, and Mass said there for the first time by Fr. G. Bampfield, B.A. (October 12). In 1891–92 the mission was served from Harrow, and in 1894–98 from Boxmoor. The Assumptionist Fathers have now charge of the mission.

RIPON, YORKS (*Leeds*). St. Wilfrid.

In 1732 Fr. Jas. Skelton lived at Markington, near Ripon, and attended the Catholics of the district. He died at Raventoft, Yorks, March 28, 1760. The present mission dates from about 1850. The present church was opened April 1862 ; architect, E. W. Pugin ; size, 104 ft. by 88 ft. The coloured window over the Lady Altar was presented by the Sparrow family. A stone high altar was erected January 1884.

Priests.

Rev. Robt. Garstang, 1850 till after 1858.
„ P. Canon Vavasour, 1862.
„ James Canon Gordon, 1888.
„ Xavier de Vacht, 1892 and to date.

RISHTON, near BLACKBURN, LANCS (*Salford*). St. Charles.

The mission was started in 1886, and on November 8, 1896, the new school chapel was opened. The Catholic population is estimated at about 890.

Priests.

Rev. John Aukes, 1886.
„ J. Lathouwers, 1892.
„ W. L. Fowler, here in 1897.
„ J. Higgins, here in 1904.

RIXTON, near MANCHESTER (*Liverpool*). St. Michael.

The church was opened on Easter Monday 1831. A great number of protestants attended High Mass on this occasion, and listened with marked attention to the sermon of Fr. Vincent Glover, of Seel Street, Liverpool. For some years the mission was united to that of Woolstan by order of the Vicar Apostolic, as the one at Rixton was too poor to maintain itself. The Benedictines served the church for many years till 1874, when Fr. J. O'Meara was appointed. He died 1898, and was succeeded by the present Fr. J. Thomé. The chapel at Rixton Hall is said to have been long served by the Franciscans, though no mention of this is made in the history of their 'province.'

ROCHDALE, LANCS (*Salford*). St. John the Baptist.

Fr. Walmesley started the mission of Rochdale in 1830, and in October 1860 the present church and school-house were opened. The former consisted of 'a plain but elegant brick structure,' capable of accommodating 500 persons. Catholic population 2,600.

Priests.

Rev. H. Walmesley, 1830.
„ W. Turner, 1831.
„ H. Walmesley, 1833.
„ Edw. Brown, 1835.
„ Jn. Dowling, 1840.
„ Edw. Canon O'Neill, 1874.
„ John Canon Boulaye, 1895.
„ John Canon Galbois, here in 1897.
„ Hy. Chipp, 1898.

ROCHDALE, LANCS (*Salford*). St. Patrick, Watt Street.

The church was opened by Bishop Turner, October 13, 1861. Catholic population 2,600 (1906).

Priests.

Rev. Michael Moriarty, 1861.

„ Thos. Cusack, 1898.

„ Richard Campion, 1903 to date.

ROCK FERRY, BIRKENHEAD, CHESHIRE (*Shrewsbury*). St. Anne.

In 1862 the Fathers Oblates of Mary Immaculate purchased a site for church and monastery near the railway· station, and in November 1864 the residential portion of the building was complete. Mass was said for the first time in the temporary chapel adjoining on November 20, 1864, by Bishop Brown, of Shrewsbury, who also preached (Is. lvi.). Schools were built in 1872. The church, designed by Cuthbert Pugin, was commenced May 9, 1875, and opened July 29, 1877. The high altar and stained-glass window were presented by the late J. Glover, Esq., of Bebington, the pulpit by Mr. de Bulnes, the font by Miss Tickle, and the Lady Altar by Mr. D. McCarthy, of Tranmere.

Priests.

Rev. J. Egan, 1862.

„ C. Jolivet (now V.A. Natal), 1865.

„ E. Bradshaw, 1867.

„ J. King, 1868.

„ W. Ryan, 1869.

„ J. King, 1873.

„ R. d'Alton, 1879.

„ Anthony Gaughren (V.A. Orange River Colony), 1882.

„ Thos. Dawson, 1886.

„ P. Newman, 1889.

„ J. O'Rourke, 1898.

ROEHAMPTON, S.W. (*Southwark*). St. Joseph.

This church, which is in the Early English style, was opened in May 1881. The seating capacity is for 200 persons. A handsome decorated iron rood screen, with figures of Our Lord on the Cross, St. Joseph and Our Lady, separates the chancel from the nave. The peal of bells is by Messrs. Lewis. There is a memorial brass in the church to Mrs. Garcia, a benefactress. The handsome lich-gate at the entrance of the church was erected in 1882. The tabernacle and massive altar candlesticks were the gift of Mrs. Lyne-Stephens. The stations of the Cross are by Westlake, R.A. Mr. F. A. Walters was the architect of the building. The consecration took place Tuesday, July 24, 1883, by the Bishop of Portsmouth, Dr. Vertue, in place of the Bishop of Southwark. The mission is served by the Jesuit Fathers.

ROMFORD, ESSEX (*Westminster*).

It is said that there was a Catholic chapel at Dagnam, or Dagenham, Park, near here, at the commencement of the eighteenth century, and that Mass was often said here, especially when the mansion was rented by Lady Derwentwater during the imprisonment of the earl, her husband, in the Tower (1716). The house afterwards passed to Sir R. Neave, Bart., and was pulled down about 1771 to make way for the modern residence. The present mission of Romford dates from May 6, 1856, when the church—the gift of Wm. Bernard, twelfth Lord Petre—was consecrated by Cardinal Wiseman.

The building is described as a very good specimen of a Gothic village church, with open roof, stone altar. Mr. Nicholls, architect. The carved stone high altar was the gift of the Hon. Mrs. Clifford.

Priests.

Rev. J. B. Colomb, 1856.
„ Joseph Drew.
„ H. Tilley, 1885 to date.

ROMSEY, HANTS (*Portsmouth*). Our Lady of Reparation.

The mission was established under the present rector, the Rev. C. Pondurand, in 1891. St. Joseph's Orphanage, for boys from three to fourteen years of age, is situated here, and is under the direction of the Sœurs de la Sagesse. The establishment was opened 1895.

N.B.—A convent of nuns (Benedictines) was founded here by Edward the Elder, son of Alfred the Great, 910. It was granted by Henry VIII. to John Bellow and R. Pigot.

ROSS, HEREFORDSHIRE (*Newport*). The Most Blessed Sacrament.

A room was hired in the Swan Hotel, Ross, and Mass said there once a month from June 1845. The visiting chaplain was the priest of Courtfield. On other Sundays prayers were read by one of the congregation. From Sunday, November 22, 1846, Mass was said regularly every week, and shortly after this a large room was hired as a chapel. The temporary church in the Gloucester Road was opened February 1861. Much of the money for the building was collected on the Continent by the Rev. Dr. Farrant.

Priests.

Rev. J. Reeve and Dawson, 1845.
„ A. Neary, 1847.
(No priests named till 1862, when the mission was served in conjunction with Courtfield ; Fr. E. Madden, rector.)
„ Hy. J. Marshall, D.D.,1867
„ P. Fotheringham, 1879 and to 1892.
(Mission vacant 1893.)
„ S. J. Capron, 1894.
„ F. Van Blerk, here in 1897.
„ H. J. Delhaise, 1898.
„ M. J. Kernan, 1903 to date.

ROTHERHAM, YORKS (*Leeds*). St. Bede.

When the mission was started in 1841 Mass was said ' in very mean premises,' held on lease, which expired in September the same year. The congregation then consisted mainly of poor labourers. The site of the present church was the munificent gift of B. Badger, Esq., a protestant gentleman. The style of the building—opened in the spring of 1842—is Early English ; cost, about £1,000. For some years after 1841 the mission was served from Sheffield.

Priests.

Rev. W. Smith, 1845.
„ Joseph Hill, 1863.
„ Jacob Illingworth, 1867.
„ Thos. Eyre, V.F., 1874 to date.

ROTHERHITHE, or **REDRIFF, LONDON, S.E.** (*Southwark*). St. Joseph.

For several years after 1793 the ' Laity's Directory ' advertised the Bermondsey mission as being in Salisbury Street, Rotherhithe (*see*

BERMONDSEY). The Rotherhithe mission proper was not commenced till 1855, when Fr. J. Lawes, of Bermondsey, used to say Mass on Sundays at Stroud Cottage, Trinity Road. In 1858 Rotherhithe became a separate mission. A large house and site in Rotherhithe Street were purchased, and three of the rooms were transformed into a chapel. The church was opened on July 2, 1861, by Bishop Grant. The style is Early English. The building was described at the time as the 'model of what a small church for such a mission ought to be.' The seating capacity was for 500. Edmund Kelly, Esq., was the architect. Cost of erection £1,000. Mr. Pereira was a great benefactor to the mission. The resident priests at Rotherhithe after Father Lawes were: the Rev. P. H. Van de Voorde and Mgr. Dennis, afterwards of West Grinstead (1863–64), Rev. E. J. Clery (1864-78); Rev. C. Kimpé (1878–92); Rev. J. Haynes (1892–1903); Revs. F. Wilderspin and J. Sheen (1904). The old church having long ceased to be central, a new school chapel was opened in Paradise Street, Rotherhithe, in October 1892. For several years prior to this, an early Mass had been said on Sundays at the old schools in Neptune Street. The fine schools in Paradise Street, built during the rectorate of Fr. J. Haynes, served as a chapel till 1903, when the present adjoining church was erected by Lady Renouf in memory of her husband, the late Sir Peter Le Page Renouf, the distinguished Egyptologist. The style of the building is Romanesque, from the designs of Mr. F. W. Tasker. When the mission was moved to Paradise Street, the old church and presbytery in Rotherhithe Street became the Convent of the Nuns of the Sacred Hearts of Jesus and Mary, who conduct a home of refuge for girls.

ROTHERWAS, HEREFORDSHIRE (*Newport*). Our Lady of the Assumption.

This old mission was originally served by the Jesuit chaplains to the ancient Catholic family of Bodenham, whose estate is in the immediate neighbourhood. The first chaplain of the society was Fr. Thos. Hildeyard, S.J., who died April 10, 1746. He was a learned natural philosopher. No mention is made of the mission in the 'Laity's Directory' for 1824, but in 1825 Fr. Patrick Morran is given as the resident priest. In 1835 the post was vacant. A very successful mission was given at Rotherwas in September 1881 by the Redemptorist Fathers, at which time the congregation is described as being composed mostly of agricultural labourers. In 1852 the Catholic population was about ninety.

Priests.

Rev. G. Stasiewiecz, D.D., 1851.
,, W. Burke, 1853.
    (Mission vacant 1856.)
,, Abbé Pauchet, 1857.
,, Edw. Feeny, here in 1862.
,, Benedict Canon Blount, 1863.
,, James Comerford, 1866.
,, T. O'Connor, 1874.
,, E. O'Dwyer, 1877.
,, W. Driffield, 1879.
    Alfred Canon Wilson, O.S.B., 1893
,, J. Vendé, here in 1897 to date.

ROTTINGDEAN, SUSSEX (*Southwark*).

The Sisters of St. Martha established a convent in the parish 1903. The chapel is open to the public.

ROYTON, LANCS (*Salford*). SS. Aidan and Oswald.

A school chapel was opened Sunday, November 27, 1880, on a site generously given by Sir J. P. Radcliffe, Bart. The accommodation is for 400 persons on Sundays and for 300 children on weekdays. The sermon on the evening of the opening was preached by Bishop Hedley, O.S.B. For some years the mission was served from Shaw. Catholic population 900.
Priests.
Rev. J. M. Willemse, 1885.
„ R. D. McIntosh, 1892.
., Jos. Hayes, here in 1897.
„ Timothy Cusack, 1898 to date.

RUDDING PARK, near KNARESBORO', YORKS (*Leeds*). The Holy Family.

The mission was established 1874, under Fr. J. Lawless, chaplain to Sir Joseph Radcliffe, Bart. The present Gothic church was commenced April 26, 1877, and opened August 1, 1879, by Bishop Cornthwaite, of Leeds.
Priests.
Rev. J. Lawless, 1874.
„ Victor Natu, 1877.
„ James Downes, 1885.
„ Xavier de Vacht, 1888.
„ Francis Wood, 1892 to date.

RUGBY, WARWICKSHIRE (*Birmingham*). St. Mary.

In 1843 a room in Chapel Street was fitted up for Catholic worship by Fr. Jn. Nickolds. Four years later the present church was erected by Washington Hibbert, Esq., of Bilton Grange, and opened September 8, 1847, by Bishop Wareing, V.A.E.D. Bishop Gillis, of Edinburgh, preached (1 Cor. iii. 16). Bishop Ullathorne gave a discourse in the evening to a crowded congregation, including many protestants. In 1849 the Catholics of the district numbered about 800. The church was enlarged in 1864, and consecrated 1882. From about 1860 the mission has been under the Fathers of Charity.
Priests.
Rev. Jn. Nickolds, 1843.
„ Stephen Bruno, 1852.
„ Richard Richardson, 1855.
„ Moses Furlong, 1857.
„ Dominic Cavalli, 1860.
„ A. Rinolfi, 1863.
„ Dominic Gazzola, 1867 to date.

RUGELEY, STAFFS (*Birmingham*). SS. Joseph and Etheldreda.

There were about 400 Catholics living here in 1847. The nearest mission then was at Bellamour, where there was a private chapel. When the estate was sold to protestants, the chapel was closed. After this Fr. T. Green, of Tixall—six miles distant—used to come over to Rugeley on Sundays and say Mass. In Advent 1847 Fr. J. Grenside hired the Town Hall at Rugeley as a place of worship, and did much to put the mission on a firm footing. The protestant opposition was then very bitter. The school-house was built in 1847, the presbytery in 1848, and the church between 1849 and 1851. Canon T. Duckett, who was appointed to

Z

Rugeley in 1860, celebrated the silver jubilee of his pastorate there in April 1885. During his rectorate he did much for the interior decoration of the church, and the mission made great strides under his care. This worthy priest died May 1906, and was succeeded by Fr. F. Ryan, D.D., the present incumbent.

RUNCORN, CHESHIRE (*Shrewsbury*). St. Edward.

In 1844 Catholics of the place numbered 300, but the bulk of the inhabitants were 'remarkable for their anti-Catholic ideas.' Fr. Gerald Ward, who was priest of the mission at this time, used to say Mass in a hay-loft fitted up as a chapel. He opened a night school in his own house, where instruction was given every evening by himself and his sister to some sixty poor children. A room in an hotel was afterwards hired for service on Sundays, but on May 11, 1845, Fr. Ward received notice to quit. The want of a church was met in July 1846, when the present building was opened. In 1866 the schools were erected, and in 1888 the chapel of 1846 added to them. Since then Mass &c. has been said in an iron building.

Priests.

Rev. Edw. Carter, 1842.
  „ Gerald Ward, 1843.
  „ Jas. Carr, 1850.
  „ Michael Power, 1858.
  „ Denis Maguire, 1860.
  „ Jos. Daly, 1876.
  „ Wm. Fennelly, 1876.
  „ Jn. Gastaldi, D.D., 1887.
  „ H. B. Gore, 1897.
  „ J. Chambers, 1899.
  „ Hugh Donlevy, 1903 to date.

RYDE, ISLE OF WIGHT (*Portsmouth*). St. Mary.

The Countess of Clare defrayed the cost of building the church (1844-46). Mr. Hansom was the architect. The building was consecrated May 21, 1863. Owing to serious decay, the Caen stone dressings were replaced by others of Portland stone (1879-81) at the instance of the rector, Fr. (now Bishop) Cahill. About the same time a fine stained-glass east window was put up in memory of the noble foundress.

Priests.

Rev. Jn. Telford, 1846.
  „ John Baptist Cahill (Bishop Auxiliary of Portsmouth May 1, 1900; translated to Portsmouth August 30, 1900). 1866.
  „ Wm. Canon Cotter, M.R., 1901. Consecrated Bishop-coadjutor of Portsmouth March 19, 1905.

RYE, SUSSEX (*Southwark*).

From about 1860, Mass was said here in a private house once a month from St. Leonards. The town has always been known since the Reformation for its 'ultra-protestantism,' though it is not a little curious that the corporation seal is 'perhaps the most Papal in the whole kingdom.' It consists of an enshrined figure of the Madonna and Child, with the legend, 'Ave Maria, gratia plena, Dominus tecum' (*see* notice by Maurice Walsh, Esq., J.P., in the *Hastings Observer*, September —, 1900). The present church of St. Walburga, in the Early English style, was opened by Bishop Bourne, of Southwark, Thursday, August 30, 1900; Canon Scoles, architect; accommodation for about 120 persons; cost of erection, about £800. Over the altar of white marble hangs an oil painting by Charles Ffoulkes, Esq., of Rye. The opening ceremony was attended by the mayor (Councillor F. Jarrett) and corporation of the town. Fr. Dominic Crescitelli is the present rector, and first resident priest of the mission.

RYHOPE, DURHAM (*Hexham and Newcastle*). St. Patrick.

The chapel was opened in 1897, and served from Seaham Harbour till 1902. The Rev. Eugene McGarrity is the first and present rector.

S

SACRISTON, DURHAM (*Hexham and Newcastle*). SS. Michael and Bede.

The mission was started in 1867, and for some years Mass was said in a chapel in the presbytery. The new church was opened on Sunday, June 5, 1881, by the Bishop of Hexham and Newcastle. The building, which was erected mainly by the exertions of Fr. M. Gilligan, consists of 'a simple, unpretending structure of red bricks,' capable of accommodating 400 persons. The cost of erection was £1,000.

Priests.

Rev. M. Gilligan, 1870 to 1891.

„ H. Gillow, 1891.

„ Edward Costello, 1897 to date.

SAFFRON WALDEN, ESSEX (*Westminster*). Our Lady of Compassion.

In April 1906 the Westminster Diocesan Missionaries purchased 'The Close,' High Street, and opened a chapel, which was soon too small for the congregation. The new church, opened September 1906, is an enlargement of the old stable block of the house, the new portions being constructed mainly of 'stout rough hewn out timbers, weather boarded outside.' The roof is covered with old tiles and is surmounted with 'a charming turret.' The altar and triptych are of English brown oak. Mr. W. J. Devlin was the architect. Fr. C. Chase, formerly Captain 21st Lancers, is the head priest of the mission.

ST. AGNES, CORNWALL (*Plymouth*).

For several years Fr. A. McKay, of Camborne, used to say Mass occasionally on Sundays at St. Agnes, 'in the kitchen of an Irish labourer's cottage.' Finally, in 1882, Mr. Pike, of Camborne, generously defrayed the cost of a church, which was opened by Fr. McKay, in the absence of the Bishop, on Sunday, August 13, 1882. The mission is served from Camborne.

ST. ALBANS, HERTS. SS. Alban and Stephen.

The mission dates from 1840, when a small chapel was opened. Prior to that time sick calls &c. were attended to by a priest from St. Edmund's College, Old Hall. On the feast of Corpus Christi, 1840, Mass was said for the first time since the Reformation, the altar being a common deal table. Fr. Stephen Ward was the priest on this occasion. He was succeeded by Fr. W. Mills in 1847. From 1852 to 1854 the mission is described as 'vacant.' No mention is made of it in the ' Catholic Directory' from 1857 to 1861. In 1867 it was served from Barnet once a month. In 1877 the south aisle of the church was opened by Cardinal Manning. The altar end was closed by a timber hoarding, afterwards replaced by a brick wall. A room in the priests' house served as a sacristy. The site of the church was presented by Major Gape. By 1885 the church was no longer large enough to contain the congregation; during harvest time as many as forty or fifty Irish labourers might have been seen kneeling outside. The missionaries of the Sacred Heart have now charge of the mission.

ST. ANNE'S - ON - SEA, LANCS (*Liverpool*). Our Lady Star of the Sea.

In June 1890 a portion of the present church was opened for worship. This happy result was mainly brought about by Canon James Taylor, assisted by the Duke of Norfolk and the Clifton family. New schools, for the accommodation of 130 children, were opened on September 14, 1896. The first rector of the mission was Canon James Lennon, president of Ushaw College, from 1886 to 1890. The present incumbent is Fr. Joseph Roche.

ST. HELENS, LANCS (*Liverpool*). Blessed Mary Immaculate, Blackbrook.

The first priest at Blackbrook was Fr. W. Barton, *alias* Gerard, who came in 1674. He died 1728,

and by will left two chalices to the mission. In September 1728 Fr. Martin was appointed. In 1741 Fr. Thos. Parkinson was at the mission. He died March 7, 1751, aged thirty-eight. Fr. P. Butler, the next priest, received a pension from Jas. Orrell, Esq., and with the money erected a chapel. He died December 9, 1777, aged fifty-two. For six months Fr. J. Bradshaw attended the mission, and after him Fr. John Orrell was rector till 1810. The next priests were : Ralph Platt, 1812-14 ; Jos. Orrell, 1814-20; Thos. Hodgson, 1820-36 ; C. Brigham, 1836 ; John Lund, 1836-38 ; James Abraham, 1838-50. The church and school were erected in 1849 on a site presented by John Smith, Esq. The new infants' school was erected August 1892, and the Convent of Mercy opened May 8, 1893.

Priests since 1850.

Rev. John Canon Walker, 1850.
„ John Flynn, 1853.
„ David Lawler, 1878.
„ Edw. O'Sullivan, M.R., 1881 to date.

ST. HELENS. St. Thomas of Canterbury, Windleshaw.

The ancient chantry here was erected by Sir Thos. Gerard, of Bryn, *temp.* Henry VI. It was suppressed 1548. Many Catholics were interred near here during the penal times, notably in 1611. On October 2, 1892, a school chapel was commenced on a site near the old chantry, presented by Lord Gerard, the lineal descendant of the warrior Sir Thomas Gerard. The building was opened May 28, 1893. Mass is said every Friday for the Gerard family. Fr. James Welsby was the first priest of the mission.

ST. HELENS, LANCS. Holy Cross.
The church site was given to the
Society of Jesus by Wm. P. Cotham,
Esq., in 1860, and the building was
opened, May 3, 1862. The style is
Decorated Gothic; size, 164 ft.
by 60 ft. ; seating accommoda-
tion for about 1,000 ; architect,
Mr. Scoles.

Priests.

Rev. Jos. Lazenby, 1862.
„ Thos. Williams, 1866.
„ Geo. Noble, in 1871.
„ Joseph Lightbound, 1877.
„ Richard Cardwell, in 1882 to
  1892.
„ Wm. Shapter, 1892.
„ Jas. Fanning, in 1897.
„ Timothy Courtenay, 1898.
„ John Procter, 1904.

ST. HELENS, LANCS. St. Joseph's.
The mission was established in
1862, and served from Sutton by
the Passionist Fathers till about
1876. The first place of worship
was a school chapel, superseded by
the present church, opened in 1878.

Priests.

Rev. Richard Baynes, 1876.
„ Patrick Byrne, 1882.
„ John Tomlinson, 1888.
„ James Hayes, 1893.
„ John Barry, 1899 to date.

ST. HELENS, LANCS. St. Mary,
Lowe House.
Before the opening of the mission,
Mass was said at Eccleston Hall.
On the death of J. Gorsuch Eccleston, Esq., in 1742, his widow removed to Cowley Hill, where she
died at an advanced age in 1793.
The Rev. J. Beaumont, S.J., was
priest at Cowley till his death in
1773. Before her death, Mrs. Eccles-

ton purchased Lowe House estate,
and presented it to the Jesuit
Fathers. Fr. Barrow built a chapel
here in 1793, and served the mission till his death in 1813. After
this Fr. J. P. Pains and Fr. Marmaduke Stone took charge of the
mission. Fr. Pains died in 1834,
after having enlarged the chapel.
Fr. Charles Irvine, S.J., added the
transepts to the old Lowe House
chapel about 1837. In 1858 a
tower was built, at the cost of
about £1,500. The number of baptisms registered in 1785 was 22;
in 1815, 45 ; in 1831, 120 ; in 1844,
210 ; in 1854, 410 ; in 1862, 500.

Priests from 1860.

Rev. Thos. Ullathorne.
„ Thos. Browne, in 1891.
„ Joseph Kenny, 1894.
„ Chas. Widdowson, in 1898.
„ Wm. Crofton, in 1904.

ST. IVES, CORNWALL (*Plymouth*).
The Sacred Heart and St. Gertrude.
About the end of the eighteenth
century, a certain Franciscan friar
' used to say Mass for the fisher-
men in the little half-ruined chapel
of St. Leonard, on the quay '
(*Tablet*, April 9, 1881, p. 579).
From this it may be presumed
that the isolation of the place
afforded protection to local Catholics against the expiring penal
laws. It may be remarked that
ancient Celtic crucifixes of granite
and holy wells exist all over Cornwall, untouched by the Reformation and venerated by all classes of
people. The mission is at present
under the care of Fr. P. Corr,
C.R.L.

ST. JOHN'S WOOD, LONDON, N.W. (*Westminster*). Our Lady, Grove Road.

The church was built, 1833-36, by the Misses Louise and Jessie Gallini. They are buried in the church. Miss Jessie Gallini was born 1761, and died November 13, 1844. On Sunday, June 8, 1845, 250 persons were confirmed in the church by Bishop Griffiths, V.A.L.D. The sanctuary was 'handsomely embellished' by Mr. Sang in 1846 with arabesques and Christian symbolic emblems. The Countess Dowager of Shrewsbury was interred beneath the church in February 1847. In June 1837, the schools were opened by Fr. J. O'Neal. About 300 children were educated, and the more destitute clothed. The teaching was put into the hands of an Order of nuns from Ireland. In October 1884, the church, after undergoing considerable repairs, was solemnly reopened by Cardinal Manning. A new altar, reredos, and tabernacle were added at the same time.

Priests.

Rev. James Canon O'Neal, 1835.
„ Wm. Burke, 1870.
„ Philip Cavanagh, 1874.
„ E. Taylor, 1876.
„ Philip Cavanagh (second time), 1884.
„ Geo. Canon Delaney, 1890 to date.

ST. LEONARDS-ON-SEA, SUSSEX (*Southwark*). St. Thomas of Canterbury and the English Martyrs.

On the death of Lady Stanley of Puddington, Fr. John Jones, of the Bavarian Chapel, Warwick Street, London, received a house and sixteen acres of land, 'for religious purposes,' at St. Leonards-on-Sea (1844). Fr. Jones appealed to the Catholic clergy, nobility, and gentry of the United Kingdom for funds to raise a church, convent, and cemetery. As the result of this appeal a splendid church, 'one of Pugin's gems,' was built, but, owing to circumstances, left unroofed for upwards of ten years. It was then completed, and opened as the chapel of the Holy Child Jesus Nuns, who had been introduced into the London District by Bishop (afterwards Cardinal) Wiseman. During the interval, Mass was said to the congregation in the room of a large house facing the sea. The temporary chapel was dedicated to the Holy Souls. The new church, in the Early English style, was commenced August 21, 1865, and opened May 24, 1866. A splendid altar of Caen stone and green serpentine marble was presented by Alexander Shea, Esq. At Christmas 1886 the entire building was destroyed by fire. A temporary iron chapel, erected February 1887, did duty till the opening of the present fine church in July 1889. The style is Lancet Gothic, the interior of the building bearing a strong likeness to that of Munich Cathedral.

Priests.

Rev. F. Lythgoe, S.J., 1846.
„ T. Richardson, 1847.
„ — Asperti, D.D., 1849.
„ Pius Melia, D.D., 1850.
„ John Butt, 1854.
„ John Bamber, 1857.
„ John Foy, 1858.
„ Thos. Ottley, 1893 to date.

ST. MARGARET'S BAY, near DOVER (*Southwark*).

The Annonciades Nuns of Boulogne, recently expelled from

France by the Law of Associations, have opened a convent here for French and English pupils. The chapel is open to the public.

ST. MARY CHURCH, DEVON (Plymouth). Our Lady Help of Christians.

The mission was commenced in 1865, when the chapel was served from Torquay. Fr. B. Brownlow, afterwards Bishop of Plymouth, was priest in 1867. The church was partially completed and opened in 1867. It was entirely finished in February 1881 by the addition of three bays and a series of vaulted arches. The family of the founder of the Lady Chapel have a mortuary crypt beneath the west end of the south aisle. The church is that of the Dominican Convent (Third Order), but is open to the public, and the chaplain serves the mission.

Priests.
Rev. B. Canon Brownlow, 1867.
„ Mgr. John S. Lapôtre, 1887 and to date.

ST. MARY CRAY, KENT (Southwark).

Until 1875, the district of St. Mary Cray was included in the mission of Chislehurst. Fr. Gangia and Canon Todd, of the last-named place, took great interest in the few Catholics of the Crays, and it was probably through them that a school was opened about 1860. The first resident priest of the mission was Fr. Edward Ryan, who came in the early part of 1875 and stayed about eighteen months. His successor, Fr. James Connelly, built the presbytery. He left in 1884, being followed by

Fr. James Carroll, who remained till 1886. Then, till 1892, the Rev. Patrick Gaughren was priest. In the above-mentioned year Fr. Carroll returned, and has been priest of the mission ever since. He built the present church in 1895 ; the style is early fourteenth-century Gothic. The estimated Catholic population of the district is about 400. We have been informed by Fr. Carroll that about seventy years ago there existed a 'holy well' near St. Mary Cray, which was much frequented by Irish harvesters on Sunday afternoons as a suitable place for reciting the rosary. Nothing is known precisely as to the origin of the well, which was destroyed during the construction of the London, Chatham, and Dover Railway. The water, which was medicinal, contained iron and arsenic in solution, and was in great request as a panacea for sick cattle and dogs.

SALE, near MANCHESTER, CHESHIRE (Shrewsbury). St. Joseph.

The chapel was opened for worship on a site purchased by Fr. Alcock, of Altringham, August 6, 1866. The chapel, 'a very neat building,' was opened by Bishop Brown, of Shrewsbury, August 5, 1868. The present church was opened May 10, 1885. The schools were erected 1898, and the presbytery house purchased 1889. Catholic population in 1903, about 800.

Priests.
Rev. J. Berry, 1853, ⎫ Served mission from Altrincham.
„ W. Walton, ⎭
„ H. Alcock, 1860.
„ H. Alcock, 1863.
„ Canon Crawley, 1870 to date.

SALFORD. St. Charles.

In 1828 a room was hired in Union Street as a Sunday school in connection with St. Mary's, Mulberry Street. In 1843 it was transferred to the then recently established church of St. John's. A school was built in Church Street in 1858, and Mass said there for the first time on November 7. The school chapel served the district till the place became a separate mission under Fr. R. Smith in 1892. On the feast of St. Charles 1895 a large school chapel, to cost £4,000, was commenced on a site at the corner of Gerald Road and Whit Lane. The building was solemnly opened July 19, 1896.

SALFORD, MANCHESTER, LANCS. St. John's Cathedral.

In 1843, a school chapel was erected on the site of the present cathedral, and Fr. Jn. Billington appointed to the mission. He died October 10, 1845. On August 9, 1848, the present cathedral was opened by Bishop Briggs, Vicar Apostolic of Yorkshire. About two hundred clergy attended the ceremony, the sermon being preached by Bishop (afterwards Cardinal) Wiseman. Matthew Hadfield, Esq., of Sheffield, was the architect of the building. On July 25, 1851, Dr. Turner, the first bishop of the newly created see of Salford, was consecrated in the cathedral by Cardinal Wiseman. The building was consecrated by Bishop Vaughan June 14, 1890, and the fabric thoroughly cleaned and renovated 1905. The number of the congregation is estimated at 8,400 (1905).

SALISBURY, WILTS (*Clifton*). **St. Osmund.**

The Hon. Thomas, brother of Lord Arundell, who had a house here in 1779, maintained a chaplain, who attended to the few Catholics of the district. A regular mission was established at Salisbury in 1793 by the Abbé Nicholas Begin, an *émigré*. He died March 16, 1826. The Abbé J. B. Marest also laboured here for a time. He afterwards became chaplain to the nuns of Canford (*q.v.*), and died at Valognes, Normandy, February 3, 1850, aged eighty-two. The present church of St. Osmund at Salisbury was built 1847–48, the foundation stone being laid by Bishop Ullathorne and Lord Arundell of Wardour. The generous donor of the church was Mr. Lambert, a Catholic gentleman. The consecration, by Bishop Ullathorne, took place September 6, 1848. The style is Decorated Gothic, from the design of A. Welby Pugin, who resided at Salisbury for a short time. A fine altar of carved oak was erected in honour of the 'Sacred Heart June 1895. In November of the same year a handsome antique oak screen, some three hundred years old, was placed in position before the Lady Altar. It belonged to one of the neighbouring churches in pre-Reformation times. The church was enlarged in 1894. The mission was 'vacant' in 1827. In 1828 Fr. M. O'Connor was priest. The clergy after him were:—

Rev. J. Butterfield, 1832.
 ,,   Anthony McDermot, 1833.
 ,,   Charles Cook, 1835.
 ,,   F. Lynch, 1840.
 ,,   E. Kenny, 1850.
 ,,   Pat. Kelly, 1851.
 ,,   H. Green, 1855.
 ,,   J. Clarke, 1861.
 ,,   Lewis Coelenbier, 1864.

Rev. Peter Seddon, 1867.

  „ George Canon Crook, 1871.

  „ Dominic Hubert and Francis Gallais, 1891.

  „ John Archdeacon, 1896.

  „ James Groomes, 1901 to date.

SALTASH, CORNWALL (Plymouth). Our Lady.

The Order of Friars Minor of the French Province of St. Louis Bishop, O.S.F., established the church and friary of St. Mary of the Angels here in 1884. The house was a filiation from Clevedon, Somerset, Père Denis being the guardian. The Franciscans resigned the mission 1896, after which the church was served by Fr. Edward O'Dea. Fr. Augustine Morford is the present rector.

SAMLESBURY, PRESTON, LANCS (Salford). St. Mary.

In 1575 the protestant Bishop of Chester reported John Southworth, Knt., and his family to the Privy Council as 'obstinate and recusant.' Six years later Sir John was imprisoned in the New Fleet, Manchester, for harbouring Edmund Campion, the Jesuit, at Samlesbury. Fr. Southworth, his son or grandson, suffered at Tyburn for the Faith in 1654. In 1690 Mr. Hardin, alias Hawarden, served the mission. Bishop Smith confirmed here in 1709. Many Catholics of the district were 'presented' to the grand jury as non-jurors and recusants in 1715. Fr. W. Tootell was priest at Samlesbury in 1749. The old chapel was at Lower Hall, and was dedicated to St. Chad. Having become ruinous, it was rebuilt about 1817 by Fr. J. Bell.

In the penal times Mass was often said in Bessa Wood, near Samlesbury, and among the relics treasured at the present church of St. Mary is an old viaticum pyx, dated 1695, and a chasuble some five hundred years old.

Priests since 1852.

Rev. Wm. Fayer, 1852.

  „ Richard Gerrard, 1876.

  „ Mgr. Wm Hill, 1901 to date.

SCARBOROUGH, YORKS (Middlesbrough). St. Peter.

In 1836 the Catholics of Scarborough comprised but 'three or four respectable families and a few Irish.' The chapel was a poor, mean building hidden behind some old tenements. When Bishop Ullathorne was a boy, in 1815, a priest only came to Scarborough once in every six weeks. 'Mr. Haydock, the editor of "Haydock's Bible," came once in three months; and Mr. Woodcock, of Egton Bridge, also came once in three months. They were both Douai priests, and as they generally dined at our house I used to be much entertained with their college stories' (Dr. Ullathorne, 'Autobiography'). Fr. J. Leyne seems to have been the first resident priest at Scarborough (1828). The next priest, Fr. J. Walker, greatly improved the chapel, and started a good Sunday school for the children. About this time many protestants began to attend the chapel, and conversions were numerous. Fr. Walker turned part of his house into a school for day pupils. By 1842 Scarborough had become a popular seaside resort. One of the constant visitors was the Catholic naturalist Charles Waterton, who has left a quaintly written essay on the attractions of the place. The new church, which, as the *Hull Advertiser* remarked, reflected 'infinite credit on the liberality and zeal of the congregation,' was opened by Cardinal Wiseman in July 1858. The Hon. and Right Rev. Bishop Clifford, of Clifton, sang the Mass, which was attended by a crowded congregation. Several of the bishops and Catholic peers were also present. The Cardinal's discourse 'was one of those lucid, forcible, and eloquent sermons which have rendered his Eminence not only popular, but illustrious, throughout Europe.' The style of the church is Geometrical Gothic.

Priests since 1835.

Rev. John Canon Walker, 1835.

  ,,   Arthur Riddell, 1874 (Bishop of Northampton 1880).

  ,,   James Canon Dolan, 1880 and to date.

SCARISBRICK, LANCS (*Liverpool*).

At the 'Old Hall,' the ancestral seat of the Scarisbricks, situated in a park some 430 acres in extent, there was always a chapel and resident priest. The Jesuits had charge of the mission. The Scarisbrick family have been lords of the manor for upwards of seven centuries. Fr. John Smith, S.J., was chaplain at Scarisbrick early in the eighteenth century, and Fr. Nicholas Furniers in 1751. Fr. Scarisbrick, who died in 1788, bequeathed the property to the Eccleston family, who henceforth resided here. On the death of Lady Scarisbrick, in 1872, the property went to the Marquis de Casteja, who assumed the name of Scarisbrick by royal licence. The Old Hall was pulled down many years ago, and replaced by a handsome Gothic structure by A. W. Pugin, but the fine oak wainscot and other ancient details were incorporated in the new building. On December 18, 1887, the present church, dedicated to St. Elizabeth, was commenced. The style is Gothic, the seating capacity of the building being for 500. The opening took place April 28, 1889. Messrs. Pugin were the architects. The Marchioness de Brandos Casteja, who defrayed the cost of erection, lies interred at Scarisbrick. The first bell of the peal was presented by the Count in 1890.

SCARTHINGWELL, near TADCASTER, YORKS (*Leeds*). The Immaculate Conception.

A mission was established in 1852, when Mass was said on Sundays in a hired room. The number of Catholics then at Scarthingwell was about forty. The present church was opened June 8, 1854, by Cardinal Wiseman. The bell of the church was blessed by Bishop Briggs, of Beverley, June 14, 1857, on which occasion Mr. Constable Maxwell, the munificent donor of the church, received a signed address of thanks. In 1858 the number of Easter communicants was 135. The schools of the mission were opened by H. C. Maxwell, Esq., on Thursday, July 22, 1858. In 1889 the congregation numbered between three and four hundred.

Priests.

Rev. Chas. O'Neill, 1852.

  ,,   Hy. Walker, 1860.

  ,,   Jn. O'Dwyer, 1863.

  ,,   James Guthrie, 1867.

  ,,   Jn. Scott, here in 1875.

  ,,   Thos. Worthy, 1877.

  ,,   Hubert Offermann, 1884.

    D. J. Collins, 1895 to date.

SCLERDER, POLPERRO, CORN-WALL (*Plymouth*).[1]

The Rev. Sir Henry Trelawney, Bart., was converted to the Faith about 1815, and after his death at Lavino, Italy, February 24, 1834, his daughters, Mary and Anne, established the mission at Trelawney, 1842. The Rev. Mark Oleron was the first priest. On the death of Miss Anne Trelawney, 1860, the oratory at Trelawney would appear to have been closed, and a regular mission established at Sclerder under the care of the Franciscans, who, however, did not long remain. In 1875 the place was served from Plymouth. Two years later Mr. B. de Barry acquired the late house of the Order, and fitted up the chapel once more.

Rectors since 1882.

Rev. Alex. Cruikshank, D.D., 1882.
  „   Augustine Béteille, here in 1891.
  „   Edward Baste, 1893 to date.

SCORTON, LANCS (*Liverpool*). St. James.

The origin of this mission is obscure. The first resident priest of the place was Fr. John Sergeant, 'a man of good social parts,' who was settled here at the time of the Rebellion of 1745. Two soldiers were sent from Preston to arrest him, but he entertained them so well that they 'vowed they would not arrest so good a fellow,' and so returned without fulfilling their mission. Fr. Sergeant built a small thatched chapel for his congregation, and was succeeded in September 1795 by Fr. James Lawrenson, who officiated at Scorton till 1826. The

next priests were : Frs. J. Dixon (1826-30), J. Woodcock (1830-36), T. Gillet (1836-38), R. Turpin (1838-1863). The chapel was subsequently enlarged, improved, and slated. It belonged to the Duke of Hamilton, and when that nobleman was introduced to the Pope he told his Holiness that he believed he was the only protestant nobleman in the kingdom to own a Catholic church. When his Grace disposed of his Lancashire property he reserved a small portion, together with the chapel site, which he sold on very liberal terms to Fr. Turpin. The new church of St. Mary and St. James was founded in August 1860, and opened in 1861. The style is Decorated Gothic, and the building will seat about 300 persons. Messrs. Hansom & Son, of Clifton, designed the structure, which cost about £2,500. The Catholic population in and about Scorton in 1860 was about 300. Fr. Robt. Turpin was succeeded as rector in 1863 by Canon Joseph Ilsley, D.D.; Fr. Austin Splaine, 1871; Fr. Patrick Flynn, 1888; Fr. Jn. Blackoe, 1901 to date.

SCORTON, YORKS (*Middlesbrough*). St. John of God.

The Fathers of the Institute of St. John of God (Brothers Hospitallers)—approved by Pope St. Pius V. in 1572 'for the spiritual and temporal good of the sick, infirm, and poor'—established an institution at Scorton in 1880. They were invited to the place by a gentleman who purchased the old abbey of St. Clare and presented it to them for use as a hospital for the sick poor. The building will accommodate about 100 patients.

---

[1] Sclerder is Cornish Celtic for 'light.'

The church of the monastery serves the mission, Mass on Sundays being (1904) at 10 A.M. and afternoon service at 3. The house occupied by the community was formerly known as St. Clare's Abbey, and was the residence of the Bower family from 1717 to 1800. From 1807 to 1857, it was a convent of Poor Clares, who erected a school and chapel. The nuns, on quitting the place, went to Darlington.

SCUNTHORPE, LINCS (Nottingham). The Holy Souls.

The increase of population owing to the development of the iron-working industry led to a mission being established here in 1897. The chapel is a small one, but sufficient at present for the needs of the congregation.

Priests.
Rev. Rupert Macaulay, 1897.
„ J. Hooker, 1899.
„ Chas. Kerin, 1903.
„ H. Lindeboom, 1905.

SEACOMBE, CHESHIRE (Shrewsbury). Our Lady Star of the Sea and St. Joseph.

The mission was set on foot in 1860 by Canon Joseph Sherwood, of Beverley, who said Mass in one of the upper rooms of his residence in Chapel Street. Catholics then numbered about thirty. Before the end of the year a chapel was built. The schools, erected in 1875, served as a chapel on Sundays and holy days till August 1889, when the present Gothic church was opened. The cost of erection (£5,000) was largely, if

not entirely, defrayed by a generous benefactor. A new school was opened in 1902. The congregation is now about 2,600.

Priests.
Rev. Joseph Canon Sherwood, 1860.
„ T. Degen, 1860.
„ J. Jenkins, 1862.
„ J. Jones, 1864.
„ F. Lynch, 1868.
„ E. Lynch, 1878.
„ W. Dallow, 1883.
„ Canon Marsden, V.G., 1885.
„ Canon Singleton, V.F., 1887.

SEAFORD, SUSSEX (Southwark). St. Francis of Sales.

When Bishop Bower, of Chichester, visited Seaford in 1724, the parish contained 'seventy families, no Papist; three Presbyterians.' The ancient parish church at this time had fallen into a deplorable state of neglect. The present mission was commenced about 1899, when Bishop Bourne, of Southwark, built a country house on the outskirts of the town and erected a chapel adjoining. This building, which in style approaches the Classic, will accommodate about 120 persons. In 1902 the house and chapel were acquired by the Sisters of Providence of Rouen, expelled from France. The services at the chapel, which is open to the public, are conducted by one of the Assumptionist Fathers from the adjacent mission of Newhaven.

SEAFORTH, LANCS (Liverpool).

In 1884 a disused stable and coach-house were acquired and transformed into a chapel. The congregation at the outset amounted to 300. On October 5, 1890, a new school chapel was opened by Bishop O'Reilly. The foundation stone of. the new church was laid May 22, 1898, and the building opened February 10, 1901. Seating for 600. The Catholic population is about 2,000.

Priests.

Rev. Patrick Murphy, 1884.

„　Jn. Seed, 1889 to date.

SEAHAM HARBOUR, DURHAM
(Hexham and Newcastle). St. Mary Magdalen.

For some years before 1860 Mass was said on Sundays in a store-room over a stable. The congregation — mostly miners and their families—came in such numbers 'as almost to cause suffocation.' After much difficulty about finding a site, one was obtained from Earl Vane. The first stone was laid by the Bishop of Hexham July 22, 1869, and the building, a plain structure for 500 persons, was opened July 1870. A new church was commenced August 25, 1906. The style is Romanesque ; material used, concrete blocks ; accommodation for about 500. Estimated cost about £2,700. The Catholic population of the district is about 2,000.

Priests.

Rev. Robt. Belaney, 1860.

„　Wm. Gaskell, 1864 (died 1868).

„　Michael Greene, 1870.

„　Joseph Fawell, 1884.

„　James Hayes, 1891 and to date.

SEDGLEY, STAFFS *(Birmingham).* St. Chad and All Saints.

The mission is described as a filiation from Wolverhampton. The

mission was established in 1789, and must not be confounded with the older one at the adjacent Sedgley Park, now represented (as a college) by Cotton Hall *(q.v.).* The first priest at Sedgley was the Rev. J. Perry. His successor, the Rev. T. Tysan, erected at his own expense the 'elegant and commodious church,' for 400 persons, opened in 1823. The building was not consecrated till September 2, 1891. Adjoining the church is, or was, a cemetery.

Priests.

Rev. J. Perry, 1789.

„　T. Tysan, 1820 (?).

„　Jn. Day (assistant), 1860.

„　Philip Hendren, 1866.

„　Chas. Malfait, 1874.

„　Jn. Kelly, 1895 to date.

SEDGLEY PARK, *see* OAKA-MOOR *(Staffordshire).*

SELBY, YORKS *(Leeds).* St. Mary.

This mission dates from 1791, in a room licensed for the purpose in accordance with the Catholic Relief Act of that year. No register was kept till 1822. The present church, opened May 16, 1839, was erected at the expense of the Hon. E. Petre, M.P. Fr. Albert Underhill was rector here for several years prior to 1802, when he went to Leeds.

The remains of the Benedictine Abbey, founded by William the Conqueror 1069, were destroyed by fire October 1906.

Priests since 1822.

Rev. Geo. Best, 1822.

„　Jn. Rigby, 1853.

„　Andrew Burns, 1874.

„　James Canon Gordon, 1904 to date.

SELLY PARK, BIRMINGHAM (*Birmingham*). St. Edward.

A school chapel was founded here in 1889, and served the mission till the opening of the present church in 1902 (commenced October 28, 1901). The cost was about £4,000. Among the benefactors to the fund was Mr. Olivieri. Prior to the erection of the school chapel, the chapel of St. Paul's Convent (Sisters of Charity) was open to the public, and the spiritual wants of local Catholics were attended to by the chaplain.

Priests.

Rev. E. Hymers, 1889.
  ,, T. Fitzpatrick, 1891.
  ,, Matthias O'Rourke, 1895.
  ,, Vincent Keating, 1899.

SETTLE, YORKS (*Leeds*). St. Mary and St. Michael.

The church was opened March 20, 1864.

Priests.

Rev. E. Woodall, 1864.
  ,, Thos. Bradley, 1891.
  ,, Thos. Parkin, 1897 to date.

SEVENOAKS, KENT (*Southwark*). St. Thomas of Canterbury.

The mission was established June 1870, but no notice of the place appeared in the 'Catholic Directory' till 1881. The iron chapel was opened by Bishop Danell Wednesday, October 20, of the preceding year. In pre-Reformation times the locality was famous for its devotion to St. Edith, daughter of the Saxon King Edgar, and on April 21, 1888, a carved statue of the saint was unveiled in the church

by Bishop Butt. The present structure, in the purest Norman style, designed by Mr. F. A. Walters, was opened in 1896. It consists of a chancel and half nave, and is intended as a memorial to Cardinal Manning, who for many years lived in the neighbourhood.

Priests.

Rev. Ignatius Lazzari.
  ,, Wm. Cunningham, 1892 to date.

SHAFTESBURY, DORSET (*Plymouth*).

A chapel was opened at Belmont House, Shaftesbury, by the Oblates of the Sacred Heart, Christmas 1894. Before this time Wardour and Marnhull were the nearest neighbouring missions. Shaftesbury was at first served from the latter place by Fr. Benedict Grillet.

Priests.

Rev. Fr. E. Baron, 1897.
  ,, Jas. Berry, 1898.
  ,, Jerome Boutin, 1899.
  ,, Peter Sivienne, 1902.

SHANKLIN, ISLE OF WIGHT (*Portsmouth*). Oratory of the Sacred Heart.

A mission was established in June 1888, mainly through the efforts of Sir P. Rose, Mrs. Hinton, of the Royal Spa Hotel, Mr. W. H. Curtan, and other Catholic residents. The chapel was in a house at the corner of Atheley and Sandown Roads, near the railway station. A temporary iron church was opened Tuesday, August 28, 1888, thanks to the generosity of Sir P. Rose. The celebrant was Mgr. Cahill, now

Bishop of Portsmouth. Bishop Vertue preached. The first stone of the new church was laid Monday, October 15, 1906. The style is fourteenth-century Gothic, consisting of nave, two aisles, and three chapels. A number of stones from ancient abbeys in Great Britain and Ireland are to be incorporated in the porch. B. Williamson, Esq., is the architect.

SHAW, OLDHAM, LANCS (Salford). St. Joseph.

An old building was purchased and opened as church and school in August 1874. Fr. Baetings was the first rector. Fr. T. Cusack, the present rector, who came here in December 1887, effected many improvements and built the presbytery. A handsome school chapel, to take the place of the old building, was opened May 10, 1896, by the Bishop of Salford.

SHEERNESS (Southwark). SS. Henry and Elizabeth.

The church, which was opened by Bishop Grant, of Southwark, September 14, 1865, is a 'mixture of Early English and Pointed Decorated.' The architect was E. W. Pugin, and the cost of the building, which will accommodate about 500 persons, was £3,700. A handsome octagonal stone pulpit, supported on marble columns, was inaugurated Sunday, February 31, 1886, in memory of the Catholic naval and military officers and men who lost their lives during the Egyptian and Soudan campaigns. A mural tablet inscribed with the names of the deceased is placed near the pulpit.

Fr. T. Moynihan was priest at Sheerness from 1880 till his death in September 1890. He was greatly beloved by all the congregation, and his funeral was attended by over 150 seamen, marines, and artillerymen, in whose spiritual and temporal welfare the good Father had always shown himself warmly interested. Fr. T. Smith is the present rector (1906).

SHEFFIELD, YORKS (Leeds). St. Mary.

The 'Lord's House,' a residence of the Dukes of Norfolk, in Friargate, Norfolk Row, had a chapel in the penal times. In 1814 a public chapel was erected, and enlarged 1837. During January 1847 'proposals were made for a new church, after the style of the noble cross church of Heckington, in Lincolnshire.' Fr. Pratt was mainly instrumental in forwarding the work of erection, and the church was opened September 1850. The cost of building was about £11,563. Owing to the outstanding debt, the building was not consecrated till June 1889, when the ceremony was performed by Bishop Knight for the Bishop of Leeds. The Duke of Norfolk and Henry Munster, Esq., were generous benefactors to the mission.

Recent Priests.

Rev. — Pratt (died February 17, 1849).
,, Matthew Kavanagh, 1849.
,, Edmund Canon Scully, 1850.
,, William Canon Fisher, 1855.
,, Samuel Canon Walshaw, 1867.
,, James Canon Gordon, 1895.
,, Oswald Canon Dolan, 1889 to date.

SHEFFIELD, YORKS. St. Catherine.

The first stone of the building was laid August 3, 1884, and the church was opened in November of the same year. Mr. C. Hadfield was the architect. Schools were opened 1876. Fr. Luke Burke was the first resident priest, 1894, and till after 1898. Fr. Patrick Hickey is the present rector.

SHEFFORD, BEDS (*Northampton*).

A family named Noddings kept the Faith alive here during the early and middle part of the eighteenth century. Mass was said occasionally in their house, formerly a butcher's shop. Mary Noddings, who died 1783, left her property to found a regular mission. The old chapel, erected in 1791, was 'behind some cottages, and only approached by a narrow passage.' By 1869 the floor was sunken low, the roof gaping, and the whole place thoroughly unsafe. The new church was commenced in October 1882, and consecrated July 3, 1884. The old chapel serves as the sacristy. Fine stained-glass windows were presented by Mrs. Lyne-Stephens, J. Eyston, Esq., &c. Mr. S. J. Nichol was the architect. The first priests at Shefford were Revs. S. Robinson, 1778; J. Barnwall, 1783; Chris. Taylor, 1786. This priest was a profound scholar, and when in Rome was much esteemed by the Pope. He died 1812. The Abbé Potier succeeded. Canon Wm. Collier, appointed in 1869, founded the orphanage, 1869-70.

SHEPHERD'S BUSH, LONDON, W. (*Westminster*).

In 1889 the mission was started by the opening of a temporary chapel at 33 Askew Crescent, the residence of Fr. A. H. Pownall, first priest of the mission. A temporary church was afterwards fitted up at 47 Rylett Road, and continued to do duty as a place of worship till the opening of the present fine Gothic edifice in Ashchurch Grove, April 5, 1904. The architects were Canon Scoles, of Basingstoke, and G. Raymond, the accommodation of the building being for about 400. On Sunday, November 13, 1904, the first confirmation given in the church by Archbishop Bourne, about eighty candidates being presented for the reception of the sacrament. The first rector of the mission was Fr. A. H. Pownall, who was succeeded in 1892 by his brother Fr. Bernard Pownall, the present incumbent.

SHEPSHED, LEICESTERSHIRE (*Nottingham*). St. Winefride.

Mission founded 1842, and for a time served from Osgathorpe by Fr. Gentili, D.D. The schools were opened 1854 at the expense of A. de Lisle, Esq., of Gaṛendon Manor. New infant schools were inaugurated 1896, the number of pupils being about 132.

Priests.
Rev. L. Gentili, D.D., 1842.
  ,, F. Segnini, 1846.
  ,, W. Lockhart, 1848.
  ,, P. Hutton, 1850.
  ,, N. Lorain, 1852.
  ,, F. Luke, 1856.
  (Served from Grâce Dieu Manor 1862.)

A A

Rev. Thos. Gillet, 1864.
„   Fr. Augustine (Henry Collins).
„   A. Canon Martens, here in 1871 and to date.

SHEPTON MALLET, SOMERSET
(*Clifton*).   St. Michael.

Fr. J. Brewer, S.J., originated the mission 1765, and served it till his death in 1797. His successor, Fr. Jas. Hussey, built the presbytery and a chapel dedicated to St. Nicholas, 1801-4. The same year the Visitation Nuns of Rouen were settled here by Mrs. Cuthbert Tunstall. They removed to Westbury-on-Trym 1831. Fr. Coombes, D.D., was rector from 1810 to 1849, when he retired to Downside. Since then the priests have been:—Rev. Hy. Swale, 1850; R. Havers, 1853; Jas. Dawson, 1856; Canon Shattock, 1858; Robt. Dunham, 1867; Jn. Fanning, 1875. The centenary of the mission was kept in October 1895, though why not in 1865 does not appear. Fr. Geo. Johnson is the present rector.

SHERBORNE, DORSET (*Plymouth*).   Sacred Heart and St. Aldhelm.

In 1891 the chapel was at Cliff Cottage, Marston Road, and was served from Yeovil by Carmelite Fathers. The new church, designed by Fr. Scholes, of Yeovil, was commenced April 5, 1893, and opened 1894. Provost Brownlow, afterwards Bishop · of Clifton,

preached on this occasion, his theme being the life and labours of St. Aldhelm, Bishop of Sherborne (died 709).

Priests.

Rev. Jos. Hearne, 1892.
„   Mgr. Vincent Coletti, 1894.
„   Francis Shepherd, here in 1897 and to date.

SHIFNAL, SALOP (*Shrewsbury*).
St. Mary.

A school chapel was opened here on October 7, 1860, by Lord Stafford, who generously defrayed the cost of the building. Mass was sung by Fr. Thos. Green, of Aldenham. At first, the mission was served on Sundays by Fr. James Jenkins, of Madeley. The building, which is Gothic, was designed by Mr. Buckler, of Oxford. Mass was said during the penal times at the old manor house belonging to the Jerningham family. The chalice in use at the church is an ancient one, bearing the inscription ' Restore me to Sheafnall, in Shropshire.' Lord Herries of Everingham, Yorks, into whose possession it came, returned it to the mission about thirty years ago.

Priests after 1866.

Rev. T. A. Crowther, December 1866.
„   T. Degen, 1870.
„   R. McCarte, 1871.
„   J. O'Dwyer and P. Deery, 1877.
„   D. Maguire, 1879.
„   J. Gastaldi, D.D., 1883.
„   G. Boen, 1884.
„   P. O'Reilly, 1885.
„   A. Bowen, 1889.
„   T. O'Connor, 1898.

SHIPLEY, near BRADFORD, YORKS (*Leeds*). SS. Mary and Walburga. The mission dates from August 13, 1851.

Dr. Cornthwaite, Bishop of Beverley, visited the mission on Sunday, December 6, 1863. The 'chapel' was a rented room in a public-house, capable of holding about 300. The congregation was estimated at double that number. Fr. Henry Walker was the first priest of the mission. The school chapel was opened in August 25, 1867; style, Gothic; dimensions, 84 ft. by 30 ft. Presbytery erected at the same time. £900 of the total cost was subscribed by the congregation.

Priests.

Rev. Hy. Walker, 1863.
„ Edward Walmesley, 1874.
„ James Glover, 1877.
„ Jos. Geary, 1882.
„ Sidney Morgan, 1888 and till 1897.
„ Denis O'Sullivan, 1898 and to date.

SHIREBROOK, DERBYSHIRE (*Nottingham*). St. Joseph.

The chapel was opened 1904, and Mass is said there alternately on Sundays at nine and eleven. The Rev. Chas. Froes is rector.

SHIREHAMPTON, near BRISTOL, SOMERSET (*Clifton*). St. Bernard.

The church was commenced Thursday, September 25, 1902, and completed in 1903. The style is fourteenth-century Gothic; architect, Mr. Doran Webb, of Salisbury. A mission was started in the neigh-bourhood in 1901 by Fr. F. H. Mather, services being held in a room which soon became inadequate. The mission also includes the adjoining port of Avonmouth, frequented by many Catholic sailors. The church of St. Bernard was intended as a memorial to the late Bishop Brownlow, of Clifton.

SHOREHAM, SUSSEX (*Southwark*). St. Peter.

Through the kind assistance of the Duke of Norfolk, a house was acquired for a mission station 1869. Afterwards a stable was transformed into a school chapel, and opened for worship December 1870. The present church (thirteenth-century Gothic) was erected by Mina Duchess of Norfolk, and opened by Bishop Danell, of Southwark, August 11, 1875. The mission for many years after its establishment was served from Worthing.

Priests.

Rev. H. Whiteside, 1870.
„ W. Linnett, 1877.
„ E. Martin, 1880.
„ Joseph Wilhelm, D.D., 1886.
„ Daniel Ferris, D.D., 1899.
„ Robt. Christall, 1903 to date.

SHORNCLIFFE, near FOLKESTONE, KENT (*Southwark*).

The iron garrison church was erected in 1894 by the late Fr. Chas. Keatinge, Chaplain to the Forces, and will accommodate about 200. It is under the care of the resident military chaplain for the time being, the presbytery being at Sandgate.

Priests.

Rev. Chas. Keatinge, 1894.
„ Thos. Foran, 1897.
„ E. M. Morgan, 1905 to date.

SHREWSBURY, SHROPSHIRE.
Cathedral Church of Our Lady
Help of Christians.

The Cloughs of Myndtown and
the Beringtons of Moat Hall were
the chief Catholics about Shrewsbury in the seventeenth century.
In 1676 the number of 'Papists'
in the town was returned at eight.
Mass was said at Moat Hall during
this troubled period, and occasionally at the town residence of the
Beringtons in the square before
St. Alkmund's Church. No public
chapel appears till April 1777, when
one was opened by Fr. Corne. After
1791 many French refugees were
hospitably entertained at Dothill
Park, and one of these, the Abbé
Louis Lemaitre, served the Shrewsbury mission from 1818–22. He
was a French Benedictine of Douai,
and died June 16, 1822, aged sixty-
five. His brother Stephen, who
predeceased him in 1818, had likewise served the Shrewsbury mission. Fr. S. Jones, priest from
1824–33, enlarged the chapel, where
a marble tablet recalls his memory.
In 1840 a great number of Irish
labourers employed by the Great
Western Railway Company settled
in the town, and during the rioting
occasioned by the restoration of the
hierarchy in 1851, a strong body-
guard of these stalwarts saved the
chapel and presbytery from destruction. The city, now the
see of a Catholic bishop, was
presented with a fine cathedral
by Bertram seventeenth Earl of
Shrewsbury. It was commenced
December 12, 1853, and finished
1867. The splendid east window,
pulpit, and stations of the Cross
were given by Canon Cholmondeley.
The Sacred Heart altar is a memorial of Bishop Brown, first Bishop
of Shrewsbury. The chapel of St.
Winefride was erected by F. Burke,
Esq., at a cost of £2,000.

Administrators.

Rev. Hy. Hopkins, 1867.
„ Hy. Walker, 1869.
„ Edw. Lynch, 1872.
Very Rev. Samuel Webster Allen
(Bishop of Shrewsbury June 16,
1897), 1874.

SICKLINGHALL, YORKS (*Leeds*).
The Immaculate Conception.

About 1851, Sicklinghall was
merely ' an obscure protestant village.' The few Catholics there
attended Mass at Storkhold Park,
the residence of Peter Middleton,
Esq. When this chapel was closed,
Mr. Middleton built the beautiful
Gothic church, and presented it to
the Fathers Oblates of Mary Immaculate (August 30, 1854). A
monastery was erected, and made
the novitiate of the congregation.
Under the direction of the Fathers
the mission has made great progress, and it is reported that the
Corpus Christi procession has come
to be looked upon by the inhabitants as a great annual event.

Priests.

Rev. Gustave Richard, 1854.
„ Joseph Arnoux, 1858.
„ Lys Marie, 1861.
„ Joseph Arnoux, 1863.
„ William Laffan, 1867.
„ Patrick Brady, 1871.
„ Hilarius Lenoir, here in 1875.
„ Patrick Newman, 1878.
„ Michael Brody, here in 1883.
„ Thos. Dawson, 1885.

Rev. Richard D'Alton, 1890.
„ James Gibney, 1894.
„ W. Browne, 1898.
„ James Comerford, 1904.

SIDCUP, KENT (*Southwark*). St. Lawrence of Canterbury.

The Hon. Thomas Howard, brother of Lord Arundell, who died here in June 1781, had a domestic chapel at Sidcup, but who the priest was does not appear. The present mission dates from 1902, when St. Joseph's Convent, in the Hatherley Road, was established, the chapel of which for some time served the mission. Fr. E. Julien was the first priest. In the summer of 1903, the Missionary Fathers of the Sacred Heart took over the spiritual care of the congregation, which numbers about 200. The present church was opened August 16, 1906, by Bishop Amigo, of Southwark. The congregation numbers about 200.

SIDMOUTH, DEVON (*Plymouth*). Convent of the Assumption.

Mass was said for the first time at Sidmouth on Easter Sunday 1881, by the Jesuit Fathers exiled from France under the Ferry laws. In the afternoon another large congregation of Catholics and protestants assembled to hear the fine discourse of Fr. Petit, S.J., and assist at Benediction. The chapel of the convent, founded in 1884, serves the mission. The building was enlarged and reopened December 13, 1904.

SILEBY, LEICESTERSHIRE (*Nottingham*). St. Gregory.

This mission was founded about 1876 by Fr. Wm. Lewthwaite, M.A. (Oxon.), who built the school chapel. For many years the place was served from Ratcliffe College. In 1900 the chapel was served from Syston. The Rev. Michael Callery, the present rector, was appointed 1903.

SILVERTOWN, LONDON, E. (*Westminster*). Our Lady and St. Edward, Tate Street.

With the sanction of Cardinal Manning, a house for a chapel was hired near the railway station (3 Mickleburg Terrace), and on Sunday, May 8, 1887, a school for religious instruction was opened by Fr. T. Prendergast, of St. Margaret's, Barking Road. Mass was said here for the first time on Sunday, June 19, 1887, by Fr. T. Ring, who was appointed resident priest of the new mission. Sixty adults and fifteen children ' were packed into the small space available,' and in the afternoon about 122 children received prizes for good attendance at the Sunday school during the past five weeks. The new school chapel, the gift of a generous benefactor, was opened Thursday, December 22, 1887. The building accommodates 400 persons. A new church, of Classic design, was commenced in August 1891, and opened during the course of 1892. The foundation stone was laid by the Bishop of *Amycla*. The architect of the new building was F. W. Tasker, Esq. The cost of erection was about £5,000. New schools, for 500 children, were opened by Cardinal Vaughan in October 1895.

SITTINGBOURNE, KENT (*Southwark*). The Sacred Heart.

On Sunday, June 26, 1893, Fr. E. O'Sullivan, who had but recently been appointed to this newly established mission, held an open-air service, at which at least 800 persons were present. The next day, Monday, Bishop Butt, of Southwark, made an official visit— the first Catholic episcopal visitation since that of Archbishop Warham, of Canterbury, in 1511—and confirmed a large number of persons. At the open-air meeting the previous evening, the audience was addressed by a Mr. Watts, a convert, for many years an energetic Baptist minister, and a student under C. H. Spurgeon. Mr. Watts's powerful address, on the almost endless varieties of protestantism and the unity of the Catholic Church, produced a great impression. In 1902, the fine Gothic church, dedicated to the Sacred Heart, was consecrated and opened by Bishop Bourne, of Southwark. The funds requisite for the building were collected by Fr. O'Sullivan by means of wholesale and often humorous advertising. The number of Catholics at Sittingbourne is about 300.

SKEGNESS, LINCOLNSHIRE (*Nottingham*). The Sacred Heart and Our Lady of the Holy Souls.

In July 1880, Fr. H. T. Sabela opened a chapel in a barn at Skegness, which was kindly placed at his disposal by the proprietor of the Sea View Hotel. The first Mass, on Sunday, July 18, was attended by a large congregation, chiefly protestants. In 1883 the mission was served from Sleaford. No mention is made of a mission here in 1891, 1893, 1894, but in 1897 a school chapel was announced as being 'in course of erection.' The opening took place September 29, 1898. Frs. P. Sabela and H. Capron were the priests in charge. In 1898 it was Fr. J. Davis, the present incumbent.

SKELMERSDALE, LANCS (*Liverpool*). St. Richard, Liverpool Road.

The first stone of the church (Gothic) was laid in August 1864 by Bishop Goss, of Liverpool, and the building was opened in 1865. W. Rotherham, Esq., of Skelmersdale, defrayed the cost of erection. In 1870 a school for 150 children was opened, and enlarged 1880. The presbytery was erected 1887. The Catholic population is about 850.

Priests.

Rev. W. Stirzaker, 1866.
„ Edw. Blackoe, 1899.

SKERTON, LANCASTER. St. Peter's, *see* **LANCASTER.**

SKERTON, LANCASTER (*Liverpool*). St. Joseph.

This second mission was opened 1896 as a chapel of ease to St. Peter's. Skerton is a flourishing suburb joined to Lancaster by a bridge.

Priests.

Rev. Philip O'Bryen, 1896.
„ Thos. Murphy, 1905 to date.

SKIPTON, YORKS (*Leeds*). St. Stephen.

The first stone of the church was laid by Sir Charles Tempest, Bart., in 1836, and the building was opened September 15, 1842. The style is Early Gothic; accommodation for about sixty. Before the erection of the church the nearest mission was at Broughton Hall, the seat of the Tempest family (*q.v.*).

Priests.

Rev. Rd. Boyle, 1843.
  „ Thos. Tempest, 1844.
  „ John Milner, 1846.
  „ Sir Geo. Bridges, Bart., S.J., 1856.
  „ H. James, S.J., 1858.
  „ John Gosford, S.J., 1862.
  „ Alfred White, S.J., 1864.
  „ Joseph Johnson, 1867.
  „ Anthony Benincassa, S.J., here 1872.
  „ Rd. Sharp, S.J., 1875 to date.

SLEAFORD, LINCOLNSHIRE (*Nottingham*). Our Lady of Good Counsel.

In August 1879 Fr. Sabela started the mission of Sleaford by preaching open-air discourses to the Irish harvesters. 'We well remember the day when Fr. Sabela made his first appearance in our midst, and we believe he was the first Roman Catholic priest that has pleaded for his Church in this town since the Reformation. A waggon was his pulpit, a blue sky his cathedral vaults ' (*Sleaford Gazette*, January 1, 1880). In December 1880 he purchased a fine site in Jermyn Street from J. T. Marston, Esq., for £600. The new school chapel was opened June 1, 1882, by the Bishop of Nottingham, who sang the High Mass. The altar, designed by Boulton, of Cheltenham, was the gift of a generous lady. The school chapel was supplanted by a church in June 1889. The style is Gothic. An oil painting by Canon Sabela, the founder, representing Our Lady of Good Counsel, hangs over the high altar. The building, which will seat 200 persons, cost £1,500. On Sunday, August 12, 1906, the Jubilee of the mission was celebrated by a High Mass and public procession. Fr. W. Lieber is the present priest.

SLINDON, near ARUNDEL, SUSSEX (*Southwark*). St. Richard.

At Slindon House, now the property of the Leslie family, Mass was offered up throughout the penal times in a secret chapel under the roof. In close proximity were three secret hiding-places. Fr. J. Silviera, who was priest at Slindon about 1834, buried a man who remembered pursuivants coming to Slindon House to arrest Fr. Molyneux, who, however, eluded the search. This Fr. Molyneux served the mission from 1765 to 1778. A little later, the house was the residence of Anthony Earl of Newburgh, grandson of the Hon. Charles Radcliffe, titular third Earl of Derwentwater, executed in 1746 in virtue of the attainder passed upon him in 1715 for his share in the Jacobite rebellion of that year.[1] Lord Newburgh, who was a pious Catholic nobleman, died without issue 1814. His widow, who

[1] He escaped out of Newgate, and, going to France, rose to the rank of colonel in the French service. He was captured at sea in 1745, while on his way to Scotland to join Prince Charles Edward. The House of Lords in 1786 (?) declared that the earldom of Newburgh was not affected by the Derwentwater attainder, and his grandson succeeded to the title and estates as fourth earl.

survived till 1861, was greatly beloved by the poor of Slindon for her kindness and active benevolence. She is buried in the church. Many relics of the Derwentwater family are preserved by the Leslies, who now own the estate. The first stone of the present Catholic church at Slindon was laid by Bishop Grant, of Southwark, on September 7, 1865. The site, as well as that of the adjoining cemetery, was given by Colonel Leslie. The style is Gothic, and the accommodation for about 300. Canon Mark Tierney, the historian of Arundel, was incumbent here from about 1821 to 1824, when he became chaplain to the Duke of Norfolk.

Priests since 1825.

Rev. Jn. White.
„ Jos. Silviera, 1829.
„ Jn. Sheehan, 1847.
„ Thos. Richardson, here in 1871.
„ Thos. Malpass, 1879.
„ Thos. Fleming, here in 1883.
„ Francis O'Callaghan, here in 1897.
„ Thos. Whelahan, 1904.
„ J. Duggan, 1906.

SLOUGH, BUCKS (*Northampton*). St. Ethelbert.

Through the exertions of Fr. J. Clementi, chaplain at Baylis House, a chapel was opened here in November 1885. The building was blessed and High Mass sung by the Bishop of Northampton. Collections for a new church were commenced in 1892. It was intended that the building should be a memorial of the landing of St. Augustine in 597. Pope Leo XIII., by special letter, blessed all those who aided in the work.

SMETHWICK, STAFFS (*Birmingham*). St. Philip.

In 1863 Fr. J. Flanagan took up his residence in Smethwick, and, having collected about £400, he made additions to the existing schoolroom, and so provided the congregation with a fairly commodious chapel. The number of Catholics in and about Smethwick was then about 700, 'mostly of the manufacturing and labouring class.' The number of children attending the school was 130. It may be mentioned here that the mission of Smethwick was founded by Fr. E. Caswall, of the Birmingham Oratory, and consolidated by 'the patience and exertions of the Rev. J. S. Flanagan.' The old chapel having long outgrown the needs of the congregation, a new church was opened in 1893.

Priests.

Rev. J. Flanagan, 1863.
„ Thos. Scott, 1867.
„ Chas. Ryder, here in 1883 and to date.

SOHO, LONDON, W.C. (*Westminster*). St. Patrick's.

In October 1791—the year of the second Catholic Relief Act—a number of Catholic gentlemen met in Covent Garden 'to consider the most effectual means of establishing a chapel, to be called St. Patrick's, on a liberal and permanent foundation.' As the result of this, a large building in Sutton Street—formerly used as dancing and supper rooms under the auspices of the celebrated Madame Cornelys—was taken and fitted up as chapel, and solemnly opened September 29, 1792, by Bishop Douglass, V.A.L.D. The first priest was the famous scholar and wit Fr. Arthur O'Leary, O.S.F., for some time chaplain to the Spanish Embassy. He died 1802, aged seventy-three. A monument was erected to his memory in St. Pancras Churchyard by his friend the Marquis of Hastings, and there is another memorial to him in the present St. Patrick's Church. The old chapel, which did duty down to 1891, was a plain, unpretentious structure, with gallery and lofty pulpit—not unlike the church in Lincoln's Inn Fields. The lease was renewed in 1853, but as early as 1848 a fund was started for the erection of a new church. The matter of building was seriously taken in hand by Fr. Thomas Barge, rector from 1860 till his death, October 13, 1885. The old church having become unsafe, the first stone of the new edifice was laid June 18, 1891, and on St. Patrick's Day 1893 the building was opened. The style is Italian, or Renaissance, an imposing feature of the structure being a red brick campanile rising to a height of 125 ft. The altar rails and pulpit are of marble. The Lady chapel contains a beautiful *pietà* and pictures by Van Dyck and Carlo Dolci. The congregation of St. Patrick's, which in 1803 was about 2,000, is now about three times that number. Schools in connection with the mission were established in 1803, and patronised by such illustrious persons as H.R.H. the Duke of Sussex and Daniel O'Connell. They were transferred to Tudor Place, Tottenham Court Road, in 1852. New schools, for 741 children, were opened in Great Chapel Street, Oxford Street, in February 1888. Since 1885, Dean George Langton Vere has been rector of the mission, the history of which he has given in an interesting pamphlet.

SOLIHULL, WARWICKSHIRE (*Birmingham*). St. Augustine of England.

This mission was formerly served by the Franciscans. For some time prior to 1758 it was 'a residence,' and 'in full working order.' It was probably founded in 1750. In 1761, Eliz. Palmer left the interest on £20 to the incumbent for five Masses. Wm. Collins, Esq., in 1815 left the rents of some lands to the mission, and about the same time a bequest of £200 came from Anne Barron. Further legacies came from the Lewin family in 1821 and Mrs. Eliz. Green 1824. The present church opened Wednesday, January 6, 1839. The building (50 ft. by 42 ft.) is 'plain pure Gothic,' from designs by A. W. Pugin. On the occasion of the opening ' an argumentative discourse ' on the Holy Sacrifice was preached by Fr. McDonnell.

Priests.

Fr. Thos. Hall, *alias* Lawrence Loraine, O.S.F., 1725-38. This missioner laboured for upwards of twelve years in the Solihull district, during which time he reconciled a great many persons to the Church. Died 1783 or 1784.

The following were also missioners in this district at the undermentioned dates:—

Rev. Bernard Yates, O.S.F., 1746.
„ Bernardine Browne, 1749.
„ Geo. Lancaster, 1755.
„ Anselm White, 1758.
„ Henry Bishop, 1758.
„ Placid Payne, 1764.
„ Charles Julians, 1767.
„ James Howse, 1785.
„ Pacificus Nutt, 1787.
„ Angelus Ingram, 1793.
„ Paschal Harrison, 1806 (?).
„ Henry Wareing, 1812.
„ James Sumner, 1818.
„ James Millward, 1821.

Rev. Bernardine Davidson, 1833.
The above were all Franciscans.

Seculars.

Rev. J. Ilsley, 1836.
„   John Lycett, 1840.
„   E. Hodson, 1852.
„   Michael Canon O'Sullivan, 1877.
„   James Canon McCave, 1892.
„   Michael Glancey 1899 to date.

SOMERS TOWN, LONDON, N.W.
(*Westminster*). St. Aloysius, Clarendon Square.

The chapel was erected in 1808 by the Abbé Carron, an *émigré* priest, who did much for London Catholicity in his day. The façade is of Greek design, relieved with pilasters. The interior contains monuments to the founder and his assistant, the Abbé Nerinckx, and also the Bishop de St. Pol de Léon, who died in 1806. The schools were built in 1822. The church has been several times repaired and redecorated, notably in 1850, when the altar and sanctuary were adorned with elaborate arabesques. On the whole, the building is interesting as a good example of church architecture of the time when English Catholics were emerging from penal laws into the happy epoch of the 'second spring.' The Catholic population of the district is about 4,000.

Priests.

Rev. Abbé Carron, 1808.
„   Abbé Nerinckx, 1815.
„   Walter McAvila, 1855.
„   James Bamber, 1857.
„   Alfred Dolman, 1861.
„   Mgr. Henry Grosch, 1902 to date.

SOULDERN, OXFORDSHIRE (*Birmingham*). St. Joseph.

The mission is described as one of considerable antiquity. It was supported by the Cox family of Broxwood, some of whom figure on the list of Catholic non-jurors of 1715. The revived mission dates from 1852, when a chapel was established by Dr. Dolman, a well-known Catholic physician of the district, and served from Hethe till 1868. Shortly afterwards the chapel was transferred to an upper room of the manor house. The present church, 'after the plan of old English parish churches,' was opened February 2, 1870, by Canon O'Sullivan, V.G., for Bishop Ullathorne. Among the crowded congregation present were Mrs. Dolman, the munificent donor of the church, Major and Mrs. Cox, Captain Stapleton &c. The altar rails of the sanctuary are from the old chapel of the penal times. Fr. Samuel Glossop is the first and present rector.

SOUTHAM, near RUGBY, WARWICKSHIRE (*Birmingham*). Our Lady and St. Wulstan.

The Sisters of the Poor Child Jesus, expelled from Germany by the Falk laws, came to England 'almost penniless' in 1875, and opened a convent at Southam. Here they carry on their special work—the rescue and training of orphan girls. The present convent was erected about 1880, at a cost of £1,500. The chapel is open to the public.

Priests.

Rev. Fredk. When, 1875.

„ Jos. Struif, 1882.

„ A. Crane, 1888.

„ Hugh Taylor, here in 1891.

„ Cornelius Klomp, 1897.

„ Jn. Nock, 1904.

SOUTHAMPTON (*Portsmouth*). St. Edmund's.

A temporary iron church was opened in the Avenue, Southampton, within the grounds of the premises formerly known as Archer's Lodge (May 1884). The building was for 300 persons. Fr. E. Rivara was the first priest. The site was given by the nuns of the adjacent convent of the Sacred Heart. The present church, in the fourteenth-century Gothic style, consisting of nave, sanctuary, Lady Chapel, sacristies, and organ loft, was commenced June 21, 1888. The west rose window is one of the largest in England. The cost of erection came to about £6,000. The solemn opening took place in November 1889. Fr. P. O'Connell is the present rector.

SOUTHBANK, YORKS, NORTH RIDING (*Middlesbrough*). St. Peter.

Canon Holland, of Middlesbrough, was appointed to the mission, then just commenced, in 1874. By his energy he raised sufficient funds to build the church. He also erected a school, 1880. He also built the school chapel at Grangetown, where a population of some 4,000 had sprung up. Canon Holland was frequently appealed to by both masters and men to intervene in strikes, and his judgment was often the means of preventing or ending these disastrous commercial struggles. On leaving for the mission of Thirsk in September 1885, Canon Graham, the next priest, was presented by the people of Southbank with a handsome parting gift as a mark of their appreciation of his public services. 'The beautiful new church' was opened November 1905. Bishop Lacy confirmed 400 persons here September 23, 1906.

Priests since 1885.

Rev. John Canon Doud.

„ Bernard McCabe, 1892.

„ James Nolan, 1901 to date.

SOUTHEND, ESSEX (*Westminster*). Our Lady Help of Christians and St. Helen.

When the mission was started here in 1862, a chapel was fitted up at 3 Capel Terrace. The present church was opened by Archbishop Manning, October 1869. The style of the building is Early English. A large proportion of the cost of erection was defrayed by Miss Tasker. Mr. Thos. Goodman was the architect. Mixed elementary schools taught by Sisters of Notre Dame were established 1899 ; average attendance in 1900, 165. A south aisle and Lady Chapel were added to the church in 1899, and an oak organ-gallery October 1906.

Priests.

Rev. John Moore, 1862 till 1891.

„ Thos. Denny, 1891.

„ Patrick McKenna, 1895.

SOUTHHILL, CHORLEY, LANCS (*Liverpool*). St. Chad.

The locality is said to have been formerly known as Slatedelph. A chapel was built here in the reign of James II. from a fund left by Fr. Richard Birket, a secular priest, who had been sentenced to imprisonment during the Oates plot. The chapel stood on land belonging to Mr. Gerard, of Heigham, and was seized by the Government after the Jacobite rebellion of 1715. Another chapel was afterwards set up in a garret of the house belonging to Matthew Talbot, Esq., of Wheelton. It was opened about 1728 or 1729, and was served by Jesuits. Fr. Charles Morphy, S.J., was here 1730 *et seq.* A party of priest-catchers was once sent to arrest him, but he mollified them by his kindness, and they left him unmolested. His successor, Fr. Wm. Gillibrand (1747) opened a school, which seems to have been well attended. It was continued by Fr. Jn. Richardson, the next priest. Bishop Matthew Gibson, V.A., confirmed sixty-eight persons here 1784, at which time the congregation was estimated at about 260. Fr. George Clarkson was priest at this time. Bishop Wm. Gibson gave confirmation at the new chapel, 1793, to 110 persons. This chapel was erected 1791, and is still in use. Fr. Clarkson died 1813, and was succeeded by Fr. Francis Massey, who served the mission till his death in August 1822, aged forty. The priests after him have been :

Rev. Jn. Weston, 1822.
„ Jn. Fairclough, 1828.
„ Jn. Beaumont, 1832.
„ James Berry, 1857.
„ John Doherty, 1867.
„ Thos. Tobin, here 1872.
„ Geo. Holden, 1888 to date.

SOUTHPORT, LANCS (*Liverpool*).
St. Mary.
In 1838 Southport was described as 'a favourite watering-place.'

The previous year the mission was commenced by Fr. Vincent J. Eyre. Prior to this the nearest chapel was six miles distant (Ormskirk ?).
Priests.
Rev. V. J. Eyre, 1837.
„ J. Newsham, 1840.
„ John Hill, 1845.
„ J. Canon Abraham, 1851.
„ Henry Cooke, 1860.
„ Patrick Cahill, 1890 to date.

SOUTHSEA, HANTS (*Portsmouth*).
St. Swithun, Saxe Weimar Road.
The mission was commenced in July 1884, when Bishop Vertue, of Portsmouth, purchased a site at a cost of £1,000 and erected a temporary iron church upon it capable of holding about 300 persons. The present church was opened in 1891.
Priests.
Rev. C. Arthur, here in 1891.
„ Jn. O'Donoghue, 1894.
„ Albert Coughlan, 1897.
„ Isidore Kuner, 1904.

SOUTH SHIELDS, DURHAM (*Hexham and Newcastle*). St. Bede.
The Tynemouth district at the commencement of the last century was served for several years by the Abbé Aubin Donniville, an *émigré*. The present mission of South Shields dates from 1849, when the church was opened (October). The church, in the Westoe Road, was opened August 22, 1876. Mgr. Capel preached on the occasion. A considerable portion of the cost of erection is said to have been subscribed by the working-class congregation.

Priests.

Rev. Rd. Singleton, 1849.
„ Edmund Kelly, 1853.
„ W. Markland, 1866.
„ Geo. Waterton, here 1871.
„ D. Ramsay, 1882.
„ Thos. O'Connor, 1888.
„ Michael Canon Greene, 1889.
„ Geo. Burton, 1895.
„ John Chapman, 1902.
„ Richard Vaughan, 1904 to date.

SOUTHWARK, LONDON, S.E. St. George's Cathedral.

In the year 1786, or, according to some, 1783, Fr. Thomas Walsh, a Douai priest, opened a retired chapel in Bandy Leg Walk (now Little Guildford Street), Southwark. In 1788 he was joined by Fr. John Thayer, a convert American, who had recently been ordained at St. Sulpice, Paris. Fr. Thayer worked zealously, and built schools for girls and boys. In 1790 he was recalled to America by Dr. Carrol, first Catholic Bishop of Baltimore. Three years later 'a large and grand chapel' (designed by Mr. James Taylor, the architect of Ushaw College) in the London Road took the place of the old Mass-house in Bandy Leg Walk. A solemn Requiem Mass for the unfortunate Louis XVI. of France was sung here in February 1793 —alleged to be the first of the kind in London outside an ambassador's chapel since the time of James II. This chapel and the adjoining clergy-house formed a very plain building, 'the interior oblong and the approach shaded with yews.' The furniture was very plain—high pulpit, straight-backed benches, and wooden high altar, surmounted by a fine paint-ing of the Crucifixion—attributed to Murillo—now in the sacristy of the cathedral. In 1817 the mission became the chapel of the Belgian Embassy. The congregation numbered 5,000 in 1814, and the clergy of the church had to attend sick calls &c. as far south as Mitcham! In 1829 the Catholics of the mission had risen to about 15,000. Fr. Thomas Doyle, who came to St. George's in 1819, founded the 'Guild of Our Blessed Lady and St. George the Martyr' in 1840. Several years prior to this, he had commenced collecting for a new church to take the place of the old crowded-out chapel. He travelled through a large part of England and the Continent, receiving contributions from princes and peasants. The design of the present structure was drawn by A. W. Pugin, and the first stone laid September 8, 1840, on a fine site in the Westminster Bridge Road. The opening took place July 4, 1848, amidst a vast concourse of Catholics, both clerical and lay. The sermon at the High Mass was preached by Bishop (afterwards Cardinal) Wiseman. In 1851 the Cardinal delivered lectures at St. George's to 'crowds of persons of all religions' on the restored hierarchy. The church was now the cathedral of the diocese of Southwark, Dr. Thomas Grant being the first bishop (1851–70). Fr. Doyle, who was created provost of the new chapter, died June 6, 1879, aged eighty-six. The cathedral was freed from debt and consecrated by Bishop Butt in 1894. Of late years, several stained-glass windows, representing St. Thomas of Canterbury, St. George, the thirteenth centenary celebration of St. Augustine's landing at Ebbsfleet, Thanet, &c.,

have been put up. The funereal monuments include that of the Hon. Edward Petre, M.P., a great benefactor to St. George's, who died 1848; also recumbent effigies in memory of Provost Doyle and Dr. Danell, second Bishop of Southwark (d. 1881). There is also a fine memorial brass to Fr. John Wheble, an Army chaplain, who died at Balaclava during the Crimean war (November 3, 1854). Near the entrance on the left stands a superb bronze crucifix, designed by Michael Angelo, and once the property of Napoleon the Great. The Knill Chantry, a fine example of A. Pugin's skill, is close to the Blessed Sacrament Chapel.

SOUTHWOLD, SUFFOLK (Northampton). The Sacred Heart.

The mission was established in 1897, in what is described as ' the most non-Catholic county of England.' The district served is one of immense area (forty miles by twelve miles), and the chapel is only a disused fishing-net shed! Fr. H. Mason, the priest-in-charge, is making great efforts to erect church and schools. When first established, the chapel was in the manor house, and was known as St. Peter's Oratory.

SPALDING, LINCOLNSHIRE (Nottingham). The Immaculate Conception and St. Norbert.

The mission of Spalding was founded through the exertions of Fr. T. Van Biesen, of the Premonstratensian Order. About 1876 the church was built, at the expense of I. Young, Esq., and, later, a convent and schools. In May 1881 a handsome stained-glass window by Hardman was erected in the church in memory of Fr. Van Biesen's jubilee. It may be remarked that before the Reformation upwards of thirty parishes in Lincolnshire were served by priests of the Premonstratensian Order, which had five abbeys, two priories, and one convent in England. Fr. Van Biesen was rector till after 1898, when he was succeeded by Fr. E. C. Tyck. A handsome coloured window, representing St. Frederick and St. Herman Joseph of the Norbertine Order, was presented to the church in May 1906 by the Bishop of Namur.

SPANISH PLACE, LONDON, W. (Westminster). St. James.

This mission, as the name implies, was formerly the chapel of the Spanish Embassy. The Embassy chapel was not always on its present site; in 1736 it was in Ormond Street, but was transferred to Manchester Square in 1792. About 1767, the chapel was within the ambassador's house. In 1792 ' the old chapel ' was erected, mainly through the instrumentality of Dr. Hussey, F.R.S., ' a man of great genius and enlightened piety.' He became chaplain to the embassy 1784, and in 1795 was chosen first president of Maynooth and Bishop of Waterford. The chapel, designed by Bonomi, was in the Basilica style, with galleries transversing the pillars, and is described as ' a very fair specimen of Italian architecture.' The altar-piece, ' The Descent from the Cross,' formerly belonged to a Flemish convent. A belfry and fine-toned bell were erected at the expense of the congregation in 1850. Considerable

structural alterations took place about this time, the galleries being removed and a new aisle added to the Epistle side. In 1827, the Spanish Government withdrew the pension hitherto allowed the chaplains; but, as the congregation was mainly a wealthy one, the loss was not keenly felt. The old chapel having long become inadequate, the site of the present building in George Street, just by Spanish Place was purchased in 1880. The foundation stone was laid in June 1887, and the church—in the Gothic style, from designs by Goldie—was opened September 29, 1890. High Mass was sung by Bishop Patterson, and the sermon preached by Fr. Lockhart, of the Oratory, the Spanish ambassador and full suite being present on this auspicious occasion. The name of Provost M. Barry will long be associated with this centre of Catholicity, as it was here he laboured during a rectorate of many years, and it was his energy that mainly got together the large sum required for the building of the present fine church.

SPETCHLEY, WORCESTER (*Birmingham*). St. John the Baptist.

Spetchley Park, near Worcester, is the residence of the Berkeley family, and was long served by the Jesuit Fathers of St. George's, Worcester. Thos. Berkeley, Esq., was converted to the Faith in the reign of Charles I., for which monarch he and his family were great sufferers. The earliest missioner at Spetchley was Fr. Charles Wilson, about 1691. His successor was Fr. Nicholas Griffin, 1693. Fr. Thos. Philips, chaplain here 1763, was the author of the 'Life of Cardinal Pole.' Fr. Thos. Falkner,

probably his successor, had formerly been a surgeon in the Royal Navy, and had made several voyages to South America, where he was converted to the Faith 1731. He is the author of a treatise on American drugs and a 'Description of Patagonia.' The Jesuits retired from the Spetchley mission 1855, and it has since been conducted by seculars. It may be of interest to recall the fact that Robt. Berkeley, Esq. (1711–1804) was perhaps the first Catholic to call the attention of his countrymen to the cruelty and folly of the penal laws (1778).

Priests since 1824.

Rev. Jn. Lycett, ——.
„ R. O'Higgins, 1840.
„ Henry Mahon, 1842.
„ Geo. Clifford, 1847.
„ Matthew McCann, 1853.
„ A. Delarue, 1856.
„ Fredk. Jones, 1877.
„ Hugh Taylor, 1879.
„ Jn. Nock, 1884.
„ Jn. Piris, 1888.
„ J. McCarthy, 1895.
„ James Kearney, 1899.
„ Walter Höfler, 1903 to date.

SPETTISBURY, BLANDFORD, DORSET (*Plymouth*). St. Monica's Priory.

The Augustinian nuns of Louvain settled here at Christmas 1799. Their chapel served the mission till the opening of the present church, September 8, 1830. For some time a small chapel at Blandford served as a second place of worship for Catholics in the district. It was opened by Fr. Towsey 1804, and served by the Abbé Pierre Moulins. Fr. Joseph Lee succeeded him 1814. In 1856 a convent of Augustinian nuns adjoined the church. Next year it was made over to the Bridgettine community, and renamed

Sion House. By 1891 the house was a priory of the Canons Regular of St. John Lateran. In October 1906 the Nuns of St. Ursula acquired the premises.

Priests.

Rev. Abbé Pierre Moulins, 1799.

„ Jos. Lee, 1814.

„ L. Calderbank, 1839 or 1840.

„ Thos. Lynch, 1849.

„ E. Kenny, 1851.

„ W. Canon Agar, 1854.

„ Joseph Canon Parke, 1862.

„ John Sabbé, 1867.

„ Wm. Walsh, here in 1875.

„ Joseph Matthews, 1877.

„ Fredk. Edwards, 1879.

„ F. Downing, here in 1883.

„ Anthony Allaria, D.D., here in 1891 and to date.

SPILSBY, LINCS (*Nottingham*). Our Lady and the English Martyrs. This locality was once perhaps the most Catholic spot in England. The Pilgrimage of Grace started here in 1536, and four centuries before the district was hallowed by the presence of St. Gilbert of Sempringham. So completely, however, had the Faith died out in these parts, owing to nearly three centuries of penal laws, that when one of the ' natives ' was told that a Catholic priest was coming to live in the village, the old lady exclaimed : ' A Catholic priest ! Lor', sir, I didn't think there was such things as them nowadays !' (anecdote in the *Tablet*, October 30, 1897). For some years prior to 1896, Mass was said occasionally in a small chapel at Skendleby Hall, but in the spring of 1896 Fr. Gilbert Bull commenced a regular mission at Spilsby. In 1897 a public hall was rented for services, and on Sunday,

October 24, the first High Mass since the reign of Queen Mary I. was celebrated by Fr. Bull. About forty persons were present, mostly protestants. In the evening the hall was filled to overflowing, the sermon on this occasion being a simple explanation of the nature and claims of the Catholic Church. About March 1899 a site for a church was secured, and building operations commenced. The church was opened the following year. Fr. H. Lindeboom is the present rector.

SPITALFIELDS, LONDON, E. (*Westminster*). St. Anne.

A meeting was held in the boys' schoolroom, Spicer Street, on May 13, 1850, to devise ways and means for the erection of a church. The number of children in the day school at that time was 200, and in the Sunday school 400. Mass was said on Sundays in the largest class-room. The church of St. Anne, erected by the Marist Fathers in charge of the mission 1855, to hold 1,400 persons, was already too small for the congregation in 1858. The present rector added the nave, chancel, and high altar. The church was reopened after the enlargement Sunday, September 11, 1904.

Priests.

Rev. Jos. Quiblier, 1850.

„ C. Bernin, 1852.

„ Cyrus Champion, 1854.

„ Stephen Chaurain, 1857.

„ Anatole Police, 1888.

„ Leo Thomas, 1890.

„ Matthew Kearney, 1892.

„ James Goggan, 1894.

„ Michael Walters, 1897.

STACKSTEADS, near MANCHES-TER, LANCS (*Salford*). St. Joseph.

The mission was established in 1892. The Catholic population in 1902 was reckoned at 1,200. The schools are well attended. There is a chapel of ease at Newchurch.

Priests.

Rev. Geo. Sparkes, 1892.
  ,, James Ryan, 1896 to date.

STAFFORD (*Birmingham*). St. Austin.

After the Reformation, the chief seat of Catholicity near Stafford was at St. Thomas' Priory, two miles east of the town, the seat of the ancient family of Fowler. Walter Fowler, Esq., the last of his race, died in 1716 without heirs male, and the estate was subsequently sold to Sarah Duchess of Marlborough. This Walter Fowler succeeded his father in 1681. His chaplain was Fr. Daniel Fitter, a Lisbonian priest, who during the reign of James II. opened a school for Catholics at Stafford. He died February 6, 1700, aged seventy-two, leaving £300 for 'charitable purposes.' The money passed into the power of his nephew, Lord Fauconberg, who, 'conforming to the Established Church' in 1730, refused to pay the interest on the money, thus adding, as was said of him, 'the crime of theft to that of apostasy.' From 1716 to 1733, the chapel at Stafford was under several priests, including Fr. George Witham, afterwards Bishop of *Marcopolis* and Vicar-Apostolic, and Fr. Simon Berington. In the last-named year, the Jerninghams of Cossy opened a chapel at Stafford. It was long only served as occasion demanded, but in 1783 Fr. Thomas Barnaby took up his residence permanently in the town. His successor built St. Austin's Chapel, in the 'Forebridge,' on a site given by Thos. Berington, Esq. It was opened July 31, 1791. In 1813, Fr. Price made this building the transept of a Gothic church. Later on Geo. Jerningham, Esq., who had established his claim to the earldom of Stafford before the House of Lords, purchased the oak stalls in Lichfield Cathedral and gave them to the Catholic church of Stafford. Fr. Price built schools in 1818, and ended his long and useful life June 1831. Under his ministrations the Catholics of Stafford increased to 140. His successor, Fr. Huddlestone, was a man of great public spirit. In 1833 he obtained from Lord Melbourne, after much difficulty, the reprieve of two Irishmen wrongfully sentenced to transportation for an alleged assault. The foundation stone of the new church at Stafford was laid May 26, 1861, by the Vicar-General of the Birmingham diocese, in place of the Bishop. It was opened on July 16, 1862. The church is a neat building in the Decorated Gothic style, from the design of E. W. Pugin. The total cost was about £3,000. Lord Stafford, Mr. Serjeant Bellasis, and Mr. Whitgreave of Moseley—a descendant of Charles II.'s protector after Worcester—were the principal benefactors of the new church.

Priests after Fr. Huddlestone.

Rev. Francis Kerril Amherst, 1856 (Bishop of Northampton 1858-80).
  ,, John Wyse, 1858.
  ,, Michael Canon O'Sullivan, 1859.
  ,, John Fanning, 1866.
  ,, James Nary, 1871.
  ,, Edward Canon Acton, D.D., 1872.

B B

Rev. John Canon Hawksford, D.D., 1880.

„ Louis Torrond, 1884.
„ Canon Acton (second time), 1885.
„ James Keating, 1899.

STAINES, MIDDLESEX (*Westminster*). Our Lady of the Rosary.

The mission was established here in 1890 by the late Canon George Akers, of Hampton Wick, from which place it was served till the opening of the present church in the Gresham Road (1892).

Priests.

Rev. C. H. Clarke, 1892.
„ David Dewar, M.A., 1894.
„ Mgr. Dunn, 1906.

STAITHES, YORKS, NORTH RIDING (*Middlesbrough*). Our Lady Star of the Sea.

The first stone of the Gothic church was laid by the Bishop of Middlesbrough July 31, 1884. Before the erection of the church the nearest mission was at Loftus or Ugthorpe. Mgr. Witham, of Lartington Hall, was a generous donor to the building fund. ' Fr. W. S. Sullivan, of Loftus, did much to forward the erection of the church at Staithes. The building was opened Tuesday, June 9, 1885. Over the west doorway is a fine carving of Our Lady holding the Holy Child, also a boat rowed by angels. The total cost was £1,250.

Priests since 1891.

Rev. Patrick Gilsenan, 1891.
„ Charles Van Poucke, 1894.
„ John Carr, 1898.
„ Lawrence Kenefick, 1899.
David O'Connor, 1903 to date.

STALYBRIDGE, CHESHIRE (*Shrewsbury*).

The church of St. Peter was opened September 25, 1839. A Catholic school had existed in the place since about 1834. In 1866 the existing schools were enlarged, and additions were again made in 1895. A beautiful high altar was erected in the church in May 1869.

Priests.

Rev. R. Brown, 1839.
„ J. Anderton, 1840.
„ R. Hubbersty, 1848.
„ J. Anderton, 1849.
„ J. Reah, 1853.
„ Canon Egan, 1853.
„ W. Canon Hilton, 1860.
„ Mgr.Carroll,V.G.,1867(Bishop of Shrewsbury 1895-97).
„ Chris. Ryder, 1895.
„ J. O'Grady, 1898.

STAMFORD, LINCS (*Nottingham*). Our Lady and St. Augustine.

In the summer of 1845, owing to the influx of Irish harvesters, the Catholic population of Stamford was reckoned at about 1,000. Fr. O'Connor preached a sermon every Sunday in Irish and English. The old chapel having become long inadequate, a new church was commenced in January 1863, from the design of G. Goldie, of Portman Square, London. The style of the church is thirteenth-century Gothic. The opening took place on Whit Tuesday 1865. The bell tower was added later.

Priests.

Rev. T. J. O'Connor, 1845.
„ J. Daley, 1862.
„ Wm. Canon Browne, 1866.
„ Henry Basil Allies, M.R 1882.
„ John Wenham, here in 1888.
„ Joseph West 1892 to date.

STAMFORD HILL, LONDON, N. (*Westminster*). St. Ignatius.

In 1894 the Jesuits, at the request of Cardinal Vaughan, started the present college in a large mansion in the High Road, the coach-house of which formed the chapel. The college rapidly increased, and the adjoining houses had to be acquired. The present church was opened on the feast of Corpus Christi 1904. A new college for about 200 students is in course of erection, B. Williamson, Esq., architect.

Rectors.

Rev. Fr. — Pollen, 1894.
   „   Fr. Jas. Nicholson.
   „   Fr. Terence Donnelly.

STANBROOK ABBEY, near WORCESTER (*Birmingham*).

In 1623 the English Benedictine congregation founded a convent for young ladies at Cambray, under the patronage of Mgr. Vanderburgh, the archbishop. Dame Frances Gawen, a daughter of Thomas Gawen, Esq., of Norrington, Wilts, was the first abbess. During the rule of the thirteenth abbess, Dame Lucy Blyde, the convent was seized by the French Revolutionists (October 18, 1793), and the community imprisoned for two years at Compiègne. The nuns then made their way to England, where the Marchioness of Buckingham hired a house for them at 2 Hereford Street, Oxford Row, London. Dr. Brewer, O.S.B., next procured a house and convent for them at Woolton, Liverpool, and here the school was reopened. In 1807, the nuns removed to Abbots Salford, in Warwickshire. Finally, in 1838 the community migrated to Stanbrook, Powick, near Worcester, where they have since continued to flourish. The fine Gothic church, which is open to the public and serves the mission, was opened in 1864, and consecrated by Bishop Ullathorne 1871.

STANDISH, near WIGAN, LANCS (*Liverpool*). St. Mary of the Annunciation.

A chapel has existed at Standish Hall since 1574. The Standish family, who own the place and are lords of the manor, have ever been staunch to the Catholic faith. Fr. J. Darbyshire, O.P., was priest here in 1727. By 1883 the old chapel had become very decayed and quite insufficient for the congregation. On May 18, 1884, a new church was opened by the Bishop of Liverpool. Henry Standish, Esq., was the chief benefactor to the mission. The sermon at the opening was preached by Canon Carr (Rev. xxi. 5).

Priests since 1825.

Rev. — Jenkins.
   „   — Duck, 1827.
   „   — Greenough, 1832.
   „   Richard Tyrer, 1839 or 1840.
   „   Wm. Placid Corlett, 1863.
   „   Richard Barry, here in 1875 and till 1893.
   „   Alfred Walmsley, 1893 to date.

STANLEY, DURHAM (*Hexham and Newcastle*). St. Joseph.

A school chapel was opened 1872, and served from Burnopfield till 1879. The present church, in the Gothic style, was commenced in 1901, and opened in 1902. A cemetery was laid out and blessed shortly after the establishment of the mission.

Priests.

Rev. Richard Hannan, 1879.

„ Andrew Keenan, 1882.

„ James Thompson, 1890 to date.

STAPEHILL, DORSET (*Plymouth*). Our Lady of Dolours.

This place is regarded as one of the oldest missions in England, the record of post-Reformation Catholicity going back as far as 1637. The Jesuits appear to have served the chapel, and even—owing to the seclusion of the place—to have kept a school. Fr. Michael Jenison, S.J., was here 1680-90. The record of chaplains, however, is almost non-existent. Fr. John Couche was priest of the place for several years before 1802. In that year a convent of Cistercian nuns exiled by the French Revolution settled at Stapehill. There was also about this time some talk of making the mission a novitiate for the Society of Jesus. Lord Arundell of Wardour, who owned property in the district, was the patron of the mission. The church was consecrated July 16, 1851, by Bishop Ullathorne. The style is Gothic, from the design of C. Hansom.

N.B.—The school kept by the Jesuits was discovered by an informer, and had to be suppressed, 1724. From about 1750 a Mr. Stafford carried on a preparatory school here for boys intended for Douai College.

Priests since 1825.

Rev. Abbé Palemon (*d.* 1851, aged eighty).

„ Francis Hawkins, 1851.

„ John Dunne, 1858.

„ John Magini, 1862 (Francis Hawkins, second priest).

Rev. David Walsh, 1867.

„ Stephen Barron, rector 1883.

„ H. Augustine Collins, here 1884 to date.

STAUNTON HALL, NOTTINGHAM (*Nottingham*).

This ancient mansion, the ancestral residence of the Staunton family—a stock settled in Nottinghamshire before the Conquest—has for some years past been leased by Redmond Cafferata, Esq., a Catholic. There is a domestic oratory in the house, served on Sundays and holy days from the cathedral, Nottingham.

STAVELEY, DERBYSHIRE (*Nottingham*).

Fr. Thos. Beveridge, S.J., *alias* Thomas Robinson (1583 – 1658), who laboured for many years in Lancashire, was educated here. It appears that there were several 'schismatic Catholicks' in the neighbourhood, but no priest or chapel. The present mission only dates from about 1885.

Priests.

Rev. Robt. Dunham, 1885.

„ Charles Kerin, 1888.

„ W. Reginald Winder, 1890 to date.

STELLA, DURHAM (*Hexham and Newcastle*). St. Mary and St. Thomas Aquinas.

After the Reformation, Stella Hall became the property of the Tempests. In 1598 Nicholas Tempest was denounced to Burleigh as 'that great recusant' by Tobie Matthews, Bishop of Durham, and heavily fined. This same Nicholas was created baronet by James I., 1622. The last of the family, Sir Thomas, died 1692, when the property passed to his son - in - law, Lord Widdrington, attainted 1715, but restored in property 1733. On the death of his only son, *s.p.*, 1774, the estate passed to the Eyres and Towneleys, and from them to the Standishes, the present holders. Several of the Tempests were distinguished as ecclesiastics, notably Abbot Tempest, of Lambspring († 1729), Robt. Tempest, S.J. († 1640), &c. The old domestic chapel of the Hall having become insufficient, a new Gothic church, designed by Green, and measuring 68 ft. by $33\frac{1}{2}$ ft., was opened October 12, 1843, by Bishop Penswick, V.A. £500 of the building expenses was collected by Fr. T. Eyre, a former chaplain at the Hall, and a large sum was also contributed by Mrs. Dunn of Hedgefield. On July 12, 1846, Bishop Riddell confirmed eighty-four persons here. In September 1859, the Redemptorists gave a mission in the church 'to crowds of Catholics and Protestants.'

Priests since 1736.

Rev. T. Greenwell, 1736-48.
,, — Gibson, 1784.
,, T. Eyre, 1787.
,, T. Story, 1792.
,, W. Hall, —.
,, Jn. Glover, 1829.
,, Thos. Witham, 1831.
,, Mgr. Vincent Eyre, 1839-40.
,, Thos. Parker, 1846.
,, Ralph Canon Platt, 1847.
,, Arsenius Watson, 1857.
,, Henry Canon Wrennall, 1866 to date.

STOCK, near INGATESTONE, ESSEX. Our Lady of Mount Carmel.

The mission was established 1866-7, at Lillystone Hall. The present chapel was opened 1880. Number of congregation, about a hundred. Average attendance at school (mixed), about forty.

Priests.

Rev. Thos. Fallside, 1870.
,, Wm. H. Cologan, 1877 to date.

STOCKPORT, CHESHIRE (*Shrewsbury*). SS. Philip and James.

Mass was first said here in recent times on July 22, 1798, in a room in Windmill Street, by Fr. R. Thompson, of St. Chad's, Manchester. In 1799 Fr. J. Blundell took up his residence in the town, and in 1801 he purchased land for chapel, presbytery, and school. The chapel was opened May 1, 1803. The building was enlarged during the incumbency of Fr. W. Keily (1825-38). In 1851 a mechanics' institute was purchased and transformed into a church under the title of St. Michael. It was closed 1882. The two chapels were attacked by a ' No Popery' mob in 1852, and much damage done. The sum of £1,700 was paid to the Catholic authorities by the corporation in compensation. In 1799 the congregation was about 400. In 1846, during the ' mission ' given by Fr. Gaudentius, over 1,200 went to Holy Communion. New schools were built 1868-69. A site for a new church was acquired 1900.

Priests.

Rev. R. Thompson, 1798.
,, J. Blundell, 1799.
,, Wm. Keily, 1825.
,, Thos. Newsham, 1838.
,, Randolph Canon Frith, 1844.
,, Hy. Hopkins, 1879.
,, Fredk. Waterhouse, 1883.
,, James Abram, 1898.

STOCKPORT, CHESHIRE. St. Joseph's.

The foundation stone was laid March 19, 1861, and the building was opened June 25, 1862. Samuel Grimshaw, Esq., of Errwood Hall, gave £500 towards the building fund, to which Alderman Waterhouse contributed £133 and Canon Frith, of SS. Philip and James, £50. In 1882 a splendid painted window, costing £200, was erected at the part cost of John Evans, Esq. The high altar was decorated in November 1883, and the organ gallery extended.

N.B.—A temporary school was opened 1845. A second set of schools, costing £3,700, was erected 1858–59. Among the speakers at the inauguration of the building were Lord Edward Howard, M.P. (Arundel) and a Mr. Coppock, a prominent citizen who had signed the Stockport petition in favour of Catholic emancipation in 1829.

Priests.

Rev. P. Lahaye, 1862.
„ W. Fennelly, 1865.
„ J. Robinson, 1871.
„ T. Ratcliffe, 1889.
„ T. Canon Moloney, 1891.

STOCKTON-ON-TEES, DURHAM (*Hexham and Newcastle*). St. Mary.

The foundation of the mission is set down at 1783. A note of the register states that 'the Rev. Thomas Story died on Friday evening, 13 Sept. 1822, having recd. all the rites of the Church. *Req. in pace.*' The church was erected 1842.

Priests from 1822.

Rev. Joseph Curr.
„ Joseph Render, 1826.
„ C. Cornthwaite, 1848.
„ Richard Singleton, 1852.

Rev. Joseph Cullen, 1856.
„ John Carlile, here in 1871, and till 1899.
„ Robt. Taylerson, 1899 to date.

STOCKWELL, near CLAPHAM, LONDON, S.E. (*Southwark*). SS. Francis of Sales and Gertrude.

The church was built 1902–3, and Mass said there for the first time on Rosary Sunday 1903. The style is Romanesque, from the design of the late F. W. Tasker. The seating capacity of the building is for about 250. Fr. F. E. Pritchard is the incumbent of the mission, which largely owes its establishment to the generosity of an anonymous benefactress.

N.B.—Tradition asserts that Stockwell derives its name from St. Simon Stock (died 1265), who lived for many years in a hollow tree beside one of the many 'wells' or springs that once abounded in this neighbourhood.

STOKE NAYLAND, SUFFOLK. St. Edmund King and Martyr.

The ancient family of Giffard was long the mainstay of Catholicity in this district. Francis Giffard, Esq., was created a baronet by Charles I. in 1627, and several members of the family entered the Society of Jesus. The earliest missioner here was Fr. Wm. Copley, S.J. (1697). Fr. Francis Mannock, O.S.B., author of 'The Poor Man's Catechism,' died at Giffard Hall after many years' labour in the locality 1764. The last of the family was the Rev. Sir George Mannock, S.J. (1724–87), who was killed by the overturning of the

Dover mail-coach near Dartford while proceeding to France to end his days—as he imagined, not fore-seeing the impending Revolution—in peace. For greater security Sir George always dressed in the height of fashion, with ruffles, sword, &c. The last Jesuit priest at the Hall was Fr. Chas. Thompson, S.J. (1790). After the death of the last baronet the property passed to Wm. Comyns, Esq., and in 1819 to Patrick Power, Esq., both gentle-men taking the name of Mannock. In the descendants of the last-named the property now remains. In the autumn of 1842 Giffard Hall was leased from P. Mannock, Esq., by Bishop Wareing, and opened as the Seminary of St. Felix for ecclesiastical aspirants. The esta-blishment was removed to North-ampton in 1845. The Rev. Joseph North, afterwards Canon of South-wark and Missionary Rector of Greenwich, was the rector. A public chapel was erected in the parish of Stoke in 1826.

Priests at Stoke Nayland.

Rev. Michael Trovell, 1826.
„ Joseph North, 1840.
„ Mathias Lane, 1851.
„ Philip Murphy, 1888.
„ Geo. Miles, 1890 to date.

STOKE NEWINGTON, LONDON, N. (*Westminster*). Our Lady of Good Counsel.

A temporary church was opened January 12, 1888, by Bishop Weathers. Bishop Patterson preached on the Epiphany to a crowded congregation.

Priest.

Rev. H. Cutajar, 1891 and to date.

STOKE-ON-TRENT, STAFFS (*Bir-mingham*). Our Lady of Angels and St. Peter's Chains.

This mission would appear to have been started in 1841 from Lane End. The place at that time was described as 'a stronghold of protestantism, where the Catholic religion could not find a place to cover her head.' So rapid, how-ever, was the growth of the old religion that at a Catholic reunion held at the mission on Novem-ber 23, 1846, no fewer than 600 were present. The chapel was also declared to be too small for the congregation. In 1857 the present church, in the Gothic style, was erected. The building was con-secrated in 1885.

Priests.—Till 1850 the mission was served first from Lane End and then from Longton. The first resident priest was the Rev. W. Grosvenor, 1851 ; Jn. Dowling, 1855 ; J. S. Northcote, 1857 ; Francis Dent, before 1862 ; Laurence Peach, before 1874 ; J. S. Northcote, D.D. (second time), 1883. Canon North-cote, who is Provost of Birming-ham, is the well-known author of 'Mary in the Gospels,' and trans-lator of 'Roma Sotteranea'—a treatise on the Catacombs.

STOKESLEY, NORTHALLER-TON, YORKS (*Middlesbrough*). St. Joseph.

The mission was founded 1860. The temporary chapel was sup-planted in May 1873 by the exist-ing church (63 ft. by 24 ft.), designed by Goldie. £1,000 of the cost of erection was given by an anonymous benefactor. The mis-sion was formerly dedicated to St. Philip Neri.

Priests.

Rev. Wm. A. Wilson, 1860.

„ Lawrence McGonnell, 1877.

„ Patrick Hennessey, 1888.

„ John Coulon, 1890 to date.

Rev. E. S. Canon Bathurst (second time), 1882.

„ Francis Clayton, 1900 to date.

STONE, STAFFS (*Birmingham*). The Immaculate Conception and St. Dominic.

In 1823 a mission was established at Aston, two miles from Stone, and served first by a single priest, afterwards by Franciscans, and then by the Passionists. In 1843 Fr. Dominic, who received John Henry (afterwards Cardinal) Newman into the Church, hired a room in a public-house at Stone, and used this as a chapel on Sundays. The same year he started the Catholic schools, on a site given by James Beech, Esq., of Elmhurst House. In 1852 Mr. Beech, who was the chief Catholic of the place, gave some cottages near the school to the Dominican Sisters, who established a convent there. Next year the nave and aisles of the present spacious church of St. Dominic were opened for worship. The style is Pointed Gothic, from the design of Mr. E. Bird, of Hammersmith. The cost of the church, convent, and presbytery was upwards of £40,000. The church, which will accommodate about 700 persons, was consecrated on Wednesday, February 4, 1863, by Bishop Ullathorne.

Priests since 1850.

Mission served from Aston Hall till 1853.

Rev. W. Trenow, 1854.

„ Eyre Stuart Bathurst, 1858.

„ J. Maltus, 1862.

„ Lewis Thompson, 1876.

„ James Spencer Canon Northcote, 1879.

STONOR, HENLEY-ON-THAMES, OXFORDSHIRE (*Birmingham*). The Holy Trinity.

The chapel at Stonor is a pre-Reformation one, having been founded before the reign of King Henry VI. Stonor derives its name from the Stonor family of Stonor Park.[1] In 1383 Sir Thomas de Camoys was created Baron Camoys by Richard II., but the title was in abeyance from 1433 to 1839. During the reign of Elizabeth a secret printing-press for the publication of Catholic controversial works was set up at Stonor Park for a short time. Owing to the fidelity of the family to the ancient Church, the Faith was maintained at Stonor throughout the dreary years of persecution. The registers, however, only date from 1758. The first priest's name to be recorded is that of Fr. Joseph Strickland, in 1790. The next was Fr. Geo. Gildart, 1791, who was succeeded in 1796 by the Abbé J. B. Mortuaire. This priest held the chaplaincy till his death in

[1] The Stonor family has produced two ecclesiastics of note : (1) Monsignor Stonor, who resided in Rome in 1778 and wrote an able reply to some of the charges against Christianity brought by Gibbon in his *Decline and Fall* ; (2) the Hon. and Rt. Rev. Edmund Stonor, Archbishop of *Trebizond*, born 1831. His Grace, who is among the most distinguished of the foreign prelates in Rome, also holds the office of Dean of the Chapter of St. John Lateran.

September 1830. He was succeeded by Fr. C. Comberbach, latterly of St. Anne's Hill, Chertsey (*q.v.*). Fr. Henry Birks came in 1849, and held the incumbency for nearly twenty years. His successor was Fr. Alex. Comberbach. The next priest was Fr. John Ullathorne, who was succeeded in 1879 by Fr. Wm. Stone. Since then the priests have been:

Rev. Thos. Keates, 1883.
„ Austin Beech, 1887.
„ Hugh Taylor, 1889.
„ Wm. Dobell, 1890.
„ Hugh Taylor, 1898.
„ James O'Hanlon, 1899.
„ J. Emery, 1903.
„ James Perry, 1904 to date.

STONYHURST, near **BLACKBURN**, **LANCS** (*Salford*).

The original mansion of Stonyhurst formerly belonged to the ancient Catholic family of Shireburne. The last male representative of this stock was Sir Nicholas Shireburne, Bart., who died *circa* 1711. His estates passed to his only daughter, Maria Winifreda, Duchess of Norfolk, and after her death in 1768 to William Weld, Esq., of Lulworth Castle, Dorset. Upon the expulsion of the Jesuits and their pupils from the English College of Liège by the Revolutionists in 1794, Thomas Weld, Esq., who had studied under the Fathers, offered Stonyhurst to his old preceptors, and thus the old English Catholic school of St. Omer's and Liège returned to its native shores after a lapse of exactly 202 years. The college made rapid progress, and during the period of its existence in England has educated the sons of the prime Catholic nobility and gentry. Charles Waterton, the

naturalist, and Richard Lalor Sheil, the barrister and Parliamentary orator, were students here. The splendid Observatory became one of the Board of Trade's northern meteorological stations in 1865-6. The number of boys in residence at Stonyhurst averages about 300. The West or Community Wing was erected 1877-8. The centre block of class study and lecture rooms was opened 1883. The centenary of the foundation of the college in England was celebrated amidst great rejoicings in July 1894. From 1794 till 1797, the boys' chapel served also for the Catholics of the neighbourhood, but in the last-named year Fr. Wright converted the stables into a church for the people, and this continued to be the place of worship till the opening of the present church in 1835, during the rectorate of Fr. Richard Parker. The architect of the new building was J. J. Scoles, who based his design on the plan of King's College Chapel, Cambridge. The building was consecrated by Bishop Briggs, June 23, 1835, and opened with much pomp next day. The sanctuary and side altars were decorated by F. S. Barff in 1853. A new altar of great beauty—the anonymous gift of an old Stonyhurst boy—was used for the first time on Whit Sunday 1893. The treasury of Stonyhurst Church is rich in relics and antique 'church stuff.' Chief among these may be mentioned: (1) A thorn from Our Lord's Crown, formerly belonging to Mary Queen of Scots. (2) A relic of the True Cross, once kept in the Tower of London among the Royal jewels. It came into the possession of Fr. E. Lusher, S.J., who received it from Mrs. Pudsey, one of whose family was

Clerk of the Green Cloth. (3) A cap, seal, gold crucifix, and 'George,' once the property of the Blessed Thomas More. (4) Chalices used in the penal times. (5) A cope used by Henry VIII. at the Field of the Cloth of Gold. (6) A richly embroidered chasuble presented to St. Omer's by James II., &c. &c.

Rectors of Stonyhurst College.
Rev. Marmaduke Stone, 1794.
„ Nicholas Sewell, 1808.
„ John Weld, 1813.
„ Chas. Plowden, 1817.
„ Joseph Tristram, 1819.
„ Richard Norris, 1827.
„ Richard Parker, 1832.
„ James Brownbill, 1836.
„ Francis Daniel, 1839.
„ Andrew Barrow, 1842.
„ Richard Norris (second time), 1845.
„ Henry Walmesley, 1846.
„ Richard Sumner, 1847.
„ Francis Clough, 1848.
„ Joseph Johnson, 1861.
„ Chas. Henry, 1868.
„ Edward I. Purbrick, 1869.
„ Wm. Eyre, 1879.
„ Reginald Colley, 1885.
„ Herman Walmesley, 1891.
„ Joseph Browne, 1898.

STORRINGTON, SUSSEX (*Southwark*). Our Lady of England.

The Premonstratensian Order, expelled from St. Michael de Frigolet by the Ferry laws, opened a small house at Storrington in February 1882. About the same time the Duke of Norfolk generously gave the Fathers a site for a new monastery. A monumental cross to determine the site of the monastery was erected with much ceremony, Thursday, September 1882. In July 1887, the foundation of the new priory in the Gothic style, was laid by Mgr. James Carter. The health of the Queen, proposed by Captain Mostyn, of Arundel, was drunk amidst much applause and the playing of the National Anthem by the Storrington band. The monastery was opened by Bishop Butt, of Southwark, May 17, 1888. The High Mass was sung by Fr. Francis Bourne, of West Grinstead, now Archbishop of Westminster. The present church, in the Early English style, was opened November 22, 1904 ; Mr. E. Goldie was the architect.

STOURBRIDGE, WORCESTERSHIRE (*Birmingham*). Our Lady and All Saints.

The foundation of a permanent mission at Stourbridge dates from June 1823, though, several years before this, Fr. F. Martin hired a room for Mass on Sundays, when he used to come over from Oscott. He was succeeded by Fr. J. T. Barlow, the first resident priest. He built the chapel, and otherwise greatly improved the mission. His predecessor at the date of his first coming to Stourbridge found but *one* Catholic family in the place. In 1859 the congregation amounted to upwards of 1,300. As the chapel only held 250, the need of a new church was very pressing. A sufficient fund having been collected, the new church was opened by Bishop Ullathorne in September 1864. The style of the building is Decorated Gothic. The seating accommodation is for 700. The silver ornaments of the altar and tabernacle were executed by Evans, of Birmingham. Bishop Amherst, of Northampton, preached on the occasion of the opening (Gal. vi. 14).

The school accommodation of Stourbridge was so very defective that not more than eighty children could be provided for out of a number of 300, the remainder having to be turned away to grow up 'ignorant of everything except the language and vices in which the demon of the streets but too surely tutors them' (Rev. Walter Keen, of Stourbridge, *Tablet*, October 21, 1865). In consequence of this appeal new schools were shortly afterwards erected.

Priests since 1842.
Rev. Walter Keen, 1842.
„ Jas. McCave, 1876.
„ Joseph Daly, 1885.
„ F. Boulton, M.R., 1888 and to date.

STOWMARKET, SUFFOLK (*Northampton*). Our Lady of Seven Dolours.

In 1879 this mission was served from St. Mary's, Ipswich, when Mass was said on the last Sunday of the month at 11.45. In 1880 Fr. Francis Warmoll was appointed resident priest in charge of the school chapel. Fr. Warmoll established a club and library for men and boys, which was well attended. Fr. Chas. Flynn is the present rector.

STRATFORD, LONDON, E. (*Westminster*). St. Francis of Assisi.

This mission was founded as far back as 1770, though the baptismal registers only date from 1788. The chapel was afterwards removed to West Ham, on the very site where in pre-Reformation times stood the high altar of the old abbey church. In 1815 the Abbé J. F. Chevrollais,

an *émigré*, built a larger chapel 'near the turnpike' at Stratford. This good and zealous priest also established a school for upwards of 300 children. The chapel was dedicated to St. Patrick and St. Vincent of Paul. By 1859, the chapel had become far too small for the congregation, which numbered some 3,000 souls. The new church was erected in 1868, and placed in charge of the Franciscan Recollects. The fabric underwent an entire renovation in 1889. A school chapel, dedicated to St. Patrick, was opened as a chapel of ease to the church March 16, 1884, by Fr. Bede, O.S.F.

Priests since 1825.
Rev. P. J. Tyrrell.
„ J. Harrington, 1828.
„ Edmund Norris, 1830.
„ Anthony de Lima, 1844.
„ W. Smith, 1848.
„ W. Mills, 1850.
„ Jn. Moore, 1854.
„ James McQuoin, 1858.
„ David Mitchell, 1871.
„ Fr. Francis, O.S.F. (superior), 1875.
„ Fr. Aidan (guardian), 1883.
„ Fr. Cuthbert (guardian), 1891.
„ Fr. Antoine (guardian), 1894.
„ Fr. Peter (guardian), 1897.
„ Fr. Athanasius (guardian), 1904.

STRATFORD - ON - AVON, WARWICKSHIRE (*Birmingham*). St. Gregory the Great.

Fr. J. Short, of Wootton Wawen, who visited Stratford-on-Avon occasionally for some time prior to 1849, reported that 'there were many Catholics in the town and surrounding villages.' The nearest chapel was then nine miles distant. Fr. Short hired a room in the house of a recent convert, and said Mass there on Sundays. Bishop Walsh, Vicar Apostolic of the Midland District, took great interest in the new foundation, and shortly before his death he visited Stratford-on-Avon and blessed the chapel. In 1851, the place was still served from Wootton Wawen, but on September 19 of the following year, a chapel was opened, and placed under the direction of Fr. Alfred Dayman. This place of worship was superseded by the fine church in the Warwick Road, opened October 23, 1866.

Priests.

Rev. Alf. Dayman, 1852.
    (Vacant 1858.)
  ,, Chas. Hollahan, 1862.
  ,, Henry Lane, 1864.
  ,, Michael Sinnott, 1866.
  ,, W. Benedict Purton, 1870.
  ,, James Spears, 1877.
  ,, E. J. Stutter, 1879.
  ,, John Stuart, 1888.
  ,, Ar. O'Hare, O.S.B., here in 1891.
  ,, Geo. Fazakerley, 1892.
  ,, Bernard Thomas, O.S.B., 1897.
  ,, James Atherton, O.S.B., 1904.

STREATHAM, LONDON, S.W. (*Southwark*). The English Martyrs.

Russell House, Streatham, formerly used as a protestant institution, was fitted up as a Catholic mission-house, and Mass said there for the first time on Friday, May 6, 1888—the feast of the English Martyrs—by Canon McGrath, of Camberwell. The temporary chapel could accommodate about 100 persons. The building of the present handsome church of the English Martyrs was commenced on a site within the grounds of Russell House, and at the junction of the Mitcham and Tooting Bec Roads. The foundation stone was 'well and truly laid' by Bishop Butt, of Southwark, on May 4, 1892. The style of the church, which is very ornate, is fourteenth-century Gothic; seating for 650 persons. Above the arches of the nave are carved stone figures of the English martyrs. The east window and the others of the church are fitted with richly stained glass. The subjects of most of these are the martyrs of the Church. The donor of this truly magnificent church, which forms one of the ornamental buildings of Streatham, was R. Measures, Esq., a great benefactor of the mission. The church was opened by Cardinal Vaughan, Tuesday, May 4, 1893. His Eminence preached during the High Mass. Fr. W. Lloyd has been rector of the mission since its permanent foundation.

STRETFORD, MANCHESTER, LANCS (*Salford*). St. Anne, Chester Road.

Prior to 1859, this mission was served from Trafford Hall, the seat of the ancient Catholic family of Trafford. In the above year, a temporary chapel was opened at Stretford pending the erection of a new church. Provost Croskell was appointed resident priest (November 1859). The church, opened November 22, 1863, was the gift of Sir Humphrey de Trafford, Bart. The building, which cost £5,000, was designed by E. W. Pugin, in the Geometrical Decorated style of Gothic. The magnificent altar and reredos were given by Lady Annette de Trafford. Bishop Turner conse-crated the church June 18, 1867. Catholic population, 500 (1906).

Priests.

Rev. Provost Croskell, 1859.
(Served from Barton 1862.)
„ Matthias Canon Formby, 1864 till 1892.
„ John Canon Beesly, 1893.

STROOD, near **ROCHESTER**, **KENT** (*Southwark*).

A convent of nuns was opened here in the summer of 1904. The chapel is at present served by the Jesuit Fathers of Higham, and affords Mass and the Sacraments to Catholics of the locality, who hitherto had no mission nearer than Chatham. It is hoped that a school may shortly be opened in connection with the convent, as there are already some fifty Catho-lic children without means of in-struction in their own faith.

STROUD, **GLOUCESTERSHIRE** (*Clifton*). The Immaculate Con-ception.

The Dominicans started a mission at Stroud in February 1856, and the following May 27 Archbishop Errington laid the first stone of the church of the Immaculate Con-ception. The opening took place August 20, 1857. Fr. Bernard Morewood, O.P., the first priest of the mission, did much to extend Catholicity in the neighbourhood. By 1859 the mission contained a wooden church, convent, and day school, and when the Hon. and Rt. Rev. Bishop Clifford gave confirma-tion in April of that year there were over fifty candidates. In October 1888 the present church was com-menced, and completed 1889.

Priests.

Rev. Bernard Morewood, 1858.
„ Joseph Portley, 1861.
„ Robert Paul Stapleton, O.P., 1864.
„ F. Wilberforce, 1867.
„ Joseph Portley, 1874.
„ Cuthbert Wolseley, O.P., here in 1883.
„ E. Buckler, 1885.
„ Wilfrid Lescher, O.P., here in 1891.
„ Lawrence Peach, O.P., here in 1897.
„ Ambrose Smith, O.P., 1904.

STROUD GREEN, LONDON, N. (*Westminster*). St. Peter in Chains, Womersley Road.

In July 1892 the Catholics of Stroud Green, Crouch Hill, and Finsbury Park—about 200—were stated to be 'sadly in need of a church.' On August 31, 1893, a meeting was held at Hornsey Rise to consider the feasibility of starting a mission. Fr. Philip, rector of St. Joseph's Retreat, Highgate, presided. Stroud Green was even at this time largely a rural suburb, with cornfields on what are now 'slopes covered with houses.' The mission which re-sulted from the above-mentioned deliberations and exertions was made over to the Canons Regular of St. John Lateran, who have erected a fine church in the place. The building, designed by Canon Scoles, was opened Tuesday, Octo-ber 21, 1902.

STUDLEY, **WARWICKSHIRE** (*Birmingham*). St. Mary.

Mass was first said here August 6, 1851, but no mention of priest or mission is made till 1854. The church, in the Gothic style, was opened January 27, 1853. A new altar, reredos, and chancel were added to the church, December 1882, at the cost of an anonymous benefactor. In December 1885, three fine stone statues of the Sacred Heart, St. Joseph, and Our Lady were presented to the church by A. B. Wall, Esq., of Cheltenham.

Priests.

Rev. J. B. Duck, 1854.
„   Nicholas Hodgson, 1856.
„   Thos. Edmund Caldwell, 1862.
„   John Dunstan Breen, 1871.
„   Jn. Bernard Caldwell, 1879, and till 1891.
„   Bernard Romanus Thomas, 1892.
„   Essington Ross, 1893 and till after 1898.
„   Bernard Romanus Thomas, 1904.

SUDBURY, SUFFOLK (*Northampton*). Our Lady and St. John the Evangelist.

The ancient and knightly family of Martin of Long Melford, near here, maintained a chapel at their residence down to the apostasy of the then head of the family, about 1761. The present mission dates from 1880. The temporary chapel in Church Street was attended by Fr. Geo. Bampfield, founder of the Institute of St. Andrew. Bishop Riddell confirmed here for the first time November 15 of the same year. The present Gothic church was opened December 12, 1895. Under the building is a long hall, used occasionally for meetings &c.

Some Priests at Long Melford.

Rev. Jn. Vivian and Rev. Jn. Maddox, 1586.
„   John Martin, O.P., 1701.
„   Jn. Martin, S.J. (uncle), 1702.
„   Jn. Martin, O.P., 1705–12.
„   Jn. Martin, S.J., 1712–17.

Priests at Sudbury.

Rev. Geo. Bampfield, B.A., 1880.
„   V. d'Apreda, 1881.
„   Wm. Fippard, 1891.
„   Augustine Peacock, 1895 to date.

SUNBURY, MIDDLESEX (*Westminster*). St. Ignatius.

A mission was started here in 1861, and served from North Hyde. In 1864 it was served from Hounslow. During August 1867, Fr. J. Browne, who had recently been appointed priest of the place, appealed in the Catholic press for assistance to build a church. Next year, the present thirteenth-century-Gothic structure, consisting of nave, aisle, and chancel, was commenced. It was opened by Archbishop Manning, Trinity Sunday, 1869. The cost of erection was about £1,400. A census taken in 1868 estimated the Catholic population of Sunbury at 600–700. Fr. Browne was rector till after 1883. Fr. Jn. Davis was his successor. Fr. Thos. Davis is the present incumbent.

SUNDERLAND, DURHAM (*Hexham and Newcastle*). St. Mary.

In 1835 Fr. P. Kearney, of Maynooth, was appointed priest. The chapel and house, a neat brick building, 'too small for the congregation,' stood in a retired spot in Bridge Street, near the river. The congregation then numbered some 400. In 1844 a new chapel was built by Fr. Kearney. The Catholics of Sunderland then amounted to 600. The schools some time prior to this were put under the care of the Christian Brothers, who on February 24, 1846, were presented by the parents of the children with a handsome silver ciborium and folio missal in recognition of their excellent work. The fifty-first anniversary of the opening of St. Mary's was celebrated August 15, 1886. The Mayor of Sunderland was among those present at the High Mass, which was offered by Fr. Robert Kerr.

Priests.

Rev. P. Canon Kearney, 1835.
„ John Bamber, 1857.
„ P. Wade, 1876.
„ Chas. Turnerelli, 1879-97.
„ Thos. Smith, 1898 to date.

SUNDERLAND, DURHAM. St. Patrick's.

The church was commenced March 17, 1860, and opened early in 1861. Style, Early English; accommodation for 1,800.

Priests.

Rev. Wm. Markland, 1863.
„ Jos. Fawell, here 1872.
„ Jeremiah Foran, 1882 and till after 1898.
„ Mark Habell, 1904.

SURBITON, SURREY (*Southwark*). St. Raphael, Portsmouth Road.

The church was erected by the late Mr. Alex. Raphael, sometime M.P. for St. Albans. This gentleman, who died November 17, 1850, aged seventy-five, was created

shortly before his death a Knight of St. Sylvester by Pius IX. The church is in the 'Constantinian' style of architecture, from the design by Mr. Parker. It was opened in September 1850. The building, which was proprietary, passed by descent to the Countess of Mexborough, who, after a temporary disagreement with the Bishop of Southwark, during which time the church was closed, made final arrangements before her death by which the church was again opened for services (1898). The cost of the structure was £10,000, and another £1,500 was spent on internal decorations by the late Countess.

Priests.

Rev. Jeremiah Donovan, 1850.
„ H. Clark, 1852.
„ J. Ainsworth, 1855.
„ W. G. Morley, 1880.
„ Emile du Plerny, 1899 to date.

SUTTON, LANCS (*Liverpool*). St. Anne's.

The Passionist monastery and church of St. Anne were built in 1850 by John Smith, Esq., a wealthy railway contractor of Sutton. Mr. Smith died June 10, 1863, aged sixty-nine, and was buried in the crypt of the church, which was opened in October 1853. The schools were built in 1867, and enlarged in 1870 and 1884. The stations of the Cross were erected in 1893 by Wm. Borrows, Esq., in memory of his brother. The new Lady Altar and statue, put up in 1894, were given by R. Grimshaw, Esq. The bodies of Fr. Dominic, who received Cardinal Newman into the Church, and the Hon.

Fr. Ignatius Spencer, are buried beneath the chapel of St. Paul of the Cross.

SUTTON, SURREY (*Southwark*). Our Lady of the Rosary.

In 1881 the Premonstratensian Fathers opened a mission in the Cheam Road, and in February 1882 an iron chapel was erected. Mass was said on the 16th by Canon David, of Croydon, and Bishop Patterson preached (St. Luke viii. 5). The Premonstratensians resigned the mission towards the end of the year, when Fr. D. Ferris, D.D., was appointed. The present church, in the Carshalton Road, was opened in 1887. It was originally intended for a school, but this having been provided by the nuns of the Carshalton Convent (Daughters of the Cross), the architect, Mr. Ingress Bell, ingeniously altered his plan to suit the present purpose. The Catholic population of Sutton is about 450.

Priests.

Rev. D. Ferris, D.D., 1882.
„   J. Hayes, 1899.
„   J. Canon Keatinge, 1904.
„   H. Canon Cafferata, 1905.

SUTTON COLDFIELD, WARWICKSHIRE (*Birmingham*). The Holy Family.

The church was opened October 21, 1834. The style is simple Gothic. The High Mass at the opening was celebrated by Fr. Pope. Dr. Weedal, of Oscott, preached. The site was obtained from a society of 'General Bap-

tists,' a 'neat presbytery' being erected about the same time.

Priests.

Rev. J. Moore, 1835–52.
        (Served from Oscott 1853 and 1855.)
„   J. B. Gowing, 1856.
„   John Harkness, 1858, and till 1882.
        (Vacant 1883.)
„   James Rigby, 1885 and to date.

SUTTON PARK, near **GUILDFORD, SURREY** (*Southwark*). St. Edward the Confessor.

This notable house was erected between 1520 and 1530 by Sir Richard Weston, a devoted supporter of Queen Catherine of Aragon, whose badge yet remains carved and sculptured on many parts of the old house. Sir Richard, who was a Knight of the Bath and Under-Treasurer of England, accompanied King Henry VIII. to the 'Field of the Cloth of Gold.' In spite of this and other marks of the royal favour, one of his sons was executed in 1536 for an alleged intrigue with Anne Boleyn. Sir Henry Weston, son of this latter unfortunate gentleman, enjoyed the friendship of Queen Elizabeth, who more than once visited Sutton Park. She even allowed Sir Henry to retain a priest in his house, for the Westons were staunch Catholics. The old house still stands almost as Sir Richard erected it. The last of the Westons was Melior Mary, who died in 1782. She bequeathed the estate to John Webbe, Esq., a near relation, who thereupon assumed the additional name of Weston. The estates are now owned by the Salvins, another old

Catholic family, who inherited them from the Webb-Westons. According to tradition, Mass had been continuously said, ' more or less openly,' at Sutton Park till the opening of the new church in the Park in 1876. The priests in charge of the mission acted outwardly as bailiffs of the family, ' by reason of the laws.' Their names and dates of service and death are preserved among the archives of the mission. After the French Revolution several of the *émigré* clergy did duty here. One of them subsequently became Archbishop of Tours. Several are buried in Merrow Churchyard, others at Send and at Sutton Place. Among the various items of ' church stuff ' preserved at Sutton Park are a chasuble-cross worked with a curious picture of Sutton Park as it was in the sixteenth century, a processional cross, and big bell dated 1530. During the rectorship of Fr. Sidden, a pre-Reformation sanctus bell was stolen from the chapel by burglars (1840). In 1867, Fr. J. D. Mooney was priest here, and in 1869 Fr. Ed. Cahill, brother of the present Bishop of Portsmouth (1904). Canon Lalor was the next priest (1871); Fr. Timothy Donovan in 1872; Fr. Robert Smith in 1873; Fr. Reynaert in 1874. The present church, in the Gothic style, was built between September 20, 1875, and September 27, 1876, when it was solemnly opened by Bishop Danell. The architect was Mr. James Harris, of Woking. The Lady Altar was built by Captain and Mrs. Charles Salvin, in memory of their daughter. Fr. Reynaert was succeeded in 1878 by Fr. Malpas, who the same year was superseded by the Rev. Dr. Conway, who remained in charge of the church till 1903. His successor was Fr.

H. Clutton. Fr. H. Hinsley, D.D., is the present rector.[1]

SWANAGE, DORSET (*Plymouth*). The Holy Ghost and St. Edward K.M.

For some short time prior to 1903 the mission was served from Spettisbury, the chapel being at Sunnydown. On Tuesday, August 9, 1904, a handsome church was opened by Abbot Allaria, of the Canons Regular, by whom the mission is served. The church is erected on the De Mulham estate.

SWINBURN, NORTHUMBERLAND (*Hexham and Newcastle*). St. Mary.

Swinburn Castle, the seat of the ancient Catholic family of Riddell, was one of the places served by the Jesuit Fathers from the ' College ' or residence of St. John the Evangelist, Durham. The district, for greater security, was known as ' Mrs. Durham,' but we have not been able to discover any items relating to the early history of the Swinburn mission. Priests have been stationed here regularly since 1690. During many years of the eighteenth century the chapel was served by Fr. Nicholas Saunderson,

[1] The late owner of Sutton Park, Captain Salvin, discovered in the priests' hiding-place in the basement a case of relics containing the bones of St. William, Archbishop of York, the Blessed Cuthbert Mayne, protomartyr of Douai (1578); likewise some old warrants of 1591 authorising the searching of recusants' houses for priests, a fine old pewter chalice, &c. The house and estate of Sutton Park are at present rented by Lord Northcliff (Sir Alfred Harmsworth).

C C

who died at Alnwick 1790. The present church was erected in 1841, and is in the Gothic style.

Priests since 1825.

Rev. James Higginson.
„ James Prest, 1829.
„ Peter Allanson, 1831.
„ E. Glassbrook, 1876.
„ Raphael Nenci, D.D., 1882 to date.

SWINDON, WILTS (*Clifton*). The Holy Rood.

A room was hired for Mass on Sundays by the Bishop of Clifton, 1851. In 1858 Catholics numbered 150. A site for a church was procured that year with much difficulty, as prejudice against Catholics was very great. A school chapel was opened in 1859, but as late as 1881 a debt of £450 lay on the mission. A census of Catholics in 1882 returned the number at 300. 'The St. John's Free Christian Church' was acquired in 1881, and opened as a Catholic place of worship by Bishop Clifford February 8, 1882. A noteworthy sermon was preached during the Mass by Father Grant, S.J., on the ecclesiastical glories of Swindon in Catholic times. This adapted building having become inadequate, the present church was commenced in 1904, and opened 1905. During the building a temporary place of worship was fitted up in Holy Rood Hall.

Priests.

From 1851 to 1856 the mission was served from Fairford.

Rev. Jas. Clarke, 1857.
„ John Corbishley, 1872.
„ Jn. Kennedy, 1874.
„ Herman Eikerling, here in 1883.

Rev. W. Otty, here in 1888.
„ James Lonergan, 1892 to after 1898.
„ James O'Shaughnessy, 1904.

SWINTON, MANCHESTER (*Salford*). St. Mary of the Immaculate Conception.

This stone Gothic church, consisting of nave, chancel, and two chapels, to accommodate 700 persons, was built at the expense of Daniel Lee, Esq., K.St.G., and opened by Bishop Turner August 14, 1859. Mr. Chas. Holt was the architect. Canon Wood, who was rector from 1877 to 1901, did much to consolidate local Catholicity, and, moreover, obtained 'many concessions and privileges' for the Catholic children in the Swinton Industrial Schools.

Priests.

Rev. Peter de Blon, 1863.
„ James Hayes, 1866.
„ Chas. Wood, 1877.
„ A. O'Rourke, 1893 to date.

SWYNNERTON PARK, STAFFS (*Birmingham*). Our Lady of the Assumption.

The estate came to the Fitzherbert family by the marriage of Wm. Fitzherbert, Esq., with Elizabeth, daughter and co-heiress of Humphrey Swynnerton, Esq., *circa* 1551. Prior to the erection of the present church (November 1868–1869) the chapel was in the Hall. The style of the new building is between Early English and Decorated, from design by Gilbert Blount. The plan includes a chancel, aisle, belfry, and tribune for the family. Cost of erection, about £4,000. Our Blessed Lady and St. Thomas the Apostle was the ancient title of the mission.

Rectors since 1824.

Rev. — Jones, 1823 (?)
„ Wm. Richmond, 1826.
„ Jn. Harkness, 1844.
„ Hy. Walker, 1857.
„ Thos. Revill, 1861.
„ Wm. Butler, 1867.
„ Geo. Smith, 1879 to date.

SYDENHAM, LONDON, S.E.
(*Southwark*). Our Lady and St. Philip.

Mass was first said here in recent times in the house of a Spanish resident, and on March 17, 1872, a temporary iron church was opened by Canon A. Bethell. For several years the mission served Beckenham, Penge, &c. A portion of the present church was opened Tuesday, December 12, 1882, by Bishop Coffin, of Southwark. Fr. W. Addis was incumbent at this time. The church (thirteenth-century Gothic) was designed by Mr. F. A. Walters. Fr. Joseph Minnett, the present rector, succeeded Fr. M. Gifkins (now of South Bermondsey) in 1893. The St. Philip's mixed schools accommodate about 100 pupils.

T

TADCASTER, YORKS (*Leeds*). St. Joseph.

A temporary chapel was established here in 1865. In 1868 the congregation was estimated to be about 300. The present church was opened August 31, 1869, by Bishop Cornthwaite, of Beverley. The style is fourteenth-century Gothic, from design by Goldie. Fr. P. Vavasour contributed most of the building fund. The mission was served from Hazelwood till 1897, when the Rev. Jn. Bradley, the present rector, was appointed.

TAMWORTH, STAFFS (*Birmingham*). St. John the Baptist.

The Comberford family, of Comberford Hall, two miles from Tamworth, had a chapel and priest during the epoch of the penal laws. The last member of this ancient family, Captain Comberford, a Royalist officer in the great Civil War, *temp.* Charles I., died in 1671. The Catholics of Tamworth were then ministered to by Fr. A. Bromwich, of Oscott. Mass was occasionally said at Tamworth, first in the house of Mr. Cowley, a weaver, and afterwards at Mr. Birch's, a basket-maker. The mission became once more independent in 1789, when a chapel was erected. In

1829 Fr. Kirk, of Lichfield, built a chapel, in the Grecian style, on a site procured from Sir Robert Peel. It was opened June 24, 1830, by Bishop Walsh. For some years the mission was served alternately from Lichfield and Oscott. Fr. J. Kelly, who died March 19, 1876, was rector for fifty years. On Sunday, June 27, 1880, the fiftieth anniversary of the dedication of the church was celebrated, and in commemoration of this event the fabric of the church was completely renovated and restored. A new pulpit was erected in the church, August 1906.

Priest since 1876.
Rev. Henry Norris, 1876 to date.

TARPORLEY, CHESHIRE (*Shrewsbury.*) *See* APPENDIX.

TAUNTON, SOMERSET (*Clifton*). St. George.

A chapel was opened in East Street, Taunton, in 1782 by Fr. G. Baudoin. In June 1808, some Franciscan nuns founded the convent of Our Lady of the Seven Dolours, near the town. They preserve in their chapel the arm-bone of the Ven. Thos. Bullaker, O.S.F., who suffered for the Faith at Exeter in 1642.[1] In 1821 a large chapel was opened by Bishop Baines (July 3). Thos. Clifton, Esq., of Lytham, defrayed the cost of erection. This building was superseded by the present church, in the Decorated Gothic style, opened by Bishop Vaughan in April 1860. The splendid east window was the gift of G. Maycock, Esq. Canon John Mitchell was priest of the church from 1852 to 1899, when he was succeeded by Canon Iles. Fr. G. Bailey is the present rector.

TEIGNMOUTH, DEVON (Plymouth). Our Lady and St. Patrick.

The Abbé Le Prêtre and the Abbé Le Verrier ministered to the Catholics of Teignmouth from about 1794 till their return to France — the first in 1803 and the second in 1815. After this Ugbrooke Park, the seat of Lord Clifford of Chudleigh, was the nearest mission. In April 1848 Fr. C. Lomax hired a room at West Teignmouth, and said Mass there on Sundays. In July 1854 the first stone of the new church was laid. C. Hansom drew the plans, and much of the cost of erection was defrayed by the Hon. W. Stourton. The building was opened in December 1854 by Bishop Errington, of Plymouth. Fr. H. Brigham, S.J., was the first priest. In 1878 (July 4) a new church was erected close to the site of the old edifice, which had been purchased by the Great Western Railway Company for extension purposes. Messrs. Hansom were the architects, the cost of erection being about £4,000. The high altar was

presented by Lord and Lady Clifford of Chudleigh, the Lady Chapel by Mrs. Tozer, the bell and pulpit by the late Miss Dease. The bell-turret was built at the expense of Mrs. Homes. The organ was acquired in January 1882.

Priests since 1866.

Rev. Patrick O'Brien, 1866.
„ John Parker, 1888.
„ Wm. Dawson, here in 1891 and to date.

TEIGNMOUTH, DEVON. St. Joseph's.

The Redemptorists purchased Buckeridge House, Teignmouth, in 1875, as the novitiate of the congregation. In 1880 the present building was erected. Bishop Coffin, of Southwark, who was a member of the congregation, is buried in the cemetery adjoining (April 1885). A few years ago the house was acquired by the Sisters of Notre Dame, who have opened a high school for girls.

TEWKESBURY, GLOUCESTERSHIRE (Clifton). St. Joseph.

The Wakeman family, whose ancestral seat was at Beckford, about five miles from Tewkesbury, had a chapel in their house during the times of persecution. Sir Geo. Wakeman, M.D., physician to Queen Catherine of Braganza, who was tried for his life during the Oates plot, was a member of this family. The mission was alternately served by Benedictines and Jesuits. Fr. Isaac Gibson, S.J., died here in 1738, and was succeeded by the Hon. and Rev. Jn. Dormer, S.J. Dom Placid Bennet, O.S.B., was here from 1783 to 1792. Then secular clergy served the mission till 1831, when the Benedic-

[1] He was arrested while saying Mass at the house of Mrs. Powell, daughter of Sir Henry Browne, son of the Lord Viscount Montague.

tines were again restored. When the Kemerton mission (*q.v.*) was started, the domestic chapel at Beckford would appear to have ceased to be used by externs. The Kemerton church (opened July 18, 1843) was the nearest Catholic place of worship till 1870, when the present church in The Mythe was opened by the Bishop of Clifton.

Priests since 1843.

Rev. S. Day, 1843.
„   P. Ridgeway, 1848.
„   Thos. Fenn, 1879 to date.

THATTO HEATH, LANCS (*Liverpool*). St. Augustine's.

A school chapel was opened 1894. The present church, in the Early English style, for 450 persons, was commenced August 21, 1905, from designs by E. Quirke. Fr. Joseph Walmsley is the first and present rector.

THETFORD, SUFFOLK (*Northampton*). St. Mary.

This town, which is partly in Norfolk and partly in Suffolk, was anciently the seat of a bishopric, removed to Norwich 1096. The place was formerly the burial-place of the Dukes of Norfolk, the last to be interred here being Thos. Howard, Earl of Surrey, the victor of Flodden Field, who died 1524. After the Reformation, the town was visited from time to time by the Jesuits, but no record of a regular mission appears to exist (Foley, ' Records, S.J ,' Series XII.). The present mission was started about November 1825 by Fr. John Holden, who remained here till the close of 1839, when he left to join the Society of Jesus. His farewell address to his congrega-

tion was published in the *Orthodox Journal* for February 29, 1840. The chapel and mission-house were erected by this excellent and zealous priest. New schools were started June 1879. Lord and Lady Clifford and the late Madame Lyne-Stephens were great benefactors to the mission.

Priests since 1840.

Rev. R. Gates, 1839.
„   M. Lane, 1845.
„   — Quinlevan, 1849.
„   Jn. Taylor, 1851.
„   Walstan Smith, 1876.
„   Peter Ward, 1882.
„   Geoffrey Brennan, 1884 to date.

THIRSK, YORKS (*Middlesbrough*). All Saints.

The site was purchased March 1865, and the church opened May 23, 1867, by Bishop Cornthwaite, of Beverley. Style, Early English ; dimensions, 81 ft. by 25 ft. ; cost of erection, £1,500. Stations of the Cross were presented by John Wallis, Esq. For the earlier history of local Catholicity in the district, *see* KILVINGTON.

Priests.

Rev. M. Fryer, 1865.
„   Luke Burke, 1870.
„   Alfred Galli, 1877.
„   C. Trant, 1879.
„   E. Kennedy, 1882.
„   Thomas Canon Holland, 1885.
„   Lawrence McGonnell, 1888.
„   Chas. Donovan, 1890.
„   Geoffrey Cremer, 1902.

THORNABY - ON - TEES, YORKS (*Middlesbrough*).

Formerly known as South Stockton. Site for church and schools was obtained, and a temporary chapel erected 1871. By 1875 a school chapel had been built.

Priests.

Rev. Wm. Breitbach, 1871

„ Gerald Canon Shanahan, 1877 to date.

THORNDON HALL, ESSEX. *See* **BRENTWOOD.**

THORNLEY, DURHAM (*Hexham and Newcastle*). St. Godric.

This locality has been well described as a place ' consecrated by the sufferings and sacrifices of our Catholic forefathers during the enforcement of the penal enactments.' In those times Catholics used to hear Mass in a rude chapel cut in the limestone rock in Glen Hardwick. Traces of the ledge used as an altar were visible in 1850, but the place was then in a dangerous condition. The Maire family of Hardwick kept a priest and priest's hiding-place in an attic chimney of the house. The present church was built in 1850, and opened by Bishop Hogarth in September of that year. Fr. R. Suffield, priest of the mission, sang the Mass. For some years the mission was served alternately with Sedgefield.

Priests.

Rev. W Markland, 1856.

„ Henry Wrennall, 1858. (Served from Sedgefield 1862.)

„ James Crolly, 1864.

„ Joseph Kennedy, 1866.

„ James Ross, 1872.

„ Jeremiah Foran, here in 1875.

„ John Baptist Bulletti, 1882.

„ James Smits, 1888 and till 1897.

„ M. J. Haggarty, 1898.

„ Wm. Toner, 1903 to date.

THORNTON HEATH, LONDON, S.W. (*Southwark*).

The West Croydon mission was sometimes referred to as the Thornton Heath mission in the early sixties of last century. The district, then quite country, is now almost covered with houses. The present church, in the Beulah Road, was formerly a dissenting place of worship known as ' The Temple,' and was erected by an ex-Freemason. The mission was opened in May 1905. Fr. Edward Mostyn, rector.

THROPTON, NORTHUMBERLAND (*Hexham and Newcastle*). All Saints.

The mission is said to have been founded in 1700, but we have come across no details of its early history. Fr. John Midford, the second priest at Thropton, died about 1750. Fr. Lucas Potts succeeded him, and remained till his death, August 16, 1787. His successor, Fr. Robt. Hensworth, came August 22, 1788. The Hall, where presumably the chapel stood, was pulled down June 4, 1811. Fr. Thos. Stout came on the mission here 1797, and died July 26, 1828, aged sixty-two. The next priests are:—

Rev. Joseph Albot, 1829.

„ Geo. Corless, D.D., 1840 till 1852.

(Mission vacant 1852.)

„ Jas. Hubbersty, 1853.

„ Thos. Ord, 1866.

„ Francis Hogan, 1901.

The foundation of the present church is due to the Robson family of Thropton Hall. One of the stock, Matthew Robson, had a horse, valued at £7, taken from him by the Jacobites in 1715, for which compensation was paid him at

Alnwick Sessions. Another, Geo. Robson, built Thropton Bridge, 1810–11. Fr. Joseph Robson, another of the family, died at Hethe, August 26, 1870.

THURNHAM, LANCS (*Liverpool*). SS. Thomas and Elizabeth. Fr. J. Swarbrick was priest here about 1711. He was arrested at the time of the Jacobite rising of 1715, and sentenced to death March 1716, but died the day before the one fixed for execution. He laboured with great zeal among his fellow prisoners, many of whom were Catholics. The old chapel, ' a conventicle-looking building,' was erected 1810. The present church was commenced March 1847, and consecrated by Bishop Brown, V.A., August 29, 1848. £1,000 of the building fund required was collected by Fr. Thos. Crowe, and the rest was generously made up by Miss Dalton of Thurnham Hall.

Priests.

Rev. J. Foster, 1785.
„ Thos. Crowe, 1824.
„ J. Shepherd, 1848.
„ W. Ball, 1852.
„ J. Swarbrick, 1857.
„ R. Billington, 1889.
„ T. Keeley, 1889.
„ P. Byrne, 1895 to date.

TICHBORNE, HANTS (*Portsmouth*). St. Margaret of Scotland. The ancient Catholic family resident here since Saxon times is said to derive its name from *de Ytchingborne* (or of ' the Itching River '). In the reign of Henry I.

Sir Roger Tichborne married Mabella, heiress of Lymerston, Isle of Wight, the originator of the famous ' Tichborne Dole,' or annual gift of bread to the poor, since commuted to alms in money. The baronetcy of the family dates from the time of James I., who conferred that honour on Sir Benjamin Tichborne. A regular mission has been maintained here since about 1633, when it was included in the Jesuit circuit of St. Thomas of Canterbury, known for security as ' Mrs. Hants.' Fr. Robt. Tempest, S.J., was here 1636–40, and Fr. Robt. Hill, S.J., 1669–92. This latter priest figures in the picture of the ' Dole ' by Tilbourg preserved at Tichborne House. Several members of the family were priests of the Society— viz. Sir John Tichborne, S.J., 1743; Fr. Michael Tichborne, 1751; Fr. John Tichborne, 1772. Several priests of the Franciscan Order also served the mission during the eighteenth century, as Fr. Paul Atkinson, 1698; Frs. John Beaumont and Ravenhill, 1758. In recent times the chaplains have been as follows:—

Rev. C. Peters, 1824.
„ Laurence Byron, 1831.
„ Henry Philips, 1833.
„ Jn. Tilt, 1846.
„ Amadeus Guidez, 1851.
„ Eugene Reardon, 1853.
„ Jn. Fegan, 1860.
„ Joseph Styles, 1863.
„ Thos. Quinn, 1866.
„ Francis Weale, 1882.
„ Jn. Wyse, 1885.
„ Jn. Trumble, 1892.
„ Laurence Doran, 1897.
„ Louis Canon Hall, 1899 to date.

TIDESWELL, DERBYSHIRE (*Nottingham*). The Immaculate Heart of Mary.

The mission was started on Saturday, September 12, 1885, and the next day Bishop Bagshawe, of Nottingham, made his first visitation of the temporary chapel which was set up in Bagshawe Hall. In April 1886 the first chapel was found to be too small, and another was fitted up in the 'Middle Room of the "Rising Sun" Factory.' The Catholic school was opened by Fr. J. J. Hooker, the resident priest, in October 1887. The number of Catholics at Tideswell in 1882 is said to have been only three. In 1887 it was over thirty. Eight children entered the school on the day of opening. Fr. Hooker was rector till after 1894. In 1897 the mission was served from Matlock Bridge. Fr. Thos. Parkinson was rector 1898. In 1904 the mission was served from Hathersage.

TILBURY, ESSEX (*Westminster*). Our Lady Star of the Sea.

At the commencement of 1887, Cardinal Manning placed Canon Keens, of Grays, 'under obedience to begin at once the building of a school chapel for the poor children and people at Tilbury.' The first stone of the school chapel was laid Tuesday, May 24, 1887, by Canon Keens. The building was opened in September the same year by Cardinal Manning. From 1891 till 1898 the mission was served from Grays. Fr. Joseph Upton is the present rector.

TISBURY, WILTS (*Clifton*). The Sacred Heart.

The church was opened in 1898 on a site between the railway station and High Street, given by Lady Arundell of Wardour. The foundation stone was laid October 13, 1897, by the Bishop of Clifton. The style is Early English. The stone and marble used in the construction were presented by Lord and Lady Arundell. Architect, Canon Scoles, of Yeovil. Exclusive of altars and fittings, the cost of erection was about £1,750. The solemn opening took place Thursday, November 3, 1898. The mission is served from Wardour.

TIVERTON, DEVON (*Plymouth*). St. John.

The Chichesters of Arlington persevered in the Faith of their forefathers until the representative of this ancient family, John Palmer Chichester, read his recantation in Exeter Cathedral, about the year 1795. After this, his brother Charles, a staunch Catholic, retired to Calverleigh, and opened a chapel there. One of the chaplains, the Abbé Jean Moutier, left a fund for the endowment of a mission at Tiverton. The first stone was laid by Bishop Baines, September 6, 1836. On May 13, 1838, Mass was said in the schoolroom, and the church was opened for worship May 19, 1839.

Priests.

Rev. Hy. Innes, left 1795 (last chaplain at Arlington; died at Ballogie, N.B., 1833, æt. 86).

„ Abbé H. Marquant, 1802.

„ Abbé Renoult, 1808.

„ Paul Fournier, 1811.

„ Jean Moutier, 1819.

Rev. Barnabé Yraizoz, 1831.
„ Jas. Lyons, 1835.
„ Thos. Costello, 1837.
„ Thos. Danson, 1842.
„ Thos. Rooker, 1842.
„ Herbert Woolett, 1846.
„ Thos. Shattock, 1846.
„ Wm. Sheehy, 1846.
„ Hy. Reily, 1848.
„ Hy. Keary, 1848.
„ Jn. Fanning, 1848.
„ Jn. Ryan, 1850.
„ Michael Carroll, 1850.
„ Thos. Fenn, 1863.
„ Joseph Bunn, 1867.
„ David Coleman, 1874.
„ Francis Gallini, 1877.
„ David Coleman, 1879.
„ Bernard Wade, 1885.
„ William Walsh, 1888.
„ E. Damen, 1904.

TODMORDEN, LANCS (*Salford*).
St. Joseph.
The church was opened October 4, 1868, and has at present (1906) a congregation of about 500.
Priests.
Rev. Thos. Francis Kelly, 1868.
„ Henry Dobbelaire, 1874.
„ C. Huybers, 1879.
    (Vacant 1883.)
„ Salvatore Carruccio, 1884.
„ Thos. Chronnell, 1890.
„ P. Joyner, 1892.
„ J. Willemse, 1893.
„ Thos. Durnan, 1895.
„ Francis Oakes, 1903.
„ Hermann Bruning, 1904 to
    date.

TONBRIDGE, KENT (*Southwark*).
Corpus Christi.
There were reported to be many Catholic labourers in this district 1839-40. The existing mission, however, only dates from 1896, when a temporary chapel was opened in the Waterloo Road, and served from Tunbridge Wells. The church in Lyons Crescent, opened 1904, was built by Mrs. Fenwick, and is a good example of Romanesque. Accommodation for about 200.
Priests.
Rev. Geo. Scott, 1900.
„ James Walsh, 1904.

TOOTING, LONDON, S.W. (*Southwark*).
Till about 1897, the chapel of St. Joseph's College, Upper Tooting Park, served the Catholics of the locality for Mass. On the removal of the college to Denmark Hill, Mass was said every Sunday at Holly Lodge, the residence of — Stowel, Esq., by Fr. R. Bullesbach, of Balham. About 1899 Fr. Bullesbach came to live at Tooting. A chapel was opened at Hereford Lodge, a large, old-fashioned mansion in the Mitcham Road, which also served as the presbytery. The much-needed Catholic schools were opened by Bishop Bourne, of Southwark, in 1903. The number of Catholics at Tooting is about 2,000, the population of late years having greatly increased owing to the building in the neighbourhood of thousands of small houses, which have turned a rural outskirt of London into a densely populated suburb. The number of children attending the school is about 400. Fr. Wm. Allanson, D.D., rector since 1904, was succeeded in September 1906 by Fr. G. Williams, late of Walworth.

TORQUAY, DEVON (*Plymouth*).
The Assumption.

Tor Abbey (Premonstratensian) passed after the Reformation into the possession of the Earls of Londonderry, one of whom sold it in 1678 to Sir George Cary, a devout Catholic, and partisan of Charles I. in the then recent Civil War. The chapel of Tor Abbey served the Devonshire Catholics for miles round. John Britton and Edward Wedlake Brayley, in their 'Beauties of England and Wales,' vol. iv., thus describe the chapel as it was in 1803 : 'The Roman Catholic chapel attached to the house [Tor Abbey] is ornamented with a superb altar and paraphernalia, on each side of which are paintings ; one represents the Crucified Saviour, the other the Blessed Virgin. The end of this chapel projecting into the garden is completely vested with ivy.' This latter was probably one of the secretive precautions of the penal times, then just past. The mission was long served by the Jesuits. The chapel was rebuilt 1779. Fr. McDonnell, who was incumbent here in 1842, is said to have found the congregation 'only a handful.' By 1850 Torquay had become a fashionable watering-place. A site for a church was given by Robt. Cary, Esq., of Tor Abbey, and on April 3, 1853, the first stone was laid by Bishop Errington, of Plymouth. The building (Decorated Gothic) was consecrated February 17, 1854. C. Hansom was the architect.

Priests since 1670.
Rev. Robt. Hill, *alias* Turner, 1670.
  ,, Jn. Lewis, *alias* Kemys, 1685.
  ,, — Vincent, 1709.
  ,, Jn. Beaumont, 1739 (?)
  ,, Ch. Needham, 1745.
  ,, Jn. Halford, 1788.
  ,, Abbé Thebault, 1796 (?)

Rev. Abbé Moriland, 1800.
  ,, Abbé Michel.
  ,, Abbé Gabriel Le Hericy, 1808.
  ,, Abbé Normand, 1816.
  ,, Abbé Jean Coupé, 1817.
  ,, Wm. Pursell, 1820.
  ,, Jn. M'Enery, 1822.
  ,, Jn. Williams, 1830.
  ,, Jn. Larkan, 1834.
  ,, Jn. M'Donnell, 1834.
  ,, — Griffiths, 1834.
  ,, Abbé Signole, 1836.
  ,, Ch. Fisher, 1839.
  ,, Pat. Woods, 1841.
  ,, Wm. Sheehy, 1844.
  ,, Thos. Danson, 1846.
  ,, Maurice Canon Power, 1846.
  ,, Edw. Canon Windeyer, 1860.
  ,, Joseph Bunn, 1874.
  ,, John A. Charles, 1877.
  ,, Geo. Canon Poole, 1888 to date.

TOTNES, DEVON (*Plymouth*).
Our Lady and St. George.

In 1788 Edward Cary, Esq., purchased the Follaton estate, near Totnes, and made it his residence. A chapel was opened in the house, and here the Rev. Charles Timings officiated from 1801 till his death in 1832, aged seventy-five. The next priests were : Revs. James Larkin, 1836 ; Henry Philips, 1837; P. A. Hogan, 1838 ; W. Carrol, 1840 ; Canon Robt. Platt, 1846. This latter remained till 1860, after which the chapel appears to have been closed. In 1898 Fr. Wilfrid Schneider, O.S.B., started a mission at Totnes. Mass was at first said at Follaton House, but in 1901 a site was obtained and a temporary chapel erected 1902. A wooden bell-tower was added in August 1906. The mission is served from Buckfastleigh Abbey.

TOTTENHAM, LONDON, N. (*Westminster*). St. Francis of Sales.

At the close of the eighteenth century Tottenham became noted for the number of its lodging-houses, chiefly frequented by persons from Ireland. In 1792 many French emigrants took up their abode here. In 1793 the Abbé Cheireux, afterwards Cardinal Archbishop of Bordeaux, being at this time tutor to a protestant family at Tottenham, hired a house in Tottenham Terrace, Queen Street, where he said Mass on Sundays till his departure for America in 1796. The Abbé Filiaires, his successor, died in 1801. The Abbé Salmon, who took his place, soon went to Chatham, but the Abbé Le Tellier, who came next, erected, at his own expense, a large chapel in Queen Street. This, in 1826, was superseded by another chapel, in Chapel Place, White Hart Lane, erected by the Countess de Montesquieu. The solemn opening took place on May 6, 1827. Fr. T. H. Ewart was priest of Tottenham from 1827 till his death, March 29, 1856. In September 1880, the chapel was broken into, and the sacred vessels stolen. By this time the building had become 'old and unsafe.' The first stone of the new church was laid in August 1881 by Cardinal Manning. F. W. Tasker was the architect. The cost of erection was about £1,900.

Priests since 1856.

Rev. Hilarius Dale, 1856.
„ Michael Driscoll, 1861.
„ Daniel Woolett, 1863.
„ H. Bradbee, 1876.
„ Francis Bayly, 1882.
„ James Martyn, 1899.

N.B.—The Abbé Le Tellier, who erected the chapel in Queen Street, was suspended in 1818 by the Vicar Apostolic Bishop Poynter, for refusing his adhesion to the declaration required of the French clergy against Blanchardism. He submitted in 1834, being probably the last supporter in England of that curious petty schism.

TOW LOW, DURHAM (*Hexham and Newcastle*). Our Lady and St. Joseph.

Church erected 1869.

Priests.

Rev. Wm. Taylor Smith, 1869.
„ J. R. Wood, 1890.
„ Matthew Culley, 1898.
„ Henry Dix, 1901 to date.

TOWER HILL, LONDON, E. (*Westminster*). Church of the English Martyrs.

The temporary church, consisting of a 'cast-iron skeleton filled in with bricks and roofed with an imitation of oak,' was opened on Tuesday, December 12, 1865, by Archbishop Manning. The style was 'Builders' Gothic.' The present fine church, in the fourteenth-century style of Gothic, was erected 1876. A large portion of the cost of erection was defrayed by the Carthusians of the Grande Chartreuse, in memory of their Fathers martyred in London 1535. The congregation, owing to the supplanting of dwelling-houses by offices and warehouses, is decreasing. The Oblates of Mary Immaculate have charge of the mission. The pulpit was presented in February 1877 by a descendant of the Blessed Thomas More.

TREDEGAR, MONMOUTHSHIRE
(*Newport*). The Immaculate Conception.

Mass was first said here, in recent times, in June 1860, the 'chapel' being a room over a public-house. A plain brick school chapel was erected July 3, 1860. In 1864, a chancel was added and a presbytery built. Bishop Brown, of Newport, preached at the reopening, October 17, 1865. The number of Catholics in 1862 was about 1,500. The mission was served from Rhymney till 1863.

Priests.
Rev. J. O'Sullivan, 1863.
„ Wm. Williams, 1871.
„ P. Degen, 1884.
„ Wm. O'Dwyer, 1892.
„ M. O'Donoghue, 1897.
„ H. Parlin, 1904.

TRIMDON, DURHAM (*Hexham and Newcastle*). St. William.

The growth of population in consequence of the development of the lead-mining industry made a mission necessary, and one was established here in 1861. The school chapel was opened by Bishop Hogarth January 17, 1864. For some time it was served from Sedgefield. The Rev. M. W. Gibson was here many years, but left about 1877, after which the mission was served from Cornforth till 1902, when the present rector, Fr. Denis Hughes, was appointed.

TROWBRIDGE, WILTS (*Clifton*). St. John Baptist.

In 1875 a humble chapel was opened at the back of the 'Hope and Anchor' inn and served from Prior Park by Fr. J. Hearne. A small church, designed by Canon Scoles, and costing about £700,

was opened by the Bishop of Clifton June 27, 1876.

Priests.
Rev. J. Hearne, 1875.
„ John Archdeacon, 1882.
„ Arnold Matthews, 1885.
„ Michael McCarthy, 1888.
„ Emile Van Dale, 1890.
„ David Mulcahy, 1892.
„ E. A. G. Arundell, 1893.
„ Michael Delany, 1898.
„ Edward Graham, 1900.
  (Served from St. Mary's, Bath, 1902.)
„ D. G. Hubert, 1903 to date.

TRURO, CORNWALL (*Plymouth*).

A temporary chapel was opened in 1882. In the spring of 1884, a freehold site for a church was purchased on Chapel Hill from Mr. F. G. Enys, and a church erected at a cost of £2,000. The patron is St. Piran, whose statue stands over the main entrance of the building, which was opened in June 1885.[1] The style is Early English, the dimensions being 38 ft. by 18 ft. The high altar has a reredos of carved wood. Three coupled lancet windows on the south side light the building. Fr. John Grainger defrayed the cost of erection. From 1891 till after 1898 the mission was served from Bodmin. Fr. Gaudentius Holden, C.R.L., was priest in 1904.

TUDHOE, near DURHAM (*Hexham and Newcastle*). St. Charles.

Fr. Arthur Story kept an 'academy for young gentlemen' here

---

[1] St. Piran was one of the Irish missionaries to Cornwall, A.D. 410. He is identified with St. Kieran, of Cape Clear Island. He has always been regarded in Cornwall as the patron of the tinners, and his feast is still observed by them.

about 1790. It was closed at the time of the establishment of Stony-hurst College, in 1794, though many of the Douai students pursued their studies here before proceeding to Crook Hall. In the neighbourhood of Tudhoe there exist traces of no fewer than four chapels where Mass was said during the penal times. The mission, which was discontinued after the opening of the chapel at Croxdale Hall, was solemnly reopened 'by command of the Bishop of Hexham in November 1858.' By the generosity of Mr. Salvin of Burn, a clergy-house and temporary chapel (in a loft) were provided for the resident priest. Mass was said occasionally on weekdays about 1857, and in November 1858 the place became a permanent mission, when for some years Mass was said in the school-house. The present 'pure Gothic' church was built by Marmaduke Salvin, Esq. (June 1869–October 1870). In September 1883 very considerable additions were made to the building 'by moving the large gable of the nave and adding two more bays to the length of it.' A baptistery, bell, and rose window of stained glass were also presented to the church at the same time by Mr. Salvin.

Priests since 1859.
Rev. Canon Humble, 1859.
„ Joseph Canon Watson, 1866.

TUNBRIDGE WELLS, KENT (*Southwark*). St. Augustine's.
Many wealthy Catholics used to resort here towards the end of the eighteenth and beginning of the nineteenth century. About 1806 Mass was said on Sundays during the season by the chaplain of the Jerningham family. No regular chapel was built till 1838, when the present structure was opened by Bishop Griffiths. The style is Classical; accommodation for about 300. In June 1887, a costly antique altar of coloured marbles was erected by Canon Searle. The altar-piece, a fine painting by Murillo of the Blessed Virgin and Holy Child, was purchased at the Chancellor House sale. The sanctuary was tastefully painted and decorated a few years ago, during the incumbency of Fr. C. Stapley. The church was consecrated by Bishop Amigo of Southwark, on Thursday, December 13, 1906.

Priests.
Rev. Randall Lythgoe, 1838.
„ Wm. Rowe, 1840.
„ Thos. Clarke, 1860.
„ Joseph Canon Searle, 1866 till his death, 1899.
„ Chas. Stapley, 1899.
„ James Canon Keatinge, 1905 to date.
N.B.—The extinct mission of Soberton, in Hampshire, was mainly supported by 'a small copyhold estate called "Kirby's" with a farm-house, part of which was used by the priest for a chapel and residence.' It was supposed to have been given by a Miss Jane Cotton, who became Mrs. Bright, and was vested in the Lords Arundell of Wardour. When the Soberton mission was closed, 1839, the funds of this estate were used for the foundation of the Tunbridge Wells mission. (See Foley, 'Records, S.J.,' vol. xii.)

TUNSTALL, STAFFS (*Birmingham*). St. Mary.
Mission founded 1853, and served from Cobridge till 1854, when Fr. Henry Davey was appointed resident priest. New schools were erected, 1903, at a cost of £5,000,

The old school chapel was opened December 21, 1869, and the present church, in the Early English style, September 1873. The accommodation is for 300; architect, Goldie. In the centre of the apse is a fine memorial window to the late General Beckwith, of Silksworth Hall.

Priests.

Rev. Henry Davey, 1854.
„ Wm. Berry, 1858.
„ Clement Harris, here 1872.
„ John Fox, 1884.
„ Edward Plaetsier, 1892.
„ Wm. Sutherland, 1899.
„ P. J. Ryan, 1904.

TURTON, LANCS (*Salford*). St. Aldhelm's.

In March 1890 Fr. Ivo Steyaert, of Tottington, started the mission here at the request of Bishop Vaughan. Mass was said for the first time in the temporary chapel on June 4, 1891, the number of Catholics in the district being at that time about 100. The present church was opened in 1902. Fr. Steyaert was rector till after 1900; Emilius Rumes, 1901, Fr. Wilfrid Hampson in 1904; Fr. Michael Pappalardo, 1906.

TWICKENHAM, MIDDLESEX (*Westminster*). St. James.

A crowded meeting of Catholic residents was held at the Alma Hotel, Twickenham, on Wednesday evening, January 30, 1884, under Canon Geo. Akers, to consider the subject of establishing a mission in the town. The new mission was started on Sunday, May 11, 1884, when Mass was said in a house close to the railway station by Fr. Godfrey. Cardinal Manning presented an altar stone and chalice to the temporary chapel. The new church was opened Saturday, July 25, 1885. It is situated in the historic quarter of Pope's Grove. Mr. James de Lacy Towle was the munificent donor. The building is in the Early English style. The lancet windows over the high altar are filled with stained glass depicting scenes in the life of St. James. The side altars of Our Lady and the Sacred Heart in the transepts were carved by Henry Hillier, of Bath, who was drowned while bathing in the Thames the day after the opening of the church, aged twenty-one years. The church was solemnly consecrated by Cardinal Manning in July 1887, in the presence of the Comte and Comtesse de Paris, the Prince of Mantua, and a large congregation.

Priests.

Rev. Geo. Canon Akers, 1884.
„ Michael Ryan, 1885.
„ Edmund English, here 1889 and to date.

TYLDESLEY, LANCS (*Liverpool*). The Sacred Heart.

The mission was opened May 7, 1865, but for some years the chapel was ' an extremely inconvenient, inadequate building ' at the back of Chapel Square. In June 1868 the present church was begun, and the building was opened October 31, 1869. The style is Early English; accommodation for about 450.

Priests.

Rev. James Lennon, 1865.
„ James Dawber, 1870.
„ Richard O'Neill, here in 1875 and to date.

TYNE DOCK, SOUTH SHIELDS, DURHAM (*Hexham and Newcastle*). SS. Peter and Paul.

The first church, opened in 1884, was an 'incommodious structure,' and has recently been superseded by a handsome Romanesque church, situated 'in a very commanding position.' The formal opening took place July 1906.

Priests.

Rev. James Kirwan, 1884.
„ Robt. Taylerson, 1891.
„ James Bradley, 1900 to date.

TYNEMOUTH, NORTHUMBERLAND (*Hexham and Newcastle*). Our Lady and St. Oswin.

In April 1850 the Brothers of St. Vincent of Paul started a Sunday school at 'New York,' a village near Tynemouth. In August 1871 a temporary chapel was opened at the rear of the house occupied by Bishop Bewick, of Hexham and Newcastle. Exclusive of the military, Catholics numbered 150 in 1886. About £300 was collected by Fr. Geo. Howe in 1887, and on September 8, 1889, the first stone of the present church was laid. The building was opened June 1, 1890. A notable feature of the interior is the splendid east window, representing the Crucifixion.

Priests.

Rev. John Canon Bewick, 1871 (Bishop of Hexham and Newcastle 1882 ; died October 29, 1886).
„ Geo. Howe, 1882 to date.

U

UCKFIELD, SUSSEX (*South-wark*). St. Philip Neri.

The mission in this ' growing and romantically situated town ' was established by Fr. Philip Fletcher, M.A., founder of the ' Guild of Our Lady of Ransom.' The iron church, opened 1885, will accommodate about 100. The schools (mixed) have an average attendance of forty-eight. St. Philip's Orphanage for girls, under the direction of the Sisters of Mercy, was opened here in 1896.

Priests.

Rev. P. Fletcher, M.A., 1885.
,, A. J. Wallace, 1891.
,, W. Allanson, 1892.
,, Thos. Revill, 1893.
,, Thos. Goodwin, 1894.
,, F. Angelo, O.S.F.C., 1897.
,, Stephen Wray, 1902.
,, Geo. Fanning, 1903.

UGBROOKE, DEVON (*Plymouth*). St. Cyprian.

According to Dr. Oliver (' Collections') the chapel was ' dedicated to Protestant worship ' by Bishop Sparrow, of Exeter, July 17, 1671. On the conversion of Thomas first Lord Clifford to the Faith, a little later, the chapel was fitted up with becoming splendour for Catholic worship. The first synod of the then recently created see of Plymouth was held here February 7, 1854.

Priests.

Rev. Thos. Risdon, *alias* Blewett, S.J., 1701.
,, Dominic Derbyshire, O.P., 1735.
,, James Price, O.S.B., 1757.
,, James Frost, O.S.F., 1758.
,, William Strickland, S.J., 1766.
Joseph Reeve, S.J., 1767. This devout and learned man was the author of the well-known ' History of the Holy Bible ' and ' The History of the Christian Church.'
,, Felix Vauquelin, an *émigré*, 1794. Returned to France 1816, and died V.G. of Rouen 1840.
,, James Lawrenson, 1816.
,, James Brownbill, S.J., 1830.
,, Wm. Cotham, S.J., 1834.
,, Chas. Lomax, S.J., 1845.
,, Henry Brigham, S.J., 1856.
,, Patrick Walsh, 1860.
,, Mgr. Thos. Reekie, 1876.
,, H. J. Dowsett, 1901 to date.

UGTHORPE, YORKS (*Middlesbrough*). St. Anne.

The date of the founding of this mission is given as 1629, and it was long served in conjunction with Whitby (*q.v.*). Fr. Nicholas Post-

D D

gate, or Posket, who [suffered for the Faith at York August 7, 1679, was a native of Ugthorpe, as was also Thomas Ward, author of the 'Cantos of the Reformation.' After Fr. Postgate's martyrdom Fr. Jn. Marsh, a priest 'of excellent wit, parts, and zeal,' laboured in the district. Eighty-four persons from Ugthorpe and Egton were confirmed by Bishop Williams in May 1728. In 1730 Fr. Jn. Harvey, *alias* Rivett, opened a school for boys at Ugthorpe, but it was closed during the Jacobite rising of 1745, and Fr. Harvey, with another priest, Sir Wm. Anderton, were indicted at the York Assizes. They were convicted 'of recusancy,' but after a short imprisonment released. Some say the school was reopened in 1747, but this is doubtful. A chapel was opened in 1768, and a second one in 1810. The congregation was computed at over 170 in 1773. The place was very poor, and regarded by priests in the North as 'a purgatory of a mission.' The present church was opened by Cardinal Wiseman in September 1857, the old chapel being converted into a school. A stone pulpit was presented by W. Middleton, Esq., and a fine altar by Bishop Briggs. Other benefactors were Charles Langdale, Esq., — Lawson, Esq., and W. Falkinbridge, Esq.

Priests.

Rev. N. Postgate, 1629 (martyred 1679).
„ Jn. Marsh, 1685.
„ Jn. Harvey, *alias* Rivett, 1729.
„ Thos. Shepherd, 1746.
„ Edw. Ball, 1747.
     Mission probably vacant 1757-67.
„ Jn. Bradshaw, 1767.
„ Thos. Ferby, 1774.
„ Jn. Marsland, 1777.

Rev. Henry Dennett, 1787.
„ Thos. Talbot, 1788 (in conjunction with Egton Bridge).
„ Geo. Leo. Haydock, 1803.
„ Nicholas Rigby, 1835 (died rector 1889).
„ Edmund Hickey, here 1883 (rector 1889).
„ Hy. Reynolds, 1891.
„ Richard Lewis, 1893.
„ Patrick McKernan, 1904 to date.

ULSHAW BRIDGE, MIDDLEHAM, YORKS (*Middlesbrough*). SS. Simon and Jude.

The mission would appear to have been founded early in the eighteenth century through the auspices of the ancient Catholic family, the Scropes of Danby. Owing to the laws, Mass was said secretly at various places in the district, where there seem to have been not a few Catholics. Fr. Frank Oakley, S.J. (1742-54), Fr. F. Wappeller, S.J. (1758-64), and Fr. Boone, S.J., were noted for their zeal in the locality, and their labours were rewarded by many conversions. In 1788, a plain chapel was built, and this building, with a few subsequent improvements, served the mission till the opening of the present Gothic church, June 10, 1868.

ULVERSTON, LANCS (*Liverpool*). St. Mary of Furness.

Fr. Thos. Barton, *alias* Hervey, was here in 1678. He was often sought after by the pursuivants, but eluded arrest, and died in Maryland 1696. His successor at Ulverston, Fr. Clement Smith, 'for two years lived in a house without light or fire for fear of the pursuivants.' He died 1695, aged thirty-eight. In 1755 Mass was said at Swarthmoor Hall, and in 1777 in the fifth house from the present church. The Abbé Everard, of Bordeaux, built the chapel about 1806. Fr. Bartholomew McHugh enlarged the building, the additions being formed of stones brought from Furness Abbey. The opening took place September 9, 1823. He also built schools at Tarnside. These were replaced by modern ones 1887. The present Gothic church, for 600 persons, was commenced August 15, 1893, and opened by Bishop Whiteside August 21, 1895.

Priests from 1750.

Rev. Thos. West (author of ' Antiquities of Furness ').
„ Abbé Everard, 1800 (Archbishop of Cashel 1816).
„ B. McHugh (secular), 1818.
„ Jn. Morris, S.J., 1844.
„ Alf. Weld, S.J., 1855.
„ Wm. Cobb, S.J., 1855.
„ R. Corr, S.J., 1856.
„ B. Jarrett, S.J., 1856.
Seculars.
„ Peter Laverty, 1863.
„ Wm. Massey, 1877.
„ P. Laverty (second time), 1886.
„ Thos. Allan, 1887 to date.

UPTON HALL, CHESHIRE (*Shrewsbury*). Sacred Heart of Jesus.

Upton Hall was purchased in 1863 by the nuns of the Order of Faithful Companions of Jesus, and here Mass was said on Sundays for the benefit of local Catholics. In 1871 a large barn was turned into a chapel, and opened by the Bishop on December 8 of the same year. In addition to their day school, the nuns also conduct night classes for both boys and girls. The first priest at Upton Hall was Fr. Roger McCarte.

Priests.

Rev. Roger McCarte, 1863.
„ J. Quinn, 1867.
„ John O'Callaghan, 1874.
„ D. Harrington, 1877.
„ Chas. Coelenbier, 1879.
„ Wilfrid Canon Dallow, here in 1885 to date.

UPTON-ON-SEVERN, WORCESTERSHIRE (*Birmingham*). St. Joseph.

Hanley Castle, Hill End, was the ancestral seat of the Bartlett family, who maintained a chapel in their house. In 1765 Fr. Felix Bartlett, S.J., brother of the proprietor, was chaplain. He died at Worcester 1777, aged sixty-nine (Foley, ' Records, S.J.,' vol. xii.) The church was consecrated August 9, 1846, by Bishop (afterwards Cardinal) Wiseman. The cost of erection was defrayed by John Vincent Gandolfi Hornyold, Esq., of Blackmore Park. The opening took place on Thursday, August 20. The church, which is in the Gothic style, is modelled after the parish church of Skelton, Yorks. There are three altars. The body of St. Aurelius, martyr, is interred in a handsome shrine beneath the sanctuary.

Priests since 1825.

Rev. Edw. Winter.
„ Thos. O'Keefe, 1841.
„ A. Lempfried, 1844.
„ J. B. Lans, 1846.
„ Francis Fairfax, 1852.
„ Thos. Canon Flanagan, V.F., 1855.
(Served from Hanley 1862, 1864.)
„ Augustine Lempfried, 1866 till 1889 (first time 1844),

Rev. Cornelius Klomp, 1890.
„ C. Zambra, 1897.
„ N. H. Higginson, 1899.
„ A. Hellé, 1901 to date.

URMSTON, LANCS (*Salford*). The English Martyrs.
Mission established 1891. Gothic church. Congregation about 340. Schools improved and playground enlarged 1905.
Priests.
Rev. Francis Newton, 1891.
„ Francis Beulink, 1894.
„ M. A. Holohan, 1898.
„ Wm. Thompson, 1900.
„ Chas. Rothwell, 1903 to date.

USHAW, DURHAM (*Hexham and Newcastle*). St. Cuthbert's College.
This seat of learning shares with St. Edmund's College, Old Hall, Herts, the academical successorship of the renowned college of Douai, founded by Cardinal Allen in 1568. As is well known, that venerable institution was suppressed by the French Revolutionists in 1793, and the professors and students, after a short but rigorous imprisonment at Dourlens, made their way to England, where collegiate studies were resumed on October 15, 1794, at Crook Hall, Durham. This old mansion, which had been in the family of Geo. Baker, Esq., of Ellemore, since 1640, was ' a plain rectangular block, built of stone.' Dr. Lingard, the historian, who was Professor of Moral and Natural Philosophy at the college from 1795 to 1811, thus apostrophises the place :

May Crook's blest soil and verdant plains
Be my retreat in trembling age,
When warned by death's approaching pains
To quit the world's tumultuous stage.

In July 1808 the community of Crook, which now numbered about forty persons, removed to more commodious quarters at Ushaw, which had recently been erected from designs by Mr. James Taylor, of Islington. From this time forward the progress of the college has never flagged. The splendid Gothic church supplanted the old chapel in 1847, and two years later the spacious exhibition hall, library, and study places were erected. Besides these developments, others too numerous to mention have occurred of late years to make Ushaw one of the greatest Catholic educational establishments of the century. The jubilee of the Ushaw foundation was celebrated in July 1858, in the presence of a distinguished gathering, presided over by Cardinal Wiseman, whose touching drama, ' The Hidden Gem,' was acted by some of the students in honour of the event. This noteworthy incident was quite eclipsed in October 1894, when the centenary of the college was signalised by an assemblage of the Catholic hierarchy and distinguished laity. Among those present were Archbishop Eyre, of Glasgow, who had been a student at the college in 1826. From the foundation at Crook in 1794 to the celebration of the centenary in 1894, upwards of 800 priests were ordained at the college for the mission. Ushaw was affiliated to the London University in 1840, and since that time many of its alumni have obtained the highest honours in the Arts examinations. Among its distinguished lay students may be mentioned the eminent barrister, Mr. Serjeant Shee, created a judge of the Queen's Bench in 1864, being the first Catholic lawyer to be so honoured since the reign of James II. The presidents of Ushaw since the commencement have been as follows:

Rev. Thos. Eyre, 1794–1810.
„ John Gillow, June 1811 to February 1828.
„ Thos. Youens, D.D., 1828–33.
„ John Briggs, D.D. (consecrated Bishop of *Trachis* 1833; left Ushaw 1836).
, Dr. Youens (second time), August 1836 to February 1837.
„ Mgr. Charles Newsham, D.D., May 1837 to February 1863.
„ Mgr. Robert Tate, D.D., 1863 to August 1876.
., Francis Wilkinson, D.D., 1876–77.
„ Bishop Chadwick, 1877 to October 1878.
, Mgr. Wm. Wrennall, D.D., 1878 to November 1885.
„ Wm. Canon Dunderdale, January 1886 to October 1887.
„ James Lennon, D.D., 1886 (resigned 1890).
, Bishop Wilkinson, 1890 to date.

USHAW, DURHAM. (*See also above.*) The Church of St. Cuthbert. The old building by A. W. Pugin, erected in 1847, was pulled down in 1882 to make way for the present magnificent structure by Messrs. Dunn and Hansom. The foundation stone was laid by Archbishop Eyre, and the building solemnly blessed October 4, 1884, by Bishop Bewick, of Hexham and Newcastle. The style is Decorated Gothic. The stained-glass windows representing SS. Cuthbert, Chad, Wilfrid, &c., are very rich, while the stalls and benches are of oak, beautifully carved. The high altar, designed by the late P. P. Pugin, was the gift of the late Canon Wm. Taylor Smith. Among the treasures of the sacristy may be noted a portion of the Holy Cross, the ring of St. Cuthbert,[1] richly chased chalice of Pope Gregory XVI., a pre-Reformation chasuble, once the property of Bishop Walton, who died in 1780, &c.

USK, MONMOUTHSHIRE (*Newport*). St. Francis Xavier.
A chapel and mission-house were opened here October 14, 1847. Catholics of the district numbered about seventy. By 1852 a school had been erected, and the congregation increased to 138. In 1858 Catholics were estimated at 200; in 1862, 250.

Priests.
Rev. A. M. Baldacconi, LL.D., 1847.
„ J. Arquis, 1849.
„ P. Canon Dawson, V.G, 1853.
„ J. Canon Wilson, V.G., 1855.
„ Thos. Croft, 1874.
„ Joseph Hurley, 1899.
„ Isidore Heneka, 1901 to date.

[1] The ring of Cuthbert was given by Viscount Montague to Bishop Smith, of *Chalcedon*, V.A., 1625, and by him bequeathed to the English Canonesses of Paris. In 1858 these nuns presented it to Cardinal Wiseman, who gave it as a jubilee gift to the college. The ring is worn by the Bishops of Hexham and Newcastle on the day of their consecration.

UTTOXETER, STAFFS (*Birmingham*). St. Mary.

This mission was founded, 1839, by George Canon Morgan, D.D., who sold his paternal estate to erect the chapel. He served the mission till 1843, when he was recalled to Oscott. He was again rector of Uttoxeter 1849-52. In the latter year he became president of Oscott.

Priests.

Rev. Geo. Canon Morgan, 1839.
„ James Harkness, 1843.
„ Clement Jeffries, 1844.
„ C. Cook, 1847.
„ Geo. Canon Morgan 1849 (second time).
„ Jos. Abbot, 1852.
„ Peter Holland, 1854.
„ John McGahren, 1874 and to date.

UXBRIDGE, MIDDLESEX (*Westminster*). Our Lady of Lourdes and St. Michael.

There are scarcely any traces of Catholicity here after the establishment of Protestantism in England. Wm. Griffiths, Esq., of Southland House, near Uxbridge, was a great protector of priests about 1581, and his mansion—a moated grange—was 'full of shifting places' and secret recesses where the persecuted missionaries could abide and baffle pursuit. There was also a covered way under the moat by which escape could be made. Fr. Campion and Fr. Parsons had a conference at Southlands in 1580 on the subject of the English mission and the spiritual wants of the recusants. The next item of Catholicity in connection with Uxbridge occurs in 1812, when the body of the Catholic Duchess of Buckingham rested here on its way to Stowe. Office for the dead was recited in the mortuary chapel, and Mass celebrated for the repose of the soul. The actual mission was founded in 1892, when a temporary chapel was opened in Lawn Road. The congregation is estimated at 150 ; average attendance of children of St. Mary's Schools, about sixty. When first started the mission was served from West Drayton.

Priests.

Rev. James Hazell, 1896.
„ John Brady, 1897 to date.

V

VAUXHALL, LONDON, S.E. *(Southwark).* St. Anne.

The locality, formerly known as Foxhall (see Addison's 'Spectator'), is said to derive its name from Guy Faux, the conspirator, who, as tradition asserts, owned an estate here. A Catholic school was opened in the district in 1864. The premises are now a shop close to the Wesleyan school. Miss Troy was the mistress. In July 1866 a school for girls and infants was started by the Notre Dame nuns. Another for boys in Vauxhall Walk followed in January 1872, Mr. W. Troy being appointed headmaster. Through the initiative of Bishop Butt, Mass was said in the boys' school on Sundays, starting with Sunday, November 28, 1886. In 1891 a property in Upper Kennington Lane and Harleyford Road was acquired by the diocese, and next year (January 1892) Fr. W. F. Brown and Fr. D. Moloney were placed in charge of the now independent mission. In February 1893 the new schools, for 625 children, were opened, at a cost of £4,350. The debt was paid off in 1899 owing to a legacy having been left the diocese by Miss Emily King, of Norwood, 'for certain purposes.' The first stone of the present fine Gothic church was laid by Bishop Bourne, of Southwark, November 3, 1900, and the nave was opened for worship January 31, 1903. The sanctuary and high altar were completed at Easter the same year. Mr. F. A. Walters was the architect. A handsome stone and marble altar was presented by Mr. W. J. Sandford, and a stone font by Mr. E. P. O'Reilly, of Cape Town, in memory of his late wife, a former organist at the school chapel. Mgr. W. F. Brown, V.G., is the first and present rector of the mission.

VENTNOR, ISLE OF WIGHT *(Portsmouth).* Our Lady and St. Wilfrid.

In September 1863 Mass was said at Apsley Cottage, in the High Street, by Fr. Victor Duke. The chapel, though small, was splendidly furnished with vestments, chalice, monstrance, statues of Our Lady and St. Joseph, &c.—the gifts of such benefactors as the Chevalier de Zulueta, Mr. and Mrs. Gilbert A'Becket, Mrs. Roope, Mrs. Grace, &c. The chapel was afterwards moved to 'a room over a shop where a good old lady used to vend apples and sweets.' On December 2, 1864, a house was taken in Devonshire Terrace, and a room fitted up for Mass &c. The present church was opened in May 1871.

Priests.

Rev. T. Fryer, 1864.

,,   Frederick Bowles, 1866.

,,   Justin Mooney, here in 1871.

,,   James Duggan, here in 1879.

,,   P. Trumble, 1885.

Rev. Geo. Dolman, 1890.

,,   Francis Drew, 1891.

,,   W. Dawson, 1893.

,,   Louis Canon Hall, 1896.

,,   Stephen Mongan, D.D., 1898 to date.

W

WADHURST, SUSSEX (*Southwark*).

The Fathers of Charity opened their novitiate here in 1881, in ' a beautiful Gothic building in the midst of wooded grounds, designed by Mr. Bernard Whelan. The Institute of Charity was founded in 1828 by the Abbate Antonio Rosmini Serbati, the ideologist philosopher; hence the members are often spoken of as Rosminians. The rule was approved by Pope Gregory XVI. in 1838, and the Fathers devote themselves to every kind of ' work of charity, spiritual, intellectual, or corporal, under the direction of obedience.' Father Joseph Hirst was the first rector at Wadhurst.

WAKEFIELD, YORKS (*Leeds*). St. Austin.

The chapel was opened March 4, 1828, ' at which time there were but twenty-nine communicants.' Fr. J. Morris, S.J., was the priest of the mission. In the registers, which date from 1828, he signs himself sometimes as ' Catholic Vicar of Wakefield.' He remained till 1844, when he retired to Birkenhead, where he died October 10, 1855. In November 1880, ' extensive alterations and additions ' were made to the chapel from plans prepared by Hansom. The height and length were increased, a new chancel added, as well as a Lady Chapel and baptistery. The cost of the extension &c. was about £2,000.

Rectors.

Rev. J. Morris, 1828.
„ Francis Jarrett, 1844.
„ John Baron, 1854.
„ Richard Cooper, here in 1871.
„ Geo. Lambert, 1877.
„ Walter Lomax, 1882.
„ Martin Everard, 1889.
„ John O'Reilly, 1890.
„ John E. Moore, 1892.
„ Isaac Lee, 1897.
„ Joseph O'Gorman, 1904.

WALKER, NEWCASTLE-ON-TYNE (*Hexham and Newcastle*). St. Anthony of Padua.

The ancient Catholic family of Lawson, who resided near here, had a chapel and resident chaplains all through the penal times. In the Civil War Sir H. Lawson, in common with the rest of the Catholic nobility and gentry, sided with King Charles I., and would have lost his estates but for the intervention of the first Earl of Carlisle with Cromwell. The domestic chapel of the Lawsons was dedicated to St. Anthony of Padua, and this name was given to the present church at the time of its opening (September 18, 1860).

Before this, the many Catholics of Walker had to attend Mass at Newcastle. The cost of the new church, which was designed by Archibald Dunn, was about £1,500. The jubilee of the church was celebrated in September 1885. A new memorial side altar was erected in the church, March 1906. It was the gift of Mrs. Elizabeth Cassidy. A fine stained glass window was presented about the same time by Miss McGlade.

Priests.

Rev. James Foran, 1859.

„ Henry Berry, 1877.

„ John McNerney, 1879.

„ Michael Bourke, 1881.

„ Henry Berry (second time), 1889 to date.

WALLSEND, NORTHUMBERLAND (*Hexham and Newcastle*). St. Columba.

The chapel was opened 1879, and served from Willington Quay till about the end of 1884. As early as 1850 Fr. Cullen, of North Shields, referred to the fact of there being ' many Catholics ' at Wallsend, but no mission was established till nearly thirty years later.

Priests.

Rev. M. Devane, 1885.

„ Edw. Walsh, 1890 to date.

WALMER, KENT (*Southwark*). The Sacred Heart.

This mission is served by the convent of the Visitation, Roselands. On the expulsion of the nuns from the convents of Himmelsthur, Hildesheim, and Ostrowo, Posen, by the *Kulturkampf* of Bismarck, 1875, Cardinal Ledochowski, Archbishop of Posen, advised the exiles to settle in England. The Sisters opened a high-class boarding school at Upper Walmer. Lady Georgiana Fullerton greatly assisted the new establishment, which is now in a very flourishing condition. The chaplain since the foundation has been the Very Rev. Mgr. Daniewski.

WALSALL, STAFFS (*Birmingham*).

This mission was at the commencement of the eighteenth century, and for long after, served from Oscott (*q.v.*). In 1782 Fr. P. Parry, priest at Oscott, became infirm and could not attend to the Catholics at Walsall. This caused many persons to fall away from the Faith. The next priests at Oscott, however, worked so vigorously that Catholics at Walsall greatly increased, and the assembly room of the Dragon Inn was hired for Mass on Sundays. On December 11, 1812, a regular chapel was fitted up and served from Bloxwich. About this time Fr. Martyn gave Sunday evening lectures on the Catholic religion, which resulted in numerous conversions. The foundation stone of the new chapel was laid August 16, 1825, by Fr. J. Abbott, deputed by Bishop Milner. Mr. and Mrs. Cox presented the site, and J. Bagnall, Esq., one of the congregation, gave £500 to the building fund, which was also most generously contributed to by the Earl of Shrewsbury. The edifice was opened May 10, 1827, by Bishop Walsh, the sermon being preached by Dr. Weedall, of Oscott. A charity school for a hundred children was built a little later. Fr. Martyn was succeeded in 1840 by Frs. R. Bagnall and J. Daniel.

The priests after this were Frs. W. Lovi and M. Payne. The number of the faithful so greatly increased that a second church, dedicated to St. Patrick, was opened in 1856, and put under the care of Fr. W. Dunne. The fine schools in connection with this latter mission were opened as recently as 1902, the foundation stone having been laid on November 19, 1901, by Sir A. D. Hayter, Bart., M.P., in the presence of a large assemblage. Fr. E. P. Delaney was priest at this time.

population of the district is over 3,000; average school attendance, about 200.

Priests.

Rev. E. Barron, 1849.
  ,,   Raphael Melia, D.D., 1854.
  ,,   Pius Melia, 1857.
  ,,   Anthony Ball, 1863.
  ,,   Raymund Stanfield, 1866.
  ,,   Francis Rhing, here 1871.
  ,,   Daniel Canty, 1885.
  ,,   Thos. Walsh, 1890.
  ,,   Martin Brannigan, 1898 to date.

WALTHAM CROSS, HERTS (*Westminster*). The Immaculate Conception and St. Joseph.

The mission owes its foundation to the late Fr. G. Bampfield, B.A., who said Mass here for the first time about May 1862. Two years later he opened a school chapel capable of accommodating 300 persons (September 1864).

Recent Priests.

Rev. G. Bampfield, 1860.
  ,,   David Hickey, 1866.
  ,,   Thomas Regan, 1871.
  ,,   Reginald Tuke, here in 1874.
  ,,   Edward Bronsgeest, 1879 and to date.

WALTHAMSTOW, LONDON, N.E. (*Westminster*). St. George.

The old church was opened August 15, 1849, on a site given by Captain Collard, a protestant. The style was fourteenth-century, from design by Wardell Schools were erected about the same time. The old church was little better than a school chapel, with open roof and bell-cot; accommodation for about 180. The present 'handsome and commodious' church was opened in 1901. The Catholic

WALTON, LIVERPOOL. St Francis de Sales.

In 1884 Fr. Smith was commissioned to undertake the formation of the mission. He opened a chapel in a disused stable belonging to a Mr. Morgan, who supplied all the necessary fittings. In 1885 a site for a school chapel was secured, and in October 1887 this was formally opened. The upper portion of the building, accommodating 500 persons, serves as a chapel Among the presents to the mission at the opening of the school were a handsome monstrance set with gems, chalice, and sanctuary lamp from Mrs. Hawthorne. The bell for the turret, a fine cope, and Mass vestment were given by other benefactors. The cost of building the chapel and schools was £2,550 A new school was opened, April 1894. The Catholic population is about 300.

WALTON-LE-DALE, LANCS (*Salford*). St. Patrick.

The school chapel was opened December 20, 1857, Fr. J. Proctor being the first priest. A cemetery

ENGLISH CATHOLIC MISSIONS

attached to the mission was part of a Cistercian property in pre-Reformation times, and was known more recently as 'Monks Meadow.' In August 1862, the Bishop of Salford confirmed a hundred persons in the chapel, this being the first time a Catholic bishop had visited the place for three hundred years. The school chapel was superseded by the present fine church, in the Decorated style of Gothic, opened October 9, 1880, by Bishop Hedley, of Newport. The accommodation is for 500. Messrs. Pugin were the architects.

Priests.

Rev. J. Proctor, 1857.
„ John Carroll, O.S.B., 1866.
„ Jas. Poole, O.S.B., here in 1872.
„ Geo. R. Turner, O.S.B., 1879 and to date.

WALTON-ON-THAMES, SURREY (*Southwark*).

The church, a plain Romanesque building, was opened May 16, 1906, when Mass was said by Fr. E. du Plerney, rector of St. Raphael's, Surbiton. Over fifty persons were present out of an estimated congregation of nearly a hundred. It is served from Surbiton.

WALTON-ON-THE-HILL, LANCS (*Liverpool*). The Blessed Sacrament.

Fazakerley House, the ancient seat of the Fazakerley family, stood in this parish, and is described as being 'full of hiding-places.' The chapel served the mission. The last male representative of the family was the late John Fazakerley, M.P. The modern mission of Walton dates from 1872, when a chapel was fitted up in

a barn—kindly lent by Mr. C. Harvey, a protestant—and used for the first time on October 20 of that year. Catholics of the district then numbered about forty. Between June 1876 and June 1878 the present church was built, at a cost of £6,000. The style is Early English. Commodious schools were opened August 1880, and enlarged 1897.

Priests.

Rev. J. Nugent, 1872.
„ James Cross, 1892.
„ Thos. Browne, 1893.
„ James Kay, 1899 to date.

WALWORTH, LONDON, S.E. (*Southwark*). The English Martyrs.

Like most other districts of South London, Walworth was a rural village a hundred years ago. By 1840, however, it was a thickly populated quarter of the Metropolis. Prior to the establishment of the present mission, the district was attended by clergy from St. George's, though as far back as 1843 or 1844 a demand for a chapel was made in the columns of the Catholic press. In 1889 a census of Catholics in the district was carried out under the direction of Fr. Reeks, John Newton, Esq., of Old Kent Road, &c. Shortly after this, Bishop Butt took a house in Northampton Place, where religious instruction was given to children on Sunday afternoons. Then a room over a shop (29 North Street) was hired, and finally 'two miserable dilapidated cottages' (Dean's Buildings). A boys' and girls' school, designed by Mr. Leonard Stokes, was opened March 10, 1890, and on the following Sunday Mass was said in one of the class-rooms of the building. This 'school chapel' continued till the opening of the present fine church, early in 1903. The style is Early English, from design by the late F. W. Tasker, Esq. The high altar is surmounted by a life-size crucifix, and there is a large and handsomely built Lady Chapel. Cost of erection, about £5,500. A fine presbytery, in the Georgian style, adjoins the church. The title of the church is appropriate, as in the neighbourhood several of the English martyrs obtained their crowns—viz. Ven. Griffith Clarke, Vicar of Wandsworth (1539) ; Ven. Nicholas Waire, O.S.F. (1539) ; Ven. John Jones, *alias* Buckley (1598) ; Ven. John Rigby (1600) ; John Pybush (1601).

Priests.

Rev. Joseph Reeks, 1889.
„ A. Doubleday, 1893.
„ Peter Amigo, 1900 (consecrated Bishop of Southwark March 25, 1904).
„ Geo. Newton, 1904 to date.

WALWORTH, S.E. St. Alban, Herring Street.
This mission is served from the Church of the English Martyrs. The church, in the Romanesque style, was opened 1905 ; accommodation for about 200. The altar and baldachino are of wood, painted white and gilded. A double row of columns separate the nave and aisles. The most noteworthy feature of the interior is a curious statue of the patron saint. The estimated number of the congregation is about 800.

WANDSWORTH, LONDON, S.W. (*Southwark*). St. Thomas of Canterbury.
The mission was started in 1841. The district was then a rural suburb, the number of Catholics amounting to seventy. The chapel was a small room, 20 ft. by 14 ft. The cost of the new chapel was £900, of which £300 was given by Bishop Griffiths, V.A.L. This chapel, ' a new and elegant structure in the Perpendicular style,' was opened on the feast of St. Winefride, 1847. The site of the building had been occupied by a convent in pre-Reformation times. Mass was celebrated by Fr. J. Sisk, the sermon being preached by Bishop Wiseman. Bishop Morris, of Troy, preached in the evening on the verse, ' Remember the days of old.' E. W. Pugin was the architect. The establishment of the Wandsworth mission was largely due to the Rev. Don Claudio Lopez, a Spanish priest, who was the means of drawing the scattered congregation — mostly Irish field labourers — together. The next priests were the celebrated Father Hodgson and the Rev. Dr. De Lima, chaplain to a wealthy Catholic family at Wimbledon. Fr. J. Bower, the next priest, bought the site for the church. He was succeeded by Fr. Denis Sheahan, who in 1854 went out to the Crimea, where he died while ministering as chaplain to the Catholic soldiers there. In 1856 the Catholics of Wandsworth had increased to about 400. Frs. Brosnan and Flannery were the next priests after Fr. Sheahan. On the opening of the Wandsworth Prison the spiritual care of the Catholic prisoners was entrusted to the priest of the Wandsworth mission, Fr. H. D. Galeran being the first Catholic chaplain. The present fine church of St. Thomas was commenced in September 1893, during the rectorate of Fr. E. Murnane, now of Bermondsey.

The building is still unfinished. The style of the church, which is at the corner of the Richmond and Santos Roads, is Decorated Gothic. Mr. E Goldie, of Kensington, was the architect. Fr. Cooney, the present incumbent, has done much for the interior decoration of the church.

N.B.—A Catholic boys' school existed at Wandsworth in 1792. It was at Bridgefield House, and was kept by a Mr. John Bloodworth, an alumnus of Sedgley Park.

WANDSWORTH, EAST HILL (*Southwark*). St. Mary Magdalen.

In December 1902 Bishop Bourne, of Southwark, offered the charge of this new mission to the Salesian Fathers of Battersea. The new chapel was opened, February 22, 1903, but for several months the mission was served from West Battersea. Fr. Hawarden has had charge of the district since the opening of the chapel On September 8, 1905, the first stone of the present church was laid by Canon E. St. John, in the absence of Bishop Amigo. The building was opened October 25, 1906. The interior is very ornate, a carved oak pulpit and fine reredos being especially noteworthy. The style of the church is a species of Byzantine. A good Catholic secondary school in connection with the mission was opened by Fr. Macey, Provincial S.C., during the course of 1903.

WAPPENBURY, WARWICK-SHIRE (*Birmingham*). St. Anne.

The earliest reference to this mission that we have been able to discover occurs in 1795, when Lord Clifford came into the property. His lordship built the chapel and presbytery—a great boon to local Catholics, who hitherto had worshipped in a barn, part of which served as the priest's residence! The Clifford chapel was used down to 1849, when the present church of St. Anne was erected. For many years the priest at Leamington also did duty here on Sundays, but in 1841 Fr. R. Marsh was resident priest. He in his turn attended to Catholics at Kenilworth (*q.v.*).

Priests after Fr. Marsh.
Rev. James Millward, 1857.
„   Walter Lovi, 1871.
„   Wm. Penny, here in 1874.
„   Vincent Holcroft, 1881 till 1892.
„   Patrick Holden, 1892 to date.

WAPPING, LONDON, E. (*Westminster*) St. Patrick's.

In December 1899 the Catholic population of the district was estimated at 2,600. The mission was separated from Commercial Road and opened at Christmas 1871. Present church opened in 1879. The schools were built in 1896, about £2,000 of the cost being subscribed by collection. The outstanding debt of £3,000 was cleared by a generous benefactor, who in 1899 completed the sanctuary of the church and provided new benches and altar rails. The mural decorations, frescoes, and pictures of the church are in keeping with the Roman architecture of the rest of the building. The fine high altar is adorned by a large idealistic picture of the Crucifixion.

Priests.
Rev. Fr. Angelo Lucas, 1871.
„   Fr. Beckley, 1882 to date.

WARDOUR CASTLE, TISBURY, WILTS (*Clifton*). All Saints.

The old castle ot the Arundell family was dismantled by its noble owners shortly after its famous siege by the Parliamentarian forces (1644). Till the erection of the present church, an oratory among the ruins served as a Catholic chapel. In 1774, Henry eighth Lord Arundell, commenced the present church (95 ft. by 40 ft.), and the building was blessed by Bishop Walmesley, October 31, 1776, ' with a pomp unprecedented since the restoration of Catholic faith in the reign of Queen Mary of England.' The body of the building was designed by Quarenghi, a Venetian, the galleries and sanctuary by Sir John Soane. The congregation was long considered to be the largest out of London. A cemetery was consecrated 1836.

Priests.

Rev. Wm. Smith, S.J. (died 1658).
  ,, Richard Mason, O.S.F., 1662.
  ,, Jn. Weldon, S.J., 1710.
  ,, Thos. Fairfax, S.J., 17—.
  ,, Richard Holland, S.J., 1716.
  ,, Hubert Hacon, S.J., 1734.
  ,, Michael Poole, S.J., 1740.
  ,, Robt. Constable, S.J., 1746.
  ,, Jn. Jenison, S.J., 1759.
  ,, Augus. Jenison, 1774.
  ,, Chas. Forrester, 1775.
  ,, Jos. Clossette, S.J., 1781.
  ,, Edw. Wheble, 1781.
  ,, Edw. Nichell, S.J., 1788.
  ,, Jean Marest, 1817.
  ,, F. Postlewhite, 1817.
  ,, Richard Parker, S.J., 1820.
  ,, Jas. Carr, S.J., 1832.
  ,, Jas. Laurenson, S.J., 1832.
  ,, Jn. Grimstone, S.J., 1853.
  ,, Ralph Cooper, S.J., 1855.
  ,, Hy. Walmesley, S.J., 1857.
  ,, E. Theophilus Hood, S.J., 1860.
  ,, Justin Dupuy, S.J., 1886.
  ,, Jn. Graham, 1896.

WARE, HERTS (*Westminster*). St. Joseph.

The mission is described as being founded between 1832 and 1840. The chapel was in French Horn Lane. Mass was presumably only said on Sundays, as the priest in charge resided at this time at 5 Artillery Street, Bishopsgate, London. The other priests who served it were Frs. Fredk. Inglis, Wil. Watson, Fredk. Elwell, Wm. Smith, and J. L. Miller. The mission is not mentioned in the 'Directory' at all some years. At present (1905) it is served on the second Sunday of the month from Hertford.

WAREHAM, DORSET (*Plymouth*). St. Michael's.

The Westport property was sold to Dr. Blackston for £3,000 in January 1888, and almost immediately transformed into a Passionist monastery. The church was commenced April 1889, the Duke of Norfolk laying the foundation stone. The building, which was erected at the cost of Mr. and Mrs. Brodrick, of Brighton, was opened Tuesday, November 19, 1889. The style is Early Gothic. The accommodation is for about 275 persons; cost of erection, about £1,500. A reredos in the fourteenth-century style of Gothic was presented to the church in June 1890 by Mrs. Limbert.

WARLEY, near BRENTWOOD, ESSEX (*Westminster*). Holy Cross and All Saints.

The church was designed by F. W. Tasker, and opened by Cardinal Manning, October 1881. Countess Tasker gave generously to the building fund, and the site for the presbytery was presented by F. Campbell, Esq.

Priests.

Rev. Francis Stanfield, 1881.
„ Thomas Walsh, 1884.
„ Moncrieff Smyth, 1889.
„ Thos. Burnett, 1896 to date.

WARRINGTON, LANCS (*Liverpool*). St. Alban.

About 1755, a room in the Feathers Inn, Friargate, served as a chapel. Fr. Shuttleworth, O.S.B., the priest, died in 1774. As far back as 1584, Fr. James Bell was executed at Lancaster for exercising his priestly functions at Warrington. In 1772, the Catholic chapel was a large hall in Dallam Lane, now occupied by the Methodists. Fr. Bradshaw in 1776 built a new chapel off Bewsey Street. A large chapel was opened November 13, 1823, by Bishop Baines. Dr. Molyneux, the incumbent of the chapel, presented the mission with a fifteenth-century chasuble, embroidered with a figure of Thomas Earl of Lancaster. Dr. Molyneux died in 1860, and was succeeded by Fr. Hall. In 1890 the church was reseated and a new Lady Altar erected. Four stained-glass windows were unveiled by Abbot Gasquet, O.S.B., September 30, 1900. Electric light was installed October 1902.

WARRINGTON, LANCS. St. Benedict's School Chapel, Oxford Lane. Opened 1896.

WARRINGTON, LANCS. Sacred Heart, Liverpool Road.

Stone laid June 3, 1894, by Mgr. Carr, V.G. Opened October 6, 1895. Style, Early English. Accommodation, 600 persons. Messrs. Sinnott & Powell architects. New schools, for 300 children, opened February 7, 1898, by Bishop Whiteside. Catholic population, about 1,050.

WARRINGTON, LANCS. St. Mary.

The church (Early English) was erected by Abbot Bury, O.S.B., assisted by John Ashton, Esq. The opening, by Bishop O'Reilly, took place August 30, 1877. Schools for 800 children were built about the same time. In January 1899 the Sisters of the Holy Cross and Passion opened a convent in the parish. The estimated Catholic population is about 3,350.

WARWICK (*Birmingham*). St. Mary Immaculate.

The place was a residence of the Franciscans during the penal times, but we have come across no details of any regular mission. There was no chapel in the place as late as 1857, sick calls, &c., being attended by the priest from Hampton-on-the-Hill. About this time, Fr. Thos. Long appealed for funds to build a chapel. According to his account, there were 300 Catholics in the town. In 1860 the present church was built under the auspices of Mgr. Longman, chaplain to Lord Dormer. The building was redecorated at a cost of £300 in May 1893. The sanctuary is adorned with pictures representing the ecclesiastical history of Warwick.

New schools, for 100 children, were built 1904-5.

Priests.

Rev. Louis Groom, 1860.
„ John Wyse, 1863.
„ Edward Charles Acton, D.D., 1866.
„ Joseph Kelly, 1872.
„ J. Nary, 1891.
„ Alfred Hall, 1892 to date.

WARWICKBRIDGE, near CARLISLE, CUMBERLAND (*Hexham and Newcastle*). St. Mary.

This mission dates from about 1719, and has always been served by Benedictines. The old chapel, erected 1774, having become inadequate, the present building, in the thirteenth - century Gothic style, was opened November 1841. Three of the copes used on this occasion formerly belonged to Henry Stafford, Duke of Buckingham, beheaded in 1521. The erection of the church — designed by A. W. Pugin—was mainly due to Fr. Wm. Ryan, O.S.B.

Priests since 1824.

Rev. A. Ryding, 1820 (?).
„ W. Dale, 1835.
„ Wm. Ryan, 1840.
„ Francis Giles, 1876.
„ Thos. J. Barnett, 1895 to date.

WARWICK STREET, LONDON, W. (*Westminster*).

The old chapel originally belonged to the Portuguese Embassy, and the arms of Portugal were emblazoned on the ceiling at the time of its destruction by the Gordon rioters in 1780. When this lamentable event occurred, however, the chapel belonged to the Bavarian Ambassador, 'a prince of smugglers,' according to Horace Walpole (letter to Sir Horace Mann, June 5, 1780). Great quantities of contraband goods were found concealed in his house. After the riots a new chapel was built, 'similar to the majority of the older Methodist conventicles.' This unpleasing state of things was subsequently greatly improved, the cumbrous galleries being curtailed and the sanctuary and altar decorated. The altar-piece of the Assumption is by the famous sculptor J. Carew. The registers of the chapel date from 1747, but the mission was established in 1730 in connection with the Portuguese Embassy. It passed over to the Bavarian minister about 1747-48. The present church was built in 1788. It is still much the same in appearance as it was at the time of opening. The florid music and professional singing of the choir long attracted large congregations on Sundays and the chief festivals. A new sanctuary was added and the interior handsomely redecorated December 1876 to January 1877. After the proclamation of the German Empire, 1871, the Bavarian Embassy in London ceased, and the prayers on Sundays were henceforward said for Queen Victoria instead of the King of Bavaria. Fr. Jas. Archer, the great preacher, was 'chaplain' here in 1805.

WASHINGTON, DURHAM (*Hexham and Newcastle*). Our Lady Immaculate.

A Gothic school chapel for about 700 persons was opened by Bishop Hogarth 1863. For some years after the opening, the mission was served from Houghton. The pre-

E E

sent church, in the Decorated Gothic style, designed by Dunn & Hansom, the architects of the school chapel, was opened in September 1878. Dimensions, 96 ft. by 24 ft.; accommodation for 500 Until about 1881 the title of the church was St. Joseph and St. Aloysius.

Priests.

Rev. Francis Cambours, 1866.
„   Fredk. Poupaert, 1879.
„   Henry Mackin, 1898 to date

WATERLOO, LIVERPOOL. St. Thomas of Canterbury.

A temporary chapel was opened November 1, 1868, by Bishop Goss. The first stone of the church was laid by Cardinal Manning, August 24, 1875. The opening took place August 19, 1877. Consecration, September 14, 1892. The schools were opened April 1872, and enlarged September 1883. New sacristies were erected 1894.

Priests.

Rev. Albert Bennett, 1868.
„   Edmund Walsh, 1902 to date.

WATERLOO, LONDON, S.E. (*Southwark*). St. Patrick's, Cornwall Road.

This mission was established in 1897 mainly to counteract the non-Catholic influence of the St. Patrick's Benevolent Society Schools in Stamford Street, which, founded as far back as 1784, have educated hundreds of Irish children with no reference to their religion. An attempt was made in the ' early forties ' of the last century by Provost Doyle, of St. George's, to give the Catholic children of these schools some instruction weekly in

the cathedral, but, needless to say, the experiment failed utterly. In 1896, Bishop Butt, of Southwark, and Canon E. St. John took the matter in hand. Schools for boys and girls were commenced in Cornwall Road, and opened November 1, 1897, by Bishop Bourne in the presence of Cardinal Vaughan, the Duke of Norfolk, Canon J. Keatinge, etc. The number of children on the books at the outset was fifty ; it is now over 300. The school chapel accommodates about 200, but as the Catholic population of the district is estimated at 1,700 the need of a suitable church becomes apparent. Over 300 children are receiving instruction in the school, which is under the able tuition of the Misses Thompson.

Priests in Charge of the Mission.

Rev. Basil Gaisford, 1897.
„   Hugh Fickling, 1899.
„   Francis Ellis, 1900.
„   Mgr. Coote, D.C.L., 1901-2.
„   Bernard W. Kelly, 1902.
„   Wm. McLaughlin, 1904.
„   Fr. Cassels, 1905.

WATERLOOVILLE,   HANTS (*Portsmouth*).

The chapel, attached to the convent of the Sisters of Charity, was opened to the public on the feast of the Epiphany 1886. Before that time, Catholics of the district had to go to Havant to hear Mass. The Sisters started their convent at Waterlooville in October 1885. Fr. Lee was the first chaplain. No mention is made of the mission in the ' Catholic Directory ' till 1898, when Fr. William Dawson was rector. The next rectors have been : Rev. James Brown, 1899 ; Rev. John Molloy, 1903.

WATFORD, HERTS (*Westminster*). The Holy Rood, Market Street.

After many futile attempts to start a mission here, Fr. G. Bampfield, B.A., succeeded in opening a permanent chapel in Carey Place, September 1863. For some time the mission was served from Waltham Cross. The present church, for 500 persons, was built at the expense of S. Taprell-Holland, Esq., of Otterspool. The building was commenced August 1889, and opened September 16, 1890, by Bishop Weathers. Style, Decorated Gothic ; architect, J. F. Bentley. The old chapel of the Sacred Heart and St. John the Evangelist serves as a chapel of ease to the church of Holy Rood.

Priests.

Rev. Samuel Swanston, 1883.
„ Michael Ryan, 1889.
„ Geo. B. Cox, 1893.
„ Thos. Regan, 1895.
„ Joseph Keating, 1903 to date.

WATH-UPON-DEARNE, YORKS (*Leeds*). St. Joseph.

The mission was established in 1877, when Fr. C. Locke was appointed resident priest. In November of the same year the church and presbytery (Perpendicular Gothic) were commenced, at the expense of Mrs. Cadman and Mr. and Mrs. B. Nicholson. The building, which seats 300, was opened in 1879. The fine east window of five lights was the gift of Mrs. Gerard Young.

Priests.

Rev. C. Locke, 1877.
„ Daniel Murphy, 1903 to date.

WAVERTREE, LIVERPOOL (*Liverpool*). Our Lady of Good Help.

The mission was started in March 1871, when the old town hall and baths were purchased and transformed into a chapel and school. The present fine church, in the Decorated Gothic style, was opened May 1, 1887, by the Bishop of Liverpool. The accommodation is for 800 ; cost of erection, £6,000. Messrs. Sinnott were the architects.

Priests.

Rev. Henry Finch, 1871.
„ Peter Morgan, 1903 to date.

WEALDSTONE, MIDDLESEX (*Westminster*). St. Joseph.

The mission was established in 1901, and is in charge of the Salvatorian Fathers (Society of the Divine Saviour). The temporary chapel was at ' The Elms,' Harrow Weald Road. Estimated Catholic population, about 550. The mission is described as ' a growing one.' The new church was opened Sunday, June 24, 1906.

Priests.

Rev. Odo Distel, 1901.
„ F. Haertl, 1905.

WEDNESBURY, STAFFS (*Birmingham*). St. Mary.

The Catholic population was estimated at 1,000 in 1849. Fr. Crewe, of Bilston, acquired a site for a church 1848, and in 1850 Fr. George Montgomery (B.A. Trinity College, Dublin) came to the mission, and built a chapel mainly at his own expense. The building was opened June 22, 1852. Having got into difficulties through financing emigrants, he was forced to sell his valuable library, 1866. By 1872 the chapel had the appearance of 'a mere tumble-down barn,' and the present building was commenced May 1873, and opened 1874. The style is Early English; accommodation for 500. Much of the cost was defrayed by the rector, Fr. S. E. Bathurst, who also paid for the erection of the schools, opened in 1873 at a cost of £2,000.

Priests.

Rev. George Montgomery, 1850.
   „   S. E. Bathurst, 1866.
   „   Stephen Johnson, 1877.
   „   Frederick Keating, 1888.
   „   John Piris, 1898 to date.

WELD BANK. St. Gregory. *See* **CHORLEY.**

WELLINGBOROUGH, NORTHAMPTONSHIRE (*Northampton*). Our Lady of the Sacred Heart.

The mission was established in 1881, but in July 1882, in spite of the appeals of the priest, Fr. B. Murray, the 'chapel' was still a garret—small and stifling. The foundation stone of the new church was laid on the Tuesday after the Assumption 1885 by the Bishop of Northampton. The building was opened Thursday, September 2, 1886. Seating capacity for 400 persons. The stained-glass windows, by Westlake, and the interior decorations of the structure are very rich. The prevailing style is late fourteenth-century Gothic. S. J. Nicholl, of London, was the architect. A splendid marble and onyx altar was presented to the church in September

1893 by H. C. Burnham, Esq., 'as a thankoffering for his conversion to the true faith.'

WELLINGORE HALL, LINCS (*Nottingham*). St. Augustine.

On the conversion of Ralph H. C. Nevile, Esq., graduate of Trinity College, Cambridge, to the Faith, about 1874, a chapel was established at Wellingore Hall, the family seat, and this has continued to serve the mission. The Nevile family, who have been resident at Walcot, Northampton, and Wellingore Hall for generations, are a branch of the Neviles Lords of Raby, who became Earls of Westmorland (title extinct 1571).

Priests.

Rev. H. Sabela, 1874.
   „   H. Swale, 1877.
   „   Albert Op Broek, 1882.
   „   John Dickenson, 1885.
      (Served from elsewhere 1890–1902.)
   „   John   Bernard   Caldwell, O.S.B., 1904 to date.

WELLINGTON,   SHROPSHIRE (*Shrewsbury*). St. Patrick.

At the time of the French Revolution, a number of refugee clergy were most kindly entertained at Dothill Park, near Wellington, by the Forester family, and one of these priests, the Abbé Lemaitre, is reported to have attended to the few Catholics in the district. After his death or return to France, about 1818, the priest at Madeley served the place occasionally. In 1834 Fr. D. Morton opened a chapel in a shed behind the 'Duke's Head' Inn. St. Patrick's Church was commenced 1836, and opened June 19, 1838. In 1885 a bell-tower and façade were added. The schools were built in 1856.

Priests.

Rev. D. Morton, 1834.
„ C. Jeffries, 1842.
„ A. Lempfried, 1848.
„ F. McGrath, 1849.
„ W. Molloy, 1849.
„ L. Kelly, 1851.
„ J. Oliver, 1853.
„ J. Jenkins, 1861.
„ A. Gavois, 1863.
„ Hy. Walker, 1866.
„ F. Waterhouse, 1869.
„ R. Hilton, 1871.
„ J. Hackett, 1873.
„ C. Langdon, 1880.
„ R. Silva, 1882.
„ A. Tremmery, 1886.
„ B. Thompson, 1895.

WELLS, SOMERSET (*Clifton*). SS. Joseph and Teresa.

In the seventeenth and eighteenth centuries, Wells was one of the places served by the Jesuit ' college ' or residence of St. Francis Xavier. Fr. John Scudamore, S.J., who died at Bristol, was missioner in the district for a time. In 1875 the Carmelite nuns of Plymouth settled here, and their chapel, opened October 17, 1877, served the mission till the erection of the present church, by Mr. and Mrs. Mercier of Alston Hall. The building was consecrated 1890. A notable feature of the interior is the handsome altar and reredos of stone and coloured marbles, designed by Canon Scoles.

Priests since 1875.

Rev. J. W. Townsend, 1875.
„ Canon Neve, D.D., 1879.
„ Jos. Butcher, 1881.
„ John Bérard, here in 1888.
„ Daniel Boyle, 1891.
„ C. Chandler, 1896 to date.

WEMBLEY, MIDDLESEX (*Westminster*). St. Joseph.

The mission was formed 1901, at Elm Cottage, the first priest being the present rector, the Rev. J. Egan. The Catholic cemetery in the district contains the bodies of the dead disinterred at Moorfields (*q.v.*) when the old church was demolished in November 1899. Since 1904 the mission has been at Perivale House, London Road.

WEOBLEY, HEREFORDSHIRE (*Newport*). St. Thomas of Hereford.

The ancient mission was at Sarnesfield Court, the ancestral seat of the Monington family. The estate is now owned by the Salvins of Croxdale.[1] For a long time the Jesuit Fathers served the chapel, but at the end of the eighteenth century (1797), an attempt was made to establish a Franciscan novitiate here, but without success. The chapel at Sarnesfield was superseded in 1834 by the present one at Weobley, which, together with the mission-house, was erected mainly at the expense of Mr. and Mrs. Monington of Sarnesfield. Catholics at this time numbered about ninety. A schoolhouse was built in 1849.

N.B.—During the *furore* of the Oates plot, Fr. Charles Carne, S.J., chaplain to the Moningtons at Sarnesfield, was tried before Chief Justice Scroggs at the Hereford

---

[1] The property passed about thirty years ago to Marmaduke Salvin, Esq., in virtue of the marriage of his kinswoman Bridget Webb to John Monington, Esq., of Sarnesfield. See Burke, *Landed Gentry* (Salvin of Croxdale).

Summer Assizes, August 4, 1679. Wonderful to relate, the prisoner was acquitted !

Priests.

Rev. Leo. Hadden, O.S.F., 1787.
„ Peter Chanteloup, 1800 (?).
„ J. Carbery, 1834.
„ S. Calderbank, 1835.
„ J. Duck, 1837.
„ Jas. Dullard, 1840.
„ M. Sinnot, 1842.
„ P. Hewitt, 1848.
„ T. Rolling, 1852.
„ Edmund Caldwell, 1855.
„ C. B. Quinn, 1861.
„ David Lambe, here 1871.
„ James Tunny, 1877.
„ Rev. Chas. Kerin, 1879.
„ Hy. Canon Mackey, 1882.
„ Wm. Bulbeck, 1891.
„ Thos. Lonergan, 1895.
„ Thos. P. Hartly Russell, 1903 to date.

WESHAM, PRESTON, LANCS (*Liverpool*). St. Joseph.

The mission was established out of funds left for the purpose by Fr. Thos. Billington († May 20, 1880) and his sister Mrs. Gibson († December 18, 1880). The site of the church — consecrated March 18, 1886—was formerly occupied by 'Wesham Cross.' It may be remarked that early in the last century the few Catholics round about Wesham were attended by the priest of Mowbreck Hall. In 1809 the number of communicants at Mowbreck was 270. In 1887 the number at Wesham was over 300. The school, for 192 children, was opened February 10, 1890, and a Catholic cemetery was consecrated by the Bishop of Liverpool, Sunday, September 22, 1895. The church was redecorated and the high altar finished 1899.

Priests.

Rev. Mgr. Wm. Wrennall, D.D.
„ Fredk. D'Heuter, 1897 to date.

WESTBOROUGH, near GRANTHAM, LINCS (*Nottingham*). Our Lady of Mercy.

The church was opened in August 1888. For five years previous to that date, Fr. Sabela conducted services in the Swan Inn, Long Bennington, for the benefit of the Irish harvesters. In 1887 a Methodist chapel was purchased, and transformed into a Catholic church. The mission is served from Grantham.

WEST BRIDGFORD (*Nottingham*).

When the mission was commenced in 1897 Mass was said in a temporary chapel in the cricket pavilion by Fr. Francis Hayes, the first incumbent. In 1904 the chapel was served from the cathedral, Nottingham.

WEST BROMWICH, STAFFS (*Birmingham*). St. Michael and the Holy Angels.

The church was dedicated and opened November 21, 1832, by Bishop Walsh, V.A. Dr. Weedal, of Oscott, preached. Before the opening of the Gothic church, a hired dissenting chapel did duty as a place of Catholic worship for several years. During this time, Fr. Martyn, of Walsall, used to officiate on Sundays, but after the opening of the new church the Hon. Fr. G.

Spencer was appointed first resident priest. On Sunday, December 22, 1834, Bishop Walsh confirmed 110 persons at West Bromwich, of whom seventy were converts. During May 1845 lectures on Catholic faith and practice were given in the church on Sunday evenings by Fr. G. Bent to counteract the effect of the anti-Maynooth Grant meetings, held at a neighbouring Wesleyan chapel. Some thousands of persons attended Fr. Bent's discourses, and numerous conversions were the result. The church of 1832 gave place in March 1877 to the present fine structure in the High Street, built mainly through the exertions of Fr. J. Daly, who collected most of the funds (£3,000), in New York. The mission will ever be associated with the initial labours of Fr. Spencer for the 'conversion of England,' and it is to his memory that the church now standing was erected.

Priests.

Rev. Hon. George (Ignatius) Spencer, 1834.
  ,, George Bent, 1840.
  ,, Thos. Revill, 1850.
  ,, John Wyse, 1860.
  ,, Louis Groom, 1863.
  ,, Joseph Daly, M.R., 1874.
  ,, Edward Plaetsier, here in 1883 till 1891.
  ,, John Fox, M.R., 1891 to date.

WESTBURY-ON-TRYM, near **BRISTOL** (*Clifton*). Convent of Mercy.

This convent is conducted by the Sisters of Mercy, and stands at the end of the Clifton Downs. The Sisters devote themselves to the work of education, the school being recognised by the Board of Education. The chapel is open to the public, and for the time being serves the mission. The house was formerly the convent of the Visitation nuns, who settled here in 1831. The fine chapel was commenced 1834, and opened December 1835. The Visitation community quitted the place for Harrow-on-the-Hill in 1896.

WESTBY, KIRKHAM, LANCS (*Liverpool*). St. Anne.

The Cliftons of Lytham kept the Faith alive in the district during the penal times, and many of the family figure on the recusant rolls. The chapel, opened May 1742, was closed in 1845 after the defection of Squire Clifton from the Faith. In 1859, Miss Dalton of Thurnham Hall purchased a site from Colonel Clifton, and a new church, in the Early English style, was opened by Bishop Goss in August 1860. The building, which holds about 400, was designed by E. W. Pugin. Buttresses and iron columns to strengthen the church were erected 1889-90, and a new organ gallery added. The building was consecrated by Bishop Whiteside, November 8, 1900.

N.B.—The baptismal register dates from October 15, 1761. The old chapel after its closure was used as a barn.

Priests since 1825.

Rev. Thos. Pennington.
  ,, Geo. Haydock, 1830.
  ,, Jn. Dixon, 1831-45.
    (Mission closed 1845; reopened about 1860.)
  ,, Wm. Ball, 1860.
  ,, Thos. Dawson, 1877.
  ,, Joseph Lowe, here in 1883 till 1892.
  ,, Geo. Park, 1892 to date.

WEST CORNFORTH, DURHAM

(*Hexham and Newcastle*). SS. Joseph, Patrick, and Cuthbert.

When the foundation stone of the church was laid, June 30, 1873, by Bishop Chadwick, the district was reported to contain ' a vast number of Catholics.' The site was the gift of James Morrison, Esq., of Newcastle-on-Tyne. The building, which measures 122 ft. in length, is of stone, and Gothic in design, from plan by R. Robinson. The opening took place October 18, 1875.

Priests.

Rev. Matthew Gibson, 1875.

„ Edward Walsh, 1881.

„ John Sheehan, 1889 to date.

WEST DERBY ROAD, LIVERPOOL

(*Liverpool*). St. Paul.

In 1716 Thos. Smith, High Constable of West Derby, reported to the Commissioners for Forfeited Estates that there was ' one Mr. Wolfall, who is reputed to exercise his functions as a Popish priest at a place called Newhall, in West Derby.' This priest was the Rev. Thos. Wolfall, who was ordained at Rome in 1699,. and served the district till his death in 1720. The present mission of West Derby dates from September 24, 1865, when a school chapel was opened by Bishop Goss. E. W. Pugin was the architect; cost of erection, £3,500. The church was opened November 21, 1880. According to an estimate, the Catholic population is about 700.

Priests since 1880.

Rev. Richard Clarkson.

„ Wm. Leeming, 1891 to date.

WEST DRAYTON, MIDDLESEX

(*Westminster*). St. Catherine the Martyr.

The first chapel of the mission was ' a poor stable ' (1867). Only forty persons could be admitted at one time, so that some 130 had to kneel outside during Mass. The church was opened September 30, 1869, by Archbishop Manning, who preached to a crowded congregation (Rev. xii. 7). The style is fourteenth-century Gothic; dimensions, 85 ft. by 48 ft. The building was consecrated September 29, 1893. Mixed schools, established 1867, had an average attendance of sixty-six in 1899–1900. The congregation numbers about 200 (1906).

Priests.

Rev. P. F. Elkins, 1867.

„ Michael Wren, 1868 till 1896.

„ Patrick O'Connell, 1896.

„ Charles Tubbs, 1902.

„ W. Donelan, 1904.

WEST GRINSTEAD, SUSSEX

(*Southwark*). Our Lady of Consolation and St. Francis.

The adherence of the Caryll family to the ancient faith made West Grinstead a focus of Catholicity as far back as the reign of Queen Elizabeth. The remoteness of the locality, hidden among the Sussex woods, also tended to favour the exercise of the proscribed religion. In 1688, Richard Caryll, Esq., was created Baron Durford by James II.—after the Revolution. The son of this gentleman was the friend of Pope, apostrophised by the poet in the well-known line,

This verse to Caryll, Muse, is due.

In 1755, John Caryll, grandson of Richard, went to Italy to enter the service of Prince Charles

Edward Stuart. He is the 'Lord Caryll' referred to in the letters of that unhappy prince and his adherents. This gentleman, before leaving England, made over the ancestral mansion to Bishop Challoner, V.A.L.D., for the use of the mission at West Grinstead. The house, which dates from about the period of the Restoration, has one or two hiding-places for priests. Near it, in more recent times, stood the old domestic chapel, adorned with Ionic pillars, which served the mission till the erection of the present church, by the late Mgr. Dennis, about 1879. The style of the building is French Gothic ; the interior is adorned with heraldic devices of the several benefactors. The congregation numbers about 300. The present rector is Fr. R. Measures.

N.B.—The Ven. Arthur Bell, O.S.F., who suffered for the Faith at Tyburn December 11, 1643, was on the mission at West Grinstead for a short period. His chalice and one or two other articles belonging to him are preserved in the sacristy of the church.

WEST HARTLEPOOL, DURHAM (*Hexham and Newcastle*). St. Joseph.

The mission was described in 1862 as 'a new station served from St. Mary's.' Fr. Peter Harivel had charge of the chapel at this time. The church was opened November 13, 1867.

Priests.

Rev. James Shea, 1869.
„ James Crolly, 1879.
„ Michael Greene, 1885.
„ Wm. Wickwar, 1888 (?) to date.

WEST HOUGHTON, LANCS (*Salford*). The Sacred Heart of Jesus.

A chapel was opened September 14, 1873, the mission being served from Bolton. It became independent about 1877, when the Rev. Peter Maringer was appointed. The present fine church was opened by Bishop Bilsborrow November 14, 1894. Estimated Catholic population of the district, about 1,000.

Priests.

Rev. Peter Maringer, 1877.
„ Jn. Willemse, 1882.
„ Wilfrid Hampson, 1885.
„ G. S. Mitchell, 1888.
„ Thos. Keelan, 1892.
„ Wm. Palmer, 1893.
„ Fredk. Beulink, 1898.
„ Adolphus Coelenbier, 1899 to date.

WEST KIRKBY, CHESHIRE (*Shrewsbury*). St. Agnes.

The church was opened July 18, 1897, by Bishop Allen. Before this time, the district was included in the mission of Our Lady's, Birkenhead. Catholic population, 250.

WESTMINSTER, LONDON, S.W. SS. Peter and Edward, Palace Street.

The Oblates of St. Charles commenced the mission here 1857-58. The first school was a disused theatre on the site of the present St. James's Park Station. The church was entered down a flight of steps, but, by the ingenuity of Mr. J. Bentley, this was afterwards altered to the present interior arrangement. The school-room is now under the church. Fr. Cyril Forster has been rector since 1881.

WESTMINSTER, LONDON, S.W.

A chapel was opened in York Street 1792, and closed 1799. In 1803, another was started in Great Smith Street, and 'served by the chaplains of the Neapolitan Embassy.' Like the first, the mission could not be supported, and was closed 1806. A third attempt, at 7 Dartmouth Street, was more successful, and on Sunday, November 13, 1813, the congregation migrated to a large permanent chapel in Romney Terrace, Marlborough Square. This building was due to Fr. Wm. Hurst, who served the mission till 1817, when he left for Trinidad, W.I. He likewise built schools for boys and girls. In 1824 the congregation was estimated at 2,000. After the restoration of the hierarchy, Cardinal Wiseman made over the mission to the Jesuits, by whom the church was considerably enlarged. It was long known as St. Mary's, Horseferry Road, but was closed 1903 on the opening of the Westminster Cathedral (q.v.).

Priests.

Rev. W. Hurst, 1811.
„ — Sumner, 1817.
„ Lewis Havard, 1820 (?)
„ Mgr. Anthony Magee, 1831.
„ Wm. Rowe, 1851.
„ Jas. Corry, 1855.
„ W. Cardwell, 1860.
„ Geo. Lambert, 1863.
„ Richard Cooper, 1867.
„ Vincent Bond, here 1871.
„ Robt. Whitty, 1876.
„ John Hartell, 1879.
„ F. Scoles, 1882.
„ Hy. Martin, 1887.
„ Jn. Beall, 1895.

WESTMINSTER CATHEDRAL.

The Westminster Cathedral, Ashley Place. It was one of the last wishes of Cardinal Wiseman that a 'cathedral might be erected for the Metropolitan See of Westminster.' On May 25, 1865, a meeting of Catholics in London, presided over by Dr. Manning, resolved to carry this pious desire into effect, and in 1867 a site was purchased in Carlisle Place, Westminster, for £16,500. Additional land was purchased in 1868, and plans prepared. The old site, purchased in 1867 and 1868, was sold to the Building Securities Company, and a more advantageous one obtained. Part of this ground was once covered by the Tothill Fields Prison. This purchase was effected by the Westminster Land Company, a business company of distinguished Catholic laymen, acting on behalf of Cardinal Manning. Little if anything was done after this till the accession of Cardinal Vaughan to the archiepiscopal see (April 1892), when his Eminence commissioned the late J. F. Bentley, Esq., F.R.I.B.A., to prepare plans for the cathedral. Mr. Bentley spent some months in foreign travel, carefully collecting ideas from the architectural masterpieces of the past, and on June 29, 1895, the foundation stone was laid. The ceremony was one of the most imposing ever witnessed in the annals of Catholic London. Two cardinals, surrounded by several of the Catholic hierarchy of England, the representatives of both religious and secular clergy and the distinguished laity, took part in the solemn function. The Mass on this occasion was celebrated by Cardinal Logue, Archbishop of Armagh. The style of the cathedral is Byzantine, which flourished at Constantinople and throughout Eastern Europe generally from A.D. 325 to 1450. Its leading characteristics are 'simple roofs, flat domes rising from square spaces and carried on massive piers, unbroken arched soffits, and barrel vaults.' The interiors are adorned with coloured marbles, gildings, and mosaics. The dimensions of the cathedral are as follows : total internal length 342 ft. ; width across nave, aisles, and side chapels, 148 ft.; height of the three domes, 112 ft. The chapels comprise : (1) Lady Chapel, (2) Chapel of the Blessed Sacrament, (3) English Martyrs, (4) Holy Souls, &c. The pulpit and baptismal font are fine examples of Byzantine decoration. A block of grey Cornish granite, weighing twelve tons, forms the high altar. It was presented by the Hon. George Saville. The vast sacristy, with its spacious oak presses for vestments &c., well reflects the magnitude of the church it is designed to serve. A striking object of the interior of the cathedral is the huge painted cross suspended from the central dome over the chancel. The graceful campanile, towering to a height of 284 ft., commands a view over several of the home counties. The lamented death of Cardinal Vaughan, in June 1903, may be said to have hurried on in an extraordinary way the work he had so much at heart. His solemn requiem amidst the rugged grandeur of the unfinished cathedral shell, which was attended by an enormous crowd of Catholics, both lay and clerical, was regarded as the official opening of the building. There is now a regularly appointed Sunday and daily service, under the direction of a numerous staff of clergy. The fine baldachino, consisting of an arch of white marble supported by eight *Verona* marble columns, was completed in the autumn of 1906.

WESTON-SUPER-MARE (*Clifton*). St. Joseph.

According to the Rev. Dr. Coombs, O.S.B., of Downside, Mass was said as far back as 1744 at Meadgate, close to this place, but by whom does not appear. The ' Mass-house ' was used as a public-house in 1857. In 1851, the Jesuit Fathers hired a large room in the town for Mass on Sundays. In 1854, Fr. Van de Voorde was priest of the mission. After several years' struggling with the initial difficulties of a new foundation, the pastor and congregation had the satisfaction of witnessing the erection of the present church in 1859. The edifice is a neat Gothic building capable of holding about 300 persons. The mission was long served from the cathedral, Clifton.

Priests.

Rev. Van de Voorde, 1854.

„ Maurice Canon Power, 1863.

„ John P. Bouvier, 1879 till 1898.

„ Eustace Canon Barron, 1898 to date.

WEST RASEN, LINCS (*Nottingham*).

The old chapel on the estate of the Constable family long served the mission. After the last Jacobite rebellion, 1746, the house was raided by the sheriff's officers in pursuit of Sir Marmaduke Langdale, Bart., and the chaplain was only saved from capture by hiding in some loose hay. The orchard of the estate served as a cemetery for the few local Catholics, whose dead were refused burial in the neighbouring parish church of All Saints. In 1872, the present church of Our Lady of the Rosary was opened by Thos. Young, Esq., K.S.G. This old Catholic family settled at West Rasen shortly after the Restoration, and in 1793 Isaac Young, Esq., purchased the parish and manor of Kingerby, near West Rasen, and with it the old mansion and chapel of the Constables. The mission is served from Market Rasen.

WEYBRIDGE, SURREY (*Southwark*). St. Charles.

The ancient mission was at Woburn Park, about a mile and a half from the present church, the ancestral seat of the Southcote family, which died out in 1783. The estates then passed to Lord Petre, and in or about 1815 to Sir John Aubyn (by purchase). This last gentleman, who was a protestant, discontinued the Catholic chapel in the house, but built another for his Catholic tenantry and others near the lodge gates. After some years' tenure by Lord Kilmorey, the Park again passed to the Petre family, in the person of Mgr. Lord Petre, who conducted a high-class boys' school there from 1876 to 1884, when the estate was sold to the Josephite Fathers of St. George's College, Croydon. They transferred their excellent educational establishment from the latter place to Weybridge in the autumn of the last-named year. The chapel of the college is thus the canonical representative of the old domestic chapel which kept alive the Faith in this district during the penal times. The Dominicans served Woburn for upwards of 300 years. Fr. Short, O.P., was priest here from 1750 till 1800, and Fr. Castrick, O.P., from 1800 to 1815. Fr. Potier, the next priest, removed the mission to Weybridge, where for nineteen years he continued to say Mass in his house for the benefit of the few Catholics round about. In January 1835 the mission was taken over by seculars, the first of these being Fr. Corr. In 1836, James Taylor, Esq., a wealthy Catholic architect of the neighbourhood, built a small chapel—now the sacristy of the church. It was opened by Bishop Bramston. The place was so small that not more than a dozen persons could be accommodated in it at one time! The present fine Gothic church of St. Charles Borromeo was built by Catherine Taylor, and opened by Cardinal Manning August 31, 1881. The interior is very ornate. King Louis Philippe and his queen were buried in this church, but the bodies were removed to France in 1876. The Duchesse de Nemours, a cousin of the late Queen Victoria, lies interred here beneath a beautifully chiselled tomb, as also does the late Comte de Paris, father of the present Duke of Orleans. On the epistle side of the church are two memorial tablets—one to the Duke de Fitz-James, a descendant of James II., and the other to Mr. Hubert Wolseley, of the Imperial Light Horse, who was killed at the battle of Elandslaagte, South Africa, November 1899. He was cousin of Field-Marshal Lord Wolseley, and for some time a student at the neighbouring Catholic college, St. George's, Woburn Park. The first confirmation at Weybridge took place in 1837. The Catholic population of the place is now about 300. The clergy in succession at Weybridge in recent times have been :—

Rev. Fr. Corr, 1835.
„ Fr. Bowman, 1835-41.
„ Fr. J. Welch, 1841-50.
„ Fr. Sidden, September–November 1850.
„ Fr. Kerm, November 1850-August 1851.
„ Fr. Hodgson, 1851-55.
„ Fr. J. McDonald, 1855-60.
„ Fr. Van Reeth, 1860-61.
„ Fr. Glennie, 1861-62.
„ Fr. Whyte, 1862-63.
„ Fr. C. Comberbach, 1863-67.
„ Canon Glennie (second time), 1867-78.
„ Fr. Richardson, 1878-87.
„ Fr. McDaniel, 1887-98.
„ Canon McGrath, 1898-1905.
„ Thos. B. Scannell, D.D., 1905 to date.

WEYMOUTH, DORSET (*Plymouth*). St. Augustine.

The Abbé Dubuisson, who settled here as a teacher of French about 1795, fitted up a chapel in a retired room for the use of the few Catholic residents and visitors. Bishop Baines, coadjutor to Bishop Collingridge, V.A., rented a house, No. 4 Belvedere, in 1823, and undertook the spiritual care of the district. Fr. P. Hartley in 1831 procured a site for a church, and the building (56 ft. by 20 ft.) was opened October 22, 1835. A series of lectures on the Church delivered in the chapel by the unfortunate Fr. Butler did much to turn the attention of protestants to the Catholic claims.

Priests.

Rev. Abbé Dubuisson, 1795 (retired 1822).
„ James Macdonnell, 1822.
Bishop Baines, 1822.

Rev. Francis Edgeworth, 1824.
„ Peter Hartley, 1829.
„ Joseph Dwyer, 1835.
„ Thomas Butler, D.D., 1837.
„ — Murphy, 1838.
„ Thomas Canon Tilbury, 1840.
„ James Dawson, 1856.
„ William Walsh, 1860.
„ John Charles, 1863.
„ Richard Meager, 1877.
„ Patrick Canon O'Brien, 1893.
„ David Barry, 1899 to date.

WHITBY, YORKS (*Middlesbrough*). St. Hilda.

In 1774 there were about fifteen Catholics at Whitby, which number increased to seventy by 1805, principally owing to the labours of the Abbé Gilbert, an *émigré* priest. Between 1790 and 1805, Mass was said at various private houses, but in April of the last-named year a chapel was opened. A debt of £700 remained on the building as late as 1822. At this time, Mass ('prayers') on Sunday was at ten o'clock, while on holy days 'Benediction, with incense,' was advertised. Fr. George Haydock was the priest. The old chapel having become inadequate, the foundation stone of the present church was laid on July 21, 1866. The building was opened in November 1867. The style is that of the eleventh and twelfth centuries. The church consists of nave and aisles, to accommodate 400. Two of the fine stained-glass windows are in memory of deceased members of the Lawson and Turnbull families. The schools, for 300 children, were opened, Easter Tuesday 1877. The number of Catholics in the district, which was only about fifteen in 1774, had increased to 184 in 1815—a strong proof of the missionary zeal of the Abbé Gilbert.

Priests.

Rev. Abbé Nicholas Gilbert, 1794.
„ George Haydock, 1816.
„ Robert Tate, 1830.
„ William Parker, 1832.
„ Richard Brown, 1835.
„ J. Conaty, 1837.
„ Charles Pratt, 1842.
„ Jos. Curr, 1844.
„ — McMahon, 1846.
„ George Keasley, 1848.
„ John Glover, 1860 (?).
„ Hy. Walker, 1874.
„ Jos. Canon Molloy, 1882.
„ W. Sullivan, 1885.
„ Benjamin Canon Randerson, here in 1889.
„ James Nolan, 1897.
„ Bernard McCabe, 1901 to date.

WHITECHAPEL (*Westminster*). German Church of St. Boniface.

The German church was removed from St. Thomas' Lane, City, where it had been since 1808, to Whitechapel in 1870. The first building having become ruinous, another was erected in 1875, and opened when partially complete. It was finished by the addition of a spire in July 1882. The style is Basilican. The pilasters between the windows are painted, after the manner of the Dusseldorf school, with life-size figures of SS. Peter, Paul, Christopher, Conrad, Henry, Engelbert, Boniface, &c. Mr. Bower was the artist. The altar rails and pulpit are handsomely carved. The Emperors of Austria and Germany contributed £50 each towards the completion of the building. The priests of the diocese

of Treves gave £400 for the same purpose. The architect of the building was Mr. Young.

WHITECHURCH, SALOP (*Shrews- bury*). St. George.

The mission was established as a ' station ' in 1863 by Fr. H. Alcock, of Crewe. In 1856-57 Frs. Jas. Kenny and Michael Power resided in the parish for a time, but the mission was again attached to Crewe 1858. The present chapel was opened on Whit Monday 1878. Fr. Thomas Bolton came as first resident priest of late years (1892), and in 1898 he was succeeded by Fr. Firmin de Vos, the present rector.

WHITEHAVEN, CUMBERLAND (*Hexham and Newcastle*). St. Begh's.

The Benedictines have been in charge of this mission since 1706. The chapel became the 'mother church' both of Cumberland and the Isle of Man. The old chapel was in Duke Street, opposite the colliery, but the house is now occupied by a society of Free- masons. The second chapel was opened in 1834, on a site given to the priest—Father Holdings—by Lord Lonsdale in recognition of his efforts in dissuading his lordship's Irish colliers from joining illegal unions, &c. The town council also offered a piece of plate, but this the priest respectfully declined. The chapel of 1834 is now used as a school. In 1861, a site for a new church was obtained on very ad- vantageous terms from the Lord Lonsdale of the day, and on it was built the third and present church. The cost was defrayed by the late Mr. Richard Cousins, the plans being prepared by the younger Pugin. The interior was beautifully redecorated in December 1899. The former patron of the mission was St. Gregory, but the title was afterwards changed to that of St. Begh or Bees, an Irish abbess who founded a convent at Copeland, near Carlisle, A.D. 630. From 1841 to 1854 another chapel existed in the town as auxiliary to the mother church. The title was St. Mary.

Priests.

Rev. Robert Daniell, 1751–59.
„ William Holding, 1825.
„ Gregory Holden, 1831.
„ William Holden, 1848.
„ Thomas Shepherd, 1855.
„ Edward Lynass, 1860.
„ Jas. Rowley, here in 1874.
„ Hubert Murphy, here in 1888 and to date.

WHITEWELL, YORKS, WEST RIDING (*Leeds*). St. Hubert.

Before the erection of the present church in May 1865, Catholics attended the domestic chapel of Richard Eastwood, Esq., of Thorneyholme. The nearest Catholic church was at Chipping, seven miles distant. The present church of Whitewell is in the Early English style. Mr. A. W. Pugin was the architect. The seating accommodation is for 100 persons, and the cost of erection was £700. For some time after the opening, the building was used on weekdays as a school.

Priests.

Rev. Alfred Watson, here in 1875.
„ John Bulletti, 1877.
„ J. Daine, 1879.
„ Walter Baggaley, here in 1883.

Rev. Francis Higgins, 1885.
„ Gustave Thonon, 1895 to date.

WHITSON COURT, near NEW-PORT, MONMOUTHSHIRE (*Newport*).

The convent of the Most Holy Sacrament was opened here 1903. Chapel open to the public. Fr. J. Perrin, chaplain.

WHITSTABLE, KENT (*Southwark*).

St. Vincent's Orphanage for little boys is described as being founded 'about five or six years ago.' The first school—a small house accommodating about thirty children—was relinquished for the present fine structure at the corner of Church Street Road, opened towards the end of 1901. The school, which meets 'all the modern requirements of the Home Office inspectors,' is under the care of the Sisters of Mercy. The chapel, on the ground floor, led to the formation of the mission, being attended by the Passionist Fathers from Herne Bay. A new church was opened by Bishop Amigo, of Southwark, Sunday, July 22, 1906. Fr. Hyacinth, C.P., is the present priest of the mission.

WHITTINGHAM, NORTHUMBER-LAND (*Hexham and Newcastle*). Our Lady Immaculate.

This mission is a continuation of the old Callaly chapel, which was founded as far back as the twelfth century. It owed its origin, and protection during the penal laws that followed the Reformation, to the Clavering family. On the death of Edward J. Clavering, Esq., in 1876, the Callaly estate was sold, and the mission removed to Whittingham. The site of the new church was obtained from the Earl of Ravensworth; the cost of erection was defrayed by Sir Henry and Lady Bedingfeld, who also provided for the maintenance of the fabric and resident priest. The church and presbytery, in the Norman style, were finished in February 1881, and on March 1 of that year Fr. C. Ickenroth took up his residence in the mission. The fine stained-glass window over the high altar was the gift of Mrs. Clavering, who died February 13, 1881, at Tynemouth. She left £600 for the benefit of the mission.

Priests.

Rev. C. Ickenroth, 1881.
  ,, Patrick Walsh, 1882.
  ,, Wm. Taylor here in 1888 till after 1900.
  ,, Matthew Culley, 1903 to date.

Callaly Castle, Northumberland, 'the seat of the ancient Catholic and loyal family of Clavering,' was served by the Jesuits. The family sprang from the Veseys, Lords of Alnwick and the Laceys, Earls of Lincoln, and were seated at Callaly from about the time of Henry III. Several of its numbers entered the Society of Jesus, viz. Thos. Clavering, S.J., confessor to the English Benedictine nuns at Pontoise (died 1694), and Fr. Ralph Clavering. Sir John Clavering, a distinguished Royalist officer, died a prisoner in London for his loyalty to Charles I. The last Jesuit chaplain at the castle was Fr. Joseph Dunn, who left for the Preston mission 1775.

WHITWICK, LEICESTERSHIRE (*Nottingham*). Holy Cross.

The old church and cemetery were consecrated by Bishop Walsh, V.A., October 12, 1837. Fr. O. Woolfrey was the first incumbent. The building (Gothic) accommodated about 200. The first stone of the new church was laid Wednesday, May 17, 1905, by Bishop Brindle, D.S.O. The building, which will be opened in about a year, is for 500 persons, the estimated cost being £5,000.

Priests.

Rev. S. Whitaker, 1840.
  ,, R. Cousinier, 1845.
  ,, F. Signini, 1849.
  ,, Ignatius Sisk, 1853.
  ,, Geo. Bent, 1860.
  ,, Angelus Van Paemel, 1866.
  ,, John Jackson, 1884.
  ,, Michael O'Reilly, 1888 to date.

WHITWORTH, LANCS (*Salford*). Our Immaculate Mother and St. Anselm.

For some years prior to 1860, Mass was said every Sunday in an upper room of the Hare and Hounds Inn. In the above year, Fr. Millward, finding this 'chapel' too small, hired a large apartment belonging to the Co-operative Society. A wooden chapel was built in 1862, and a cottage close by fitted up as a school and presbytery. After one or two more such makeshifts, a church was opened October 10, 1869, at a cost of about £3,000. A tower, with clock and peal of bells, was added to the church about 1878. The clock is now lighted at night at the public expense

Priests.

Rev. John Millward, 1860.

„ Chas. Wood, here in 1874.

„ Adrian Egglemeers, 1877 till 1893.

„ Robt. Smith, 1893.

„ A. Van der Beck, 1895.

„ Thos. Dillon, 1904 to date.

WIDNES, LANCS (*Liverpool*). St. Bede, Appleton.

The place takes its name from the Appleton family of Fenilstreet, afterwards represented by the Hawardens and Gillibrands. In the sixteenth century, a secret chapel was maintained at Fenilstreet House, and a priest kept in constant residence. A public chapel was opened in 1750. For over a century, the mission of Appleton served that of Widnes, which had no church of its own till 1865. The old chapel at Appleton was superseded by the present church, erected in 1847 at a cost of £4,000.

Priests.

Rev. Mr. Barlow, 1657.

„ Wm. Hawarden (convicted of recusancy at Lancaster 1716 ; he died at Widnes).

„ Edw. Hawarden, 1717 ?

„ Thos. Hawarden, V.G. (*d.* 1746).

„ Hy. Gillow, 1821.

„ Geo. Fisher, 1848.

„ Thos. Finegan, 1876 to date.

WIDNES, LANCS. St. Mary, Lugsdale Road.

In 1862 the Catholic population was over 2,000. The first priest of the mission was Fr. D. Malkerns, but the chapel was only a large room accommodating at the most 100 persons. On Sunday, October 30, 1864, the first stone of the Gothic church was laid by Bishop Goss, of Liverpool. The seating capacity is for about 500. The cost of erection was upwards of £3,100. Until the opening of the church (September 1865), Mass was said in the schools erected by Fr. Fisher. Excluding the chancel, which was added later, the cost of the building was £2,700. The ground was given by John Hutchinson, Esq. The new church of St. Patrick, West Bank Street, was commenced in May 1887, and opened Sunday, June 24, 1888. The style is Early Gothic. The seating accommodation is for 700. Messrs. J. & B. Synott were the architects. The Catholic population of Widnes in 1887 was estimated at 8,300. New schools were opened May 3, 1893.

WIGAN, LANCS (*Liverpool*). St. John.

This mission, like most of those in Lancashire, was anciently served by the Jesuit Fathers. In the reign of James II. a chapel and school were opened, and well attended. Even the mayor and corporation were present at Mass on several occasions. In 1687, Bishop Leyburn confirmed 1,318 persons at Wigan. The chapel was destroyed by a mob at the Revolution of 1688. The earliest missioner recorded is Fr. J. Canell, S.J., who died at Wigan 1722, *æt.* 73. The Rev. Sir Pyers Mostyn, Bart., S.J., was the next priest ; he died August 29, 1735, *æt.* 45. Fr. C. Brockholes, S.J., who succeeded, built the chapel and presbytery under the same roof about 1740. The cost of erection was defrayed out of his own *peculium*, or income. In 1750,

F F

Catholics in Wigan numbered 300, the general confessions being about sixty. A second chapel was erected 1819-20, and is in the Italian style. Fine altar rails of marble and alabaster were added to the sanctuary November 1891. The interior was redecorated and reopened October 1849.

Priests since 1824.

Rev. — Newsham, —.
„ John Hagarty, 1829.
„ J. Cattanach, 1835.
„ Malachy Clarke, 1837.
„ Edw. Morron, 1840.
„ John Hearne, 1844.
„ Maurice Mann, 1848.
„ Thos. Seed, 1852.
„ Thos. Hill, 1860.
„ Jos. Gradwell, here in 1871 till 1891.
„ Vincent Bond, 1891.
„ Fredk. O'Hare, 1893.
„ Joseph Lightbound, 1895.
„ Walter Strappini, 1897.
„ Patrick Hoyden, 1900.
„ Joseph Flynn, 1903 to date.

WIGAN, LANCS. St. Joseph's.
The mission was established in October 1870. In January 1871, a Methodist chapel was acquired, and three years later schools for 800 children were opened at a cost of £2,000. The present church was opened July 1878, on the site of the old chapel. The building, which measures 87 ft. by 60 ft., cost about £5,647.

Priests.

Rev. J. Lamon, 1870.
„ E. Grennan, 1881.
„ John Chapman, 1884.
„ Hugh Kavanagh, 1888.
„ Michael Quirke, 1891.
„ Timothy Sheehan, 1895 to date.

WIGAN, LANCS. St. Patrick.
The schools were built 1846, and the church in 1847. This latter is a cruciform Gothic structure, notable for a fine painted window of the Crucifixion by Wailes. In March 1846 Fr. Mathew, 'the Apostle of Temperance,' gave the pledge to thousands of persons in the town. The mission was for many years served from St. John's.

Priests.

Rev. Hugh Nugent, 1860.
„ J. Banks, 1877.
„ Joseph Fagan, 1882.
„ Dagobert Sommer, 1884 to date.

WIGTON, CUMBERLAND (*Hexham and Newcastle*).
The mission was described as an 'infant' one in 1830. The chapel was an 'unsuitable attic,' and the congregation, which numbered above 300, 'poor weavers and mechanics.' After an uphill struggle of two years, Fr. John Dowdall was enabled to erect a chapel, opened June 1, 1837, by Bishop Briggs, V.A.N.D. Mr. and Mrs. Howard of Corby Castle contributed liberally to the building fund. Schools to accommodate 120 children were erected 1854-55. The present Gothic church, designed by Bonomi, was opened 1847, and enlarged 1857. The altar-piece is a good copy of Raphael's 'Christ Falling under the Cross.' Church reopened after renovation, September 1898.

Priests.

Rev. John Dowdall.
„ Edmund Kelly, 1840.
„ Nicholas Canon Brown, 1852.
„ Francis Moverley, 1866.
„ James Rooney, here in 1875.

Rev. Edmund Barnett, here in 1883.

Michael Bourke, here in 1889 and to date.

WILLENHALL, near WOLVERHAMPTON, STAFFS (*Birmingham*). St. Mary.

Prior to the establishment of the mission, the place was served from Bilston. About 1875, the district became an independent mission. Fr. G. Onions, who was appointed priest in 1875, did much for the spiritual welfare of his poor and straggling congregation. At his death in September 1880, aged thirty-seven, he was a member of the local school board, and much valued in the neighbourhood for his business capacity, not to mention his genial and witty disposition.

Priests.

Rev. Geo. Onions, 1875.

„ John Donworth, 1880.

„ Timothy Burke, 1884.

„ James Giblin, here in 1889.

„ Arthur Villiers, 1891.

„ Patrick O'Toole, 1893.

„ Walter Hanley, 1895 to date.

WILLESDEN, LONDON, N.W. (*Westminster*). Our Lady of Willesden.

The mission was opened Sunday, February 6, 1886, in a temporary chapel at 6 St. Ann's Terrace. Mass was said by Fr. Bernard Ward, now president of St. Edmund's College. Fr. Stanfield preached at the evening service to a congregation of seventy. On May 17 following, an iron church for 160 persons was opened at Manor Park by Cardinal Manning. The Rev. Lord Archibald Douglas sang the Mass, and his Eminence preached (Acts i. 11). The school was commenced in October 1887, the first stone being laid by Bishop Patterson. In 1905 the average attendance was 180. A permanent church is about to be erected.

Priests.

Rev. Geo. Cologan, 1886.

„ Henry Casserly, 1903 to date.

WILLESDEN GREEN, LONDON, N.W. St. Catherine.

The foundation.stone of the church in the Linacre Road was laid June 1906 by Lady E. Talbot. Fr. Bernard Vaughan preached on this occasion (Matt. xv. 16). The church, to accommodate about 350 persons, was opened by Archbishop Bourne, August 5, 1906. The mission, which was commenced 1903, at 59 Chapter Road, is under the care of the Westminster Diocesan Missionaries.

WILLINGTON, NORTHUMBERLAND (*Hexham and Newcastle*). Our Lady and St. Aidan.

Fr. H. Riley in December 1865 estimated the number of Catholics there at about 1,000. The 'chapel' was a room in a public-house. Confessions were heard in a small one-roomed cottage, which also served as a Sunday school, and afterwards as a temporary day school. The school chapel, dedicated to Our Lady and St. Aidan, was commenced Saturday, December 2, 1865. This building served its twofold purpose down to 1874, when the present church was erected.

F F 2

Priests.

Rev. H. Riley, 1865.
„ Robt. Sharples, 1867.
„ Wm. Perrin, 1871.
„ John McNerney, 1874.
„ Aloysius Hosten, here in 1877 till 1896.
„ Gerard Van Kippersluis, 1896.
„ Aloysius Hosten (second time), 1898.
„ Fredk. Savory, 1900 to date.

WILLOWS, KIRKHAM, LANCS (*Liverpool*).

The mission dates from 1762, when Fr. Robt. Westby established the chapel at Mowbreck. The baptismal register commences 1775. Bishop Gibson confirmed fifty-five persons here 1784. The old chapel and presbytery were built at the Willows by Fr. Irving 1890. His brother, Fr. Thomas Irving, who took the name of Sherburne, opened the cemetery 1814. A school was erected in 1826 by Thos. Daniel, a Catholic clockmaker. In 1845, Pugin's grand church was built. Its peal of bells was the first heard from a Catholic church in England since the Reformation. New schools were erected 1871, and enlarged 1889 and 1893. The sanctuary of the church was improved and new stations of the Cross erected 1897. The baptisms, which were thirteen in 1776, were eighty-six in 1886. The Catholic population is about 1,000.

Priests.

Rev. Robt. Westby, 1762.
„ Robt. Bannister, 1775.
„ W. Irving, 1803.
„ Thomas Sherburne (Irving), 1813 till 1854.
„ J. Swarbrick, 1854.
„ Provost Fk. Hines, 1857 (removed to South Kerton 1895).
„ F. Gillow, 1895.

WILMSLOW, CHESHIRE (*Shrewsbury*). St. Teresa.

The mission was founded 1871, and the church opened 1875.

Priests.

Rev. J. Coulston, 1871.
„ G. B. Canon Clegg, 1889.
„ Richard Heffernan, 1892.
„ Henry Canon Hopkins, 1895.
„ Edward Byrne, 1901.

WIMBLEDON, SURREY (*Southwark*). The Sacred Heart.

Fifty years ago the mission at Wandsworth was often referred to as of Wimbledon. There was no mission in the town till 1878. Before this time, the nearest church was at Roehampton. A private chapel, dedicated to SS. Jerome and Agnes, at Cottenham Park was served by the Jesuits from Roehampton. In December 1882 a school chapel was opened in Russell Road, under the title of Our Lady Help of Christians. The first stone of the present magnificent church was laid in July 1886. The style is Decorated Gothic. The exterior is of flint and Ancaster stone. Architect, F. A. Walters, Esq. The church is admirably situated on the slope of a hill in Upper Wimbledon, and commanding a magnificent view of the surrounding country. The nave of the building was opened for worship by Bishop Butt, of Southwark, on the titular feast of the mission ('The Sacred Heart'), June 1887. Fr. Sebastian Bowden, of the Oratory, preached. The cost of the building was generously defrayed by Madame Arundrup, one of the congregation. A noteworthy feature of the interior is the chapel of St. Ignatius, adorned with mural paintings representing the principal events of his life.

WIMBLEDON (SOUTH), SURREY.
St. Winefride.

A new Romanesque church, also served by the Jesuits, was opened November 3, 1905, by Bishop Amigo of Southwark. It is situated in the Morden Road, and accommodates about 400. The rich altar and reredos, adorned with statues of saints, are the gift of an anonymous benefactress.

WINCANTON, SOMERSET (Clifton). St. Luke's.

The mission was started on the Saturday before Pentecost 1881, and by October the same year the present church was opened for worship. The first priest at Wincanton was Fr. Cotham, who at the outset said Mass in a room lent by one of his parishioners. At the opening of the church, High Mass was sung by the Prior of Downside, the sermon being preached by the Hon. Fr. W. J. Clifford, S.J. The Order of Discalced Carmelites erected their priory, dedicated to St. Luke, at Wincanton in 1883, during the superiorship of Fr. E. Sharples, O.C.D. The novitiate of the Order in England is centred here. The new monastery was commenced May 7, 1888, and opened in August 1889. The cost was £2,200. On the day of opening, twenty-six persons were confirmed by the Hon. and Right Rev. Bishop Clifford, of Clifton, this number being more than the whole congregation at the outset of the mission.

Priests.

Rev. Edmund Sharples, 1881.
„ Edward Badger, 1884.
„ Sebastian Colin, 1891.
„ Edward Badger (second time), 1895.
„ Benedict Zimmerman, 1900 to date.

WINCHESTER, HANTS (Portsmouth).

The Benedictine traditions and glories of this historic city were preserved after the Reformation at various secluded spots in the county, which during the times of persecution afforded spiritual comfort to the little band of Hampshire Catholics. At Punsholt, or Ponshall, the seat of Thos. Loveden, Esq., died in 1610 Fr. Sigebert Buckley, the last Benedictine monk of Westminster. A year before his death, he had the happiness of seeing the 'monastery of Westminster' titularly restored by Paul V. Stoke Charity, in the same county, witnessed the labours of Fr. Francis Morgan, O.S.B. (1600–69), titular Prior of Winchester. The first monk resident in Winchester itself after the Reformation was Fr. Wm. Ambrose Brown, 'Procurator of the South Province,' who served the mission from 1717 till 1741. The next priests were Fr. Thos. Sheppard (1741–45) and Fr. Wm. Metcalfe (1758–59). The chapel and presbytery were in an old mansion—still standing—called Hyde House, in the north part of Winchester. In August 1767 the names of the inmates were 'taken down,' presumably with a view to prosecution, there being a perfect epidemic of 'priest-informing' from that year till 1769. In 1777, the mission would appear to have been served by seculars. One of the priests there at that time was Fr. John Milner, afterwards Bishop of *Castabala*, the well-known historian of the city. The 'King's House,' which had often been used as a place of confinement for prisoners of war, was in 1792-93 used as a house of residence for a large number of French clergy exiled by the Revolution. On December 6, 1792, a new chapel in 'the carpenter's style of Gothic' was opened for service. A mural tablet on one of its walls recalls the gratitude of the French clergy for the hospitality afforded them by the Government of King George III. The Benedictine nuns, exiled by the Revolution, settled in the town shortly after the opening of the convent. After some fifty years' residence at the 'Bishop's House,' they removed to East Bergholt, in Suffolk. Until the opening of the Catholic schools by Fr. Ignatius Collingridge, about 1849, the good nuns, although by constitution a contemplative Order, taught some children in an extemporised schoolroom. The schools, erected by Fr. Collingridge, were used till the opening of the present fine buildings in 1899, during Canon Gunning's rectorate. Fr. Collingridge was a strenuous advocate of religious equality for Catholics not only in the Army and Navy, but also the prisons, and during his tenure of the Winchester mission (1848–62) had a long and well-known correspondence with the Hampshire justices on the subject, with the result that much injustice was ultimately removed.

Priests since 1824.

Rev. T. White, 1824.
„ James Delaney, 1826.
„ C. Picquot, D.D., 1846.
„ Ignatius Collingridge, M.R., 1848.
„ Peter Canon Collingridge, M.R., 1862.
„ Ignatius Collingridge (second time) 1865 (?). (He retired from active missionary work in 1883, but continued to hold the title of rector of the church till 1889, when he was succeeded by his

coadjutor, Canon Luke Gunning, the present incumbent.

WINDERMERE, WESTMORLAND (*Hexham and Newcastle*). St. Herbert.

The idea of building a church at Windermere was carried into effect by Canon Curry, of Dodding Green, Kendal, who zealously attended to the spiritual wants of Catholics in the district. The first stone of the building was laid by Bishop Bewick, of Hexham and Newcastle, September 4, 1883. Mr. R. Walker was the architect. The opening of the building took place June 1884. The style is Gothic.

Priests.

Rev. W. Stevenson, 1884.
„ John Bamber, 1888.
„ Joseph Fawell, 1889 to date.

WINDLESHAW. *See* **ST. HELENS**, ST. THOMAS OF CANTERBURY.

WINDSOR, BERKS (*Portsmouth*). St. Edward.

'It is not surprising,' remarks the writer of the 'Catholic Handbook' (London, 1857), 'that the influence of the English sovereign should prevent the Catholic religion being professed for many years in this locality,' *i.e.* since the Reformation. On April 21, 1686, Fr. Nicholas Cross, or Lacroix, O.S.F., who had been confessor to Ann Hyde, Duchess of York, preached at Windsor Castle on 'the joys of Heaven' before Queen Mary of

Modena, consort of James II. Very early in the nineteenth century, Mass was occasionally offered up in the house of Lady Mannock at Datchet, a mile from Windsor. It is, however, probable that Fr. John Phillips, *alias* Samuel Goltier, a Lisbonian priest who died near Windsor September 13, 1727, may have served a permanent mission in this locality. In 1810, John Riley, Esq., turned a room of his house at Windsor into a chapel, where Mass was said weekly down to the time of his death in 1817. After this the Abbé Duclos, an *émigré*, and professor of French at Eton College, said Mass at his own house, ' quietly and almost surreptitiously, for fear of giving offence to the authorities.' Finally Wm. Riley, Esq., only son of the above-mentioned John Riley, being unable to procure a site in Windsor, built a chapel on his own property at Clewer Green. The building, which was dedicated to St. John the Baptist, was opened in 1826, and placed under the care of Fr. C. Comberbach, long afterwards chaplain to Lady Holland at St. Anne's Hill, Chertsey. He died 1890 aged ninety-two years. The next priest, Fr. J. F. Wilkinson, had the honour of being presented to King William IV. by Lord Melbourne in 1835. The chapel was enlarged by a tribune in 1844, on the occasion of King Louis Philippe's visit to England. Fr. Wilkinson was succeeded in 1854 by Fr. Augustus Applegath, during whose long incumbency of more than twenty years the old chapel at Clewer Green was abandoned for the present fine church in the Alma Road, Windsor, opened in 1868. The Rev. J. Longmotto, M.R., is the present rector.

WISBECH, CAMBRIDGESHIRE

(Northampton). Our Lady and St. Charles Borromeo.

Wisbech Castle was the scene of the long imprisonment of Bishop Watson, of Lincoln, deposed by the Government of Elizabeth for opposing the changes in religion. The mission was started from Lynn in 1840, when ' a very decent little chapel ' was erected ' by the zeal and liberality of Mr. Mantegani.' Who this individual was is not stated. At first, Mass was said once a month. On the other Sundays prayers were read by one of the congregation from the ' Garden of the Soul.' After Mass or prayers, the children were catechised for half an hour. The congregation about this time amounted to some twenty persons. In 1847 it had risen to seventy. A school was opened in December 1862.

Priests.

Rev. Thos. Canon Fox, 1852 till after 1858.

(Mission served from Lynn 1862.)

„ Henry Colpman, 1863 till 1899.

„ Geo. Page, 1899 to date.

WISBECH HIGH FEN, CAMBRIDGESHIRE.

The chapel of St. Patrick was opened March 30, 1862, as auxiliary to the mother church, from which it is still served.

WITHAM, ESSEX *(Westminster)*.

The Holy Family.

The property known as Abbots Witham was granted by Henry VIII. at the dissolution to Geo. Tresham, Esq., from whom it passed to the Southcotes. Sir

John Southcote, judge of the Queen's Bench under Elizabeth, was known, despite his position, for his staunch Catholicity. He died 1585, and was buried in Witham parish church. The last of his descendants owned Woburn Farm (see WEYBRIDGE). About 1770, the manor of Abbots was rented by Lord Stourton, and it was at this time that the mission was commenced by his chaplain, Fr. Barnes.[1] A public chapel was probably erected after the second Relief Act of 1791. The Abbé Armand Benard, who was 'chaplain' here for many years, died at Witham Place, August 18, 1826. Fr. McDonnell, the next priest, was succeeded about 1840 by Fr. Wm. Woods. In 1844 Fr. Jn. Kaye was incumbent. Two years later there would appear to have been no resident chaplain, but Mass was said every Sunday at ten o'clock. In May 1851, the foundation stone of the present church was laid by Cardinal Wiseman, and the building was opened by his Eminence towards the end of the same year. The church was constructed to accommodate about 200 persons, and is described by a contemporary journal as one of 'quiet, unpretentious beauty.' The priest of the mission at this time was Fr. Joseph da Silva Tavares, D.D. The number of Catholics in the locality was then estimated at eighty. Fr. Wm. Baines, who came after Fr. Tavares in 1854, held the incumbency for nearly thirty years. The late Fr. Angelo Lucas died in June 1902, and was succeeded

[1] Mention is made of Lord Stourton and his chaplain, Fr. Barnes, in Mrs. Barnewall's interesting narrative of her grandfather's conversion (A Hundred Years Ago, Burns and Oates).

by Canon Reginald Tuke, M.R., the present rector.

WITHINGTON, LANCS (Salford). St. Cuthbert.

The present church was partially erected 1881-82, and completed November 23, 1902. The style is Lombardo-Byzantine, the arrangement cruciform. The cost of building the nave, which was opened for worship in September 1881, was £2,400, of which sum Mr. Lavery generously gave £1,000. The first priest at Withington was Fr. Seth Clarkson, who was succeeded by Fr. F. Lawless. The next priests have been:

Rev. Robert Smith, 1890.
  ,,   Francis Daniel, 1892.
  ,,   Henry Newton, 1895.
  ,,   James Rowntree, 1897 to date.

WITHNELL, LANCS (Liverpool). St. Joseph.

The school chapel was opened December 14, 1884. The number of Catholic children in the village and neighbourhood then amounted to sixty-five. Before the opening of the chapel, the nearest church was at South Hill, near Chorley. The Catholic population is now about 350.

Priests.

Rev. Wm. Moore, 1885.
  ,,   Peter Kane, 1887.
  ,,   Michael Flynn, 1889.
  ,,   Wm. Bradshaw, 1895.
  ,,   Edward O'Reilly, 1903 to date.

WITTON PARK, DURHAM (Hexham and Newcastle). St. Chad.

This mission was served from Bishop Auckland till about December 1881, when it was placed under Fr. Francis Kuyte. During the 'mission' given here in April 1882 by Frs. Barry and Shee upwards of 775 persons approached the sacraments.

Priests.

Rev. Francis Kuyte, 1881.
(Mission served from Wolsingham 1889.)
„ Henry Cadogan, 1890.
„ Wm. Drysdale, 1893.
„ R. Myler, 1898 to date.

WOKING, SURREY (*Southwark*). St. Dunstan.

The mission proper was established in 1895, when for some time Mass was said on Sundays and holy days at the residence of Mrs. Mostyn. In 1898, an iron chapel, capable of accommodating about 100, was erected in Percy Street, by Fr. W. Allanson, D.D., who also built the presbytery. Before the erection of the chapel, civilians were admitted to Mass on Sundays at the Inkerman Barracks.

Priests.

Rev. F. Wilderspin, 1896.
„ James Connell, 1897.
„ W. Allanson, D.D., 1898.
„ Joseph Livesey, 1905 to date.

WOKING, SURREY. Inkerman Barracks.

The convict prison formerly existing here had Catholic chaplains from about 1863, the first being Fr. T. Donovan, who resided at Maybury Villa. The chapel was dedicated to St. Dunstan. The prison was transformed into a barracks in 1895, since which time the Catholic soldiers have been attended by a special chaplain.

WOLSINGHAM, DURHAM (*Hexham and Newcastle*). St. Thomas of Canterbury.

In January 1849, Fr. Thos. Wilkinson, now Bishop of Hexham and Newcastle, hired a hay-loft and stable at Wolsingham, and converted the former into a chapel and the latter a school. The mission then embraced the districts of Tow Law, Crook, and Willington. The church, designed by J. Hansom, was commenced in 1853, and opened September 5, 1854, by Bishop Hogarth. The golden jubilee of the church was celebrated in October 1904, when High Mass was sung by Mgr. Corbishley, and a powerful sermon on the Blessed Sacrament preached to a crowded congregation by Fr. Nicholson.

Priests.

Rev. Thos. Wilkinson, 1849.
„ Robt. Orrell, 1860.
(Mission served from Tow Law for many years.)
„ Richard Collins, 1886.
„ Wm. Taylor Canon Smith, 1890.
„ E. McGarrity, 1892.
„ M. Moloney, 1894.
„ A. Wilkinson, 1897.

WOLVERHAMPTON, STAFFS (*Birmingham*). SS. Peter and Paul.

In 1743 Peter Giffard, Esq., of Chillington, built a large mansion at Wolverhampton called 'The Great House,' where a chapel was fitted up. Mr. Green, a Catholic residing in the town, used long afterwards to relate the difficulties experienced by Catholics at this time in attending Mass. ' We were obliged to steal our way in small parties, or, rather, singly, and by different and circuitous routes, to avoid observation and the consequences which often attended detection.' In 1765, Bishop Hornyold adorned the chapel with Italian stucco work. The house, it may be remarked, was built as a residence for priests and a boarding establishment for Catholics. Lady Teynham and her daughter, Mr. and Mrs. Manby of Essex, &c., were among the residents. In 1804, Bishop Milner made the house his abode as Vicar Apostolic of the Midland District. In 1813, Fr. Walter Blount enlarged the chapel gallery. Bishop Walsh made other additions, so that, by the reopening on May 8, 1828, the building represented the letter T. Nave and transept were added in 1855, and chancel in 1880. A burial ground for Catholics was laid out near the chapel about this time. Bishop Milner, who died April 19, 1826, is interred in the crypt. On November 20, 1849, St. George's and St. Patrick's Schools were opened by Bishop Ullathorne, V.A. The church was consecrated in 1885. The new Sacred Heart chapel and sacristies were opened October 17, 1901. A striking feature of the chapel is the handsome marble altar and Italian Renaissance reredos, in the centre of which is displayed a picture of the Sacred Heart—a devotion which Bishop Milner did much to spread in England.

Priests since 1775.

Rev. Joseph Berington, *Sacrae Theologiae Licentiatus* (Douai), 1775. Fr. Berington was the eminent author

of the ' Literary History of the Middle Ages.' Died at Buckland Farringdon 1827.

Rev. John Carter, 1776.
  „   Morgan D'Arcy, 1803.
  „   W. Blount, 1804. President of Sedgley Park, 1821–36.
  „   W. Benson, 1821.
  „   P. O'Sullivan, 1831.
  „   Peter Davies, 1851.
  „   J. Fanning, 1853.
  „   Geo. Canon Duckett, 1855.
  „   Edward B. Hymers, 1898. President of St. Wilfrid's, Oakamoor, 1903.
  „   John Hopwood, D.D., 1903 to date.

WOLVERHAMPTON, STAFFS. St. Patrick's.

This handsome Gothic church, for about 700 worshippers, the foundation stone of which was laid by Bishop Ullathorne in June 1866, was chiefly intended for the great number of Irish in the town. The cost was about £4,000. Fr. W. Hall was priest of the mission at the time of the erection of this church.

WOLVERHAMPTON, STAFFS. SS. Mary and John, Snow Hill.

Erected 1855. The Whitgreave family of Mosely and the Duke of Cleveland gave £300 and £100 respectively towards the site. The cost of the building was about £2,000.

WOLVERTON, BUCKS (*Northampton*). St. Francis of Sales.

The mission was commenced October 1865, the chapel being ' a club-room of a public-house,' used during the week as a meeting place for some workmen of the 'Grand Boiler Association'! The few Catholics of the place had not seen a priest for years, and the rising generation were wholly ignorant of even the rudiments of their religion. A site was secured, and the present church opened Trinity Sunday 1867, upon which occasion Bishop Amherst pontificated, and preached to a considerable congregation.

Priests.

Rev. W. Blackman, 1865.

„ Geo. Stokes, 1873 till after 1883.

„ H. W. Parkes, here in 1889 till after 1900.

„ Augustine O'Sullivan, 1904 to date.

WOLVEY, WARWICKSHIRE (*Birmingham*). Our Lady of Ransom and St. Thomas of Canterbury.

A chapel was opened at Wolvey Hall, the residence of H. F. J. Coape-Arnold, Esq., in Holy Week 1890. Before the opening of the mission Mr. Coape-Arnold had instituted lectures on Catholic subjects in the neighbourhood. The first Mass was said by Fr. Francis, a Premonstratensian of Weston. On the evening of Easter Sunday, Fr. Leslie, S J., addressed a crowded audience at the Hall on the spiritual benefits to be derived from a Catholic mission. The first stone of the present church was laid by Bishop Ilsley, of Birmingham, September 15, 1890, and the building—erected at the sole expense of Mr. Coape-Arnold—was opened in 1891.

Priests.

Rev. Austin Richardson, 1890.

„ F. Salins, 1895.

„ Henry Yeo, 1897.

„ Cornelius Klomp, 1899. (Mission served from Harborne 1904.)

WONERSH, near GUILDFORD, SURREY (*Southwark*).

St. John's Diocesan Seminary was commenced at Henfield, near Brighton, by the late Bishop Butt in the August of 1889. The house was an old compact mansion near the parish church. The village of Henfield is famous for being the birthplace of the illustrious Catholic divine, the Rev. Dr. Stapleton, of Louvain († 1599). Fr. Bourne, now Archbishop of Westminster, was the first rector, the number of students at the outset being about twelve. The idea of a separate diocesan seminary had long been before the Southwark authorities, and Bishop Danell first appealed for funds to start one in 1874. At first, Clapham was selected as the site, but ultimately abandoned as being too much in London. In August 1889, the foundation stone of the seminary at Wonersh was laid by Bishop Butt, and in 1891 the building was occupied by the students from Henfield. The style of the edifice is that of the Queen Anne period, from a design of Mr. F. A. Walters, F.S.A. The oblong Romanesque chapel opened on May 4, 1896, in the presence of Cardinal Vaughan, Bishop Butt, Bishop Bourne, &c., was the gift of Mr. Brodrick, of Brighton. In addition to the high altar, which has been lately adorned by the addition of a handsome baldachino and a splendid marble reredos, displaying mosaic figures of the patron saints of the seminary, there are several side altars. The Lady Chapel, with its alabaster altar and reredos, adorned with pictures in *opus sectile*, is also well worthy of attention. A handsome organ, by Bishop, has recently been added to the chapel. The number of students for the priesthood at present amounts to about ninety. These are divided into seniors and juniors, the former comprising the divines and philosophers and the latter the 'humanitarians.' The junior course of study culminates in the Arts examination of the London University, in which great success has been achieved. The rectors of St. John's have been: (1) Bishop (now Archbishop) Bourne (1889-97); (2) Fr. G. Barrett, D.D., now of Richmond, Surrey (1897-99); (3) Mgr. Joseph Butt, 1900 to date.

WOODCHESTER, GLOUCESTER-SHIRE (*Clifton*). The Annunciation.

William Leigh, Esq., late scholar of Brasenose College, Oxford, purchased Woodchester Park from Lord Ducie in 1846, and as a thankoffering for his conversion to Catholicism resolved to make it over to a religious Order. The church which he built, together with the adjoining monastery, were inaugurated by Bishop Hendren, October 10, 1849. The sermon was preached by Bishop Wiseman. The Passionist Fathers had the house for a time, but in 1850 it was made over to the Dominicans, of which Order it is now a priory. The church, built from a Gothic design by Charles Hansom, is a

splendid specimen of ecclesiastical architecture, and the romantic scenery of the locality displays its structural beauty to great advantage. A conspicuous object of the interior is the tomb of the pious founder, surmounted by his sculptured effigy representing him in his robes as a Knight of Malta. The cathedral at Adelaide, Australia, is another example of his pious munificence.

Priors.

Very Rev. S. A. Procter, 1853.
,, ,, J. D. Aylward, 1855.
,, ,, H. L. Gonin, 1857.
,, ,, Samuel Procter, 1863.
,, ,, Wilfrid Lescher, 1866.
,, ,, Lewis Weldow, 1870.
,, ,, F. Paul Stapleton, 1874.
,, ,, G. Kelly, 1885.
,, ,, Thos. R. Laws, in 1889.
,, ,, Wilfrid Lescher, 1890.
,, ,, Antoninus Williams, 1894.
,, ,, Gabriel Whitacre, 1896.
,, ,, Ambrose Smith, 1898.
,, ,, Vincent McNabb, 1904.

WOODFORD GREEN, ESSEX (*Westminster*). St. Thomas of Canterbury.

The church site was presented by the Dowager Duchess of Newcastle, and the stone laid by Cardinal Vaughan in May 1895. The building, which is in the Early English style, will accommodate 700 persons. Canon Scoles was the architect. The opening and consecration took place in July 1896.

Rev. Fathers Guardian (*O.S.F.*).
Rev. Fr. Peter Baptist, 1896.
,, John Forrest, 1899.
,, Fr. Mathias, 1903

WOOD GREEN, LONDON, N. (*Westminster*). St. Paul.

The mission was established December 24, 1882, Mass being said in the dining-room of a private house. The next chapel was extemporised from a stable, and the wants of a tabernacle and ciborium rendered the reservation of the Blessed Sacrament impossible. An iron church was erected shortly afterwards, and used till the opening of the existing fine church, in the Early English style (1904). The congregation numbers about 1,000.

Priests.

Rev. Geo. Cox, 1882.

„ John Nicholson, 1903.

WOODHALL SPA, LINCS (*Nottingham*).

A site for a church was secured and a temporary chapel established 1895. Mass was said here every Tuesday during the summer months by Fr. P. Sabela, of Grantham. A school chapel was opened 1896. Fr. Eugene Goddard, resident priest 1899 to date.

WOODLANE, STAFFS (*Birmingham*). St. Francis of Sales.

In the early part of the eighteenth century Mrs. Mary Ann Howard, of Hoare Cross, Woodlane, had a chapel in her house and a resident chaplain, Fr. Thomas Berington, Dean of the old English Chapter in 1748. After the death of Mrs. Howard the estate went to the Hon. C. Talbot, a brother of Bishop Talbot, coadjutor to Bishop Challoner. He died in 1766. In 1793 the property was sold to H. Meynell, Esq., with the exception of a small portion, upon which Charles

fifteenth Earl of Shrewsbury built a chapel and presbytery. Fr. Thomas Flynn was priest of the mission at this time. He was succeeded in 1797 by Fr. Gasper Bricknall, who greatly improved the house and chapel. He died May 6, 1833, and was buried beneath the chapel. He was succeeded by Fr. J. Jeffries, who remained till about 1852. The next priest, Fr. P. O'Sullivan, was rector for nearly thirty years. Fr. J. Parker is the present incumbent.

WOOLER, NORTHUMBERLAND (*Hexham and Newcastle*). St. Ninian's.

Fr. Alexius Whalley, O.S.F., was residing here in 1808, but whether privately or in charge of a mission does not appear. The present mission dates from 1843, when a chapel was opened over a malt kiln. A 'mission-house' was erected 1847, and Mass said there once a month. The house was destroyed by fire 1857, while the rector, Fr. Chadwick, was giving a mission at Preston. A subscription was raised and the place rebuilt 1859.

Priests.

Rev. Edw. Smith, 1843.

„ Geo. Meynell, 1846.

„ E. Consett, 1850.

„ James Chadwick, 1852 (Bishop of Hexham and Newcastle 1866–82).

„ Robt. Suffield, 1852.

„ Jn. Carlile, 1860.

„ Denis Buckley, here 1871 and till 1892.

„ Ignatius Beale, 1893. (Served from Lowick 1894–1903.)

„ Denis O'Kelly, 1903 to date.

WOOLHAMPTON, BERKS (*Portsmouth*). Douai Abbey.

Woolhampton Lodge is described as 'the last remnant of the great estates which the [Earls of] Fingal at one time owned in England.' The property, however, was not baronial. Arthur James seventh Earl of Fingall merely inherited the Woolhampton estate on marrying Henrietta, daughter of William Woolascot, Esq. Lord Fingall resided at Woolhampton till 1779, when he retired to Killeen Castle, co. Meath. The estate at Woolhampton was sold to Mr. Crewe of Bolesworth Castle, in Cheshire, father of the third Viscountess Falmouth. The chapel and a portion of the land appear to have been excepted from the deed of sale. In 1825, the priest in charge of the mission was Fr. Thomas Webster. In 1830, the incumbency was vacant, but the following year Fr. Stephen Dambrine, the son of a French *émigré* gentleman, was appointed incumbent. The chapel at this time 'was a miserable place, and his residence a still more wretched hovel.' In 1846, Arthur Earl of Fingall gave the site of the present church, and the building, in the Tudor style, was opened May 11, 1848. On the advice of Fr. Robert Hodgson, Canon Dambrine opened a small school with a view to training boys for the priesthood. By 1854 the institution had become St. Mary's College, with 100 pupils. Canon Dambrine died May 27, 1855. Canon Crookall, V.G., the next president, did much to advance the educational reputation of the place, and in this he was ably assisted by the above-mentioned Fr. Hodgson, an excellent disciplinarian and spiritual director. The school has received a fresh impetus at the present day owing to its acquisition in 1903 by the English Benedictine Fathers of St. Edmund's College, Douai, recently expelled by the persecuting policy of the anti-Christian Government of France. The title of ' Douai Abbey,' by which the college is known, serves as a link to connect the institution with the old *alma mater* in the nursery of martyrs and confessors 'beyond the sea.'

WOOLMER, near **LIPHOOK, HANTS** (*Portsmouth*). The Immaculate Conception.

The mission was established in 1870. Confirmation was first administered at the school chapel in November 1885.

Priests.

Rev. John Warner, 1870.
„ Abbot Burder, 1877.
„ F. Pius, O.S.F.C., 1879.
„ Geo. Mayne, here in 1883.
„ James Daly, 1885.
„ Geo. Dolman, 1890.
„ John Edmund Wallace, 1891.
„ James Daly, 1893.
„ Cuthbert Winder, 1895.
„ Emmanuel Rivara, 1901 to date.

WOOLSTAN, HANTS (*Portsmouth*). St. Patrick.

The mission dates from 1879. A new school chapel was built, August 1883. The stone was laid by Fr. H. P. Kelly for the Bishop of Portsmouth. The accommodation of the building was for 300. Architect, Mr. Leonard Stokes. The number of children attending the school in 1883 was eighty. The mission was served from Netley from 1879 till after 1886.

Rectors.

Rev. Albert Coughlan, here in 1889.

„ Joseph Hayes, 1892.
„ John Molloy, 1893.
„ Patrick Kelly, 1895.
„ Stephen Mongan, 1896.
„ Francis O'Farrell, 1897.
„ John Hayes.

WOOLSTAN, WARRINGTON, LANCS (*Liverpool*). St. Peter.

Till about the beginning of the last century, the mission was served by the chapel at Woolstan Hall. The foundation stone of the present church was laid February 19, 1834, by Edward Statham, and the building was opened July 2, 1835. Many protestants in the district contributed to the building fund. Priests here since 1834 have been:—

Rev. H. Sharples.

„ Jn. Carter (died March 16, 1875).
„ Jn. Gardner, 1875–84.
„ Wm. Walsh, 1884–86.
„ Thos. Dawson, 1886–88.
„ Thos. Myerscough, 1888.
„ Joseph Lowe, 1895 to date.

WOOLTON MUCH (*Liverpool*). St. Mary.

The chapel of Woolton Hall, which was served by Benedictines was frequented by local Catholics before the establishment of the present mission in 1765, when Fr. Cateral built the chapel and presbytery. It was enlarged in 1828 by Fr. Phillips, but in 1860 was supplanted by the present church, erected by Abbot Burchall, O.S.B. Schools were built 1870, and the church enlarged 1878.

St. Mary's Hall, for Catholic social gatherings &c. was built in 1884 by Fr. Prest. Various stained-glass windows were put up in the church 1897–98, and a cemetery consecrated about the same time.

WOOLWICH, KENT (*Southwark*). St. Peter, New Road.

The mission was started in St. Mary Street, near the dockyard. Two Blanchardist abbés were there early in the last century (1805 ?).[1] The mission was attended from London 1816–25. The old chapel accommodated 400, and by 1842 the congregation was estimated at 3,000. On February 12, 1841, the Board of Ordnance made over to the priest of the mission, Fr. Coles, a freehold site for a new church. The number of Catholic soldiers in the garrison was at this time about 500. By dint of strenuous efforts, the present church was commenced October 20, 1842, and opened by Bishop Griffiths October 26, 1843. The style is Decorated Gothic, from designs by A. W. Pugin ; accommodation for about 2,000. A stone image of St. Peter surmounts the entrance door. An addition was made to the presbytery in 1870, and a chancel opened by Bishop

[1] 'Blanchardism' was the name given to a schism occasioned amongst the French *émigré* clergy by the Abbé Blanchard. The Blanchardists refused to recognise the Concordat of 1801 between Napoleon and Pius VII., and adhered to the old pre-Revolution hierarchy. The English Vicars Apostolic required a repudiation of 'Blanchardism' from all French priests holding faculties in the country, and lists of those who subscribed were published yearly in the *Laity's Directory* and *Catholic Directory* down to as late as 1848.

Butt in August 1887. The jubilee of the church was celebrated in November 1893. The Catholic population in 1904 was computed to be about 5,000.

Priests.

Rev. James Delaney, 1816.
„ J. Staples, 1826.
„ W. Nightingale, 1835.
„ Cornelius Coles, 1840.
„ Jeremiah Cotter, 1860.
„ Seraph Fieu, 1889.
„ Joseph Reeks, 1893.
„ Arthur Doubleday, B.A., 1900.

WOOTON WAWEN, near **BIRMINGHAM, WARWICKSHIRE.** Our Lady and St. Benedict.

Opened Tuesday, November 29, 1904, by the Bishop of Birmingham. The site of the church was given by Lady Smythe and Mrs. Haydock of Acton Burnell. Until the opening of the church, Catholics worshipped at the domestic chapel of Wootton Wawen Hall, which has only recently been acquired by G. Capewell Hughes, Esq., from the Smythes of Acton Burnell. This gentleman, although a protestant, has behaved with great generosity to the mission, the fine bell of the new church being his gift. The mission of Wootton Wawen is one of the oldest in England. For many years after 1677 the Jesuit Fathers were here as chaplains to the Carrington family at the Hall. Fr. Henry Kemp was priest in 1710. Nothing, however, is known precisely of the early history of this mission. After the Jesuits left the place the Benedictines took charge of the chapel, and have since continued to minister to the spiritual wants of the local Catholics.

Rectors since 1824.

Rev. James Deday.
„ Joseph Short, 1840.
„ Peter Hewitt, 1851.
„ John Alphonsus Morrall, 1871.
„ Robert Green, here in 1888.
„ Thos. McCabe, 1892 to date.

WORCESTER (*Birmingham*). St. George, Sansome Place.

This mission was established about 1685, and has ever since been served by the Jesuits. The registers date from May 9, 1685, with the entry of the baptism of Francis Smith. The second records that 'Mrs. Parsons was reconciled to ye Church of Rome ye 1685 ye of [*sic*] and departed this life soone after, having received all ye rites of ye Church, and was buried at Ruardine.' Between 1686 and 1712, about thirty persons were reconciled to the Church; from 1721 to 1746 about sixty. Fifty-one persons were confirmed here May 14, 1780, by the Hon. and Right Rev. Bishop Talbot, and sixty-one on November 2, 1788, by Bishop Charles Berington. Dr. Thos. Attwood left at his death in September 1765, £200 for the use of the mission, which also benefited by various bequests made by the Misses Ann and Eliz. Hill (1788 and 1799), Stephen Smith, Esq. (£200, 1777), Thos. Bowyer, Esq. (£300, 1822), &c. The old mission chapel was too small for the congregation, 1828. The present one, in the Grecian style, measuring 84 ft. by 40 ft., and designed by Mr. Rowe, was opened July 16, 1829, by Bishop Walsh. Transepts, sanctuary, and chapels of Our Lady and St. Joseph were

added in 1880 (June). The sarco-
phagus-shaped altar of marble and
alabaster is surmounted by a fine
copy of Raphael's 'Transfiguration.' A splendid set of bronze
candlesticks was presented to the
church by the Earl of Shrewsbury
at the time of opening. The
schools were founded in 1830, and
two years later had an attendance
of eighty children. Alderman H. A.
Leicester, the first Catholic mayor
of Worcester since the Reformation, was elected 1904.

Rectors.

Fr. Oldcorne, the martyr, and
Fr. Lister laboured in the district
from about 1595 to 1603. After
this no missioners are recorded till
1648, since which time the supply
has been continuous, as follows:—
Rev. Edw. Beswick, 1648-80.
„ Henry Humberston, 1686.
„ C. Hanne (?).
„ ' Mr. Butler, O.S.B.' (?)
„ Wm. Case (died 1747, æt. 57).
„ John Baynham.
„ Thos. Sanders (died Novem-
    ber 12, 1790, æt. 66).
„ Joseph Williams (died 1797,
    æt. 53).
„ Andrew Robinson (died 1826,
    æt. 85).
„ John Morris, 1826.
„ Joseph Tristram, 1832.
„ John Rigby, 1838.
„ Francis Brownbill, 1842.
„ Francis Chadwick, 1843.
„ Bernard Jarrett, 1844.
„ Henry Beeston, 1845.
„ Hy. Walmesley, 1848.
„ Jn. Bird, 1851.
„ James Laurenson, 1854.
„ Wm. Waterworth, 1860. (Fr.
    Waterworth was the emi-
    nent author of 'England
    and the Holy See.')
„ Joseph Foxwell, 1879.
„ John Turner, 1888.
„ T. Knight, 1891.

Rev. C. Karslake, 1893.
„ A. Charnley, 1895.
„ T. Lyons, 1898.
„ E. Kernan, 1899 to date
    (1904).

WORCESTER PARK, SURREY
(*Southwark*). St. Matthias.

The name of this rising village
is derived from that of a mansion
in the neighbourhood bestowed by
Charles II. on the Duchess of
Cleveland. The Catholic Church,
begun July 1906, was opened for
worship Rosary Sunday, October 7,
of the same year. The style is
Romanesque, the materials used
being chiefly red brick with Kentish rag-stone dressings. Accommodation for about sixty-five. The
chief feature of the interior is the
high altar surmounted by a painted
and gilded baldachino, and adorned
with a well-painted triptych representing the Assumption of Our
Lady, St. Matthias, and St. Bernard. The massive brass candlesticks, of old Flemish design, are
also well worthy of note. The
architect of the building was Mr.
Benedict Williamson; builders,
Messrs. Godson, of Kilburn. The
mission is served from St. Anthony's, North Cheam, by the Rev.
Bernard W. Kelly.

WORKINGTON, CUMBERLAND
(*Hexham and Newcastle*). Our
Lady Star of the Sea and St.
Michael.

The mission was separated from
Whitehaven in 1810. The first
chapel was a room totally inadequate for the even then considerable congregation. Half an
acre of land was shortly afterwards

G G

given for a chapel by Joseph Curwen, Esq., member of a protestant family that inherited Workington Hall towards the end of the eighteenth century. Fr. Rishton, O.S.B., was the first priest of the mission. In 1831, one of his successors, Fr. Glassebrooke opened 'a school for young gentlemen,' which had considerable success. The enormous growth of the Catholic and general population of the place owing to great developments in the iron, steel, and coal industries, made a new church absolutely necessary. The first stone of the new cruciform church (159 ft. by 63 ft.) was laid by the Bishop of Hexham October 9, 1873, and the building was opened 1876. E. W. Pugin was the architect; cost of erection, about £8,400. A new pipe organ was installed May 27, 1906, towards the cost of which Mr. Andrew Carnegie, the millionaire, contributed £300.

Priests.

Rev. Thos. Rishton, 1810.
,, A. Abrams E. Glassebrooke, 1831.
,, H. J. Sutton, 1841.
,, R. Sanderson, 1842.
,, J. Ginnevan, 1843.
,, Francis Williams, 1844.
,, C. Clifton (abbot), 1845 till 1891. (Several assistant priests after 1874.)
,, Neville Vincent Wilson, 1891.
,, Francis B. Hutchinson, 1892.
,, Michael Elphege Duggan.
,, J. Standish, 1901 to date.

WORKSOP, NOTTS (*Nottingham*). St. Mary.

The manor of Worksop passed to the Dukes of Norfolk, *temp.* Elizabeth. The constant presence of a chapel and priest and

the protection of the Howard family kept the Faith strong in the district. In 1830 Catholics are described as being 'very numerous in the neighbourhood.' Fr. Gerard Saltmash, who was chaplain here for some years after 1705, might have been V.A. of the Western District but for an unfounded accusation of Jansenism. The old chapel, near the manor house, built towards the end of the eighteenth century, served the mission till the opening of the present church in 1839. The site, described as 'well chosen,' was given by the Duke of Norfolk. Mr. Hadfield was the architect, the size of the building being 72 ft. by 27 ft.

Priests since 1825.

Rev. J. Jones, —.
,, Chas. W. Tasker, 1860.
,, Geo. Bent, 1866.
,, Wm. Canon Croft, here 1871.
,, Jas. Canon Griffin, 1876.
,, Michael Canon Fryer, 1884 to date.

WORTHING, SUSSEX (*Southwark*). Our Lady of the Angels.

From about 1862 till the opening of the church in 1864, Mass was said at the convent of Notre Dame de Sion, the chapel of which was open to the public. The priest at this time was Fr. M. P. Fannan, afterwards of Deptford. A new chancel and transept—added to the building by T. Gaisford, Esq.—were opened by Bishop Danell November 12, 1873. The stone and marble altar of the transept was the gift of Edmund Coffin, Esq. The east window of three lights has representations of Our Lady, St. Peter, and St. Thomas. Fr. James Purdon has been rector since 1869.

WREKENTON, DURHAM (*Hexham and Newcastle*). St. Oswald. The mission was commenced 1884, and served from Birtley till 1892. Fr. Joseph Kershaw, O.S.B., was priest here 1893–1901; Fr. Peter Wulstan Fossato, O.S.B., 1901 to date.

WRIGHTINGTON HALL, LANCS (*Liverpool*). The domestic chapel served the district during the penal times and down to the opening of the present chapel in 1806. The Dicconson family have been seated at the Hall since 1652, and it is to their protection that the preservation of the Faith in the district is in large measure due. Bishop Dicconson (1670–1752), V.A. of the Northern District, was a member of this family, as was also Wm. Dicconson, Esq., tutor to the Chevalier de St. George, commonly called the Old Pretender.

Priests since 1820.

Rev. L. Cooper, —.
  ,, T. Margison, 1852.
  ,, Geo. Rigby, 1892.
  ,, John Melling, 1893 to date.

WROXHAM HALL, NORWICH (*Northampton*). SS. Michael and Helen. The mission was established in 1870 by E. S. Trafford, Esq. Fr. C. Kemp, the first rector, died November 22, 1882, and was succeeded by Fr. Michael Burke. The next priests were:—

Rev. Andrew Morgan, 1897.
  ,, Henry Stanley, 1899 to date.

WROXTON ABBEY, near BANBURY, OXFORDSHIRE (*Birmingham*). A priory of Augustinian canons was founded here by Michael Belet in the reign of Henry III., and granted by Henry VIII. at the dissolution to Sir Thos. Pope. The present mission was established at Wroxton Abbey in 1885.

Priests.

Rev. Jn. Rieter, 1885.
  ,, J. F. Roche, 1888.
  ,, Augustus Petre, 1891.
  ,, A. Hellé, 1895.
  ,, N. H. Higginson, 1901.
  ,, Francis Sutherland, 1904 to date.

WYCLIFFE, YORKS (*Middlesbrough*). St. Mary. The domestic chapel of the Tunstall family served the mission as far back as the reign of James II. Fr. E. Parkinson, a Lisbonian, was missioner here from 1688 till his death, April 7, 1735. Bishop Witham in 1724 recommended him to Propaganda as a fit candidate for the episcopate, but the advice was not acted upon. The next priest was Fr. Joseph Holden (1735–43). He was a doctor of the Sorbonne, and after leaving Wycliffe became superior of St. Gregory's Seminary, Paris, where he had a misunderstanding with the archbishop on account of a suspicion of Jansenism. The register of Wycliffe commences 1743, but till about 1791 no priest's name occurs. The old chapel was built 1743, probably at the initiative of Fr. Holden. The present church was opened in October 1849. The building is a neat structure, though 'without much pretension to architectural display.' The east win-

dow, by Wailes, has representations
of the Lamb of God, the Evangelists, St. Charles Borromeo, &c.
Cuthbert Watson, Esq., defrayed
most of the cost of erection.

N.B.—The Tunstall family, the
ancient patrons of the mission,
became extinct on the death of
Marmaduke Tunstall, Esq., F.R.S.
(1790). His estates finally went to
the Sheldons.

Priests since 1824.
Rev. T. Sanderson.
  ,,   Jn. Woodcock, 1827.
  ,,   Jn. Bradshaw, 1833.
  ,,   S. Walshaw, 1855.
  ,,   Geo. Brunner, 1866.
  ,,   C. O'Neill, here 1872.
  ,,   Provost Walker, 1882.
  ,,   Geo. Brunner, 1885.
  ,,   Peter Kennedy, 1896.
  ,,   C. Donovan, 1901 to date.

453

Y

YARM, or YARUM, YORKS (Middlesbrough). St. Mary.

The ancient Catholic family of Meynell were formerly the patrons of this mission, which was served by the Jesuit 'college' or residence of St. Michael the Archangel. Fr. Thos. Nandyke, S.J., died at Yarm March 17, 1793, aged sixty-seven. His successor, Fr. P. Potier, O.P., was here till 1812. The chapel was built 1795. The priest in 1824 was Fr. J. Bradley, who served the mission till his death in October 1853. He was succeeded by Fr. Mathew Kavanagh. On May 3, 1860, the new church of St. Mary was opened by the Bishop of Beverley. The building, of Gothic design, was erected at the expense of Thos. Meynell, Esq., of the Fryerage, York. Messrs. Hadfield & Goldie were the architects. In September 1886 Fr. J. Doud, formerly incumbent at Yarm, was, on his promotion to a canonry of Middlesbrough Cathedral, presented by the congregation with his official robes, 'as a fitting mark of their esteem for him.'

Rectors since 1865.

Rev. Geo. Keasley, 1865 (died at Scorton 1890, æt. 88).
,, John Canon Doud, 1885.
,, Thos. Canon Holland, 1888 and to date.

YARMOUTH, NORFOLK (Northampton). St. Mary.

The mission is described as 'vacant' in the 'Laity's Directory' of 1825, but in 1826 the resident priest was Fr. Joseph Tate. Mass was at that time said in a hired room. In 1827 a plain chapel was erected, which did duty till October 1850, when the present church was opened in the Regent Road. The foundation of this church was largely due to the zeal and energy of Fr. W. Cobb, S.J. The inaugural Mass was celebrated by Bishop Wareing. The Rev. Don Claudio Lopez, priest of the mission, established the mortuary guild in 1849. In March 1857, a handsome window was unveiled in the church to the memory of Fr. Lythgoe, S.J., a truly apostolic priest of this mission. Fr. E. Rigby, S.J., is at present the chief priest at St. Mary's.

YEALAND, CARNFORTH, LANCS (Liverpool). St. Mary.

The mission was founded 1782 by Geo. Townley, Esq., of Leighton Hall. Before this time Mass was said at the residence of the Gillows. The present chapel was built by R. T. Gillow, Esq., J.P., and consecrated August 4, 1852. The style is Early English; dimensions, 76 ft. by 20 ft.; cost of erection, about £1,200.

Priests.

Rev. Michael Wharton, 1782.
„ Basil Barrett, 1809. (He wrote the 'Life of Cardinal Ximenes' while a priest here.)
„ H. Banister, 1818.
„ Hy. Rutter, 1820.
„ Joseph Maini, 1834.
„ Wm. Henderson, 1848.
„ Joseph Parker, 1888.
„ James Birchall, 1892 to date.

YEOVIL, SOMERSETSHIBE (*Clifton*). The Holy Ghost.

On June 24, 1888, an ancient chantry, situated near the west end of the parish church, was opened for service as a Catholic chapel. After the Reformation the building fell into neglect but about 1820 was altered and opened as a charity school. A large congregation assembled on the day of its inauguration as a place of Catholic worship, 1888, and among the decorations of the chapel was a fine pre-Reformation crucifix formerly on the old town cross. The Hon. Dr. Clifford, Bishop of Clifton, preached (1 Peter iii.). The chantry did duty till the opening and consecration of the present commodious church (May 17, 1899), designed by Canon Alexander Scoles, rector of the mission from 1888 to 1901. Fr. Louis Valluet is the present rector.

YORK (*Leeds*). St. Mary's Convent, Micklegate Bar.

Yorkshire shares with Lancashire and Staffordshire the honour of being one of the Catholic counties of England. In its manor houses and old halls the proscribed faith lingered on long after the rest of the nation had succumbed to the 'great apostasy.' In 1604, just after the accession of James I., the number of persons convicted of 'Romish recusancy' was 20,000 in the West Riding of Yorkshire alone. In York itself, the establishment of a permanent mission dates from the foundation of St. Mary's Convent, Micklegate Bar, in 1680, by Mrs. Bedingfeld, who also erected the Benedictine convent at Hammersmith. The nuns wore the ordinary gentlewomen's dress of the period, and devoted themselves to the education of the daughters of the Catholic nobility and gentry. In 1745, during the rebellion of Prince Charles Edward, the convent was threatened with repression by the Government, but the storm subsided, and the famous Laurence Sterne, author of the 'Sentimental Journey' &c., who had done his best to close the convent, became its fast friend. From 1710 to about 1800 the chaplains of the convent were Jesuits, and these also served the York mission. In 1796 the Abbé Ludovic Dehenne was chaplain, and remained till about 1811. The convent chapel ceased to serve the mission about the time of the opening of St. Wilfrid's second chapel in 1 02.

YORK. (*Middlesbrough*). St. George.

This church, in the Decorated style, was opened by Bishop Briggs September 4, 1850. Architect, Hansom; accommodation for about 700. For some years after the opening the church was served from Little Blake Street (St. Wilfrid's). It may be remarked that on the day the foundation stone was laid (October 25, 1849) the event was marked by a public procession, the first since the establishment of the Reformation.

Priests.

Rev. Charles A. O'Neill, 1861.
„ Thos. Canon Harrison, 1864.
„ Thomas Holland, 1867.
„ Michael Fryer, 1874.
„ John Concemius, 1882.
„ James Canon Brady, 1885.
„ Patrick Cronin, 1902.

YORK (*Leeds*). Church of the English Martyrs, Blossom Street.

This mission was opened in 1882, for the benefit of ' some 500 Catholics in that part of the city.' The place of worship was at first a couple of granaries, one of them forming a school. Mgr. Canon Goldie was the first priest of the new foundation.[1] He was succeeded in 1896 by Fr. Oswald Dolan, who was followed in 1898 by James Canon Gordon. Fr. Geo. Machell is the present rector (1904).

YORK (*Middlesbrough*). St. Wilfrid's.

The first chapel, in Little Blake Street, was founded about 1760. The register commences 1771 (January 12). Bishop Douglass,

[1] The martyrs of York were Margaret Clitheroe (1586), Fr. Hy. Walpole (1595), Fr. Postgate (1679), Fr. Thos. Thwing (1680).

V.A.L.D., was priest here from 1776 to 1790, the year of his consecration. Dr. Lingard, the historian, was ordained in the chapel by Bishop Gibson, V.A.N.D., 1795. The second chapel was erected by subscription, and opened 1802. It was of 'modern architecture' in style, and 'much admired for elegance.' The organ cost £500. Fr. Wm. Croskell was probably rector at this time. His successor, Fr. Benedict Rayment, was incumbent from 1811 till his death in 1842. The same year a meeting, presided over by Bishop Briggs and the Hon. W. Stourton, resolved on the erection 'of a really fine church.' Nothing was done, however, till July 1862, when the old dilapidated chapel was removed and the present church commenced. It was opened by Cardinal Wiseman June 2, 1864, amidst a great gathering of the Northern clergy and laity, including most of the Catholic bishops and nobility. The style is 'French Gothic,' from designs by Goldie. The seating accommodation is the same as that of the old chapel—about 7,000. Cost of erection, about £10,000.

Priests since 1842.

Rev. Thos. Billington, V.G. (died 1849).[1]
„ Provost Joseph Render, V.G. (died 1881).
„ Wm. Canon Browne, 1881.
„ Provost Chas. Dawson, here in 1888 to date.

[1] Fr. T. Billington was greatly esteemed in York, and at his death the bell of the historic minster was tolled by order of the dean, who publicly referred to the deceased as ' a Christian clergyman '—much to the annoyance of the *Church and State Gazette.*

APPENDIX

ACOCKS GREEN, WARWICK-SHIRE (*Birmingham*).

An 'academy' was kept here 1819–22 by a Mr. Grant, a former student of St. Omer's College. Mass was probably said in the house during this time by an *émigré* priest. The present mission dates from 1905. During that year, Wilton House and adjoining property in the Warwick Road were purchased and opened as the Convent of Our Lady of Compassion. A temporary wood and iron chapel serves the mission. The Rev. John Gibbons is the chaplain.

BIRMINGHAM. Holy Family, Coventry Road, Small Heath.

This mission was started from St. Anne's, Easter Sunday, 1901. For two years and a half the chapel was in a workshop in Green Lane. The school, a well-equipped two-story building, was opened in September 1903, after 'some local opposition.' The chapel was used for the first time Sunday, September 27 of the same year, but the day school not until January 11, 1904.

Priest.

Rev. James Wright.

BIRMINGHAM. St. John, George Street, Balsall Heath.

The mission was started as a chapel of ease to St. Anne's, 1896. The church, which consists of nave and Sacred Heart Chapel, was opened by Cardinal Vaughan. The high altar is very rich in marble and mosaics.

Priests.

Served from St. Anne's by Fr. J. P. Dowling, 1896.

Rev. C. Haskew, 1903.

„ G. Bunce, 1904 to date.

CLAPHAM, S.W. St. Vincent of Paul (*Southwark*).

The presbytery and temporary chapel were opened at 5 Altenburg Gardens, Clapham Common, north side, 1903. The foundation stone of the church was laid by Bishop Amigo, Saturday, July 28, 1906.

Priest.

Rev. George Grady, 1903 to date.

TARPORLEY, CHESHIRE (*Shrewsbury*).

Mass was said here for the first time of late years on Sunday November 18, 1906, by Fr. J. Chambers of St. Werburgh's, Chester. The chapel was a 'commodious room' kindly lent by Mr. Martin Goulding, about fifty persons being present.

Spottiswoode & Co. Ltd., Printers, New-street Square, London.